An Overview of Co... ...*...tivities*

Other Publications of the European Platform on Conflict Prevention
and Transformation/European Centre for Conflict Prevention

Prevention and Management of Violent Conflicts
An International Directory - 1998 Edition

Conflict Prevention Newsletter
a quarterly publication

People Building Peace
35 Inspiring Stories from Around the World - May 1999

European Platform for Conflict Prevention and Transformation/
European Centre for Conflict Prevention
P.O. Box 14069
3508 SC Utrecht
The Netherlands
Tel +31 30 253 7528
Fax +31 30 253 7529
Email euconflict@euconflict.org
http://www.euconflict.org

Searching for Peace in Africa

An Overview of Conflict Prevention and Management Activities

Includes

- Surveys of 31 Violent Conflicts
- A Directory of 120 African and international NGOs
- Many introductory articles on thematic and regional trends

Editors **Monique Mekenkamp, Paul van Tongeren** and **Hans van de Veen**

A publication of the European Platform for Conflict Prevention and Transformation in cooperation with the African Centre for the Constructive Resolution of Disputes

Financially supported by the **Ministry of Foreign Affairs of the Netherlands**

Visit our Website at www.euconflict.org

With an average of 26,000 visitors per month to date, the European Platform's website has proven to be a popular source of information for people from all over the world. Most of the information offered in this publication - including the Surveys of Conflict Prevention as well as the Directory section - is also available on our website. Additional information can be easily accessed via the hypertext links to the homepages of relevant organisations. Moreover, the website information on conflict prevention and management activities related to the main violent conflicts in Africa will be updated on a regular basis, increasing its accuracy. To further enhance the quality of the information provided, we invite readers of this publication as well as visitors to the website to let us know your opinion of the information and to inform us about possible adjustments or corrections.

© 1999, European Platform for Conflict Prevention and Transformation
Utrecht, the Netherlands

ISBN 90 5727 03 31

US$ 30

Editing and production Bureau M&O, Amsterdam
Set and designed by Karel Meijer, MMS Grafisch Werk
Cover photography Wim van Capellen/Lineair (front), Henny van der Graaf (back)
Printed by Haasbeek, Alphen a/d Rijn

Contents

Appendices

Acknowledgements

In your hands is a publication that would not have been possible to produce without the support, advice and contributions of many people from all over the world. To those who have worked on this project since the summer of 1998, we take this opportunity to express our thanks.

The European Platform's 1998 International Directory included fourteen pilot Surveys of Conflict Prevention and Management Activities. These texts were given a warm welcome by many people who are confronted in their daily routine with the issues of violent conflict and the search for solutions. It was therefore decided to go on with this work and produce surveys of all main violent conflicts in the world. At the seminar 'Strategies in Conflict Prevention,' June 12-14, 1998 in Soesterberg, the Netherlands, support for the project was expressed by, amongst others, Kevin Clements (International Alert), John McDonald (Institute for Multi-Track Diplomacy), John Marks (Search for Common Ground) and Mari Fitzduff (INCORE). In particular, Kevin Clements has been most constructive throughout the project.

Another seminar that was instrumental in developing the project was the Consultative Networking Meeting in Africa, organised by the Africa Dialogue Center on September 21-22, 1998, in Arusha, Tanzania. It was here that the idea was born of combining the Conflict Prevention Surveys with the Directory-section (with profiles of organisations active in the field of conflict prevention/management) and to produce one publication per continent.

Several other international experts have also shared their expertise with us: Janet Durno (Canadian Peacebuilding Coordinating Committee), Joyce Neu (International Negotiation Network of the Carter Center), David Nyheim (FEWER), Charles Radcliff (International Crisis Group), Luc Reychler (Leuven University, Belgium), Bethuel Kiplagat (Africa Peace Forum) and Tom Woodhouse (Bradford University).

We are very much indebted to the Netherlands' Ministry of Foreign Affairs who made this project possible by providing the financial support for this publication, as well as a following publication on violent conflicts in Europe.

In a short space of time, several authors have contributed introductory articles on different issues, Connie Peck (UNITAR), Hussein Solomon (ACCORD), Chris Lansberg and Shaun Mackay (Centre for Policy Studies, South Africa), and Fitzroy Nation (freelance journalist).

Each group of surveys on specific conflicts in one of the African regions is preceded by two introductory articles. Michael Lund (Creative Associates International) looks at recent developments in the five sub-regions and their relevance in terms of de-escalating violent conflict. The other set of introductory articles focus more on recent conflict dynamics from a regional perspective. The authors are Arend Jan Termeulen (political scientist), Hizkias Assefa (international mediator), John Amoda (Department of Peace Studies, New York), Véronique Parqué and Filip Reyntjes (Centre for the Study of the Great Lakes, Belgium), and Hussein Solomon (ACCORD).

Most of the actual surveys were written by experienced journalists who travelled extensively in the countries and regions they cover: Jos van Beurden, Anne Graumans, Jos Havermans, Reinoud Leenders, Bram Posthumus, and Hans van de Veen. Some surveys were written by staff of the European Centre, Anneke Galama, Monique Mekenkamp, Emmy Toonen, and edited extensively by Hans van de Veen.

Academic Associates PeaceWork in Nigeria is responsible for the five texts on conflicts in Nigeria, which were written by Judith Asuni, Raphael Chima Ekeh, Akin Akinteye, Shedrack Gaya Best, Oronto Douglas and Doifie Ola. Barnett Rubin (Center for Preventive Action) wrote the introductory article and edited the Nigerian surveys.

Besides the journalists and staff of the European Centre, several other people have contributed to the conflict surveys by providing background material and documents. Berto Jongman, PIOOM Institute provided academic input and wrote background articles for some conflicts. Lucas van de Broek (MSF The Netherlands) contributed to the Burundi survey.

The draft surveys were sent to several experts who were invited to give comments and make suggestions. We wish to thank those that have contributed substantively to the final versions of the surveys: Roel Meijer, Eric Goldstein, Mark Salter, John Entelis, Fransisco Tunga, Laurie Nathan, John Stewart, Christian Scherrer, Jan van Eck, Francois Verschave, Andreas Mehler, Maria van den Boer, Jan van Criekinge, Hans Determeijer, Sue Williams, Stephan Marysse, Raymond Kitevu, Ibrahim Allam, Saad Eddin Said, Kebede Asrat, Bea Stolte, Dekha Ibrahim, Abdulai Napoleon, Alex Gerbrandy, Gill Nevins, Roy van der Drift, Sabala Kizito, Stephen Ellis, Hussein Solomon, John Hanlon, Bineta Diop, Ali Osman, Karthi Govender, Mary de Haas, Hadi Guma Gadal, Yvonne Heselmans, David Smock, Yves Del Monaco, Paul Aarts, Cedric de Coning and Suzanne Scholte.

Following research into African organisations by Anneke Galama, questionnaires were sent to some 175 organisations. Based on this preliminary research and the replies to the questionnaires, she collected initial information for the profiles. This information was processed into final profiles by Jim Wake.

As always, the cooperation with Hans van de Veen and the team at Bureau M&O was both productive and pleasant. The practical organisation of a publication such as this can safely be entrusted to his care and he has been very helpful in developing the project in general. We therefore want to express our deepest thanks. We believe that through this cooperation between our Centre and many leading experts within and outside the region as well as the group of journalists, this publication gets its unique character and - we hope - its value. We also thank Karel Meyer for his layout work and Niall Martin for the English copy corrections.

We want to express our sincere gratitude to ACCORD (African Centre for the Constructive Resolution of Disputes) Durban, South Africa whose cooperation has been invaluable. In particular we want to thank Vasu Gounden for his advice and constructive comments and suggestions, Hussein Solomon for his regional overview of southern Africa and the various articles and background material he sent us regularly, and Hayden Allen for his help with several organisational issues and his always prompt response and familiar 'Greetings from ACCORD!' Furthermore we thank Hussein Solomon, Napoleon Abdulai, and Karthi Govender for their comments on several of the draft surveys.

And last but not least the staff of the European Centre, the backbone of this project. In particular thanks to Guido de Graaf Bierbrauwer and Juliette Verhoeven for their flexibility and precision in proof-reading. Further, thanks are due to Anneke Galama for her valuable assistance and involvement in this project and her independent and optimistic working spirit, and to Emmy Toonen for her research into West African conflicts and her supportiveness for the project and the Centre.

Paul van Tongeren, *executive director, project director*
Monique Mekenkamp, *project co-ordinator*

Introduction

'Who will bring peace to Africa?' This was the question posed by a despairing editorial in the January 16, 1999 edition of the international magazine, *The Economist*. 'From north to south, east to west, large swaths of the continent are at war, but almost all efforts at pacification have come to naught', the editorial continued.

Believe the headlines and one would think that the entire continent of Africa is perpetually engulfed in armed conflict. True, Africa has been judged to be 'the most warring region on the planet', with some thirty wars being fought on its soil since 1970, the majority of them intra-state. According to the figures of the human rights research organisation, PIOOM, in 1998 there were some 200 violent and armed conflicts taking place world-wide. Of these, 72 were in Africa, by far the highest number of conflicts in a separate continent. But it is essential to realise that there is also another Africa, an Africa where people are living in peace and harmony with each other and their neighbours.

Another common misapprehension about the subject of war and conflict in Africa is the notion that Africa's conflicts are 'tribal' wars. For one thing, the term 'tribal' is inaccurate and pejorative, a term that would never be used to describe the warring factions in northern regions (Kosovo or Northern Ireland, for instance). For another reason, the origins and nature of conflicts in African nations are as complex as they are in other parts of the world. They cannot be explained simplistically, as the many case studies in this publication make clear.

The failure of the international press to give fair and realistic coverage to the terrible events in Rwanda in the first months of 1994, is just another example, of the West's distorted view of Africa. The fact that for several weeks the slaughther was widely portrayed as resulting from ancient tribal feuds illustrates the depth to which Western stereotypical perceptions of Africa are ingrained in the media's consciousness. Of course, obtaining accurate information was not easy - especially at the beginning of the crisis - but a more accurate analysis could easily have been made by closer consultation with Rwandan experts and human rights and refugee organisations at that time. The Western media's failure to report adequately on the genocide in Rwanda possibly contributed to international indifference and inaction.

The African continent has in recent years suffered a disproportionate share of the world's violent conflict. The ten major conflicts in the past 25 years have claimed the lives of between 3.8 and 6.8 million people - which is between 2.4 and 4.4 per cent of the continent's total population. Moreover, beyond the mortality figures, these conflicts have caused immense suffering among the survivors: refugees, internally displaced persons, the traumatised and the victims of landmines. Whole societies have been wrecked and development has been set back years.

The editorial in *The Economist* focused on the failure of outside intervention in Africa. The Nigerian-led regional intervention force was at that time receiving a fearful drubbing at the hands of a rag-tail rebel movement in the tiny Sierra Leone. The United Nations was contemplating the complete withdrawal of its monitoring force in Angola, leaving the country to face total war once again. 'To send foreign soldiers', the magazine lamented, 'whether African or not, to intervene in any of the continent's manifold disputes looks even more hopeless, even more foolish.'

A few months later, Western countries intervened in the war in Kosovo, Yugoslavia. This led to bitter complaints from the side of African people about what they saw as the West's biased and ethnocentric attitude. 'As Western bombs rain on Yugoslavia, dozens of wars of greater magnitude have been simmering for decades in Africa with little interest being shown in an unipolar world', journalist Gumisai Mutume wrote in the magazine *TerraViva*. 'Oppressed minorities, millions of refugees, and those enduring dictatorships, warlords and striking poverty in Sierra Leone, the Democratic Republic of Congo, Angola and other countries would be elated to receive some attention from the international community.'

In his article, Mutume also quotes South African Institute of International Affairs' director Greg Mills, saying that 'this is a time when the international community appears intent on trying to wash its hands of large-scale multilateral involvement in Africa's seemingly unending conflicts.' Mills also notes the existence of 'a policy trend quaintly termed the promotion of African solutions and capacity to solve African problems.'

Whether or not it is the result of a trend in international politics' to cynically balance the pros and cons of intervention, the shift towards a more regional and even local approach could signal a very positive development for the continent. Debating the meaning of the frequently used phrase, 'the African renaissance', Chris Landsberg and Shaun Mackay of the Johannesburg-based Centre for Policy Studies in one of the introductory chapters in this publication quote South Africa's new leader Thabo Mbeki. He recently warned his fellow-African leaders that they should no longer pretend that undemocratic practices are somehow more acceptable merely because they are occurring in Africa rather than in Nicaragua or Yugoslavia. Or that the 'ethnic cleansing' practices in several African conflicts are less important than those occurring in Europe, even if the varying reactions of the international community may seem to suggest this. 'It will not help Africa to look to those nations to change their attitudes,' Landsberg and Mackay conclude, 'it is Africans themselves who must lead the fight to change these perceptions.'

In another introductory chapter, journalist Fitzroy Nation quotes South African conflict resolution specialist Professor Jannie Malan's observation that many time-proven methods of conflict resolution originated on African soil: 'The conflict resolution expertise that has developed in Africa incorporates insights and skills acquired during the years of traditional leadership, colonial rule, and new independence.'

Indeed, the 1990s have seen a range of the kind of initiatives which point to a future for the continent marked as much by attempts at reconciliation as by the explosive conflicts that have tarnished its image and reputation. Many of these inspiring examples of local peace building have been documented in the publication *People Building Peace,* which was published by the European Centre for Conflict Prevention in May 1999 (the Centre acts as the Secretariat of the European Platform). Several more examples can be found in the Surveys of Conflict Prevention in this publication.

Concentrate on the local capacity for peace, is the message which sounds both loud and clear, and the international community should do far more than it does today to help strengthen these capacities. Non-governmental organisations play an increasingly important role in this field. In many conflict situations, NGOs, such as churches and women's groups, have shown their ability to bring about conflict resolution and reconciliation at the community level. Business-groups and scholarly institutions within civil society have also been actively studying and disseminating knowledge about conflict prevention and resolution. In many cases they have been supported by international NGOs which focus on conflict resolution.

Networks of conflict prevention organisations have recently sprung up in large numbers in Africa - a trend described here in a separate chapter - partly based on the growing awareness that more and more conflicts have regional implications or even suck in neighbouring countries to the conflict. This suggests the need for a greater bonding of organisations, and the sharing of common experiences.

In yet another introductory chapter in this publication, Connie Peck strongly pleads for the creation of UN Regional Centres for Sustainable Peace, to provide a conflict prevention mechanism that would build a strategic partnership for the provision of assistance in dispute resolution and good governance aimed at preventing conflicts. These Centres would liase closely with the relevant regional organisations as well as conflict resolution and governance NGOs, research institutions and think tanks in the region. They should combine the functions of research, policy advice, training and offering a meeting place to all people sincerely working for peace in the region.

To reduce and overcome the ongoing violence - in Africa, as well in many other places in the world - it is necessary for many more civilian actors, both inside and outside of the conflict zones, to engage themselves in the field of conflict prevention. By virtue of their non-governmental and non-military approaches, these actors from civil society are comparatively well placed to contribute to the prevention and transformation of violent conflicts vis-à-vis more formal and state-based institutions. But while the, nevertheless essential, contributions by states and multilateral agencies are discussed and coordinated in many networks and fora, the activities of NGOs in this field are still much less systematically linked to each other and lack effective structures of mutual support.

This awareness led to the creation of the European Platform on Conflict Prevention and Transformation, a few years ago.

One of the Platform's main goals is to provide comprehensive support for the conflict prevention and transformation activities of civilian actors. The European Platform also strives to help create a strong and active network between - if possible - all the players in the field, as an important step towards achieving synergetic effects and to overcoming the weakness of small and isolated actors.

One of the main problems confronting people and organisations working for peace is the lack of information about the many initiatives that have been and are currently being undertaken. Nor is sufficient information available about persons and institutions that have gained expertise in this field which is specifically related to particular regions or countries. The number of organisations involved in conflict prevention - particularly humanitarian and development NGOs - has grown immensely, as has the scope of their activities. However, there is a rising tide of complaints about a flagrant lack of communication and co-ordination.

The present publication - the first in a multi-annual project - should be seen in this light. The main part of this book consists of a large amount of so-called Surveys of Conflict Prevention and Management Activities, as well as a Directory of some 120 organisations which are involved in peace building and transformation activities in Africa.

The Surveys provide a brief background analysis of 33 of the main violent conflicts in Africa. The choice of these specific conflicts has been based on the list of High-Intensity and Low-Intensity Conflicts on the continent, as identified by the World Conflict and Human Rights Map 1998, produced by the Interdisciplinary Research Programme on Causes of Human Rights Violations (PIOOM). Also the yearly publication *States in Armed Conflict* of the Department of Peace & Conflict Studies of Uppsala University has been consulted.

Introductory articles provide the Surveys with a regional analysis. But the primary focus is on surveying the activities of key local and international actors to contain and transform the violent conflict. In the Directory section short summaries of the activities as well as addresses, contacts, etc. of some 100 of the main African NGOs in the field of conflict prevention are given, as well as information on twenty important international organisations.

The first objective of this project is to provide information on Who Does What? Practical information on important publications, resource contacts, websites and databases is added to this. A third objective is of a more evaluative nature. The Surveys aim to offer insight into existing possibilities for successful conflict prevention and transformation activities in different situations. This in turn fosters our fourth objective, which is to help organisations to better attune and harmonise their activities, and work together in order to develop a more effective approach. A further objective is to give a voice to African NGOs, by working in cooperation with and drawing upon the expertise of local people. The potential of those organisations to act as intermediares between the civil society in the conflict areas and international organisations should be much more fully exploited.

Putting all this information together has been a Herculean labour in which many people from all over the world have participated. Draft versions of the Surveys were published on the Platform's website, and readers were asked to react with additional information or comments. The many reactions have certainly contributed to improving the quality of the information. Still, we are the first to recognise that there are weak or even blank spots in the information given here. That's why we prefer to see this exercise as an ongoing process. All Surveys will be available on our website, and via the hypertext links to the URLs of relevant organisations, users will be able to find additional information. These website-texts will be updated on a regular basis, increasing the accuracy of the information. We also hope to publish an updated and improved version of this book within two years.

Finally, we aim to provide a practical follow-up to the collection of information combined in the Surveys by organising policy seminars on specific conflict areas. Starting in the Netherlands, the Platform then plans to organise further seminars in other Western countries as well as in the conflict areas themselves. The meetings should offer all those who want to enhance the possibilities for peace in specific areas - local people as well as those from other areas - the chance to debate the analysis given in the Surveys, as well as the policy options and recommendations.

As stated earlier, this publication marks the start of an ongoing project. In the coming years it is our intention to publish Surveys of Conflict Prevention and Management Activities for all the main conflicts in other regions in the world, as well as Directories of the main actors. Europe will be the first in line, with publication scheduled for mid-2000.

We would not have started this immense task without the sincere believe that there is a clear need for this kind of information. This project should act as a bridge between intergovernmental organisations, governments, NGOs, academic institutions, networks, and resource persons and serve the final objective of facilitating exchanges between these different groups and bringing them closer together, hopefully thereby contributing to lasting peace in those places where it is so badly needed.

Paul van Tongeren, *executive director European Centre for Conflict Prevention*

Part I
Reflections

The meaning and content of the 'African Renaissance'

Wake up, Africa!

The idea of a renewal, rejuvenation or rebirth in Africa is not a new one. Many African leaders such as Kwame Nkruma, Chief Obafemi Awolowo, Jomo Kenyata, Julius Nyerere, South Africans Chief Albert Luthuli, Robert Sobukwe and more recently, Steven Bantu Biko, have espoused this notion of continental renaissance. But ever since South African president, Thabo Mbeki, dared some two and a half years ago to do what in some circles is considered political suicide, by venturing to suggest that there can be a renewal in this dark continent, the term 'African Renaissance' has increasingly become a part of the South African - even African - political lexicon. And while the idea of an African Renaissance is the subject of considerable, and at times heated debate, it does seem to be a major public relations scoop simply because it has got the world talking ◆

By **Chris Landsberg and Shaun Mackay***

The phrase owes its popularity in South Africa, and further afield, as much to the praise it has received as to the vilification that has been heaped upon it. Some see the African Renaissance as a wake-up call by those who firmly believe Africa's time has come; others see it as an empty policy vessel desperately yearning to be filled with substance; and still others see it as an attempted modernisation of the Pan-Africanism of yesteryear.

But, whatever the real rationales behind the articulation of the purported Renaissance, the idea is at the forefront of many a dinner conversation, political rallying cries, and even scholarly investigation.

Even more importantly, it has begun to fire the imagination of many African intellectuals and leaders in the political, business and social spheres. Today, the sound of the call to revival, like the proverbial African drumbeat, reverberates far beyond South Africa's boundaries. From Cape to Cairo, Washington to London, Tokyo to Delhi, Rio to Kingston, the African Renaissance has captured the African and international imagination.

Because he is the architect of the very idea - and had the foresight to perceive of an African Renaissance - some have billed South Africa's newly elected president Thabo Mbeki, the man who has the unenviable task of having to fill Nelson Mandela's gigantic shoes, an 'African visionary', an activist president destined to take his place among the greats of the continent. But visionaries are necessarily dreamers, those who prophesy, and Mbeki does not strike us as an exception. And yet, the prophet and dreamer has begun to fill the vessel with concrete policy ideas.

Thabo Mbeki has recently started to punt the idea of 'the 21st Century as the African Century'. He believes in a Renaissance based on 'the establishment of genuine and stable democracies in Africa'. He is of the opinion that 'history teaches us that the one-party states and the military governments will not work'. Mbeki's Renaissance is a call for Africans to resist all tyranny, oppose all attempts to deny liberty by resorting to demagogy, repulse the temptation to describe African life as the ability to live on charity, engage in the fight to secure the emancipation of the African women, and reassert the fundamental concept that we are our own liberators from oppression, under-development, poverty, and the perpetuation of an experience from 'slavery, to colonisation, to apartheid, to dependence on alms'.

Mbeki is pleading that Africa should

reintegrate itself into the global economy, and participate in a 'New World Order' that will have as its pillars 'the elimination of poverty in all its forms, as well as the consequent human conflict and degradation; achieving sustainable development, universally leading to shared prosperity; ending war and conflict in and between countries; and abolishing weapons of mass destruction'.

President Mbeki seeks to concretise 'the will of the people of Africa to liberate themselves from corrupt, unaccountable and undemocratic regimes'. According to the president, 'a new indigenous and energised African movement for the liberation of the continent has surely emerged'.

It is therefore clear that the term 'African Renaissance' as espoused by Thabo Mbeki does have some tangible meaning. Mbeki for one believes that what has been described as 'lofty words on a politician's wish list' can, and should be turned into the awakening of a slumbering continent. More importantly, Mbeki is of the view that this continent, variously described by European writers as 'this savage land', 'the derelict continent', 'the coming anarchy', and the 'heart of darkness', is capable of being resurrected from the ashes of the many conflicts its shores have played host to.

Some have tended to take the classical meaning of the word 'renaissance' and have interpreted it to be a call for a revival of the arts and letters and science and technology in the African context - a harking back to some golden age when these were supposedly at their Zenith; clearly Mbeki subscribes to this idea as well, but this is only one element of a broader scheme of things. Many observers, including President Mbeki, suggest that the African Renaissance also means recapturing the values, virtues and cultures of Africa as they existed before the intervention of the colonialists. Based on these values and cultures, we then can see the beginnings that may lead this continent to an unprecedented growth in ideas, arts and letters, science and technology and African culture. But, this approach should not fail to recognise that not everything that happened in Africa before the advent of colonialism was necessarily good or that everything that happened after the advent

'Having shrugged off the yoke of colonialism and apartheid, Africa must now face the enemy within.'

was necessarily bad. Furthermore, we can imagine the pitfalls involved in trying to determine what is truly African in nature. More importantly, how do we 'unscramble the egg' so that we inculcate these wholly African values and cultures into the masses of Africans? And who, at the end of the day are these Africans and what are the factors which define them as such?

The latter question is important because it will decide which values and cultures we adopt. Does Swahili, based generously on Arabic, qualify, as being African? Does Afrikaans, spoken nowhere else but in Africa's most southern tip, but with more than a dab of Dutch, qualify? Do the Arabic clothes adorning some of Kenya's coast dwellers, qualify as part of African culture?

As is evident, this approach engenders more questions than answers. But this is not to say that we should not do exactly this. It is the approach we take when we begin to reconstruct our past and decide which traditions we need to revive and develop and which we need to exorcise, that is important.

Others, ourselves included, tend to see Mr Mbeki's invocations of Africa's great achievements before the colonial age as merely pointing to the fact that Africa is capable of greatness; a greatness unconnected to foreign interventions. It is a greatness of its own. If Africa could achieve such greatness in the past then she is surely capable of this in the future, such evocations say. After all, as Mr Mbeki has pointed out: out of Africa, mankind was born, the great courts of Timbuktu, the library at Alexandria and the Egyptian pyramids at which all the world still wonders. It is sometimes necessary to remind the world, and Africans in particular, that civil wars, corruption and famine are not the only things that Africa has given the world. The African Renaissance is an idea that confounds the coming anarchists and the Afro-pessimists.

But if the African Renaissance is to succeed, it will also need to be a forward looking vision rather than an exclusively backward-looking one. This approach says that we need to decide on those things that we believe are good in our past and our present and to emulate and diffuse the continent with these. Those are the qualities that we can use and build upon to revive the continent and its people and become an intellectual and economic powerhouse that can take its place proudly among the rest of the world. But the converse is also true: we need to decide once and for all what is bad in our continent and vow to take a stand against it wherever and whenever it should rear its head.

May we be so bold as to suggest that the time has come when together African nations and their leaders need to commit to an agreed list of broad principles and objectives which they should then hold as inviolate. And where a leader who has agreed to abide by these principles breaks any of them, she or he must expect that action will be taken by the other signatories. This will take us a major step forward to giving true meaning to the idea of 'African solutions for African problems'; it will help to lay the foundations for a real Pax Africana or the African Peace.

African leaders, Thabo Mbeki has cautioned, should no longer pretend that undemocratic practices are somehow more acceptable merely because they are occurring in Africa rather than in Nicaragua or Yugoslavia. That is the kind of logic seemingly employed by those powers in the West who invade and attack Yugoslavia because of the 'ethnic cleansing' taking place there. Yet many of these same nations stood idly by while the massacre of entire tribes took place in Rwanda and Burundi and the invisible war in Angola. Somehow the 'ethnic cleansing' which occurred there did not seem as important to them as that occurring in Europe - and did not warrant the type of action taken in Cassava, where these nations put at risk some of their finest young men and women to protect the lives of the persecuted. The logic appears to be that the kind of behaviour can be expected from and, therefore, tolerated in Africa but not from among

the ranks of the 'civilised' and 'free' world.

'Ethnic cleansing' is more acceptable in Africa, it seems, than it is in Europe. It will not help Africa to look to those nations to change their attitudes: it is Africans themselves who must lead in the fight to change these perceptions. Nobody else will do it for Africa. And chief among the methods of combatting this is simply not to accept it; not to sit idly by while whole tribes and ethnic groups are slaughtered in the name of patriotism, defence of democracy or anything else. Africans should take charge of, and responsibility for, the continent's ills and challenges. And South Africa, and other powers like a democratising Nigeria, who hold some moral authority for the moment, should be at the forefront of this revolution.

Reconciliation and the African Renaissance

One of the positive aspects of South Africa's transition from apartheid and white minority domination to democracy is that it has put the issue of democracy and reconciliation firmly on the agenda in Africa. To be sure, it is an agenda item that is not necessarily shared by all political elites and powers in Africa, but it is one that is beginning to focus the political minds. The unleashing of the African continent's potential stands squarely as the guiding principle of this renaissance.

In South Africa, the strong Africanist overtones of the renaissance doctrine, seemingly out of kilter with the ANC's traditional philosophy of non-racialism, has given rise to fears of an exclusionist policy focused on blacks and discriminating against others. These fears have been reinforced by the type of policies and legislation that the South African government has adopted to address the historic imbalances in socio-economic conditions between black and white.

As a consequence, these seemingly disparate doctrines - intersecting as they do at this juncture in South Africa's history - have sent mixed signals to the country's minorities, particularly to sectors of the white community. While reconciliation told whites that they were an essential part of the 'rainbow nation', Africanism tends to suggest that they are

MONROVIA, LIBERIA

Ron Giling/Lineair

parliament illustrates he recognises that if the Renaissance is to succeed, at home at least, he has got to take all South Africans along for the ride with him. But there are some distortions that he has to deal with. For one thing, economic power and the high-level skills are still mainly in the hands of white South Africans. The enormity of the tasks demanded by the Renaissance will require all the economic power and skills that this country, and indeed the continent, can muster. So the ownership of the Renaissance in South Africa, must rest with all South Africans and they must be made to feel that they are part of this regeneration of the continent: that they are part of the solution rather than part of the problem. The African Renaissance needs to navigate a careful path that avoids whatever racial undertones, unconscious or otherwise, that may be emanating from it.

excluded from this Renaissance and breeds uncertainty about their future.

But Thabo Mbeki has already personally challenged this narrow definition of the African Renaissance and Africanism. Mbeki has argued that this is an interpretation of the Renaissance by those people who want to opt out of participating in the new South Africa. He clearly knows that this vision of the Renaissance cannot be allowed to become the dominant one in the minds of minorities, for if this happens, there is a strong possibility that they will become disaffected as citizens and consequently dismissive of the philosophy.

Thabo Mbeki's inauguration address, and his first State of the Nation address to

More recently, President Mbeki has significantly tried to lean towards the kind of reconciliation that was the trademark of the Mandela era: 'I think that the people of South Africa recognise the fact that all of them are South African. I think that is a matter that is fundamental to the willingness and the capacity to accommodate one another. South Africa belongs to all who live in it. I'm saying that I believe, that indeed all of us believe, that South Africa belongs to all of us.' This sounds like Mandela in full stride and seems fashioned to assure those sceptical of the Africanist message that they are indeed a part of Mbeki's African Renaissance.

Black consciousness and the Renaissance

At least one early aspect of the African Renaissance in South Africa can be traced to the black consciousness philosophy which gained currency during the darkest days of apartheid. Even today this philosophy urges Africans to become aware of their self-worth, to fight to restore their pride, and to take their place as equals in an ever contracting world. This is the Renaissance of the African Id: the upliftment from a position of mental colonisation to an assertion of the African self. It is, in short, a reclaiming of the African mind.

In South Africa perhaps the greatest challenge for this aspect of the Renaissance is to effect a movement away from a 'victim mentality' where everything that goes wrong is blamed on the apartheid oppressors of the past. Prominent black commentators such as Thami Mazwai, realising that we can never move forward unless we break these shackles, have called for blacks to move on, unhindered by the baggage of the past, to claim their place as Africans and fully-fledged citizens of the world. Having shrugged off the yoke of colonialism and apartheid, Africa must now face the enemy within. The ability is there but is the resolve?

The Renaissance and the reclaiming of the moral high ground

There can be little doubt that Africa is a continent weighed down by the anguish of too many civil wars, too many greedy despots and too much debt to the International Monetary Fund (IMF) and the World Bank. In too many African countries the word 'democracy' is but a rumour and hunger and privation are constant visitors at too many tables. Corruption has become a cancer that must be rooted out lest the Renaissance is killed in its infancy.

Collectively, Africans might be poor but they are rich in human, natural and mineral resources. In the past these resources were used in large measure to enrich other economies; part of the Renaissance should entail the use of these resources to benefit Africa. The huge debts owed to the IMF and the World Bank ensures that Africa remains colonised; that much of her wealth is still being used for the benefit of foreign lands. Africans are beginning to question the morality of an African country struggling to uplift itself, spending more on servicing its IMF debts than it spends on education, health and welfare combined. They are calling for the IMF and the World Bank to revisit, along with African leaders, the crippling debts of African countries that have only added to their woes, and renegotiate these so that there is more room for manoeuvre. According to *The Economist* the thirty African countries deepest in debt spend as much on debt interest as on health and education combined. In Tanzania, for instance, the government devotes three times more to debt servicing than to education, on which spending has dropped two-thirds in a decade. And these institutions appear at last to be listening.

But Africans are themselves not without blame for the continent's plight. African leaders also need to realise that it will be throwing good money after bad if the savings effected by these renegotiations are simply diverted to the pockets of yet another corrupt despot. Western donors and debtors want to have the reassurance that the money they are putting into African countries is not being used to line the pockets of greedy despots as has too often been the case in the past. The time has passed when Africans could expect their bona fides to be accepted blindly, for the recent history of the continent testifies against them in this regard. Africa's hour is at hand; the burden of proof is upon it. Demonstrating these bona fides means a paradigm shift for many African political leaders: increasingly the West and the IMF see it as democracy and political stability. And rightly so.

Instability

And just when it seemed as if the wars in Africa were subsiding, the conflict in the Democratic Republic of the Congo, Niger, Sudan and Angola have flared. The Congo conflict, which now involves more than eight African countries, has become Africa's own 'First World War'. It clearly holds the potential of plunging that entire sub-region into a war. These are issues that the Renaissance movement will have to address if we want to see a rebirth in Africa. The ascension to power in Africa cannot continue to be effected through the barrel of a gun - over the bodies of innocent citizens.

For the African elites particularly, it will be easier to slip back into the old ways, especially when the going gets as tough as it is apt to in times of transformation. This will need to be resisted, lest corruption and despotism become the defining features of this continent. But in order to diminish the forces of despotism effectively, we need a strong and independent civil society to thrive in Africa. Countries such as South Africa and Nigeria, where the organs of civil society are strong, should be encouraged to export their organisations to other states on the continent. The risks will be enormous, the sacrifices great, but if our civil society organs are committed to the Renaissance then they have little choice but to bite the bullet and replicate like a virus through Africa.

Who is an African?

Considerable debate has ensued, particularly in academic circles, on the definition of the term 'African'; about how an African is defined and what criteria should be used in arriving at such definition. Race, ethnicity, continent of birth, citizenship, language, allegiance to the continent, and other such factors have all at various times been quoted as some of the primary criteria in the consideration of whom an African is. Still no end seems in sight and a common definition remains elusive. This is, no doubt, an important debate since it seeks to define who will own the process and be its chief beneficiaries. The difficulty with this debate is that the concept can end up as an exclusivist one that will alienate sections of the South African citizenry. Ironically, it could also alienate sectors of the international community, such as the many African-Americans who regard themselves as Africans.

It is not the intention here to get caught in an circular debate about who an African is. The focus should instead be clearly on the objectives that the rebirth hopes to achieve. In this way the Renaissance can be made to be a more inclusivist movement. We should accept that all in Africa must be prepared to work towards the upliftment of the country and the continent, the eradication of hunger and poverty, and the creation of skills and jobs. At the end of the day

the poorest of the poor must benefit. Africa as a whole must be the winner.

South Africa and the Renaissance
Economic growth

In South Africa it is through its macro-economic policy - Growth, Employment and Redistribution (Gear) - that the government aims to create the conditions for sustained job creation and the reduction of inequality through the creation of conditions for sustained economic growth. It aims to create these conditions through a competitive and outward-oriented economy. But, as many of its critics have pointed out, much of the success of such strategy will hang on the decisive and determined implementation of what will be 'bitter but necessary medicine' for the economy. In this the government has been constrained, inter alia, by its labour constituency. Thabo Mbeki's government will have to invest considerable human capital in convincing the trade union COSATU of the merits of this strategy despite its short term effects on labour. It will not be helped in this by the recent financial crisis that originated in the East and then moved on to Russia and Brazil. But more than this, it will have to provide a safety net for the fall-out that is characteristic of such changes in macro-economic policy. It will have to ensure that it does not forsake the social objectives while trying to attain its budgetary stringency.

Greater racial equity

In South Africa the socio-economic stratifications, as Mr Mbeki was at pains to point out recently, continue to be mainly along racial lines. The president has thus labelled South Africa a country of two nations: one poor and chronically underdeveloped, and mainly black; and the other wealthy and enjoying 'First World' standards and mainly white. An examination of the Johannesburg Stock Exchange reveals that only about six per cent of all listed companies have black majority ownership (10,3 per cent if companies in which blacks have major - but not controlling - shareholdings is taken into consideration). And in many cases the ownership of these shares are precariously balanced between the new black owners and the

'In order to diminish the forces of despotism effectively, we need a strong and independent civil society to thrive in Africa.'

banks and finance houses that have bankrolled the deals. A considerable number of these are now under threat following the recent falls on the stock markets.

But that stratification is also between the employed and the unemployed, regardless of race, although (as is to be expected) the vast majority of the unemployed are black.

Within the country, racial equity and redistribution of economic resources are being pursued primarily through 'employment equity' (the government's affirmative action policy) and 'black economic empowerment' (where large blocs of shares in white-owned companies are sold to black people - often at discounted prices). But the government has not been content to leave these programmes to the goodwill of the private sector and market forces. They have adopted the Malaysian strategy of direct intervention in the private sector to force compliance with these goals through legislation and incentives. Legislation in the form of the Employment Equity Act (which forces companies to provide for racial equity in the workplace) and governments procurement and tender policies (which encourage small black business and partnerships between emergent black business and established white business) are at the heart of these efforts.

Employment equity is, of course, of no avail if the targeted groups do not have the necessary skills. Human development and skills training are therefore of primary importance and programmes in partnership with the private sector are being put into place.

Xenophobia
If the xenophobia sweeping through parts of South Africa is anything to go by, this Renaissance is not off to a very good start. South Africans cannot at once expect to be both at the forefront of the rebirth of the continent and persecute fellow Africans simply because they are different. South Africans have short memories. It was not long ago that black South Africans were being persecuted, driven from their homes, incarcerated and - yes - even killed, merely because they too were different. And in numerous cases it was to the open arms of the very homelands of those we would now persecute that the brave men and women who led this country's struggle for democracy, fled. This is not to argue that our borders should be thrown open for all and sundry. A good immigration policy is necessary that does not trample on the human rights of others.

But more than this. If the tide of immigrants seeking jobs and security in South Africa is to be reversed, then the success of the rebirth is critical. One of the core objectives of the Renaissance must be the stimulation of economic growth and the creation of wealth and job opportunities in more than just South Africa and Egypt. The economy of Mozambique, for instance, is now growing and creating jobs - but the conflict in the country had to be resolved first. This means that fewer people from that country will need to jump the border fence into South Africa to seek a living.

Much of the xenophobia in South Africa centres around the scarcity of jobs. The rallying cry for these xenophobes is often 'these foreigners are taking our jobs away'. If the South African economy grows and begins to become a net creator of jobs rather than a net loser of jobs as is the case at present, this will ease some of the tension around foreign job seekers from the rest of Africa. Furthermore, the reduction in oppressive governments, periodic civil wars and coups that help to drive the citizens of the affected countries to more stable countries such as South Africa, will all help to reduce the xenophobic tendency that has reared its ugly head in South Africa.

African economic unity
The external leg of Mbeki's vision entails the integration of Africa economically. Initiatives such as West-African ECOWAS and the Southern African SADC free trade protocol, aimed at establishing EU-type free trade areas,

need to be duplicated and expanded. This will, to an extent, result in more integration of African economies across borders as the regional communities pool political and economic resources to create bigger markets, attracting larger capital flows and spurring industrial development. With a coordinated plan for sharing resources across borders, Africa can take its rightful place in the world trading community. An impediment in this scenario is that some economies in Africa are better developed than others and tend to dominate the relationship resulting in squabbling, bitterness and sometimes failure. South Africa in SADC and Nigeria in ECOWAS are examples.

The white ex-owners of empowerment companies (several of whom also own the banks and finance houses) have accumulated considerable capital from these deals - capital that they can use to invest in other business. This money could just as easily be spent abroad as in Africa. In the short term it might make sense to spend it abroad where there is much more stability for the investor. But such an attitude ignores the potential of Africa alongside countries like China as one of the last great emerging markets of our time. It is true that the risks are greater here but the returns too can only be greater.

To quote Mbeki: 'The time has come for the world to suspend its disbelief - Africa is on the rise again'. Let us give this Renaissance a chance. Let us not stand on the sidelines and criticise and find fault. The tide of history is turning and it is Africa's turn to stand tall and proud. Every one of us needs to put our shoulders to the wheel and propel this revival. And we need to start at home. Poverty, joblessness and economic growth must be at the top of our lists. Corruption, despotism and nepotism must be consigned to the dustbins of our history - where they belong.

Regardless of the outcome, at least we will have tried to implement what has truly been an African vision. At least it will have been a failure or success, as the case may be, that we can call all our own. Freedom brings with it the burden of proof: proof that those who through the ages held that Africa and this our nation at her southernmost tip would never be able to run a modern economy, were wrong. Africa's moment of truth is at hand; the burden of proof is upon it.

*   **Chris Landsberg and Shaun Mackay are policy analysts at the Johannesburg-based Centre for Policy Studies.**

A Continent at War, and in Discourse

Africa's shaped like a question mark;
Africa's got the answer!

old African song

A seemingly endless sequence of conflicts - full-blown border disputes, internecine civil wars, genocidal ethnic clashes - have combined to frame Africa's image as the continent of conflict. Less known is the tradition, in places quite deeply imbedded, of resolving disputes through broad-based dialogue ◆ By Fitzroy Nation*

Africa's approach to conflict resolution, says South African conflict resolution specialist Professor Jannie Malan, is special because of the 'emphasis on relationships'. Potential and actual conflicts are understood in their social context. They are normally addressed in the environment where they are emerging or have emerged. The expertise of elders of both genders is tapped. Not as arbitrators, or in individual capacities, but as family member, or neighbourhood sage - knowledgeable of the social context of the disputants. Communal endorsement of dispute resolution is also important.

Despite the conflict resolution expertise on the continent however, 'Africa's past history and current news contain tragic reports of conflict - small and large scale, brief and protracted, detrimental and devastating. In spite of all the common-sensical and wise ways of preventing and resolving conflict, there always seem to be individuals and groups who wilfully remain unwilling to make use of them.'

A landmark report to the United Nations Security Council in 1997 by Secretary-General Kofi Annan, underlined the perception that the level of conflict, and their enduring nature, made Africa a major challenge to efforts to achieve global peace, prosperity and human rights.

More than thirty wars have been fought in Africa since 1970. Most of these have been intra-state in origin. In 1996, fourteen of the 53 countries of Africa were afflicted by armed conflicts. This accounted for more than half of all war-related deaths world wide. These conflicts produced eight million refugees, returnees and displaced persons. The continent's long-term stability has been undermined. Nonetheless, that is one side of a coin which features on its obverse, evidence of initiatives which have prevented the escalation of some of those conflicts - and prevented others from developing into full-blown crises.

As Annan told the council: 'Today in many parts of Africa, efforts to break with the patterns of the past are at last beginning to succeed.'

In other words, conflicts abound; so too cease-fires and agreements.

Transition

In places where potential and existing conflicts have been successfully defused, such success has almost been taken for granted. Nelson Mandela's departure from office in South Africa in 1999, and his replacement by Thabo Mbeki following general elections, seemed like 'normal' developments. But the transition that led to this phase of relative political stability has variously been termed a 'miracle' and 'negotiated revolution'.

'There was nothing inevitable about it - in fact, at various stages of this process, the prospects of peaceful progress or civil war were balanced on a knife-edge,' according to Peter Gastrow, Cape Town Director of the Institute for Security Studies, an independent applied policy research body.

Gastrow, writing in *People Building Peace*, a recent publication of the European Centre for Conflict Prevention[1], says the change resulted from 'a daring experiment in conflict resolution on a national scale'.

Nelson Mandela's release from prison in February 1990 came amid numbing political violence. Some 1,400 people had been killed the previous year. Mandela's release raised expectations. Violence continued: the death toll rose to 3,699 in 1990.

Eventually, realisation that it was in everybody's interest to end the violence - religious and business groups, political parties, the public at large - spurred the preparations that led to a National Peace Convention. Out of that process, the 'miracle' of political change occurred in 1994.

That convention was symbolically important. It brought leaders of warring political groups to the same table. A Peace Accord was signed providing for the establishment of a network of representative peace committees at national, regional, and local levels. That Accord developed a 'peace culture'.

Ideological commitment to the idea of 'political tolerance' was secured from the key political actors. Procedures and mechanisms for crisis management were established. The South African elite, as well as ordinary communities, played a role. So too did trade unions, churches, business and traditional leaders, and other civil society structures. By the time of the multi-party elections on April 26 1994, violence had subsided.

Gastrow, who played a key role in the peace promotion efforts, says though the country still has immense problems, the legacy of the momentum developed and sustained in the period between 1990 and 1994 is that it offered evidence that South Africans 'have it within themselves to pull together and overcome ... crises.'

Participation

Continent-wide, the Organization of African Unity (OAU), based in the Ethiopian capital, Addis Ababa, has been trying since the beginning of the nineties, to promote the idea of internally-generated initiatives. In 1990, the OAU agreed a Declaration 'to work together towards the peaceful and speedy resolution of all conflicts.' This was followed by agreement on a Mechanism for dealing with conflict - in all its stages, before emergence and after resolution.

'The Mechanism came into being as a truly indigenous initiative,' notes Malan. 'It endorses Africa's commitment to be the principal architect of its own destiny.'

That requires spreading the net of participation as wide as possible.

Explaining the involvement of business groups in South Africa's political transition, Theuns Eloff, Chief Executive of the National Business Initiative, makes the point that its command of resources and inherent ability to manage complex issues efficiently (logistics, management, organisation and information technology) made involvement of business crucial to South Africa's political transition from violence to peace, and from apartheid to democracy. That involvement began in the mid-eighties, with businessmen making secret trips overseas to meet leaders of the banned African National Congress (ANC).

Business groups became 'honest brokers' and 'shuttle diplomats', moving between different groups involved in conflict. They had an organisational role in the peace process. With political transition achieved, the business community is trying to get its teeth into measures aimed at achieving a successful socio-economic change and prevent South Africa from being 'catapulted back into conflict', says Eloff. Through the National Business Initiative (NBI) launched in March 1995 by Mandela, business groups have taken initiatives in areas such as education and training, local government capacity building, housing, and local economic development.

Early in 1999, a Business Trust was formed 'to accelerate the creation of jobs and the development of human capacity in South Africa, while building productive relationships between business and government, and demonstrating the commitment of business to South Africa's success.'

Through the Trust, senior business leaders and officials of the government plan to mobilise US$ 165 million over five years. Listed companies have been asked to contribute 0.15 per cent of market capitalisation and non-listed companies two percent of after-tax profits of one year. Tourism and education are the two specific areas chosen for focus. 'Business has a moral obligation to be a constructive and loyal part of civil society,' notes Eloff, 'as well as the broader national framework. This calls for partnerships with government. On the other hand, as business needs a stable environment in which to operate, it is clearly in its own long-term interest to ensure that this environment is created and/or maintained.'

Completing the coordinated series of actions - some merely symbolic, others quite concrete - which have sustained the country's emergence from apartheid, South Africa followed the examples of Chile, Argentina, Guatemala and El Salvador, and confronted its history. The mechanism used was called the Truth and Reconciliation Commission. Through its proceedings, torturer faced tortured. Political prisoner looked into the eye of jailor. Victims of police brutality eyeballed those who administered beatings.

Proceedings were held in an atmosphere of tension and generated some of its own. Yet the Commission serves a distinct purpose in societies emerging out of a period of protracted violence, according to Michelle Parlevliet, Program Manager of the Human Rights and Conflict Management Training Program at the Centre for Conflict Resolution in South Africa. In fact, writing in *People Building Peace,* Parlevliet says recognition is growing that redressing past violations can reassert the rule of law, create awareness of human rights, and legitimise structures of governance.

In the process, conditions in which serious crimes occurred could be altered. 'While the past cannot be undone, it may be possible to mitigate its negative impact on society,' notes Parlevliet. And the involvement of the public and civil society helps increase the democratic value of the truth-telling process. 'Non-governmental organisations often have a wealth of material on past human rights violations that will aid investigations by a commission,' observes Parlevliet.

'They can further be involved in collecting statements, providing information to the public, and supporting witnesses. The role of the media is also relevant in this regard, especially when the activities of a commission are conducted in public. Reporting can extend a commission's reach and accessibility considerably, yet if the media lack independence it may also undermine the truth telling process.' Truth commissions cannot in themselves institute change. But they can create an environment in which other measures are more likely to gain a foothold.

A sensitive issue

Ethnic conflicts still ravage the African continent. Rwanda has had its genocide; neighbouring Burundi is shadowed by the fear of being next. In 1993, conflict between Tutsis and Hutus left 50,000 dead. In previous decades, there had been hundreds of thousands of deaths, and many refugees, the result of clashes between the two groups.

NGO initiatives in Burundi are focused on prevention. Rwanda serves as the example. Thus radio is used to spread reconciliation rather than for the promotion of hatred and fear as happened in the neighbouring state. At Studio Ijambo, a radio outlet established in 1995 by Common Ground Productions - part of the Washington-based Search for Common Ground - reporter Adrian Sindayigaya says, 'the purpose ... is to try to be as objective as possible'.

Sindayigaya, a Hutu, is among thirty members of the multi-ethnic staff. Eight paired Hutu-Tutsi reporting teams gather material for three weekly news programs broadcast in French and Kirundi. 'Here in Burundi, telling lies has become widespread' says Agnes Nindorera, who form a reporting team with Sindayigaya. 'This is part of the reason for the current crisis. By informing people and by telling the truth, we are helping Burundi find a path towards peace - a peace in which people are led by the facts, and not by the lies of the politicians.'

Studio Ijambo, located in Bujumbura, the capital, was set up after extensive consultations involving NGOs and government counterparts. In addition to opening the radio production studio, Common Ground promoted a scheme involving women in a peace drive, and a forum for political dialogue.

Ethnic identification is a sensitive, emotional issue, and one that is easily manipulated, observes Sam Kobia, former General Secretary of the National Council of Churches of Kenya (NCCK). 'Ethnicity can become part of the transition phenomena when people do not know how to relate swiftly and correctly to rapid political change. In such times of uncertainty, it is easy to politicise ethnicity and build a support base from it.'

Perhaps as many as 300,000 people have been displaced due to ethnic violence in Kenya. The country has more than forty distinct ethnic groups. Dozens of languages are spoken. Its border lines, imposed by an outside colonial power, results in a central government asserting authority across ethnic divides. However, the NCCK believes much of the ethnic violence that has plagued Kenya in recent years has its roots in politics.

An umbrella organisation for Christian churches in Kenya, the NCCK has a long record of working to spur development at the economic and political as well as spiritual levels. Its Peace and Reconciliation Project, undertaken to help overcome the consequences of this ethnic conflict, has shifted focus from relief and rehabilitation to peace and reconciliation.

Area Peace and Rehabilitation Committees (APRCs) have been set up with members drawn from a cross section of local people, including representatives of the local leadership, churches, NGOs, young people, and women. In fact, the success of the program has been premised on the active participation of the local population.

Hundreds of Good Neighbourliness Seminars have been organised. These were opened to elders, local opinion leaders, politicians, educators, community workers, government workers, and members of other important groups and local level bodies. Discussion was encouraged on causes of local conflicts. Meetings were held exclusively for women to give them a chance to participate in ways that wouldn't have been possible in mixed seminars. Similar attention was given to the young. Participants were challenged to re-evaluate the values that resulted in them perceiving 'the other' as enemy, and encouraged not to allow others to manipulate them into acts of violence, but to channel their energies into more constructive activities. Out of those seminars, Village Peace Committees were established with members drawn from both the

'Involvement of an elder from a family, village or clan allows the disputants to move away from accusations and counter-accusations, to soothe hurt feelings and reach a compromise that may help improve future relationships.'

displaced persons and those who had remained in their villages.

Jannie Malan, head of Research at the African Centre for the Constructive Resolution of Disputes (ACCORD), says getting elders in particular to talk about conflict, marks the resolution of conflicts in Africa as part of a 'continuum of social life'. Involvement of an elder from a family, village or clan allows the disputants to move away from accusations and counter-accusations, to soothe hurt feelings and reach a compromise that may help improve future relationships.

Malan says promising signs have been identified, of 'local initiatives to cooperate in cross-stitching ways which ignore ethnicity', with several of these attributed to women.

Equitable sharing of limited resources

Many of the classic elements in which African conflicts are framed - ethnic differences, inadequate resources, arbitrarily set colonial borders - are present in Wajir, a huge barren region of Kenya close to the border of Ethiopia and Somalia. The Ogaden, Ajuran and Degodia clans occupy the area. They make a living from herding camels, sheep and goats. The region is neglected by central government. It lacks essential services. Drought is prevalent. Clashes between the clans over land encroachment and violation of political space was the order of the day. Until a successful peace initiative began in the early nineties.

A group of women suffering from violence fatigue formed the Wajir Peace Group. Reviving basic methods of conflict resolution used in pre-colonial times, the group encouraged the equitable sharing of the limited resources - one underlying basis for mistrust and violence. The community became involved. Young people. NGOs. Government departments. Students and elders. Christians and Muslims.

By the middle of the decade, a process of healing had led to the setting up of the Wajir Peace and Development Committee comprising members of parliament, religious leaders, businessmen, NGO workers, the security forces, women and clan elders. A Rapid Response Team was formed. It comprised community leaders - elders, religious leaders and security officers. Mandated to move into any part of the district to diffuse tension and mediate in case of conflict or violence, the body was a success, managing to tackle the roots of poverty. Drought data was collected and analysed. Food was distributed to the affected area.

'Drought is one of the major contributors to poverty, and poverty is also one of the contributors to the escalation of conflict to violence,' says Dekha Ibrahim Abdi, one of the founders of the Wajir Peace Group. 'Anticipating the drought and early intervention has saved lives and also livelihood of the people affected.'

That was among the critical areas identified by Annan in his Security Council speech. To consolidate peace and prevent recurrence of armed confrontation, he said, 'a multifaceted approach, covering diplomatic, political and economic factors, must be adopted.' That needs adequate finance.

What, indeed, is peace without economic well-being? In Somalia - one of the African nations stuck with the image of anarchy and destruction, often cited as an example of a 'failed state' - the Life & Peace Institute (LPI) has been trying to find the balance between the two elements. An international and ecumenical peace research institute, LPI has supported locally based peace processes in Somalia since 1992. Its primary approach to peace building has been to empower local actors.

'The approach starts at the community level, eventually aiming to lay the foundations for regional and national reconciliation,' says Susanne Thurfjell from that organisation. 'It is partly through the women on the ground that LPI fully came to realise the need for a more holistic approach to peace work. Peace is not an abstract but it has to make a difference in the lives of people. As one woman expressed it in a workshop: "We cannot just have peace, we also need life!" Peace has to take the form of a peaceful and non-violent society with respect for all people irrespective of age, sex, religion, ethnicity or clan belonging.'

Yet, these small victories in Somalia remain just that - examples of possibilities. Somalia still has no central government.

Flame of Peace

Mali in West Africa, one of the least developed and poorest countries in the world, had a central government that was considered by some to be far too powerful - and distant. The one-party rule of President Moussa Traoré (1968-1991) was particularly repressive and corrupt. Development was skewered in favour of the south. Northern Mali remained mired in a poverty. Long periods of drought made matters worse.

As early as the fifties, secessionist moves had been made by the Touaregs and Arabs who occupy the northern regions. In 1990, a rebellion was launched by Mali's northern peoples against what they said was 28 years of central government oppression.

The rebellion in the north coincided with protests in the capital Bamako itself, against Traoré's rule. A peace accord was signed with the rebels in 1991 and there were moves towards multi-party democracy. Still the violence continued. The Movement Populaire de Liberation de l'Azawad (MPLA) rebel group, already split into separate Touareg and Arab factions, was splintered even further. Anarchy and banditry prevailed in the north. Traore was eventually arrested, in 1991, and Mali shifted towards multi-party democracy.

A 'National Pact' signed in April 1992 gave the north a 'special status' and provided for demobilisation of armed rebels. Conditions improved for short periods, then deteriorated. People fled the continuing fighting and banditry, seeking refuge in neighbouring countries, or moving to the south.

A civilian administration headed by President Alpha Oumar Konaré brought hope, but not much change in the dismal economic picture. Fighting continued.

Into this already explosive mix an anti-banditry armed movement - Ganda Koy (Masters of the Land) was launched. The new government recognised it could not impose a military solution. Local and international actors worked with the warring parties, seeking ways of re-establishing the rule of law. Some measure of success was achieved only when a series of local level meetings, convened in 1994, followed the pattern already used to effect transition to democracy following the 1991 popular revolution.

In effect, the normal boundaries of the western democratic process were expanded. African tradition was invoked. Hundreds of meetings took place between 1994 and 1996, involving political parties, government, trade unions, religious groups, NGOs, local leaders, women's organisations, social groups, economic cooperatives and associations, and other institutional representatives of civil society.

For its part, the government promised to reform the military, and improve communication within the force and between it and civil society. Both security and development were considered crucial to achieve stability in the north: those involved in peacemaking efforts described this as 'security first'. This followed from the logic that the armed civilian population would only give up its weapons if they believed that the security forces were capable of defending their families.

'As a modern state, Mali needs to add to its ancestral heritage of dialogue, a modern institutional infrastructure which demonstrates there is a real democratic process taking place,' said President Alpha Oumar Konaré on 8th June 1994, as he launched the series of regional Concertations.

The Konaré administration offered to extend more power to local authorities in the north. Seven hundred locally elected 'communes' were established throughout Mali.

Robin-Edward Poulton, Senior Research

Fellow at the United Nations Institute for Disarmament Research, who has worked on conflict resolution for many years in West Africa, describes the Konaré approach as 'ambitious' and 'visionary'. Most African states will flourish in the 21st century 'only if they are able to reconcile the need for broader economic or monetary unions with the pressure from local groups to assume their cultural identities,' Poulton concludes. 'Decentralisation is the new framework which will make people responsible for their own lives, for mobilising national resources and using them locally for productive investment.'

On March 27, 1996, Konaré, Ghanaian President Jerry Rawlings (chairman of the ECOWAS at that time), leaders of the Mouvements et Fronts Unifiés de l'Azaouad (the MFUA, uniting the various rebel factions) and Ganda Koy, and a large delegation of international observers gathered in Timbuktu for the highly symbolic destruction of all collected weapons in what was called a 'Flame of Peace'.

The weapons were stacked into a giant pyramid, doused with fuel, and then ignited by the presidents of Mali and Ghana. The rival movements issued a joint declaration in which they affirmed the indivisibility of Mali, pledged their support to the Malian constitution, renounced the use of violence, exhorted their fellow African fighters across the continent to 'celebrate their own Flame of Peace', and finally, proclaimed the irrevocable dissolution of their respective organisations.

Lessons learned

Africa is vast and diverse. So too the conflict resolution challenges confronting it. These unfold against a varied geographical and historical background. 'The sources of conflict in Africa reflect this diversity and complexity,' notes Kofi Annan. 'Some sources are purely internal, some reflect the dynamics of a particular sub-region, and some have important international dimensions.'

Nonetheless, they have some common themes and experiences.

Territorial units carved out at the Congress of Berlin in 1885 resulted in newly independent nations inheriting new lands which defy any attempt at national unity. The difficult issues of governance this created, has been compounded by the tendency to over-centralise power.

'The nature of political power in many African States, together with the real and perceived consequences of capturing and maintaining power, is a key source of conflict across the continent,' Annan commented in his report to the UN Security Council. 'It is frequently the case that political victory assumes a 'winner-takes-all' form with respect to wealth and resources, patronage, and the prestige and prerogatives of office. A communal sense of advantage or disadvantage is often closely linked to this phenomenon, which is heightened in many cases by reliance on centralised and highly personalised forms of governance.'

At the grassroots level, questions have long been raised about the nature of the democratic systems fashioned since the colonial period. Such concerns are also echoed in the objectives set by the continental political body, the Organization of African Unity (OAU) -

encouragement of political reform, economic development and greater social opportunities for all within the broader set of goals of which negotiations form a part.

Professor Jannie Malan says in fact many time-proven methods of conflict resolution originated on African soil. Some of these are ancient. Others, more rooted in contemporary experiences and practices, have scored successes.

'After its long and eventful history Africa can indeed make most significant contributions to the field of conflict resolution,' writes Malan in the ACCORD publication *Conflict Resolution Wisdom from Africa*. 'The conflict resolution expertise that has developed in Africa incorporates insights and skills acquired during the years of traditional leadership, colonial rule, and new independence.'

Indeed, the nineties have seen a range of the kinds of initiatives which point to a future for the continent marked as much by attempts at reconciliation as the explosive conflicts that have tarnished its image and reputation.

*   **Fitzroy Nation is a former editor of the Third World press agency IPS and is currently working as a freelance journalist, based in the Netherlands**

1   People Building Peace - 35 Inspiring Stories from Around the World. A publication of the European Centre for Conflict Prevention in cooperation with IFOR and the Coexistence Initiative of State of the World Forum. Utrecht/the Netherlands, May 1999.

In short - 16 lessons learned

In People Building Peace - a recent publication of the European Centre for Conflict Prevention - 35 stories of successful peace-building from around the world are described and analysed. Out of this, a list of sixteen lessons learned resulted. Here they are, in summary.*

1. Involve as many people and sectors as possible in peace building

It is an obvious point but one which is, nevertheless, frequently overlooked: it is essential that as many sectors of society as possible be included in any peace-building process.

2. Strengthen local capacities for peace

If efforts to prevent, resolve and transform violent conflict are to be effective in the long-term, they must be based on the active participation of local civil groups committed to building peace. Strengthening such 'local capacities for peace' may take many forms, including education and training, nurturing the volunteer spirit in society and highlighting the work of local peacemakers in the media. Granting basic human rights such as freedom of speech and press and freedom to organise oneself are prerequisites for including the different civil organisations in the peace process.

3. Conceive peace building and reconciliation as a process

Peace is not an abstract goal but a process. It must be built-up over a long period of time. Building peace must be an organic process, growing at all levels of society. Peace cannot be built just through exclusive conclaves of the leaders of the conflicting parties. The idea of 'historic agreements as a stepping stone to peace' has proven to be wrong on too many occasions. Long-term strategic relationships should be built which reach across the dividing lines of conflict in society.

4. Change and transform the conflict pattern: create hope

A common feature of many stories of successful peace building is that they succeeded in breaking the logic of war. Successful initiatives create hope and stimulate people to disengage themselves from war. By inspiring others these initiatives have an extremely important spin-off effect.

5. Create dialogue

Stimulate a feeling of interdependence, emphasise common identities and help people to understand the other side's position. Private peace making should focus on 'humanising the enemy'. The most effective dialogue often occurs when each side forcefully advocates its position and then listens to its opponent. It should be recognised that people can communicate with each other, but may not be ready for a dialogue. Much creativity is needed to bring the parties together for a first round of talks.

6. Promote education and enhance professionalisation

Educational programmes should stimulate the universal awareness of coexistence, tolerance and reconciliation. Those involved in the peace-building process must be thoroughly prepared and trained. Professionalisation of peace building can enhance its effectiveness.

7. Exchange experiences

Promote international exchanges between peacemakers from conflict regions. Learning from each other's experiences inspires innovative approaches.

8. Include local authorities

The decentralised approach of grassroots and community-based organisations has resulted in many successes.

9. Strengthen coalition building between civil organisations

The effectiveness of civil activity is often hampered by a lack of co-ordination between groups operating in similar fields. As a result, scarce resources are wasted through duplication of tasks and failure to achieve synergy. There is a great need to create civil networks and/or platforms that promote coalition- and constituency-building.

10. Institution building

To sustain peace building and reconciliation, institution building should be stimulated at all levels of society and at the international level.

11. Make 'Conflict Impact Assessment' a requirement

In order to maximise the benefits of development aid, dispensing bodies - governmental, inter-governmental and private- should be required to assess and report on the likely impact of their developmentaid policies in terms of whether they will heighten or reduce the risks of violent conflicts.

12. Role of the corporate sector

The potential role of the corporate sector in peace building is still not widely recognised. However, just as business can exacerbate tensions and fuel conflict, so it can contribute to building peace and security.

13. Role of donors

The role of donors can extend beyond the simple provision of financial support for projects. Donors can provide an extra impulse in the peace-building process by stimulating conferences, agenda setting, and developing directories.

14. Prioritise Early Warning and Early Response

That prevention is better than cure is a truth which needs to be better observed in practice. Civil organisations, governments and inter-governmental bodies should dedicate much more attention and resources to prevention, as opposed to reacting to violent conflict. In particular, this should include generating the political will needed for early responses to potential conflict situations both present and future.

15. Promote an integrative approach to peace building and reconciliation by using a combination of approaches

The construction of a stable peace in the northern part of Mali was not the result of any single action. It followed from a complex of efforts to rebuild trust, to address legitimate grievances, to reward combatants who chose to give up the fight, and to build incentives into the peace process that would assure the continued commitment of people on both sides of the conflict.

An integrated framework towards peace building should include
- a coherent and comprehensive approach by all actors;
- partnerships between, and the coordination of, the various members of the international community and the national government;
- a broad consensus on a strategy and related set of interventions;
- careful balancing of macroeconomic and political objectives, and
- the necessary financial resources.

16. Mainstream multi-track diplomacy

Peace processes should combine official as well as non-official approaches. Official diplomacy is usually most effective when it is linked to official processes and channels. For this, contacts as well as the exchange of information and experiences between both approaches should be frequent and structural.

---

*   This 16-point list is also based on an outline of guidelines and principles from the Institute for Multi-Track Diplomacy, as well as the 'Agenda for Peace and Justice for the 21st century' of the Hague Appeal for Peace and the Strategic Plan developed by the Coexistence Initiative of State of the World Forum.

Analysing Conflicts

Africa faces the monumental challenge of attempting to hold in check the forces that are wreaking havoc on the continent. Effective conflict analysis is one small step towards an Africa which can live up to its full potential of peace and prosperity[1] ◆ By Hussein Solomon*

Future historians will certainly view the twentieth century as one of the bloodiest in the record of humanity's struggle against its more primordial instincts. From the bloody plains of Armenia to the trench warfare of World War I, the gas chambers of Auschwitz and Dachau, the killing-fields of East Timor, Cambodia and Sudan and now Angola and Yugoslavia, the twentieth century has seen mans' inhumanity to man descend to new depths of depravity. In total some 160 million people lost their lives as a result of war, genocide and state killings[2]. In 1996 alone, Rupesinghe and Anderlini[3] note that nineteen major internal conflicts were being fought world-wide, with a further 42 lower-intensity and 74 lethal violent political conflicts.

Africa contributed more than its fair share to this century's warfare. Of the 48 genocides and 'politicides' registered throughout the world between 1945 and 1995, twenty took place in Africa. In the same period, an estimated eight million people were killed in Africa as a direct result of war[4].

These horrendous statistics reveal the challenge we all face: to effectively analyse violent conflicts or potential violent conflicts with a view to channelling them along more non-violent trajectories. To borrow a phrase from Kumar Rupesinghe, the goal of such conflict analysis is not conflict termination but conflict transformation. The reason for this is that conflict is an integral part of human relations and cannot be entirely eliminated. Indeed, under certain circumstances conflict can be a positive force. The purpose of such conflict analysis, then, is to aid in the ending of the violent expression of conflict and to have it re-channelled through such institutional arrangements as regular elections or procedures at the International Court of Justice in The Hague.

The purpose of this chapter is to provide a brief overview of steps towards effective conflict analysis. I will explain some aspects of the methodology employed by ACCORD's Early Warning System in its analysis of conflicts and potential conflicts.

Caveat

Our discussion of conflict analysis needs to be preceded with a caveat. There is a tendency to reduce complex social and political analysis into CNN-style 'sound-bites' - into easily consumable stereotypical phrases. Two such examples illustrate the point.

First, amongst academics and policy-makers there is a growing tendency to view inter-state conflicts as being replaced by intra-state conflicts. On closer inspection, however one finds that such a dichotomy is false; that historically there has been a strong interaction between these two forms of conflict and that this interaction continues today. Surveying the current state of Africa it is clear that several rebel movements - be they Jonas Savimbi's UNITA in Angola or Joseph Kony's Lord's Resistance Army in Uganda - would cease to exist in the absence of external support.

Second, there is a tendency in certain circles in Washington and in certain other Western capitals to equate 'Islamic fundamentalism' with terrorism. When African governments internalise these positions the consequences are disastrous. This sort of 'pseudo-analysis' does not deepen our understanding of why 'Islamic fundamentalist' Sudan would support the efforts of the 'Christian fundamentalist' Lord's Resistance Army to topple the secular government of Uganda's Yoweri Museveni. Equating 'Islamic fundamentalism' with terrorism effectively problematises over one billion of the world's Muslims and could in the long-term result in a self-fulfilling prophecy. Commenting on this, Rupesinghe and Anderlini[6] note that 'Islamic fundamentalism':

'... is a popular reaction to western cultural domination and the West's support of often corrupt regimes. It is also a reaction to the increasing disparity between the rich and the poor in these areas. In Bosnia, the emergence of extremist Islamic groups is, in part, a consequence of the Muslim population's anger at what they perceived as western indifference to their plight. For the Chechens, on the other hand, the promotion of Islam as part of a new national identity is a means of distancing themselves from their former Russian rulers ... Care must be taken, however, not to oversimplify the issues through injudicious stereotyping.... The Islamic world is made up of a patchwork of nations, cultures, languages and histories. The danger is that by focussing on Islam itself, rather than on its politicisation by governments (and groups) this perceived threat could become a self-fulfilling prophecy'.

Many other cases can be used to illustrate what's at issue here, but I believe that the point has been made: over-simplistic analysis and injudicious stereotyping needs to be avoided in any conflict analysis.

The art of conflict analyses

A concomitant of the above point is the fact that we need to accept that the emergence of violent conflict is often the result of complex processes, often with deep historical roots. Following Barry Buzan's typology, ACCORD's Early Warning System views conflict as the result of five sources of insecurity: political, economic, military, environmental and socio-cultural variables.

Often in our analysis we are prone to emphasise the political and military dimensions of a conflict at the expense of other variables which are often more deep-seated and drive violent conflicts more directly. According to Stanley Samarasinghe[7] a functional correlation exists between poverty and conflict. Consider in this regard the following statistics:

- In the past fifteen years, about fifteen of the world's twenty poorest countries have experienced violent conflict.

'Preventive diplomacy has focused on short-term cessation of hostilities between parties for too long.'

- About half of the world's low income countries are either engaged in conflict or are in the process of transition from conflict.
- Almost every low income country shares at least one border with a country in conflict if it is not embroiled in its own conflict.
- In the 1990s about seventy million of the world's poor have been displaced from their homes as a result of conflict. In Africa, alone, about one-third of the countries have produced refugees.

Supporting this view and relating poverty to the occurrence of the 1994 genocide in Rwanda, Rupesinghe and Anderlini[8] note that the poor Central African country was faced with a rapidly increasing population and decreasing agricultural productivity. The situation was exacerbated by a drop in tea and coffee prices in the late 1980s and structural adjustment policies in 1990 leading to even harsher living conditions. These developments eroded the government's legitimacy in the eyes of the people. Although these factors in themselves did not create sufficient conditions for the outbreak of civil war or the genocide of 1994, the authors point out that they were instrumental within the wider context. They contributed to the build-up of tensions in a country with a history of social and ethnic divisions and violence.

In addition to identifying a set of causes for violent conflict, good conflict analysis is boosted by applying a time frame to the course of the conflict. According to Stanley Samarasinghe[9], any violent conflict has five basic phases. He distinguishes the Pre-Conflict Phase; the Conflict Emergence Phase; the Conflict and Crisis Phase, which is characterised by chaos and complex emergencies; the Conflict Settlement Phase; and the Post-Conflict Phase.

A question that might be asked at this point is what factors need to be taken into account when demarcating a particular conflict into phases or plotting the crisis life-cycle on a graph. In the search for an answer to the question as to how one can distinguish between different conflict phases, we can again resort to Rupesinghe and Anderlini[10], who identified the following determining factors in making a gradation of conflicts:

Table 1: Factors Affecting the Gradation of Conflict

- The intensity of grievances
- Parties' awareness of differences and separate identities
- Parties' perception and attitude towards each other
- Level of political mobilisation and organisation behind parties
- Extent of polarisation
- Amount of hostile behaviour
- Extent that parties use or threaten the use of arms
- Number of issues in dispute
- Number of parties supportive of each side
- Intensity of emotion and level of psychological investment in parties' positions and views of the world
- Amount of direct interaction and communication the parties have with one another
- Cohesion between leaders of respective parties and their constituencies

To this categorisation, I would like to add:
- The ability of existing institutions *in the society* to effectively redress the grievances of the parties and effectively resolve the conflict.

Two relevant phases

For the purposes of conflict analysis, the first two phases as listed by Samarasinghe are most relevant. The pre-conflict phase, according to Samarasinghe[11], represents conditions that are normal to the society concerned. At this stage, he says, disputes between groups do not result in violence. Samarasinghe: 'If the country has democratic institutions such as a freely elected legislature with minority representation and a free media, protest will be channelled peacefully through such institutional channels.'

In the conflict-emergence phase disputes become more evident and protesting groups more vocal and militant. Protest can take many forms, including boycotts, strikes, and mass demonstrations. The degree of violence that such protest entails, according to Samarasinghe's scheme, would depend on the specific conditions that prevail in the country. If the country has a democratic tradition less violence can be anticipated. If the political conditions are more authoritarian a higher level of violence can be anticipated. This phase distinguishes itself from the conflict and crisis phase in that violence, should it occur in this phase, is sporadic and random rather than organised and regular.

From analysis to action

It is during this second phase too that an effective Early Warning System should start monitoring the situation. Early warning, in my view, is concerned with forecasting the potential for violent conflict and framing an appropriate response that seeks not only to resolve the current conflict but also to create conditions that would result in sustainable peace. I think that preventive diplomacy has focused on short-term cessation of hostilities between parties for too long. As a result, the international community is often surprised when hostilities flare up again. The various attempts at peace in Angola are possibly the archetypal example of this phenomenon on the African continent. Addressing the root causes of a conflict is necessarily a longer-term project but its contribution towards sustainable peace can be more significant.

For an Early Warning System to be effective, it needs to be practicable. Despite alluding to the fact that Buzan's five sources of insecurity seen in a historical context are essential in understanding the origins and nature of violent conflicts, this is too broad to measure in an Early Warning System. Thus this categorisation needs to be subdivided and criteria to be measured need to be established. Once again Rupesinghe and Anderlini[12] provide us with some of the indicators which can be practically measured. Their indicators, which are captured in Table 2,

Table 2: Possible Indicators for Early Warning

Political and Leadership Issues	Criteria to be Measured
Regime capacity	Duration, democracy/autocracy, revenue as share of gross domestic product
Characteristics of the elite	Ethnic and religious base, revolutionary leadership, exclusionary ideology
Political and economic cleavages	Extent and degree of group discrimination, group separation, income inequality
Conflictual political cultures	Revolution or ethnic war/ genocide/ politicide, low level conflict in past 15 years
International influence	Military intervention, shifts in interstate conflict/ cooperation instability/ conflict in neighbouring countries
Economic and Environmental Issues	Level of pollution, impact on indigenous livelihood
Demographic and Societal Issues	
Population pressure	Density, total change in five years, youth bulge, cropland and labour force in agriculture
Ethno-linguistic diversity	Diversity, history of suppression
Militarisation of society	Military expenditure, five-year change in arms import, military vs medical personnel
Economic strength	Level and change in per capita income and consumption
Quality of life	Access to safe drinking water, food supplies, infant mortality
Constraints on resource base	Water depletion, soil degradation, famine
Government's economic management	Change in revenue and public sector debt, level of inflation, capital outflows, government reserves
Economic openness and trade	Import + export/GDP, direct foreign investment
International economic aid	Existence of IMF stand-by loan, other external aid

vary from a regime's capacity to effectively run a country and its economy, the specific characteristics of the ruling elite, to the level of economic openness and international aid.

Whilst such a list is not exhaustive, it does provide us with some idea of the kind of criteria which need to be measured in a given conflict situation. It is important to recognise that the criteria used will determine the kind of interpretation or analysis that results from the process. This, in turn, would determine the kind of conflict resolution tools one will employ in a given situation, be it informal consultation, civilian fact-finding missions, arms embargoes and other punitive sanctions, or military confidence-building measures. Conflict analysis and early warning, it should be noted, are tools for action aimed at the immediate cessation of hostilities between parties as well as creating conditions of a sustainable peace.

* Hussein Solomon is currently Research Manager at the African Centre for the Constructive Resolution of Disputes (ACCORD). In this capacity his primary responsibility is to manage ACCORD's Early Warning System and generate Early Warning Reports. Previously he was Senior Researher at the Institute for Security Studies and Research Fellow at the Centre for Southern African Studies.

1   A more extended version of this article was presented as a paper to the Workshop on Advanced Negotiation, Mediation and Facilitation Skills. Organised by the OAU, ACCORD and CMG. 24 May 1999.

2   Newsweek International, December 7, 1998.

3   K. Rupesinghe and S.N. Anderlini (1998). Civil Wars, Civil Peace: An Introduction to Conflict Resolution. London. Pluto Press, p. 2.

4   L. Reychler (1997). 'Conflicts in Africa - the issues of control and prevention', in Report of the Commission on African Regions in Crisis, Conflicts in Africa: An Analysis of Crises and Crisis Prevention Measures. Brussels. European Institute for Research and Information on Peace and Security, p. 17.

5   Rupesinghe and Anderlini, op.cit., pp. 10-11.

6   B. Buzan (1991). People, States and Fear: An Agenda for International Security Studies in the Post-Cold War Era. New York. Harvester-Wheatsheaf.

7   S.W. Samarasinghe (ed). Conflict Management Throughout the Crisis Life Cycle. Mimeo, p. 2.

8   Rupesinghe and Anderlini, op.cit., p. 12.

9   Samarasinghe, op.cit., p. 1.

10   Rupesinghe and Anderlini, op.cit., p. 67.

11   Samarasinghe, op.cit., p. 1

12   Rupesinghe and Anderlini, op.cit., p. 77.

A More Strategic Partnership for Preventing and Resolving Conflict

With the end of the Cold War, the United Nations and regional organisations were called upon to assume greater responsibility for conflict resolution and prevention than ever before. But due to the changing nature of conflict which was now mostly *within* states, a significant problem was posed for inter-governmental organisations which were designed to manage disputes *between* states and whose charters specifically prohibited them from 'interfering in the internal affairs' of their members. This new situation meant that the UN and regional organisations had to reconsider how to meet this new challenge. It also led to ongoing debate about which kind of organisation is best-placed to carry out conflict prevention and resolution - the UN, regional or sub-regional organisations or NGOs. An either-or approach, however, is not very helpful. What is needed is careful consideration of the comparative advantage of each and how they could work together more effectively to achieve a more strategic partnership. A brief review of the advantages and disadvantages should help to illustrate this point ◆ *By* **Connie Peck***

The United Nations

As the only global inter-governmental organisation whose function is the peaceful settlement of disputes, the UN has a number of potential advantages. One is that all of its members have agreed to resolve their disputes peacefully, to respect human rights, to work for social and economic justice, to practice tolerance, and to live together in peace. Because some regions do not have regional organisations, and because a number of states that are UN member do not belong to any regional organisation, the coverage of the UN is greater than that of regional organisations.

A second advantage is that the UN provides the most comprehensive dispute settlement system available, with a full range of organs (the Secretary-General, the International Court of Justice and the Security Council) and a wide array of methods (from good offices through peace keeping and peace enforcement). This system embodies three distinct approaches to dispute settlement - an interest-based approach; a rights-based approach; and a power-based approach, with each corresponding roughly to the organs of the United Nations - good offices of the Secretary-General and his Special

Representatives representing the organisation's interest-based approach; the International Court of Justice and the UN human rights machinery representing its rights-based approach; and the Security Council and its potential responses under Chapter VII representing its power-based approach.

The power-based instruments, however, are sometimes a double-edge sword. In some cases, they encourage members to abide by their obligation to resolve their disputes peacefully, but in others, they may actually discourage states from availing themselves of other parts of the system. For example, members may not use the Secretary-General's good offices because they are worried that the Security Council might become involved. However, it is not only the Security Council's power-based instruments which are of concern, but also the Council's Great Power privileges (e.g., permanent membership and the veto) and perceived lack of adequate representation. Some member states also feel that the Security Council acts inconsistently and in the self-interest of its permanent members.

Another factor is that the basic medium of discourse and action within the UN system is that of governments. The advantage is that the various activities of the United Nations constantly put pressure on governments to conform to international norms. But because governments have bilateral and multilateral relationships outside the UN system, they also bring political baggage to their interactions within the UN, which can lead to political trade-offs against principles of the Charter, and to inconsistent decision-making, motivated by national or coalitional interests rather than 'the greater good'.

Another drawback is that the UN remains largely focused on crisis management rather than on conflict prevention. Although it has improved its collection and analysis of information about potential problems, there is still no effective mechanism for early assistance in conflict prevention. The number of Special and Personal Representatives and Envoys of the Secretary-General has increased in recent years, but most are still engaged after a conflict has erupted (i.e., to carry out peace making and peace keeping) rather than for conflict prevention.

In spite of these problems, the UN has more institutional experience than any other organisation in attempting to prevent and resolve conflict. Its human and financial resources, although small in relation to its enormous mandate, are considerably greater than those of regional or non-governmental organisations. In theory, however, the UN should be able to develop a more proactive, quiet approach to conflict prevention, which could gradually win the confidence of its members.

Regional organisations

Chapter VIII of the UN Charter not only includes regional organisations and arrangements as part of the UN system, but also explicitly encourages their development in furthering the aims of the Charter. Like the UN, however, regional organisations have advantages and disadvantages. One advantage is that they are likely to be familiar with the actors in a dispute, as well as with the situation on the ground and how it is developing. Proximity itself can make a situation more salient. Neighbours are likely to take a greater interest in conflict prevention in an adjacent state if they fear that

'Increasing resources for conflict prevention and shifting the focus to a more preventive, assistance approach could go a long way to helping member states of the UN and regional organisations work more effectively to ameliorate the many existing and potential conflicts besetting all regions of the world.'

fighting could spread or result in uncontrolled flows of arms or refugees through their territory. On the other hand, neighbours sometimes have a vested interest in a dispute, such as when members of an aggrieved group in a neighbouring state are ethnic 'kin'.

In terms of long-term conflict prevention and resolution, regional organisations can apply even more pressure than the United Nations because of the importance of regional relationships. Regional politics, however, sometimes play a less-helpful role. Regional cleavages can cause some governments to favour one side while other governments favour the other side, which can widen a dispute. Regional hegemonies can also use their weight to unduly influence decision-making within the organisation. Of course, similarity of norms and values among states in a region and a low level of conflict within a regional organisation may promote consensus and overcome such problems. However, regional norms and values can sometimes evolve in a manner that deviates from universal norms. In certain instances, for example, a majority of governments might agree to condone or overlook certain abuses by a member state in the interests of regional harmony.

Finally, most regional organisations have even more meagre human and financial resources than the UN, which necessarily limits their reach and effectiveness.

The two regional organisations which have been working the hardest on developing a capacity in conflict prevention are the OAU and the OSCE. Since the OAU Mechanism on Conflict Prevention, Management and Resolution will be dealt with elsewhere in this book, the section below will briefly review the approach taken by the OSCE High Commissioner on National Minorities, since this represents the most developed regional mechanism for preventive diplomacy to date.

The High Commissioner offers assistance to OSCE participating states in preventing conflict based on minority issues. Using a proactive, quiet approach, he visits countries where he has concerns, and through discussions with all concerned, seeks to understand the basis for minority grievances, and then to offer specific recommendations to governments for changes to legislation, regulation or practice, which can effectively address these grievances. He also provides advice on how to reduce tension and carry out structural reform, including how to establish an ongoing process of dialogue within societies, through the creation of mechanisms, such as ombudsmen, special offices for minority questions, and national commissions on ethnic and language questions.

The High Commissioner's informal, quiet approach, which typically does not involve either 'early warning' or formal mediation, overcomes the traditional opposition of governments to preventive diplomacy within states, since it avoids 'internationalising' the problem and bypasses governments' concern over recognising and legitimising leaders of disaffected minority movements. As the government is never required to sit down at the table with the leaders of these groups, it does not have to formally recognise them. It is simply asked to listen to and consider seriously the suggestions of the High Commissioner. In most of the cases he has dealt with, governments *have* listened to his advice and implemented the necessary reforms to ameliorate ethnic tensions, thus avoiding violent conflict. The High Commissioner has operated since 1992 and his success demonstrates that *even having one person of*

knowledge, stature and skill, carrying out preventive diplomacy on a daily basis can be cost-effective. Moreover, the world's most active preventive diplomacy mechanism operates with a staff of only seven advisers and a budget of just over one million dollars. Certainly, this model demonstrates that preventive diplomacy is possible and suggests that the UN or other regional organisations might consider how they could adopt such a mechanism to their own needs.

Non-Governmental Organisations

Conflict resolution NGOs tend to be less constrained than Inter-Governmental Organisations (IGOs) in being able to relate freely to the non-governmental parties involved in a dispute (although governments sometimes discourage such dialogue). They sometimes, however, also operate at the official level as third party intermediaries, as Sant' Egidio did in Mozambique, and as the FAFO Institute for Applied Social Science did with the Oslo Peace Process. Other NGOs work at the level of Track Two Diplomacy, bringing together, in an unofficial capacity, influential members of the policy-making community or those who have other forms of access to decision-makers for 'problem-solving workshops'. A limited number of NGOs, such as The Carter Center and its International Negotiation Network, are also working in the realm of 'Track One and a Half', finding a path between official and unofficial approaches.

With their work in the field, many NGOs (including churches and women's groups) have the ability to bring about conflict resolution and reconciliation at the community level, as various organisations are currently attempting to do in South Africa. NGOs and scholarly institutions within civil society have also been actively studying and disseminating knowledge about conflict prevention and resolution, helping IGOs develop their capacity and even evaluating IGO action and proposing reform.

Another advantage of NGOs is that they can take many forms and play many roles. Their multidimensional character and flexibility allow them to highlight specific problems and work on issues in ways that IGOs usually cannot. Local

NGOs and those that work extensively in the field are often more aware than IGOs of the root causes of problems. In some cases, however, they do not have the same face validity with governments as IGOs and the lack of accreditation for NGOs and the possibility of their acting inappropriately remain as problems. Finally, NGOs are often even more resource-poor than the UN or regional organisations and are usually dependent entirely on voluntary contributions, making their staying power more tenuous.

Complementarity of the three models

Given the respective advantages and disadvantages described above, the potential exists for the formation of a more strategic coalition of actors, whose work could complement and augment one another. Indeed, cooperation between the UN, regional organisations and NGOs has begun to increase. A number of cooperative agreements have been signed between the UN and regional organisations and three meetings have taken place over the last five years between the Secretaries-General of the UN and regional organisations (followed recently by one meeting at the middle level) from which recommendations for greater cooperation have emerged. In some cases, UN staff members already regularly attend important meetings of regional organisations and vice versa.

The UN and some regional organisations have also agreed upon a division of responsibility, with one organisation taking the lead in some instances and the other in other cases. In a few situations, the UN and regional organisations have organised joint peace missions or jointly appointed Special Representatives. Recently, a senior UN political officer was posted to Addis to coordinate with OAU Headquarters to ensure greater communication.

In 1998, a meeting hosted by the Canadian Department of Foreign Affairs and Trade and the Canadian International Development Center and coorganised by UNITAR, the Carnegie Commission for Preventing Deadly Conflict and the International Peace Academy (IPA) brought together *for the first time* those working in conflict

'In spite of some promising developments, many problems still exist between the UN, regional organisations and NGOs and, all too often, these organisations still do not coordinate properly, occasionally even appearing to actively obstruct one another.'

prevention from the UN, regional organisations, and NGOs to share their developing ideas and to discuss obstacles and outcomes. A Visiting Fellowship Programme is now being planned to allow those working in conflict prevention to visit one another's institutions to promote mutual learning about different approaches.

The International Peace Academy, through its Vienna and New York Seminars, and UNITAR and IPA jointly, through their Fellowship Programme in Peacemaking and Preventive Diplomacy and UNITAR's Senior Seminar in Peacemaking and Preventive Diplomacy, bring together UN staff, personnel from regional organisations and conflict resolution NGOs and scholars to develop and refine the practice of conflict prevention and resolution.

Also, over the past few years, several NGOs have played an important role as consultants to regional organisations. The International Peace Academy has, for example, played a major part in helping the OAU develop its Mechanism for Conflict Prevention, Management and Resolution by hosting a number of strategic meetings to stimulate creative thinking and policy development within the OAU. The Council for Security Cooperation in the Asian-Pacific Region (a coalition of academic institutions) has been working closely with ASEAN, to assist in policy development for the ASEAN Regional Forum, including its approach to conflict prevention.

However, in spite of these promising

developments, many problems still exist between the UN, regional organisations and NGOs and, all too often, these organisations still do not coordinate properly, occasionally even appearing to actively obstruct one another. A problem of *diffusion of responsibility* also sometimes occurs, when the UN Security Council believes a situation should be handled by the regional organisation and the regional organisation abdicates responsibility to the UN. Other times, two or more actors become involved in an uncoordinated manner and work at cross-purposes. Equally problematic are bureaucratic jealousies and inter-institutional rivalries, which can plague efforts at coordination, exacerbate problems and waste time.

Providing more effective regional assistance

Potentially, all three kinds of organisations could be substantially developed in terms of conflict prevention and a much more coordinated approach adopted. Ideally, the advantages and disadvantages of each should be carefully considered in every situation and organisations should work cooperatively, delineating how tasks should be divided, and how work should be integrated. Such a multilayered approach will require careful coordination, which would be facilitated by proximity.

One way to expand and build on the emerging efforts would be for regional organisations and the UN to join together in a closer partnership to provide assistance in conflict prevention at a regional level, in cooperation with local and international conflict resolution NGOs. Elsewhere (in my book *Sustainable Peace: The Role of the UN and Regional Organisations in Preventing Conflict*), I have provided a detailed discussion on how UN Regional Centres for Sustainable Peace could be established (as an extension of the Department of Political Affairs to the regional level) to provide a conflict prevention mechanism that would build a strategic partnership to provide assistance in dispute resolution and good governance aimed at preventing conflict.

Such Centres would need small teams of expert staff to provide full-time quiet assistance

in conflict prevention and good governance to those wishing to avail themselves of it - following the example set by the OSCE High Commissioner and the OSCE Office for Human Rights and Democratic Institutions.

Expert knowledge and skill would be *fundamental* to the work of these programs. Senior staff, with specialist knowledge and experience in dispute settlement and governance, would be required, along with regional or country experts, who are well-versed in the cultural, historical and political perspectives of actors in the region.

Regional Centres would also maintain close cooperation with the relevant regional or sub-regional organisation. Working together would allow both organisations to pool their expertise, use their comparative advantages and be better informed about individual situations, as well as about the overall causes of conflict within a region. A joint approach would also provide an opportunity to share responsibility and truly coordinate activities.

Further, UN Centres could liaise closely with conflict resolution and governance NGOs, as well as with research institutions and think tanks in the region, to extend their knowledge-base and reach into all levels of civil society. This would ensure that learning proceeds in both directions - i.e., bottom-up as well as top-down - so that the constructive ideas of those at all levels are heard and incorporated into solutions which are acceptable and well-tailored to local concerns, culture and circumstances. Equally important would be the *horizontal transfer of knowledge and experience within each region*. Those within the region who have found solutions to their local problems or have developed relatively successful models for good governance could be tapped to assist others in this endeavour.

NGOs with appropriate expertise in conflict resolution could help to provide assistance in dispute resolution at the community level - training local actors in problem solving and establishing local fora for dialogue. NGOs and other civil society groups could keep the Centres informed of local issues which might need other kinds of attention.

High profile individuals with the necessary status and political expertise could be used to extend the Centres' influence upward into the highest levels of government by convening meetings between decision-makers and regional and international scholars to identify and analyse emerging or existing regional or sub-regional problems, and to consider a range of possible solutions. Such individuals could also work quietly, behind-the-scenes, with government leaders, to urge them to move in the direction of addressing minority concerns and providing good governance.

Strategic cooperation between the UN, regional and sub-regional organisations and NGOs could also be expected to have a synergetic effect. Increasing resources for conflict prevention and shifting the focus to a more preventive, assistance approach could go a long way to helping member states of the UN and regional organisations work more effectively to ameliorate the many existing and potential conflicts besetting all regions of the world.

*   **Dr. Connie Peck is the Senior Coordinator of the Programme on Peacemaking and Preventive Diplomacy at the United Nations Institute for Training and Research where she organises advanced training programmes and seminars on topics related to conflict prevention and resolution for middle and senior level UN staff, diplomats, and staff from regional organisations. She is the author of eight books and numerous journal articles. Her most recent book, Sustainable Peace: The Role of the UN and Regional Organisations in Preventing Conflicts, elaborates further on the ideas outlined in this section.**

Africanets: No Boundaries

Networks of conflict prevention organisations have cast a blanket of peace building across Africa. In the process, civil society on the continent is developing less of a narrow national focus, and becoming more sub-regional, regional, and even Pan-African in character and outlook ◆ *By* **Fitzroy Nation**

Participating in a network not only increases the efficiency of the member organisations' efforts, it also makes the individual organisations more sensitive to the scope of the problems and solutions they are working on. Experience has shown that the staff of NGOs that are engaged in a network feel encouraged to gain a better overview of the problem area and also pay more attention to what other organisations are doing. This enhances continual reflection on their own organisation's performance and mandate. It makes people more aware of both the strengths and the limitations of their own organisation. Membership of a network has often given rise to beneficial internal organisational changes that might not have been considered were it not for the link to a network.

There are, of course, also disadvantages and pitfalls. Closer ties among NGOs can intensify rivalry and competition in fund-raising. Networks sometimes tend to keep looking for more partners, which may undermine their existence. History has shown that big networks have short life spans, because as the number of partners grows, mutual dependence and cohesion wither.

Nevertheless, networks have sprung up in such large numbers over the last decade - and Africa is no exception here - that they now have gained recognition as a separate category of activity, alongside NGOs, multilateral organisations and governmental actors.

One reason for the rapid growth of networks is the growing awareness that conflicts do not respect physical borders. Frequently two countries, and on occasions a whole group of countries, get sucked in. That recommends a greater bonding of organisations, and the sharing of common experiences. The wide availability and relative ease of use of communications technologies is also a spur.

With a computer, email and modem even small NGOs operating on a shoestring budget, can acquire a higher profile than previously - and become more effective by linking with counterparts.

Information and experiences can be exchanged. Minutes of meetings and research reports downloaded with relative ease. Email messages criss-cross borders without danger of Big Brother style monitoring by hostile governments. Workshops can be organised. Joint programs planned.

Sometimes these networks are highly formalised. The trend has both South-South and North-South elements. In other instances, they function merely as a kind of virtual community, the high-tech age equivalent of regular gatherings around a cup of coffee or tea to share ideas and develop strategies. Organisations are as varied in name as the range of activities in which they are engaged. From Life & Peace Institute, operators of a major conflict transformation program in the Horn of Africa, to Synergies Africa, which, as its name suggests, works on a variety of cooperation programs with NGOs in ten countries of West Africa.

An NGO equivalent of a regional organisation

West Africa Network for Peacebuilding (WANEP) typifies the trend. Launched in 1997, this organisation could be called the NGO equivalent of ECOWAS, the association of regional states, which, in an effort to reduce conflict in the region intervened in Liberia and Sierra Leone. WANEP enables groups and organisations involved in peace building to exchange experiences and information on issues such as human rights, conflict resolution/ transformation, social, religious, and political reconciliation, and peace building.

'ECOWAS's intervention in a world that is moving towards regional politics, stimulated thoughts of other possible non-military and non-political initiatives that could enable civil communities to add their voices to the political, economic and social evolution that their societies are undergoing,' said a communiqué issued after the February 1998 meeting at which WANEP was launched. 'The introduction of non-governmental organisations in realpolitic was the second motivating factor. Non-governmental organisations have, in the last fifteen years, become a major socio-political factor in the world. Through non-governmental organisations, civil society now has the opportunity to contribute to the administration of their own lives and their society's.'

A team of West African peace practitioners, Africans studying in the United States, and a few expatriates working in Africa began the drive that led to WANEP. They were supported by the Nairobi Peace Initiative, the Institute for Peacebuilding (IFP), and the Winston Foundation for World Peace.

The September 1998 meeting at which the body was formally launched, lasted for two days. WANEP strives to promote West African cultural and religious values as resources for peace building. Initially, the body included eight peace-building institutions representing countries in the region. Membership was opened to members of national networks of NGOs, as well as single organisations and individuals. WANEP's activities seek to forge personal and professional relationships, allow for cross-fertilisation of ideas and expertise, exchange research programs, and intervention in social, religious and political conflicts in West Africa.

Many of the networks being set up in Africa are interlinked - networks of networks, so to speak. Thus WANEP is among the members of FEWER - the Forum on Early Warning and Early Response - which is itself a model of the kinds of networks spreading their influence continent-wide. Twenty-two international NGOs, academics, lobbyists, UN agencies and governments joined forces to set up FEWER.

In 1996 an international study of the events leading to the 1994 Rwandan genocide, revealed that the United Nations and many governments had received ample warning of the impending violence. But lack of coordination between the different sectors involved, and gaps in the response structures, resulted in nothing substantial being done to prevent the outcome.

As a knowledge exchange network allowing for the sharing of experiences in areas like early warning, conflict prevention and conflict resolution, FEWER believes it can help avoid such lapses occurring in the future. A multi-sectoral and multi-disciplinary body combining various organisations with interest in Asia, Africa, North America, and East and West Europe, FEWER's goals include providing support for early warning networks.

One of FEWER's objectives is to add value to and complement existing early warning systems and processes. It attempts to make research more policy-relevant and useful to local actors and supports local and regionally managed early warning activities in areas of conflict. In effect, FEWER is an organisation of organisations. Its membership includes regional as well as international bodies. Among them is the *Africa Peace Forum,* based in Nairobi, a conflict prevention NGO with activities on the ground in the Great Lakes and the Horn of Africa - research (particularly on arms transfers) and early warning in the Great Lakes.

Another member of FEWER is the *Conseil National des ONG pour le Developpement du DRC (CNONGD)* a network of eleven human rights, development and peace NGOs located in the Democratic Republic of Congo. CNONGD's goal is to strengthen civil society and democracy in the DRC. Its mission is to support the activities of its members by providing education, training, and technical assistance.

ACCORD (South Africa), Inter Africa Group (Ethiopia), International Resource Group and Nairobi Peace Initiative (Kenya) are also associated with FEWER.

The involvement in Africa of bodies like the *International Resource Group (IRG)* offers prospects for strengthening the roots and branches of NGOs even further, as well as reinforcing the principles guiding their work. IRG is a special interest group of National University Telecommunications Network of the USA. Its thesis is that existing social systems throughout the world need direction, support and encouragement in coming to terms with the emerging global society. Through its involvement with African NGOs, IRG seeks to offer a forum through which discussion and understanding can take place relative to the development of the goals, priorities, values and philosophies needed to implement and govern global learning efforts. The particular focus of the IRG is the role and application of technology in this increasingly interdependent global society.

African Centre for the Constructive Resolution of Disputes (ACCORD), based in South Africa, seeks to encourage and further constructive resolution of conflicts by Africa's peoples and help achieve peaceful coexistence, political stability and economic progress within societies where justice and democracy prevail. ACCORD's networking activities draw fifteen universities in southern Africa into its Conflict Resolution Policy and Research Group (CRPRG). The organisation has established a Preventive Diplomacy Forum to facilitate intervention in conflicts. It also conducts training in preventive diplomacy and peace keeping.

The body now known as *Nairobi Peace Initiative (NPI)* used to be called the Nairobi Peace Group (NPG). The name change is more than window dressing: it mirrors the organisation's altered focus and new operating method. Where NPG was mainly concerned with building public awareness of the nature and consequences of African conflicts, NPI's approach is multi-disciplinary and holistic. Conflict prevention not as a separate activity, but rather as an element of peace building and conflict transformation.

NPG saw its principal role as that of a catalyst for motivating and inspiring churches, ecumenical organisations, academic institutions, NGOs and government agencies to take up peace making as an integral part of their work. NPI goes beyond raising awareness of the effects of violent conflict and engages directly in assisting parties to search for peaceful solutions. NPG embarked on its new course in 1990. Now, in its new incarnation as NPI, the organisation is considered an indigenous African peace resource organisation. NPI also seeks to build local capacity through training people in conflict situations in peace making and peace-building skills relevant to their respective communities.

Its projects have been undertaken in Angola, Burundi, Ethiopia, Ghana, Kenya, Liberia, Mozambique, Rwanda, Somalia, South Africa and Sudan. NPI works with civil society organisations throughout the continent: NGOs, church-based and community organisations and specialised conflict resolution organisations in Africa. The organisation also cooperates with the Eastern Mennonite University in the USA and Justapaz in Colombia.

The Horn of Africa

In the conflict zone that is the Horn of Africa, a variety of networks have been developed, stringing together various groups operating in the region. Some, like the *Inter Africa Group*, based in Addis Ababa, are engaged in awareness raising projects. A non-partisan body, Inter Africa operates on a regional basis to advance humanitarian principles, peace and development in the greater Horn of Africa region. Its programmes combine research, dialogue, public education and advocacy. Through expert consultations, brainstorming sessions and efforts to sensitise public opinion, the InterAfrica Group promotes greater awareness and understanding of victims of disaster and armed conflict and assists in developing national and international consensus on coherent and timely response.

Also active in that region, and adopting a networking approach, is the Sweden-based *Life & Peace Institute* (LPI). In fact, it is in the Horn of Africa that the Institute has its largest conflict transformation programme. Traditional research projects and targeted action research are combined with practical support for grassroots peace-building initiatives in Djibouti, Eritrea, Ethiopia, Somalia/ Somaliland and Sudan. Coordination of the work in Somalia/Somaliland, LPI's largest peace-building programme, is carried out from the regional office in Nairobi, Kenya. In Somalia/ Somaliland, LPI has a number of national zonal officers, trainers as well as women's coordinators.

In collaboration with the Pastoral and

Environmental Network in the Horn of Africa (PENHA), Life & Peace Institute has explored different ways of structuring economic relationships in the Horn.

Great Lakes

In Central Africa, the *Great Lakes Policy Forum*, established in the wake of the Rwanda genocide of 1994, is the joint networking initiative of the Center for Preventive Action (CPA), based in the United States, along with Refugees International, Search for Common Ground, and the Johns Hopkins School of Advanced International Studies.

'The Great Lakes Policy Forum enables international actors working to prevent further violence in the region to exchange information, coordinate strategies, evaluate their activities, and advocate policies to the US and other governments,' says one of its documents. Monthly meetings are held in Washington, D.C. This body also cooperates closely with the EuroForum on the Great Lakes in Brussels, a body set up by CPA and the European Centre for Common Ground to improve transatlantic cooperation in the region. Great Lakes Policy Forum has the advantage of joining together NGO staff, as well as staff from various agencies of the US government, and international organisations. Because of that broad composition, the Forum is viewed as having the ability to influence North American and European policy in the region.

Southern Africa

Further to the south, in South Africa itself, the *Centre for Conflict Resolution* has as its primary focus the promotion of peace in that country and elsewhere using constructive, creative and cooperative approaches to conflict resolution and reduction of violence. The centre, an independent institute associated with the University of Cape Town, seeks to contribute towards a just peace in South and southern Africa.

To that end, it provides third-party assistance in the resolution of political and community conflict, equips people with conflict management skills, promotes public awareness of the value of constructive conflict resolution, promotes

democratic values, and advocates disarmament and demilitarisation. Mediation, training, education and research are among the Centre's main activities. Its emphasis is on capacity-building at grassroots level. Centre staff have been deeply involved in the transition to a democratic South Africa. They served as monitors, trainers, mediators and policy advisors in Peace Accord Structures and several key commissions.

In the post-apartheid era the emphasis has shifted to include other African countries, especially in the Southern and Great Lakes regions. A new focus is on training senior African officials in constructively managing conflict. In order to reduce reliance on foreign donors, the Centre today puts greater emphasis on generating its own income.

International organisations

With a board consisting of former prime ministers, presidents and foreign ministers, as well as prominent figures from business and the media, the *International Crisis Group* (ICG) operates in Africa at a different level. Its aim: reinforcing the capacity and resolve of the international community to head off crises before they develop into full-blown humanitarian disasters. Founded in 1995, the Brussels-based body is dedicated to fact-finding, monitoring, early warning, training and lobbying with governments and media to help improve the situation in countries such as Burundi, Nigeria and Sierra Leone.

The approach adopted by ICG depends on the nature of an impending crisis. In certain instances, it will seek to give greater prominence to information already gathered by other NGOs in the field. Elsewhere, Group staff may be posted to a country for a period, to consult widely and produce analyses. High-profile visits to potential crisis zones by the Group's board members, may also form part of that strategy.

ICG identifies countries on the road to crisis and engages with all relevant players (government, military, opposition groups, business, relief NGOs and religious, ethnic and other groups). Then strategic, integrated policy proposals are developed, aimed at strengthening stability and avoiding the development of crisis.

Finally, the international community is alerted to the risk of crisis, thus bringing pressure to bear on governments, international organisations and relevant sections of the business community to take preventive and remedial action.

Based in Geneva, but with strong African roots, *Synergies Africa* wants to enhance the continent's capacities to manage its own conflicts. It does this through close cooperation with local NGOs, associations and institutions. Through a program called Rencontre Régionale de Concertation des Chefs Traditionnels de l'Afrique, Synergies Africa aims to set up mechanisms for permanent consultation among traditional rulers of regions within the boundaries of present-day state, government, and civil society. The organisation runs a variety of programmes in ten countries of West Africa - Benin, Burkina Faso, Cameroon, Chad, Côte d'Ivoir, Ghana, Mali, Niger, Nigeria and Togo - as well as in Burundi. Workshops in Burundi brought together politicians and intellectuals. Women and journalists have also been specially targeted.

International Alert, which has as its specific mission the prevention and resolution of violent internal conflict, has its own independent programmes in Africa, and is also part of various networking initiatives involving other bodies. In the Great Lakes region, the London-based body has established a small conflict resolution programme in recent years. It has also worked to sustain peace - in Burundi, and to a lesser degree, in Rwanda. International Alert has also done work in Liberia, and is examining other potential areas - Ghana and Nigeria.

Operating out of Washington DC, *Search for Common Ground* works directly on the ground in a variety of conflict-resolution initiatives. The international non-profit body (and its Brussels-based counterpart, European Centre for Common Ground) emphasises the use of cooperative solutions and long-term commitment. It has a permanent presence in conflict areas, eight fully operational offices in various parts of the world, include three in Africa - Liberia, Burundi and Angola.

Eighteen different tools for conflict resolution and prevention have been fine-tuned by Search for Common Ground. These include traditional methods and approaches and the less standard joint TV and radio productions, investigative reporting, community organising, convening professional groups and promoting cooperation among NGOs, governments and international organisations.

GERDDES-AFRICA (Research Group on the Democratic, Economic and Social Development of Africa) has a mandate to match the impression conveyed by its name. From its headquarters in Cotonou, Benin, the organisation aims to do no less than spread its message across the entire continent. GERDDES-AFRICA sees itself as the first non-partisan Pan-African democratic movement.

Constituted as a non partisan panafrican body, it was set up in 1990 by African intellectuals. GERDDES-AFRICA functions at two levels. National chapters exist in 32 countries of Western, Central, Eastern and Southern Africa, with more than 2,000 members. The objective is to become continent-wide by 2000.

The organisation says of itself that it is 'neither a political party nor.. against political parties'. It promotes democracy in the service of social and economic development - that is, to mobilise productive forces to change society, improving living conditions and well-being of members of that society. Participation of all local communities in the decision-making process as well as the realisation of development-related activities, is central to its approach. The organisation has trained thousands of electoral agents and elections observers in West and Central Africa, observed elections in several countries, and participated in various mediation efforts.

RANGAPC, French acronym for the *African Non Governmental Network on the Preventive Alert of Conflicts*, was created by GERDDES as a specialised data collecting institution. Its programmes embrace twenty countries in Africa. There are plans to widen this reach. Essentially, RANGAPC is repository for data on economic and social events that could cause damage to society. It keeps an updated list of African resource-persons who are specialists in political and social mediation at the national and regional levels. RANGAPC has already carried out 170 projects and launched many political interventions to prevent conflict.

It faces a variety of difficulties, not least of which is the absence of studies on the political and socio-economic realities of countries where mediation is necessary - Congo, Mali, Niger and Senegal. The program also has a resource shortage, and problems related to lack of adequate training and shortage of civil society members.

ETHNO-NET AFRICA was set up to support the efforts of the Organization of African Unity's (OAU) Division for Conflict Prevention, Management and Resolution to deal with ethnic conflicts which have increased in importance and intensity since the collapse of the Berlin Wall and disintegration of the Soviet Union and Yugoslavia. An urgent need existed for basic research and strategic case studies of societies in conflict and for seeking endurable sustainable solutions to these conflicts. ETHNO-NET AFRICA is seen as a global initiative towards monitoring, evaluating and providing an early warning system of latent ethnic conflicts.

In this regard, ETHNO-NET constitutes a Pan African network of scholars engaged in comparative research, coordinating isolated initiatives by various institutions or scholars, and addressing ethnic issues in a more comprehensive, constructive, comparative and regional perspective. Common denominators are sought. Lessons are drawn from experiences in specific countries and regions. ETHNO-NET also attempts to fill existing gaps in knowledge and understanding of issues of ethnicity and culture as well as questions of conflict and conflict resolution and prevention

It also seeks to enhance capacity building in a number of African universities through the training of a critical pool of young scholars in the domain of ethnicity, and in the conduct of serious comparative research. The network wants to monitor and evaluate ethnic conflicts and design and implement an early warning system for the prevention of disastrous ethnic conflicts in a selected number of countries.

In order to attain these objectives, the project coordinates and sustains the activities of isolated scholars/researchers and institutions currently addressing the questions of ethnicity and ethnic conflicts at the national or regional level. It also seeks to enhance and strengthen research

capacities of scholars/researchers.

Through comparative research, an electronic database and a documentation centre on ethnicity accessible to scholars and others will be created. It uses the latest computer software for data collection and analysis.

The network will also compile a database of African scholars and other members of civil society who can support conflict management processes in Africa. ETHNO-NET AFRICA has also set itself a monitoring and evaluation function, acting as a regional observatory and as an early warning system, monitoring, documenting, analysing and making information available to decision-makers, researchers, teachers, NGOs, human rights activists, lawyers, opinion leaders and to others seeking better ways of mitigating ethnic conflicts or finding lasting solutions.

Global Coalition for Africa (GCA) combines North-South cooperation in forging policy consensus on development priorities among African governments, their northern partners, and non-governmental groups working in and on Africa.

Its leadership includes African leaders as well as prominent figures from Europe and North America. The GCA Secretariat is located in Washington, D.C. It emerged out of a meeting in July 1990 of African policy makers and representatives of the international community held in Maastricht, the Netherlands to discuss priority areas in Africa's development, and the future of development cooperation. Their discussions resulted in a proposal to create a forum that would follow-up and implement the concept of a 'global coalition for Africa'.

They envisioned it as a 'continuing association of interested parties, which would bring together representatives of African governments, bilateral donors, regional and multilateral agencies, and other development partners in Africa', to 'examine the full range of development issues' in Africa, discuss and agree on programs of action, and monitor the results. It is thus a forum where decision-makers from African countries and the international community can discuss issues of current relevance to Africa's development, reach consensus, and then return to their own organisations to implement agreed actions.

African Heads of State meeting in Addis Ababa, Ethiopia, in July 1990, and again in Abuja, Nigeria, in June 1991, endorsed the proposal to form the Coalition. GCA started operations in 1991. The Coalition is based on the premise that Africa can grow only from within, but that to do so it needs outside support. Thus it seeks to improve the evolving working partnership between Africa and the North. The GCA itself is not a donor organisation, nor does it manage assistance programs. It seeks instead to act as a catalyst for action by both sides to the partnership. Almost all African governments, donor agencies and international groups involved in Africa took part in setting up the GCA. Its ultimate governing body is a Plenary of all members which meets approximately every five years. In the interim, the Coalition's work is guided by the Policy Forum which meets annually.

In conclusion

Most of these networks seem to comply with the advice offered by experts regarding the need for networks to choose a regional focus and establish close contacts with policy-makers. Anton Ivanov *(Advanced Networking: a conceptual approach to NGO-based Early Response strategies in Conflict Prevention,* October, 1997), and others who have studied the subject, like former Australian Foreign Minister Gareth Evans, say in a regionally oriented setting cooperating NGOs can do what they are good at: provide access to local knowledge, backed up by a transnational structure and apparatus. This combination is ideal for enhancing effective practical action.

NGO networks are also advised to limit themselves in the scope of the problems they deal with and are advised to provide policy-makers with political options in order for early warning to be followed by practical preventive measures. Some other recommendations when setting up a network are to set clear goals about one wants to achieve by setting up the network. Proper awareness of the limitations of organisations' abilities is also important.

In the process of establishing a network, partners will inevitably encounter difficulties. Selecting good partners in other countries can be difficult, considering the variety of organisations eligible for a conflict prevention network. There are no formal criteria. Organisations such as research institutes and development, humanitarian, peace and human rights organisations may all be interesting partners. Once the connections are made, it may sometimes also be hard to maintain smooth cooperation between people of very different professional and cultural backgrounds. Establishing an open network without formal membership or membership fees is probably the best way to reduce these difficulties, as experience within the FEWER network has shown.

Bridging differences in vision and mandate is another challenge that members of a network will have to cope with, as well as the fear of competition on the market for donations. Annoyance may arise when organisations specialised in conflict resolution discover that big development NGOs or research institutes see conflict resolution as just one of their many tasks. Their counterpart in the bigger organisations may often be unavailable for consultation because he or she is overloaded with other assignments. Developing a close relationship and direct contact could be the way to overcome this problem.

Still, there can be no doubt that 'networks play an important complementary role in defusing tension and preventing conflict,' as Jos Havermans concludes in *Prevention and Management of Violent Conflicts: An International Directory, 1998 edition.* 'National governments have in many cases proven to be incapable of stemming upcoming domestic violence. Large international organisations such as the UN often lack efficiency because of bureaucracy or politically imposed limitations. With an informal structure, focusing on one particular region (they) appear to have a good chance of making a useful contribution to the prevention of violent conflict.'

Part II
Surveys of Conflict Prevention

Introduction

Sub-Regional Approaches to African Conflict Prevention and Resolution

Since the end of the Cold War reduced the stakes that major powers had in competing for influence in Africa and outside aid to the continent declined, 'African solutions for African problems' has been a watchword in policy discussions regarding the region. This theme of African self-reliance has been carried a step further in the notion of an imminent, largely home grown 'African Renaissance.' In this view, a new dawn is reflected in the recent ascendance of enlightened and skilful African leaders such as Isais Afewerke of Eritrea, Meles Zenawi in Ethiopia, Yoweru Museveni of Uganda, Paul Kigame of Rwanda, Nelson Mandela of South Africa, and most recently, Olusegun Obusanjo of Nigeria. All democratically elected, pragmatic in their economic views, but combining vision with political savvy, these leaders will empower their nations, the argument goes, to compete more effectively in the era of globalisation and thus achieve economic growth. Their similar views and good relations with one another also allow them to resolve their nations' mutual disputes so as to restore stability to the war-torn continent ◆ By Michael S. Lund*

To many, such talk of an 'African renaissance' may sound dubious to say the least, in view of the recent outbreak and spread of new conflicts between some of the very countries, such as Ethiopia, Eritrea, Rwanda and Uganda, in which leaders who are listed above are currently in power, and also in view of statistics showing the continuing stagnation of many African economies. Yet, as recently as the Summer 1999 issue of the *Harvard International Review*, Ugandan President Museveni defends the 'renaissance' idea by characterising the recent conflicts as simply the 'residues of unresolved past problems,' 'the last kicks of a dying order, and the birth pangs of a new one.' In his view, bloody internal conflicts such as in Rwanda and the earlier struggle he waged in Uganda simply reflect how regenerative forces are transforming feudal, undemocratic societies into meritocratic, democratic ones. The conflicts are not cause for pessimism but signs of hope, because forceful overthrow is often the only way to get rid of unjust regimes who follow the old beliefs and policies.

Be that as it may, a leading subtheme in Museveni's and other recent analyses is that

Africa's 53 states, many of whom are small in terms of geography, must overcome the economic isolation and political fragmentation bequeathed to them by their colonial borders. Instead, they need stronger links of regional cooperation in economics, diplomacy, and even politics.

Of course, the notion of African regional cooperation has been advocated before. It is as old as the vision of Pan-Africanism that Kwame Nkrumah of Ghana espoused in the early years of the independence era, when he argued that the formerly dependent colonies needed to pool their resources and energies if they were to survive economically and politically in their new environment of states. The spirit of African cooperation also inspired the formation of the continent-wide Organization of African Unity (OAU) in 1963, and a host of other experiments in African regional economic cooperation since then.

In fact, the OAU has had some success in achieving agreement among African states with regard to their relations with one another and increasingly, with respect to their internal affairs. Its Charter's protection of the inviolability of the existing state borders has helped avoid inter-state wars, although many African conflicts still were handled through informal ad hoc means outside the OAU. Unfortunately, being largely a club among heads of state, OAU norms for many years discouraged any significant multi-national efforts to address internal practices, disputes and conflicts, and thus tolerated some horrible abuses of their own societies by leaders such as Idi Amin, because it favoured states over opposition elements of any kind within states. The exceptions were the OAU's support for liberation struggles in the remaining colonies and the fight against apartheid.

In the 1990's, however, the OAU shifted to somewhat more emphasis on supporting democratisation, such as through doing election monitoring; providing good offices for disputes that might lead to conflicts; sponsoring mediation of open conflicts through sending out special envoys; and sending observer missions to places in distress. In 1993, it adopted a mechanism for early warning, conflict prevention and management to be run within the Secretariat.

From a global perspective, the OAU is a 'regional' organisation. African regionalism usually defines the continent as a whole as the region in question. But more recently, more and more attention has been paid to sub-continental areas, or sub-regions, within Africa as an appropriate focus for cooperation. In the last five years, several sub-regional organisations have expanded their memberships and their functions. The Southern African Development Community (SADC) now includes Congo and Mauritius, the InterGovernmental Authority on Development (IGAD) includes Uganda, a revived East African community may include Rwanda and Burundi, and Common Market for Eastern and Southern Africa (COMESA) extends from Egypt all down the east coast, as well as Angola, except for South Africa. Renewed interest and increasing energy is not only being focussed on existing sub-regional trade organisations such as COMESA as means to improve African economic performance, but sub-regional organisations such as the Economic Community of West African States (ECOWAS), IGAD, and SADC are expanding from the original concerns

such as trade and drought to conflict meditation, early warning, and regional peacekeeping forces. Some are also adopting institutionalised procedures for these new functions.

Undoubtedly, much of the revitalised interest in African regionalism has been inspired by recent widely heralded steps being taken in the continent just to the north, especially perhaps by cethe European Union (EU) and the 53-nation Organisation for Security and Cooperation in Europe (OSCE). The former has not only taken bold steps toward market and monetary integration, but is also dedicated to evolving a Common Foreign and Security Policy. During the Cold War, the latter, as the CSCE, formulated a number of agreed-on norms adopted as conventions regarding arms control and security, democracy, and human rights. These then helped to rally the civil societies in eastern and central Europe and among the republics of the former Soviet Union as their struggling popular movements were seeking more autonomy and political change within their respective crumbling communist societies. More recently, the more formalised OSCE has sent a special envoy and observer missions right into many member states in order to work directly with the governments and opposition groups in dealing with minority problems and internal conflicts. A host of articles and seminars have discussed whether the original CSCE model - involving periodic governmental and non-governmental discussions of several 'baskets' of issues and aimed at evolving basic principles of agreement - and the newer more institutionalised OSCE, are applicable to other regions, such as Africa, the Mediterranean, and East Asia. A key idea that has undergirded both these European trends is that of cooperative security, in which domestic matters of human rights, democracy, and development are regarded as integral to traditional inter-state security goals as ways to achieve lasting stability and peace.

International actors outside of Africa have also organised their actions toward Africa more along regional lines. Perhaps the most significant external regional approach was inaugurated in 1975, when the first Lomé Convention was signed between the members of the European Economic Community and their respective former colonies plus some other African, Caribbean and Pacific Countries (ACP). This was followed by three other Lomé Conventions, each of which ran for a five-year period, with the exception of Lomé IV, which runs for ten years and expires in the year 2000. Initially intended to support the economies of the ACP countries by ensuring the price stability of their major exports, one of the major objectives of the Lomé conventions is to promote closer economic integration among African states and to foster movement toward democracy. Other Western actors have their regional initiatives as well, such as the United States' launching in 1994 of a 'Greater Horn of Africa Initiative' for the ten countries of the Horn of Africa and East Africa. About the same time, France and Great Britain started a conflict prevention initiative for West Africa. The UN, OAU, EU, and US have appointed special envoys to deal with the current conflicts in central Africa and other African conflicts.

The new subregionalism has been advocated in three differing forms: economic, diplomatic and political. Although not always stated explicitly, each of these varieties is believed to hold distinct advantages and each has behind it a strategy or theory with respect to conflict prevention or conflict resolution.

Economic Cooperation
First, regional *economic* cooperation through inter-state trade, common market, and multi-national development agreements is intended to achieve the economies of scale in production and the larger markets that Africa's many small economies do not make possible. By stimulating new or expanded commerce such agreements are expected to boost the economic growth of African countries. The increased wealth that results will reduce root causes of conflicts such as poverty and create new stakes in the widening prosperity. The resulting new ranks of African businessmen and workers will insist on the need for maintaining peace in order to ensure continuing economic growth. With respect to the approach it takes to addressing conflict, such policies reflect the theory of functional cooperation with regard to how to achieve peace and a conflict strategy of 'structural prevention.'

Diplomacy and Security Cooperation
African regional cooperation is also approached through the strengthening of inter-governmental *diplomatic* and conflict resolution functions, including peacekeeping, of inter-state organisations such as the OAU. Because the effects of many recent intra-state conflicts often spill over into neighbouring countries, and the sources of these intra-state conflicts are often external, regional approaches have to be taken toward preventing and containing them. Through holding regular multi-lateral consultations, adopting confidence building agreements, and taking joint actions, regional organisations can often mediate and resolve existing conflicts as well as head off newly emerging crises and conflicts. Regional governments are thought to have the advantage of being most affected by conflicts in their region and thus being more motivated to act than outsiders will tend to be. They also can understand the local situation better than distant outsiders (other such arguments are mentioned in the chapter by Connie Peck). This approach reflects the idea of 'direct prevention.'

Civil Society and Governance
Although it is most visible and developed within the bounds of individual states, the third form which regionalism has taken recently concerns *civil society* activity. This idea sees autonomous non-governmental organisations (NGOs) in African societies - trade unions, business associations, religious groups, social service organisations, and advocacy groups devoted to promoting democracy and protecting human rights - as a grassroots-based social force that can pressure governments to increasingly open up politics to wider participation and institutionalised democracy. Democracy then reduces conflicts because democracies tend to treat their citizens more fairly and do not tend to fight one another. NGOs can also monitor their governments' performance in areas such as upholding democracy, human rights, rule of law, and international agreements. The regional version of this idea envisions transnational networks of like-minded NGOs that are connected with each other across their nations' borders. Forming larger, more powerful regional

constituencies for peace can restrain hostile tendencies in their respective governments and outweigh the influence of more belligerent groups within their respective societies.

Initial Conclusions from the Sub-regional Chapters

Because of the new interest in sub-regional processes in Africa, the following chapters in this volume look at the recent developments at the sub-regional level in the five sub-regions of Africa, in terms of their possible significance for African conflict management and prevention. These articles resist the temptation either to subscribe to broad characterisations of Africa such as the notion of an African Renaissance or to dismiss this motif as simply another public relations 'buzzword,' and presuming the recent wars are merely another cycle of chronic African conflict. Instead, the chapters look more closely at what actually has been done under sub-regionalism recently, the results of these efforts, and the limits and obstacles they have encountered. They then offer what may be promising next steps. Wherever fitting, the chapters seek to address major developments occurring within the three areas of a) strengthening economic cooperation, b) international diplomacy and security cooperation, and c) civil society activity to promote norms of governance such as human rights and democracy.

The brief treatments of sub-regional developments in the five sub-regional articles can not provide definitive conclusions. But here are some tentative observations arising from them that may stimulate policy discussion, help to guide the setting of priorities, and more in-depth research.

1. The five African sub-regions vary greatly in the extent they share a sense of sub-regional interests and have institutionalised it, or they even engage at all in inter-governmental processes. A rough ranking of them on this dimension might place Southern Africa, still experiencing a region-wide rapprochement and relatively free of conflicts, as the most institutionalised sub-region at one of the spectrum. North Africa, although relatively free of conflicts and sharing political ties to the larger Arab community, is nevertheless barely engaged as a distinct sub-region, and thus lies at the other end of the spectrum. West Africa, the Horn of Africa, and Central Africa, all of them coping with several conflicts, lie in between, in that order.

The process whereby the more institutionalised regions reach their present development seems to go through certain general stages. Sub-regional organisations are usually founded initially for the purpose of economic cooperation but conflicts emerging in their region lead some to broaden in function so they can now take on new diplomatic tasks in conflict mediation. This may be followed among the more advanced entities by steps to institutionalise their conflict prevention and mediation capacities such as early warning systems, and in some cases, take steps toward preparing regional peacekeeping forces. Most recently, such organisations may also have begun to discuss the adoption of common norms concerning internal matters of governance, such as democracy and human rights.

The degree of development appears to be related to, among other factors, whether a hegemonic state exists and acts as an engine for sub-regional collaboration, such as Nigeria and South Africa have done. Thus, keeping the momentum going of the more developed sub-regional organisations will require maintaining the support and leadership provided by these hegemonic states.

2. But although trade and economics was the first realm in which sub-regional cooperation was tried, many of the organisations created for that purpose either disbanded or have failed to achieve their objectives of significantly lowering trade protections. This may be due largely to the unequal advantages enjoyed by the stronger economies in a sub-region and the continued resort to existing advantageous bilateral trade relations in view of the dependencies of the economies on a few vulnerable products. As a result, however, the potential benefits for conflict prevention that may possibly flow from sub-regional economic cooperation simply have not been realised so far.

Even where inter-state economic agreements do operate in a sub-region, such as West Africa, such organisations do not seem to be sufficient to prevent or contain the eruption of violent conflicts in the same regions, at least of internal sources of turmoil. More data would be required to test this impression, and it would still be difficult to measure whether such agreements reduce what would otherwise be a higher potential for inter-state or internal conflicts or help to restrain them some when they do arise. But evidently, regional economic ties have not become a significant disincentive to conflict.

This regional tool has been rather ignored as a method for conflict prevention. To reap its possible benefits in that regard, more vigorous efforts need to be made to open up national economies and discourage economic nationalism (with appropriate compensating policies), and to promote joint development programmes to achieve economies of scale.

3. As to the results of regional diplomacy and security cooperation, one of the most useful purposes served by sub-regional organisations, as with the OAU, is the regular venue they have provided in which governments can begin dialogue about outstanding problems and disputes. These organisations also seem to have been particularly effective mainly in preventing interstate conflicts. These should be understood in the strict technical sense, however, of invasions of a neighbouring state by another state's army, but not applying to the common practice of harbouring or supporting insurgencies against neighbouring states.

As to internal conflicts, however, the record is much more mixed. Contrary to what might be assumed, sub-regional organisations did not necessarily respond to brewing disputes in their area that could escalate into violence, any earlier than other types of third parties did. All third parties, whether close to or remote from a conflict, have tended to wait until they have reached the crisis or mid-conflict stage before getting significantly engaged. (There have been exceptions, such as when the OAU responded promptly to the post-election crisis in Congo-Brazzaville in 1993.) Sub-regional organisations also did not tackle every significant conflict in their own neighbourhoods even at the crisis stage; other actors - the UN, OAU, major powers, track two diplomats - were also active. In short, sub-regional organisations remain simply one of several kinds of players that may or may not choose to engage in mediating any given conflict. However, if a significant sub-regional organisation does operate in an area, other third parties may tend to feel more obliged to work with it or through it to resolve conflicts, rather than operate entirely independently. Thus, strengthening these organisations may help to increase the coordination and coherence among internal and external third parties.

4. Whether a mediator was a sub-regional organisation or some other type of governmental or non-governmental third party does not seem to determine their effectiveness in bringing an end to conflicts. Outside actors have had as much success as inside actors. No one regional actor consistently was successful, in fact few were at all. The explanations of effectiveness lie elsewhere. This outcome seems to have to do less with who was involved than with whether the conflicting parties were open to negotiations because of stalemates, and can no longer gain significantly from military action. Another powerful factor is whether the third parties were able to exert considerable pressure on them through carrots, or more usually sticks such as through sanctions or military intervention itself.

But high levels of escalation usually mean a conflict has become militarised, very destructive, and very difficult to stop. Because counteractions are then difficult to mount for lack of political support and sanctions often have many unintended consequences, if sub-regional organisations are going to play increasing roles regarding the conflicts in their area, then more emphasis needs to be placed on strengthening their capacities for early preventive actions, rather than rely only on the most coercive actions at later stages.

From this point of view, the current initiatives to develop Africa-wide or sub-regional peacekeeping forces - such as the African Crisis Response Initiative under which the US, the United Kingdom and France will provide peacekeeping training to battalion sized military units volunteered by African nations - seem to miss an important point. Unless these forces could clearly be used in preventive deployment rather than simply 'crisis response,' this movement has tended to skip over and pre-empt the importance of strengthening African capabilities for the more cost-effective methods of conflict prevention, whose aim is to avoid in the first place the need for forceful interventions at relatively late stages of conflicts.

5. However, sub-regional organisations recently have undertaken peacekeeping and peace enforcement actions toward conflicts in their areas, and those may be the only recourse in certain situations. But these actions were often far from adequately authorised, fully supported, and impartial in their execution. Instead they reflected too narrowly the political goals and national interests of a major government or coalition of governments within the sub-region. While these interventions may have had value in containing violence, the lack of full legitimacy discredits the overall advance of sub-regional cooperation. Thus, an important policy priority is to gain deeper sub-regional agreement on common criteria and procedures for deciding when intervention under the auspices of the organisation by some members into the affairs of others is warranted.

6. Recent national conflicts have arisen, to be sure, in the soil of impoverishment and political domination, but of late, such grievances often appear to be simply exploited politically by competing alternative elites who gain access to weapons as a means to gain political power and control of economic assets, rather than to be the cause of popularly-based movements aimed at a society's injustices. Because such challenges often start from insurgencies that are aided by neighbouring states, another avenue for reducing the incidence of internal conflicts through sub-regional organisations may be to secure tighter mutual agreement and the means of censure around norms that prohibit such acts of external abetting or support of armed subversion, as well as the usurpation of power through coups. This rather conservative inter-state confidence-building measure risks

shielding incumbents from threats to their power and thus allowing for its abuse, but it also can provide those in office to build stronger, more legitimate states in a climate of relative security. And such a regional measure could be complemented by more consistent and concerted application of human rights and democratisation standards as conditions in aid programs by external donors.

7. The initiatives in regional diplomacy show that leaders of states often have great difficulty in working productively together, due to their personal rivalries, the competing political interests of their governments, and the disputes and tensions that may persist regarding inter-security. Thus, with the rationale that peace is too important to be left to the diplomats, NGOs have increasingly become involved in various kinds of peace efforts. In some instances, prominent private individuals and international or national NGOs have sought to facilitate peace settlements, with varying results depending mainly on the factors mentioned under 4 above. But such 'track-two' diplomacy is often given token adherence or sidelined by the main players.

A more fruitful avenue for increasing the role of civil society NGOs in peace and conflict matters involves mobilising broad national constituencies for advocacy and delivery of human rights, rule of law, democracy, and dispute resolution functions by government and other actors in society, and providing monitoring of government practices and groups behaviour that threaten those values. At the same time, even in countries where NGO activity as a whole is quite extensive, such as in Kenya and Uganda, this kind of presence and pressure is severely limited so far because of government policies, varied NGO agendas, the limited scale and scope of initiatives, disunity and competition, funding difficulties, and sustainability. Cross-regional civil society contact and joint activities are even more limited.

In sum, civil society-building is by far the least developed form of sub-regionalism, and even within states, it would be unwise to look to this realm alone as a powerful engine for significant domestic political change soon. Such efforts should be approached as long-term strategies. They are needed complements to the peace settlements that are mainly prompted by military or political stalemates, but they rarely can be immediate solvents of current conflicts.

At the same time, however, carefully designed and focussed cross-regional civil society initiatives might make a little go a long way by breaking a mold. Initiatives to bring together NGOs from several countries to develop platforms regarding internal subversion, human rights practices, military reform, inter-group

tolerance, and other such pertinent problems - the equivalent of the national assemblies or conventions that have been held within countries - might prove quite influential in shaping international discourse and constraining undisciplined rulers. This might take the form of a quasi-official CSCE Helsinki Process-like activity whereby representatives of governments and civil society actors convene to hammer out codes of principles in specified fields, monitor their respective societies and governments, and reconvene to measure compliance.

---

*   Michael S. Lund is an international relations consultant, and senior associate, Creative Associates International Inc., in Washington, D.C., where he is conducting research on effective approaches to conflict prevention. At the United States Institute of Peace he served as senior scholar (1994-1995) and director of the Jennings Randolph fellowship program (1987-1993), his work focusing on political development, conflict resolution, and multilateral organisations in sub-Saharan Africa and Europe.

References

Deng, Francis M. and Terrence Lyons, eds. *African Reckoning: A Quest for Good Governance*. Washington, DC: Brookings Institution Press, 1998

Museveni, Yoweri, ' Birth Pangs: Africa in the Coming Millenium,' *Harvard International Review*, Summer, 1999, P 76-80

Olusegun Obasanjo, and Felix G.N. Mosha, eds. *Africa: Rise to Challenge*. Africa Leadership Forum, 1992

Connie Peck, *Sustainable Peace: The Role of the UN and Regional Organizations in Preventing Conflict*. .Lanham, Maryland: Rowman and Littlefield, 1998

Torduff, William, *Government and Politics in Africa*, Third Edition, Bloomington, Indiana University Press, 1997

North Africa

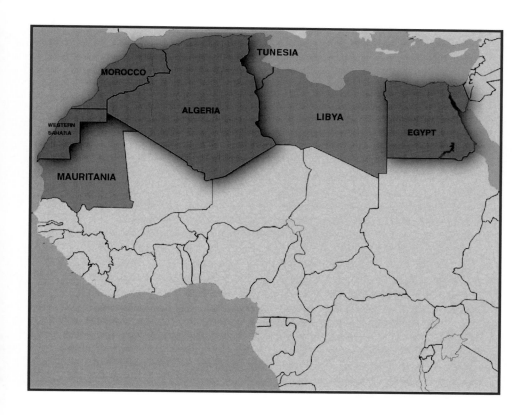

Civil Society, a Victim of Confrontations between State and Islam

The different political organisations representing Islam were the most important opponents of the regimes and the political and military elites within the region of North Africa in the past two decades. The clash between the various Islamic groups and the ruling regimes is a potential source of future conflict in the region. Although the origins and development of Islamic organisations are mainly to be explained within the national context, the Islamic challenge has regional implications especially with regard to state intervention ♦ *By* **Arend Jan Termeulen***

The most violent conflict between Islam and the state took place in Algeria where in 1992 a military *coup d'etat* intended to overturn the political success of the *Front Islamique du Salut* (FIS) resulted in a bloody civil war. The effects of the Algerian conflict were largely borne by Algerian civilians, 100,000 of whom were killed while the rest of the population suffered the trauma of witnessing the most horrible atrocities. At the same time the regional consequences and implications of the Algerian civil war are numerous.

Tunisia

Like Egypt, Tunisia legitimised its crackdown on its own Islamic opposition groups in the 1990s by referring to the ongoing Algerian tragedy. However, one should be wary of reducing Egyptian and Tunisian state policies to a 'simple state versus Islamist dynamic'. In a Machiavellian manner, both states presented their repressive policies as the only way to defeat the evil of Islam. This had serious consequences for the autonomous space of muscular civil society organisations in both countries as the record of human rights movements, women organisations, professional syndicates and the press shows.

In Tunisia after three years of political reforms and national reconciliation, president Ben Ali's regime successfully cracked down on the Islamic opposition, Ennahda, in the early 1990s. In successive actions thousands of Islamic militants were arrested and often held in custody for an indefinite time without trial. The Tunisian human rights organisation *Ligue*

Tunisienne des Droits de l'Homme (LTDH) and its international counterparts Amnesty International and Human Rights Watch repeatedly accused the Tunisian state of torture and other violations of the human rights of Islamic activists. Most of the Islamic leadership went into exile; Rachid al-Ghannouchi, for instance, travelled to London after the elections of 1989 from which Ennahda was excluded. One observer called this Ennahda's 'offshore operation'. From metropolitan Europe the exiled Islamic leadership tried to guide the remnants of a once powerful party and warned the regime that unless all parties were allowed in the political system Algerian-style violence would be the result. However, these and other threats only increased the regime's determination to defeat the Islamic enemy. It also encouraged the regime to emphasise the international dimension of the problem. Echoing Egypt's president, Mubarak, Ben Ali demanded that European states, especially Great Britain, take tougher action against Islamic 'terrorists' and expel their Islamic refugees. Tunisia supported Egypt's initiatives of regional conferences aimed at creating and guiding a common regional front against Islamic 'terrorism'.

Ben Ali's repressive policies and actions were not limited to Islamic groups. Along with Ennahda, the communist party (POCT) was also outlawed. At the same time other secular opposition parties, even when represented in parliament such as the *Mouvement des Démocrates Socialistes* (MDS) and civil society organisations were denied the freedom of autonomous operation. The state revived its cooptation policies and seduced leading personalities in civil organisations into joining state initiatives. Moreover, lawyers who defended Islamic prisoners were arrested on dubious charges and according to Amnesty International the Tunisian government intimidated human rights activists. The media were particularly affected by state intervention. Foreign correspondents were denied access to Tunisia or were expelled, laws were fabricated to strictly control the use of satellite dishes, and in October 1996 *Reporters sans Frontières* condemned the regime for stifling the press. On the other hand, although civil society organisations have experienced a difficult time, they still exist and function. Even the LTDH has ample room to manoeuvre and publish very critical reports accusing the regime of violating human rights. It is a positive sign that, as one observer notes, a vast network of civil society associations exist that are 'training civilians in civility'. This may challenge the de-liberalisation tendencies and force state elites to open up the political process.

However, it is difficult to foresee a return to real democratisation in the near future. Ben Ali's retreat into authoritarianism has stabilised his regime. The pro-government party *Rassemblement Institutionel Democratique* (RCD) dominates Parliament and the few cosmetic political reforms will not prevent the RCD from further orchestrating the political system. Most importantly, returning to the political liberalisation of the late 1980s revives the issue of tolerating a legal Islamic opposition party, the very issue that initiated Ben Ali's retreat to repression. It is still possible for Ben Ali to elicit the support of many Tunisians and sometimes even elements within civil society such as some women's groups, by referring to events in neighbouring Algeria. Many Tunisians remember that in 1987 Ben Ali saved the country from political and economic chaos and the threat of civil war. Moreover, the fact that Ben Ali has a secure grasp of power is also explained by the relatively successful liberal economic policies, sustained by the IMF structural adjustments programmes. The middle classes are particularly anxious about the chaos evident in Algeria. As in Egypt, liberal economic policies can go hand in hand with political authoritarianism. However, this success story of economic reforms needs to be put in perspective. The continuing high levels of (youth) unemployment and the uneven economic development, which is largely at the cost of lower income groups and rural regions, are the side products of the structural adjustment programmes. In the longer run this may destabilise the Ben Ali regime. Whether this will imply more or less democracy remains to be seen.

Egypt

Like the Tunisian regime, the Egyptian state has legitimised its struggle against the Islamic challenge by referring to the civil war in Algeria. In the early 1990s the state started a military campaign against two militant Islamic opposition groups, the Jihad and Jama'at, which were responsible for various assaults and bloody attacks especially in the south. After the horrific killing of 58 tourists in Luxor in November 1997, a terrorist assault that was claimed by the Jama'at, military operations against the Islamic forces were intensified. Apart from security problems the state was anxious to protect income from tourism from further erosion. Most commentators agree that by late 1997, in military terms at least, radical Islam had been defeated. Its organisational infrastructure had been destroyed, and its leadership was either imprisoned or in exile. This view was confirmed by the various calls for unilateral cease-fires and negotiations from the imprisoned Jihad and Jama'at leadership, an offer of dialogue the government refused. The success of the state's military campaign had its price, however. Since 1992 the war between the security forces and Islamic militants has caused the death of about 1,200 people (police officers and suspected Islamic activists). Local and international human rights organisations voiced concern over the mass detention of Islamic activists (approximately 20,000 alleged Islamic activists have been detained as political prisoners), trials in military courts, repeated reports of torture, death sentences and executions, and 'collective punishments' of villages accused of 'hiding' Islamic radicals.

The state's tougher approach to Islam is not limited to its radical wing. The more moderate Muslim Brotherhood (MB) also became a repeated target of state repression. On the eve of the 1995 elections, for instance, more than 1,000 MB members and sympathisers were arrested. In an obvious attempt to marginalise the MB, the regime accused its members of creating a common front with the radical Islamic groups. This demonstrated that the regime had abandoned its strategy of accommodating the mb and returned to repressive tactics. This move was entirely consistent with the more general tendency towards political de-liberalisation that Egypt experienced in the 1990s. Opposition parties and civil society organisations were the main victims, secular and Islamic alike. Further signs of this worrying tendency toward political de-liberalisation include the rigged elections of 1995 in which the pro-government National Democratic Party (NDP) scored an unheard-of victory; state policies directed at closing down the autonomous space of professional syndicates of lawyers and others; and the various attacks upon the Egyptian press, which compared to regional standards still enjoyed a remarkable freedom and autonomy. Like the Tunisian regime, the Egyptian state has, in the words of one observer, 'used the image of an Islamist threat to inspire fear and slow the pace of democracy.'

An assessment of the likely development of Egyptian Islamism must take three facts into account. First, the state seems to have managed to defeat Islamic radicalism. However, this victory is purely military. Egyptian and other human right activists express fears that the 20,000 Islamic political prisoners, the largest ever political prison population in Egypt, will inevitably be radicalised in the tough regime of Egyptian prisons. If this view proves correct, the menace of radical Islam is far from over and the state's repressive policies will encourage rather than prevent the production of an 'Algerian monster'. Secondly, and in the longer term perhaps even more importantly, the regime has changed its policy of accommodating the moderate Islamism of the MB into one of repression. Many observers inside and outside Egypt fear that interventionist state actions against moderate Islamic organisations

ultimately breed extremism. Also non-Islamic Egyptian intellectuals have attacked the state for continuously denying any place within the political system for what is potentially Egypt's largest opposition movement. In their view cooptation and accommodation are far better political instruments to control moderate Islamism than sheer repression. Finally, the role of economics needs to be considered. Economic reform and IMF sponsored structural adjustment programmes may have benefited the middle classes and the affluent, however, the economic position of the lower income groups has deteriorated as food and other subsidies were reduced and high levels of unemployment continue. One observer even sees a partial explanation of Egypt's political de-liberalisation in the state's desire to contain opposition to the economic reforms and liberalisation. Hence, as in Tunisia, economic liberalisation may cause political de-liberalisation.

Libya

Libya is also watching events inside Algeria very closely. Qaddafi's authoritarian state has a record of brutally repressing all opposition forces within and outside the country. In fact Islamic groups were the only viable political opposition within the country apart from the dissatisfied groups within the army, which envy the prerogatives and increasing power enjoyed by Qaddafi's fellow tribesmen. The Islamic challenge gained in strength in the mid-1990s when several new organisations were established. Islamic opposition increased to the point where it seriously threatened to destabilise Qaddafi's regime. Various attacks on state property by Islamic organisations initiated violent confrontations between Islamic militants and security forces, especially in the Cyrenaica region where the Islamic movement originated. In February 1996 Qaddafi himself survived an assassination attempt by Islamic militants. The state reacted by arresting hundreds of Islamic activists and by placing the mosques, the traditional bases of militant Islamic organisations, more firmly under state supervision.

These facts notwithstanding, little reliable information is available about Libya's Islamic opposition. It is unclear why the challenge of Islamic movements should have intensified in the mid-1990s. Some suggest a link with the UN sanctions against Libya following the country's alleged involvement in the Lockerbie tragedy. Other observers have noted that Libya's international isolation mostly triggered protest within the army. Popular support for the various militant Islamic groups that have emerged is difficult to estimate, although it is widely believed that the Militant Islamic Group, which is supposed to have links with the GIA in Algeria, appears to be the most important. Moreover, it is suggested that the Islamic resources are limited, a fact that seems to suggest there is no significant support from Saudi Arabia or other Gulf monarchies. Finally, there seems to be little evidence of cooperation between the different Islamic organisations or between the Islamic organisations and the secular opposition.

From a regional perspective, Libya's approach to Islam was ambiguous until the mid 1990s; Algeria complained about Libya's unclear relationship with the Algerian Islamic opposition of the FIS and Libya maintained cordial relations with Sudan's Islamic regime, which denied any support for the Islamic movement in Libya. In the second half of the 1990s this situation was changing. Confronted with its own Islamic challenge and international isolation because of UN sanctions, Libya tried to improve its relations within the region by adopting a tougher stand against Islamic 'terrorism'. At the same time its relations with Sudan were soured when Libya expelled thousands of Sudanese migrant workers. Relations between Algeria and Libya were increasingly focused on cooperation over security matters to contain Islamic militancy. In April 1996 both countries signed a security agreement to cooperate in the struggle against Islamic groups. The previously strained relations with Tunisia also improved. On several occasions Egypt even claimed that Libya was a crucial bulwark against the spread of militant Islam inside the region. However, the Egyptian-Libyan love affair was mainly born out of economic considerations. Egypt desperately wants to resettle one million Egyptian farmers on Libyan lands to be irrigated by the Great Man Made River project.

It is difficult to predict scenarios for the future development of the Libyan Islamic opposition and the stability of Qaddafi's authoritarian state. Despite the state's intermittent repression of Islam, reports of an Islamic challenge continue to appear. In June 1998, for example, the Libyan Islamic Martyrs Movement, a militant section of the Libyan Islamic opposition close to Egypt's Jihad, claimed responsibility for an assassination attempt against Qaddafi. However, it remains very difficult to assess the real strength of the Islamic opposition groups. The strength of the regime has also been increased by the lifting of the UN sanctions after Libya finally agreed to extradite the two Libyan suspects in the Lockerbie case to a Scottish court in the Netherlands in April 1999.

Morocco
In contrast to the above cases, in Morocco repressive state practices declined in the 1990s. Since the general amnesty in 1991, civil society organisations have started to develop a degree of autonomy and operational freedom. As long as the implicit rules of the game are respected - for example, refraining from spontaneous demonstrations and not criticising the king - human rights movements, women's organisations, youth groups and cultural associations have been given the space to operate. The government of Abderrahmane Youssoufi, which was formed, in early 1998 after the parliamentary elections of November 1997, has also contributed to the new liberal image of Morocco. Youssoufi became the first left-wing Prime Minister and his personal experience as a leading human rights activist and active involvement in the leftist opposition created great expectations of further political openings among many Moroccans. Nevertheless, the powers of the new government should not be overestimated. First, the Kutla coalition is rather fragile. Second, the omnipotence of the king is largely untouched. Inside the government, Hassan II's wishes were - untill his recent death - represented by his interior minister, Driss Basri, who, ironically, was responsible for the repression in the 1970s that jailed and exiled Youssoufi. In fact many Moroccans are disappointed about the actual

EGYPT, CAIRO

DICK ROSS/LINEAIR

state's cooptation strategy. As an alleged descendant of the Prophet Muhammad, Hassan II had considerable religious authority. Consequently, the king was able to give a religious legitimacy to his political power and present Morocco as a 'fundamentalist' state - that is, as a state governed in accordance with the regime's construction of Moroccan traditions. All this contributed to the hegemony of the Moroccan state and helped steal a march on the Islamic movement. Although Morocco also closely monitored the events in neighbouring Algeria it was nevertheless much more confident in its repression of its radical Islamist opposition and avoided resorting to naked violence.

An assessment of Morocco's political future may focus on two points. Since Hassan II's recent death, the continuation of an effective monarchy into the twenty-first century depends on a smooth succession of the Moroccan throne. However, the succession issue is still unresolved. Heir Sidi Ahmed does not possess his father's aura of authority and is engaged in a power struggle with his brother Rachid.

Secondly, since Hassan II tied the question of his legitimacy with the continued occupation (rejoining the Moroccan homeland, Morocco would claim) of the Western Sahara, the development of the dispute between Morocco and Polisario over the Western Sahara is of the utmost importance. However, apart from Moroccan political anxieties and desires, a solution to this prolonged conflict is also needed in order to resolve the issue of the 165,000 Sahrawi refugees that are currently living under

accomplishments of the government after its first year in power.

Within this context of political liberalisation, the position of the Moroccan Islamic opposition is ambivalent. The Moroccan regime is trying to coopt the moderate sections of the Islamic opposition while repressing the more radical branches. Thus, the radical Islamic party of Abdessalam Yassin, Justice and Charity, is still banned, while a more moderate Islamic party, Justice and Development, holds ten seats in the 325-seat parliament. In comparison to the other North African states, the Moroccan regime was less exposed to attacks from radical Islam. The main reason for this was the success of the extremely harsh conditions in refugee camps in Tindouf (Algeria). Besides Moroccan concerns and Sahrawi needs and aspirations, the dispute has wider implications as a solution could have positive consequences for the region as a whole. Relations between Algeria and Morocco, for instance, are still hindered by Morocco's continuing occupation of the Western Sahara and Algeria's support for Polisario, although a careful rapprochement between Algeria and Morocco is underway. A settlement of the West Saharan dispute may trigger wider regional cooperation that could be institutionalised under the umbrella of a revived Arab Maghreb Union (AMU). Non-member state Egypt has already expressed interest in joining the AMU.

Although in spring 1999, Polisario and Morocco finally agreed to implement the United Nations supervised referendum on the future of Western Sahara in July 2000, Morocco's record of delaying tactics since 1991 makes the actual implementation of the referendum highly uncertain. Another bad omen are the many provisions, especially about voter registration, that Morocco has formulated as a condition for accepting Kofi Annan's proposals, and these have in fact already severely compromised Polisario's position. A good sign, on the other hand, is the appointment of the top American diplomat Bob Eagleton as the head of the UN operation in Western Sahara (MINURSO). Eagleton's appointment can be read as a token of UN determination to push for a solution.

For the Moroccan regime the outcome of the referendum is a delicate issue. The surrender of West Saharan sovereignty to Polisario would certainly mean a blow to the regime's credibility in the eyes of many Moroccans and it is a risk the regime does not dare to take. On the other hand, from a financial point of view the withdrawal of the Moroccan army would save more than US$ 1 million a day, making a significant contribution to easing the burden of Morocco's external debt of US$ 22 billion. Moreover, a peaceful settlement of the dispute - albeit against Morocco's original designs - could add to Morocco's international prestige and attract foreign investment, which would increase the political stability of the regime. In this scenario, the strategy of domestic democratisation to attract foreign capital is enlarged by regional peaceful conflict resolution.

Algeria

Recent developments in Algeria are dominated by the (rigged) election of Bouteflika as President in April 1999 and his subsequent policy of 'national reconciliation' that resulted in a Law of 'Civil Harmony', which was presented to the Algerian Parliament in July 1999. The main provision of this new law was the amnesty for several thousand Islamic activists who had not been found guilty of murder or rape. At the same time, Bouteflika promised to protect the security forces against investigations into their involvement in the violence of the past seven years.

These developments followed a period of relative de-escalation. Firstly, the parliamentary elections of June 1997, from which the *Front Islamique du Salut* (FIS) was excluded, but in which constitutional Islamic parties secured 103 seats (27 per cent of the total), helped foster political normalisation. Secondly, FIS leader Abbasi Madani's release from prison in July 1997 was interpreted by many as another sign of attempts at reconciliation by the Algerian regime. Then, in September 1997 the military wing of the FIS, the *Armée Islamique du Salut* (AIS) declared a unilateral truce. The main consequence of the change in tactics by the AIS were the joint military actions of the army and ais against the *Groupes Islamiques Armee* (GIA). FIS leaders were embarrassed by the brutal mass attacks on civilians by GIA militants. Fearing that popular support would be lost, most FIS leaders supported the joint actions against their Islamic rivals. Observers were more puzzled by the reasons for the military's deal with the ais. Most analysts emphasised that army leaders acknowledged the military advantages of joining forces with the AIS, while some observers also noticed the beginning of a common political front between the FIS and the military, which also contained Islamic sympathisers, especially in the lower echelons. Some observers acknowledged that such a political front could develop into a 'Sudanese scenario' in which other political parties would eventually be excluded from the political platforms and the FIS would be in charge of the administration while the military continued to rule. However, this view fails to take full account of the internal divide within the upper echelons of the army. This split within the military elite was exemplified by the fight between president Zeroual - who headed the so-called conciliators, a group within the army that aspired to some kind of political trusteeship with the Islamic groups - and his top two generals, chief of staff, Mohamed Lamari, and head of the security services, Tawfik Mediene, who headed the 'eradicators'. The 'eradicators' favour a strategy of brutal suppression of the Islamic movement. In addition to these two groups, and further complicating the picture, there is the shadowy figure of General Khaled Nezzar, the most powerful man behind the show.

Initially the military results of the army-AIS alliance were hardly noticeable as GIA's military power remained unbroken. December 1997 and January 1998 (Ramadan) were two of the most violent months since 1992. The violence and counter-violence of groups of armed civilians (the so-called patriots), armed by an army that was utterly unprepared for the kind of guerrilla warfare started by GIA militants exacerbated the national crisis. At the same time the Algerian press confirmed rumours that, in some cases, local functionaries (mayors) were directly responsible for the violence. The regions south of Algiers in particular were turned into Algerian 'Killing Fields'. Political parties such as Hocine Ait Ahmed's *Front des Forces Socialistes* (FFS) and human rights organisations including Amnesty International and Human Rights Watch warned that the proliferation of arms could 'add to the violence and deepen existing tribal and other divisions within society'. This 'privatisation of the violence' would ultimately lead to the tribalisation of the nation state, warned Ait Ahmed. This evokes images of the Lebanese civil war where after years of fighting violence took on a dynamic of its own.

After early 1998, however, there were signs that GIA's military power was diminishing as its hit and run actions decreased dramatically. However, GIA was far from destroyed. Some leaders continued to publish threats to internationalise the violence and bring Europe

into the conflict. Moreover, although less frequent, the killings inside Algeria continued. One of these killings, the assassination of Berber singer and songwriter Lounès Matoub in June 1998, illustrated the inflammable ethnic dimension of the national crisis. Matoub had been a severe critic of the Arabisation policies, which had resulted in the Arabic-only law that went into effect just after his death. By promoting Arabic at the expense of the Berber language (*Tamazight*) and French, the regime tried to show its Arab and Islamic credentials towards the Arab educated Algerian youth and the Islamic movement. This enraged Berber cultural and political groups who wanted the regime to acknowledge Berber cultural identity as part of national Algerian identity and *Tamazight* as one of the national languages. Matoub's assassination and the new laws triggered angry anti-government protests among the Berber youth, especially in Kabylia. The establishment of a new militant Berber political group, the Armed Berber Movement, confirmed the potential for ethnic conflict.

Although the Algerian civil war seems to have ended, the conflict between the state and society is far from resolved. At first sight, the state's designs for political institutionalisation and Bouteflika's announcement of national reconciliation encourage hope that the violence is over and the process of renewing trust between state and society is underway. However, there are several reasons to be more pessimistic. Firstly, Bouteflika's rigged election supports the conclusion of one observer that 'political institutionalisation is one thing; democratisation is quite another'. Secondly, the law of 'Civil Harmony' is rather ambiguous. To start with, amnesty will only be granted to those Islamic activists who are not guilty of killings and other atrocities. The question arises who judges whom on the basis of what evidence, under which circumstances is it to be collected and over what period? Thirdly, an important component of Bouteflika's amnesty deal is the protection of the security forces from scrutiny. The fact that the security forces are backed-up by the most authoritative agent of the state in this way seems to confirm reports by various local and international human rights organisations that the state apparatus took part in the violence. This means that the question of who is guilty and who is innocent cannot be properly answered. This does little to accommodate the needs of a population that suffered from the violence and experienced the most horrible atrocities. Unlike South Africa, where a commission sponsored by the government investigated the violence during apartheid (the so-called commission for truth or *Waarheidscommissie*), the Algerian population is being given the impression that state officials who took part in the violence will get away scot-free. Political and social nihilism and lasting psychological damage may well be the undesirable consequences. In the short term, Algeria's future will be decided by the military who remain the power brokers *par excellence*. Two scenarios seem possible. First, in the 'Turkish scenario', political institutionalisation is continued and the military only intervenes when the 'secular' constitution is in danger. Whether in this scenario a renamed FIS will be allowed legal status remains to be seen. At first sight Bouteflika's national reconciliation and amnesty laws seem to confirm the likelihood of this scenario. However, a second scenario, the 'Sudanese option', is not impossible if one recalls the cooperation between the army and the AIS after the latter had declared a unilateral truce. In this scenario, Bouteflika's amnesty for Islamic activists appears to be one of the results of a premeditated deal between the army and the FIS of which the other consequence may well be a power sharing between the army and the Islamic movement *à la* Sudan. One may wonder, however, how this scenario fits with the still powerful military wing of the 'eradicators'.

Conclusion

Although this regional survey of Islam in North Africa confirms the view that Islamic manifestations are mainly to be understood within the national constellation of political and social forces, some general conclusions can be drawn from recent developments. Firstly, in all the North African countries the Islamic groups are potentially the most powerful opposition, with the possible exception of Morocco. The (violent) confrontation between political Islam and the state produces the most serious test

cases for conflict management in the North African region as the civil war in Algeria has shown most clearly. Again, the Moroccan case appears to be an exception as, in Morocco, the politics of succession and the dispute over the Western Sahara possess a far greater potential for future conflicts.

Secondly, the state applies different strategies to contain the Islamic challenge; cooptation and repression in the Moroccan case, political repression and armed confrontation in the other cases, although the Algerian regime has recently opted for coopting the moderate Islamic groups in a process of political institutionalisation, while at the same time it has formed a military alliance with the ais.

Thirdly, the most radical representatives of Islam are on the defensive (Morocco, Algeria) or are (temporarily?) defeated (Egypt, Tunisia). Due to a lack of reliable information a sound conclusion about the prospects of radical Islam in Libya is hard to make. In Egypt and Tunisia the more moderate forms of Islam are also repressed.

Fourthly, in the confrontation between the state and Islamic groups, civil society is a common victim. The state's political de-liberalisation tends to decrease the autonomous space of civil society organisations as the Egyptian and Tunisian cases show. In Morocco, on the other hand, tendencies towards political liberalisation and a mushrooming civil society occur simultaneously with the cooptation of moderate Islamic groups and the repression of the more militant organisations.

Policy recommendations

From a political perspective it is important that we analyse Islam in North Africa not solely as a security problem. This simply reproduces a discourse of state elites that not only represses the violent and non-violent manifestations of Islamism but uses the Islamic 'threat' as a pretext to curtail burgeoning civil society. This is all the more threatening for political and social stability as most of the region lacks a meaningful democratic political party system for which autonomous civil society organisations can act as a substitute. Furthermore, there seems to be no simple 'trade off between democracy and Islamic fundamentalism.' The history of the region shows no examples of an Islamic party bringing to power an anti-democratic regime via the ballot box. Not even the FIS scored an absolute majority in the cancelled elections of 1991. Political cooptation of Islamic parties in democratic institutions may have a moderating effect upon their political behaviour and tactics. At the same time the strengthening of 'progressive' civil society organisations is needed to challenge socially undesirable views such as the prohibition on women assuming public roles, and to protect the rights of religious and ethnic minorities. Moreover, elections should be critically monitored, as political institutionalisation is not synonymous with democracy, as manufactured election results prove. At the same time the process of the international monitoring of elections needs scrutiny for two diverging reasons: to challenge the claims of the regime that international monitoring attacks the national sovereignty of the state, and, secondly, to decrease the possibilities of legitimising the state's electoral engineering. Finally, as local and international human rights organisations have emphasised, a continuous condemnation of all forms of violence and abuses of human rights, either committed by Islamic organisations, security forces, or armed civilians, is necessary. In the specific case of Algeria an independent investigation of the killings and atrocities during the civil war is highly recommended. This research may take place under the responsibility of the UN High Commissioner on Human Rights. This investigation will support psychiatric solutions to traumatic experiences and sustain the socialisation of a new generation.

From an economic point of view a critical assessment of the different structural adjustment programmes is necessary. Although liberal economic reforms have produced some very positive results, their negative consequences should not be underestimated. High unemployment figures and uneven economic development carry the seeds for social and political conflict. Evidence from the Egyptian and Tunisian cases suggests that economic liberalisation may cause political de-liberalisation. The example of Morocco, on the other hand, seems to indicate that economic and political liberalisation can go hand in hand.

Attention needs to be paid to the possibilities of institutionalised regional cooperation as these forms of cooperation may tend to soften inter-state rivalries and reduce the potential for political and military conflict. Regional economic integration may enhance the chances of importing foreign capital, which may support the reduction of high debt burdens and the negative impact of structural adjustment. Moreover, it may stimulate economic cooperation with the European Union within the institutional cadres of the Euro-Mediterranean Partnership Agreement (Euromed). At the same time, the European Union can use Euromed's clause on human rights to protest against human rights abuses in the North African region, although in the past the eu has rarely used this clause. A possible institutional applicant for this type of regional conflict management may be a revived Arab Maghreb Union (AMU). However, unless the Western Sahara dispute is resolved the prospects for real cooperation within AMU remain bleak. This may serve as an additional reason to solve the dispute between Morocco and Polisario. To accomplish this, diplomatic efforts are needed to force Morocco to give up its delaying tactics and submit to the implementation of the referendum.

---

*   Arend Jan Termeulen is a political scientist at the University of Amsterdam, the Netherlands. He is preparing a Ph.D on the Islamic and nationalist construction of Tunisian authenticity in the modern history of Tunisia (1867-1987). He is an editor of the academic journal Sharqiyyât and has published on Islamism, nationalism, and political developments in North Africa in academic journals and readers, encyclopaedias, and the press.*

Solidarity without Cooperation

North Africa includes the countries from Morocco in the West through Algeria, Tunisia, and Libya to Egypt in the East. Within that, the Maghreb is often used to describe Morocco, Algeria, Tunisia, and Libya. These countries' shared Arabic language and culture provide a strong platform for relations among its peoples, as does Islam. They also had similar colonial experiences, and hold common interests regarding the conflict with Israel. The region's states are generally at peace with one another, and Algeria is the only country that has experienced a major violent internal conflict recently ◆ *By* Michael S. Lund

Nevertheless, the countries of North Africa have several demographic, economic, political, and international problems that could generate violent intra-state or inter-state conflicts in the region in the short or medium term. Although the growth rate of the population in the area may be slowing somewhat, it has more than doubled in the past thirty years, and its societies have a high proportion of youth seeking jobs in the labour market. Though there has been some economic growth in recent years, unemployment rates have ranged from 18 to 25 per cent. Population growth has also kept national food self-sufficiency low, and generated high rates of urbanisation, with the associated strain on municipal services and the decline of traditional social controls. The frustration felt by many unemployed in the cities could take violent forms, and religious extremism could spread due to the allure it holds out of restoring a kind of normative order.

The current trend toward economic liberalisation could further strain the North African economies. Lacking as yet adequate levels of education and literacy, food, urban water supply, basic public hygiene, and housing, these countries' economic reforms such as privatisation, loosened trade protections, and lower taxes will variously mean more competition from imported products, high costs for business restructurings, more bankrupted industries and further unemployment, reduced government spending, fewer social services, and wider socio-economic disparities, at least in the short term. Reform could simply advantage certain elites or classes without spreading the new economic opportunities more widely, thus

delegitimising the governments that sponsor these policies. Underlying inter-group divisions could rise to the surface that exist between Islamic religious traditions and between it and other faiths, as well as among ethnic groups and clans.

These domestic sources of potential social unrest could lead to violence or repression because the governments in the region have relied in different degrees on traditional authority, autocracy, one-partyism, and military authoritarianism as the means for maintaining social cohesion and political order. Functioning institutions and processes are generally lacking that could shift the existing political support systems for maintaining the loyalty of elites and masses to more participatory forms of political representation, such as effective parliaments, and to government by laws rather than patronage. Without enforceable guarantees of political rights and protection of opposition forces and minorities, destabilising pressures for rapid change could provoke old habits of repression from incumbent regimes or could provoke populist-based extremist majorities or minorities with violent revolutionary aims and authoritarian tendencies of their own. In sum, the societies are not generally well-prepared for undertaking a necessarily peaceful process of economic, social and political transition.

The most notable and powerful manifestation of Islamic radicalism occurred in Algeria in December, 1991, when the Government's renunciation of the election results, in anticipation of a victory by the Islamic Salvation Front (FIS), began what became a bloody civil war that resisted numerous initiatives to conclude it. Political Islamism has arisen in Egypt and some in Tunisia as well, though less so in Morocco, due perhaps to the respect for royal authority, a more cohesive population, and a more tolerant government stance towards civil society organisations.

Inter-state conflicts also threaten over water, oil or mineral resources, and unresolved boundary issues. The Middle Eastern and North African countries include many of the most militarised states in the world in terms of defence expenditures. As long as the Arab countries oppose a militarily superior Israeli state, regional or sub-regional arms control or disarmament will not make headway. Instead, an incentive or an excuse exists for Arab states to counterbalance Israel by keeping men in arms and for regimes such as Libya to try to develop weapons of mass destruction. On the other hand, Israel will not reduce its own military might.

The militarisation of the region derives not solely from the Arab-Israeli conflict. Despite their cultural and political bonds, many Arab states maintain mutual military rivalries and suspicions. Potential inter-state conflicts in the region include Egypt versus Libya, and Egypt versus Sudan and Ethiopia regarding the Nile.

The Euro-Mediterranean Partnership

A number of organisations and processes to increase intra-regional economic cooperation have originated from within the region. Among the states of Mauritania, Morocco, Algeria, Tunisia and Libya, the desire for economic development following colonialism provided an impetus for increasing their economic coordination. The Union of the Arab Maghreb (UAM) created in 1989, held a second summit and a conference on security in 1990. But the UAM soon failed because of the Algeria crisis, political differences such as between Morocco and the others over the Western Sahara issue, and economic disputes. Libya withdrew when the UAM countries complied with the UN sanctions against Libya. The UAM also suffered from the Maghreb states' attempts to develop favourable bilateral relations with European states. Other regional initiatives affecting North Africa include the Mediterranean Forum and the Middle East and North Africa Economic Summits (MENA).

The latter has held annual summits since 1994 aimed at promoting the economic liberalisation agenda in order to enhance the climate for business and international investment.

But undoubtedly the most ambitious and comprehensive regional initiatives which has considerable potential to affect future stability and cooperation in North Africa was initiated principally by actors from outside the region. The Euro-Mediterranean Partnership (EMP) was established between the European Union (EU) and the non-EU Mediterranean states in 1995. It encompasses all the countries in North Africa except Libya, as well as all countries of the EU, the Balkans and the Near East that border on the sea.

Beginning in the early 1990's, the member states of the (then) European Community (EC) became concerned about a number of problems in the countries on the southern rim of the Mediterranean and their impact on Europe. These worries included the increased movement of immigrants from the region into southern Europe, fears of civic unrest within the countries, the possible export of radicalism and terrorism to Europe, the U.S. confrontation with Libya, and Middle East tensions. Possible inter-state wars could disrupt the flow of oil and reduce trade and thus seriously harm the basic economies of Europe, and they could divide Europe in terms of their joining different sides.

Thus, in 1991, the EC announced a financial aid programme for eight Mediterranean countries in order to enhance stability in the region. Subsequently, the European Union (EU) sought to develop a Mediterranean policy as part of its overall desire for a Common Foreign and Security Policy (CFSP). The Barcelona Declaration of November 1995 announced the intent of the EU to create the EMP as a way to contribute in a comprehensive way to the stability, prosperity and development of the Mediterranean region, largely through development cooperation. It was adopted by the fifteen EU member states and eleven non-EU Mediterranean states (Algeria, Cyprus, Egypt, Israel, Jordan, Lebanon, Malta, Morocco, Syria, Tunisia, and Turkey), plus the Palestinian authorities. The EMP was to monitor developments in the region with a view to possible threats to security and launching a range of pro-active development, trade and security programs that can be described as forms of conflict prevention. For the non-EU countries, the main perceived advantage of the EMP was the possible opportunity to expand trade relations with the EU.

The EMP embodies not only a regional approach to the sources of potential conflicts, but also a shift away from a donor-recipient concept to one of mutual action, a multi-track strategy of conflict prevention potentially involving many instruments, a combination of region-wide and specific bilateral Association agreements, a non-governmental or transnational dimension, and a long-term perspective that recognises the need for an ongoing focus on the structural sources of conflicts. Initiatives were proposed in three principal areas: economic cooperation and trade, security cooperation, and civil society concerns such as human rights and cultural and social relations.

Economic Cooperation

The most extensive provisions concern economic development and financial cooperation, including the improvement of infrastructure, the integration of environmental concerns into development, and the creation of a free trade area by 2010. The EU partner committed itself to increase its financial assistance to the region in order to promote local business development and to improve living conditions by increasing employment, and it allocated 4,685 million European Currency Units (ECU) for those purposes from 1995 to 1999.

Diplomacy and Security Cooperation

The EMP security partnership commits the signatories to a political dialogue to strengthen their cooperation in addressing terrorism and illicit arms transfers and in promoting regional security. The EMP did not envision setting up any regional military capabilities such as peacekeeping forces, however.

Governance and Civil Society

A political plank of the agreement involves commitment to the rule of law, democracy, human rights, equal rights of peoples, and the right to self-determination (sic). A final aspect recognised the contribution that civil society can make through transnational partnerships in social, cultural and scientific affairs.

Achievements

By 1996, the initial euphoria about how the Middle East peace process could boost the EMP gave way to fears that the stalled process could undermine it. The second meeting of the Euro-Med partners in Malta in April, 1997 revealed that little progress had been made in implementing its work programmes. An ad hoc ministers' meeting in Palermo in June 1998 sought to renew their countries' commitment and give the partnership new momentum, but a specific implementation plan was postponed until the third Ministerial Conference in Stuttgart in April 1999.

As of 1998, no specific institutional organs or policies had been created to concretise the aspirations of the Barcelona Declaration. Many of the proposed civil society exchange programmes at the human, cultural, scientific, technological, and business levels had not been put into effect. Where they have started, they are not established on an ongoing basis. In short, the concrete implementation of central ingredients in the Euro-Med vision so far has been very slow.

Still, the EMP has made some modest progress. This EU effort to define its relationship with its southern periphery has perhaps emboldened new efforts among the Maghreb states themselves to rekindle their efforts to develop closer regional links. In November 1997, Morocco and Tunisia took a small step by agreeing to jointly study the possibility of creating a free trade zone by 2005.

In the area of civil society, the EU's MEDA Democracy programme made six million ECU available in 1996 for projects by European and Mediterranean NGOs, foundations, churches, human rights organisations, women's groups, and other bodies. Euro-Med networks have been established in higher education, print and electronic media, and local government development.

One significant transnational civil society effort flowing from this effort is the Euro-

Mediterranean Study Commission (EuroMeSCo), started in 1996. Comprised of working groups of European, Egyptian, Algerian, Maltese, Tunisian, and Moroccan analysts, this project has been analysing in depth and discussing a number of topics that are key, directly or indirectly to conflict prevention in North Africa and thus faced the members of the EMP. Their studies include the social ramifications of economic liberalisation; legal and governmental conditions conducive to foreign investment; domestic civil society development on behalf of democratisation, human rights, and professional governmental administration; cross-regional and North-South civil society relations; the rise of extremism in both regions and cross-cultural understanding; political cooperation regarding migration, drug-trafficking, terrorism, and the Middle East Peace Process; common global interests such as UN reform; and institutional capacities in support of the Barcelona process. EuroMeSCo seeks to formulate well-informed and realistic policy recommendations that seek to take into account the current political climate in the Mediterranean and Middle East regions and to disseminate them to relevant professionals and government policymakers.

A number of nationally-based NGOs have been created throughout the region in recent years that are dedicated to improving understanding and practices regarding human rights and democracy in the Arab world. The first International Conference of the Arab Human Rights Movement was held in Casablanca in April 1999.

Obstacles

The overall lack of vigorous movement by the EMP stems from several impediments. Some of these concern the nature of North Africa as a focus for regional activity:

- North Africa countries are shaped less by any distinct regional common identity of their own, or their links to the African continent, than by their cultural and political ties with their fellow Arab countries in the wider Middle East region with its centre to the East.
- The highly statist and military basis on which their political regimes often rest for their

power discourage significant moves not only toward domestic democratic and economic development and foreign investment, but also toward regional cooperation. Few meaningful ties have emerged around economic, political or security issues, either in the form of trade or formal regional organisations. The pressure of increased competition in the world economy does not favour regional cooperation among countries which traditionally have not been highly diversified and are so dependent on bilateral trade relations.

- The forging of new relationships, not to mention the creation of new mechanisms and taking of actions with respect to potential new conflicts, have been severely hampered by the several continuing military and political conflicts among the countries in the Mediterranean region or between them and outside powers - particularly the recurring tensions between Greece and Turkey over Cyprus and the Aegean islands, the creation of Turkish-Israeli defence cooperation, the internal strife in Algeria, the UN review of sanctions against Libya, the unresolved Western Sahara dispute, not to mention the Arab-Israeli conflict. Thus, more regional conflict management must take place before regional conflict prevention can take root.
- Despite its wide geographic coverage, many of the countries that affect or threaten the security of the EMP countries, such as Iraq, Iran and Sudan, are not in the EMP. This weakens the ability of the EMP per se to act with regard to dealing with such issues, such as through possible diplomatic interventions.
- The EMP faces formidable competition from other external actors if it aspires to carve out a major role in crisis prevention with respect to several of the region's potential future threats to security, such as the tensions between Egypt and Libya. The EMP reflects the view that in the long run at least, the EU is the most significant international actor to be able to act consistently toward the problems of the region, in view of the US's concentration on the Arab-Israeli conflict and Gulf region. But active roles are already being played with regard to current crises, such as the Middle

East peace process, by other state and multilateral actors such as the U.S., the Arab League, and NATO. Because the latter are much more influential in the region with respect to these current preoccupations, the EMP may continue to be kept out of many of the most important issue areas concerning regional security by the existing international division of labour in diplomacy.

- At least on economic issues, greater horizontal cooperation under the UAM may have conflicted with vertical integration of the Maghreb states with Europe.

Several of the obstacles to the EMP have to do with intra-EU policies, politics and perceptions:

- Aid priorities are in conflict within the EU. Its northern members have focused mainly on Central and Eastern Europe and Central Asia, whereas the southern EU members such as Spain, Portugal and Italy who promoted the EMP are more concerned about the Mediterranean region and have even developed their own Mediterranean policies. But EU aid to the East far outstrips that to the South. The Central and Eastern European countries have the political advantage of being prospective EU members. With the new EU commitments now in Kosovo and continuing instability in the Balkans and Russia, these trade-offs are likely to become even tougher in the years to come.
- The EU's policy emphasis so far has been put on the protecting the EU's borders rather than development programmes in the region to address the sources of out-migration. But the former efforts would become utterly fruitless if the latter are not undertaken.
- The EU's redefinition of the Maghreb as including Libya and Mauritania may have weakened a narrower Maghreb unity.

In the absence of a more coherent and vigorously pursued EU common policy toward the Mediterranean, the Euro-Med partnership so far lacks sufficient credibility, and the non-EU partners tend to look to other actors in the region, such as the U.S. or the UN.

Finally, obstacles arise out of the relationships between the northern and southern members of the EMP:

- Northern members tend to stress trade toward the South, whereas the southern members emphasise financial aid.
- Interdependence between the EU countries and the southern Mediterranean countries is asymmetrical - the latter are more dependent on the former, than vice-versa. Their links with the northern partners create few incentives for cooperating among themselves, unless the EU specifically encourages that.
- Ambiguity exists between the EU and the southern Mediterranean members as to whether the security risks and threats that the EMP should address refer mainly to the threat of spillover into Europe from southern problems, such as migrants resulting from underdevelopment or the exporting of terrorism, or mainly to those problems concern threats to security arising from within the region itself, such as inter-state military conflicts and domestic threats to stability, as well as European policies toward North Africa and its emigrants in Europe. This conceptual difference concerning security has undermined the notion of equal partnership.
- This unresolved difference arises from the original asymmetry that was built into the formation of the EMP with respect to where the main source of the problems of possible regional conflict are assumed to lie. Despite the negotiated formation of what is officially described as an equal partnership, the southern partners, because of their lack of democracy, stability and development, are regarded as more in need of some kind of 'treatment' through various forms of intervention than are the northern members. Notwithstanding the existence of problems in the northern countries such as xenophobic discrimination of immigrants and remaining conflicts such as Northern Ireland, the degree of difference that may exist on this dimension do not obviate the necessity of approaching this imbalance sensitively and mutually, so as not to perpetuate a source of intra-EMP resentment that blocks vigorous cooperation.

- Continued distrust, distorted images, and prejudices exist between Europe and the southern Mediterranean regions at the mass popular and the leadership and professional levels, and these barriers will block an EMP role in establishing a cooperative security regime and doing direct conflict prevention. Although the western countries are not seen as enemies, there is a widely shared weariness toward the intentions, power, and potential consequences that lie behind the northern states' apparent moves to advance their cultural and political visions unilaterally, such as reflected in the EU's CFSP and NATO's expansion. Fostered by such events as the Gulf War of 1990-91, Iraq's disarmament, Europeans' alleged hostility toward Arab migrants, the view is that the West's policies could possibly be carried out by military actions or political coercion.
- A related barrier to the EMP's ability to advance the prevention of potential internal conflicts through either diplomatic or structural measures, not to mention military actions, is the policy viewpoint of the southern members that such policies can constitute unacceptable interference in domestic affairs - another version of colonial or neo-colonial intrusion.
- The relationship between the northern and southern members lacks the presumption that there will be increasing integration, such as lies behind the relationship of the EU to Eastern and Central Europe, even the Balkans. For example, the notion that an OSCE-like High Commissioner for National Minorities could move about the region addressing inter-ethnic and human rights issues would be out of the question.

All in all, notwithstanding the eventual promise of a regional approach, the differences within the region, the developments outside it that greatly influence its southern members, internal EU divisions and its limited instruments and current influence, the existing diplomatic monopolies in the region, and other factors add up to serious limitations on how much regional cooperation through the EMP can be expected in this region very soon.

Nevertheless, the EMP's shortcomings have to be judged from a larger perspective before the value of the Euro-Med Partnership is assessed. Any multi-lateral initiative covering so many countries and issues cannot be expected to produce quick results. The appropriate criteria lie with whether meaningful results will emerge in the long run. If the EU members themselves, with their common values and institutions, have not yet evolved the Common Foreign and Security Policy they have desired, it should not be expected that working together with would-be partners in the southern Mediterranean who may have even more differences between them and with the EU, should produce visible results very soon.

But the immediate future may actually provide the EMP with opportunities to act where other actors have not or cannot. Despite the barriers with respect to regional security in a short-term sense, the door appears to be open with regard to the EMP's goals of long-term structural prevention. But this role should avoid any overbearing emphasis on quickly changing political institutions and policy practices, and focus mainly on increasing development aid that will increase growth without worsening social imbalances, expanding trade opportunities in equitable ways, and improving the technical capabilities of governments and other actors.

More fundamentally, the EMP has begun to supercede the past reliance solely on North-South relations through bilateral state-to-state diplomacy and trade by its sheer creation of a region-wide venue in which the interrelated national and international issues affecting regional security - development, social issues, arms control, cultural relations, and so on - can be discussed together, as they should. And the EMP has affirmed the goal of an integrated security and development policy, begun to create institutional apparatus or a process to carry it out, and tapped into the region's states' latent desires for more regional autonomy and a regional forum. This means it is in a strong position to activate these institutions, if and when the political environment becomes more favourable.

Ways forward

- For the EMP to take advantage of its opportunities requires the dominant partner, the EU, to take the leadership role and in particular, to continue to promote development and other initiatives. To do this, the EU must pursue its goal of developing an integrated Common Foreign and Security Policy more vigorously. To achieve a strategy that is conflict preventive in reality, rather than only in rhetoric, intra-EU policy coordination has to be enhanced with respect to its policies toward regions such as the southern Mediterranean that are threatened by increased instability and conflict. This applies, for example, to the relations between development cooperation and trade policies. The latter may worsen economic dislocations, at least in the short run, thus making it more necessary and difficult if not impossible, for the former to provide compensating protections and benefits, such as through supporting new enterprise development and social safety nets.
- To sustain the momentum behind EU concerns toward the southern Mediterranean, the individual EU states most concerned - Portugal, Spain, France, Italy and Greece - have to work together in taking the leadership of the EU effort and need to persuade the northern members of the benefits for them all.
- Rather than expect progress on the political and security tracks to occur before the Euro-Med is credible and can make progress in other realms, priority emphasis should be placed to the economic, social and cultural opportunities that might be more feasible for now, so that confidence in the overall vision of comprehensive security and in the EU's commitment to it is sustained.
- The Euro-Med Partnership needs to gain more institutional form and take more concrete visible steps in the short and medium term.
- While doing the above, strenuous efforts should be made to resolve the several outstanding current conflicts, such as the Western Sahara, that are blocking the EMP's ability to make major strides.
- To become effective in regional security issues, the EMP needs to create some link with the U.S., such as was envisioned in the EMP's precursor idea, the Conference for Security and Cooperation in the Mediterranean (CSCM), obviously inspired by the Conference for Security and Cooperation in Europe (CSCE).
- One bold initiative that might jumpstart a wider civil society dialogue is to convene a series of CSCE-like pan-Mediterranean civil society conferences on selected issues where modest agreements and concrete steps can be taken. A product of such a process could be a Charter of Peace and Security in which certain basic principles and codes of conduct for states are laid down and promulgated.

References

Roberto Aliboni, *Conflict Prevention in the Euro-Mediterranean Context.* Unpublished paper written for the EuroMesCo process, 24 pages. no date

Roberto Aliboni, Abdel Monem Said Aly, and Alvaro De Vasconcelos, *EuroMesCo: Working Group on Political and Security Cooperation, and Working Group on Arms Control, Confidence Building and Conflict Prevention.* Joint Report, 63 pages. April, 1997

Susanne Baier-Allen, *Conflict Prevention through Development Cooperation: The EU Approach in the Maghreb.* Pp. 32-47 in Peter Cross and Guenola Rasamoelina, eds., Conflict Prevention Policy of the European Union: Recent Engagements, Future Instruments Yearbook 1998-99 of the SWP-Conflict Prevention Network (Baden-Baden: Nomos Verlagsgessellschaft, 1999)

Laura Guazzone, *Managing Security in the Mediterranean Region: Problems, Tools, and Institutions.* Unpublished paper written for the EuroMesCo process, 23 pages, no date

Yannis A. Stivachtis, *European Union's Mediterranean Policy: An Assessment.* Schiller International University, no date. 50 pages

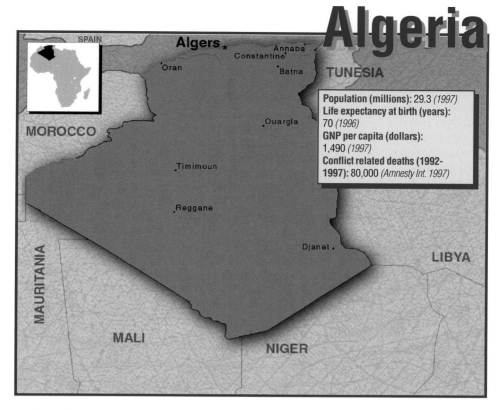

Population (millions): 29.3 *(1997)*
Life expectancy at birth (years):
70 *(1996)*
GNP per capita (dollars):
1,490 *(1997)*
Conflict related deaths (1992-
1997): 80,000 *(Amnesty Int. 1997)*

Civilians Trampled in a State of Turmoil

Following the cancellation in 1992 of Algeria's first free parliamentary elections since independence, a war between government forces and numerous armed Islamic groups has resulted in some 80,000 casualties. Although the large-scale assault on human rights in Algeria is rooted in a range of factors originating in the failure of political institutionalisation, the violence has now reached a stage of self-perpetuation where cause and effect can no longer be easily identified. Mainly as a result of Algerian nationalist sentiments, attempts to manage the conflict through external intervention have been rare and largely unsuccessful. A political solution is unlikely as long as the stalemate between government forces and armed groups persists. However, the first initiatives of the newly elected president, Abdelaziz Bouteflika, as well as the reactions of important sectors among the Islamic groups, give reason for some optimism ◆ *By* **Reinoud Leenders**

Following mass rioting in 1988, triggered by the failure of the state to address a widespread socio-economic malaise, by 1990 Algeria had developed from an authoritarian state into an - albeit restricted - multiparty system under reforms carried out by President Chadli Bendjadid. The first municipal and provincial elections held in 1990 were won by

the Front islamique du salut (FIS), an Islamic party, while the *Front de liberation national* (FLN), previously the ruling party, obtained only 28 per cent of the votes. In December 1991, the FIS obtained 47 per cent of the votes in the first round of the first free parliamentary elections held since independence in 1962. Shocked by this result, the military subsequently cancelled the second round of the elections and arrested thousands of FIS supporters and their leaders.

The High State Council, comprising military officers and political appointees, was formed to formally rule the country. Mohamad Boudiaf presided over the council but was killed in June 1992 by a member of the security forces, allegedly because he intended to crack-down on widespread state corruption. He was succeeded by Ali Kafi (July 1992-January 1994) and Liamine Zeroual. Due to the political clampdown, some Islamic groups opted for armed strategies while other groups that had already carried out armed operations earlier became more prominent. When one radical wing of the FIS declared a Jihad against the military regime and the latter refused to reverse its decisions concerning the elections, a war broke out that, to date, continues to claim the lives of government personnel, Islamic gunmen and civilians.

Although observers disagree in their analyses about the causes of the outbreak of hostilities or place differing emphases on particular factors, the main reason for the conflict can perhaps best be summarised by pointing out the deficiencies of political institutionalisation since 1962. In the words of one observer, Hugh Roberts, post-independence Algeria has been marked by the fact that the 'formal distribution of political responsibility does not correspond to the actual distribution of power'.

The failure of state-building had its roots in the political set-up which emerged immediately after independence when the historical leadership of the resistance against French colonial rule was outmanoeuvred by the military. The latter formed a coalition with state bureaucrats and the remains of the FLN which became Algeria's sole political party. Rampant corruption and conflicts between different clans rendered state institutions practically dysfunctional, contributing to the failure of development policies. This problem became particularly acute with the fall in gas- and oil prices in 1986 as hydrocarbons accounted for 57 per cent of government revenues. The collapse of the oil price and ineffective measures to remedy the crisis caused a dramatic fall in living standards, increasing unemployment (it was estimated that by 1990, seventy per cent of the labour force under thirty years was out of work), and shortages in adequate and affordable housing. A package of economic reform policies to relieve the state's debt burden, initiated in collaboration with the IMF in 1989, disproportionately hit the poor and exacerbated the atmosphere of general crisis. In these circumstances, another issue that was left unresolved by the country's ruling coalition, the role of Islam, gained political significance.

Islam had played an important factor in the struggle for independence against the French as witnessed by the close relationship between the FLN and the Association of Reformist Ulama, a grouping of Muslim clerics founded in 1931. Following independence, the FLN disassociated itself from this Islamic-nationalist current and began advocating a largely secularist and 'socialist' state ideology. When the revolutionary legitimacy of the ruling elite began to fade, many began to feel alienated from the political system. The slowly emerging fault line between a secularist elite and under-privileged groups was accentuated by a school and university system that, in terms of job opportunities and social status, privileged those educated in French and deprived others who were educated in Arabic from real prospects of social mobility.

In the late 1980s, the FIS effectively capitalised on all of these different sources of discontent with the regime. Operating a network of mosques and Islamic centres, the FIS also increased its popularity by providing an alternative to cash-starved state institutions in offering social services. However, the rising power of the FIS, and symbolic concessions made by the regime such as the Arabisation of the education system, alarmed the Berber minority that forms about 20 to 25 per cent of the total population and is concentrated in the Kabylia region. Berber political and cultural organisations have subsequently stepped up their campaigns for the recognition of their main language, Tamazight, and opposed the Islamic movement that has explicitly linked its drive for Islamisation to further Arabisation.

The main adversaries in the armed conflict are, on the one hand, numerous armed Islamic groups and, on the other hand, the security forces and armed civilian groups allied with them. The two most powerful men in the military are believed to be Lt. General Mohammad Lamari and the head of the military security forces, Mohammad Mediene. The FIS has been increasingly marginalised following the arrest of its long-time leaders Abbasi Madani and Ali Belhadj in June 1991. Armed Islamic groups include the *Armee islamique du salut* (AIS), the military wing of the FIS comprising an estimated 10,000 men, and a loose organisation of different militant and armed groups known as the *Groupes islamiques armes* (GIA), comprising an estimated 2,500 to 10,000 men. The groups falling under the umbrella of the GIA are usually headed by an 'Emir', a military commander, and a 'Caliph', his political guide. They target state officials, journalists, artists, musicians and other civilians. The GIA are reported to engage in black-market operations and mafia practices which enable them to sustain their military activities. Armed groups are also believed to be involved in private corporations that replaced privatised and/or destroyed state-run enterprises, in order to finance their operations. Some of the armed groups' members, the 'Mudjahedin', are believed to have received military training during the war in Afghanistan. They have also reportedly been involved in armed operations in Morocco, Bosnia and Yemen.

Apart from the FLN, political parties with some significant following include the *Front des forces socialistes* (FFS), a secularist and mainly Berber-supported party revived in 1989 and led by Hocine Ait Ahmed, the *Mouvement pour la Democratie en Algerie* (MDA), created in 1985 by exiled FLN-leader and former President Ahmed Ben Bella, and the *Rassemblement pour la culture et la democratie* (RCD), a Berber party with minor support led by Said Saadi and legalised in 1989, and two legalised Islamic parties that are more or less loyal to the regime.

Conflict Dynamics

The Algerian government has persisted in regarding the conflict solely as a 'security problem' posed by the challenge of 'terrorist groups' that have to be eradicated by all necessary means. At the same time, the government has claimed that the security situation is 'under control' and that the violence is 'residual'. However, within the armed forces there are splits between '*eradicateurs*', favouring the hard-line position, and those in favour of guided negotiations with opponents of the regime to stop the violence. These splits have been complicated by divisions between clans and officers with their own supporters, as shown by accusations between several factions reported in the Algerian press since the summer of 1998. The FIS has advocated the establishment of an 'Islamic state', in line with Islamic law, but has made statements in favour of parliamentary democracy, although its adherence to liberal principles remains ambiguous. It took part in the 'National Contract', negotiated in Rome (see below), that offered a blue-print for a peaceful transition to democracy. The GIA have opposed any form of reconciliation and aim at the violent overthrow of the state but, with little prospect of achieving this aim, seem to be content with exploiting the situation in their own interests. The FFS and MDA oppose the military regime, criticise its violations of human rights and public liberties and have pressed for recognition of the FIS as a condition of normalisation. The RCD initially adopted a stance in line with that of the '*eradicateurs*' but seems to have opted for a more reconciliatory approach since it participated in the 'National Contract'.

Although individual killings by both government forces and armed groups have been responsible for most of the casualties, since the beginning of 1997 massacres of innocent civilians have become systematic, thereby transforming the conflict into one of indiscriminate and self-perpetuating violence. Most of the massacres were committed in a systematic and organised manner in villages in areas around the capital, in the Algiers, Blida and Medeain regions. The largest massacres occurred in Sidi Rais, south of Algiers, in August 1997, claiming the lives of up to 300 people, and in Relizane, in December 1997, claiming the lives of over 400 people. Little is known about the reasons for these acts of violence, or the identity of their perpetrators. They may have resulted from GIA members' frustration at their inability to continue hitting state targets. Others have explained the massacres as being land grabs, banditry, local vendettas or the settling of old scores. Often the massacres took place in close proximity to government forces who failed to intervene and let the perpetuators leave the scene after they committed their crimes. This has fed suspicions that security forces, for one reason or another, were actually actively involved in the killings. In another development, armed groups have started to fight each other, possibly in bids to control certain areas and to raise illegal 'taxes' and generate other economic gains. The proliferation of Islamic armed factions and sub-factions, armed gangs, and paramilitary 'self-defence units' has further contributed to a situation where it is no longer clear which aims are being pursued or for what reasons groups have fallen out amongst each other.

Since his election as president in November 1995, and bolstered in his powers by constitutional amendments in 1996, Zeroual seems to have followed a three-track strategy to restore a minimum of stability within the conditions set by the military. Firstly, the government has initiated a major economic reform programme by privatising state enterprises, cutting expenditure on state subsidies and creating favourable conditions for foreign investments to increase economic growth and living standards. Secondly, the government stepped up its security measures against Islamic insurgents, arresting and killing thousands of its armed opponents. Thirdly, Zeroual initiated a dialogue with 'acceptable' opposition parties and made provision for new local and parliamentary elections that provided a minimum of political participation. In September 1996, these efforts resulted in a 'national reconciliation pact', boycotted by the FFS. Probably as a result of pressure by more hard-line army officers, the dialogue excluded the FIS and the GIA.

Parliamentary elections took place in June 1997 with a majority of seats being gained by the FLN and another pro-government party. Legalised Islamic parties (the FIS was again excluded) gained about 25 per cent of the seats. The elections were widely believed to have been rigged. In July 1997, FIS-leader Abbasi Madani was released from prison but was again placed under house arrest two months later after he had sent an open letter to the UN Secretary-General.

Abdelkader Hachani, another detained FIS-leader, was released in July 1997 after being sentenced to five and a half years, the term he had already served. In response to Zeroual's limited political opening, the AIS declared a unilateral truce in September 1997 and started joint military operations with the army against the GIA. In November local elections took place, resulting in a distribution of power similar to that of the parliamentary elections. Some observers speculated that Zeroual wanted to allow for a limited degree of pluralism within a framework controlled by the government parties and continuing military tutelage. However, the major power-holders within the military seem to have disapproved of this strategy. Frustrated by the obstacles the military put in his way, Zeroual announced his resignation in September 1998. Shortly before the presidential elections held on April 15, 1999, six candidates, mostly from the opposition, withdrew in protest against alleged vote rigging and election fraud. Consequently, the only remaining candidate, Abdelaziz Bouteflika, a former foreign affairs minister, was elected but voter turnout seems to have been extremely low. Bouteflika, reportedly supported by the more moderate factions in the army and by the FLN, immediately promised to hold a 'dialogue excluding nobody' and to steer the country towards 'national reconciliation'. Six weeks after his appointment, Bouteflika hinted on May 29, 1999 that he would support a national referendum on reconciliation and a general amnesty for those involved in the conflict, excluding those charged with murder. In reply, the leadership of both the FIS and AIS expressed their 'total and unconditional support to stop the battle', leaving members of the GIA and other armed groups as the main actors in their armed conflict with the security forces and the government at large.

Government sources estimated the number of fatalities as 26,000. However, Amnesty International's figure of 80,000 killed has been widely accepted as more realistic. According to Amnesty International, in 1996 the victims included over 100 foreign nationals. Most of the casualties were civilian victims of arbitrary killings, massacres and extra-judicial executions. The only estimate of material damage currently available refers to an unspecified but large number of factories being destroyed by 1995, resulting in 45,000 workers losing their jobs. Other victims include those tortured by government forces, 'disappeared' persons (estimated by Amnesty International in 1999 to number 3,000), imprisoned journalists, about sixty journalists killed by Islamic groups since 1993, and detainees killed in prison. Tens of thousands, if not hundreds of thousands of civilians have been forced to flee or to go into hiding out of fear of arrest or violence by the parties involved in the conflict.

Official Conflict Management

Following five years of inaction, the *United Nations* expressed its desire to become involved in efforts to manage the conflict when, in August 1997, UN Secretary-General Kofi Annan stated that 'words are no longer enough' to bring about a peaceful solution in Algeria. However, in March 1998, urgent requests by Annan and the UN High Commissioner on Human Rights, Mary Robinson, to the Algerian government to allow an investigative mission by the UN Special Rapporteur on Extrajudicial, Summary or Arbitrary Executions and the UN Special Rapporteur on Torture were rejected. Neither rapporteurs has succeeded in gaining access to Algeria since 1993. In the 1998 session of the UN Commission on Human Rights - a body of eighteen independent experts - the situation in Algeria was discussed for the first time after the Algerian state submitted a report on its obligations concerning civil and political rights. As a result of mounting pressure, in July 1998 the Algerian government invited a UN team headed by former Portuguese President Mario Soares to visit the country, but denied it an 'investigative or fact-finding mandate'. Lacking a clearly defined mandate, the team stayed for about two weeks in the country and talked to trade union leaders, opposition parties, women's groups, lawyers and a small number of victims of the conflict.

Meanwhile, the Human Rights' Commission concluded in a report issued in August 1998 that allegations of the involvement of security forces in the massacres were persistent enough to warrant an international inquiry. The

Commission also condemned grave violations of human rights by government forces. One month later, Soares and his panel had toned-down the language of their report considerably. It repeated the government's talk of 'terrorism' and failed to condemn violations by the government. Only the report's calls for reform of the security forces and the judiciary indicated indirectly that along with armed groups, the Algerian government bears responsibility for human rights abuses. The UN panel report was blasted by Amnesty International as a 'whitewash'. Other UN organisations to have taken a stand on the crisis in Algeria include UNICEF which, in November 1997, condemned the 'relentless civilian killings in Algeria' with specific reference to children. *The Organisation of African Unity (OAU)*, of which Algeria is historically a highly influential member, has failed to play any role in efforts to stop the violence. In November 1994, its African Commission on Human and Peoples' Rights adopted a resolution on Algeria, expressing concern about extra-judicial executions, torture and arbitrary detention and calling upon the world community to 'mobilize and support democratic forces in Algeria and abroad in their efforts to restore peace, the rule of law, and respect for human rights in Algeria'. However, this resolution was dropped in March 1995, undoubtedly as a result of Algerian pressure not to intervene in its domestic affairs. The *Arab League* has also refrained from making any attempt at conflict resolution. Instead, it has merely supported the Algerian government and accepted its stress on combating 'terrorism' with all means.

The *European Union* temporarily froze its economic and humanitarian assistance to Algeria following the abrogation of the 1992 elections but the freeze was short-lived. Negotiations, ongoing since 1995, concerning the Euro-Mediterranean Partnership Agreement (EUROMED), which contains a clause on human rights, failed to discuss issues related to conflict management and human rights in the Algerian crisis. In 1996 and 1997 the EU called for a 'political dialogue' and 'condemnation of terrorism' from the UN Human Rights Commission, but refrained from referring to the Algerian state's responsibility for human rights violations. Since 1997 the EU seems to have sought a more active role. In September 1997, the European Parliament (EP) recommended 'international protection' for Algerian asylum-seekers who would be at risk if they were forced to return to their country. However, EU members continue to reject Algerian asylumseekers on the basis that 'it could not be proved that they were in danger' or that 'it could not be proved that they could not obtain protection from the authorities of their country'. An exact number of Algerians having requested and/or granted political asylum in member-states of the EU has not been made public.

In November 1997, the EP organised a closed hearing on the conflict and the human rights situation in Algeria which was attended by Algerian lawyers, journalists and relatives of the 'disappeared'. In January 1998, three EU foreign ministers visited Algiers and called upon the Algerian government to allow UN Special Rapporteurs to visit the country. In February 1998, a delegation of the EP went to Algeria in a visit that was carefully programmed by the Algerian authorities. Surprisingly, the delegation failed to call for an international investigation into the violence nor did it condemn human rights abuses by government forces. What was left of the delegation's credibility was lost when its members refused to open a letter sent by the FIS during a press conference and set fire to it in their hotel toilet.

After the November 1995 election of President Zeroual, the *Algerian government* initiated a dialogue with several secular and legalised Islamic political parties, excluding the FIS and GIA, in an attempt to bolster its credibility. These efforts led to a unilateral truce by the AIS in September 1997. However, the dialogues failed to bring about meaningful political participation, let alone a peaceful solution, and there are suspicions that these efforts merely served to outmanoeuvre or divide the regime's opponents. The government established in 1992 the *Observatoire nationale des Droits de l'Homme* to report on human rights violations in the country. However, the Observatoire seems to view its role largely as defending the government rather than human

rights. It has repeatedly stated that human rights violations by government forces have been limited in number and that these incidents were immediately followed up by judiciary action. The government also opened centres run by the National Commission for the Preservation and promotion of Women for victims of rape by 'terrorists'. Moreover, since 1998 citizens can report the 'disappearance' of their relatives at offices established all over the country.

Other 'NGOs' set up and sponsored by the government are those that purport to speak in the name of victims of 'terrorism'. These organisations include *Djezairouna, Sumoud* and the *Association nationale des familles victimes de terrorisme*. In a controversial move to enable citizens to defend themselves against 'terrorists', the state has since 1995 set up civilian militias comprising some 150 to 200,000 armed citizens. But rather than managing the conflict, this move severely exacerbated the situation resulting in the proliferation of armed groups settling scores in local and tribal disputes, extra-judicial killings and complete anarchy.

Until 1995, *France* largely subscribed to the view of the Algerian government that the conflict can only be addressed by ruthlessly repressing the violence of Islamic groups. This stand was reflected in France's own crackdown on suspected Islamic militants residing in France following the hijacking of an aircraft of Air France in December 1994, resulting in three casualties, and the bombings by the GIA in Paris in 1995-6, which killed twelve civilians. However, at the end of 1994, the late French President François Mitterrand proposed a EU-sponsored peace conference. The Algerian government's rejection of this proposal on the grounds that it constituted an interference in its domestic affairs made France adopt a more careful and distanced approach, claiming neutrality in the conflict. France says it no longer supplies weapons to Algeria although bilateral credits and loans amounting to about US$ 1 billion per year have continued. Since 1996 France has appeared to acknowledge that there is no military solution to the conflict but it has continued to prevent the EU formulating more active policies towards the Algerian crisis.

ALGERIA, ALGERS: Freedom monument

PHOTO MICHAEL MOGENSEN/LINEAIR

The *United States* has developed a closer interest in Algeria since American companies stepped up their investments in the Algerian oil and gas sectors in 1994. In 1995, the GIA was added to the blacklist of 'terrorist organisations' prepared by the US State Department. In February 1998, Algerian MPs were invited by the US Congress to receive training in parliamentary democracy. In Spring 1998, US Assistant Secretary of State for Near East Affairs Martin Indyk went to Algiers and called upon the Algerian government to allow access for UN rapporteurs to investigate the massacres. The US threatened to support a resolution in the UN Human Rights' Commission critical of the Algerian government. Following a strong rebuff from the Algerian government, calls for an international inquiry have not been pursued. Meanwhile, the US seems to have tightened its relations with the Algerian government as illustrated by joint US-Algerian military exercises at the end of 1998.

Multi-Track Diplomacy

Although the 1989 Constitution allows NGOs, under some conditions, to operate freely, in practice NGOs, even when legalised, have been severely hindered if not blocked in their efforts to manage the conflict. The Roman Catholic Sant 'Egidio community in Rome undertook a major attempt to facilitate peace talks between all parties involved and to act as an intermediary in their conflicts. International NGOs also suffered from the lack of civil liberties as they were particularly targeted by the government's hostile attitude towards any external intervention in the conflict. Under these difficult circumstances some Algerian NGOs continued to operate, largely by advocating a peaceful solution to the conflict. They were supported by international NGOs which conducted fact-finding missions when possible, sent delegations and urged, on the one hand, the Algerian government and armed groups to respect basic human rights and, on the other hand, called upon the international community to launch an international inquiry into the violence.

Domestic
The International Service for Human Rights and the Latin American Federation of Associations of Relatives of Disappeared Detainees gathered

with the *Committee of Relatives of the Disappeared of Algeria* in a workshop on the 'disappeared' in Algeria held in September 1998. They submitted 477 dossiers of documented cases of 'disappearances' to the UN Working Group on Enforced and Involuntary Disappearances. The Committee of Relatives of the Disappeared of Algeria is a loose organisation that has been active since the summer of 1998. Aided by Amnesty International and the Federation Internationale des Droits de l'Homme (FIDH), it sent delegates to several European countries where they held conferences to draw attention to the problem of the 'disappeared'. The organisation also started to organise weekly demonstrations in Algeria which are attended by hundreds of mothers. A request by the Committee for formal recognition has been denied.

Another Algerian NGO involved in conflict management is the *Rassemblement d'action jeunesse* (RAJ), an organisation founded in 1992. The RAJ provided human rights education to youth all over the country, assisted them in searching for employment, and lobbied the government to start a dialogue between all the parties involved in the conflict. Following the first massacres in 1995, the RAJ produced a manifesto for peace and collected over 20,000 signatures in a few days. It has also organised an all-night concert for peace which was attended by more than 11,000 young people. The activities of the RAJ were subsequently curtailed by government forces despite its legal recognition in 1993.

Algeria has two major human rights organisations; *the League algeriene pour les droits de l'homme* (LADH) and the *League algeriene pour la defense des droits de l'homme* (LADDH). The difficult circumstances under which both organisations operate were highlighted in June 1994 when Yousef Fathallah, the president of the LADH was murdered. Both organisations claim complete independence but their members and activities are far from non-partisan. On several occasions Algerian intellectuals and politicians, including former Foreign Prime-Minister Mouloud Hamrouche, FIS-leader Abdelkader Hachani and LADDH president Ali Yahya, have made a 'call for peace' by issuing written statements. Numerous major mass demonstrations have taken place: in October 1994, in protest against the violence in general, in 1997 following the rigged local elections, and in June 1998 in protest against the murder of Berber Rai-singer Matoub Lounes.

The Algerian press has been remarkably vocal and informative, given, on the one hand, the government's harassment, prosecution, imprisonment, and monopolistic control of paper supplies and printing presses. On the other hand, journalists have been a target of deadly assaults from Islamic activists, although no new attacks have occurred since 1996. The Algerian press has been a major source of news on the conflict, but it has also been used by factions within the military and civilian government elites as a platform to promote their own views and discredit opponents. Consequently, factual news reporting is far from reliable, as illustrated by contradictions within various newspapers' accounts of major incidents of violence. International human rights activists see the daily *La Tribune* and *El-Watan* as the most reliable and non-partisan news sources from Algeria.

International
In November 1994, the *Sant 'Egidio community*, which had earlier been involved in the peace process in Mozambique, invited all parties in the conflict, including the government and the FIS, for peace talks in Rome. Of the various parties, only the government declined the offer. In January 1995, the parties involved launched a 'National Contract' that denounced all forms of violence while calling for a cease-fire, recognition of the FIS, recognition of the Tamazight language, the release of all political detainees, and convening of a national conference to establish a transitional government in preparation of free and democratic elections. The initiative was flatly rejected by the government.

Amnesty International has taken the main initiative in exposing the scope of human rights violations by government forces and armed groups in Algeria. Until 1997, when the organisation was banned from entry, Amnesty International conducted fact-finding missions that were documented in several reports.

Human Rights Watch and the FIDH also conducted visits to Algeria to record human rights violations. An attempt by the FIDH to observe a trial in July 1997 failed when they were denied access to the court. *Reporters sans frontièrers* (RSF) and the *Committee to Protect Journalists* also published reports. A delegation of the latter organisation, headed by CNN-reporter Peter Arnett, went in October 1998 on its first fact-finding mission and met with Communications' minister Habib Chawki, to discuss, amongst other cases, the 'disappearance' of two Algerian journalists and the suspension of permits for several daily newspapers. Amnesty International and Human Rights Watch both briefed the UN Human Rights Commission on the situation in Algeria. The organisations mentioned here issued joint statements in October 1997 and April 1998, in both cases to persuade the world community at large and the UN in particular to immediately launch an international inquiry into the violence.

In 1998 a group of leading Algerian and European intellectuals, including Pierre Bourdieu and historian Mohamed Harbi, formed the *International Committee for Peace, Democracy, and Human Rights in Algeria*. In an attempt to advise the UN panel led by Soares on which issues needed to be addressed during their visit, the Committee issued its first declaration just before the panel's departure for Algeria.

Numerous other international NGOs have called upon the Algerian government to end human rights violations and respect public liberties. They include the World Organisation against Torture, Article 19, the International Federation of Journalists, International Pen, the International Press Institute, and the World Press Freedom Committee.

The *International Crisis Group* began monitoring the situation in Algeria at the end of 1997 with the aim of identifying 'practical ways in which the international community can contribute to a lasting resolution of the Algerian crisis'. In March 1998 it issued its first report on Algeria. This contained a series of recommendations emphasising the importance of press freedoms.

The *International Red Cross Committee* has been unable to visit the country since 1992 due to restrictions imposed by the Algerian government. Other humanitarian organisations have also been denied the access needed to provide relief to victims of the conflict.

Reflection
The lack of access to Algeria and inability to freely investigate the human rights abuses have been the major obstacles to a successful intervention by international NGOs. The peace talks in Rome, and the government's refusal to accept any mediation attempts by outsiders, clearly illustrated that Algerian national pride is a serious obstacle to foreign interventions. Undoubtedly, this position has been fed by Algeria's traumatic colonial experience. It has been suggested that Algeria's excellent connections in the UN and the OAU have been an additional reason for the failure of the very few serious international attempts to manage the conflict. The country's reliance on oil- and gas reserves can be seen as a third reason of why the government has been able to lock itself off from outside critique and suggestions. However, the talks in Rome had some positive effect in that they forced the regime to initiate its own 'national reconciliation pact', even if this initiative lacked sincerity. Furthermore, in spite of the obstacles faced by human rights organisations, they have succeeded, especially since 1997, in drawing attention to the humanitarian crisis in Algeria.

More generally, the Algerian regime's hostile attitude towards outside offers of mediation has raised awareness that the conflict cannot be seen as a simple trade-off between democracy and Islamic fundamentalism. The unprecedented scale of the violence committed contributed to the fact that UN could no longer ignore the situation in Algeria. However, since the UN agreed to send a mission on terms dictated by the Algerian government, the call for an international inquiry has lost momentum. Given the lack of public liberties, Algerian NGOs have only made little achievements in their efforts to manage the conflict. An important exception is the Committee of Relatives of the Disappeared of Algeria. Since it launched its campaigns in the summer of 1998, the issue of the 'disappearances' has become much talked about in Algeria, with even the press and members of Parliament raising questions about the fate of the 'disappeared'.

Prospects

Partly because of the hidden nature of the conflict and the opacity of behind the scenes power struggles, analysts outline several contradictory scenarios for Algeria's future development. A genuine peace settlement has in this context only rarely been considered as realistic. Others believe that the conflict has reached a stalemate. Most observers have therefore predicted a protracted armed conflict with parts of the country controlled by armed groups and other parts by government forces. It has also been suggested that this may ultimately lead to an 'Afghan scenario'; a disintegration of the state and a division of the country into de-facto 'emirates' and state-controlled areas. Others believe it more likely that some 'Turkish scenario' will develop wherein some political participation will be allowed but with the military continuing to play a major political role. Alternatively, a 'Sudanese scenario' may evolve in which the military will strike a deal with Islamic armed groups, largely at the expense of all other parties involved.

Recent FIS and AIS support for Bouteflika's suggestions concerning a national referendum on reconciliation and an amnesty, suggest that these two groups will accept any opening even at the cost of changing their names and leaving their long-time leaders in prison or under house arrest. An alliance between Bouteflika, military moderates and these two Islamic groups may become instrumental in neutralising the violence committed by the GIA and other armed groups. However, the validity of such future projections is difficult to assess as observers already disagree over what will happen in the very near future. Some regard Bouteflika's room of manoeuvrability as equally limited due to military hard-liners who, as with their ejection of former president Zeroual, may continue to dominate the political process. Other observers, such as Ignacio Ramonet of Le Monde Diplomatique, have described Bouteflika's initiatives as serious and unprecedented.

Recommendations

International human rights organisations, including the UN Human Rights Committee, have recommended that both the Algerian government and armed groups take immediate and concrete measures to stop violations of human rights. The Algerian government has been urged to ensure that prompt, independent and impartial investigations are carried out into all cases of human rights abuses and to bring those responsible to justice. The government has also been urged to disband all paramilitary militias and ensure that all security operations are carried out only by law-enforcement personnel who have received the necessary training and who can be held accountable to their superiors. The Algerian government was also urged to lift censorship of reports on the conflict, ensure freedom of expression and to end the politically motivated financial pressure against local newspapers. One international NGO, the International Crisis Group, has urged the European Union to take the occasion of its negotiations with the Algerian government over EUROMED to demand an end to press restrictions and the monopolisation of printing facilities.

The UN has been advised to set up a credible, international inquiry into the massacres and other human rights abuses by using the existing UN-machinery and by appointing a Special Rapporteur on Algeria. The Organisation of African Unity has also been advised to play a more active and supporting role in this context. The EU has been advised to further distance itself from the French position towards Algeria, and start giving greater encouragement to Algerian politicians and NGOs committed to a peaceful solution, if possible under the social and humanitarian provisions of EUROMED. Others have recommended any third party wanting to contribute to conflictmanagement in Algeria to take into account the country's colonial past and related sensitivities in order to render its efforts more effective.

Background document provided by Berto Jongmans/PIOOM

Service Information

Newsletters and Periodicals
La Tribune (Algerian French-language daily):
see also: latribune-online.com/
El-Watan (Algerian French-language daily): see
also: www.elwatan.com/
Le Monde Diplomatique (much reporting by
Algerian journalists and intellectuals), see also:
www.monde-diplomatique.fr/
Maghreb-Machrek
Peuples Mediterranees
The Maghreb Review

Reports
Amnesty International
- Algeria: Civilian Population Caught in a
  Spiral of Violence. November 1997
- Algeria: Fear and Silence - A Hidden
  Human Rights Crisis. November 1996
Human Rights Watch
- Algeria: Violations of Civil and Political
  Rights - A Briefing Paper for the UN
  Human Rights Committee. July 1998
- Algeria: Neither Among the Living nor the
  Dead. February 1998
- Algeria: Elections in the Shadow of
  Violence and Repression. June 1997
International Crisis Group
- Algerie: La Crise de la Presse, Octobre-
  Decembre 1998, 11 January 1999
- Algeria, Between Death Threats and
  Censorship, 31 March 1998
Reporters Sans Frontières
- Algerie: Les violations de la liberte de la
  presse, de 1992-98. May 1998
United Nations
- Algeria: Report of Eminent Panel, July-
  August 1998: UN Department of Public
  Information, September 1998
UNHCR
- Background Paper on Refugees and
  Asylum Seekers from Algeria, Centre for
  Documentation and Research. October
  1995
Council on Foreign Relations (US)
- Algeria's Struggle for Democracy,
  Prospects for Incremental Change, Studies

Department Occasional Paper Series,
prepared by Mona Yacoubian. November
1997

Other Publications
Algeria: The Next Fundamentalist State?
Graham E. Fuller. Rand Corporation, 1996
L'Algerie dans la Guerre. Remy Leveau (ed).
1995
La Guerre civile en Algerie - 1990-1998. Luis
Martinez. 1998
*Between Ballots and Bullets - Algeria's Transition
From Authoritarianism*. William B. Quandt.
Brookings Institute, 1998
L'Egypte et L'Algerie au Peril de la liberalisation.
Alain Roussillon. 1996
The Agony of Algeria. Martin Stone. Columbia
University Press, 1997

Selected Internet Sites
www.north-africa.com/ (Maghreb Weekly
Monitor, on subscription only)
www.santegidio.org/ (Sant' Egidio community
in Rome)
www.fisalgeria.org/ (FIS)
www.derechos.org/human-rights/mena/alg.html
(Human Rights Reports)
www.waac.org/ (World Algeria Action
Coalition, containing news, articles and
reports)
*userpage.fu-berlin.de/~yusuf/algeria-
watch/ondhrap.htm* (Observatoire Nationale des
Droits de l'Hommes)
*members.tripod.com/~AlgeriaWatch/InstitutionsA
ndOrganizations.html* (Algeria Watch
International)

Resource Contacts
Boudj Aghechir, president LADDH, Algiers
(can be contacted via Amnesty International)
Abdennour Ali-Yahia, president LADH, Algiers
(can be contacted via Amnesty Int.)
Moustapha Bouchachi, Algerian lawyer and
human rights activist, Algiers University.
Universite d'Alger-Centre, 2, Rue Didouche
Mourad, Algiers, Algeria.

John P. Entelis, Fordham University USA, tel: 1-71-88173953, Fordham University, Lincoln Center New York, New York 10023, USA
Hugh Roberts, London School of Economics, Tel. +44 1 71 4057 686.
Mark Salter, Life and Peace Inrstitute. Email: mark.salter@life-peace.org

Organisations
Algeria Watch International
P.O.BOX 27423
West Allis, Wisconsin, 53227, USA
Tel: +1 610 634 0810
Fax: + -610 695 5636
Email: bouzid@slu.tr.unisys.com

Data on the following organisations can be found in the Directory section:
Rassemblement d'Action Jeunesse (RAJ)
Saint Egidio
Amnesty International
Human Right Watch
International Crisis Group

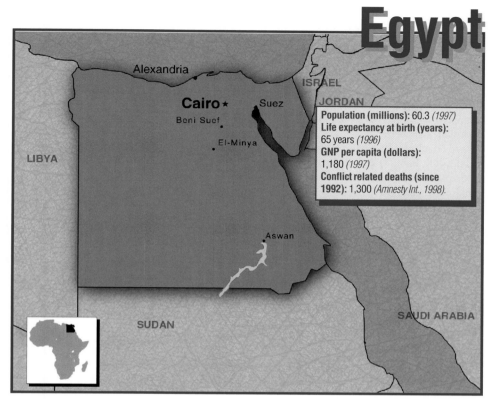

Egypt

Population (millions): 60.3 *(1997)*
Life expectancy at birth (years):
65 years *(1996)*
GNP per capita (dollars):
1,180 *(1997)*
Conflict related deaths (since
1992): 1,300 *(Amnesty Int., 1998).*

State Control versus Armed Islamic Groups

A multifaceted conflict between the Egyptian state and numerous Islamic opposition groups culminated in armed confrontations and deteriorating security conditions in 1992. All parties in the conflict have pointed at international factors complicating the current political situation, but the disagreements and violence seem to be primarily of a domestic nature. International attempts to mediate and/or manage the conflict have therefore been rare, with most initiatives being taken in Egypt itself, but generally with little success. Although structural solutions to the conflict may not be in sight, observers largely agree that armed Islamic groups are on the losing side as a result of the heavy military force applied by the state ◆ *By* **Reinoud Leenders**

The conflict within Egypt can be politically explained, on the one hand, by the persistent refusal of the Egyptian government since the 1950s to allow the Islamic opposition to fully participate in the country's constitutional political life and, on the other hand, by the Islamic movement's ambiguity in denouncing the use of violence in achieving its aim of 'islamising' society. Moreover, the escalation of the conflict is closely related to socio-economic imbalances and the continuing failure of the state to address widespread poverty and relative deprivation.

Following the 1952 revolution by the 'Free Officers', a state of emergency was proclaimed and all political parties were banned in 1953-54. The leader of the Free Officers, Mohamad Naguib, was deposed in 1954 and Egypt's new president, Gamal Abdul-Nasser, launched a one-party political system that from 1962

93

transformed into the Egyptian 'Arab socialist Republic'. While all 'acceptable' political and social forces were supposed to be represented in the 'National Rally', later renamed the 'Socialist Union', the Muslim Brotherhood, a large movement with several hundreds of thousand members, became the target of political exclusion and state repression. Thousands of alleged members of the group were imprisoned for allegedly wanting to overthrow the regime by participating in the movement's 'secret cells'. Most of them remained in prison until the early 1970s when Abdul-Nasser's successor, Anwar al-Sadat, initiated his 'Reform Movement' that aimed at boosting economic growth and partly reversing the authoritarian policies of the former era.

In 1966, the Muslim Brotherhood's spiritual leader Sayyid al-Qutb and other activists were executed on charges of treason for conspiring against the state. As a result, important sections of the Brotherhood radicalised and split from the mainstream Islamic movement. The main source of disagreement within the Egyptian Islamic movement has since been the use of force to bring about political change and the Islamisation of society. The Muslim Brotherhood continued to adhere to a gradual and non-violent approach, and enjoys support among wide sections of society, including its upper class and state bureaucrats. Among the two most important breakaway factions advocating and committing violence are the Gama'a al-Islamiyya and the Jihad movement that mostly recruit from lower middle class sections of society and students at Egypt's universities and technical scientific institutions. Both radical groups are also reported to have recruited members in the army and security forces.

Under the new regime of Anwar al-Sadat, these factions formed clandestine organisations aiming at the violent ousting of what they perceived as a 'secular' and 'infidel' regime. Sadat calculated that some truce had to be reached with the more moderate factions, not least to counter the strong leftist opposition to his policies of economic liberalisation. To achieve this goal, several accommodating measures were taken, including banning 'reformist' books, novels and other publications

on Islam or referring to Islamic themes. Even English translations of the Koran were banned, including the translation by UK publishing house Penguin which is allowed in conservative Moslim countries like Saudi Arabia.

Sadat also allowed a few political currents to organise themselves as political parties, some of them incorporating Islamic activists. But Sadat found himself under mounting criticism from the secular and Islamic opposition for his peace overtures towards Israel, his friendly foreign policies towards the West, continuing violations of the freedom of speech and freedom of association, widening income inequalities, and the regime's perceived 'secular' character. Sadat responded with repression and the arrest of over a thousand leading opposition figures. Many newspapers and magazines were closed and over a hundred journalists were dismissed. In 1981 Sadat was killed by a member of al-Jihad. Attempts by other Jihad members to capitalise on the resulting chaos in the country and to overthrow the regime failed and hundreds of militant activists were arrested.

The new president, Hosni Mubarak, soon restored the accommodation policy towards the Muslim Brotherhood and secular opposition forces. Muslim Brothers were allowed to participate and ultimately take over the leadership of several professional syndicates, which, with parliamentary life more heavily controlled, increasingly began to operate as an alternative platform for political expression. Moreover, the Muslim Brotherhood was tolerated in setting up alliances with legal parties, thus enabling it to occupy a limited number of seats in parliament.

However, this tendency began to be reversed from the late 1980s when more militant Islamic groupings increasingly made themselves heard through their spectacular attacks on state symbols and leading politicians. In 1987, two assassination attempts, one against the Interior minister and a second against a director of a state-owned publishing house, failed. In 1990, Rifa'at al-Mahjub, the speaker of the Parliament, and his body-guards were killed in an attack by armed Islamic activists. Another assassination attempt was carried out, but failed, against hard-line Interior minister Zaki Badr. Some clashes, although limited in scale, broke out in the south and, closer to Cairo, Fayum. Gradually, political liberties became increasingly restricted and the government began justifying its ban on political gatherings, conferences and publications by referring to the uneasy security situation.

Conflict Dynamics

In 1992, intense armed conflicts broke out, with thousands of troops fighting numerous secret Islamic groupings. These clashes took place mainly in Upper Egypt and have continued, with varying degrees of intensity, up to the present day. In many respects the conflict has gained alarming proportions (see: Tawfiz Ibrahim, 1994).

Firstly, the scale of armed conflicts widened with the army and security forces using helicopters, heavy armour and more troops to repress or retaliate against violent attacks by Islamic armed groups. Especially in 1993, major army operations were carried out in Imbaba (a poor neighbourhood of Cairo), Asyut, Dayrut and in the Aswan area, followed by mass arrests of suspected Islamic militants. Secondly, whereas the clashes were formerly confined to certain restricted areas (Cairo, Giza, Bani Swayf, Asyut, Minya, Fayum and Suhaq), the conflict now spread throughout virtually the whole country. Thirdly, while the Gama'a and al-Jihad had initially restricted their targets to security and police forces, and politicians, they now broadened their range of targets to include tourists, intellectuals and members of Egypt's Coptic minority.

In June 1992, Farag Fawda, a secularist writer, was killed because he was suspected of having ties with Israel. Responsibility for the attack was claimed by al-Jihad. In May 1992, armed Islamic activists also killed thirteen Copts in the Asyut province. Failed assassination attempts were carried out against Safwat al-Sharif (the minister of Information), in April 1993, and Hassan al-Alfi (the minister of Interior), in August 1993. Fourthly, Egyptian volunteers who had joined the Mujahidin guerrilla war against the Soviet occupation of Afghanistan returned to Egypt where they joined the ranks of armed Islamic groups. This led to a professionalisation of their operations. Fifthly,

the government demanded more powers to fight the 'terrorism' it was facing. Thus, in addition to the already sweeping powers given to security and army forces by the prolonged state of emergency, in 1992 an 'anti-terrorism' legislation was promulgated. The law introduced the death penalty for members of 'terrorist organisations' and gave additional powers to the security forces to fight 'terrorism' with all means.

The main victims of the armed operations undertaken by Islamic militants have been security personnel, some members of Egypt's Coptic minority, state officials, and foreign tourists, all targeted in hit-and-run assaults. Human rights concerns have also been voiced about the security forces' operations to counter 'terrorism' which include imposing 'collective punishment' on villages allegedly sheltering Islamic militants. Trials have been grossly unfair and failed to meet both Egyptian and international legal standards. In these circumstances, human rights organisations are especially concerned over the death sentences imposed on 85 'terrorists' since 1992, of which 64 executions have been carried out. During the same period, approximately 20,000 other alleged Islamic activists have been held as political prisoners.

In 1994 the Egyptian Human Rights Organisation documented twenty cases of 'disappearances', cases of torture, police brutality, incommunicado detention, and the arrest of family members of suspected Islamic activists. Extra-judicial executions by police forces were also reported. For example, in 1993 eight suspected Islamic activists were shot dead after being captured during a police raid on a mosque in Aswan. Many attacks carried out by armed Islamic groups were in direct response to such practices. On the other hand, killings and violence by Islamic armed groups of innocent civilians have been equally denounced as gross violations of human rights.

Following the killing of 58 tourists in Luxor in the south of Egypt, in November 1997, for which responsibility was claimed by the Gama'a, the state stepped up its security campaign against Islamic armed groups and slowly gained the upper-hand in the conflict. The number of armed attacks has since decreased while al-Jihad and the Gama'a are believed to have failed to recruit new members. Consequently, imprisoned leaders of both groups have been forced to indirectly acknowledge military defeat and denounce the use of further violence.

In 1997, for the first time, imprisoned Islamic leaders called for a general cease-fire and negotiations with the government. This call was publicly supported in October 1998 by Sheikh 'Omar 'Abd al-Rahman, the spiritual leader of the Gama'a who was serving a prison term in the United States. Although the government has denied any rapprochement, in 1998 it silently freed 5,000 imprisoned members of the Gama'a. In April 1999 it released another 1,200 members, among whom several senior activists.

However, the position taken on the use of violence by splinter groups of the Gama'a based in Europe and Afghanistan has remained ambiguous. Shortly after the cease-fire initiative of the Gama'a, supporters of Al-Jihad in exile issued a statement saying it will continue its armed struggle to turn Egypt into a strict Islamic state. In December 1998, al-Jihad even promised to wage a 'long battle' against the United States which it sees as an enemy of Islam. Such reluctance to surrender may explain why these activists continue to be sentenced to death, as illustrated last April when nine al-Jihad members, all residing outside Egypt, were given the death sentence while 107 others, half of them in absentia, received life sentences.

Official Conflict Management

United Nations efforts to contribute to conflict management have been limited to monitoring the human rights situation in Egypt and pressing the Egyptian government to comply with international standards of basic human rights. In 1993, the UN Human Rights Committee and the Committee against Torture called upon the Egyptian government to lift the state of emergency in force since 1981 which gives exceptional powers to security forces and special courts.

Both *European official donors* and the *United States* have largely refrained from linking their aid to Egypt to an improvement in the country's human rights record or to the formulation of any

policies of conflict management. For example, the United States has generally refrained from making its aid to Egypt (amounting to US$ 1.3 billion worth of arms and military training annually for 20 years in addition to US$ 775 million in economic aid in 1998) conditional on human rights improvements. However, during an official visit by Egypt's president Hosni Mubarak to Washington, June 1999, the Clinton administration put some pressure on Egypt by describing its new restrictive law on NGOs (see below) as 'a step in the wrong direction'.

Regionally, two initiatives have been taken to combat 'terrorism' in Egypt, both of which see the challenge of Islamic fundamentalism merely as a security issue. Firstly, Egypt is an active and founding member of a summit organisation set up by the ministers of the Interior of several Arab countries which was developed in the early 1990s. The aim is to achieve closer coordination between security services and exchanging information on the activities and whereabouts of Islamic activists. In practice, cooperation has been extended to include taking a common stand against international human rights organisations that criticised Egypt's and other countries' internal security policies. In line with these attempts at closer cooperation, 1,000 suspected Islamic activists were reportedly extradited to Egypt in 1998 by other Arab member states of the summit organisation.

Secondly, in 1996 a conference was held in Sharm el-Sheikh (Egypt), the 'Summit of Peacemakers', following several bomb attacks in Jerusalem by Palestinian Islamic groups. Participants included most Arab countries and Israel, the EU and the US. Here too, preparations were made for closer coordination of intelligence and security operations to curb 'terrorist' organisations, including Egyptian groups, which oppose the current Middle East peace process and their architects.

The Egyptian government continues to stress that local armed Islamic groups are being sponsored and trained by neighbouring countries including Sudan and Iran. Semi-official Egyptian newspapers have also laid similar charges against groups based in Saudi Arabia. Such allegations have seriously disturbed Egypt's relations with these countries. No

EGYPT, DAKHLA: Coran Schoolgirls

PHOTO DICK ROSS/LINEAIR

concrete evidence of these foreign links has been made public. In October 1998 an attempt was made to overcome major differences with Sudan, including the latter's alleged support of armed Islamic groups, by way of several meetings between the Egyptian and Sudanese ministers of Foreign Affairs. It was agreed as a first step in further confidence-building to refrain from raising media campaigns against each other.

In a further development, in September 1998, the British government adopted a law banning refugees, including Egyptian Islamic activists, from raising funds and/or organising their armed activities on British soil. Extradition of Islamic suspects residing mainly in the UK and France, as generally but not explicitly demanded by Egypt, has not been considered. However, other governments have become more cooperative since al-Jihad members are believed to have been involved in 1998's bombings of the American embassies in Kenya and Tanzania. Dozens of suspects were handed over to the Egyptian government by Albania, Azerbadjian, Ecuador, South Africa, Saudi Arabia, the United Arab Emirates, Yemen and Libya. Most of those extradited received harsh sentences, largely following unfair trials. More generally, the Egyptian government does not seem to be prepared to open up the political process to opposition forces, including more moderate Islamic groups.

Multi-Track Diplomacy
Domestic

Local NGOs in Egypt have been relatively free to operate for a long time, despite the fact that the state has maintained its powers to curb their activities and carry out arbitrary arrests of activists associated with NGOs. However, in Spring 1999 a new law on civil associations was passed in Parliament that is likely to seriously encroach upon the NGOs freedom to organise and act. Ambiguously, the new law bans private groups from working to affect government policy or union activity. It gives the Ministry of Social Affairs powers to disband boards of directors while NGOs now have to seek permission from the government before accepting foreign donations. The new law sets prison terms of up to two years for violations of vaguely formulated offences such as 'threatening law, public morality, order and national unity'. As yet the

97

law has not officially come into force as, to date, it has not appeared in the government's Official Gazette.

Moreover, despite Egypt's large number of NGOs, it should be noted that many of these are simply an office run by a single person. Some of Egypt's 'semi-NGOs', the professional syndicates, have long been among the most active groups advocating respect for human rights. But since the government promulgated a law setting tight restrictions on their internal election procedures in 1993, the syndicates have practically been taken over by government appointees.

Few NGOs, either internationally or locally, have tried to contribute directly to conflict management and/or prevention in Egypt. But strategies of advocacy, primarily by raising awareness of human rights and calling on all parties to the conflict to refrain from violence, have been undertaken by several local human rights groups, at least one private think-tank and secularist political parties. At least one regional NGO and one Egyptian NGO have been involved in capacity-building by, respectively, training lawyers and facilitating the reintegration of former armed Islamic activists into society.

At least one international NGO has been involved in attempts to introduce conflict resolution methods to local NGOs. More moderate Islamic forces have tried to mediate, via discreet diplomacy, between armed Islamic groups and the government. International human rights organisations have undertaken numerous fact-finding missions, registering gross human rights violations by both sides in the conflict, resulting in detailed and comprehensive reports.

The most active exponent of Egypt's human rights movement is the *Egyptian Organization for Human Rights (EOHR)*, affiliated to the Arab Organisation for Human Rights (AOHR), which conducts excellent research on human rights issues, publishes reports and assists victims of human rights abuses and their lawyers.

Other human rights organisations include the Centre for Human Rights and Legal Aid, the El Nadim Centre for the Management and Rehabilitation of Victims of Violence, the Centre of Women's Issues, the Association of Human

Rights Advocates, the Cairo Institute for Human Rights Studies, the Regional Program for Human Rights Activists and the Land Centre for Human Rights.

Some of Egypt's political parties have also been involved in human rights advocacy and have called for a peaceful solution of the conflict. A leftist coalition of secular opposition forces, the Tagammu party, has organised symposia and raised awareness campaigns on human rights and the use of non-violent means to achieve political ends. It has also expressed its strong opposition to the state's Islamisation of society which it views as playing into the hands of violent Islamic groups. On several occasions, Egypt's legalised opposition parties, have made joint appeals to the government to address the country's over-stretched crisis of political participation. In 1997, opposition parties released 'the Programme for Democratic, Political and Constitutional Reforms' which centred around the need to adopt a political system that ensures a peaceful sharing and transfer of power. In April 1999, four licensed parties in addition to the outlawed Muslim Brotherhood and the Communist Party released a joint petition stressing the need to introduce urgent and basic political reforms, especially with regard to the method of electing the head of state.

The officially banned *Muslim Brotherhood* is reported to have brokered local cease-fires between militant Islamic groups and security forces, mainly in the early 1990s. Possibly as a result of the mediation efforts by the Muslim Brotherhood, informal contacts with the government were established in 1993. However, militant Muslims reportedly interpreted this attempt at rapprochement as a sign of weakness on the part of the government and, subsequently, stepped up their violent attacks.

The Muslim Brotherhood is also involved in the activities of a think-tank run by the prominent Islamic judge Tariq al-Bishri. It publishes an annual report on human rights and democracy in Egypt, the 'Nation in a Year', modelled on a similar annual report by the semi-state sponsored Al-Ahram Centre for Political and Strategic Studies. More recently, the Muslim Brotherhood has begun publishing leaflets advocating the use of non-violent means to bring about social change.

International

The *Arab Organization for Human Rights (AOHR)*, founded in Cyprus in 1983, provides technical assistance and training facilities to lawyers and a platform for discussing human rights and the legal profession in Arab countries, including Egypt. The Arab Lawyers' Union is engaged in similar activities.

Most promising, perhaps, have been the activities of the Cairo-based *Ibn Khaldun Centre*, which publishes a magazine called *Civil Society* and is involved in local development projects and democracy awareness campaigns. The Centre advocates a 'peaceful and constructive way of dealing with Islamic militants through a strategy of 'inclusion'. The Centre has provided former Islamic militants with financial aid and guidance to set up their own small-scale businesses and facilitate their reintegration into society.

Search For Common Ground in the Middle East, an international NGO with its head office in Washington, has tried to introduce conflict resolution methods to local NGOs and other groups in civil society. In 1997 it launched a Conflict Resolution Working Group in Egypt, providing training for journalists, social workers, students and lecturers and labour activists. Follow-up workshops were held in 1998. Search for Common Ground closely cooperates with an Egyptian NGO, the *National Center for Middle East Studies.*

Fact-finding missions were undertaken by *Amnesty International* and *Human Rights Watch,* collecting testimonies from victims of violence committed by government forces, including torture and mass-reprisals following Islamic attacks, and of violence committed by armed Islamic groups. Their reports have made human rights violations in Egypt among the best documented in the region.

In the United States, American Coptic organisations and right wing Christian groups, working with conservative congressional sponsors of the Freedom from Religious Persecution Act, sent a strongly worded letter in February 1999 signed by 93 American legislators, calling the Egyptian government to

set up an independent investigation into allegations of torture of Coptic Egyptians arrested in a small village in the Nile delta in August 1998. These demands were supported by other human rights organisations, including Human Rights Watch. However, unlike American Christian activists, most human rights organisations tend to see the conflict in Egypt more as a general human rights crisis than as a clear case of religious persecution.

Generally, the potentially positive effects of most of these and other NGO activities have been severely curtailed by repressive policies carried out by the Egyptian government that continues to regard the conflict as a mere security problem. According to one observer, the government's hostile attitude to private initiatives has also been fed by its fear of mass-scale protests against the socio-economic consequences of its economic liberalisation programme. (see: Kienle, 1998)

Most NGOs therefore have encountered government efforts to obstruct their activities. On the one hand, Egypt's human rights movement has been described by Human Rights Watch as 'one of the most dynamic and sophisticated in the Arab world'. But the government has not legalised the EOHR, and security forces have repeatedly tried to obstruct the activities of the organisation. At the end of 1998, its secretary-general Hafez Abu Sa'ada was arrested for having protested against the government's handling of conflicts within the Coptic community in the north of the country. Shortly after, Abu Sa'ada was jailed for fifteen days on the grounds that he had accepted a donation from the British government without the Egyptian government's approval. The board of directors of the EOHR decided to return the donation to the British government to facilitate the release of Abu Sa'ada. A report prepared by the EOHR on torture by security and police forces was banned.

The influence of political parties have been similarly curtailed, by arbitrary and discriminatory legalisation of their formal status, vote-rigging during elections and the financial superiority of the government party NDP, limiting the audience reached by alternative voices. Regionally, the AOHR has become increasingly a target of the Arab governments' policies that rely on force rather than on peaceful methods of conflict resolution. The Egyptian government's attitude towards more moderate Islamic members of the Muslim Brotherhood has obstructed the latter's mediation attempts. The government continued to reject the Muslim Brotherhood's requests to become a legal political party. In 1996, a group of young dissidents within the Muslim Brotherhood set up the Wassat party, which stressed liberal-democratic principles, apparently in a quest to leave behind the Muslim Brotherhood's ambiguous reputation concerning respect for democratic rules and principles. The party was not legalised, however, and its members were prosecuted.

Prospects

Most independent observers have stressed that the Egyptian government's reliance on military force to fight 'terrorism' is in the long run likely to be counter-productive. Excluding any Islamic tendency from the country's constitutional politics will only invite them to opt for less peaceful means to advocate their aim of Islamizing society.

Furthermore, the government's strategy of paying lip-service to certain Islamic party principles, such as raising obstacles for women wanting to play an active role in civil society on perceived 'Islamic' grounds, has actually increased the popular appeal of Islamic hard-liners, making further ideological concessions difficult to avoid. (Karam, 1998) For example, by banning secular women's organisations, like Nawal al-Sa'dawi's Arab Women's Solidarity Association, which campaigned against the country's women-unfriendly personal status law, the state has actively contributed to the Islamisation of the women's debate.

A consensus has emerged that the current status-quo wherein Islamic armed groups are less able to launch new attacks will produce some degree of armoured political stability, at least temporarily. Armed Islamic groups have also been reported to have lost support among their earlier constituencies. However, in the long term, most observers emphasise that Egypt should come to terms with its crises of political

participation and the negative socio-economic effects of economic liberalisation if the country is ever to solve the armed conflict between the state and Islamic armed groups. However, immediate solutions for both crises do not seem likely. Pressure by Western donors to speed up economic liberalisation and a retreat of the state from its welfare functions is likely to further exacerbate income disparities. In terms of political participation, liberties continue to be curtailed and access to the decision-making centre of the presidency is more restricted than ever before. Egyptians will go to the polls in Autumn 1999 in another round of presidential 'elections' for which Mubarak is the only candidate.

Recommendations

Virtually all human rights organisations mentioned above, in particular Human Rights Watch, Amnesty International and the Arab Organisation for Human Rights, have called upon both the Egyptian state and Islamic armed groups to immediately stop using arbitrary violence in order to achieve greater respect for human rights at large. They have equally called upon armed Islamic groups to publicly revoke all death threats without further delay.

Moreover, the Egyptian state has been called upon to harmonise its legal system with international law, particularly in the field of women's rights, to strengthen both more moderate Islamic groups and alternative voices in civil society. Likewise, NGOs active in the field of human rights should be given more freedom to operate as their activists and members may check opposition forces opting for violent methods. Some independent observers have advised the Egyptian state to allow more moderate Islamic forces, like the Muslim Brotherhood, to participate in the country's constitutional political framework in order to counter the appeal of armed opposition. It has also been stressed that the Egyptian state, and international financial organisations involved in Egypt's economic restructuring programme, should set up social funds to cushion the effects of privatisation and cuts on state subsidies on the poor.

Service Information

Newsletters and Periodicals
Al-Ahram Weekly (English version of main Egyptian daily Al-Ahram)
Al-Wassat (London-based Arabic weekly with excellent Egypt coverage)
Civil Society Bulletin (monthly on human rights and democracy in Egypt), Ibn Khaldun Centre
Middle East International (bimonthly on regional politics incl. excellent coverage of Egypt)
Middle East Report (quarterly containing semi-academic articles on regional affairs, including Egypt)

Reports
Amnesty International
- Human Rights Abuses by Armed Groups, 1998
- Women targeted by Association, 1997
- Indefinite Detention and Systematic Torture - the Forgotten Victims, 1996
- Deaths in Custody, 1995
- Human Rights Defenders under Threat, 1994

Article 19
- The Egyptian predicament - Islamists, the State and Censorship, 8/97

Egyptian Organisation for Human Rights
- A Crime without Punishment - Torture in Egypt, 12/93

Human Rights Watch
- Hostage-Taking and Intimidation by Security Forces, 1995
- Violations of Freedom of Religious Belief and Expression of the Christian Minority, 1994

Other Publications
Political Islam - Religion and Politics in the Arab World, by Nazih Ayubi. Routledge, 1991
Sadat and After - Struggles for Egypt's Political Soul, by Raymond W.Baker. Harvard University Press, 1990
Egypt, Islam and Democracy - Twelve critical essays, by S. Eddin Ibrahim. American University in Cairo Press, 1996
Women, Islamisms and the State - Contemporary

Feminism in Egypt, by A.M. Karam. St. Martins Press, 1998
The Prophet and the Pharao - Muslim Extremism in Egypt, by Gilles Kepel. University of California Press, 1985
More than a Response to Islamism - The Political Deliberalization of Egypt in the 1990s, by Eberhard Kienle. In: Middle East Journal, vol 52, no 2, Spring 1998
The Struggle of State and Civil Society in Egypt - Professional Organisations and Egypt's Careful Steps towards Democracy, by Reinoud Leenders. Middle East Associates paper series, Amsterdam, 1996
La violence Politique en Egypte, by Hasanayn Tawfiz Ibrahim. In: Le phenomene de la violence politique: perspectives comparatistes et paradigme egyptien, P. Dupret (ed), Dossiers du Cedej, Cairo, 1994
The State of Religion in Egypt, by D. Rashwan (ed). Annual report prepared by the Al-Ahram Centre for Political and Strategic Studies
The Nation in a Year, by T. El-Bishri a.o. (eds). Annual report related to democratisation, religion and human rights in Egypt prepared by researchers close to the Muslim Brotherhood (in Arabic).

Selected Internet Sites
www.acpss.org (Al-Ahram Centre for Political and Strategic Sudies)
www.ned.org/page_3/icds (Civil Society Bulletin)
www.chrla.org/ (Egyptian Centre for Human Rights)
www.frcu.eun.eg (Egyptian Human Rights Network homepage)
www.uk.sis.gov.eg (State Information Service)
www.eohr.org.eg/ (Egyptian Organisation for Human Rights)
www.menc.edu/menic/centers.htlm (Centre for Middle Eastern Studies, University of Texas)
www.mideastnet.com/ups/ (review Egyptian press)
www.almurabeton.org/ (al-Gama'a al-Islamiyya in exile)
www.aohr.org (Arab Org. for Human Rights)

Resource Contacts

Paul Aarts - University of Amsterdam, the Netherlands, email aarts@pscw.uva.nl
Ibrahim Allam - executive director Arab organisation for Human Rights
Saad Eddin Ibrahim - American University of Cairo and director of Ibn Khaldun Center
Eberhard Kienle - School of Oriental and African Studies, London University, email ek@soas.ac.uk
Dia'a Rashwan, Al-Ahram Centre for Political and Strategic Studies

Mustapha Kamal al-Sayyid - University of Cairo, Faculty of Economics and Political Science Gama'a Street, Giza - Cairo

Data on the following organisations can be found in the Directory section:
Ibn Khaldun
National Centre for Middle East Studies
Amnesty International
Human Right Watch

The Western Sahara

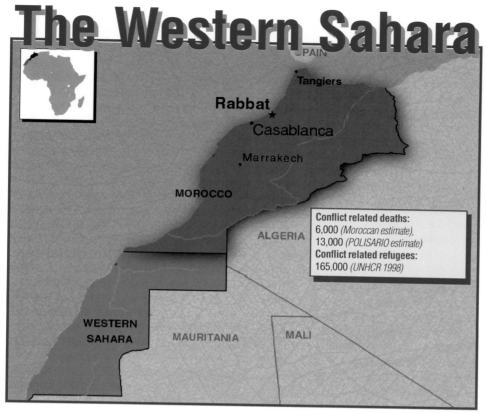

Conflict related deaths:
6,000 (Moroccan estimate),
13,000 (POLISARIO estimate)
Conflict related refugees:
165,000 (UNHCR 1998)

Africa's Last Colony

Ever since the Spanish withdrawal from the Western Sahara in 1976, the Western Sahara has been disputed between a Sahrawi liberation movement, that declared an independent 'Sahrawi state', and neighbouring Morocco, which claims sovereignty over what it regards as its 'southern province'. Armed clashes came to a halt in 1988 but UN preparations for holding a referendum and to grant the original inhabitants of the region the right to self-determination begun in 1991 have so far failed to produce a lasting settlement. Continuing failure to hold a free and fair referendum increases the likelihood that armed conflict will resume ◆ *By* **Reinoud Leenders**

Bringing to an end the period of Spanish colonial rule in the Western Sahara which dated back to 1884, Spain began preparing a referendum for the inhabitants of the region to determine the final status of the territory in 1974. However, armed hostilities broke out a year later when Morocco sent 350,000 'volunteers' into the Western Sahara in advance of the Moroccan army, even before the Spanish withdrawal. As a result of this 'Green March', over 100,000 Sahrawis fled to neighbouring

Algeria, taking refuge in camps hastily set up in Tindouf. A liberation movement, POLISARIO (Frente Popular Para La Liberacion De Saguia El Hamra Y Rio Do Oro), set up in 1973 to fight Spanish colonial rule, began a series of guerrilla attacks.

Smaller refugee communities are based in Mauritania, the Canarian Islands and Spain. Algeria supported POLISARIO mainly because of its continuing border disputes with Morocco elsewhere. Mauritania, a secondary party to the conflict, briefly occupied the south of the territory but following a coup in 1979 renounced all its claims to the Western Sahara.

Other secondary parties to the conflict include France and the United States who indirectly opposed the creation of a separate state in the territory by providing military support to Morocco. More generally, both Western powers have largely refrained from putting pressure on Morocco over the Western Sahara issue as Morocco is regarded as an important ally in the region. However, formally both France and the United States have expressed support for the UN-sponsored peace process and the holding of a referendum to let the Sahrawis themselves decide on the status of the disputed territory.

In spite of Morocco's effective control of the region through its heavy military presence, armed clashes escalated into a full-blown war, especially between 1982-85 during which POLISARIO guerrillas claimed to have killed 5,673 Moroccan soldiers. But a 2,500 kilometre wall of sand, electronic detectors and mines surrounding the Western Sahara prevented any further progress in POLISARIO's attempts to take control of the territory. In 1988, following the first direct contacts between the two parties, both Morocco and POLISARIO announced a cease-fire. POLISARIO, however, has pointedly left its options open and says that it will resume armed operations as soon as peaceful means are deemed to be exhausted and unable to help obtaining effective independence of its 'Sahrawi Arab Democratic Republic', declared in 1976 and, by 1998, recognised by 76 countries. Until 1992, Morocco was repeatedly accused by UN-observers of violating the cease-fire.

The conflict in the Western Sahara can be regarded as a classical post-colonial independence conflict. In this respect, the Western Sahara is Africa's last remaining colony for which a lasting settlement has so far failed to be achieved. Ethnic factors in the conflict can be recognised in POLISARIO's claim to represent a separate nation different from Morocco by its descent from three ethnically and culturally distinct peoples - the Sanhaja Berbers, Bedouin Arabs and Africans who were brought to the territory as slaves. The Sahrawis speak a unique dialect of the Arabic, Hassaniya.

Domestic complications lie in the fact that Hassan II, the king of Morocco, has used his claim to the Western Sahara in a successful attempt to create unity and divert the attention of his Moroccan subjects from internal challenges to his regime which, especially in the 1970s, has experienced serious political instability. Economically, the 260,000 square kilometres of seemingly barren territory is significant given the discovery and exploitation of its lucrative natural resources, including phosphates, oil, iron and fertile and productive coastal fishing waters. Partly as a result of its control of West Sahrawi resources, Morocco has become one of the world's biggest exporters of phosphates. These are used mainly for the production of fertilisers.

Conflict Dynamics

A meeting in Marrakech between King Hassan and POLISARIO officials in 1989 marked the beginning of continuing negotiations about the territory's final status. A UN-plan for a referendum on self-determination to be held before 1992 was accepted by all parties and, accordingly, in April 1991 the UN established a special peace-keeping force, the UN Mission for the Referendum in Western Sahara (MINURSO) followed by a formal agreement on a cease-fire.

It was agreed that voter eligibility should be based on a Spanish census held in 1974. However, Morocco is reported to have sent thousands of Moroccans into the territory in order to shift the demographic balance, and thus the referendum, into its favour. Instructing these Moroccans in applying for registration as voters seems to have been a deliberate policy, as illustrated by a Moroccan government document dated January 1998 showing that local officials carefully co-ordinate and train fake applicants.

Moreover, the Moroccan authorities started hindering the deployment of MINURSO forces while they failed to withdraw half their own troops as stipulated in the cease-fire agreement. The peace process has been further frustrated by reports that Morocco had stepped up its intelligence presence in the territory, watching and arresting Sahrawis that spoke out for a fair referendum. Reports of torture, bans on demonstrations, mass arrests and 'disappearances' by Moroccan forces continued to have a negative effect on confidence-building processes between the two sides. On the other hand, in 1991, more than 300 'disappeared' Sahrawis were released, however, they received no compensation for their illegal incarceration nor was any information given on the fate of hundreds of other Sahrawis that are still reported to be missing.

In spite of its stated commitment to the peace process and the high financial costs of its military deployment in the territory, Morocco seems to hold to its position that the Western Sahara is historically part of its territory while POLISARIO is seen as an illegitimate group of secessionist terrorists. Public statements by Moroccan officials, including the late King Hassan, stressing that Morocco will never surrender the Western Sahara cast further doubts over the Kingdom's intention to let a referendum determine the final status of the territory. One explanation for this hawkish position lies in the fact that King Hassan had directly tied his legitimacy as ruler of Morocco to the Western Sahara issue, as exemplified by his 'autobiography', significantly titled *The Green March*.

Consequently, POLISARIO has repeatedly stated its disappointment with the peace process and indirectly threatened to resume its armed struggle 'to defend [the Sahrawis] right to self-determination and independence'. Meanwhile, disappointment within the ranks of POLISARIO has given way to some degree of disillusionment reflected in the defection of several Sahrawi top officials to Morocco. Some of them were included in a Moroccan negotiation team in 1993, leading to POLISARIO's refusal to attend a meeting planned in the US. Perhaps most importantly, 165,000 Sahrawi refugees remain trapped in the camps of Tindouf in Algeria where living conditions are extremely harsh with temperatures that can reach 50 degrees Celsius and with limited opportunities to generate minimum standards of health, shelter and sanitary conditions. Other victims of the conflict include 1,900 Moroccan prisoners of war held in Sahrawi prisons. In 1989, 184 elderly or ill Moroccan prisoners were released by POLISARIO but Morocco refused to take them back, arguing that this would be tantamount to

recognising POLISARIO. Morocco's attitude on this issue seems to be informed by fear that their return may negatively effect the Moroccan consensus on the Sahrawi issue.

Due to continuing disagreement between the parties regarding voter eligibility, the UN-sponsored peace process practically came to a halt and the voter registration process was formally suspended in May 1996. According to a former official within MINURSO, Frank Ruddy, these delays have cost the international community a considerable sum. Even with a reduced staff, UN presence in the territory costs some US$ 100,000 per day. In 1997, new peace talks between the two parties resulted in a series of agreements over criteria for voter eligibility and a new deadline for the referendum was set. The process of identifying voters was finally completed by MINURSO in September 1998. A total of 147,350 applicants have been interviewed by MINURSO. Although it is not yet known how many of these applications have been accepted, some sources suggest a figure of 85,000, which could be close to the 74,000 Sahrawis registered during the Spanish census of 1974. There still remain serious obstacles, such as the fate of three sub-tribes, amounting to 65,000 persons, which Morocco wants incorporated in the list of voters.

In technical terms, the dispute centres on Morocco's insistence on registering all members of a sub-tribe even if only a few of its members can be found on the Spanish census list. POLISARIO insists that at least 70 per cent of all members of a sub-tribe should be mentioned in the Spanish census to allow the whole sub-tribe to cast their votes. In more political terms, Morocco's new demands have been widely interpreted as another indication of its lack of sincerity in participating in the peace process that is designed to lead to a referendum. POLISARIO officials have stated on several occasions their willingness to resume armed struggle should Morocco ultimately fail to carry out its commitments under the agreements it has signed.

Official Conflict Management

The *United Nations* has been actively involved in attempts to settle the Western Sahara conflict since 1974 when Spain asked the international organisation to supervise a referendum to take place shortly after. In May 1975, the UN sent a fact-finding mission to the territory that found an overwhelming consensus in favour of independence and opposing integration within any neighbouring country. However, Morocco tried to forestall the referendum by referring the issue to the International Court of Justice. The Court advised in favour of the right of self-determination by the Sahrawi people in 1975.

In 1985, the UN initiated a joint mission of good offices with the Organisation of African Unity (OAU) to resolve the dispute. The resulting 'Settlement Proposals' of both organisations were accepted by Morocco and POLISARIO in 1988 and passed by the UN Security Council in 1991. A multinational peacekeeping force, MINURSO, was established to monitor a cease-fire, verify the reduction of Moroccan troops, ensure the release of all political prisoners and prisoners of war, identify and register qualified voters and organise a free and fair referendum. In an attempt to break the deadlock over voter registration, former US Secretary of State, James Baker, was appointed the UN-Secretary General's Special Envoy in March 1997. He brokered a series of agreements that became known as the 'Houston Agreements', reached between July and September 1997. The agreements included issues such as the identification of voters, troop confinement, treatment of prisoners of war and measures to resume the identification process.

However, UN operations have been severely criticised for failing to uphold a minimum of impartiality and compromising the credibility of the peace process. Reports by Human Rights Watch and declarations by former MINURSO commander Frank Ruddy have set out in detail how MINURSO has given in to demands of the Moroccan authorities concerning the voters' registration process. MINURSO is also said to have tolerated Moroccan measures that restricted Sahrawis' freedom of expression and movement during the transitional phase. Moroccan troop withdrawals have also failed to take place as stipulated in the agreements. As an illustration of the atmosphere, in at least one incident MINURSO was banned from raising an UN-flag

over its buildings in the territory by the Moroccan authorities. Instead of protesting against such aggression against the peace process, MINURSO complied. The Special UN Representative for the Western Sahara, Charles Dunbar, resigned in March 1999, reportedly out of frustration with the slow peace process. He has been replaced by the American diplomat William Eagleton. Following many delays and numerous failures to meet the time-table, MINURSO's mandate has been recently extended by the UN Security Council until July 2000 when the referendum is also planned to take place.

The *United Nations Higher Commissioner for Refugees (UNHCR)* main involvement in the Western Sahara has been to give legal protection and ensure the provision of material assistance to refugees in Tindouf, as well as to Sahrawis living in Mauritania and elsewhere. With respect to the current peace process, the UNHCR has been given the task of facilitating the voluntary return of refugees to the territory by providing transport and establishing reception centres as soon as the referendum takes place. In addition, the UNHCR assisted the construction of chicken farms in the camps in Tindouf for local consumption and profit generating in 1998.

The *Organisation of African Unity* began advocating a free referendum on the final status of the Western Sahara in the early 1970s. But as many of its members feared antagonising Western allies or weakening King Hassan's position, the OAU refrained from taking a clear position on the issue until the late 1970s. In July 1980, POLISARIO requested membership of the OAU as a sovereign state. Although 26 of the 50 members then recognised the Sahrawi state, the application was delayed as a result of Moroccan pressure. Meanwhile, an OAU proposal for a cease-fire and a referendum was rejected by Morocco. In 1982 the Sahrawi was accepted as member of the OAU, leading to serious divisions within the organisation. When POLISARIO continued to attend OAU meetings, Morocco resigned from the organisation. However, the OAU continued its role in the conflict, together with the UN-facilitated talks between the two parties in the late 1980s. Although the OAU became a co-sponsor of the 'Settlement

WESTERN SAHARA, NEAR ALGERIAN BORDER: POLISARIO Trainings camp

PHOTO HELDUR NETOCNY/LINEAIR

Proposals', its offer to supply a contingent of troops to the multinational peace keeping forces was rejected by Morocco on grounds of partiality. The OAU continues to play a low-key observer role in the identification process.

The *European Union* has kept an extremely low profile with respect to the Western Sahara issue, undoubtedly due to internal differences among its members on the conflict. It has passively supported the UN peace plan. In October 1995, the European Parliament adopted a resolution blaming Morocco for hampering the UN peace plan. But the EU also negotiated with Morocco over the fishing rights in Western Saharan territorial waters, thereby indirectly recognising its claims to sovereignty.

Multi-Track Diplomacy

Domestic

NGOs have played a limited role in attempts to address the conflict. Locally, in Morocco, their role have been strictly confined due to the state's tight control on civil society generally in addition to a widespread consensus in Morocco that the Western Sahara is and should remain an integral part of Morocco. In the occupied territories NGOs are restricted in their freedom of access and movements. In the Sahrawi refugee camps in Tindouf, and abroad, Sahrawis have established an active movement for the defence of human rights with excellent relations with international counterparts. Many groupings in Europe have lobbied their governments to put pressure on Morocco to respect the right of self-determination for the Sahrawi people.

A Sahrawi human rights organisation, *AFAPREDESA*, or Association of Sahrawi Families of Prisoners and Disappeared, set up by relatives of Sahrawi prisoners and registered in Spain, has continuously tried to sensitise the public through news bulletins and communiques concerning human rights and the peace process. It enjoys observer status at the African Commission on Human and People's Rights and made a presentation to the UN Commission on Human Rights in 1998.

The *National Union of Sahrawi Women (NUSW)* was set up in 1979 on the initiative of POLISARIO. It represents Sahrawi female members based in and outside the camps of

Tindouf and provides assistance to alleviate the suffering of women facing abductions, torture and imprisonment. Other main interests of the NUSW include improving the situation for children, the elderly and the handicapped.

Another NGO, the *Union of Sahrawi Jurists (UJS)*, is a Sahrawi initiative, grouping both Sahrawi and international jurists with the aim of sensitising international public opinion by publishing legal texts on the conflict and helping to establish a free and independent judiciary in the camps and for a future Sahrawi state.

Only one Moroccan human rights organisation, the *Association Marocaine des Droits de l'Homme (AMDH)* has taken up Sahrawi cases of human rights violations but it has refrained from commenting on the Sahrawi identity of the victims. Other Moroccan human rights groups, such as the Organisation Marocaine des Droits de l'Homme (OMDH) which is affiliated to the ruling party USFP, have systematically left out Sahrawi cases from their otherwise energetic campaigns for human rights. Moroccan NGOs that advocate the Moroccan point of view on the conflict, are rare and include the Moroccan Committee for the Regrouping of Saharan Families (Corefasa). They focus on alleged violations of human rights by POLISARIO. Such NGOs are probably in most, if not all cases, front organisations of the Moroccan state.

International
Strategies of advocacy on behalf of POLISARIO or the Sahrawi people at large have been undertaken by many European solidarity groups and one major Sahrawi human rights organisation. Strategies of capacity-building, by way of briefing Canadian armed forces for their participation in MINURSO, were undertaken by a Canadian human rights organisation that is sympathetic to the Sahrawi cause. Fact-finding missions, undertaken by three international human rights organisations, have undoubtedly contributed greatly to conflict resolution. Lastly, humanitarian aid and technical support for the refugees in Tindouf has been provided mainly by Spanish NGOs and the International Red Cross.

Dozens of *solidarity groups* based in Europe and the US have carried out public awareness-

raising campaigns, lobbied their governments, and drawn attention to the plight of the Sahrawi people. Examples of such initiatives include the British Western Sahara Campaign, the US-based Defense Forum Foundation, the French Collectif d'Initiatives pour la Reconnaissance du Sahara Occidental, the France-based Association Internationale des Juristes pour le Sahara Occidental and several pro-POLISARIO solidarity committees in Spain and joint efforts of several European workers' unions.

Perhaps the most active organsations in the field of advocacy are the *Association de soutien a un referendum libre et regulier au Sahara Occidental (ARSO)*, which has a web-site containing a well-documented history of the conflict, regular updates, bibliographies and major documents concerning the conflict, and the *Canadian Lawyers Association for International Human Rights (CLAIHR)*, that in 1994 started its 'Western Sahara Initiative', mainly to provide information on the existing legal machinery concerning the referendum. The latter organisation has also offered its expertise, in an example of capacity-building, to MINURSO by twice briefing officers of the Royal Canadian Mounted Police who were sent to the territory.

Fact-finding missions were undertaken by international NGOs including *Human Rights Watch*, resulting in a report in 1995, *Amnesty International*, resulting in a report one year later, and *CLAIHR* in 1997. On a more regular basis, AFAPREDESA has used its extensive contacts within the occupied territory to constantly warn other human rights organisations of cases where Sahrawis 'disappeared' or were arrested by Moroccan authorities. However, only Human Rights Watch has been able to actually enter the occupied territories and interview UN-staff and Sahrawi victims of human rights violations. Amnesty International also recorded human rights violations by POLISARIO within Tindouf at the end of the 1980s. This encouraged the local Sahrawi authorities in the camps of Tindouf to take measures in order to guarantee an independent judiciary, as laid down in the new Sahrawi Constitution of 1995.

Humanitarian aid, mainly to the refugees in Tindouf, has been provided by some of the solidarity groups mentioned above, the Spanish section of Engineers without Borders, established in 1991, and the International Red Cross. The latter organisation gives support to health institutions in Tindouf, allocates and distributes food in the camps, keeps detailed demographic statistics in order to determine the needs of each camp, and regularly visits Moroccan prisoners of war held by POLISARIO. It is expected to play a key-role in the release of prisoners as foreseen by the Houston Agreements. Major providers of food are the World Food Program of the UN and various humanitarian agencies of the European Union.

The direct results of the initiatives of the NGOs mentioned here are difficult to assess. Generally, advocacy strategies by solidarity groups are said as well as to have contributed to the recognition of the Sahrawi state by 76 states the fact that it has received sympathy from many others; this contrasts with the fact that, to date, no state has recognised Morocco's claim to the territory. Naturally, humanitarian aid has been indispensable for Sahrawi refugees who have no other means of support. Fact-finding missions have had the most impressive impact on the peace process. Amnesty International put considerable pressure on the Moroccan government by publicising several cases of 'disappeared' or arrested Sahrawis. In 1996, Amnesty publicised the case of a group of Sahrawis, including 'prisoner of conscience' Kelthoum Ahmed Labid El-Ouanat, who as a consequence saw their sentences reduced and were released.

According to CLAIHR and other observers, especially the report by Human Rights Watch wherein the organisation accused MINURSO of being biased towards Morocco have contributed to the decision of the UN-Secretary General to revive the peace process by appointing a new Special Representative to formalise voters' registration and broker other agreements on issues that obstruct the peace process.

Prospects

Most observers committed to the peace process have expressed little optimism about the future of the Western Sahara. The most important obstacle to the referendum seems to be the fact that King Hassan II made the

territory into one of the ideological bases of his popularity in Morocco.

At the moment of writing, it is too early to say if his successor, King Mohammed VI, will change this policy.

For Morocco, participation in the peace process seems to have become a way of appeasing international criticisms of its handling of the territory but the actual implementation of a referendum may only materialise when Morocco is certain the result will be in its favour. Human Rights Watch has noted that when MINURSO's authority is undermined by refusing to provide it with the necessary tools to organise a referendum in the near future, there is a danger that it will be forced to withdraw. The region's future, the organisation warns, may then be determined by a 'misdirected UN operation', not by a fair referendum. This could lead to a resumption of armed conflict.

CLAIHR, on the other hand, has noted that the people of the Western Sahara have never been so close to being able to exercise their right to self-determination. But delays and even suspension of the voters registration process may eventually halt the peace process altogether. POLISARIO has on several occasions stated that in such a scenario it would reconsider its military options. However, reduced Algerian military and financial support, in addition to an apparent problem of morale given recent defections, may prevent POLISARIO from immediately carrying out these threats. An unresolved but potentially violent conflict may then continue to exist.

Recommendations

There is a general consensus within the international NGO community that the only way out of the impasse is for the people of the Western Sahara to be allowed to vote in a fair and transparent referendum on self-determination. Most recommendations by independent observers have concentrated on improving MINURSO's handling of the conflict in general and the voters registration process in particular. Member states and the Security Council must ensure compliance with the Settlement proposals through direct active engagement. The UN is also advised to keep employing James Baker to ensure that the Houston Agreements retain their authority and credibility.

Although internal accountability within MINURSO has been increased by periodic reports by the UN Secretary General to the Security Council, the UN is seen as lacking an objective assessment from third parties. In this context, CLAIHR recommended the involvement of NGOs providing objective, impartial analysis as being essential in promoting transparency in the peace process which, in turn, may ensure greater compliance with the agreements.

Human Rights Watch has recommended that the UN re-examine and modify the powers of MINURSO in order to ensure a fair referendum is carried out without delay. Concrete proposals include making explicit MINURSO's mandate to protect human rights (a recommendation shared by Amnesty International); ordering an independent review of the identification process to ensure the impartiality of the process and increase transparency; calling publicly for Morocco to end the obstruction of the UN operation; ordering an investigation into allegations of MINURSO staff siding with Morocco in the identification process; and setting up clearer guidelines for the registration of voters.

Service Information

Newsletters and Periodicals

L'echo du POLISARIO (POLISARIO newsletter, Paris/France)

Sahara Info (pro-POLISARIO newsletter, Paris/France)

Newsletter Western Sahara Campaign (pro-POLISARIO, Leeds/UK)

Nouvelles Sahraouies (newsletter of Comite Suisse-Romand de Soutien au Peuple Sahraoui)

Jeune Afrique (contains detailed information on peace process in Western Sahara)

Liberation (Moroccan daily in French with regular updates on Moroccan position on Western Sahara)

Reports

Human Rights Watch
- Keeping it Secret - The United Nations Operation in the Western Sahara, October 1995

Amnesty International
- Morocco and Western Sahara, Turning the Page - Achievements and Obstacles, June 1999
- Human Rights Violations in Western Sahara, April 1996
- Morocco - The Pattern of Political Imprisonment Must End, May 1994

AFAPREDESA
- From the Heart of Darkness - Testimonies of Former Sahrawi prisoners of Moroccan Jails, Tindouf, May 20 1993

CLAIHR - Western Sahara Initiative
- Report of the Fact-Finding Mission to Algiers and the Refugee Camps, June 1997
- The Role of Non-Governmental Organisations in Contributing to Peace in the Western Sahara, June 17-19, 1998.

Michael Bhatia
- Statement Regarding the Issue of the Western Sahara before the Fourth Committee of the United Nations General Assembly, 9 October 1998

United Nations
- The Secretary General's Reports on the Situation Concerning the Western Sahara, latest: 13 May 1999

Other Publications

Historical Dictionary of Western Sahara, by Anthony G. Pazzanita & Tony Hodges. Scarecrown Press, 1994

International Dimensions of the Western Sahara Conflict, by Yahia H. Zoubir (ed). Praeger Publishers, 1993

The United Nations Failure in Resolving the Western Sahara Conflict, by Yahia H. Zoubir & Anthony G. Pazzanita. In: Middle East Journal, vol. 49, no 4, 1995

Sahara Occidental - La Confiance Perdue, by Martine de Froberville. 1996

Sahara Occidental - Les enjeux d'un conflit regional, by Khadija Mohsen-Finan. CNRS 1997

Breaking the Stalemate in the Western Sahara, by Jarat Chopra. In: International Peacekeeping, vol. 1, no 3, 1994

The United States and the Western Sahara Peace Process, by Stephen Zunes. In Mideast Policy, vol. 5, no 4, 1998

Selected Internet Sites

north-Africa.com (Maghreb Weekly Monitor)

arso.org/index.htm (comprehensive database of news and documents, Association de Soutien a un Referendum libre et regulier au Sahara Occidental)

sahara-occidental.com (Collectif d'Initiatives pour la Connaissance du Sahara Occidental)

infoweb.magi.com/~morocco/sahara.html (Moroccan government sponsored site on Western Sahara)

www.derechos.org/Afapredesa/doc/ (AFAPREDESA site in Spanish)

www.web.net/~claihr/ (Canadian Lawyers Association for International Human Rights - Western Sahara Initiative)

Resource Contacts

Michael Bhatia - Thomas J. Watson Jr Institute for International Studies, Brown University. Fax +1 401 863 1270, Email iss@brown.edu

Yves Del Monaco - human rights activist on Western Sahara yves_monaco@hotmail.com

Robert Young - project leader Western Sahara Initiative CLAIHR, Canada. Tel. +1 613 233 0398
Andy Rutherford - One World Action, London UK. Tel. +44 113 245 4786
Abdeslam Omar El-Hassan - AFRAPREDESA
Suzanne Scholte, President of the Defense Forum Foundation, Email Skswm@aol.com

Organisations
AFAPREDESA
BP DZ-Tindouf
Algerie
Tel. +213 7 932 332
Fax +213 7 931 568
Bureau de l'AFAPREDESA pour L'Europe
Paris, France
Tel/fax: +33 1 4585 1979
Email afapresa@derechos.org

CLAIHR
575 King Edward Avenue
Ottawa, Ontario K1N 6N5
Canada
Tel: + 613 233-0398
Fax: + 613 233-0671
www.web.net/~claihr/contact
Email: claihr@web.net

National Union of Sahrawi Women (NUSW)
c/o Mission de la RASD
BP 10, El Mouradia
1, Rue Rooswelt
DZ-16 000 Alger
Algerie
Tel. +213 7 931 480
Fax +213 7 931 822

Union des juristes Sahraouis
BP 12, Tindouf
Algerie
Tel/fax: +213 7 921 568

Western Sahara Campaign
Oxford Chambers
Oxford Place,
Leeds LS1 3AX
UK
Tel/fax: +44 1 1324 54786
Email:100427.3223@CompuServe.COM

Organisation marocaine des droits de l'homme (OMDH)
24 Avenue de France
Agdal, Rabat
Maroc
Tel: +212 7 770 060
Fax: +212 7 77 46 15

Data on the following organisations can be found in the Directory section:
Association Marocaine des Droits de l'Homme
Amnesty International
Human Right Watch

The Horn of Africa

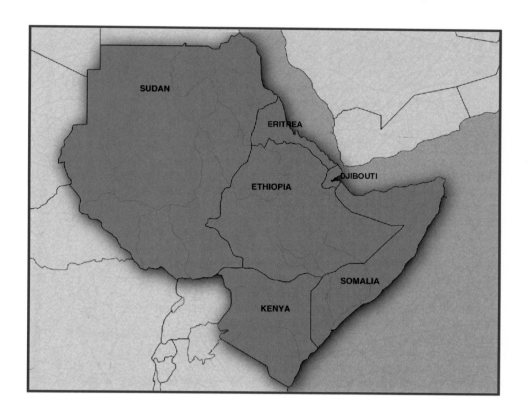

A Lack of Visionary Statesmanship and Democratic Leadership

Over the past three decades, the Horn of Africa[1] has come to represent protracted conflict and great instability. It has hosted some of the world's longest civil wars (Ethiopia and Sudan), featured a state that has totally disintegrated due to protracted civil war (Somalia), and produced a huge percentage of the world's refugees. Although some of the conflicts in the region are restricted to the specific countries therein, we will focus here on the more recent conflicts that have regional dimensions or implications ♦ By **Hizkias Assefa***

The most recent events having regional repercussions are the Ethiopian-Eritrean war, the Sudan government's gesture toward the resolution of the southern problem, the elections in Djibouti, and the continuing strife in Somalia.

The perplexing war between Ethiopia and Eritrea is now at a stalemate. Although both sides do not report their own losses and exaggerate the loss of their adversary, many estimate that at least 6,000 people might have died already. Over 350,000 have become internally displaced and about 80,000 people have been expelled from each other's countries. Both sides have spent over US$ 300 million in high technology armaments. The OAU's initiative to bring about peace between the adversaries has failed. A new initiative by a UN special envoy is underway, which so far has not been able to even get a cease-fire agreement.

In the meantime, both sides are try to weaken the other side by attempting to foment internal conflict in each other's country either through propaganda or indirect arms support to dissident elements. The Eritrean government has been encouraging and supporting the Oromo Liberation Movement to be more active in its campaign against the Ethiopian government. In retaliation, the Ethiopian government is encouraging the Eritrean Liberation Front and other Eritrean dissidents to operate from Ethiopia against the Eritrean government.

In addition to the human cost, the material destruction and the financial loss that these two very poor countries are inflicting on each other, the conflict is beginning to affect other countries

in the region, undermining the Horn of Africa's fragile hope for rehabilitation. One of the countries that is affected by this war is Djibouti. Because of the war, Ethiopia could no longer use the port of Assab and resorted to relying on the Port of Djibouti as its main access point for its imports and exports. This has not endeared Djibouti to Eritrea who sees it not only as a competitor but also as being sympathetic to Ethiopia's war effort. This, added to the fact that there are unresolved border issues between Djibouti and Eritrea has created political and military tension between the latter two countries. The mediation effort undertaken by the former president of Djibouti as part of the OAU team was rejected by Eritrea, which was seen by Djibouti as an insult.

The head office of the Intergovernmental Agency for Development (IGAD), the major regional peacemaking body, is located in Djibouti. At one time, the Secretary General, an Eritrean, was refused entry into Djibouti. Djibouti has completed its presidential elections, and the new president is expected to continue the policies of the former president Aptidon.

Sudan is also being drawn into the conflict. The government of Sudan has a longstanding feud with Eritrea over Eritrea's accusation that Sudan is exporting Moslem fundamentalism and Sudan's anger over Eritrea's support to Sudanese opposition groups who are trying to overthrow the Sudanese government. The escalation of the conflict between Ethiopia and Eritrea has given the Sudanese government an opportunity to use the situation to its benefit. In the same way that

Eritrea has been supporting Sudanese opposition groups, Sudan convened major opposition groups in Eritrea and gave them permission to organise their activities against Eritrea from Sudan. Ethiopia's tense relationship with Sudan has began to improve since both governments now see Eritrea as a common enemy.

The conflict in Somalia is becoming even more complicated and is exacerbated by the war between Eritrea and Ethiopia. There are indications that the Eritrean government is arming as well as training Somali factions and movements, such as the Aideed faction in Mogadishu and the Ogaden Liberation Movement, which are opposed to the Ethiopian government. The idea seems to be to diffuse Ethiopia's concentration on Eritrea and give it a multifront war. On the other hand, the Ethiopian government is arming those Somali factions opposed to the factions supported by the Eritreans such as those in Puntland and Morgan in Kismayu. This exacerbates the civil war and power struggle inside Somalia. The drought and the resultant famine in Somalia has not helped to dampen the factional competition and ongoing warfare.

Escalating tension between the Ethiopian government and the Oromo Liberation Movement (OLF) which is being supported by the Eritrean government is beginning to affect Kenya. On a number of occasions OLF forces have retreated into Kenya after attacking Ethiopian government forces. The Ethiopian military has pursued the OLF insurgents into Kenyan territory, thereby causing tension and even military confrontation with Kenyan forces. As a result of these repeated skirmishes with Kenyan forces on the border, relationships between the two governments are becoming more tense. Kenyan officials fear that the hundreds of millions of dollars spent by Ethiopia and Eritrea could start a regional arms race even if the war ends tomorrow.

Recent developments in Sudan with regard to the southern problem might have a positive influence on the region. The government has just announced that it wants to resolve its problem in the south by creating a transitional government in southern Sudan which will include the SPLA and which will prepare for a referendum in two years to decide whether the south should be given independence. The reaction to this proposal has generated division among southern Sudanese. Given that the SPLA is identified with the Dinka ethnic group, the joint administration of the south by Khartoum and SPLA is being opposed by some Equatorian and Nuer leaders saying that they would not want to resuscitate the post-Addis Ababa Agreement arrangement in southern Sudan where the autonomous government was reportedly dominated by Dinkas. If the problem is not resolved to the satisfaction of all parties involved, the war in the south would likely continue and the division among Southerners could intensify. A referendum and a declaration of an independent south might bring the north-south war in the Sudan to an end. However, it is not clear yet if the deep division that exists between the various ethnic groups in the south might generate another round of conflict and warfare after independence.

Prospects

Given current developments in the region, there does not seem to be much to suggest that the major conflicts in the region are going to end soon. Even if they do because of exhaustion of the combatants, it does not mean that such cessation of armed confrontation will necessarily translate into durable peace in the region. More hard work needs to be done to transform the current perceptions and attitudes of animosity, incompatibility, suspicion and hostility that exist among the elites of the region who are behind most of these conflicts.

The danger with the ongoing Eritrean and Ethiopian war is that unless stopped soon, it could develop into a very deep people-to-people hatred and violence. With the exception of southern Sudan and some instances in Somalia, most of the major conflicts in the region in the past had been between insurgents and governments and not between people like the ones witnessed in Rwanda or Burundi which have generated pogroms and mass killings.

Conflicts between insurgent groups and government can be settled on the negotiating table by agreements between the leaders. But once the conflict seeps deep and degenerates

SUDAN: A Southern Air Transport Hercules chartered by the Lutheran World Federation has landed at Panyagor, a former agricultural centre near the town of Kongor (north of Juba).

HELDUR NETOCNY/LINEAIR

into people-to-people hostility, the peace process becomes very difficult and the wounds take generations to heal. Unfortunately, most of the people that are being mobilised to hate each other in these conflicts are neighbours; have long historical, social and economic interconnections and have no choice but to continue to coexist regardless of who wins the wars. It is very tragic to inflict such deep damage to these community fabrics now and attempt to rebuild them later, when probably there may not be very much left to build upon.

Given the interconnected nature of the conflicts described above and their spillover effects, there is no doubt that their resolution would not only bring peace to the immediate protagonists but would also contribute to the improvement of relationships among all the actors in the region.

Recommendations

One of the problems facing the region in terms of generating durable peace has been the lack of visionary statesmanship and democratic leadership. In most instances, the wars in the Horn of Africa have been started by elites who then mobilise the population to join in. In many of these conflicts, it is not the combatants that are paying dearly by their lives for the armed struggles but the unarmed populations in whose names the conflicts are being waged. It is also clear that these intended ultimate beneficiaries of the wars do not have a say on whether the wars should continue or what amount of sacrifice should be extracted from them for attaining victory. It seems therefore that if mechanisms were developed that would permit free grassroots discussion and debate and the emergence of public opinion that could exert influence, the wars in the region could be significantly dampened as it will be clear that the people do not have much enthusiasm for the continuation of the conflicts. This could then create the proper environment for the search for political solutions instead of fighting till the end until victory is achieved. This suggests the encouragement and promotion of a national and regional civil society that can have a say on how these conflicts are understood and handled.

It is true that this process will not happen overnight nor will it be easy. However, a place to begin might be to target some of the different sectors of the society in the different countries of the region such as the media and opinion makers, trade and professional associations, legislators and parliamentarians, academic institutions, religious and civic institutions such as women's and youth organisations, non-governmental organisations, etc. and give them fora to express their views, concerns and proposals about these conflicts. Ironically, it might be easier to start this process regionally since it could have more international visibility and might be more difficult for the national governments to squelch the initiatives.

Of course, the methodology for such discussion and input would have to be carefully crafted. One should not have the illusion that these elements of the civil society will be cohesive or harmonious in their views and perspectives. A great deal of consensus-building and conflict resolution work has to be done among them.

Another problem in the conflict resolution and prevention efforts in the region has been the role of some governmental and non-governmental actors from outside the region. These actors have been quick to judge which side of the conflict is right and which one is wrong, and to support one side against the other either politically or materially. Needless to say, such a role by outsiders only exacerbates and perpetuates the conflicts in the Horn. A more useful role for outsiders would be to become guarantors of a process in which the regional governments as well as their citizens could have the safe space to examine different perspectives freely and openly. Such a process could allow all the involved parties to search for mutually satisfactory and durable solutions unhindered by intimidation and manipulation.

From a regional perspective, an appropriate body to undertake the function of resolution and prevention of many of the conflicts in the region would have been IGAD. However, as it currently stands, it has some very serious limitations that prevent it from being an effective actor. For

'Make IGAD a body where the public opinion from the civil society can have a hearing and influence. Some kind of a regional parliament with voices from the regional civil society might be a development in that direction.'

example, it has been attempting to mediate the Sudan conflict for close to six years. But to date, it has not succeeded in bringing about a negotiated settlement. Part of the problem is that most of the mediators in the conflict have been directly or indirectly involved in the war on the side of one of the parties against the other. With the exception of Kenya and Djibouti, the other IGAD members (Uganda, Eritrea, and Ethiopia) had taken the side of the SPLA.

Therefore, the agency does not enjoy the trust of Khartoum to effectively mediate the conflict. It is unlikely that a mediation process by third parties who are at war with one of the conflict parties or are attempting to overthrow the government of one of the conflict parties, can produce an honestly negotiated peace. It is possible that the warming of relationship between Ethiopia and Sudan might change the old alliance patterns that existed prior to the eruption of the Eritrean-Ethiopian war and the SPLA might not be able to count on Ethiopia's sympathy. However, Ethiopia's changing position to be more sympathetic to the Sudan government will not remedy the shortcomings IGAD is experiencing as a regional peace-making body in the Sudan conflict.

In the current conflict between Ethiopia and Eritrea, IGAD has been unable to take even the first steps to address the problems. There have been attempts to reinforce and strengthen IGAD. However, to the extent that the Agency is riddled with the political problem where the member governments are involved in undermining and destabilising each other, any kind of reinforcement of IGAD is not likely to increase its effectiveness.

This is not however to suggest that regional bodies or regional approaches do not have roles to play in the resolution or prevention of conflicts in the Horn of Africa. There are many justifications for a regional perspective or approach. Among others:

a) Many of the major conflicts in the Horn have been inter-connected in various ways. Thus, concentrating only on the immediate parties to the conflict without involving the other regional players in one way or another may not lead to effective and enduring resolution of the conflicts.

b) Even if the conflicts are not interconnected, many of them have causes which are similar or consequences which are regional in scope and therefore could benefit greatly from collective treatment within a regional framework.

c) Aside from the conflict resolution benefits, operating in a regional framework could have beneficial economic, political, and social spillovers.[2]

However, for IGAD to play a role in bringing these benefits of a regional approach to fruition, it must develop a new vision and operate in a different way.

A first step in reforming IGAD could be to make it a body which can promote trust among its member governments so that its intervention to resolve conflicts in the region is not seen as an initiative disguised to serve the interest of some actors at the expense of others. It must build its credibility in such a way that conflict parties in the region perceive it not as an instrument for power brokering but rather for sincere mediation and resolution of disputes. Professionalising the staff of the agency and giving it more autonomy to operate so that it is not paralysed by the politics of the member governments might be a step in the right direction.

Another element in that reform could be to make IGAD a body where the kind of public opinion from the civil society that was referred to earlier can have a hearing and influence. Some kind of a regional parliament with voices from the regional civil society might be a development in that direction.

*   Prof. Hizkias Assefa is Distinguished Fellow at the Institute of Conflict Analysis and Resolution at George Mason University and Professor of Conflict Studies at Eastern Mennonite University, both located in Virginia, USA. He also coordinates the African Peacebuilding and Reconciliation Network from Nairobi, Kenya. He has been involved in second track diplomacy in a number of civil wars in Africa as well as in facilitating grassroots based reconciliation processes in many war-torn societies. He has written many books on conflict and conflict resolution. Currently, he is working on projects entitled: Regional Approaches to the Resolution and Prevention of Conflicts in the Horn of Africa and the Great Lakes Region .

1   The traditional definition of the Horn of Africa includes Djibouti, Eritrea, Ethiopia, Somalia and Sudan. However, for purposes of this regional survey, it would be necessary to expand the definition to include Kenya since it is significantly affected by and affects a number of states within the region.

2   For more elaboration and operationalisation of this regional approach see, Hizkias Assefa, Regional Approach for the Resolution and Prevention of Conflicts in the Horn of Africa, forthcoming.

In Search of Regionalism

The Horn of Africa conventionally has been understood as including the states of Sudan, Ethiopia, Eritrea, Djibouti and Somalia. This area was usually distinguished from the countries of East Africa, Uganda, Kenya, and Tanzania. By dint of the spillover of recent conflicts such as refugees, however, the Horn has increasingly been thought of as extending from the former group, or northern tier, into the latter group, or southern tier. The notion of a 10-country 'Greater Horn of Africa' that includes all these plus Rwanda and Burundi recently has been used by the U.S. government. In this article, we focus on the original Horn region plus East Africa. Defined as such, the region encompasses countries that still differ somewhat in terms of relative level of development and the incidence of conflicts. But that contrast may be lessening ◆ *By* **Michael Lund and Wendy Betts***

The countries of this region possesses rich natural resources and educated elites, and they are linked through local cross-boundary trade, the major river basins of the Blue and White Nile, and other transportation routes. These assets could be utilised to achieve food self-sufficiency and economic growth. Yet several of these countries, especially in the northern tier, have experienced recurrent drought and resulting food shortages, and are among the very poorest economies in the world. Although Uganda has seen comparatively impressive growth in recent years, slow growth and high unemployment rates are common amid rapidly rising populations. The region's external or internal colonial histories have resulted in the educated classes sharing both Anglophonic national and regional language communities. Due to the colonial boundaries, the countries are also linked by local ethnic and linguistic communities that straddle their borders. But in part by the same token, they are politically fragmented by several ethnic groups and religions. In some, lowland pastoralist communities compete for land and resources with highland dwellers.

The potential reasons for pursuing inter-state regional cooperation to promote national development have neither been capitalised on nor kept a number of violent conflicts from breaking out in recent decades, within and between states. Many disputes and resulting tensions that could escalate continue to persist. In the northern tier, with the onset of the Ethiopia-Eritrean border war in 1998, all the states are now embroiled in active or simmering military conflicts. Most of these conflicts involve competition for influence over areas within the states, but each of them has spilled into the neighbouring countries. This takes the form both of fleeing refugees and the policies of states to support dissident groups that are opposed to the government of a neighbouring state. Such policies risk provoking state against state. Although the southern set of countries have been comparatively more stable in recent years, the potential exists for more internal turmoil there in the future. Uganda already faces several local rebellion and is engaged in the Congo War.

Recent Developments

Despite its many divisions and conflicts, a sense of regionalism has been growing slowly in this area, and small steps toward regional cooperation have been made.

Economic Cooperation
The first signs of regional cooperation in the Horn came with attempts in East Africa to coordinate economic policies and integrate economies, some predating the independence period. The East African Common Services Organisation of 1961 (EACSO) was intended to set unified policies in areas such as the post, harbours and currency, but it was hampered by the tendency of the country-based ministers who sat on its bodies to neglect regional affairs, as well as by Kenya's dominance of inter-regional

trade. After Tanzania imposed unilateral import restrictions on Kenya in 1965 and 1966, an effort was made in 1967 to revitalise economic cooperation through the creation of a regional common market under the East African Economic Community (EAEC). Despite the creation of more decentralised institutions and the removal of all trade restrictions, Kenya continued to benefit disproportionately. Trade disputes and personal differences between the unpredictable President Amin of Uganda and Tanzanian President Nyerere led to the demise of EAEC in 1977 and the closing of the Kenya-Tanzania border until 1983. Negotiations to re-establish a community began again in 1995, but agreement was hampered by suspicions of the intentions of Uganda's President Yoweri Museveni.

Some have argued that the obstacles encountered from intense economic rivalries between a few countries can be attenuated by economic agreements that are more geographically inclusive. One notable attempt involving the Horn was the Preferential Trade Area (PTA) for Eastern and Southern Africa, which was conceived in the OAU and the UN Economic Commission for Africa as a way to link several of the Horn countries to the countries to the south. Created in 1981, the PTA overlaps with the somewhat newer and similar regional economic organisation for southern Africa, SADC (see the regional article on southern Africa). But rather than forging new efforts at regional development as was SADC's goal, the emphasis in the PTA was to build on existing levels of production and regional infrastructure in order to increase regional trade. A 10-year phased programme for eliminating tariffs in designated areas would allow countries to protect their infant and strategic industries and it provided compensation and other corrective measures. The ultimate goal was the integration of the various regional communities to form an African Common Market. By 1989, the PTA had eighteen members.

The PTA was replaced in 1994 by the Common Market for Eastern and Southern Africa (COMESA). COMESA includes 21 members, including all the states from Egypt through the Horn to Zimbabwe, and Angola,

Namibia, and Madadascar, but not South Africa. (Recently, COMESA leaders accused South Africa of dumping its subsidised goods onto regional markets but closing its own market to African goods.) Observing that Africa's export trade had declined, COMESA members have cut tariffs on each other substantially, causing some increase in intra-COMESA trade. The organisation intends to eliminate all tariffs among its members by October, 2000 and to establish a common external tariff by 2004 and monetary union and free movement of peoples by 2005. COMESA meetings have urged the member states that were fighting each other to stop fighting in the interest of development, but they have been unsuccessful.

Although the Organization for African Unity (OAU) is headquartered in Addis Ababa, Ethiopia, the region's own border and civil wars and other inter-state disputes, especially between Ethiopia, Sudan, and Somalia, kept any regional cooperation from emerging among the northern Horn countries, until the late 1980's. But the primary regional organisation now active in the wider Horn region is the Inter Governmental Authority on Development (IGAD), consisting of Djibouti, Ethiopia, Eritrea, Sudan, Somalia, Uganda and Kenya. At the urging of the UN Environmental Programme, IGAD was formed in 1986 as the Inter Governmental Authority on Drought and Desertification (IGADD) with the purpose of coordinating member states' policies on desertification and other environmental issues, since the distribution of the Horn's scarce water supply is a source of potential conflict.

In 1996, IGAD's mandate was restructured to address three more ambitious priority areas: food security and environmental protection; political and humanitarian affairs, including conflict prevention and resolution; and regional economic security. The organisation receives the support of numerous western countries, including Canada, the UK, Netherlands, Norway, and the US, through the mechanism of the IGAD Partners Forum, which was formally created in 1997 out of the Friends of IGAD. Member States and donors identify and develop projects through a consultative process. The organisation secretariat is located in Djibouti.

To date, IGAD has achieved modest success in the field of water usage and food security. It was responsible, for example, in developing an Early Warning and Food Information System for the region. But efforts at broader and deeper economic cooperation have encountered a number of political obstacles, so the goal of significant economic integration in the Horn remains elusive.

Diplomacy

IGAD envisioned the possibility that environmental cooperation might be broadened into political and security matters. The fact that its successive summits provide a regular forum for communication means that potential problems and policy areas other than environmental matters can be discussed. In 1986, for example, Ethiopia and Somalia began talks aimed at détente and demilitarisation of their borders. In the early 1990s, the threat that several violent conflicts in the region would spill over into neighbouring countries, causing refugees and serious humanitarian emergencies prompted IGAD to become involved in regional political affairs and to undertake attempts at direct conflict management. The member states also recognised that these conflicts had adverse effects on its economic programmes, by diverting important resources away from development.

The most vigorous and challenging initiative was the effort begun in 1993 to actively mediate the Sudanese civil war. This consisted primarily of four of its members (Kenya, Uganda, Ethiopia and Eritrea) brokering talks between the regime in Khartoum and the rival factions of the Sudan People's Liberation Movement and Army (SPLM/A). The partners' motivation was guided in part by the support Sudan was giving to rebel groups in Eritrea, Ethiopia, and Uganda. As part of the initial talks in 1994, IGAD developed a Declaration of Principles (DOP) that emphasised the importance of national unity under a secular state but recognised the right of self-determination for the people of the south.

Disagreements over the DOP led the Sudan government to delay and withdraw from the process, however, resulting in a three-year collapse of the peace initiative. In 1995, the countries that had launched the mediation de-emphasised diplomacy and adopted instead an actively hostile approach toward the Sudan government. Believing the government was the main source of instability in the region, they supported UN sanctions against Sudan and supported the opponents of the Khartoum regime, including providing assistance to the SPLA. This raised the question of whether IGAD was any longer a body for conflict resolution or rather an alliance of four states against Sudan.

In 1997, IGAD restarted the peace talks. Two rounds were held under Kenyan leadership and a third was held in August 1998 in Addis Ababa. Despite proposals put forth by IGAD, these talks have not brought the parties to an agreement and no subsequent rounds have been held. Further talks opened in Nairobi in July 1999.

Though the Sudan war wages on, IGAD has made some progress in regard to the Sudan conflict. It succeeded in bringing the rival factions in the south closer together, a consolidation that facilitates the talks between the south and the north. More importantly, the 1994 DOP provided a framework for the negotiations. Despite its initial rejection by the Sudanese government, both sides have since accepted the DOP as a starting point for negotiations. Finally, IGAD has convinced the warring sides of the need to address and alleviate the humanitarian suffering caused by the conflict, which led to the opening of 'safe corridors' for the delivery of relief supplies.

More broadly, IGAD has succeeded in creating a spirit of dialogue and an accepted, official forum for the discussion of security issues, as seen in the 1996 expansion of its mandate. Remarkably perhaps, it has at least survived the emergence of new conflicts between its members. IGAD also provides a mechanism and conduit for coordinating assistance from the West and maintaining a concerted diplomatic strategy. Through the Partners Forum, Western countries can provide much needed resources, while allowing the peace process to continue to be an indigenous, African initiative.

IGAD has been marginally involved in the Somalia conflict, primarily by placing it on the IGAD agenda and reiterating the need for international attention. In regard to the Ethiopia-

Eritrea conflict, currently the most militarised conflict, IGAD has had no serious involvement, however.

IGAD obviously has not been successful in ending current conflicts and bringing stability to the region. IGAD's inability to foster peace and security cooperation among the countries in the Horn stems fundamentally from the persisting suspicions, geopolitical rivalries, and ideological differences among its members. In Sudan, IGAD is not seen as neutral due to cross-border conflicts between Sudan, Ethiopia, and Eritrea. The members' conflicting political interests have completely precluded any direct action in Ethiopia. The desire to undermine Ethiopia's natural hegemony in the Horn prevents effective cooperation between Ethiopia and other countries. The animosities among the northern tier countries have precluded IGAD from any serious discussion of inter-state security cooperation such as regional peacekeeping forces. Exacerbating the competition among member states is the fact that the states themselves are not consolidated. Their resulting insecurity and fear of threats to their sovereignty intensifies the efforts to strengthen themselves at the expense of the others. This regional competition prevents IGAD members from developing a coherent, consolidated approach to security issues.

Even were these differences not so intense, IGAD also has limited ability to broker an end to the Sudan civil war because of its lack of leverage over the warring parties. It lacks the resources necessary to provide incentives and disincentives to the parties. The shortage of resources implies that IGAD also would not have the means to monitor or guarantee peace should an agreement be achieved.

Civil Society Activity

The obstacles associated with the official efforts at conflict prevention and management raise the question of whether non-governmental initiatives by NGOs might expedite the termination of the region's conflicts and create a leavening influence and source of pressure that prevents internal or inter-state conflicts from being so readily pursued by rival leaders. The pertinent functions NGOs might provide include early warning, facilitating mediation, monitoring of human rights behavior and elections, confidence-building between communities, civil society development, and movement toward economic, social and political reform. It is widely believed that the current proliferation of NGOs will bring about greater democratisation of African societies. If democracy then tends to constrain a government's penchant for violent pursuit of interests, then NGOs can help conflict prevention and management.

In theory, strong regional NGOs might play a useful role in conflict management in the Horn of Africa, but so far, no significant non-governmental activity is actually being carried out that is Horn region-wide or that goes beyond a few joint projects in a few of its countries. On a regional level, NGO networks remain in very early stages of development. Most non-governmental organisations (NGOs) in the region that are devoted to democracy-building, human rights, development and conflict resolution operate within one or other of its states. Kenya has perhaps the largest number of NGOs in Africa, and Uganda also has a large number. The lack of cross-border networks prevents NGOs from formulating common recommendations and putting concerted pressure on the governments in the region to resolve their differences.

In some countries in the Horn, however, a few locally-organised NGOs operate outside occasionally their own borders. Among the most active in civil society promotion and conflict prevention and management are the All Africa Conference of Churches (AACC) in Nairobi and the InterAfrica Group (IAG) in Addis Ababa. The AACC, formed in 1958, has perhaps the most experience of the regional NGOs. This group coordinates the efforts of African churches in building tolerance and awareness at a local level. While playing an instrumental role in the negotiations that ended the Sudanese Civil War in 1972, in the current conflict, the AACC primarily has supported IGAD's efforts. The AACC has also sent peace missions to other conflict zones in Africa, such as Angola and Rwanda. Founded in 1989, the Inter-Africa Group engages in research, public education and advocacy. IAG also promotes human rights standards, encouraging governments to abide by them and citizens to mobilise in support of them. This group pursues peace-building through economic development and human rights. To this end, they work closely with IGAD to address refugee and environmental issues. Although the AACC played a role in ending the earlier civil war in Sudan, and other NGOs have achieved occasional 'track-two' advances in facilitating conflict negotiations, by and large, however, NGOs, whether regional or national, have not been able to exercise significant leverage over the main protagonists in the Horn's conflicts, such as governments and warlords. NGOs ability to pressure these actors to pursue specific peace negotiations may be related to their inability to guarantee implementation of any peace agreements reached.

The approach to the region's conflicts taken by many of the NGOs operating in the Horn is indirect. These groups work to strengthen civil society and empower the citizens to become involved in advocating for peace, such as by promoting electoral participation and monitoring elections. Thus, NGOs often have been effective in raising the awareness of aggrieved groups of the gains that can be realised by political action, and they have encouraged more popular participation in local and national politics. Local projects

Despite their potential importance, however, definite obstacles still stand in the way of many NGOs being effective agents of domestic change in their societies on behalf of civic education, human rights, and democratic reform. In the first place, most of the NGO sector in African societies is devoted not to civic political action at all, but to the delivery of services of various kinds such as in health or development, which often thus supplements government action. Or they serve primarily religious purposes. As worthy as these purposes are in their own right, they do not necessarily empower constituents to advance the cause of democracy or conflict management. Another obvious limitation is NGOs chronic lack of sufficient resources to launch major efforts, and their financial dependence on external aid. Third, NGOs need to have other NGOs as their allies in national coalitions if their influence is to

aggregate into a powerful force that can affect public policy and that requires governments to come to terms with it. Yet their financial penury does not encourage inter-NGO cooperation or coordination.

Further, NGOs need to have a conducive political climate to make much of a difference. But many governments and their political parties, which are themselves trying to establish their identity and pre-eminence, are often threatened by independent groups that advocate civic awareness and thus are hostile to the creation and functioning of NGOs, equating many of them with the political opposition. Consequently, many civil society NGOs are prohibited, and others face repeated bureaucratic hurdles. NGOs that do survive often are those that are supported, both politically and materially, by the government, but these groups then become political organisations rather than nonpartisan assistance providers or advocates. To the extent that an NGOs confidence-building capacity is linked to its neutrality and independence from the government, government support can have an adverse effect on the NGOs efficacy. On the other hand, if NGOs adopt a consistently anti-government view or ally themselves with one political faction or another, they may simply be heightening the political tensions in a society and increasing the potential for violent conflict, rather than transforming those tensions into energies for peaceful change.

Finally, NGOs in Africa are shaped greatly by their key leaders. The latter must be consistently dedicated to finding and implementing effective and ongoing strategies for mobilising constituencies behind viable social change campaigns. Yet NGOs often may be used as means of career enhancement and social mobility for various elites, such as providing platforms for entering politics.

Next Steps

For lasting stability and cooperation to begin to return to the Horn and to last, both the official and unofficial channels must reinforce the efforts of the other, creating both a top down and bottom up approach. Despite the need for dynamic civil society, however, that realistically is a long-term objective, and it may in fact be as much a result of peace as a cause of it. In the short term, peace cannot be achieved nor implemented without changing the current political and military calculations of the incumbent leaders who are most responsible for waging violent conflicts. But they are difficult for NGOs to influence. Nor will IGAD and other regional inter-governmental organisations be able to function effectively as regular means for conflict prevention and management, unless the incentives of these leaders to terminate current hostilities are substantially increased.

The shortcomings of IGAD and NGOs have led to calls for greater leverage exerted by major actors in the international community, particularly the West, such as major powers and donor organisations. Such international actors need to work together to offer peace plans that have sufficiently robust inducements to bring about different behaviour. But rather than becoming directly involved in addressing African security issues, these third party efforts should simultaneously foster the viability of African institutions. Thus, the consideration of the offered alternatives to conflict should take place within the diplomatic channels that are being gradually institutionalised by IGAD and similar regional organisations. Such entrees should also be followed up with efforts to institutionalise conflict prevention and preventive peacebuilding processes in these institutions as well.

References

As Peace Talks Start, Sudan Recruits 70,000 Soldiers. Electronic Mail and Guardian, 5 August 1998

Common Market for Eastern and Southern Africa, Website at www.comesa.int

Deng, Francis M. *Out of Sight, Out of Mind: In Sudan, African 'Kosovars' Have No Reason to Hope for Allied Help.* The Washington Post. 30 April 1999

Deng, Francis M. and Terrence Lyons, eds. *African Reckoning: A Quest for Good Governance.* Washington, DC: Brookings Institution Press, 1998

Dicklitch, Susan, *Indigenous Non-Governmental Organizations and Civil Society in Uganda: Viable Vehicles of Democratization?* University of South Carolina, Unpublished paper, 1995

IGAD Peace Initiatives Fail to Take Off Again, Africa News Service Inc. 3 May 1999

InterAfrica Group. *Social Development in the Horn of Africa: Challenges and Prospects, March 1995.'* Paper prepared for the World Summit on Social Development, March 1995, Copenhagen, Denmark

Inter-Governmental Authority on Development (IGAD). United States Department of State website, www.state.gov

Life and Peace Institute website, www.life-peace.org

Martin, Guy, *The Preferential Trade Area (PTA) for Eastern and Southern Africa: Achievements, Problems and Prospects.'*

Menkhaus, Ken and John Prendergast, *Conflict and Crisis in the Greater Horn of Africa*, Current History, May, 1999. p.213-222

Mwangi, Wagaki. *A Revitalized IGAD, But What Is In Store.'* Econews Africa, Vol. 5, No. 24, 28 November 1996.

Ndegwa, Stephen N., *The Two Faces of Civil Society.* West Hartford, Connecticut: Kumarian Pres, 1996

Prendergast, John, *Building for Peace in the Horn of Africa*, Special Report, Washington, D.C.: United Staes Institute of Peace, June 28, 1999

Smock, David R. and Chester A. Crocker, eds. *African Conflict Resolution: The U.S. Role in Peacemaking*, Washington, DC: United States Institute of Peace, 1995

Torduff, William, *Government and Politics in Africa.* Third Edition, Bloomington, Indiana University Press, 1997

UN Beefs Up Regional Peace Efforts in Sudan, Somalia, Xinhua News Agency. November 13, 1998

United Nations Environmental Program. *Report of the Regional Consultations held for the first Global Environment Outlook*, 1996

Welch, Claude E., Jr. *Protecting Human Rights in Africa: Strategies and Roles of Non-Governmental Organizations.* Philadelphia, University of Pennsylvania Press, 1995

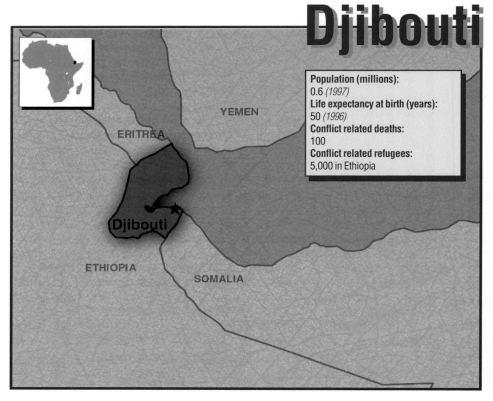

Djibouti

Population (millions):
0.6 *(1997)*
Life expectancy at birth (years):
50 *(1996)*
Conflict related deaths:
100
Conflict related refugees:
5,000 in Ethiopia

External Conflict Internalised

A ten year old, low-intensity conflict between the government of Djibouti and the armed faction of the Front pour la Restauration de l'Unité et de la Démocratie (FRUD) was aggravated by the outbreak of the Ethiopian-Eritrean border conflict in May 1998. Eritrea was quick to accuse Djibouti's Gouled Aptidon administration of siding with Ethiopia, while the government feared an alliance between the FRUD and Eritrea. Prospects for a sustainable peace are remote, even after the election of a new president. Little progress has been made with the further demobilisation of 9,000 soldiers. The rather limited and oppressed peace lobby in Djibouti is not in a position to play an effective role in pressing for an end to the conflict ◆ *By* Jos van Beurden

The impact on Djibouti of conflicts in surrounding countries is clearly reflected in the fluctuations in its population. Refugees and illegal migrants, coming from and returning to Somaliland, Ethiopia and Eritrea, have meant that total population has varied between 500,000 and 600,000. According to UN estimates, in 1998 the country sheltered some 70,000 - 100,000 refugees and illegal immigrants. Some

80 per cent of Djibouti's inhabitants live in cities, mostly in Djiboutiville.

Djiboutians are of either Somali or Afar descent. The Afar, comprising around one-third of the inhabitants of the northern part of the country, are the largest ethnic group. They have kinsmen in Eritrea and Ethiopia. The Issa, comprising almost one-third of the total population, are the second largest single group.

However, the Issaq and Gadaboursi, also of Somali descent, together form the majority of the population. They live mainly in the southern part of Djibouti. There is also a long-established Arab trading community and several thousand French expatriates. Djibouti is predominantly Islamic.

Since its independence in 1977 Djibouti has been confronted by a number of problems. Firstly, as the only country between the Mediterranean Sea and the Indian Ocean it has a significant Western military presence playing host to some 3,200 troops of its former coloniser, France. Djibouti was the operational base for French participation in the Gulf War (1991) and Operation Restore Hope for Somalia (1992). The French presence is crucial to the Djibouti economy.

Secondly, the economy of this tiny state is rendered vulnerable by its dependence upon neighbouring countries, notably Ethiopia. The growth of modern Djibouti followed the French-Ethiopian decision to build a 780 kilometre long railway to Addis Ababa, a plan made when Eritrea was an Italian colony and Ethiopia landlocked. The health of Djibouti's economy is directly related to the demand for its port facilities in Ethiopia. In Djibouti's independence year Somalia and Ethiopia fought their Ogaden War which effectively brought Ethiopian import and export activity to a standstill.

Thirdly, as part of a divide and rule policy, and fearing the association of the Somali with pan Somali-nationalism, the French administration gave preferential treatment to the nomadic Afars. The Somali, however, were dominant in Djioutiville and were often better educated and more fully integrated in the commercial life of the colony. As a result, the Issa and other Somali began to seek independence while the Afar preferred to maintain the French connection. This ethnic problem still exists today.

After independence, Hassan Gouled Aptidon, an Issa, became the country's president. At first Djibouti's national coalition was relatively united. Soon, however, this balance disappeared as Gouled Aptidon's tendency towards authoritarianism and propensity to favour his own kinsmen became apparent. The national coalition broke down in the 1980's, when a movement for effective multiparty democracy was launched. Subsequently, Gouled Aptidon's Rassemblement Populaire pour le Progrès became the target of much political unrest while the opposition was organised into the FRUD (Front pour la Restauration de l'Unité et de la Démocratie).

1991 was an eventful year in Northeast Africa. Somalian President Siad Barre was ousted. A civil war created a flow of refugees into Djibouti - some observers claim as many as 120,000. Ethiopian President Mengistu Haile Mariam was replaced by Meles Zenawi from Tigray. Many of Mengistu's sympathisers fled to the tiny city-state. The independent Eritrea became a new neighbour.

In October that year, 3,000 Afar launched an attack on government-positions in the Afar area of Abah. This marked the beginning of a three-year civil war in which ethnicity and lack of democracy were the key issues. The government employed migratory guerrilla-fighters from Ethiopia, granting them Djiboutian nationality upon conscription, and providing them with light armaments bought on the black market in Somalia and Ethiopia. Its army, swollen from 3,000 to more than 16,000 men, put down the insurrection and the whole country was placed under a general mobilisation order. Claiming that the attack was carried out by men in Ethiopian army uniforms, the government invoked French military assistance against this foreign aggression. Officially Paris only offered a team of 'observers', but there was compelling evidence of French military involvement at the time. For their part, the rebels denied that any Ethiopian Afar or former Mengistu advisors had been involved in the attack.

In 1992 the events of the previous October forced President Gouled Aptidon to make some constitutional changes and allow more political parties, but in reality he remained the sole leader of Djibouti. In 1994 the government and a faction of the Afar-led FRUD signed a Peace Accord. The rest of the FRUD, led by Ahmed Dini, continued to fight the government, accusing the president of 'tribal dictatorship'.

Conflict Dynamics

The conflict in Djibouti was low key in the first months of 1998, while prospects for a lasting solution remained absent. FRUD-underground forces carried out several small-scale attacks on army-installations in northern and western Djibouti. As in previous years, they were no real threat to the government and casualties remained limited. However, they did undermine the credibility of those within FRUD who had chosen to cooperate with the government in 1994.

President Gouled Aptidon and his nephew and heir-apparent, Ismael Omar Guelleh, were unwilling to share their power, and Afar distrust of the government remained deep-seated. During the December 1997 legislative elections, the ruling party, which had concluded a coalition with a faction of FRUD earlier in 1997, took all 65 seats in the National Assembly. Some leaders of FRUD-underground, who had been arrested in Ethiopia in September 1997 and handed over to the Djibouti-authorities, were still in jail. Presidential elections, promised for 1998, eventually took place in April 1999. Gouled Aptidon's top aide Ismael Omar Guelleh won convincingly. A week after his victory the armed faction of FRUD planted a mine in northern Djibouti, which killed seven policemen.

The government has objected strongly to France's decision to cut its troops from 3,200 to 2,600 by the year 2000 - part of the French policy to decrease its military presence throughout Africa. Djibouti requested large amounts of compensation.

In the second half of 1998 the silent civil war in Djibouti was intensified by the Ethiopian-Eritrean border conflict. Long before it came into the open, Ethiopia had begun to intensify its relations with Djibouti. In 1996 the two countries concluded an agreement to combat the Al-Ittehad al-Islam, a fundamentalist group operating from south-western Somalia. In 1997 they agreed to join their fight against smugglers and drugs trafficking. Djibouti handed over a number of Oromo refugees to the Ethiopian police.

Because of the closure of the Eritrean port of Assab for Ethiopian imports and exports, Djibouti and Ethiopia decided to work on the renovation of their joint railway. The work, funded by France and the EU, started in April 1998 and led to a sudden increase in Ethiopian transit-cargo. Later,

Ethiopia stationed troops inside Djibouti to protect lorries on the road and trains to Addis Ababa, which would otherwise be vulnerable to terrorist attack. It may also have wanted to dissuade Eritrea from making use of the armed opposition in Djibouti. During a FRUD-attack in September 1998 a plant and vehicles belonging to a French company were damaged.

At the same time Djibouti's relationship with Eritrea deteriorated significantly. In June 1998 Djibouti deployed its army to the north, where FRUD-units were based, in order to patrol its borders with Eritrea and prevent any incursion. Some French army units joined the Djiboutian troops, officially to participate in a de-mining programme. Early in 1999, France made a frigate available to patrol the coast and prevent any foreign troops landing.

In late 1998, Eritrea accused Djibouti of allowing Ethiopia to use its port for importing military equipment for use in the border conflict. Djibouti immediately severed its relations with Eritrea and recalled its ambassador. Later that year the Executive Secretary for IGAD, Tekest Ghebrai, who is an Eritrean, was refused entry into Djibouti. Apparently the five-year agreement to increase contacts and cooperation, which Djibouti and Eritrea signed in December 1997, had not sufficiently cemented the two countries together. In his capacity of IGAD-Chairman, President Gouled Aptidon tried in June to mediate in the conflict, but during the November 1998 mini-OAU-Summit in Ouagadagou on the border conflict, Gouled Aptidon was quickly rejected as mediator by Eritrea on the grounds that he was not sufficiently independent.

The damage resulting from civil unrest is serious and trade and services have deteriorated. This has resulted in the destruction of livestock, water resources, and education and health facilities. Djibouti's humanitarian aid requirements have increased significantly since the outbreak of the civil war in 1991.

Official Conflict Management

In 1991, when the civil war broke out, *France* refused to help the Gouled Government, which it considered corrupt and authoritarian, but offered to mediate with the FRUD-rebels. This resulted in an initial cease-fire in 1992. However, the government used this lull in the conflict to acquire new arms, and the war continued. When the FRUD-rebels had secured control of more than half of the country, France changed its mind and assisted the government's army by, for example, defending the town of Dikhil.

The *Gouled-Government* has made some concessions including the introduction of a multiparty system, a more decentralised administration and press freedom. The opposition has taken advantage of this limited democratic freedom, and some independent unions have been established. At the same time it saw the concessions as delaying-tactics. In the December 1994 Peace Accord these concessions were more clearly defined. The FRUD faction which continued its armed opposition to the government claimed that the Accord did nothing to bring about the demobilisation of the clan-based militia recruited by the government and that the multiparty system was subject to so many conditions that only a few were in a position to profit from it. After the April 1999 Presidential elections chairman Ahmed Dini of the FRUD armed faction stated that 'as long as there are no negotiations, there is no way of putting an end to armed struggles', indicating his willingness to have a dialogue with the new strongman.

To further aid the peace process, France, the *European Union* and the *African Development Bank* provided funding for the demobilisation and social reintegration of 8,500 soldiers. Until 1996 only 3,000 of the more than 16,000 strong army were demobilised and targets for 1996, 1997 and 1998 were not reached. The government hoped that many demobilised Issa would return to south-western Ethiopia. The Ethio-Eritrean border conflict may further interrupt demobilisation efforts.

The day before the legislative elections of December 1997, the *European Parliament* expressed 'alarm at the situation of human rights in Djibouti' and said that it was particularly anxious at the violence exercised against the members of the opposition'.

Multi-Track Diplomacy
Domestic
Before the 1977 Ogaden War between Ethiopia and Somalia and the famines which

followed the country's independence in 1977, *civilian organisations* in Djibouti were limited to a small number of interest groups, charities such as the Rotary Club and some agricultural and fishery cooperatives. Their relationship with the State was defined in a law dating from 1901. Community development organisations were established only in the 1980s. In the 1990s they began to focus increasingly on activities for the urban poor, AIDS-victims, women, refugees and on relief aid.

The reality of serious underdevelopment, a weak government and the International Monetary Fund's pressure on the government to further reduce its public spending heightens the need for a strong civil sector and increased NGO activity. Djibouti receives much development aid, notably from the European Union, the Council of Europe and France, but civil organisations are for the most part weak and often ethnically based.

Political parties and trade unions have traditionally been important forms of association in Djibouti. Over the years since independence there have been some thirty political parties, although only four of them were declared legal after 1992. However, many parties, whether they are aligned with the government, the opposition or the rebels, are plagued by a partisanship which can be traced back to ethnic and sub-ethnic affiliations. Consequently, neither the rebels, the political opposition, nor the government have a constant and stable support from their members.

Unions of Primary and Secondary Education Teachers were set up in 1993. A federation of trade unions, UDT/UGDT, was also established and includes a wide variety of professions including workers in health, telecommunications and public works. They are intended to be multi-ethnic, are not allied to any political party in the country and aim to act as a social partner for the government.

Both political parties and unions have often been the target of repression. Students protesting about inadequate scholarships in December 1998 were fired on by armed police. The government created its own unions and even forced some trade union-leaders to resign and go into exile.

Djibouti has almost no human rights organisations. Although there are some human rights activists, their work has been seriously frustrated by the security forces. Frequently the subject of legal action, French lawyers who would like to defend them are often refused entry visas.

Amnesty International, the US Government as well as associations of Djiboutians in the diaspora, especially in France, have criticised Djibouti's human rights record on numerous occasions, claiming that security forces carry out extra-judicial executions, maltreat prisoners and rape female prisoners. The freedom of the press is often limited and the authorities have been known to seize printing machinery. In 1998 several newspaper editors were imprisoned. In October 1998 French-based Djiboutians opposed to the government occupied the Djibouti Embassy in Paris. Protest organisers included three organisations of Djiboutians and one support group.

A 1995 UNDP report concluded that local NGOs play a marginal role in the socio-economic development of the country. Local NGOs are mostly unknown outside their own immediate community base. They get almost no support from the state or from donors. They lack the capacity to be real partners in the long-term development of the country. Apart from ethnic-based organisations and loyalties, Djibouti has no tradition of people organising themselves.

There are some forty local NGOs. They have a serious capacity problem and often lack a clear policy and programme. Only a few are involved with sustainable development, including advocacy and conflict resolution. Very few are multi-ethnic. *L'Association d'Entraide du Quartier 4,* an urban-based NGO in Djiboutiville, is a good example. It works closely with traditional elders. Many NGOs are local sports or cultural associations. The activities of most of the other NGOs reflect the day to day problems of Djibouti. They focus on the urban unemployed youth, on women, on Ethiopian youngsters who are to be repatriated, on HIV-patients, or on nomads who need emergency aid. In addition there are some fishing and agricultural cooperatives.

In conclusion, there is a rather limited and oppressed civil society in Djibouti, while the space for new independent initiatives is limited. The government is using a wide variety of means to pacify this form of opposition, while it strongly favours its own civil society organisations.

International
Among the ten to fifteen foreign NGOs those of religious (Christian) origin and those in the medical field are best represented. Their programmes are aligned with overall government policies. Some of the refugee populations have set up their own relief organisations. The *Somali Relief and Development Agency* is an example. These organisations often cooperate with UNHCR.

Prospects
Experts stress, that Djibouti is a young and artificial entity, where nomadic traditions often outweigh civil society initiatives. Djiboutians who try to go beyond the ethnic-individualism often meet with opposition.

The Ethiopian-Eritrea border conflict has heightened the traditional ethnic tensions. This external conflict was quickly internalised. Because France did not oppose Ethiopia's lengthy flirtation with the authoritarian Gouled Aptidon regime, it became a party in the conflict. If the Government of Djibouti accuses Eritrea of support for the armed FRUD-faction, it is entitled to invoke French military assistance.

Although Djibouti received military assistance from France to protect its territorial integrity, its relationship with its former coloniser will change in the not too distant future. Gouled Aptidon's good relations with top French politicians, including the presidents François Mitterand and Jacques Chirac, who both favour(ed) leniency towards the authoritarian Djiboutian regime, have not endeared him to the present Socialist government of Lionel Jospin. France is reviewing its African policy, and Djibouti may soon lose its place at the top of the favoured country list. This will have serious economic repercussions.

Service Information

Newsletters and Periodicals

Horn of Africa Bulletin - bi-monthly newsletter published by the Life & Peace Institute, Uppsala/Sweden

Indian Ocean Newsletter - weekly published by Indigo Publications Group, Paris/France

Inter-Africa Group News and Networking Service - Monthly Update, Inter-Africa Group, Addis Ababa/Ethiopia

Focus on the European Union and Peace-Building Efforts in the Horn of Africa - newsletter published by Saferworld/London

Reports

Bonn International Center for Conversion

- Demilitarisation, Reintegration and Conflict Prevention in the Horn of Africa - Discussion Paper, by Kees Kingma & Kiflenariam Gebrewold. July 1998

PNUD/UNDP

- Rapport de Consultation sur les ONGs a Djibouti, by Niba Houssein. October 1995

Other Publications

La Securité au Sommet, l'insecurité à la base, by François-Xavier Verschave (ed.). Dossier Noir No 12, l'Harmattan, Paris, 1998

Le Mal Djiboutien - Rivalités Ethniques et Enjeux Politiques, by Ali Coubba. Paris/L'Harmattan, 1995

The Horn of Africa - Prospects for Political Transformation, by Colin Legum. London/Research Institute for the Study of Conflict and Terrorism, 1992

Resource Conflict in the Horn of Africa, by John Markakis. SAGE Publications, London/Thousand Oaks/New Delhi, 1998

Selected Internet Sites

www.djibouti.org (Association Djibouti Espace Nomade-ADEN)

www.amb-djibouti.org (Djibouti Embassy, France)

www.arab.net/djibouti/djibouti (ArabNet on Djibouti)

192.203.180.62/mlas/djibouti.html (League of Arab States)

Resource Contacts

Mme Mariam Hassan Ali - former Secretary-General of Syndicat des Enseignants Djiboutiens du Second Degré (Teachers Union in Secondary Education), now exiled. Email: Denis.mariam@wanadoo.fr

Roger-Vincent Calatayud - lawyer of some Djiboutian ex-ministers and human rights activists. Email: rv.calatayud@wanadoo.fr

Organisations

L'Association Française des Amis des Démocrates de Djibouti (AFADD)
Tel. +33 5 62 341 083
Fax +33 5 62 513 909
Email afadd@wanadoo.fr

L'Association Djibouti Esapce Nomade (ADEN)
France
Tel. +33 1 43 989 606
Fax +33 1 43 989 602
Email aden@clubinternet.fr

Survie
57 Avenue du Maine
75014 Paris, France
Tel. +33 1 43 270 325
Fax +33 1 43 205 558

Eritrea vs Ethiopia

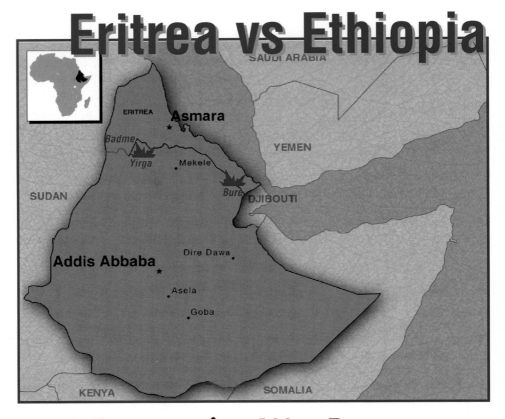

A Devastating War Between Former Friends

The eruption of the border conflict between Eritrea and Ethiopia in May 1998 took many by surprise. Underlying the conflict were Ethiopian claims that Eritrean armed forces had invaded the Yirga-triangle, which the Ethiopians considered Ethiopian territory. For its part, Eritrea maintained that Ethiopian troops had begun incursions into Eritrean territory as early as July 1997. The OAU, supported by the UN Security Council, tried to mediate. Ethiopia was quick to accept an OAU peace proposal. Eritrea did so only from late February 1999. By that time Ethiopia had recaptured the Yirga-triangle. Lacking the flexibility to find a peaceful solution, both parties continue to prepare for war. In the first half of 1999 the war flared up and thousands of soldiers died on both sides. Humanitarian and civilian organisations have little scope for contributing to the peace process. Their work is limited to incidental dialogues between citizens from both sides, appeals for a peaceful solution, silent diplomacy and helping the numerous civilian victims. The regional implications of the conflict have become increasingly serious. In July 1999 the parties began negotiations under pressure of the OAU, UN, USA and the European Union. A cease-fire was accepted. Although President Isayas Afewerki said there was reason for cautious optimism, Ethiopia rejected the peace plan early September ◆ *By* Jos van Beurden

Ethiopia
Population (millions): 60.1 *(1997)*
Life expectancy at birth (years): 49 *(1996)*
GNP per capita (dollars): 110 *(1997)*
Conflict related deaths: tens of thousands
Conflict related internally displaced persons:
330,000
Conflict related repatriated Ethiopians: 22,000
As a result of earlier conflicts many Ethiopian refugees
returned from Sudan after 1991 with some 40,000
remaining there. There are also several thousand
Ethiopian refugees in Kenya, and some in Djibouti and
Yemen. Ethiopia itself harbours 313,000 refugees:
mostly from Somalia and Somaliland; but also from
Sudan, Kenya and Djibouti.

Eritrea
Population (million): 3.8 *(1997)*
Life expectancy at birth (years): 55 *(1996)*
GNP per capita (dollar): 210 *(1997)*
Conflict related deaths: tens of thousands
Conflict related internally displaced persons:
268,000
Conflict related repatriated Eritreans: 58,000
Some 300,000 Eritreans still live in Ethiopia, although
their number continues to decrease as a result of forced
remigration. Since 1991 some 130,000 Eritrean
refugees have returned from Sudan, most of them did so
voluntarily. Some 320,000 Eritrean refugees remain in
Sudan and some in Yemen. There are some 3,000
refugees from Somalia in Eritrea.

Ethiopia and Eritrea have had long-standing, strong economic, political and cultural ties. Before gaining its independence in 1991, Eritrea was a part of Ethiopia for four decades. An account of the background and causes of their conflict can most usefully begin with Ethiopia.

Ethiopia
Ethiopia is landlocked. It has a 1,000 kilometre long border with Eritrea in the north and northeast, and elsewhere shares borders with Djibouti, Somaliland, Somalia, Kenya and Sudan. The country has a diversity of peoples, cultures and religions. It lies at two crossroads: that of the Arab world and Africa and that of the Christian and Muslim world. About forty percent of the population is Muslim, while half is Christian, the Ethiopian Orthodox Church is the most important religious institution. There are no serious religious tensions.

Since the centralisation of the administration (from 1850 onwards) most Ethiopian rulers have faced the same challenges: they have tried to further centralise their administration and expand their territory. Ethiopia has rarely presented a united front in fights with foreign aggressors and its rulers have usually combined a policy of divide and rule with a culture of intolerance and violence. Ethnic differences have often accentuated these tensions.

According to the most recent census (1984) there are 76 ethnic groups in Ethiopia. These include the Oromo, Amhara, Tigray, and Somali. Ethiopia's traditional ruling class is drawn from the Amhara and Tigray groups who have often fought each other. The Oromo, by far the largest ethnic group in the country, have traditionally felt themselves to be oppressed by the Amhara rulers. Much of the area they inhabit was conquered by the Amhara around 1850. Some Oromo also feel oppressed by the Tigray, who dominate the presently ruling Ethiopian Peoples Revolutionary Democratic Party (EPRDF) government. Others have little trouble accepting the 'ethnic federalism', the decentralisation and regionalisation of power in the country, which was introduced after 1991.

Eritrea
At the end of the nineteenth century Eritrea was colonised by Italy. In 1941 the British assumed the role of the Italians. In 1952, endorsed by a resolution, Eritrea was put into a federation with Ethiopia on an equal footing. Ten years later it was brutally annexed by Emperor Haile Selassie. This act of aggression marked the beginning of a war which was to last for three decades. During a National Convention in Ethiopia in 1991 the new Ethiopian government, led by Meles Zenawi, accepted the 'de facto' independence of Eritrea. Following an UN-supervised referendum the State of Eritrea formally acceded to independence on May 24, 1993.

Eritrea has nine ethnic groups, the Tigrinya being the largest. The population is equally divided between Christians and Muslims. Ethnic and religious tensions are negligible. The country borders Ethiopia, Sudan and Djibouti. The

133

Eritrean port of Assab, with its oil refinery, was a free port for Ethiopia until the border crisis. Eritrea's long coastline has enabled it to develop close ties with the Arab world over the centuries.

As long as they found a common enemy in the Mengitsu Haile Mariam administration, relations between the rebel organisations in Tigray/Ethiopia and Eritrea were close. After 1991 both countries continued to be led by former rebel leaders, Meles Zenawi in Ethiopia and Isayas Afewerki in Eritrea. They were personal friends. However, their friendship could not prevent the continuation of the underlying tensions created by the differing aspirations of their organisations. These tensions surfaced in 1997 when Eritrea introduced its own currency, the *nacfa*. Previously the Ethiopian *birr* had been the common currency. The new currency came to be seen as an expression of Eritrea's sovereignty and an indication of economic differences between the two countries. Ethiopia believed that the nacfa had been overvalued by Eritrea, and demanded that all financial transactions between the two countries be expressed in American dollars.

This was a serious setback for the traditionally close trading relations between the two countries. Migrants and small traders from both sides had crossed the border freely for centuries and Eritrean merchants were used to buying large parts of the coffee-harvest in Ethiopia and transporting it to one of the Red Sea ports for export. This trade ended with the de facto closure of the border. Poor families on both sides suffered severely, some losing half of their income and being forced to become dependent on relief. On both sides of the frontier police and military patrols were stepped-up and occasional armed exchanges were reported. This was the situation in early 1998.

Ethiopia - International Relations

Ethiopia's relations with its other neighbours have also been strained. Credible sources report that Ethiopian troops have been raiding the Gedo Region in south-west Somalia since 1996. Ethiopia justifies these incursions as responses to AlIttihad AlIslam, a Somali Muslim-militant group, accused of bomb attacks in Addis Ababa. In 1999 Ethiopia and Eritrea expanded the war

into Somalia, initially by arming a number of local warlords. Ethiopia then captured several towns. In June 1999 the Ethiopians captured Baidoa to the north west of Mogadishu. Baidoa had previously been held by the warlord Hussein Aideed, an ally of Eritrea.

Ethiopia's relation with Sudan remains complex. Both countries support each other's rebel factions. After the outbreak of the border conflict with Eritrea, Ethiopia and Sudan tried to normalise their relationship.

In Ethiopia's relations with its neighbours different issues are at stake. Ideology and stability seem to be central to the conflicts with the radical-Muslim government of Sudan and militant-Muslim groups in Somalia. In the conflict with Eritrea it is the demarcation of borders which is critical with economic motives also playing an important role. Many Ethiopians had great difficulty accepting the secession of their Northern Province in 1991.

Eritrea - International Relations

Eritrea has had poor relations with Sudan since 1993 when armed Muslim-radicals were reported to have entered Eritrea from Sudan. In late 1995 the two countries accused each other of harbouring and training each other's rebels. Khartoum was upset about Eritrea's decision to host the Sudanese oppositional NDA (National Democratic Alliance) in Asmara. The NDA is a coalition of the southern and northern opposition groups in Sudan. Another strain on the relation has been the continuing presence of some 320,000 Eritrean refugees in Sudan.

In late 1995 Eritrea sent troops to some of the Hanish-islands in the Red Sea, claiming they were not Yemenite but Eritrean territory. Yemen and Eritrea finally agreed to seek a decision from the Permanent Court for Arbitration. In 1998 the Court declared some islands as Yemenite, and others as Eritrean. The two parties reconciled themselves to the decision. In this conflict Eritrea combined a show of military force with willingness to accept the decisions of an internationally recognised body.

Several issues, apart from power and politics, are at stake in Eritrea's relations with its neighbours. Ideology has been at the centre of the conflict with Sudan. Eritrea adheres to a

ADDIS ABABA, ETHIOPIA: Ethiopian man, deported from Eritrea because of the war situation, is being counselled for depression

strict demarcation between state and religion. Eritrea accused Sudan of trying to export its fundamentalist revolution. In May 1999 however the two countries decided, after mediation by Qatar, to restore diplomatic relations, to live peacefully together and to refrain from adopting a policy of exporting ideologies.

In the clashes with Yemen, Djibouti and Ethiopia, the demarcation of borders has been the issue. Economic motives are also important. For example, in the conflict with Yemen, the possibility of discovering oil in the Red Sea and the potential for tourism, were contributing factors. In general, the Eritreans whose fight for independence lasted three decades, are very sensitive about any threat to their sovereignty.

Conflict Dynamics

On May 6, 1998 the Ethiopians attacked Eritrean troops in the border area. On May 8, Eritrean members of a Joint Commission, set up in 1994 to deal with border problems, arrived in Addis Ababa. They left on May 9 having made no progress. On May 12 a clash took place close to Badme and Shiraro in the 400 km2

agricultural region, the Yirga-triangle, as a result of which Eritrea recaptured the areas which it claimed Ethiopia had taken ten months earlier. Ethiopia demanded the immediate withdrawal of the Eritrean troops from an area it considered its own territory. According to Eritrea, Ethiopian government troops had occupied this Eritrean owned area in July 1997, and replaced the Eritrean administration by an Ethiopian one.

According to the Eritrean government, Ethiopian military units had invaded Eritrean territory on earlier occasions, although on a much smaller scale. The Eritrean People's Liberation Front (EPLF) had allowed the Tigray People's Liberation Front (TPLF) to use some of these areas as a base during the struggle against the Mengitsu regime in the 1980s. Eritrea claimed that it had not mentioned these incursions and occupation earlier as they were regarded as a 'crisis' between brothers.

A short while later fighting broke out on two further fronts outside the Yirga-triangle region: one near the border town of Zalembessa and another near Buri on the road to Assab. From September until the beginning of 1999 fighting was sporadic and international pressure and several mediation initiatives helped transform the conflict into a propaganda war. In the UN General Assembly, Ethiopian foreign minister Mesfin Seyoum spoke of the Eritrean leaders' 'known irrationality bordering on the insane'. Ethiopian propaganda is mostly directed towards Eritrean President Isayas Afewerki. The Eritrean propaganda is intended to isolate the Tigrayans from the other peoples in Ethiopia. It describes Ethiopia's participation in the war as a purely TPLFaffair and asserts that the TPLF wants to undo Eritrea's independence, to capture certain parts of Eritrea, including Eritrea's offshore territory, and to create an independent Tigray. In both countries the population's initial reaction of disbelief soon changed into outspoken hostility and hatred.

In late February 1999 the conflict entered a second phase. Ethiopian ground forces, supported by warplanes, mounted an offensive against Eritrean positions as a result of which Eritrea was forced to withdraw from the Yirga-triangle. Losses on both sides were much heavier. Eritrea, for example, claimed to have killed 10,000 Ethiopian combatants during a three-day battle in March 1999. In June 1999 Ethiopia claimed to have killed, wounded or captured more than 20,000 Eritrean ground troops.

The position of President Isayas Afewerki and his Popular Front for Democracy and Justice (PFDJ) - formerly EPLF - has remained unchallenged. The Presidential Office, which includes his closest associates, is the most influential body in the country. The launch of the Eritrean National Forces Alliance (ENFA) in March 1999, backed by both Ethiopia and Sudan will not prove a threat in the immediate future.

Despite the outlawed OLF calling upon the Oromo not to join the fighting 'among highlanders in the North', the conflict seems to have strengthened the position of Prime Minister Meles Zenawi and his government. More than 200,000 Ethiopians have joined the army. Among the new recruits are 31 former political detainees who, as military specialists under the previous Mengistu-regime, were released on condition that they joined the EPRD-Farmy. Outlawed opposition groups such as the OLF and the Ogaden National Liberation Front

(ONLF) are discussing the possibility of a coalition of the oppressed peoples of the Ethiopian Empire, a move which may have been inspired by Eritrea.

Both countries have well-trained ground forces and both air forces have recently been modernised although training pilots remains a problem. Because it is landlocked, Ethiopia has greater difficulty securing a fuel supply for its aircraft. It is unlikely that this conflict can be solved by military means.

Eritrea's Achilles' heel is Assab which is virtually inaccessible by road. Until the conflict it was a free port for Ethiopia, where thousands of Ethiopians were employed. By far the largest part of Assab's traffic - estimated value of US$ 300,000 per day in port fees - was transit cargo from and to Ethiopia. The port of Djibouti and, to a lesser extent, that of Berbera in Somaliland, has profited from this situation. Relations between Eritrea and Djibouti have been strained since Eritrean accusations that Djibouti has allowed Ethiopia to use its port as a conduit for arms. Djibouti has even severed diplomatic links with Eritrea.

Since the conflict began there has been a significant exodus of Eritreans from Ethiopia and Ethiopians from Eritrea. Eritrea has accused Ethiopia of the forcible detention and expulsion of 58,000 Eritreans. Ethiopia claims the number of expulsions was lower and that most were 'rank and file members of the EPLF'. The mistreatment of Eritreans in Ethiopia has been substantiated by reports from Amnesty International and UN-agencies.

Ethiopia claims that an equal number of Ethiopians have been forced to leave Eritrea and that Eritrea is guilty of the random imprisonment and mistreatment of Ethiopian residents and of taking their properties. Independent foreign observers have not substantiated this claim. Eritrea claims that some 22,000 Ethiopians left Eritrea as they could no longer find employment particularly in the harbour of Assab.

There have been civilian casualties on both sides. In May and June 1998 the Eritrean airforce bombed two towns in the Tigray Region, leaving 55 dead and 164 wounded, among whom, a large number of primary school pupils. Eritrea apologised for the civilian casualties. Ethiopia bombed Asmara airport in May/June 1998 and several South-Eritrean villages in February 1999, causing several civilian deaths.

It is possible only to estimate military losses. During the first phase (May/June 1998) thousands of soldiers died at the three fronts of Badme, Zalambessa and south of the Eritrean port of Assab. During a battle near Buri intense man to man fighting was reported. During the second phase (from February 1999 onwards) losses were much more serious. According to several independent observers there were tens of thousands of deaths on both sides. Ethiopia lost thousands of recruits during a battle near Tzerona in March 1999. Eritrea suffered heavy losses near Badme in February 1999 and near Bure in June.

In villages on both sides of the border, houses, shops and government buildings have been demolished. Although the actual extent of the economic damage remains to be calculated, a few indications can be given. Hundreds of thousands of people in the border area, who used to cross regularly as migrants or small traders have lost their livelihood. Tens of thousands of workers who have been called up for armed service are no longer employed productively. Both governments have adjusted their budgets in order to meet the costs of armed conflict. The port authorities in Assab have lost about US $ 1 billion in port fees annually. Both countries have spent considerable sums on the purchase of new military equipment from Russia, China, France, Bulgaria and the Ukraine, mostly light armaments, tanks and warplanes. More generally, most of the energy devoted to national development since independence has been diverted towards the war effort.

Official Conflict Management

Several attempts have been made to resolve the border dispute. The first attempt was brokered by the US Assistant Secretary of State for Africa, Susan Rice, and Rwandan government minister, Patrick Mazimhaka. This *US-Rwandan peace plan* contained four points:
- commitment by both parties to resolving this and any other disputes by peaceful means and renouncing force as a means of imposing solutions;
- deployment of a small observer mission to

Badme, while Eritrean forces should redeploy from Badme to positions held before May 6, 1998;
- agreement to a swift and binding delimitation and demarcation of the EthiopiaEritrea border;
- demilitarisation of the entire common border.

This plan became the basis for most other mediation efforts. All these points were accepted by Ethiopia but were difficult for Eritrea to accept. The unconditional withdrawal of Eritrean forces from Badme to positions held before hostilities broke out, remained the stumbling block.

After deliberations with Italy's Secretary of State for Africa Affairs, Rino Serri, and US President, Bill Clinton, Ethiopia and Eritrea decided on June 15, 1998 to suspend air raids.

The *Arab world*, particularly Libya, Egypt and Saudi Arabia, has also tried to bring an end to hostilities. A proposal by Libya called for a cease-fire and the deployment of an African peacekeeping force to separate the belligerents. It did not call for the withdrawal of Eritrea's troops from the contested Yirga-triangle. Eritrea welcomed the proposal, while Ethiopia clung to the terms of the US-Rwanda peace proposal. This agreement had in the interim been endorsed by the *Organisation of African Unity* (OAU), while the *UN Security Council* had in turn endorsed the OAU efforts to find a peaceful solution.

On June 18 and 19, a prestigious OAU delegation, headed by Secretary Salim Ahmed Salim and the presidents of Burkina Faso, Rwanda and Zimbabwe, visited both capitals and once more tried to convince the two governments to accept the peace plan. On October 7, US Special Envoy Anthony Lake met with the presidents of both countries. Both leaders told him they would not change their positions but agreed to continue the cease-fire until the OAU had finished its efforts.

A highpowered OAU delegation again met with the leaders of both countries in Ouagadougou, Burkina Faso on November 7 and 8, 1998. On behalf of UN Secretary General Kofi Annan, Mohamed Shanoun (in 1992 the first head of UNOSOM in Somalia) attended the meeting as an observer. The delegation brought to the table a proposal for 'A Framework Agreement for a Peaceful Settlement of the Dispute between Eritrea and Ethiopia'. Again this was rejected by Eritrea and accepted by Ethiopia. According to Eritrea the main stumbling block remained 'Ethiopia's precondition of an unconditional Eritrean withdrawal' from the Yirga-triangle. Eritrea regarded the Ouagadougou meeting as positive. 'Its recognition that the conflict did not start in May 1998 but that it goes back to July 1997 and its call for an investigation into these events is significant'.

While Ethiopia blamed the Eritreans for not accepting this proposal, Ethiopia in turn rejected Eritrea's proposals for a direct meeting between the leaders of the two countries. The publication by President Afewerki of his personal correspondence with Ethiopia's Prime Minister Meles Zenawi, in which the two leaders discussed possible solutions to the conflict, aroused considerable criticism inside the EPRDF. Meles Zenawi was pressurised into taking a tougher stand towards the Eritreans.

The OAU's final attempt at mediation took place on December 17 and 18, 1998, again in Ouagadougou. Eritrea still had a number of questions and consequently, no progress could be made. Ethiopia's Minister of Foreign Affairs, Seyoum Mesfin, concluded that the peace effort 'could be considered dead' unless the US was to bring effective pressure on the Eritrean leadership. The Eritrean authorities received an answer to their questions in late January 1999. After heavy military losses the Eritreans accepted the OAU peace framework in late February 1999.

In July 1999 the OAU, then chaired by Algeria, the UN, USA and the European Union brought the two parties together in Algiers, and finally a three tier peace proposal was formulated. The first part is OAU peace proposal, the second and third contain modalities and technical arrangements for implementation. Eritrea has accepted all three elements. Late August Ethiopia still had questions about the technical arrangements.

Multi-Track Diplomacy

Compared with countries such as Kenya or Uganda, civil society in Ethiopia in general and the NGO-sector in particular is underdeveloped. It is however stronger than in neighbouring Djibouti, Somalia, Somaliland and Sudan. Eritrea has a comparatively small civil society and a limited number of NGOs with a restricted operational scope. In early 1999 the government in Asmara requested that some NGOs, which had previously been forced to leave Eritrea, return to the country.

To date the only public criticism of the war has come from the *religious leaders* in both countries. On a number of occasions they have spoken jointly with their Islamic and Christian colleagues in the opposing camp, on other occasions they have acted separately.

In early June 1998, the Ethiopian and Eritrean bishops' conference made a common appeal to their governments to halt any armed conflict that could lead to allout war, and to settle their differences 'peacefully and expeditiously'. One week earlier, Pope John Paul had expressed his deep concern about the dispute.

Separate appeals followed slightly later. The leaders of the Ethiopian Orthodox Church, the Supreme Council of Ethiopian Muslim Affairs, the Ethiopian Catholic Church and the Ethiopian Evangelical Church Mekane, as well as a number of eminent Ethiopian elders held a joint peace meeting where they called for a peaceful solution to the conflict and asked the Eritrean government to accept the US-Rwandan Peace Proposal. In August their colleagues in Eritrea held a similar meeting which called upon the Ethiopian leaders to let innocent Eritreans in Ethiopia live in peace.

In late October and early November, church leaders and imams from both countries met for the first time since the outbreak of the conflict. In Oslo they made a common appeal for a peaceful solution.

Eritrean Christian and Muslim leaders formed a joint committee in Eritrea with the *Eritrean Relief and Rehabilitation Commission* (ERREC) in order to help the internally displaced and the Eritrean deportees from Ethiopia. They received assistance from international NGOs such as USAID, the ICRC and Norwegian Church Aid. The possibilities for cooperation of this sort already existed in Ethiopia which has a greater number of NGOs.

An Eritrean journalist, residing in the

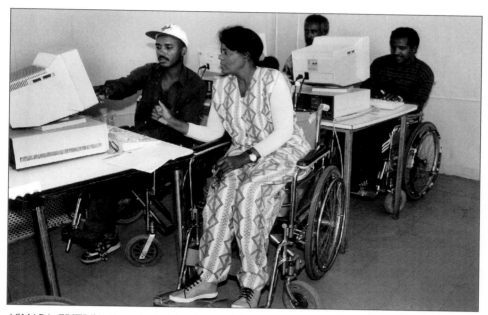

ASMARA, ERITREA: Computer training for war victims. The course is arranged by EWDFA (Eritrean War Disabled Fighter Ass.) and the ambition is to find jobs in the administration once the participants have completed the course

PHOTO: HELDUR NETOCNY/LINEAIR

Netherlands and supported by Dutch NGO, Interchurch Aid, has organised a petition signed by a significant number of wellknown figures including Nobel Prize Winners, politicians and other international celebrities, requesting both parties to solve their dispute peacefully. The call for peace, published in the *International Herald Tribune* on December 17, 1998, was widely praised without having an effect on the political leadership of either country.

There have been a number of informal initiatives to encourage dialogue between citizens from both countries. To mention some examples: Ethiopian and Eritrean journalists met in Germany. Academics from both countries have had several meetings in western countries. In Nairobi, young Eritreans and Ethiopians sat down to discuss how they would solve the border dispute. An Eritrean has started a peace email list inviting both Ethiopians and Eritreans to start a dialogue for peace.

Ethiopia: Domestic Organisations
Ethiopians ascribe Ethiopia's meagre tradition of

civil society organisations to their pronounced lack of interpersonal trust and their difficulty in organising cooperative institutions. This attitude is described as 'parochialism' and continues to feed the existing culture of intolerance, exclusion and violence. The importance of values such as tolerance and trust has been frequently emphasised. For example, a World Bank discussion paper about the reintegration of excombatants after 1991 states: 'National reconciliation, between the hitherto belligerent factions is crucial for sustainable peace. It can best be achieved by transparent policies that aim at building a relationship of trust'.

The achievements of the EPRDF-government in developing civil society have met with little acclaim. After 1991 the new government enacted laws and regulations that guaranteed respect for human rights, civil liberties and the independence of the judiciary and the press. Free universal suffrage and freedom to form parties meant that, for the first time in the country's history, competitive elections were held in Ethiopia. Ethnically-based fronts, opposition parties and civil groups occupied the new areas of the political landscape opened up by democracy.

But the new freedom did not last long, nor was it as extensive as many had hoped. Human Rights Watch/Africa published the following indictment in December 1997: 'The ruling EPRDF dominated the political system by favouring regional parties affiliated with it and clamping down on opposition groups. It also sought to dominate the emerging civil society through bureaucratic and legal restrictions and various forms of harassment of activists.'

At times the EPRDF-government has showed the same tendency towards oppression and parochialism as it predecessors. The *Ethiopian Human Rights Council* (EHRCO) has claimed that under the EPRDF government, the judicial system had collapsed and lost its independence and that the widespread violation of human rights continued in various quarters. In the conflict with Eritrea the government offers civil society organisations little alternative other than accepting the government's position.

A major conference of the Human Rights Council and Ombudsman in May 1998 typified the government's attitude. The Council and Ombudsman were acceptable as long as the government could exert some control over their activities. That the European Union paid for the conference indicates the faith of Western donors in the government's democratic intentions. The conference's conclusions were tabled for public debate from late April 1999 onwards.

In 1998 some 240 NGOs were registered. Almost half were national organisations. Due to the hostile policy environment during the previous regimes most are rather ineffective. Since 1991 several NGOs have been searching for ways of including advocacy, human rights issues and conflict prevention and management in their activities. They do so through civic education, teaching legal literacy, and providing seminars and workshops. The *Ethiopian Peace and Development Committee* is one example and there are several others.

Initially, the new leaders of the country and the NGOs had much in common, sharing in particular a focus on grassroots participation. Soon, however, the government began to voice

its criticism of both national and international NGOs (too affluent, too many overheads, too inefficient) and to tighten its grip on them.

The government began to use registration as a tool to control NGOs and other civil organisations. In 1993 all NGOs were instructed to re-register with the Disaster Prevention and Preparedness Commission (DPPC). In practice this enabled the government to get rid of some NGOs with which it seriously disagreed. One of the victims was the EHRCO. Some other NGOs whose registrations have also been refused, have had their activities brought to a virtual standstill. In 1995 the government moved the registration mandate from the DPPC to the Ministry of Justice. In the process the registration applications of a further 46 NGOs were refused. Early in 1998 the registration complications were eased somewhat. EHRCO won its case and was re-registered.

There exists a crucial disagreement between the government and many NGOs about the definition of grassroots organisations. According to the government, the *kebele* or lowest administrative unit is defined as CBO (community based organisation). It plays a central role in the decentralised development plans. All development plans are to be discussed at the kebele level, and information should go from there upwards. Yet this new role of the kebele has not been formulated in the constitution.

For many NGOs, kebele are too deeply implicated in the topdown power structure to be regarded as genuine, independent grassroots organisations. In some places the friction between the two concepts is negligible, but frequently it takes both NGOs and local officials much patience and diplomacy to work in the same area.

In order to streamline development efforts the government has encouraged the creation of Development Associations such as the Tigray Development Association (TDA), Amhara Development Association (ADA), Southern Ethiopia Peoples' Development Association (SEPDA) and Oromo Development Association (ODA). The government regards these as typical NGOs. Their main advantage over other NGOs is that they avoid aid-dependency. Since they are partially funded by the contributions of individual members, while their activities conform precisely to Federal and Regional development strategies. In the opinion of many NGOs less closely aligned with the government, these Development Associations are effectively 'parastatals'.

The history of the *Christian Relief and Development Association (CRDA)* is typical of the Ethiopian situation. In 1998 this large umbrella-organisation had a membership of 140 registered NGOs, almost half of all officially registered NGOs in Ethiopia. Formerly dominated by international NGOs, today half the membership comprises local organisations and church agencies. The CRDA wants to forge a stronger and more productive partnership between government organisations and NGOs. It has set up an NGO-Government Task Force.

So far only a few initiatives have been taken by civil society organisations or NGOs inside Ethiopia in response to the border conflict. Those of the religious leaders, mentioned above, are the most significant to date. Some of these initiatives adhere closely to the government position, calling for the unconditional withdrawal of the Eritrean forces from the Yirgatriangle. Others include more general calls for peace made in cooperation with Eritrean colleagues. An example is the Ethiopian Peace and Development Committee. Its core activities have shifted more and more towards conflict prevention and resolution, mainly in Ethiopia's marginal areas. Training, research and education are main activities.

Eritrea: Domestic Organisations

During the famine of 1973 the Orthodox Church, the Roman-Catholic Church and other churches became involved in relief work in Eritrea. During the thirty years war these church-linked organisations were mostly active in government-held areas. In the EPLF-areas, unions for workers, women and some professionals arose as well as one local NGO: the Eritrean Relief Association (ERA). This was responsible for raising funds amongst donors for food aid and development projects among the civilian population. ERA played a crucial role during the war of liberation and continues operating today as the *Eritrean Relief and Rehabilitation Commission* (ERREC).

After the EPLF-victory in 1991, the NGOs in both the government and rebel-held areas continued functioning. At the same time the government was keen to define their relation to the state and the framework within which they were to function. President Afewerki considers the state as a 'facilitator'. When the state has to approve of everything, he said in an interview in the German magazine *EPD/Entwicklungshilfe*, (9/98), then 'every participatory process in society becomes meaningless... We are a liberal disciplined society'. According to Afewerki no one in Eritrea is told what he should or should not do. 'The people here... know what they do. There is discipline, while there is also self-consciousness. This discipline is not ordered by the government, police or military, but the result of a long history'.

Eritreans know all too well what is 'done' and what is 'not done'. Those who fail to tread the line can expect heavy government censure. In fact, the governing principles of Eritrea are derived not only from the 'long history' of the region but from the wartime experience when, effectively, the same government was in power. The Presidential Office is much stronger than President Afewerki suggests above.

On several occasions the Eritrean leadership has shown itself to be highly principled. Their selfreliance and dislike of dependency upon foreign assistance have become proverbial. In the conflict with Yemen over the Hanish-islands they refused to withdraw their troops but also agreed upon arbitration and accepted the decision of the Permanent Court of Arbitration. In the border dispute with Ethiopia this attitude can be invoked as a confidence-building measure.

NGOs based on religion or ethnicity are forbidden. Such organisations are divisive, it is argued. To support this claim the Eritreans point to Sudan, where the ruling Muslim-militants ensure that the country is kept divided. Eritrea offers almost no scope for independent civil society organisations in the field of advocacy, human rights and democracy. A few years ago the *National Union of Eritrean Women* became formally independent from the ruling PFDJ-party, but it maintains close relations with the top of the PFDJ. In June 1998 a new organisation was created, *Citizens for Peace*. It publishes background information on the border conflict with Ethiopia. However, it works so closely with the Department of Information, that for an outsider it is difficult to consider it as a fully independent initiative. The organisation has been particularly concerned with documenting the forced deportation of Eritreans from Ethiopia and other Ethiopian offences.

The already limited scope for local organisations, groups or individuals, to express individual opinions has been further restricted since the outbreak of the border conflict. This restriction extends even to the Eritreans in the diaspora. Eritreans who do not accept the government's policy on the border dispute can easily become outcasts in their own community.

Ethiopia: International Organisations

So far NGO-initiatives, whether Ethiopian or international, have had little impact. National NGOs have mostly repeated government policy while international NGOs have tended to concentrate exclusively on sustainable development. Some foreign NGOs with a long history in Tigray and a close relationship with the ruling circle have spoken informally and critically with top politicians. A few have even withdrawn part of their financial support. Yet the atmosphere in which they have to work is not conducive to direct intervention.

The *Inter Africa Group*, which aims to be the voice of the citizens of Northeast Africa, is based in Addis Ababa. So far the civil war in Sudan, the conditions of NGOs and the civil society in Ethiopia and an analysis of the border conflict have been the main themes.

Eritrea: International Organisations

Eritrean government policy with respect to foreign NGOs is very strict. President Afewerki has said repeatedly, that his government has its own development programme and a clear policy towards foreign aid, gifts and loans. Aid is regarded as an 'intervention mechanism' that should enable government and citizens to solve problems themselves. Eritrea prefers fair trade and soft loans.

In 1996 foreign aid organisations received a letter in which the government announced that the period of relief and rehabilitation was over and that future projects and programmes should be geared towards development. In February 1997 the (ERREC) instructed foreign NGOs to run projects only in the fields of education and health, and in close cooperation with the Ministries concerned. Each NGO was asked to place its jeeps, machinery and other equipment into a pool, and the authorities would then decide who was entitled to use what. Early in 1998 foreign NGOs were told to close their offices. By then the UNHCR, the American CRS and World Vision had already left the country. Others were to follow.

In 1998 the border conflict forced the Eritrean government to relax the rules for foreign NGOs. It has invited both *UNHCR* and the *International Red Cross Committee* to help with the management of the 275,000 internally displaced people and the 58,000 Eritreans deported from Ethiopia. In 1999 it invited some international NGOs, which had earlier been requested to leave the country, to return to Eritrea.

International NGOs have avoided any critical public utterances about the conflict and have concentrated exclusively on their development activities. Their failure to make a consolidated appeal for a peaceful solution is in line with their policy of avoiding open criticism of the Eritrean government. Some NGOs, which were active in EPLF-held territory during the war against the Mengistu-regime, may have held private talks with Eritrean officials about the conflict.

One of the best known international NGOs is the US-based *Grassroots International*, which was set up in 1983 to provide material aid and other forms of solidarity to the then EPLF and Eritrea. Grassroots projects have included an organising and job-training programme for women. Grassroots has extensive information on Eritrea.

Prospects

The prospects of a peaceful solution are remote. Most experts fear that the conflict could drag on for quite some time and will spill over to neighbouring countries, thus increasing regional instability.

Some experts note that Ethiopia is less unified behind its leadership than Eritrea. The TPLF from Tigray, involved in a fight with its former brother with an intensity reminiscent of the bloody war in the early 1980s between the EPLF and the then Eritrean Liberation Front (ELF), might be satisfied if the border areas they claim, will be really theirs. Many Amhara-supporters of the former Mengistu regime have always regretted the secession of Eritrea. They will want to recapture Assab at the very least. Those among the Oromo, the largest ethnic group in Ethiopia, who sympathise with the outlawed Oromo Liberation Front (OLF) do not want to be involved in the border dispute. These experts also argue, that apart from the OLF-factor the border conflict has not created extra (ethnic) tensions inside Ethiopia.

Ethiopia has a rich tradition of diplomacy and is using it effectively. It has held the diplomatic initiative for most of the conflict. Eritrea's aversion to diplomacy and principled attitude is working against the interests of this foundling state. Its failure to mention Ethiopia's incursions of July 1997 until much later was a serious blunder.

International pressure on the two countries to solve their conflict peacefully has been immense and has mostly been focused on Eritrea. The United States, the OAU and the European Union want the Eritreans to relinquish their claims. It is remarkable that Eritrea's withdrawal from the contested areas is the only 'unconditional' part of the OAU-Peace Plan.

In the opinion of most experts, the atmosphere in which NGOs work in Ethiopia or Eritrea is not conducive to involvement in such sensitive matters as the border dispute. At the same time there has been a signal lack of coordinated and consolidated efforts from international NGOs, both inside Ethiopia and Eritrea with like-minded organisations in the other country, to prevent the conflict from escalating into a full-scale war. Some international NGOs are so close to the former liberation movements, i.e. the TPLF in Tigray and the EPLF in Eritrea, that they are unable to recognise their weaknesses and have turned a blind eye to the lack of democracy after 1991. It took some time before they acknowledged the inability of both regimes to solve this conflict peacefully.

Some experts compare Eritrea's attitude in this conflict with its approach to the Hanish-islands dispute. In both cases Eritrea first made a display of military force yet eventually accepted international arbitration. If it comes to arbitration in this conflict with Ethiopia, these experts believe Eritrea will accept the conclusion.

Fears are rising that the border conflict will spread beyond the two countries. The conflict has already increased tensions between Eritrea and Djibouti. France has warned both countries that it will invoke its military agreements with Djibouti if Djibouti becomes a military target for either Eritrea or Ethiopia. The two belligerents have been distributing arms to factions in Somalia. In June 1999 Ethiopian troops helped capture the strategic town of Baidoa, previously held by the Eritrean ally Hussein Aideed. Ethiopia has helped Eritrean opposition groups to form a front and take action against the Government in Asmara, while Eritrea has made similar overtures to the oppositional OLF in Ethiopia. The latter resulted in an Ethiopian army attack on OLF-units in Kenyan territory.

Recommendations

Both Ethiopia and Eritrea are taking a culture of intolerance into the 21st century. This is a root cause of the present border conflict and of both countries' inability to solve it by non-military means. Much more should be done to promote a culture of peace and reconciliation in both countries. Existing local opportunities can be used for this. For example, in Ethiopia a host of new, informal, amateur theatre groups sprang up after 1991. They often put on a mixture of popular plays and pieces devised on the basis of local problems.

Religious and other leaders from both countries should be encouraged by supporters outside Northeast Africa to continue their calls for a peaceful solution. International NGOs in both countries should be encouraged to formulate common recommendations and to put pressure on the leadership of both countries.

Service Information

Newsletters and Periodicals

Horn of Africa Bulletin, bimonthly newsletter published by the Life & Peace Institute, Uppsala/Sweden

Indian Ocean Newsletter, weekly published by Indigo Publications Group, Paris/France

InterAfrica Group News and Networking Service Monthly Update, InterAfrica Group, Addis Ababa/Ethiopia

Focus on the European Union and PeaceBuilding Efforts in the Horn of Africa, newsletter published by Saferworld/London

Reports

Amnesty International
- Ethiopia and Eritrea - Human Rights Issues in a Year of Armed Conflict. London/UK. 21 May 1999

Save the Children Fund
- Baseline Report - The Tigray Northern Highlands Food Economic Zone, with an Analysis of the Possible Effects of Eritrean Border Problems this Year, by T. Boudreau. Ethiopia/UK, 1998

Bonn International Center for Conversion
- Demilitarisation, Reintegration and Conflict Prevention in the Horn of Africa Discussion Paper, by Kees Kingma & Kiflenariam Gebrewold. July 1998

Saferworld
- Undermining Development: The European Arms Trade with the Horn of Africa and Central Africa, by William Benson. London, 1998
- Prevention of Violent Conflict and the Coherence of EU Policies towards the Horn of Africa, by Emma Visman & Emery Brusset. London, April 1998

Human Rights Watch/Africa
- Ethiopia - The Curtailment of Rights. New York 1997

Institute of Development Studies, Sussex
- The Potential for Donor Mediation in NGO-State Relations: An Ethiopian Case Study, by W. Campbell. Working Paper 33, June 1996

Other publications

Crucible of Civilization and Conflicts - Ethiopia, by H. Assefa. In: P. Anyang'Nyong'o (ed.): Arms and Daggers in the Heart of Africa - Studies on Internal Conflicts. Nairobi, Academy Science Publishers, 1993

Ethiopia NGO Country Profile 1998, by Jos van Beurden. GOM, Oegstgeest/The Netherlands, 1998

Case Studies in War-to-Peace Transition - The Demobilisation and Reintegration of Ex-Combatants in Ethiopia, Namibia, and Uganda, by N.J. Coletta, M. Kostner, I. Wiederhofer. Washington, World Bank Discussion Paper no. 331, 1996

Post-conflict Eritrea: Prospects for Reconstruction and Development, Eds. Martin Doornbos and Alemseged Tesfai. Red Sea Press, Lawrenceville, NJ, 1999

Selected Internet Sites

addistribune.ethiopiaonline.net/ (Addis Tribune)
www.eritrea.org/EIB/control/EIMain.html (Eritrean Network Information Centre: ENIC)
www.netasfrica.org/eritrea/index.html (Government of Eritrea official website)
www.ethemb.se (Embassy of Ethiopia in Sweden)
www.visafric.com (Peace email, started by Eritreans in Canada)
www.asmarino.com/asmarino (Asmarino)

Resource Persons

Jalal Abdul Latif - InterAfrica group
Lebesech Tsega - consultant Addis Abeba, fax +251 1 615 076
Hizkias Assefa - expert in international peacebuilding and mediator, Nairobi. Email: hizkias@africaonline.co.ke
Habtom Yohannes - Eritrean journalist, Amersfoort/The Netherlands, fax +31 33 4758 227. Email: habtomy@rehaas.demon.nl
Mohamed Salih - Institute of Social Studies, The Hague/The Netherlands, fax +31 70 426 0799, Email: salih@iss.nl
Bea Stolte - Dutch Interchurch Aid,

Utrecht/The Netherlands, fax +31 30 2717 814.
email: beas@dia.antenna.nl

Organisations
Grassroots International
179 Boylston St.
Boston, MA 02130 USA
Tel. +1 617 5241 400
Fax +1 617 5245 525
Email grassroots@igc.apc.org

ERREC
P.O. Box 254
Asmara
Eritrea
Tel. +291 1 182222
Fax +291 1 182970

EHRC
P.O. Box 2432
Addis Ababa
Ethiopia
Tel. +251 1 514489
Fax +251 1 514539
Email sewr@padis.gn.apc.org

CRDA
P.O. Box 5674
Ethiopia
Tel. +251 1 650100
Email crda@telecom.net.et

*Data on the following organisations can be found
in the Directory section:*
Ethiopian Peace and Development Committee
Inter Africa Group

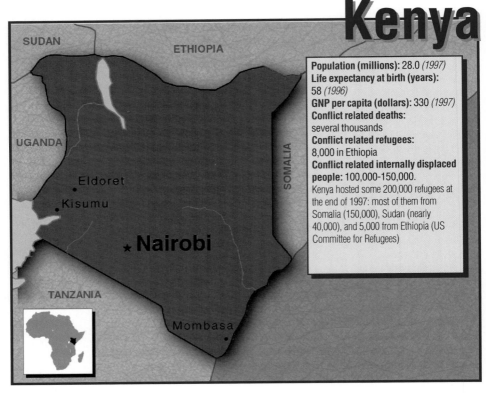

Kenya

Population (millions): 28.0 *(1997)*
Life expectancy at birth (years):
58 *(1996)*
GNP per capita (dollars): 330 *(1997)*
Conflict related deaths:
several thousands
Conflict related refugees:
8,000 in Ethiopia
Conflict related internally displaced
people: 100,000-150,000.
Kenya hosted some 200,000 refugees at
the end of 1997: most of them from
Somalia (150,000), Sudan (nearly
40,000), and 5,000 from Ethiopia (US
Committee for Refugees)

Small Scale Conflicts Could Have Major Repercussions

Although Kenya appears to be an island of stability in comparison with its neighbours, it is confronted with a range of mostly low intensity conflicts. Most of these are domestic and directly linked to the scarcity of natural resources. The weakness of the state, its corruption and the concentration of power in the hands of a few are further exacerbating factors. Other sources of conflict include crossborder guerrilla activity and cattle rustling. In most cases conflicts also have an ethnic dimension. NGOs are playing an increasingly important role in the efforts to stop the violence. However, there is no immediate prospect of an end to Kenya's many troubles ◆ *By* Jos van Beurden

A British protectorate since 1895, Kenya became independent in late 1963. Its first president, Jomo Kenyatta died in 1978 and was succeeded by Daniel Arap Moi. The transition was relatively smooth, but after an attempted coup d'état in 1982, Moi has become increasingly jealous of his power. He and his Kenyan African National Union (KANU) party began to build a strong power base around a coalition of politicians and businessmen most of whom belong to Moi's own ethnic group, the Kalenjin. For many years supporters of the president have own a majority of Kenya's media, transport, banking and tourism businesses.

The Kalenjin are one of the five major ethnic communities in Kenya. According to the 1989 census, the Kikuyu are the largest group with 21 per cent of the population, followed by the Luhya (14%), Luo (13%), Kamba (11%), and Kalenjin (11%). The latter, although usually considered one group, are in fact an amalgamation of ten peoples. There are over fourty smaller ethnic groups, including the Boran, Maasai, Samburu, Turkana, Kuria, Gusii, Somali and Taita. Most of the population adhere to traditional religions. A quarter of the population is Christian, while in the coastal areas there are many Muslims to be found as a result of the Arab influence.

President Moi is not averse to using ethnicity as a tool of government, and has played the ethnic card with particularly devastating effect in the Rift Valley province. When, after the end of the Cold War, Moi was confronted with the demand for multi-partyism, his answer was *majimboism*. According to the government, majimboism is a form of Kenyan regionalism. According to its opponents it is nothing less than a form of ethnic cleansing which has encouraged discrimination against Kikuyu in the Rift Valley province.

So the Kikuyu - and the Luo - have been excluded from the President's cabinet, while numerous smaller peoples have cabinet representation. The state has explicitly called for the expulsion of all non-Kalenjin, non-Maasai, non-Samburu, and non-Turkana from land in the Rift Valley. Many observers agree that majimboism has played a pivotal role in inciting the ethnic violence which has prevailed in the Rift Valley since 1992 and as a result of which some 250,000 Kikuyu have been forced to leave their villages. Interviews with the victims of these clashes and other evidence suggest that groups aligned with Moi assisted the Maasai and Kalenjin KANU militants by providing training, transport, and sometimes payment. Underlying these conflicts is a life and death struggle for natural resources, especially land.

Since president Moi and his KANU party held onto power in the 1997 National Assembly elections - albeit with a smaller majority than in 1992 - the situation has further deteriorated. Ethnic tensions have sharpened and the leadership's rhetoric of hatred is finding a ready audience throughout the country. Political unrest has led to a spectacular drop in the number of tourists visiting the country, with the number of visitors from Germany, Kenya's largest source market, down 80 per cent. Corruption is endemic, foreign and domestic investment has stopped, while bi- and multilateral donors have found it more and more difficult to support Moi's administration. Unemployment has skyrocketed and basic government services, such as education and health care, have deteriorated.

Outbreaks of violence are common. For example, after the 1997 elections in the Rift Valley province more than 120 people were killed, thousands displaced and hundreds of homes destroyed when members of the Kalenjin, Samburu and Pokot attacked the Kikuyu. The Kikuyu had voted overwhelmingly for the opposition in the multi-ethnic districts of Laikipia and Nakuru where they gained 90 per cent of the seats in the two districts. The well-armed murderers operated systematically with the security forces allegedly being instructed to turn a blind eye to the violence. A year passed before the government attempted to regulate land ownership for the displaced Kikuyu.

The Northeast province is another trouble spot. Here three major clans including the Kenyan Somali share the territory with a number of smaller groups. Eighty per cent of the people derive their income from herding camels, sheep and goats, and they are regularly involved in disputes over grassland, water and cattle. The continued presence of Somali refugees has exacerbated the problems faced by Kenyan Somalis. Somali bandits (shiftas) have been active in the area since the 1970s when a pan-Somali movement was defeated. Highway robberies, cattle rustling, rape, and occasional murders are unexceptional. The government has no control of the situation.

In a further outbreak of ethnic violence at least 69 people were killed and hundreds of thousands displaced in the coastal region around Mombassa in August and September 1997. The victims were again 'up country' Kikuyu from Western, Eastern and Central province, who had come to the area in search of employment or business opportunities. Leaflets warned 'non-native' families to return to their 'ancestral homes,' and gangs destroyed their houses and businesses. According to African Rights, the

147

government feared that these migrants would vote for the opposition in the December elections, and consequently decided they had to be chased away.

Kenya has also been affected by conflicts in neighbouring countries which have created significant refugee problems. Although the total number of refugees is in decline, many have still not returned to their homes and remain displaced in Kenya's urban areas.

Attempting to explain why these numerous smaller conflicts, including the increasing violence in Nairobi and other urban centres, have as yet failed to escalate into civil war, Colin K. Kahl points to Kenyan class interests which cut across ethnic lines in urban areas. Kenya's upper class includes large landowners and urban professionals, businessmen, physicians, high-ranking politicians and civil servants, and senior Kenyan associates in residential multinational corporations. One level below is an emerging and increasingly cohesive urban middle class which includes small businessmen, lower ranked government employees, nurses, teachers, artisans, mechanics, plant supervisors, and skilled factory workers. Kikuyus, the main victims in the ethnic clashes, still dominate Kenya's economy, making up the largest proportion of prominent Africans in business and agriculture. Along with Luos, Kikuyus also make up the largest segment of Kenya's middle class.

Despite the fact that their kinsmen have been murdered in the countryside, the interests of the Kikuyu and Luo members of the upper and middle classes are best served by pushing for political reform that would increase their access to the state on policy matters, not by escalating ethnic violence. Political reform would increase access for Kikuyu and Luo members of the middle class to state funds, civil service positions, etc., while violence would only bring destruction. Most Kikuyu and Luo see the problem as one of bad government and corruption, rather than evil intent.

Conflict Dynamics

In the Rift Valley province the authorities often seem to side with the perpetrators of violence. Machira Apollos of the Centre for Conflict Resolution has analysed several cases. She reports that ethnic violence frequently flares up in areas where there had previously been no serious frictions between the different communities. This is usually preceded by cattle rustling and theft by the instigators of the violence. A spiral effect is then set in motion and incidents of violence and rape, suspicion, accusation and counter-accusation increase.

The government at first denies the problem, but is forced to change its stance when the churches and media continue to publicise the situation. Finally the police are instructed to act but they arrive too late and fail to impress the victims thereby 'confirming the fear that they are state sponsored'. One witness said that 'we informed the police immediately the raiders stole our animals... but instead of following the route the raiders had taken the police went in the opposite direction despite our protestations.'

The pastoralist Pokot and Marakwet communities have shared the same region in north-west Kenya for a long time and have sometimes fought with each other. In April 1998, 500 Marakwet attacked a police post in West Pokot's Lelan Division, about 200 miles north-west of Nairobi. Two policemen were killed and three injured. This was the first attack in which security forces had been directly targeted. Hundreds of cattle were stolen or maimed. A few weeks later the violence spilled over into an area of northeastern Uganda, inhabited by the Karamajong, a people closely related to the Pokots. In July 1998 the Pokot and Uganda's Karamojong clashed over cattle. At least 84 people were killed.

In early 1998, the government moved forcefully to prevent a mass wave of refugees fleeing drought in Somalia from crossing the border. Once this flow of potential refugees was halted, the government invited the UNHCR and other humanitarian organisations to provide assistance to these individuals.

Armed raids by bandits and guerrilla activity have been reported from the Ethiopian border. In October 1998, a large group, comprising mainly Borana, raided several settlements inhabited by the ethnic Somali Degodia clan, killing at least 142 and abducting around fifty people. An estimated 17,500 cattle were stolen.

Government officials said that the majority of the attackers came from the Oromo Liberation Front (OLF), an Ethiopian rebel group. Survivors and witnesses, however, maintained that the attackers were Borana acting with Ethiopian backing. Following a new incident in January 1999 Kenya lodged a formal protest with the Ethiopian government, claiming that Ethiopian army troops had entered the country searching for fleeing OLF-rebels. At that time the OLF claimed to have carried out a surprise attack on a garrison in Ethiopia in which it killed more than sixty Ethiopian soldiers and injured or captured hundreds.

The inability of the Kenyan authorities to guarantee the safety of foreign officials adds to the overall feeling of danger. In February 1999, Kurdish rebel leader Ocalan was first allowed into the country, but then captured and flown to Turkey. In May 1998, former Rwandan Interior Minister Seth Sendashonga was assassinated along with his driver in a Nairobi suburb. Sudan People's Liberation Army (SPLA) leader John Garang was the target of a further assassination attempt in November 1998. This lack of sufficient security measures and the presence of a Muslim community to provide cover, has made Kenya a target of international terrorism. On August 7, 1998, 253 people were killed and several thousand people injured in a bomb attack on the US Embassy in Nairobi. The government provoked the 1.7 million-strong Muslim community by banning five Muslim NGOs. This was not the first occasion President Moi had challenged the Muslim community: in the 1997 elections the Islamic Party of Kenya (IPK) remained unregistered.

Official Conflict Management

Since most conflicts are domestic, no outside interference by the UN, OAU, IGAD or other international bodies has taken place. While the *Kenyan government* is sometimes accused of having an interest in the continuation of violent conflicts in the Rift Valley province, it has mediated in several cross-border conflicts. For example, the governments of Kenya and Ethiopia discussed the attacks by the Oromo Liberation Front (OLF) in early 1999.

In addition, several high level government officials and politicians organised meetings with the Ugandan authorities to try and resolve the conflict between Kenyan pastoral groups and the Ugandan Karamojong. In June 1996, the first -ever such meeting was held at Kakuma county headquarters in Kenya's Turkana district. As a result the Dodoth and the Turkana handed over stolen animals. A second (four-day) meeting was held in November 1996 to bring peace to the southern common border pastoralists in Kenya and Uganda. It was attended by Pokot from Uganda and Kenya, Sabiny, and Turkana. The high-level meeting was intended to develop the basis for regular meetings and to coordinate regional planning in these areas. One of the recommendations was the establishment of a Regional Peace Secretariat to address peace and security issues in the border areas.

However, government policy for managing violent conflicts is often a source of confusion. In May 1998, an armed gang disrupted a peace rally near the farming centre of Kitale. The rally was being held to protest against interethnic violence in the area. A grenade was thrown into the crowd and two people were subsequently wounded by arrows. Police officers did not attempt to stop the armed gang but did intervene when the crowd pursued the gang. There were over 5,000 persons in attendance.

Multi-Track Diplomacy

Democracy and good government are still remote prospects for Kenya, and Amnesty International places Kenya high on its list of countries with poor human rights records. The ill-treatment and torture of opposition activists is the norm. Although the media are relatively powerful in Kenya, criticism of President Moi, his administration and the KANU party is muted by a set of unwritten conventions. Licenses for radio and television stations or the written press can be revoked at any time. With trade unions being poorly organised, most of the criticism of the Moi regime originates among students and intellectuals. Because many people trust the church or mosque to which they belong, church and mosque-related, NGOs play an important role.

Domestic

Kenya has a surprisingly wide range of NGOs. These include many 'briefcase'-organisations, although others take their work more seriously. Kenyan NGOs tend to operate in the fields of development and advocacy, and the Moi administration has accused some advocacy outfits of supporting the opposition and engaging in covert activities. There are even questions raised about the patriotism of NGOs who receive foreign funding.

President Moi also attacked the NGOs' concept of civic education which he claims is unnecessary in Kenya. In a circular distributed in early 1998, the government indicated that NGOs sponsoring civic education are 'a threat to the security of the state and their activities must be curtailed.'

President Moi has threatened to annul the registration of so-called 'political NGOs'. However, the Government NGO Co-ordination Board has refused (!) to cooperate with the president and has withheld information indicating which NGOs are 'political'. Nevertheless, NGOs involved in civic education and advocacy are in a precarious position.

Prominent *civilian pressure groups* include churches, legal associations, university students, and private voluntary organisations advocating environmental and development causes, women's interests, and civil liberties. These groups were, and remain, the main domestic proponents of political reform. Nevertheless, although they are strongly representative of Kenya's larger ethnic clusters, the issues they raise tend to be class-based rather than communal.

Kenya has a growing number of *human rights organisations*. These include the Kenyan Human Rights Commission (KHRC), the Kenya Anti-rape Organization, the Legal Advice Centre, the Catholic Justice and Peace Commission, the National Council of Churches of Kenya (NCCK), the Release Political Prisoners pressure group, and the Centre for Governance and Development (CGD). Legal organisations concerned with human rights include the Public Law Institute, the Law Society of Kenya (LSK), the International Commission of Jurists (ICJ/Kenya) and the International Federation of Women Lawyers (FIDA/Kenya). NGOs and some opposition

parties maintain comprehensive files on human rights abuses. In addition to special reports, the KHRC produces a 'Quarterly Repression Report' cataloguing the human rights situation in the country. The Government Standing Committee on Human Rights, established in May 1996, has maintained a low profile and kept away from most pressing human rights problems.

These organisations can sometime respond quickly to crisis situations. After the ethnic cleansing in the early 1990s in the Rift Valley, some thirty NGOs affiliated to the Non-Governmental Council of Kenya organised a NGO Council Ethnic Clashes network alongside the provision of relief assistance. Later renamed the *Peace and Development Network* or Peace Net, this network sought to find solutions to societal problems which, experience elsewhere in Africa showed, if ignored were likely explode with disastrous consequences.

The influential *Protestant National Council of Churches of Kenya* (NCCK) - staff, 300; membership, six million) - and its Peace and Rehabilitation Programme also deserve special mention. The Programme was started in 1992 to help resolve several devastating conflicts in Kenya. These were initially political in nature but soon turned different ethnic communities against each other. The Programme allows the NCCK to cooperate closely with other NGOs, including Muslim organisations, and with officials at district and local level. The *Nairobi Peace Initiative* (NPI) has been a frequent partner in the training and workshops for members of parliament and others.

As Rose Barmasai and Greetje Witte-Rang have shown in separate papers, the Programme has a strong base in Kenyan society. It has evolved through three phases. During phase I (1992-1993) emergency relief was central to its activities. In phase II (1993-1996) rehabilitation and reconciliation activities were added. During phase III (1996-1999) Good Neighbourliness Workshops have been held, two hundred village level Peace Committees have been created and Peace Facilitators have been identified and trained. For the communities *bazaras* (public gatherings) have been organised in consultation with the local administration. On many occasions local government officials have been made

MUHURONI, WEST KENYA: Peter Mwaura learns his son James about the family's shamba. His family was displaced by ethnic lashes in 1992 but they returned after a few years

PHOTO CRISPIN HUGHES/LINEAIR

albeit with a smaller impact than the NCCK. The *Centre for Conflict Resolution*, based in Nakuru (between Nairobi and Eldoret), promotes constructive, creative and cooperative approaches to the prevention, management and resolution of conflicts. It carries out public education and awareness campaigns, undertakes situational analysis of the state and the nature of social conflicts in Kenya, and acts as an advocacy liaison centre for the improvement of dialogue, negotiation and mediation services.

Theatre is also used in peace promotion and conflict handling. An example is the *Amani People's Theatre* in Nairobi. Amani is Swahili for 'peace'. The Theatre group encourages people in communities, at youth conferences and at peace festivals in Kenya and countries of the Great Lakes Region to respond pro-actively to conflict. The group is particularly interested in Afro-centric models of peace-making using participatory methods of research. Recently it transformed its research and documentation division into the Institute of Interactive Arts and Peacebuilding. It has also begun an intermediate level training programme in leadership and conflict transformation for grassroots leader and people in positions of authority. So far the Amani People's Theatre has been involved in some potentially violent conflicts.

moderators of meetings encouraging them to listen to the debate. President Moi has frequently accused the NCCK of fuelling tensions in the country and on one occasion he almost banned the NCCK's Peace and Reconciliation Programme. In 1998, a slander campaign against an NCCK official was started by a pro-government magazine. In the next phase, the NCCK will, in cooperation with its national and regional partners and its own country-wide network, publish a national agenda for peace.

There are a number of other groups active,

Communities threatened by violent conflicts use internal mechanisms to deal with these conflicts far more frequently than is recognised by the outside world.

Frequently unrecognised too are the few NGOs focused on conflict prevention and management which operate far from the capital at regional and local level. A good example is the *Wajir Peace and Development Committee*, set up in 1994 in Kenya's North-eastern District. It is a multi-ethnic network of 27 governmental and non-governmental organisations representing a variety of people including businesswomen, elders and religious leaders, both Muslim and Christian. Its mandate is conflict prevention and resolution. Women play an important role. They are often better equipped than men to get meetings organised with people from all clans. They were rather instrumental in interesting local police officials in peace work. The peace group combines both traditional and modern mechanisms and conducts community training for leaders, aimed at capacity building and the creation of structures. Mediation is part of its mandate, while it also has a Rapid Response Team for conflicts, run by elders religious leaders,women and government security officials.

Muslim NGOs have felt the fullest weight of government censure. The ban on five Muslim NGOs following the bomb attack on the US Embassy in August 1998, enraged the Islamic community. The NGOs vehemently denied any complicity in the attack and representatives of the community threatened to desert the KANU and join other parties. National demonstrations were organised to protest against the government's action.

At present some NGOs are still under investigation in connection with the bombing. One of these was never properly registered and consequently had been operating illegally. While it is not clear what, if any ties, these aid organisations had with the Embassy bombing, Islamic terrorist groups - including those affiliated with Osama bin Laden - have a history of using aid groups to carry out both legitimate aid work and fund terrorist operations.

International

To date there have been no conflict resolution initiatives from international sponsors, largely because Kenyan conflicts tend to be regarded as internal affairs which are relatively insignificant in comparison to conflicts in nearby countries. The fact that the elections of 1992 and 1997,

although criticised by political groups inside Kenya, were judged as relatively free and honest by international monitors has also contributed to this neglect. The regime is regarded as legitimate. The government denies any involvement in the conflicts which makes it hard to identify the conflicting parties and to bring them to the negotiating table. There is no organised, armed resistance against the government. There is no acceptable alternative to President Moi.

Kenya's various conflicts have aroused little attention in the foreign media. The Rift Valley has been practically closed to foreign journalists in the belief that international intervention in domestic conflicts is directly linked to the amount of media coverage they receive. The North-Eastern Province is remote from the capital, and the safety of travellers cannot be guaranteed.

President Moi's consistent denial of any government involvement in the political violence, however, is becoming less and less credible. Although Kenya's foreign donors have never threatened to suspend aid as a means of ending the domestic political violence, they have supported international human rights organisations in their criticism of the Moi regime. What little public awareness exists of the conflicts in Kenya, has been generated largely by *Amnesty International, Human Rights Watch* and *African Rights*.

At present, government policies benefit certain ethnic groups and discriminate against others and the government does not do enough to solve conflicts. Foreign organisations have emphasised that economic reform and political democratisation are the most important means of ending corruption and improving standards of government. With the present economic crisis and Kenya's continuing dependency upon foreign financial support, the Moi government has come under increasing international pressure to submit to the demands of the international community. Withdrawal of this support will further destabilise the country and this could result in growing resistance to the regime.

Developments in Kenya are closely linked to developments in neighbouring countries. Any deterioration or improvement of the situation in Sudan, Ethiopia, Eritrea, Uganda, Somalia or the Great Lake Region has an immediate impact on

Kenya. Recognising this sensitivity, *ActionAid* has set up an information centre in Nairobi to monitor political events and conflicts in eastern and central Africa. In 1996, it organised an international conference in Nairobi on the crisis in the Great Lakes region. ActionAid supports the basic needs and rights of the poor, in particular pastoralist and squatter communities. Its projects are intended to improve pastoralist's and squatter's access to services, and it lobbies government and others to change policies and practices that affect their lives.

Several organisations which focus on conflict resolution in regions of Africa or parts of the continent, are based in Nairobi, Kenya. Although we are not aware of activities/projects specifically oriented towards the Kenyan situation, they could be useful because of their extensive networks, knowledge and experience. Among these are the *Life & Peace Institute Nairobi,* and the *International Resource Group on Disarmament and Security in the Horn of Africa.*

Prospects

Although some peace initiatives have been successful - the end to the conflict between the Karamojong and Kenyan pastoralists, for example - they remain fragile insofar as they depend largely on the willingness to uphold agreements. In Kenya, as in many other African countries, the possession of guns has shifted political and economic authority from clan elders to those who command the warriors' respect and these are not necessarily the elders.

In order to stop the spiral of violence, Kenyan Church leaders have urged Washington and London to put pressure on the government to commit itself to an all-party constitutional conference and draft a new constitution for Kenya. They have indicated - with the full support of human rights organisations - that if the constitution is not amended, Kenya might be gradually sucked into a cycle of civil strife similar to those in Rwanda, Burundi and Somalia.

According to Colin Kahl, the overlapping and intermingled group affiliations and interests in urban areas have helped Kenya avoid all-out civil war. Most directly, they have served to dampen the possibility of ethnic violence in urban areas, without which full-scale escalation is unlikely.

To date, Kenya's urban population has maintained substantial ties with and influence over kinsmen in the countryside. Consequently their strong preference for peaceful change over ethnic warfare may have helped limit the expansion of rural conflict. Yet even if this violence is kept below the level of a civil war, it will affect the lives of hundreds of thousands of people.

In a more pessimistic scenario, the violence could escalate into civil war before the elections of 2002. The number of violent incidents, the number of victims and the amount of damage has already increased significantly. Despite the chaos Moi's position remains unchallenged and his divide-and-rule policy is still effective. There is currently no figure in the opposition or even within KANU who could be accepted as president by the majority of Kenyans. KANU is divided, and although Moi has managed to keep the two sides together, it remains to be seen whether this fragile unity will survive to the end of his term.

Most of the land is now in Kalenjin hands and the majority of the displaced people are Kikuyu. Moi looks likely to succeed in changing the Rift Valley into an exclusively KANU/Kalenjin zone. He is likely to act on the demands of the international community for economic and political reform only with the greatest reluctance.

Recommendations

The fact that most violent confrontations in Kenya are low-intensity and are not immediately visible to outsiders, does not relieve the international community of its duty to intervene in favour of the forces of peace. There is a pressing need to find structures which facilitate a smooth transition at the end of Moi's term in office.

Most experts have stressed the need to more thoroughly and consistently address the primary problem of competition for scarce resources such as (grass)land and water. The problems of the pastoralists and their warrior-like cultures are one dimension of this competition with most governments in this region of Africa, including Kenya, tend to promote policies favouring the non-pastoral sectors of their predominantly agrarian economies at the expense of pastoral communities. Pastoralists face marginalisation and underdevelopment.

One condition for the effectiveness of continued negotiations involving local, district or national authorities and increased government presence is an effective gun control policy.

Those forces in Kenyan society which are trying to build a culture of reconciliation and peaceful coexistence in place of the current culture of division and exclusion should be recognised and encouraged. Foreign donors should seek a true partnership with these groups and respect and encourage their autonomy.

Greater recognition should be extended to the potential of women in the prevention and management of conflicts. Kenyan women could benefit greatly from the experiences of women peacemakers in other African countries, particularly South Africa.

Background document provided by Berto Jongmans/PIOOM

Service Information

Newsletters and Periodicals
Focus on the European Union and Peace-Building Efforts in the Horn of Africa (this newsletter - covering all IGAD countries, incl. Kenya) is published by Saferworld, Tel. +44 1 71 5808 886. Email: sworld@gn.apc.org
Quarterly Repression Report - Kenyan Human Rights Commission

.Reports
National Council of Churches of Kenya
- Clashes in Kenya and the Rough Road towards Democracy- Lessons and Challenges, ed. Barasa K. Nyukuri. Nairobi/Kenya. 1996 (Unpublished)
Research Institute for the Study of Conflict and Terrorism
- Kenya - Prospects for Peace and Stability, by Simon Baynham. Conflict Studies 297. London/UK. March 1997
Centre for Conflict Resolution
- Ethnicity, Violence and Democracy - The Kenyan Experience, by Machira Appollos. Nairobi/Kenya, November 1998
African Rights
- Violence at the Coast - The Human Consequences of Kenya's Crumbling Political Institutions. London/UK, October 1997
Oikos
- A Way out of Conflict - A Report on Reconciliation Activities in Projects of Partners of Dutch Church-related NGOs and the Dutch Government, by Greetje

WitteRang. Oikos, Utrecht/the Netherlands, June 1998 (casestudy on the NCCK Peace and Rehabilitation Project)
Centre for Development Research
- Contestation over Political Space - The State and Demobilisation of Party Politics in Kenya, by Karuti Kanyinga. Copenhagen/Denmark. Working Paper 98.12, November 1998

Other Publications
Conflicts in Africa - Analysis of Crisis and Prevention Measures. Dossier GRIP # 215/217. Brussels, 1997 (case-study on Kenya)
Population Growth, Environmental Degradation, and StateSponsored Violence - The Case of Kenya, by Colin H. Kahl. In: International Security, 23(2), 1998,

Selected Internet Sites
www.africaonline.co.ke/AfricaOnline/coastwk (daily newspaper Coast Week)
www.nationaudio.com/News/DailyNation/Today/index.html (Daily Nation)
www.africaonline.co.ke/AfricaOnline/ereview (Economic Review)
www.nationaudio.com/News/EastAfrican/current/index.htm (The East African)
www.kenyaweb.com/ktn/ktn.html (Kenya Television Network)
www.actionaid.org (Action Aid)

Resource Contacts
Machira Appolos - Director Centre for Conflict

Resolution, Kenya
Rose Barmasai - Peace and Reconciliation
Programme NCCK, Kenya
George Wachira - Nairobi Peace Initiative,
Kenya
Dekha Ibrahim Abdi - Wajir Peace and
Development Committee
Sabalo Kizito - Africa Peace Forum
Tom Joseph - Director Action Aid Kenya

Organisations
Action Aid Kenya
PO Box 42814
Waiyaki Way, Nairobi
Tel. +254 2 440 444
Fax 254 2 445 843
Email: thomasj@actionaidkenya.org

Action Aid Great Britain
Hamlyn House
Macdonald Rd.
London N19 5PG
Tel. +44 1 71 5617 561/5617 614
Email mail@actionaid.org.uk

*Data on the following organisations can be found
in the Directory section:*
NCCK Peace and Rehabilitation Project
International Resource Group on
Disarmament and Security in the Horn of
Africa
Life and Peace Institute Nairobi
Armani People's Theatre
Centre of Conflict Resolution
Nairobi Peace Initiative

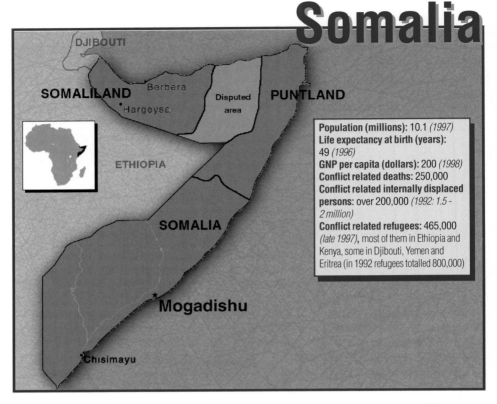

Somalia

Population (millions): 10.1 *(1997)*
Life expectancy at birth (years):
49 *(1996)*
GNP per capita (dollars): 200 *(1998)*
Conflict related deaths: 250,000
Conflict related internally displaced
persons: over 200,000 *(1992: 1.5 -
2 million)*
Conflict related refugees: 465,000
(late 1997), most of them in Ethiopia and
Kenya, some in Djibouti, Yemen and
Eritrea (in 1992 refugees totalled 800,000)

In a State of Permanent Conflict

Life in large parts of Somalia is still characterised by conflict and anarchy. Some
regions, however, have come to know relative peace and stability. The absence of a
central administration has created the opportunity for regional initiatives. Two
regions, Puntland in the north-east and Jubaland in the south-west, have set up
semi-autonomous regional administrations. With these and the self-proclaimed
republic of Somaliland (currently the most stable area in the region), the country
could become an almost stateless society where a legal framework corresponds with
the requirements of the traditional pastoral structures. Some (former) warlords have
kept positions in these regional self-administrations. As in the case of Djibouti and
Kenya, the Ethiopian-Eritrean border conflict had serious repercussions in Somalia,
where both belligerents have sought allies ◆ *By* Jos van Beurden

Somalia is situated along the Gulf of Aden and
the Indian Ocean. It faces the Arabian
peninsula with which it has had commercial and
cultural contacts for centuries. It borders
Djibouti, Ethiopia and Kenya. Most people are
nomadic pastoralists, whose livelihood is
dependent on dromedaries. Cultivation is
practised between the Juba and Shebelle rivers in
the south. Fishing is an important source of
income. According to a UN estimate 10.7 million
people are presently living in Somalia. Aid-
agencies put the total at less than seven million,
based on the number of people who receive
assistance.

The Somali people speak the same language,
Somali, and adhere to the same religion, the

Sunni-variation of Islam. They can be subdivided
into six major clan families: the Darod, Hawiye,
Issaq and Dir, which are all predominantly
nomadic, and the Digil and Rahawayn in the
inter-riverine south, who are more agricultural.
Most issues revolve around this genealogically
clan-based system with its temporary alliances
and coalitions. The Somali clan system has at
times been a source of conflict, e.g. over water
and livestock, while at other times it has
provided a basis for reconciliation.

The partition of Africa divided the greater
Somali nomadic community over five countries:
French Somaliland (now Djibouti), British
Somaliland (now Somaliland) and North-east
Kenya, Italian Somaliland (now Somalia), and
the Ethiopian Ogaden. In 1960 the French,
Ethiopian and Kenyan-British parts of the Somali
people remained outside the new state which
was created: the Somali Republic.

Initially a coalition government gave a more
or less balanced representation to the different
clans, but soon clan-based jealousies began to
create splits. In the ensuing vacuum of power,
general Mohamed Siad Barre seized control in
1969. He professed an anti-tribalist 'scientific
socialism' and received support from the then
Soviet Union. In 1977, during the war with the
pro-US Ethiopia, the two neighbours switched
sides. The strongly anti-communist US
administration could no longer tolerate
Ethiopia's new Marxist rulers and Washington
became Barre's new supporter. Moscow, which
was no longer needed in Mogadishu, filled the
vacuum and chose Mengistu Haile Mariam's
side. Barre's capricious despotism evoked more
and more opposition. Opposition groups formed
a coalition in 1990 and began fighting in many
corners of the country. They defeated Barre, who
fled the country in early 1991. That same year
another autocratic leader in north-east Africa was
forced to step down, Mengistu of Ethiopia.

Soon the thirty year-old Somali nation state
began to fall apart, and it has subsequently been
dominated by conflict and chaos. One major
opposition faction, the USC, appointed its own
chairman, Ali Mahdi Mohamed, as interim-
president. This move was rejected by the other
members of the anti-Barre coalition, some of
whom began to fight the USC. The SNM in the

north-west declared the self-styled Somaliland
Republic. Following a major split within the
USC two factions emerged, one led by Ali
Mahdi, the other by general Mohamed Farah
Aideed. These two factions have subsequently
been engaged in a bitter struggle for the control
of Mogadishu. Both warlords have a policy of
arming their supporters, without providing
leadership or a programme for securing
discipline and peace. This resulted in a state of
anarchy and terror which was most acutely felt in
the capital and surrounding areas. In most
factions members of the old Barre-regime
remained active. The dominance of warlords
strongly diminished the influence of the
traditionally important elders.

The main causes for conflict and anarchy in
Somalia can be found in the clash between the
traditional, mostly pastoral society, which is
strongly characterised by clan-individualism, and
the straitjacket of the modern state. Because of
Barre's culture of militarism this clash resulted
in considerable violence. It became more serious
because natural resources were scarce, and the
lack of justice, good governance and education
were strongly felt.

Despite their occasional talk of peace, the
issues at stake for the warlords in Somalia, are
power, money, land and other natural resources.
These natural resources include pastures, water
points, urban property and markets. The control
of the capital and other cities, of ports and
airports, of export crops such as cattle and
bananas have been permanently contested.

Many Somali refugees returned home under
UNHCR-auspices, however, this UN Agency
rarely achieves its targets. For 1998 the target
was 50,000, most of whom were supposed to
return to the self-styled Somaliland Republic.
According to the World Food Programme (WFP)
the harvest will be poor in 1999 and many
people will be in need of food aid.

Somaliland
Civil strife in Somalia began in 1988 in the
north-west region, when the SNM took control of
the area. Within two years, and after many aerial
bombardments and other atrocities, some
50,000 people had died. As warlords, especially
in the south, continued fighting for power after

Somali Parties and Factions

National Salvation Council (NSC)
The NSC brought together 26 factions in
Sodere (Ethiopia) in January 1997. All are
members of the SSA, except for the SSDF and
one SNA-faction. Its chairman is Aden
Abdullahi Nur. The NSC failed to secure the
support of Hussain Aideed.

Al-Ittihad Al-Islam (Al-Ittehad)
This radical Islamic group, inaugurated in
1992, is based in Mogadishu and is allied to
Hussein Mohamed Aideed. It is mainly
preoccupied with fighting the SNF in the
Gedo region and has shown some activity in
other regions. According to Ethiopia Al-Ittihad
fights for the independence of the Ethiopian
Ogaden, where mainly ethnic Somali are
living.

Central:

United Somali Congress (USC)
This group, based on the Hawiye ethnic
group, was formed by Ali Mahdi Mohamed in
1989 and initially also included Mohamed
Farah Aideed. Presently the group has
strongest ties with the SSA and the SNA. The
USC-leader is Ali Mahdi Mohamed, who is
recognised by his followers as the president of
the whole of Somalia. The USC controls
North-Mogadishu.

Somali Salvation Alliance (SSA)
Break away group of USC.

Rahawayn Resistance Army (RRA)
This clan-based group, allied to the SDM,
fights Aideed's militias in the Bay and Bakool
regions.

Somali Democratic Movement (SDM)
Hawiye group, opposed to Aideed and active
in Mogadishu.

Somali National Alliance (SNA)
Beakaway of the USC. Its leader is Hussein
Mohamed Aideed, who succeeded his father
Mohamed Farah Aideed after his death in
1996. Aideed controls most of south-
Mogadishu and large tracts of southern
Somalia.

Northeast:

Somali Salvation Democratic Front (SSDF)
Began in 1978 as an anti-Barre group, based
on Majerteen and Darod clans in the
northeast. It has its headquarters in Bosaso,
the harbour city in the northeast. Presently it
has two major factions, one headed by
Mohamed Abshir Muse, the other by
Abdullahi Yussuf Ahmed. The latter is the
president of the Puntland self-administration
area.

Somali People's Democratic Union (SPDU)
Was formed early 1997 in Gaalkayo as a
breakaway of the SSDF.

United Somali Party (USP)
Group involved in the creation of Puntland.

Somali National Front (SNF)
Marehan/Darod based group which mainly
fights the Al-Ittehad in Gedo region.

Southern:

Somali Patriotic Movement (SPM)
The SPM is based on the Darod clan. It was
started as an anti-Barre group in 1989. It is
based in Kismayu. Chairman is general
Mohamed Siad Hersi Morgan.

Somaliland:

Somali National Movement (SNM)
The SNM began as an Issaq, anti-Barre group
in the north-eastern former British
Somaliland. It is now the ruling party in the
self-proclaimed Republic of Somaliland. Its
leader, Mohamed Ibrahim Egal, is
Somaliland's president.

Northern Somali Alliance (NSA)
The NSA was formed in 1997 by the merger
of two other anti-SNM groups in Somaliland.

Red Flag
Group also opposed to Egal's SNM.

the overthrow of the Barre regime, the north-west set up its own administration and proclaimed the Somaliland Republic.

While international recognition was withheld for the new republic, it was from the beginning relatively peaceful. The traditional elders and community-based peace committees brought most of the armed militia under control. Each community registered the number and kind of arms in their possession and began to control their movements. In addition, a crucial initiative was taken. Practising their traditional peace-making methods, religious leaders, politicians, intellectuals, social groups, businessmen and women's groups, gathered from all over Somaliland to initiate a peace process. Between 1991 and 1993, 48 mini-conferences were held, followed by three more extensive conferences aimed at ensuring reconciliation. Somaliland has since had a central government and a social development programme has been implemented. This whole effort has been a purely local initiative, with the role of outsiders being restricted to the provision of incidental funding and acting as observers.

However, in Somaliland too, the clan question has not been fully resolved. Clans living in the Somaliland districts of Elayo and Laascano, which border north-east Somalia, feel themselves to be the victims of discrimination by the government in Hargeisa, which in their opinion is Issaq dominated. Some of them would prefer not to be part of Somaliland.

Conflict Dynamics

In the capital and most of the south the balance between warlords, their militias and other allies on the one hand, and the traditional elders and their sympathisers on the other, still favours the former. The USC of Ali Mahdi Mohamed and the SNA of Hussain Mohamed Aideed have been the most powerful by far. Each has kept control of his part of Mogadishu and its hinterland. In 1998 the two set up a joint administration for Mogadishu and began to demobilise the capital city. According to reports from the capital, the number of arms in the streets diminished visibly. Reports from southern and central Somalia were less positive. While people suffered from drought and

diseases, outlawed militiamen extorted money from them by setting up checkpoints and charging for drinking water.

The continuing violence and anarchy provided leaders in other regions of Somalia with the impetus to go their own way. In north-east Somalia this led to elections in June 1998, where a non-secessionist, regional administration for the Puntland State of Somalia was elected. Abdullahi Yussuf Ahmed was chosen as president. SPM-Chairman General Morgan and clan elders in south-west Somalia are trying to set up their own administration in Jubaland. A constitutional conference was planned for 1999.

Thus, during the past years the focus in the Somali peace and reconciliation efforts has moved from the national to the regions level. This does not imply that Somalis want to see the disintegration of their country, but that, for the time being, they have no wish for a centralised government, preferring instead regional cooperation and regional co-existence, possibly leading to a federal state based on several clan-based states. In certain areas the elders recovered some of their power, although both in Puntland and Jubaland a warlord became the leader of the region. This new trend was accepted and confirmed during conferences held in Ethiopia and Egypt, in 1996 and 1997.

There are no reliable national figures for current casualties and economic damage. Some approximate figures are available for earlier stages in the conflict. In the north-west, in the early days of the war, there were some 50,000 fatalities while, in only four months of fighting in Mogadishu between 1991 and 1992 some 30,000 people were killed. In total, a quarter of a million people may have died. To this we can add 300,000 people who died during the famine of 1992, which was significantly aggravated by the civil war. Among the wounded can be reckoned thousands of people who have survived landmine-explosions. Currently, the number of dead is relatively low.

Because of their registration by the UNHCR and the distribution of ration-cards by NGOs the number of refugees and internally displaced people is better known. Around 1990, 600,000 people had fled to Ethiopia and other countries. In 1992, their number had increased to

800,000. During the 1992 famine period between 1.5 and 2 million people were internally displaced. Many Somali, who had been residing for decades in Mogadishu returned to their villages and towns.

In the absence of a centralised administration, taxes were collected by clans. In some regions they were used for maintenance, rehabilitation or development purposes, in others the revenue went into the war effort or was used to pay the militias. Several currencies were used in different regions of the country.

Especially in the south, traditional commercial networks between rural areas and cities or ports suffered continual disruptions. The arrival of large-scale food aid in the early 1990s had a profound impact on the markets in the major urban centres, but much aid has subsequently disappeared. The ports of Mogadishu and Kismayu were mostly out of operation, while the docks in Berbera and Bosaso took over part of their tasks. The port of Bosaso which in 1991 was defunct has since grown into a thriving city with hundreds of thousands of inhabitants, attracting migrant workers from as far as Tanzania. However, Somalia's territorial waters have been consistently over-fished by foreign, often highly mechanised, fishing boats. Traditional fishermen have frequently seen their boats and nets destroyed and their fish factories looted. Occasionally, pirates have concluded deals with warlords and divided their profits. In general, insecurity is an important obstacle for food production and economic activity.

The national reconciliation conference in Baidoa, planned for February 1998 was postponed several times, and by the end of 1998 it seemed unlikely to be held. Militias, loyal to Hussein Aideed, continued to occupy Baidoa. The same factions reported to have received arms from Ethiopia accused Eritrea of supplying arms to the faction of Hussain Mohamed Aideed who could distribute them among Ethiopian dissidents.

In June 1999 Ethiopia was accused of invading Baidoa and helping to chase away Aideed. This was not Ethiopia's first incursion. In August 1996 it had sent troops to defeat the Muslim-radical Al-Itahad al-Islami and occupied sites in the border areas of Gedo. In January

1998 it withdrew 500 men together with their armoured personnel carriers and tanks, but left behind a well armed SNF. By doing so Ethiopia sharpened factional splits without defeating Al-Itahad. Nor did Ethiopian arms deliveries to General Morgan (SNF), the Rahenweyne Resistance Army (centre) and Ali Mahdi (Mogadishu) help to defeat the Muslim-radicals. Hussein Aideed, who often works in coalition with the Muslim-radical Al-Itehad, condemned this Ethiopian involvement. Ethiopia has regularly sent Special Envoys to Somaliland and Puntland.

The general insecurity and shortage of water and food in central and southern Somalia resulted in the movement of thousands of people. Since November 1998 some 5,000 Somali's have gone to the Kenyan border leading Kenya to close its border with Somalia. According to official Ethiopian sources 10,000 people crossed the border with Ethiopia. In the coastal town of Bossaso an unidentified number of internally displaced people arrived.

Somaliland

In the much more stable Somaliland Republic the Government introduced tax, banking and customs systems in 1993. The administration worked reasonably well and did its utmost to gain international recognition but with no success. As a result, its funding for reconstruction and rehabilitation is at a far lower level than in Somalia. It has, however, been visited by representatives of UN and EU-institutions, Western donors and neighbouring states.

In 1998, President Egal opposed the creation of Puntland on the grounds that its precise demarcation was not yet clear. Apart from the Bari, Nugaal and Mudug regions it might comprise the Sanaag and Sool regions of Somaliland. Early in 1999 some border clashes were reported and some hard words were exchanged between Somaliland and Puntland.

Official Conflict Management

In the last eight years, twelve peace initiatives have taken place. Some were directed at the warlords, with little success. Others concentrated on re-empowering clan elders, enlightened intellectuals and other local leaders. Some of these offered a more hopeful prospect.

From the early 1990s the *United Nations* has tried to mediate and soften the consequences of the conflict. In April 1992 UN-representative Mohamed Sahnoun arrived in Mogadishu, starting UN operations in Somalia (UNOSOM). His approach was to seek a political settlement and national reconciliation through the traditional elder-based structures. He concluded that in six months a good atmosphere had been created and many intractable issues were resolved. A cease-fire was largely respected. Ports and airports had been reopened. A chain of solidarity had begun to materialise. Moreover, Sahnoun came to a separate agreement with Somaliland and discussed an operation to reconcile the faction leaders with Ethiopian prime minister, Meles Zenawi.

Inside the UN a debate was started on the best way forward for Somalia. The UN Secretary-General, Boutros Boutros Ghali, the US and some other member states pointed to the then reigning famine and favoured a rapid intervention, while others like Sahnoun continued to support a gradual approach. The result was the replacement of Sahnoun, and the landing by 28,000 American and 1,700 French troops near Mogadishu on December 9, 1992. In Operation Restore Hope military units from Belgium, Italy, Canada, New Zealand and Australia followed soon. Later, troops jfrom Pakistan, Botswana, Tunisia, Morocco, Egypt, Nigeria, Saudi Arabia, Turkey and Djibouti joined the force. The UK sent cargo planes.

The Somali and the international community differ widely in their assessment of the UN operation which ended in 1995. The Somali were particularly critical of the UN's failure to disarm the militias, and consult the local inhabitants about the UN's plans to set up District Councils. This criticism was shared by a large number of foreign NGOs in Somalia. In addition they argued that in December 1992, when the American troops landed in Somalia, the worst of the food shortage was over.

Hussain Aideed and representatives of 25 other factions attended a peace conference in Cairo in December 1997. Inspired by the ethnic federalism and division into regions of Ethiopia, they opted for the principle of regional self-administration. They planned a national peace conference in the southern city of Baidoa for February 1998. The conference in Cairo had been preceded by a meeting in Sodere, Ethiopia, under *InterGovernmental Agency on Development (IGAD)* auspices in late 1996. A National Salvation Council was set up, but Husain Mohamed Aideed's group did not participate.

In the summer of 1998 the UN adopted this regional approach and further shifted its attention from warlords to peace-seeking civilian leaders, involving the development of regional administrations. Emerging administrations, such as those in Puntland or Jubaland, could get assistance, with the aim of finally bringing the whole country into a federal structure.

In July 1998 an international meeting was organised by the Somali Aid Coordination Body under the auspices of the *Forum of Partners of the IGAD* in Addis Ababa. Participants were mostly representatives of UN organisations, European Union member states and IGAD itself. They registered their scepticism about a July 1998 Libyan peace initiative among factions in Mogadishu and praised the Somaliland administration for its effective government, while they hailed the Puntland autonomous civilian administration as 'the most desirable option' for Somalia.

Whether this development is really positive, however, cannot be assessed in the absence of a full analysis of these regionalisation processes. Regionalism could become a means for warlords to continue exercising their power in a new context.

Multi-Track Diplomacy
Domestic

The history of indigenous NGOs in Somalia goes back to the early 1980's. During this period they emerged in the wake of the international NGOs which had entered the country to help with the influx of refugees from Ethiopia as a result of the 1977 Ogaden war. In 1988 the World Bank established a US$ 3 million fund as seed money to encourage local NGOs to implement social projects. It was administered by the Ministry of Planning. The Bank tried to diminish the hardships arising from its

Structural Adjustment Programme for Somalia but due to their limited capacity few local NGOs used the fund. In the same period USAID established a Management Unit for Supervision and Training (MUST) to support those local NGOs which were implementing agency-funded projects. Training, research, monitoring and evaluation were MUST's main tasks.

During this period and during the later civil strife, the collapse of government, public services and civic structures led to their further growth. It also caused many educated and qualified people to return from Mogadishu to their home villages and towns. The destruction they encountered was so extensive that they had little choice other than to participate in the reconstruction. This led to the birth of a variety of local NGOs. Many of them quickly disappeared, while others turned out to be more enduring.

Those which continue to operate are reported to have a relatively positive record in relief and rehabilitation. It is also remarkable that they are often focused on women. Women-owned NGOs were more visible and energetic in working for peace, building coalitions across faction lines and supporting health and nutrition programmes. In Mogadishu and Hargeisa women leaders set up extensive networks which had some impact in solving local conflicts, helped build bridges between hostile clan groups and encouraged the men to stop fighting and find alternative means of solving disputes. These initiatives were respected by both men and women.

The *Coalition of Grassroot Women's Organisations (COGWO)* is working for peace via various women's organisations in Somalia, thus crossing faction lines and linking up grassroots women's groups at many levels. Working with the displaced and with those who have lost access to income and basic resources, these organisations also worked to mitigate the negative effects of conflict on communities.

NGOs in Somalia have certain weaknesses. Most are new and inexperienced. They urgently need training in setting up an organisation, bookkeeping, etc. Some are built around individuals and their immediate relatives and are more focused on offering employment than setting up development programmes. Others are

effectively cover operations for warlords and it is sometimes difficult to distinguish between genuine and fake grassroots-organisations. As is to be expected, the development of most of these organisations has occurred on a regional basis. Most show an urban bias.

The wide range of their activities is a clear indication of the existing needs and the absence of any other bodies to fulfil these tasks. The range of concerns includes: preventive health care, growing vegetables by women, water, education, reintegration of returned female refugees, establishment of local structures, credit programmes, training fishermen, research into fish stock, conflict resolution and advocacy.

The *Peace and Human Rights Network (PHRN)* based in Mogadishu is worthy of special mention. This non-clan based organisation came into being in February 1997 when some twenty organisations attended a workshop in order to analyse the conflict situation. Among the participants were human rights organisations, the Somali Olympic Committee, other NGOs, journalists, teachers, community leaders and ex-militia members. They decided on the spot to form this network organisation. Their most conspicuous activity so far has been the organisation of a peace demonstration on March 8, 1998 which was attended by one hundred thousand people.

Given that civil society is usually thought to act as a counterbalance to the state, it is questionable whether there can be a civil society without a state. In the case of Somalia and Somaliland, however, there is a civil society and it consists of all those, who do not belong to a warlord, his militias and sympathisers and who are part of formal or informal networks.

A positive aspect of the strong (clan) individualism is the Somali people's tradition of speaking frankly on any issue. They are also willing to take sufficient time to fully discuss an issue. The final negotiations in Garowe, which led to the creation of the Puntland self-administration area, lasted two months and brought 300 clan elders and other local leaders together. It had been preceded by years of consultations and meetings.

Clan elders, traders, women's groups and NGOs have already been mentioned, but in

SOMALIA, Af Madow Peace Conference, December 1996

PHOTO SUSANNE THURFJELL/LPI

Somalia and Somaliland another important group are the media. Since the mid-1990s the presence of all sorts of archaic mimeographs and radio broadcast installations combined with the availability of computer technology and skilled journalists was a fresh impetus for this tradition. Papers and radio broadcasts were often critical and were well read or listened to. To mention an example, Radio Voice of Peace/Somalia (RVOP) broadcasts to Somalia, Somaliland and the Somali diaspora in some ten other countries. It is non-political and aims at strengthening civil society.

The strength of elders, organised traders, women, NGOs and media differs per region. In the north-east, presently Puntland, for example, traders have been reasonably supportive of efforts to stop all fighting and help build the self-administration. They need stability in order to be able to export cattle, and have an interest in reconciliation efforts. Such traders are almost absent in southern Somalia, where cultivation is the main mode of production.

In Mogadishu several informal newspapers encourage a lively debate on the future of the capital and Somalia. They bring new ideas and voice opposition to the practices of some warlords or other leaders. In Somaliland the elders are playing a vital role in the continuation of the national debate which finally led to the current situation of relative stability. The elders in the south often belong to the rich land-owning class who do not represent constituencies of small-holders.

International
International NGOs played an important role in the earlier years of the civil war. They were mostly involved in the distribution of emergency assistance. In order to do their work they were often involved in immediate conflict solving. Although there were many failures, one has to realise that they had to work under extremely difficult circumstances. A few of them deserve special mention.

From May 1991 until December 1992 the *International Committee of the Red Cross (ICRC)* was the only major relief organisation operating in Somalia. Its programme was wide-ranging. Execution and control were largely in Somali hands. The ICRC often had to negotiate levels of payment that seemed excessive to outsiders.

When it started a kitchen programme for the most needy, even its own field staff estimated a loss of 50 per cent before cooking. Yet independent evaluators doubted whether ICRC could have operated in any other way.

As the war had cut off large parts of the country from its ports and overland transport, the *Lutheran World Federation (LWF)* began an airlift of food aid in 1992. The LWF had gained wide experience in this type of operation from Ethiopia/Eritrea in the 1980's and Southern Sudan in the 1980's and 1990's. Food, medicines and other goods were flown in from Nairobi and Mombasa. Unfortunately, the needs assessment lacked an inventory of specific needs and there was insufficient co-ordination with other agencies.

The Irish NGO *Concern* arrived in Somalia in 1987, was forced in January 1991 to withdraw its expatriate field staff but returned in early 1992 because of the famine. It quickly started a supplementary feeding programme which began in Mogadishu and was later extended to other parts of the country. The food they distributed however was rather expensive and not very suitable for therapeutic feeding. Yet the building of an experienced senior local staff and the training of hundreds of local medical volunteers was a successful aspect of the programme.

Due to the continuing insecurity many international NGOs have withdrawn from Somalia and Somaliland or have never entered the area. The absence of an emergency situation and the increase in the number of local NGOs have also encouraged this 'avoidance factor'. Some foreign NGOs are restricting themselves to financing local initiatives.

Since 1992 the Life & Peace Institute, an international and ecumenical peace research institute, has supported locally based peace processes in Somalia, to begin with in a consultative role together with the UN. However, when UNOSOM left in 1995, the Institute had established an ongoing support and capacity building program all over Somalia, which later came to be extended also to Somaliland. LPI supported the so-called Boroma conference, where all clans of Somaliland were represented through their elders which - in a remarkable

Somali and participatory way - elected a government and a president.

Somaliland

The situation for local NGOs in Somaliland differs from that of their colleagues in Somalia in that they have more difficulty in getting foreign funding and support. The disadvantage is that capacity building is slow, and that more NGOs disappear due to lack of funds. An advantage of this scarcity is that NGOs in Somaliland learn better to solve their own problems.

Prospects

Experts have different opinions on the prospects of peace in Somalia and Somaliland. Some take encouragement from the absence of the state in Somalia: the space for peace initiatives from below and for a very strongly decentralised administration. This would fit in with the pre-colonial nomadic traditions of the country.

At the same time it is argued that there is a danger that warlords will try to take advantage of these initiatives. In Puntland the SSDF was marginalised for a time allowing the clan elders, grassroots organisations and local leaders to take the initiative. The SSDF then suddenly returned and initiated a platform with these civil society organisations and itself. In Jubaland General Morgan's SPM is even more closely allied with the initiative for regional self-administration.

For mediating countries such as Ethiopia, Egypt and Libya the main counterpart continues to be the warlord, as he represents power. They continue to focus on the national level of the state, i.e. a group of ministers and a president. Experts think this strategy has proven mistaken. In the most stable areas of Somalia there is no centralised administration, while new structures are arising outside the traditional patterns. Most multilateral organisations or international NGOs no longer look for a state in the first place.

All argue, that a solution to the problems should come from the Somalis themselves. Some believe that neighbouring countries should be excluded from the peace process, as they have demonstrated that they have their own agenda and interest in this conflict.

Recommendations

To present the civil war as a conflict between clan-based factions and their leaders is an oversimplification, argues African Rights in its report *Somalia Operation Restore Hope: A preliminary assessment* (May 1993). Disputes over land-ownership were a central factor in the outbreak of war and famine. They still play a role. In the case of Somalia reconciliation also means looking into contradictions between rich landowners and the landless. In southern Somalia particularly, several minority clans are severely disadvantaged in terms of their social status. Warlords control most of the land. Some clan elders represent the interests of the rich.

A guiding principle to peace-building in Somalia is 'to empower individuals and groups within the society (...) and to mobilise indigenous capacities for peace-building', writes Wolfgang Heinrich in *Building the Peace*. He mentions the example of a reconciliation conference in 1993, where the UN representatives weakened the influence of civilian representatives by having the agreement signed only by the representatives of the factions, 'who - as became evident very soon - were not the least committed to this agreement'.

In its Editorial of Nov-Dec 1998 'Somalia goes Regional', the *Horn of Africa Bulletin* writes that 'a closer look shows that the main Somali actors remain the same and we have not yet seen whether their aims and objectives have truly changed'. They fear that some old faction leaders have found a new and more becoming 'costume'.

Bringing peace to Somalia is not a quick fix. If outsiders are to be involved, they can do useful work under certain conditions. They must have a long-term commitment and willingness to give priority to indigenous conflict prevention and management. They need a thorough understanding and extensive knowledge of the local situation. They should build up relations of trust with groups and people from below, who are to carry on the peace process.

Service Information

Newsletters

Monthly newsletter of Arab Organisation for Human Rights, Cairo/Egypt

Horn of Africa Bulletin, bi-monthly newsletter published by the Life & Peace Institute, Uppsala/Sweden

Indian Ocean Newsletter, weekly published by Indigo Publications Group, Paris/France

Inter-Africa Group News and Networking Service, monthly update, Inter-Africa Group, Addis Ababa/Ethiopia

Focus on the European Union and Peace-Building Efforts in the Horn of Africa, newsletter published by Saferworld/London

Reports

Catholic Institute for International Relations
- Building Partnerships for Participatory Development. Reports of workshops held in Hargeisa and Boroma. London, 1996

United States Institute for Peace
- Removing Barricades in Somalia - Options for Peace and Rehabilitation, by Hussain Adam & Richard Ford. Washington DC, October 1998

Bonn International Center for Conversion
- Demilitarisation, Reintegration and Conflict Prevention in the Horn of Africa - Discussion Paper, by Kees Kingma & Kiflenariam Gebrewold. July 1998

Saferworld
- Undermining Development - The European Arms Trade with the Horn of Africa and Central Africa, by William Benson. London, 1998
- Prevention of Violent Conflict and the Coherence of EU Policies towards the Horn of Africa, by Emma Visman & Emery Brusset. London, April 1998

WSP Info/UNRISD
- War-torn Societies Project in Somalia, prepared by Martin Doornbos. Geneva/Switzerland, 1998

Other publications

Somalia - The Missed Opportunities, by Mohamed Sahnoun. Washington DC, USIP, 1994
Humanitarian Aid to Somalia - Evaluation Report. Netherlands Development Cooperation. The Hague, 1994
Building the Peace - Experiences of Collaborative Peacebuilding in Somalia: 1993-1996, by Wolfgang Heinrich. LPI, Uppsala, 1997
Learning from Somalia - The Lessons of Armed Humanitarian Intervention, by W. Clarke, J. Herbst (Eds.). Boulder, CO. Westview Press, 1997
Humanitarian BandAids in Sudan and Somalia Crisis Response, by J. Prendergast. London, Pluto Press, 1997
Somalia: When two Anarchies meet, by Kenneth D. Bush. In: Canada and Missions for Peace - Lessons from Nicaragua, Cambodia and Somalia. Eds. G. Wirick and R. Miller. Ottawa/Canada, International Development Research Centre. 1997.

Selected Internet Sites

www.somali.com/ (Somalia On Line)
www.etek.chalmers.se/~e3hassan/news.html (Somali News Page)
www.home.ica.net./~somalipress (Somali Press on Line)
members.tripod.com/~sepado/ (Somali NGO based in United Arab Emirates)
www.arab.net/somalia/somalia (ArabNet on Somalia)

Resource Contacts

Jalal Abdul Latif - Inter-Africa Group, Addis Ababa
Abdullah Mahmoud - Department Political Science, University of Amsterdam, fax +31 20 525 2086. Email mohamoud@pscw.uva.nl
Ahmed M. Haji-Jama - expert in Somalian affairs, notably Puntland, Toronto/Canada. Email ahajijama@globalserve.net
Rakiya Omaar - African Rights. Email omaar@global.net.co.uk
Karthi Govender - ACCORD. Email karthig@accord.org.uk
Mohamed Salih - Institute of Social Studies, The Hague/the Netherlands, fax +31 70 426 0799. Email salih@iss.nl
Dorothé Appels, NOVIB, The Hague\The Netherlands, fax +31 70 361 4461, Email dorothe.appels@novib.nl

Organisations

COGWO
P.O. Box 71135
Nairobi
Kenya
tel +252 121 5292
fax +252 121 5048
email cogwo@compuserve.com

Data on the following organisations can be found in the Directory section:
Peace and Human Rights Network
Life and Peace Institute
Inter Africa Group
Nairobi Peace Initiative
African Rights
Arab Organisation for Human Rights

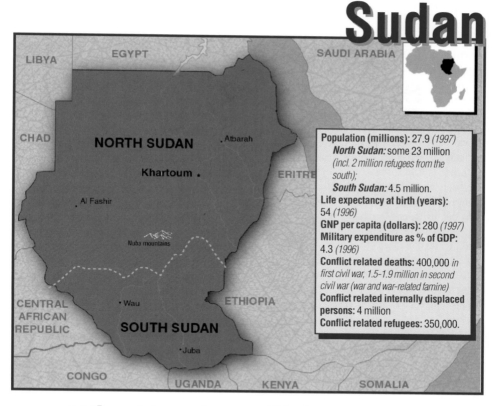

Sudan

Population (millions): 27.9 *(1997)*
North Sudan: some 23 million *(incl. 2 million refugees from the south);*
South Sudan: 4.5 million.
Life expectancy at birth (years): 54 *(1996)*
GNP per capita (dollars): 280 *(1997)*
Military expenditure as % of GDP: 4.3 *(1996)*
Conflict related deaths: 400,000 *in first civil war, 1.5-1.9 million in second civil war (war and war-related famine)*
Conflict related internally displaced persons: 4 million
Conflict related refugees: 350,000.

Map labels: LIBYA, EGYPT, SAUDI ARABIA, CHAD, NORTH SUDAN, Atbarah, Khartoum, ERITRE, Al Fashir, Nuba mountains, CENTRAL AFRICAN REPUBLIC, Wau, ETHIOPIA, SOUTH SUDAN, Juba, CONGO, UGANDA, KENYA, SOMALIA

Who Has the Will for Peace?

The massive loss of life caused by the war in Sudan far surpasses that of any civil war being waged elsewhere in the world. However, to date the international community has shown little urgency in its quest for a resolution to the conflict and a concerted, forceful lobby for peace in Sudan is still lacking. The peace initiatives undertaken since 1993 under the auspices of Sudan's neighbours - supported behind the scenes by most western countries - initially seemed promising. More recently, however, the military situation has stalemated, famine has plagued large sections of the South, and the mediation process has yielded no significant results. At the international NGO level there is a growing awareness that coordination of peace efforts is badly needed, as well as close cooperation with grassroots peacebuilding initiatives in the region. Surprisingly enough, after almost forty years of civil war indigenous conflict management mechanisms are still operational in Sudan ◆ *By* **Hans van de Veen**

Sudan is the largest country in Africa, with borders that touch Egypt, Eritrea, Ethiopia, Kenya, Uganda, Congo, Central African Republic, and Libya. It's size, along with its strategic location straddling the Nile River and abutting the Red Sea, made it a prominent target of revolving-door superpower intervention and massive arms transfers throughout the Cold War. As unstable civilian governments alternated with governments installed by military coups after independence in 1956, the country slid deeper into an economic malaise and social crisis, which has been accentuated by lengthy outbreaks of civil war.

The US alone provided successive Khartoum governments with close to US$1 billion in arms in the late 1970s and 1980s. For its part, the Soviet Union provided arms to Sudan in the early 1970s. As the Horn of Africa lost significance to the departing superpowers in the early 1990s, Sudan was allowed to wither in arms-bloated poverty.

Sudan is one of the most ethnically diverse countries in Africa, with a population estimated at close to 28 million, from 19 major linguistic groups and nearly sixhundred subgroups. Those who identify themselves as Arabs make up the largest group (40%), followed by the southern Dinka (12%), the Bejas of the north-east (7%), and West African immigrants (6%).

Like most of the former European colonies along the Sahara's southern rim - the Sahel - Sudan comprises an Arabic-speaking Muslim north and an African south which is inhabited by ethnically-diverse Christians and practitioners of traditional religions.

Since the north attained a higher level of economic development in colonial times and is home to about three-quarters of the country's population, the south feels itself to be marginalized and the victim of discrimination. Successive governments have done extremely little to ease the grievances of the south. Turning the entire country into an Islamic republic was probably the surest way to perpetuate the civil war.

In the central, eastern and western parts of the country there are numerous politically and economically marginalised groups which have not been completely Arabised or Islamicised. Since independence, rival northern parties have vied to control the country and to dominate these regions.

Sudan has known only a short period of peace since achieving independence on January 1, 1956. A mutiny in the army in the South led to the outbreak of the first civil war, which held the country in its grip from 1955 to 1972. In 1969, a military coup brought to power General Numeiry, who promised to grant limited autonomy to the south and signed a peace accord in Addis Ababa in 1972. The accord granted regional autonomy to the three southern states. In 1983 new tensions between the south and

north emerged after Numeiry announced the introduction of Islamic legislation, the Sharia. Shortly thereafter the transfer of southern garrisons to the north resulted in mutiny. The Sudan People's Liberation Army (SPLA) was set up and the second civil war began.

In 1985 Numeiry was ousted in a military coup brought about by a peaceful popular uprising. A coalition government with Umma leader Sadiq al-Mahdi as prime minister came to power after elections in 1986. An agreement with the SPLA was then concluded which included a cease-fire. Suspension of the Sharia was one of the conditions agreed upon. The National Islamic Front, which had joined the coalition in the meantime, was the first to reject the agreement. A new coalition was on the point of beginning discussions on the implementation of the agreement when the government was overthrown by Lieutenant-General Omar Hassan al Bashir on 30 June 1989.

It soon became clear that, from that moment onwards, NIF ideology was directing political developments. Support from Iran, which rushed to strengthen relations with its first sub-Saharan ally, enabled the NIF-controlled government to make massive arms purchase from China and the former Soviet republics, which it used to step up the war in the south. Ethnic militia and breakaway factions of the SPLA also received support in an effort to divide the southern opposition against itself.

In 1991 the SPLA split into two factions: the SPLA-mainstream led by John Garang de Mabior and the SPLA-United led by Riek Machar. The SPLA-United has since undergone further rifts (partly as result of Dinka-Nuer clashes). As a result of the southern rebel inter-factional fighting, government forces managed to recapture a number of garrison towns and to regain the use of some roads and communication infrastructure in 1992.

A series of cease-fires brought some respite in 1995, but negotiations to end the fighting failed to get off the ground. In April 1996, the government of Sudan entered into a political charter with six southern rebel groups. Under the terms of the accord the north and the south would remain together in a unitary state and the

Sharia and local customs would become the main sources of law.

Several leaders of rebel groups were rewarded with top government posts. However, in January 1998, one of them, Kerubino Bol, with his Dinka-based militia, defected from the government side, realigned with SPLA forces, and launched a number of surprise attacks on government forces in the Bahr al Ghazal province. In 1999 Kerubino rejoined the Sudanese government.

Contemporary Conflict Dynamics

During the early 1990s, the government of Sudan opened its doors to rebel groups from other countries. These included opposition (and mostly armed) groups from the neighbouring countries Ethiopia and Uganda, and the newly independent Eritrea, as well as radical Islamic groups from the Middle East. Because of the welcome extended to these Islamic radicals, the Sudanese regime became increasingly isolated at the international level. In 1993 the United States put Sudan on its blacklist of state-supporters of international terrorism.

In the meantime, in the north, the National Islamic Front and its allies, in an effort to consolidate control of government and enforce its vision of an Islamic state, had built up a repressive police state. The resistance towards the ruling party found an outlet when in 1995 the Eritrean government opened its doors to the Sudanese opposition. At the end of 1996 the National Democratic Alliance (NDA) - composed of the two traditional northern political parties, the Sudan Communist Party as well as several ethnically based parties - became allies or at least co-belligerents of the SPLA. Their co-ordinated attacks posed the most serious threat to the government since it came to power. The neighbouring countries of Ethiopia, Eritrea and Uganda supported the coalition openly.

The Sudan civil war thus evolved into a multi-front war - with dangerous regional implications. In 1997 the combined Sudanese opposition launched several attacks in the areas bordering Eritrea and Ethiopia as well as Uganda, which resulted in significant advances. Sudanese government officials dispute rebel claims of credit for these military advances, alleging that the campaigns were led and waged by the armed forces of the three neighbouring countries. Nevertheless, reports of the victories encouraged other NDA parties - which had no military involvement at that time - to mobilise military units to fight government forces. For its part, the government responded to this new spate of armed incursions with a call for a national mobilisation and a renewed quest for arms from its global suppliers, while charging its neighbours with invading its territory.

For some time US attempts to overthrow the Sudanese government by covertly aiding its neighbours seemed to be meeting with success, but the policy suddenly collapsed when the United States' two chief allies - Ethiopia and Eritrea - began fighting each other in May 1998. Both countries called back troops from the Sudanese borders and made peace overtures to their former enemy, Sudan. The Sudanese government reacted immediately by launching fresh attacks against the rebel movement in the eastern part of the country.

In the meantime, the humanitarian situation in several parts of the country further deteriorated. The 1998 famine in the western province of Bahr al Ghazal - instigated by the government but made worse by the indifference and incompetence of factions of the rebel movement - affected an estimated 2.6 million people, prompting the greatest UN relief operation in human history. On July 15, the SPLA announced a three-month cease-fire in the province, and opened three corridors leading to the area. The government then implemented a one-month truce, which was later extended to April 1999. However, hundreds of thousands failed to survive the catastrophe, adding to the misery of a people who have known little if any peace in their lives. The food shortage is projected to continue until late 1999.

Another seriously affected area was the Western Upper Nile which belongs to the southern Nuer tribe. This area suffered because two pro-government Nuer forces were fighting each other over political and military control of this territory, where a government-organised international consortium is drilling for oil. Some 150,000 civilians, most of them displaced by the fighting, were put at risk. The UN relief operation was unable to reach them because of the unstable military situation. In the SPLA-held areas of the central Nuba Mountains, some 20,000 people at risk were not even included in the UN's relief operation or statistics. The government's strategy in the mountains is to starve civilians into leaving the rebel areas, so it has denied any UN access. Some small civilian relief agencies have defied the ban and are trying to help the 300,000 Nuba thought to have remained in the area.

All conflict parties in this civil war have committed war crimes. The Sudanese government has engaged in indiscriminate aerial bombardments of southern population centres and still uses scorched earth tactics. In order to quell civilian resistance to government policies, torture, disappearance and summary execution are used. The government has also severely restricted relief efforts by non-governmental and UN agencies.

For their part, the southern rebel groups have also committed human rights violations. They have abducted civilians, principally women and children, from their opponents, used starvation as a means of combat and deployed children as soldiers on a massive scale.

It has been estimated (U.S. Committee for Refugees) that at least 1.9 million people in southern and central Sudan have died during the past fifteen years as a direct result of civil war or war-related famine. It is believed that at least one out of every five southern Sudanese has died as a result of the civil war, and more than 80 per cent of southern Sudan's estimated five million population have been displaced at some time since 1983. Some four million Sudanese are internally displaced, more than any other country in the world.

The prime responsibility for the suffering of the people of Sudan is shared by the government, the SPLA, and the various other militia. All of them pursue a war that, according to almost all international experts, cannot be won. While a few profit from the conflict, many more civilians suffer. Sudan seems a level enough killing field to allow the war to continue for many years, unless both sides are persuaded that their interests lie in participation in a meaningful peace process.

Official Conflict Management

There is still no end in sight to Sudan's conflict after more than thirty years of fighting. As the war and the humanitarian crisis continue, there is little momentum for serious negotiations. Both the government and the SPLA seem to have settled into a brutal routine of accepting limited cease-fires which 'buy time' for both sides. They do not necessarily represent a commitment to peace by any party. The war rages on, perpetuating the conditions for famine.

In May 1998 the Sudanese government agreed with the SPLA on a referendum that could, in theory, lead to independence. However, no attempt has been made to allow the electorate to vote on the issue. In February 1999, President Bashir once again offered independence to the south but most of those closest to the situation remain sceptical. Their scepticism is fed by the continuing delays in setting dates for a fresh round of peace negotiations in Nairobi under the auspices of the regional *Inter-Governmental Authority on Development (IGAD)*.

Most African diplomats emphasise the importance of an African solution for the problems in Sudan. From non-African countries they expect pressure on the Sudanese government to return to the negotiating table and keep its promises. The IGAD mediation efforts, involving neighbouring countries Eritrea, Ethiopia, Kenya and Uganda, as well as the support from the (western) *IGAD Partners Forum*, are in line with this.

In September 1993, the regional Inter-Governmental Authority on Drought and Development (IGADD) launched a first peace initiative and agreement was reached between the Sudanese government and the two SPLA factions for talks later that year. Renewed talks between the government and the rebels began in May 1994 but ended in deadlock in September that year when the Sudanese government rejected a Declaration of Principles out of hand. There were two breaking points: the principle of separation between state and religion and the rights of self-determination of southern Sudan and other marginalised areas.

In July 1997, the government stated that the 1994 Declaration of Principles could be taken as 'a starting point for further discussions'. At the

NIMULE, SOUTH SUDAN: John (12), second from left is a Dinka boy from Bor. He says: 'I don't want to leave here, the other boys are my brothers.' The boys from the Palotaka school are orphans or separated from their parents. The Khartoum government has bombed the area with regular intervals causing massive displacement of the civilian population.

PHOTO CRISPIN HUGHES/LINEAIR

is agreed upon and reconciliation and reconstruction become the priority.

At the beginning of 1997 the Friends of IGAD was transformed into the *IGAD Partners Forum,* part of the overall IGAD Partners Committee (principally formed by the northern donors of the countries in the region). The EU and France are new members of the Partners Forum Committee, which is presently co-chaired by Italy and Norway.

International pressure on the warring parties has increased in recent years. Practically all donors have frozen their aid to Sudan, except for emergency relief. The European Parliament dispatched a fact-finding mission in 1995. In the same year both the UN and the Commission on Human and People's Rights of the Organisation of African Unity (OAU) called for improved human rights monitoring.

Millions of people in South Sudan are extremely vulnerable because of the war and crop failures. International food relief has become an important element in the subsistence economy of southern Sudan. However, it is also seen as an asset to be taxed, confiscated, expropriated, or otherwise taken for the war effort by both the government forces and the guerrillas. Food is power in Sudan.

Since 1989 *Operation Lifeline Sudan (OLS),* co-ordinated from Nairobi, Kenya, has provided the umbrella for relief activities from the UN and over 30 international NGOs. OLS has become

end of the year the government and the SPLA returned to the IGAD negotiating table, but shortly afterwards the talks were postponed.

Following a proposal by the US government, a Western support group for IGAD was initiated in 1995: the Friends of IGAD. Members included the US, Sweden, Italy and the Netherlands. The group has been involved in discrete diplomatic peacemaking efforts and foresees an important role for itself when peace the largest air relief in history. Its overall costs since 1989 are estimated at US$3 billion. Yet, the people of southern Sudan are no better protected against famine than they were in 1989.

The root cause of this anomaly lies in the OLS agreement itself, and in the principle of 'negotiated access' that underlies all NGO operations on the ground in southern Sudan. The UN and the aid agencies are bound to seek permission from the Khartoum government and the SPLA before delivering food. The positive aspect is of course that in this way a possibility is created to distribute food in rebel-held areas. However, the destination and the quantity of food has to be cleared with both sides.

The UN is anxious to stay on good terms with both sides and is unwilling to criticise when aid is blocked. February and March 1998 were critical months for the hungry people in Bahr el Ghazal but the government refused the UN access. UN officials complained, but not too loudly. Only in April, when television began to show the horror, did the government allow the delivery of food to resume.

Donor countries face another request from the World Food Program for 1999. Many are exasperated, believing they are financing an endless war in the name of feeding the hungry. Consequently, western countries are once again searching for a political way out.

Since the American search for a 'peaceful solution' collapsed together with the outbreak of the Ethiopian-Eritrean war, the IGAD Partners Forum is once more at the forefront. Their representatives recently visited Khartoum as well as Nairobi, where the SPLA has its office. It is hoped that the present cease-fire in the south-west can be prolonged and extended towards other southern areas. The European members of the IGAD Partners Forum are hoping that a referendum on South-Sudan's future could break the present stalemate. At a meeting in Oslo in March 1999, the IGAD Partners Forum discussed the provision of financial support to a new Kenyan special envoy to 'mount a concentrated and continuous mediation effort'.

A recent review of the Kenya-led IGAD Sudan peace process, sponsored by the US Institute for Peace, suggested however that the four main IGAD-countries (Kenya, Eritrea, Ethiopia, and Uganda) disagree about the best overall solution. The Ethiopia-Eritrea conflict, and shifting regional and international alliances 'may have paralysed the IGAD secretariat', the report says. Privately, representatives of the IGAD Partners Forum express frustration about what they see as a lack of genuine commitment from the IGAD-members.

Multi-Track Diplomacy
Domestic
Surprisingly enough, after almost forty years of war, indigenous conflict management mechanisms are still operational in Sudan. Traditional, tribal structures are the oldest institutions of civil society for peace-making mediation and conflict resolution. The conflicts usually centre around cattle or pastures.

In a study for the Swedish Life & Peace Institute, Dr Raphael K. Badal found that the institutions of elders and chiefs have managed to retain their status as important socio-political factors, influencing and guiding everyday social and economic interactions within and between groups at the grassroots level. 'They appear to be the principal instruments for reconciling ethnic groups who contest such issues as grazing land, water holes, and instances of livestock raiding.' This suggests that these structures constitute a basis upon which a new civil society can be built. 'These structures might be strengthened or empowered to be more effective both in the local context with possible effect upon the nation as a whole.'

Besides these traditional structures, churches, women groups and local NGOs have a special role to play in situations where government and the international NGOs either cannot or prefer not to act. Several peace conferences and agreements have been organised in recent years by churches, women groups and community leaders, mostly to address serious intra-tribal fighting or to promote emwara (reconciliation).

It is important that those seeking peace in Sudan take not of this conclusion for it is obvious that the large-scale conflict cannot be resolved without a significant broadening of the peace process to include all segments of society. The fact that it has not been possible to stop this war, which has been going on for so long, is a very strong indication of the weaknesses of conventional diplomatic approaches that try to address peace issues exclusively through military and political leaders. It is this context that the peace endeavours of the churches in both the north - the *Sudan Council of Churches* - and in the south - *the New Sudan Council of Churches* - as well as NGOs are important.

In March 1999 the Sudan Council of Churches facilitated a successful Dinka-Nuer West Bank Peace and Reconciliation Conference, held in Bahr el Ghazal. The *Wunlit Dinka-Nuer Covenant* was signed by more than 300 Dinka and Nuer chiefs, community and church leaders, women and youth. It boldly promises an end to seven and half years of conflict between the two groups and declared a permanent cease-fire with immediate effect (the full text of the agreement is available through Sudan Infonet on its Internet Website).

The *Sudan Working Group under the All African Conference of Churches (AACC)* - based in Nairobi - monitors all peace efforts in Sudan and fulfils a special, co-ordinating role in the peace efforts of the churches.

The *Ecumenical Forum on Sudan* under the World Council of Churches (Geneva) monitors and co-ordinates all efforts by the Sudanese churches and church-based development agencies concerning peace in Sudan. Already in 1972, the Addis Ababa agreement was achieved through the mediation of the AACC and the World Council of Churches. Both organisations signed the agreement as guarantors of peace, but failed to follow through this commitment.

The *Sudanese Catholic Information Office (SCIO)* is the Press Office of the Sudanese Catholic Bishops, working in the nongovernment controlled areas of Sudan. It started in April 1995 and is located in Nairobi. SCIO disseminates information on Sudan through the publication of documents, articles, videos and radio programmes. The *Sudan Monthly Report* is distributed by email.

One of the most active indigenous NGOs is the *Sudanese Women's Voice for Peace (SWVP)*, which is involved in several peace activities from women's perspectives entailing the creation of mutual bonds between women in the communities and various traditional institutions in the war-torn areas in the south. SWVP

organises peace-building training, creates peace-demonstration centres in southern villages and supports small-scale local development projects. The organisation is based in Nairobi, Kenya, but has many active members in southern Sudan. SWVP cooperates with churches, NGOs such as Pax Christi and other women's groups.

The *Sudanese Women Association in Nairobi (SWAN)*, an organisation of women refugees from different ethnic and political groupings, aims for reconciliation and respect for human rights within the Sudanese refugee camps in Kenya. SWAN aims to contribute to the political empowerment of Sudanese women.

The *New Sudan Women Federation (NSWF)* aims to improve the human rights situation of women in the liberated areas in the south.

The *Nuba Relief, Rehabilitation and Development Society (NRRDS)* published an open letter in February 1999 addressed to UN's secretary-general Kofi Annan on the situation in the Nuba Mountains, where an estimated 200,000 people have already been denied the right of humanitarian assistance for ten years.

The Khartoum-based *Disaster Management and Refugees Studies Institute (DIMARSI)* aims 'to advocate awareness and capacity building of community leaders at grass root level on conflict resolution, peace building and human rights.' Through its peace support programme, DIMARSI is targeting local leaders for peace training. The organisation also started a national campaign to ban landmines. DIMARSI cooperates with the US Institute for Multi-Track Diplomacy and International Alert (UK).

International
Sudan Focal Point is a network of church-based development agencies which collects all kinds of information on and from Sudan. Until May 1997 it was based in Copenhagen, since then, the *Life & Peace Institute* has been the lead agency for the network. Project officers working in Europe and in the region itself monitor the situation in Sudan and the Horn region and support the churches on advocacy issues on peace, human rights, etc.

Through its Horn of Africa programme, the Swedish Life & Peace Institute has been at the forefront of efforts to fashion new and creative approaches to peace building in the region. The organisation supports grassroots peace-building initiatives in Sudan (churches, women's organisations), in the north as well as in the south. It also publishes the bimonthly Horn of Africa Bulletin and commissions research on issues such as the role of local traditional structures in peace efforts.

The *International Resource Group of Disarmament and Demobilization (IRG)* aims to stimulate a more focused and sustained exploration of alternative security structures and disarmament measures for the Horn of Africa region as a whole, including Sudan. The work of the organisation is based on the assumption that the long-term stability and prosperity of the Horn region depends on the integration of security, humanitarian, political and economic development measures. The secretariat is constituted by Arbeitsgemeinschaft Kirchlicher Entwicklungsdienst (AGKED) in Germany, Project Ploughshares at the Institute of Peace and Conflict Studies in Canada, the All African Conference of Churches - Peace Consultancy in Nairobi and the Life & Peace Institute, Sweden.

Through its Conflict Resolution Program *The Carter Center*, established by former U.S. president Jimmy Carter, closely monitors conflicts in several countries. In Sudan the organisation has been involved in dispute resolution since 1989. In March 1995, all major Sudanese parties agreed to a four-month partial cease-fire, negotiated by the Carter Center, which enabled relief workers to conduct an extensive vaccination campaign.

The *U.S. Committee for Refugees* has facilitated meetings to discuss prospects for peace in which the main Sudanese rebel leaders took part. The organisation has also regularly conducted public and private policy discussions with US officials regarding policy options vis-à-vis Sudan. In March 1999, the organisation urged the UN's Security Council to act decisively to schedule a specific date for the people of southern Sudan to vote within three years on their own political independence.

Pax Christi International has published several reports on Sudan, based partly on its own research. Its Dutch section supports local and regional peace initiatives through the Sudanese

NGO Women's Voice for Peace and the New Sudanese Council of Churches. Local capacities for peace are supported through integral programmes in which self-generating income processes are linked with trauma counselling.

The *Centre for Strategic Initiatives of Women* (CISW) joined with African women's coalitions in 1995 to found SIHA, *Strategic Initiative for the Horn of Africa*. CSIW organises conflict management training programmes in the Horn, focusing on negotiation, mediation, consensus-building, resources for peace building and follow-up actions to implement agreements. It also works to establish community peace centres where local residents of diverse backgrounds can gather to identify common objectives and plan local peace projects.

Sudan Update, an UK-based centre, publishes the Sudan Update Newsletter, but also compiles background documents for advocacy purposes and conducts research and liaison work for the media, NGOs, lawyers, parliamentarians, academics and human rights bodies.

Christian Solidarity International, an UK-based NGO, involved in a controversy over Sudan's slave trade, claims to have ransomed over 9,000 Sudanese slaves since the start of its campaign in 1995. Organisations including Human Rights Watch and Unicef have warned that the ransoming of slaves offers no solution and even makes the problem worse.

At the end of 1998, four large relief organisations, all of them with projects in Sudan, co-ordinated their efforts to advocate for a more practical approach to tackling the civil war. Aid alone, they say, will not end the disasters that have cost so many lives. Instead, a forceful and positive lobby for peace should be generated. Representatives of *Oxfam, CARE International, Médicins sans Frontières and Save the Children* met with Security Council members at Sweden's UN mission to press their campaign. 'Humanitarian assistance alone, in a political vacuum, will not solve Sudan's problems nor stop the next famine. What we need is the political will to end the war', said Guy Tousignant, secretary-general of CARE International.

The *Inter-Africa Group* organised a conference in Kampala, Uganda in February 1999 on 'Human Rights in Sudan in the Transitional Period'.

Some other NGOs with (limited) activities related to the Sudan conflict are Norwegian Church Aid, the African Centre for the Constructive Resolution of Disputes, the Institute for African Alternatives (London, UK), Lutheran World Relief, Nairobi Peace Initiative, Project Ploughshares, Dutch Interchurch Aid, Cordaid and Novib (Netherlands).

Prospects

At the beginning of 1998, the government of Sudan seemed to be completely isolated and inaccesible: besieged by its neighbours, attacked by increasingly confident rebels, the target of UN sanctions for sponsoring terrorism, and almost friendless. All that has changed. With luck, and skilful diplomacy, Sudan's Islamic government has begun to end its isolation and to win back the political initiative in the civil war.

The luck was in the discovery of oil and in the outbreak of fortuitous foreign wars. Sudan recently exported its first ever oil and hopes to its import bills by a quarter. Sudan's neighbours are now caught up in their own conflicts: Eritrea and Ethiopia with each other, and Uganda in Congo. Both Eritrea and Ethiopia are now trying to make peace with the government in Khartoum. And the Sudanese government has seized the chance to improve its image and is trying to lure leading opponents back from exile. A recent decision to allow legal opposition parties hints at a new willingness to contemplate change. On the question of southern self-determination president Bashir stated that he prefers southern secession to a continuation of the war.

So, is peace within reach? Far from it. First of all, the new regional truces are tactical, and likely to wither as old animosities resurface. Uganda still supports the southerners and the Khartoum government will continue to support Ugandan dissidents. Eritrea too, is convinced that Sudan supports its rebels as part of the Islamic agenda.

At least two fundamental internal controversies remain. The first one concerns the character of the Sudanese state. The opposition, headed by Sadiq el Mahdi, the ousted prime minister, wants a democratic, secular Sudan. The NIF-government rejects secularism and wants Islamic law to prevail.

The split between the North and the South is now probably unbridgeable, and some day a referendum on the status of the South might be held. But what South? In the beginning of 1999 the Khartoum-regime launched a major new offensive against the SPLA in the Nuba Mountains. 'Their intention is to cut us from the world so that the Nuba are not on the agenda at the coming IGAD-talks, and they can just talk about the problem of southern Sudan', a local SPLA-commander commented. He is probably right. Both the government and the opposition in the north are determined not to let the Nuba secede. Their fear is that any concession to the Nuba would encourage rebellion among the north's other marginalised peoples in Darfur (western Sudan), the Red Sea Hills and the Blue Nile province.

The leaders of these areas want to ensure a process that would result in regional self-government with a federal system for Sudan. The federal system would recognise and protect the religions, cultures, and languages of these regions, the right of people to own their own land, and other civil and political rights. As long as these demands are not recognised, even self-determination for the south would not end the war in the rest of Sudan.

Recommendations

On January 14, 1999 the *United States Institute for Peace* convened a consultation on Sudan to generate recommendations for strengthening the negotiating process and to help refine some of the issues. Representatives of the main political parties and factions in Sudan attended the meeting, although a high-level delegation representing the government in Khartoum was unable to attain visas to the US. The consultation concluded that:

- The IGAD process needs to remain the vehicle for mediation and negotiation, with Kenya continuing to take the lead.
- The process must be strengthened through international assistance to permit more effective and sustained negotiations.
- The countries of the IGAD Partners Forum including the US, along with the UN and the Organisation of African Unity, need to give the financial and technical support to make the IGAD process more effective.

- The Declaration of Principles agreed by both parties needs to frame the negotiations. By giving particular attention to the principle of self-determination for the South, the process might make more significant progress.

Ambassador Francis M. Deng, Sudan's former Minister of State, added that the northern opposition parties should be included in the IGAD negotiations, which should also address the most pressing needs in the north.

Local conflicts are on the rise in Sudan. To avoid a further 'Afghanisation' of the country, local reconciliation is of the utmost importance to create the basis for a future national reconciliation. Representation of civil actors in the IGAD negotiations seems a prerequisite. Sudanese Women's Voice for Peace, Bishop Taban of the Diocese of Torit, and the new Sudan Council of Churches have started a lobby for this integration of the civil sector within the IGAD peace process. They are supported, amongst others, by Pax Christi International, Sudan Focal Point and the Life and Peace Institute.

Service Information

Newsletters and Periodicals

Horn of Africa Bulletin - bimonthly newsletter published by the Life & Peace Institute, Uppsala/Sweden

Sudan Update - independent media review published twice monthly. www.sas. upenn.edu/African_Studies/Newsletters/menu_SD_Update

Sudan Monthly Report - published by the Sudanese Catholic Information Office (SCIO). www.peacelink.it/africa/scio/month

Sudan News and Views Newsletter (UK) - independent electronic newsletter: http://webzone1.co.uk/www/sudan/snvindex

Reports

African Rights
- Food and Power in Sudan - A Critique of Humanitarianism, 1997
- Justice in the Nuba Mountains of Sudan, 1997

Amnesty International
- Sudan - A new Clampdown on Political Opponents, 1997

Human Rights Watch
- Sudan - Global Trade, Local Impact. Arms transfers to all sides in the civil war in Sudan. Aug. 1998
- Famine in Sudan 1998 - The Human Rights Causes. March 1999

Life and Peace Institute
- Local Traditional Structures in Sudan - A base for rebuilding civil society and promoting peace and reconciliation. Dr Raphael Koba Badal. 1998

Minority Rights Group International
- Sudan: Conflict and Minorities. Peter Verney. 1995

Pax Christi International
- The French Connection. Report on the Political, Economic and Military Collaboration between Khartoum and Paris, 1995
- We have to sit down - Women, war and peace in southern Sudan. 1998

Save the Children Fund, CARE International and Oxfam GB
- Sudan: Who has the will for peace? 1998

US Committee for Refugees
- Quantifying Genocide in Southern Sudan and the Nuba Mountains, 1983-1998

USIP
- New Approaches to Peace in Sudan - Report on a USIP Consultation. 1999

Other Publications

Requiem for the Sudan - War, Drought and Disaster Relief on the Nile, by J. Millard Burr & Robert O. Collins. Westview Press, 1995

Their Brothers' Keepers - Regional Initiatives for Peace in Sudan, by Francis M. Deng (ed.). Inter-Africa Group, Addis Ababa/Ethiopia

War Of Visions - Conflicts of Identities in the Sudan, by Francis M. Deng. The Brookings Institute, 1995

Preventive Diplomacy - The Case of Sudan, by

Francis M. Deng. ACCORD, 1997
Crisis Response - Humanitarian BandAids in Sudan and Somalia, by J. Prendergast. Pluto Press, 1997.
The Politics of Liberation in South Sudan - An insiders view, by Peter Adwok Nyaba.

Selected Internet Sites

www.members.tripod.com/~SudanInfonet (Sudan Working Group-US)
www.incore.ulst.ac.uk/cds/countries/sudan (many more titles of publications and reports as well as addresses of NGOs)
www.sudan.net (Sudanese links and information, news)
http://members.aol.com/NewSudan (New Sudan Online: information on SPLM and their concepts of 'New Sudan')
i-cias.com/abubakr (Nubian Home Page)
www.sufo.demon.co.uk (UK-based Sudan Foundation)
www.columbia.edu/~tm146/Khar/UofK.html (University of Khartoum)
www.refugees.org/news/crisis/sudan.htm (US Committee for Refugees)

Resource Contacts

Alex de Waal/Rakiya Omaar - African Rights .
Francis Deng - formerly Sudan's minister of State for Foreign affairs, currently senior fellow at the Brookings Institution, US. Email: fdeng@brook.edu
El Hadi Guma Gadal - Advisor for conflict resolution and human right program DIMARSI, Khartoum.
Yvonne Heselmans - Pax Christi, Utrecht/The Netherlands . Email:paxchristi@antenna.nl
Bethuel Kiplagat - All African Conference of Churches, Nairobi/Kenya.
Abdul Mohammed - Inter-Africa Group, Addis Ababa/Ethiopia.
Jemera Rone - Sudan researcher Human Rights Watch. Email: hrwnyc@hrw.org
David R. Smock, coordinator Africa activities United States Institute for Peace .
Email: ds@usip.org
Bea Stolte - Dutch Interchurch Aid, Utrecht/The Netherlands.
Email: beas@dia.antenna.nl

Susanne Thurfjell - programme officer Life & Peace Institute, Uppsala/Sweden. Email: susanne.thurfjell@life-peace.org
Peter Verney - Sudan Update, West Yorkshire/UK. Email: sudanupdate@gn.apc.org

Organisations

New Sudan Council of Churches
P.O. Box 52802, Nairobi, Kenya
Tel: +254 2 446 966
Fax +254 2 44 715
email: nssc-nbo@maf.org

Sudan Council of Churches
Interchurch House, St. 35, New Extension, POB 469, Khartoum
Tel: +249 11 441 855/442 859

Sudanese Women Association in Nairobi
P.O. Box 67464
Nairobi, Kenya
Tel. +254 2 571 726
fax +254 2 560 329

Nuba Relief, Rehabilitation and Development Society
P.O. Box 27531
Nairobi, Kenya
Tel/fax +254 2 448 540
email NRRDS@maf.org

Data on the following organisations can be found in the Directory section:
Inter-Governmental Authority on Development (IGAD)
All African Conference of Churches (AACC)
Sudanese Catholic Information Office (SCIO)
Sudanese Women's Voice for Peace (SWVP)
Disaster Management and Refugees Studies Institute (DIMARSI)
Life and Peace Institute (LPI)
International Resource Group of Disarmament and Demobilization (IRG)
The Carter Center
Centre for Strategic Initiatives of Women (CISW)
InterAfrica Group
Nairobi Peace Initiative (NPI)
United States Institute for Peace (USIP)

Central Africa

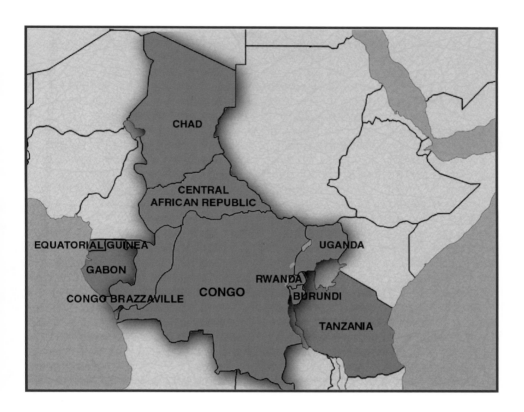

Shifting Alliances, Extraterritorial Conflicts and Conflict Management

Once seen as peripheral, enclosed and of no political or economic interest, the Great Lakes region of central Africa is today at the centre of a major geopolitical and economic shake-up with repercussions for the whole continent. Countries as far apart as southern Namibia, northern Libya, western Angola and eastern Uganda are directly involved in a regional war that knows no boundaries ♦

By Véronique Parqué and Filip Reyntjens*

Even if we look farther back in time, at for instance the unresolved problem of the Tutsi refugees who fled their country during and after the 1959-1961 revolution, the attack by the Rwanda Patriotic Front (RPF) from Uganda (1990) and the civil war that ensued, or the assassination of Burundi's democratically-elected president, which sparked the massacre of tens of thousands of people and a civil war (1993). The region's sharp destabilisation began with the Rwandan genocide that definitively put an end to the peace deal strongly backed by the international community. Kivu, which had just embarked on a fragile peace process, was overrun with almost 200,000 Burundian refugees at the end of 1993 and more than a million from Rwanda in mid-1994, when the RPF was on the brink of seizing power. That was the start of the spreading of the Burundian and Rwandan conflicts and the implosion of the state of Zaire, which was to see two wars in two years.

Although the internal conflicts of Rwanda and Burundi have had major repercussions for the stability of the entire region, and - alongside Kivu and ex-Zaire - are the site of the regional and continental conflict known as the 'Congo war' which broke out in August 1998, our comments will focus on the regionalisation of the conflicts and the attempts of international institutions, be they the UN, the EU, the OUA (Organization of African Unity) or regional organisations such as the Southern African Development Community (SADC) to resolve the regional conflict.

Regionalisation of conflicts

Regionalisation[1] has been exacerbated by three factors: the geographical proximity of the conflicts, population flows and a game of alliances. At the beginning of the 1990s, Rwanda, Burundi and two Kivu regions had a population of almost twenty million spread over a surface area of around 180,000 km2. That was around one hundred inhabitants per square kilometre, far and away the highest regional density on the continent. The population pressure was certainly greater in Rwanda and Burundi, but the Kivu regions were equally exposed to serious tensions over land, especially in the border areas of Rwanda and Burundi. Age-old population flows have made international borders porous. The nationality debate found its clearest expression in Zaire, culminating in the sudden arrival of more than a million Rwandans in mid-1994. Alliances, meanwhile, are as much 'macro' (such as the Mobutu-Habyarimana axis before April 1994) as at a 'micro' local level (in Kivu, for instance, first 'natives' against Banyarwanda, then Hutus against Tutsis).

These three factors have combined to produce a highly unstable political and military arena. However, this conflict-ridden zone cannot be divorced from a broader context. It forms a junction with two other conflicts, in Angola and Sudan. Mobutu's Zaire forms the link, for two reasons. Firstly, the Zairean state had nearly disappeared, leaving a 'gaping hole' in the porous borders with almost no armies or national administrations, very poor communications between outlying areas and the centre and between outlying areas themselves,

181

plus an informal economy. Just like nature, geopolitics hates a void. In circumstances like these, the void is filled by other players, be they insiders or outsiders. What is more, Zaire is involved in internal conflicts raging both in the region and in the continent. In the Great Lakes region it backed, passively at any rate, rebel Ugandan, Rwandan and Burundian movements, which used Zaire as the base to launch strikes against their respective countries. In Sudan, Zaire backed the Khartoum central government in its war against southern Sudanese guerrillas, especially the SPLA, which is supported by Kampala (Uganda), Asmara (Eritrea) and Addis Ababa (Ethiopia). Finally, the backing given by the Mobutu regime to UNITA rebels in Angola did not end with the Lusaka accords in 1994. Elsewhere, international allies are behind the scenes. France sided with Khartoum, the 'Hutu' rebels in Rwanda and Burundi, and UNITA; the United States with the SPLA, Eritrea, Ethiopia, Uganda, Rwanda and Angola. Alliances of convenience run along two axes: one groups France, Khartoum, Zaire, the Hutu rebels in Rwanda and Burundi, and UNITA. The other groups the United States, Eritrea, Ethiopia, the SPLA, Uganda, Rwanda and Angola. Even though these conflicts have no intrinsic link, geographical proximity to Zaire and the game of alliances have raised the spectre of a war zone stretching from Angola to Eritrea.

During the first war in the Congo (ex-Zaire) - according to the Rwandan vice-president Kagama himself, in an interview with the *Washington Post* on July 9, 1997 - the AFDL rebels' operation was directed from start to finish by the Kigali (Rwanda) regime. And though this eastern war began with an essentially Tutsi core (Banyamulenge and Rwandans), they were fast joined by Ugandan and Burundian troops, along with soldiers from Eritrea, Ethiopia, Somalia and Uganda on temporary contracts[2].

The second Congo war, which began in 1998, proved these alliances of convenience to be unstable. Kabila swept to power with the help of foreign troops, but in July 1998 he sent them home. In the days that followed Kabila's decision, eyewitnesses reported seeing large numbers of Rwandan and Ugandan troops heading across borders toward the east of the

Congo. The rebellion spread swiftly in the east as the Ugandan and Rwandan troops spearheaded the offensive. Then, on August 4, the rebel forces launched a daring airborne operation in lower Congo, west of Kinshasa. On the western front, Kabila was saved by Angolan expeditionary troops sent as reinforcements thanks to an August 19 decision by Zimbabwe, Namibia and Angola in Harare to grant a request for help under the auspices of the SADC, which the Congo had just joined. Attempts by rebel troops to invade Kinshasa were thwarted by Congolese troops and by the local population, backed by the Zimbabwean army. Angola and Zimbabwe sent thousands of reinforcements, and Namibia supplied several hundred. By the end of September 1998, Chad, Libya and Sudan were involved directly or indirectly, while several French-speaking West African countries voiced political support for Kabila, condemning the aggression against the Democratic Republic of the Congo at a summit in Libreville, Gabon on September 24, 1998. The situation rapidly deteriorated into what Susan Rice, U.S. assistant secretary of state for African affairs, called 'the first African world war'.

We only have room here to look briefly at what motivates the pro-Kabila alliance.

Angola's concerns were threefold. The 'Mobutist' generals Nzimbi and Baramoto were seen in Kigali before the war broke out and some *ancien regime* politicians openly joined the new rebellion, as did some ex-FAZ (the former Zairean army) units. Moreover, Angolan intelligence services were convinced that contacts existed between UNITA, the rebel command and its Rwandan and Ugandan patrons. In the likely event of civil war breaking out again (which was to happen a few months later), Luanda's choice was clear - even if its relations with Kabila were far from perfect.

Zimbabwe had several reasons for getting involved. The Congo owed Zimbabwe a large debt, amassed during the 1996-97 war, and the Zimbabweans feared they would never be repaid if Kabila was deposed. Secondly, Zimbabwean financiers had been trying for years to penetrate the Congolese market and invest in the mining sector, at the expense of South African companies in particular. Some Mugabe associates and high-ranking officers stood to

KINSHASA, CONGO, Rwandan fugitives

lose large amounts of money if Kabila were to fall. Finally, the 'old revolutionary' Mugabe saw in the Congolese crisis a chance to reassert some of the regional influence he had largely lost to Mandela, and to oppose the 'new leaders' like Museveni and Kagame, selected chiefly by the Americans, to the great detriment of Mugabe.

The realignments go even further. The Mai-Mai traditional warriors in the east, who fought Kabila before he came to power, now allied themselves him within an 'anti-Tutsi' coalition. In an even more spectacular volte-face, the ex-FAZ and the Interahamwe militias came over to the Kabila camp even though Kabila and his then allies had inflicted huge losses on the Rwandan Hutus less than a year earlier. The FAR (former Rwandan Hutu government troops) were brought in from neighbouring countries, rearmed, retrained and massively deployed. According to a United Nations report, 'shifting alliances in and around the DRC have unexpectedly worked to the advantage of the forces of the previous government', since the ex-FAR and the Interahamwe militias 'have now become a major component of the international alliance against the Congolese rebels and their presumed patrons, Rwanda and Uganda[3].'

Finally Sudan, which backed the Mobutu regime against the Kabila rebels, now supports Kabila against the new uprising. That has to be seen in the context of the conflict between Khartoum and Kampala.

Conflict management by international institutions

Diplomatic efforts during the first war in the Congo were ambiguous. After the Zairean regime agreed to negotiate with the rebels, the Alliance of Democratic Forces for the Liberation of Congo (AFDL) pretended to pursue a negotiated solution and the international community chose to believe it. In actual fact, after the fall of Kisangani the AFDL pursued a strategy that Museveni had already used to good effect in Uganda: 'talk and fight'. 'Talk' was part of a military strategy rather than a genuine will to reach a political agreement.

Moreover, the diplomatic drives by the Western countries involved in the conflict pulled in diverging directions. Until March 1997, the American and French agendas were so opposed and the distrust between the two powers so great that coordinated action proved impossible. America was heavily involved: fighting the Khartoum regime and keen to get rid of Mobutu, the United States actively supported their Ugandan and Rwandan allies and thus risked destabilising the entire region. France put its money on the other side, but lacked the moral authority to influence the course of events. And by the time Washington and Paris had a certain rapprochement it was too late, because Kabila felt he was within a hair's breadth of victory. He became uncontrollable at that point, an 'unguided missile' in the words of an American official. On top of that, there was no coordination between the various mediation attempts: first Kenya, then South Africa, then special envoys from the UN, the EU, the OAU, the United States, other bilateral players, and so on. At the beginning of April 1997, UN Secretary-General Kofi Annan expressed concern at the large number of mediators, saying there were 'too many cooks in this broth' and urging them to submit to the authority of UN special envoy Mohamed Sahnoun[4]. But without the support of America and therefore lacking political and military clout, Sahnoun was powerless and Kabila knew it. The 1996-1997 Congo war showed that the ability of international players to influence events in Africa has diminished sharply, to the advantage of local and regional figures who have their own agendas and the great plus-point of a political and military presence on the spot. In this sense, as Gerard Prunier has rightly pointed out[5], the importance attached to a Franco-American confrontation has definitely been overplayed, by the press in particular.

The 'international community' proved somewhat better able to mediate in the second Congo war. Numerous attempts at mediation were launched on August 8, 1998 with an urgent regional summit at Victoria Falls which brought together the heads of state of the DRC, Zimbabwe, Rwanda, Uganda, Zambia, Namibia and Tanzania. A joint mediation drive by Zambia, the OAU, the UN and the SADC managed to persuade the warring sides to seek a peace agreement (the Lusaka accord). That accord gives a central role to a UN peacekeeping force, though with the cooperation of the OAU. If the UN did not send a force, responsibility for peacekeeping would pass to the OAU. The accord spells out the tasks assigned to the peacekeeping mission: cooperating with an OAU/mixed military commision to implement the accord; observing and verifying hostilities; investigating violations of the cease-fire accord and the measures needed to enforce it; supervising the warring sides' disengagement; supervising the redeployment of forces in defensive positions in conflict zones; collecting weapons from civilians and planning and supervising the withdrawal of all foreign troops; disarming armed groups; identifying the perpetrators of crimes against humanity and other war criminals; bringing those responsible for genocide before an international tribunal; repatriation; and the reassimilation into society of members of armed groups. The agreement looks just like a classic peace accord whose central pillar is the creation of a peace-keeping force that will guarantee its implementation. It can, for instance, be compared with the Arusha accords for Rwanda, which contained similar provisions.

But there are several shadows over what could be a bright picture.

Firstly, a cease-fire was in theory supposed to have come into effect on July 11, 1999, but one of the main sides involved in the conflict, the rebels, did not sign the pact because of leadership struggles, and some of their representatives made clear that they would continue fighting. That poses two problems: first, the parties' prior consent[6] - which according to Chapter 6 of the United Nations Charter is a prerequisite for the deployment of any peacekeeping mission - is absent. Furthermore, not all are equally respecting the second condition, a cease-fire.

Secondly, the pact does not specify whether the UN-led peace-keeping mission will be in accordance with Chapter 6 or Chapter 7 of the United Nations Charter, although only the latter chapter authorises peacekeepers to use force.

RWANDA, Returning refugees

Should it transpire that not all the parties have a genuine will to implement the peace accord, as was the case in Rwanda for instance, a mandate under Chapter 6 could prove inadequate.

Thirdly, nothing is specified in terms of the composition of the mission, its strength and logistics. Given that since the failure of the peace-keeping operation in Ethiopia and later in Rwanda, no western country is willing to send troops to Africa (except perhaps for France, which since Rwanda would never be accepted as a neutral force by the combatants), one wonders which countries would take part in this mission. The vastness of the Congo, the distrust between the warring sides and the complexity of the conflict could discourage more than one member of the Security Council or potential contributor of forces.

Fourthly, the creation of an ad hoc international criminal tribunal - when the idea of setting up an International Criminal Court to try serious violations of international humanitarian law in Burundi has been the subject of constant disagreement among members of the Security Council - will not be easy. Should UN member states fail to act, it is foreseen that the OAU could carry out peace-keeping operations. That too presents problems, however. The 'mechanism of prevention, management and resolution of conflicts' installed by the OAU in 1993 has given it some influence - limited, though, by its meagre resources - in preventing and managing conflicts with mediation missions and observation forces. But it was never envisaged at the outset that the 'mechanism' would involve peace keeping. The issue was meant to be debated at the OAU summit of heads of state and government in 1998, but it was postponed. In any case, the OAU is so strapped for funds that it would be forced to appeal for donations outside the Organisation, and that too could prove problematic.

Conclusions and prospects

Experience in the Great Lakes region and elsewhere in Africa has shown that since the establishment of the 'new world order' marked by a policy of conditionality, prevention and management of conflicts, external players have turned out to have very limited influence in internal and regional situations when there is an emergency. Local, national and regional players set the agenda, which entails pursuing their own, usually short-term interests. A regional approach would therefore appear desirable, in theory. The OAU and the SADC could be the appropriate bodies. But in a war of continental dimensions, most members of the OAU or the SADC are, as we have seen, directly or indirectly involved and that significantly reduces the chances of mediation by one of the member countries.

Should Africa, for that matter, give up traditional mediation - usually conducted by a head of state, a former head of state, an incumbent president or a minister of one of the member states? The advantage of this kind of mediation is that it revolves around a political figure who has an indisputable authority in the region. But the disadvantage is the distrust over whether or not the mediator in question is acting in a purely objective way. This approach can, in certain cases, bear fruit. But where it proves impractical it would be wiser to strengthen

regional institutions such as the OAU or the SADC by endowing them with more funds, but most of all with more autonomy, with regard to member states. That would allow the institution to be viewed as a guarantor of the general interest of its members, rather than the sum of the various members' interests in the conflict.

Lastly, if these supranational public bodies prove indispensable in managing and resolving existing conflicts, they should - within a more long-term policy, not in an emergency one - be given a greater role in the prevention of developing conflicts. This could be achieved with a carefully considered social, economic and cultural policy[7] capable of bringing together all the players: the local population, civil society, bilateral and multilateral alliances, external non-governmental organisations. This way everyone could join in the building of a more tolerant society where conflict management would be an exceptional occurrence.

*   **Filip Reyntjes is professor at Antwerp University (Belgium) and President of the Centre for the Study of the Great Lakes Region of Africa. Véronique Parqué is researcher at the same Centre.**

1   For a more detailed examination see F. Reyntjens, The War of the Great Lakes: Shifting alliances and extraterritorial conflicts in central Africa (L'Harmattan, Paris, to be published.)

2   See E. Kennes, The War in the Congo in F. Reyntjens and S. Marysse, The Africa of the Great Lakes, 1997-1998 edition, Centre for research into the African Great Lakes region (L'Harmattan, Anvers and Paris, 1998, p251 onwards.)

3   United Nations Security Council, Final Report of the International Commission of Enquiry (Rwanda), November 18, 1998, S/1998/1096, paragraphs 86-87.)

4   Le Monde, April 2, 1997

5   G. Prunier, "The Kivu crisis and its consequences in the Great Lakes region" (Herodote, no. 86-87, 3rd-4th quarter 1997, p55.)

6   This requirement is based on the principles of sovereign equality and respect for territorial integrity which protects a state against any non-consensual entry by a foreign country; the principle of non-interference which prohibits any interference in the internal affairs of a country; and the principle of not resorting to violence, which forbids any foreign occupation and any interference (on this point, see O. Paye, "Peacekeeping operations and the new local disorders" in In Search of the New World Order, UN changes and challenges (Brussels, Editions Complexe, 1993, pp93-136.)

7   On the harmful effects of ill-conceived cooperation, see P. Uvin, Aiding violence, The development entreprise in Rwanda (Kumarian Press, 1998.)

A Region at War

Central Africa can be defined as the area from Chad in the north to Angola and Zambia in the south, excluding the countries of the Horn. Besides those countries, it includes Cameroon, Central African Republic, Equatorial Guinea, Gabon, Congo (Brazzaville), the Democratic Republic of Congo (DRC), Rwanda, and Burundi. Although most of these countries have links through commerce and their French or Belgian colonial and linguistic legacies and political cultures, this area's sense of regionalism and regional institutionalisation is possibly the weakest of the five that are examined in this volume ◆ *By* Michael S. Lund

The virtual absence of regionalism and a hegemonic power to promote it may be one reason why Central Africa is currently embroiled in the most extensive African inter-state war in its history. This war involves the armies of seven states with increasingly heavier weaponry. The regional war is being waged between the forces of the DRC under Laurent Kabila and several rebel forces over control of a vast country the size of most of the eastern part of the United States. Each of these sides have been joined by allies from neighbouring or nearby countries. Angola, Namibia, Zimbabwe, and Chad, with Libyan support, are backing Kabila, while Rwanda, Uganda, and Burundi have been aiding rebel factions.

Five post-Cold War internal conflicts have affected that war, and the current Congo war evolved out of three of these - in Rwanda, Burundi and the DRC's predecessor, Zaire. All these internal conflicts, and the recent one as well in Congo-Brazzaville next door, arose during periods of domestic economic and political liberalisation, and they reflect the tendency of rapid democratisation in weak states to provoke violent backlashes. From the time when we need to pick up this story, in Uganda in the 1980's, up to mid-1999, these proliferating Central Africa conflicts reveal how internal conflicts can generate armed forces who, in the absence of effective national conflict settlements and of mutual diplomatic and military restraints between states, can export conflict into neighbouring states. The spillover conflicts can then regionalise conflict even further if they threaten a wider set of neighbours and prompt them to enter the fray on one side or another, creating war between inter-state alliances.

Central Africa thus illustrates regionalism more in terms of the spread of violent civil conflicts outside their countries of origin than in terms of effective regional conflict resolution or prevention. No effective inter-state institutional mechanisms exist solely within the Central Africa region that can be activated to prevent further escalation of emerging intra-state violence, to mediate an end to escalated wars, or to contain their spillover. Nevertheless, the conflicts elicited many ad hoc and informal diplomatic mediation initiatives. Most of these were African-led efforts launched by groups of nearby states, influential heads of state, functioning sub-regional organisations outside Central Africa, or the OAU. Ancillary initiatives originated in the UN, Western governments, or NGOs from outside Africa.

Regional Mediation Efforts
The focus below is the succession of African regional diplomatic efforts that addressed the Rwanda, Burundi and Congo conflicts, respectively. As we shall see, none of the regional mediation efforts has yet succeeded in clearly resolving the civil conflicts they addressed, although peace processes have been initiated in each instance. Some reasons for their basic failure are given.

The Arusha Process and Rwanda, 1992-94
Since its independence in 1962, Rwanda has experienced recurrent confrontation between the majority Hutu community and its leaders, who had assumed power just before independence, and the minority Tutsi population and leadership. But Rwanda's most horrible confligration - and one of the most horrible

human tragedies of our time - followed a more open period of economic liberalisation and democratisation. A peace settlement through which the Hutu government and Tutsi rebels were to share power was mediated by regional leaders under the OAU, but the agreement was not effectively enforced by the UN peacekeepers and other international actors who were supposed to monitor its implementation. Instead, the deliberate subversion of the Peace Accords led to massive genocide and the take-over of the country by the rebel forces.

In 1973, a Hutu group from the north-west under President Juvenal Habyarimana took power in a military coup and established a one-party state. Hutu leaders increasingly defined the restive Tutsis within and outside the country as subversives and sought periodically to drive them out and confiscate their property. Each attempted revolt or purge produced new communities of Tutsi refugees in the surrounding countries, especially Burundi and Uganda, out of which expelled Tutsi political leaders could launch new incursions to make claim to the state.

By the late 1980's, many of the Tutsi diaspora had formed into a political movement based in Uganda refugee camps. The Rwandan Patriotic Front (RPF), and its military wing, the Rwandan Patriotic Army (RPA) was composed of Tutsi men who had learned guerrilla warfare from having served in the then-rebel National Resistance Army of Yoweri Museveni during its bid to overthrow Uganda's government. The RPA's invasion of Rwanda on October 1, 1990 began a civil war in which the RPA received support from Museveni, while Habyarimana's regime was aided by France and neighbouring Zaire under Joseph Mobutu.

From 1990 to 1993, the Habyarimana regime also came under increasing pressure from Tutsi as well as Hutu opposition parties, who were critical of the favouritism and corruption of the government. In response to oppression and helped by pressures on Habyarimana from international donors, the opposition was able to obtain acceptance of a multi-party system in June 1991. In April 1992, the opposition parties forced the Habyarimana governing party to share power in a coalition. The administration of the country was increasingly divided into spheres of

influence according to which parties were in the majority in an area.

This relative openness did not keep Habyarimana from trying to strengthen the political base of his party, the National Republican Movement for Democracy and Development (MRND), by once again appealing to the ethnic fears of Hutus and labelling Tutsis as fellow travellers who were in league with the invaders. With continuing oppression from the government, a coalition of these parties began to cooperate with the RPF by mid-1992 and were organising their own militias to protect their party members from the increasing practice of the MRND to use state security forces and its militia, the Interahamwe, to harass and kill opposition members. A campaign to criticise the government as illegitimate and to withhold taxes put the government under increasing financial pressure as it sought to counter the advances of the RPA.

As the RPA slowly gained ground but the war dragged on without victory by either side, and as the Habyarimana party faced losing political control, mediation efforts were undertaken by several regional and Western governments, under the aegis of the OAU. The Arusha Accords, signed in June 1993 and named after the nearby Tanzanian town where they were negotiated, called for a cease-fire, further political power-sharing and wholesale re-constituting of the Hutu-dominated army. Officers and enlistees of the RPF were to be integrated into a single national defence force. A UN peacekeeping force of about 2,500, including a civilian police component, would be installed to oversee transition to the new broader-based government. Although military experts recommended as many as 8,000 troops, much smaller OAU and UN military observer forces were put in place to monitor progress in the accords and look for human rights violations.

A number of factors led to delay and even active thwarting of the Accords' implementation by the government. Taking advantage of rifts between the opposition parties and the RPF, and within two of the opposition parties, Habyarimana felt strong enough to challenge the RPF politically under the banner of majority (i.e., Hutu) power. State-sponsored radio and newspaper propaganda suggested that Tutsis were dedicated to re-establishing total control and reminded Hutus of past Tutsi killings of Hutus. This message seemed to be corroborated by the events in neighbouring Burundi in October 1993, when the newly-elected Hutu president, Melchior Ndadaye, was assassinated by Tutsi army officers (see below). The Tutsi threat justified any measures of self-defence by Hutus against Rwanda's enemies and their accomplices (meaning all Tutsis and Hutus who supported the peace process). A few donors called attention to the lack of progress and ethnic demagoguery, and they withheld development assistance accordingly, but others made no clear linkage between aid and the unfolding political trends.

By late 1993, a group of high officials in the government was conspiring to reverse the Arusha peace process. Plans were put into effect to import and distribute thousands of machetes and small arms and to train Hutu men to eliminate Tutsis in certain regions. The strategy expected that when the RPA was provoked by these attacks to break the cease-fire, there would be an excuse for renewed hostilities. The murder of Belgian UN peacekeepers was expected to lead to a withdrawal of the UN military observer force (UNAMIR).

The opportunity to put the plan into action came on April 6, 1994 when a plane was mysteriously shot down that was bringing both Habyarimana and the second Hutu president of Burundi back from further talks in Arusha. Systematic massacres began by Hutu extremists of Tutsis and of Hutu moderates, about which the UN mission did nothing. When it appeared that the accords had broken down completely and the international community would not intervene to achieve order, the RPA renewed the war and by July 1994 succeeded in taking over the country. But the ethnic genocide begun in April resulted in up to 800,000 Tutsis and their sympathisers being massacred within a matter of weeks.

With a Tutsi government in power, Tutsi refugees soon began to return from Zaire, Burundi and Tanzania to which they had fled over the country's several decades of strife. Although thousands of Hutus were driven out of

the country as a result of the RPF military take-over and they filled refugee camps in eastern Zaire, they were encouraged to return. But within their ranks were many Hutus who were responsible for the massacre of Tutsis. The new government announced its intention to treat all citizens impartially and supported programs of reconciliation, but the overpopulated country's resources for housing and other basic needs came under even more severe strain. The mistrust between the two groups continues to haunt Rwanda's social and political life.

To add to the problem of accommodating the two ethnic communities, a renewed insurgency made up of expelled Hutu militants based in Zaire soon began carrying out ambushes and other attacks in the northwest areas of the country. The insurgents' stepped-up attacks on villages have sowed further ethnic animosities and put to the test the government's anti-insurgency methods in responding to the attacks. Rwanda may be returning to unstable conditions similar to 1990-94 when Hutus and Tutsi groups were jostling for control.

In sum, the inadequate enforcement of a regional peace settlement led to the re-eruption of ethnic violence on an unprecedented scale and the military victory of the rebel party to the agreement, who now preside as the government over a society that is still divided and increasingly embattled.

The Arusha Process and Burundi, 1996-99
Recurrent Hutu-Tutsi conflicts also defined the politics of post-independence Burundi and led to a civil war, but there, neither side achieved military superiority. As in Rwanda, the highest levels of genocidal violence, in October 1993, followed a period of openness within the established regime. After this eruption, several major actors from the international community sought to promote ethnic power-sharing and reconciliation. Their actions included a UN and numerous other special envoys, an OAU military observer mission, a UN commission of inquiry, many fact-finding and jawboning delegations, and an array of NGO initiatives on the ground. In 1996, the worsening conditions in the country stimulated an effort at regional diplomacy, again based in Arusha, and following

another coup, the imposition of economic sanctions by Burundi's regional neighbours. Despite this unusual degree of attention from multiple actors, and pressure from its neighbours, however, Burundi's violence escalated into civil war that still shows no signs of a cease-fire or conclusive settlement.

Following independence in 1962, increasingly Tutsi-dominated regimes discriminated against Hutus in educational opportunities and positions in the civil service and army. Despite the long-standing Tutsi dominance of government and social institutions, the numerical preponderance of Hutus, about 85 percent, made possible periodic rebellions. Burundi thus experienced coups, attempted coups and inter-communal violence in 1965, 1966, 1972, 1976, 1987, 1988, 1989, and 1991.

Although he seized power through a coup himself, in September 1987, the Tutsi President Major Pierre Buyoya responded to a new round of Hutu guerrilla killings and anti-Hutu army reprisals in 1988, and to the democratic sentiment then rising in Africa, by inaugurating an unprecedented series of economic and political reforms. These included a referendum on a new constitution and the country's first multiparty elections, set for June 1993. The two main political parties, UPRONA (Union pour le Progrès National), the longstanding government party which originated as an inter-ethnic nationalist movement, and FRODEBU (Front Démocratique de Burundi), the main Hutu party, were officially non-ethnic and include individuals of both groups. Nevertheless, they evolved into political movements that largely assert the interests of Tutsis and Hutus, respectively. The mid-1993 elections brought the decisive victory of the FRODEBU candidate Melchior Ndadaye as its first Hutu president, backed by a parliament dominated by FRODEBU.

This outcome was widely heralded as a triumph for majoritarian democracy and the dawn of a new era in Burundi politics. Although the election campaign had been deeply imbued with ethnic overtones, the new government appeared to be assuming effective control and gaining acceptance from the army and Tutsi

political leaders. Apparently, unlike Rwanda from 1990 to 1994, Burundi was making the transition to more representative government in a peaceful way.

However, on October 21, 1993, an army unit led by junior officers attacked the presidential palace and killed President Ndadaye and four other top Hutu officials. Though senior army officers claimed they faced pressure from the lower ranks, they most likely acquiesced in or supported these actions. Within hours, widespread killings mainly of Tutsis were instigated by Hutu activists in many parts of the country in the name of revenge for 'killing our president.' On their part, army paratroopers began first to rescue threatened groups, then to carry out massive reprisals against Hutu peasants and local officials, attacking civilians indiscriminately, including some Tutsis. Although the army leadership soon halted the coup and declared support for the remnant of the elected government, a massacre had been unleashed in which 50,000 to 100,000 Burundians are estimated to have been killed.

A 'collegial' government took charge in late 1993 until a new president could be elected by the parliament, as called for by the 1992 constitution. This period saw the first significant external action in direct response to Burundi's violence and its unstable politics. Under the rubric of the UN term 'preventive diplomacy,' Ambassador Ahmedou Ould Abdallah, a former Foreign minister from Mauritania, arrived in November to serve as the UN special representative (SRSG) in Burundi. Working with the government and opposition parties, the energetic envoy arranged in January and February 1994 a revision of the constitution to allow the Parliament to elect the new president and the formation of a coalition government, blessed by the army. The OAU also deployed about sixty military observers in the late spring, 1994 to monitor the behaviour of the army in the countryside.

In September 1994, the SRSG mediated an inter-ethnic power-sharing arrangement called the Convention of Government, which was the closest thing Burundi had to a peace settlement. It put the government on a provisional footing leading to elections in 1998, and gave forty-five per cent of the cabinet positions to Tutsi opposition parties. A prime minister elected by opposition parties had to countersign all presidential decisions. A National Security Council (NSC) would now approve all government decisions. Though the political leaders on the NSC were split evenly between FRODEBU and the opposition, the military representatives gave the Tutsi opposition an effective two-thirds majority and a veto over any action by the elected government. The power-sharing agreement appeased the Tutsi opposition's fears by offering it important government positions, but the concessions made many Hutus feel that the coup's results had effectively deprived the majority of its election victory, even though a Hutu was in the presidency.

In any case, despite the Convention agreement, the number of rural insurgency attacks, army reprisal campaigns, and local ethnic clashes increased. Hutu insurgents, among which the CNDD/FDD under former Interior minister Nyangoma were the most active, attacked military bases and government installations. In response, the army conducted more and more indiscriminate reprisal attacks, killing many civilians, often in joint operations with Tutsi militias. In 1995, the conflict also became increasingly regionalised. The attempt during the Rwandan genocide of the spring, 1994 to wipe out all Rwandan Tutsis and Hutu political dissidents had increased the fears of Burundi's Tutsis. The refugee and military camps of Rwandan Hutus in Zaire and Tanzania provided bases and supplies for Burundian Hutu guerrillas. On the other hand, the predominantly Tutsi armies of Rwanda and Burundi cooperated along their common border regions, reinforcing the Hutu belief in a regional Tutsi conspiracy.

The 1994 Rwandan genocide also prompted a surprising number of intergovernmental and non-governmental organisations (NGOs) to set up operations in Burundi in order to prevent 'another Rwanda.' Efforts at negotiations to achieve a cessation of hostilities were attempted by various international players. UN Secretary General Boutros-Ghali visited Burundi in July 1995 to reinforce the message of Ould Abdallah. The OAU sent several high-level delegations in

the spring and summer of 1995. The US at various times sent its national security adviser, UN representative, USAID administrator, two assistant secretaries of State, and appointed two special envoys, one for the region, and one for Burundi. The EU sent ministers.

In 1995, an effort by the UNSG to explore the possibility of a regional conference collapsed, but US former President Jimmy Carter took up this task. The Carter Center convened the presidents of all states in the region, plus Desmond Tutu and the ex-president of Mali, Amadou Toure, in Cairo in November 1995 and in Tunis in March 1996 to discuss the problems of the whole Great Lakes region. Their joint declarations agreed on a framework for refugee repatriation, an end to cross-border raids and arms trafficking, and support for the International Tribunal on Rwanda. The agreements, however, were not implemented.

In the spring of 1996, Burundi's East African neighbours then decided to try to take concerted action through a regional initiative under the leadership of former Tanzanian President Julius Nyerere. Nyerere had co-chaired the Carter Center's Tunis conference, and he had agreed to take primary responsibility for Burundi negotiations. In March, a meeting in Addis Ababa including representatives of both the UN and the OAU recognised him as lead negotiator on Burundi. Proceeding as an independent actor who had the international community's blessing, Nyerere tried in May and June to obtain a return to more representative government and to set up negotiations with the insurgents. But this approach was rejected by the Burundi Tutsi leadership.

Alarmed by Nyerere's initial inability to make progress, the major East African states then opened a summit on Burundi in Arusha, Tanzania in June 1996 - the first undertaken by the region's leaders themselves. They agreed to an all-party meeting. The states also agreed to study a request for 'security assistance' from 'Burundi.' But the very announcement of this idea led instead to the complete unravelling of whatever political consensus still remained among the 'moderates' of the two Burundi parties. Apparently, the president wanted foreign troops to come and protect him from the military, while the prime minister wanted foreign troops to support the Burundi military. Also, as the force was aimed at curbing violence by the army, Tutsi militias, and the CNDD, all opposed it.

By mid-1996, the uncontrolled methods of the army in response to continued rural violence were suggesting to more and more Hutus that Hutu President Ntibantunganya and his ostensible government were no longer able to protect them. A massacre in early July 1996 of about 300 Tutsis led to attacks on the president at the funeral of the victims as the army stood by. President Ntibantunganya sought refuge for his own safety. A political vacuum developed after the various calls for foreign intervention went unheeded, and former President Pierre Buyoya was asked to cooperate with yet another army coup on July 25, 1996.

Regional and other international actors then tried to put pressure on Buyoya to reinstate Parliament and constitutional government and on both him and the CNDD insurgency to end their fighting, enter all-party negotiations under President Nyerere and find acceptable power-sharing arrangements. In the name of defending democracy, nine East African states responded to the coup by imposing comprehensive trade and travel sanctions on Burundi, which were endorsed by the Organization of African Unity (OAU). International donors also suspended aid.

A series of further summits were convened by the regional states, with President Museveni now acknowledged as the regional spokesman. While the Buyoya government made some concessions to their pressures and with their mediation, the group became increasingly uneven in their enforcement of the sanctions. Vigorous public debate surfaced over whether to lift them as a way to provide incentives and rewards for partial fulfilment of the group's stated requirements. This debate divided the regional group into two camps, with the sanction supporters Uganda and Tanzania on one side. Because of Nyerere's support of sanctions and accusations that Tanzania was harbouring insurgents that carry out raids in Burundi, Buyoya accused him and the peace process he conducted as biased, and demanded his resignation. This atmosphere led to a virtual

breakdown of the regional process, despite a further summit in Kampala in February 1998.

However, the continuing military stalemate and debilitating humanitarian effect of the sanctions were in part responsible for opening of a new phase in the negotiations later that year. This started with an initiative by Buyoya in June 1998 to sign an internal partnership agreement between the government and Hutu-dominated National Assembly. The agreement created a coalition government and inaugurated a national dialogue process that could focus on issues between the Tutsi government and FRODEBU opposition. This hopeful sign contributed to the restarting of the Arusha Process talks, which included all the major players, including rebel factions. International donors were increasingly eager to provide humanitarian aid and several urged removal of the sanctions, but were looking for tangible progress toward a peace settlement.

In the later part of 1998, a series of sessions involving rebel delegations, the government and opposition parties appointed four committees within the Process that were each assigned to work respectively on the topics of the nature of the conflict, democracy and good governance, peace and security, and economic reconstruction and development. The forward movement in the Process and international pressure prompted the regional states to finally suspend their sanctions in January 1999, an act of virtual recognition of the Buyoya regime. Further committee and plenary sessions were held in early 1999 with the expectation that the reports of the committees could provide the basis for negotiations on a peace agreement that would begin later that year. But whether this would represent a turning point that yielded a lasting agreement still depended on the war, for which no cease-fire had yet been agreed, and the effect on the conflict of the continuing Congo regional war.

SADC and the Congo
The basic source of the two subsequent wars arising in Zaire in 1997 and in its successor the DRC a year later lay with the deterioration of the authority and reach of the Zairean state in eastern Zaire due to the longstanding corruption of the regime of the widely reviled Mobutu Sese

Seko and his bankruptcy of the state. This political and security vacuum was filled by two successive rebel movements. The longstanding malaise of the nation finally crystallised into violence when Mobutu, to shore up his influence in the east, tapped into local ethnic resentments and announced restrictions on the peoples of Tutsi descent who had actually lived there for decades. The resulting alarm among the Tutsis provided the opportunity for a Katangese politician and businessman, Laurent Kabila, to recruit an armed rebel movement that galvanised the Tutsis and other discontented groups in growing opposition to the government in Kinshasa.

But the rebellion would not have succeeded were it not for the aid and direction given by Rwandan military forces who were pressing into eastern Zaire to rid the area of the ex-Interhamwe and ex-FAR forces who had been pushed out of Rwanda after the genocide. These forces were continuing to launch insurgencies into Rwanda aimed at ultimately reinstating a Hutu government. Rwanda had objected to Mobutu's policy of tolerating the Hutu militants camps. Angola, Uganda, Burundi, Tanzania, Zambia and Eritrea also provided direct or indirect support to Kabila.

Major governments and other international actors had watched with dismay for many years how Mobutu ransacked his country's treasury and subverted the Zairean democratisation process that had begun. Thus, even though Kabila was not clearly aligned with the civilian opposition that had participated in a national conference and won seats in the Parliament, his armed rebellion was not treated as a source of yet more instability in the region nor strenuously criticised as it swept successfully across the country toward the capital. Nor were fears of a possible bloodbath in Kinshasa sufficient to engender vigorous efforts to mediate between Kabila and the ailing Mobutu.

But following his victory in May 1997, Kabila made little effort to reach out and unify the splintered democratic opposition and establish a broad-based popular government. Instead, he increasingly acted like his predecessor in repressing political rivals. In August 1998, soon after Kabila demanded that the Tutsi Rwandan

soldiers who had helped him defeat Mobutu return home, a new rebellion broke out in the East to challenge his government. Its leaders accused Kabila of corruption, cronyism, and nepotism, as well as of supporting the groups who were responsible for the Rwanda genocide and pursuing insurgencies against Rwanda, Uganda and Burundi. The rebel leadership, comprised of various political opponents of Kabila or disillusioned military officers, claimed they came from around the country and represented the Congolese people. But much of their discontent appeared related to Kabila's military promotion decisions. Kabila asserted that the rebels were supported by Rwandan and Ugandan forces who thus were committing aggression.

Through bold early moves, the rebel forces captured some key eastern towns and airlifted the rebellion to the West, quickly advancing to within striking distance of the capital Kinshasa. But although Kabila's performance in office has disappointed many observers, the rebellion against him did not pick up the broad international moral support that greeted that against the incorrigible Mobutu. Instead, Zimbabwe and Angola unexpectedly came to Kabila's aid militarily and halted the rebel's progress. Namibia, Sudan and Chad joined also.

Although denying their involvement for some time, it became evident that Rwanda and Uganda were working with the new rebels. Their intent was not to take over the Congo, however, but rather to create a wide buffer zone in the highly volatile eastern Congo to solve the still festering problem of the two insurgent movements who continued to make raids into north-west Rwanda and north-west Uganda, respectively, from Congolese soil. In ways that echoed their earlier complaints with Mobutu, Rwanda claimed that Kabila in fact was not only not containing the Hutu Interahamwe, but arming and training them.

The war shifted back to the East, where the rebel factions and their allies captured by year's end key cities in the north such as Kisangani and in the south, due to waning Angolan involvement as a result of the re-ignition of its civil war. By mid-1999, the rebels had succeeded in capturing one-third of the country, and a balance of power prevailed over a country that was divided into certain occupation zones. Although they had formed a political movement to present their political demands, the rebel movement split into three main factions in June 1999, supported by Rwanda and Uganda. These factions differed in terms of whether they wanted to pursue negotiations to achieve a transitional government, or to persist in the military struggle.

The rapid military gains by the rebels in August 1998 triggered a variety of peace initiatives at the very outset of the fighting, whose aim was a cease-fire. None of these came from within Central Africa per se. Besides missions and meetings conducted by the OAU, Libya's Colonel Khaddafi, Sant'Egidio, and other parties, the most active and sustained involvement came from the Southern Africa Development Community (SADC) in conjunction with the OAU, for the SADC members feared the conflict could lead to a region-wide war. But with some would-be mediators backing one of the protagonists, different approaches were in contention among different SADC members, based on their respective national interests and allies.

An early South African initiative headed by Nelson Mandela immediately called an emergency summit of five states which proposed a cease-fire, a conference among all the parties, a transitional government for Congo, and elections. But Kabila did not attend. While this initiative tended to be impartial as to the source of the problem, Robert Mugabe of Zimbabwe promoted a rival approach, based on his view that the rebels were at fault and SADC states must come to Kabila's aid under its Defense Protocol.

SADC asked President Chiluba of Zambia, who with Tanzania favoured a non-military solution, to act as its principal mediator. A series of meetings in the fall of 1998, in which Kabila or the rebels alternately often did not attend, no agreements were made. In July 1999, however, the Lusaka Accords sponsored by SADC were signed between the states that were supporting the various Congolese sides: the DRC, Angola, Zimbabwe, Rwanda, and Uganda. They agreed to a cease-fire, freezing their current territorial control and withdrawing, and calling on a UN peacekeeping force. But no plans were made to disarm the rebels, who did not participate in the meeting. At one point in August 1999, the Rwandan and Ugandan troops supporting different rebel groups began shelling each other in Kisangani, where there was gold and diamond booty to be had. With the fighting continuing, the rebel factions divided, blame for the conflict unaddressed, and the future of the government unresolved with Kabila still in power, it was unlikely this agreement meant either the end of the fighting or the beginning of peace negotiations that could resolve the country's political stalemate.

Conclusions
The three Central Africa conflicts suggest certain patterns with respect to the roles and effects of neighbouring and nearby countries in resolving internal conflicts in their region.

In each case, although not always, the first third parties to respond, regional states or leaders did act on emerging crises when these conflicts generated refugees, disrupted trade, and posed other threats to regional stability. Outside third parties seem to have ceded or handed more and more responsibility for mediating the conflicts to African and especially sub-regional actors. In the Congo case, they deferred to the most appropriate sub-regional organisation, SADC.

Inevitably perhaps, regional mediators brought their own regional agendas and rivalries to the table, and in several cases were openly partisan to one side or another, even mixing diplomacy with military assistance. Neither the regional actors as diplomats - nor, for that matter, any other of the multiple third parties who came on the scene to offer diplomatic services - made much headway in forging realistic peace settlements that ended armed ethnic hostilities. Even accompanying negotiations with the stick of regional sanctions took two and a half years to have some influence. Governments and rebels in the midst of conflict assumed they could win. Regional states did shape the course of the conflicts significantly, however, when they intervened on one of the sides militarily.

Where some agreement or movement to a peace process was achieved, the reason does not appear to lie with either a regional actor's propinquity or whether they were impartial facilitators. It happened when the contending armed forces appeared to face a continuing military stalemate or with losing what they had. Then, negotiations became an attractive default option for pursuing their goals.

Where peace settlements or something like them were arranged, the content or implementation of the agreements did not bring about a genuine reallocation of power. This was undermined either by covert subversion (Rwanda) or overt intimidation (Burundi). The mediators could not or did not provide the required pressure on or security guarantees against those factions that stood to lose from the change. So the latter could manipulate the situation in their own favour.

References

Stephen Buckley, *Mass Slaughter Was Avoidable, General Says*, Washington Post, February 26, 1998

Patrick Gaffney, *The International Response to Burundi: 1993-1995, Compared to Rwanda, 1990-94*. Paper for International Studies Association Meetings, San Diego, April 17, 1996

Patrick D. Gaffney, *Burundi on the Brink: The Long Somber Shadow of Ethnic Instability*, paper for UNU/WIDER project on The Political Economy of Humanitarian Emergencies

Barbara Harff, *Crisis in Rwanda*, Working Papers, Conflict and Early Warning System Project, University of Southern California, 1997

International Crisis Group, *Burundi Under Siege*, Report, April 28, 1998

International Crisis Group, *Africa's Seven Nation War*, Democratic Republic of the Congo Report No. 4, May 21, 1999

International Crisis Group, *Burundi: Internal and Regional Implications of the Suspension of Sanctions*, Burundi Report No. 3, May 4, 1999

International Crisis Group, *'Burundi: Proposals for the Resumption of Bilateral and Multilateral Cooperation*, Burundi Report No. 4, May 4, 1999

Stefan Lovgren, *'Burundi on Edge over an Invasion*, Christian Science Monitor, July 8, 1996

Michael Lund, Barnett Rubin, and Fabienne Hara, *Learning from Burundi's Failed Transition: Did International Initiatives Match the Problem?* in Barnett Rubin, ed., Cases and Strategies for Preventive Action (New York: Twentieth Century Fund, and Council on Foreign Relations, 1998)

Gerard Prunier, 'The Geopolitical Situation in the Great Lakes Area in Light of the Kivu Crisis (February 1997),' at http://www.unhcr.ch/refworld/country/writenet/wrilakes

United Nations, *Letter of the Secretary-General to the Security Council on the Situation in Burundi*, S/1995/1068, December 29, 1995

United Nations, *Report of the Secretary-General on the Situation in Burundi'*, S/1996/116, February 15, 1996, para. 44-5

United Nations, 'Report to the Security Council on the Situation in Burundi', S/1996/660, August 15, 1996

U.S. Committee on Refugees, Life after Death: Suspicion and Reintegration in Post-Genocide Rwanda, Washington, D.C. February, 1998

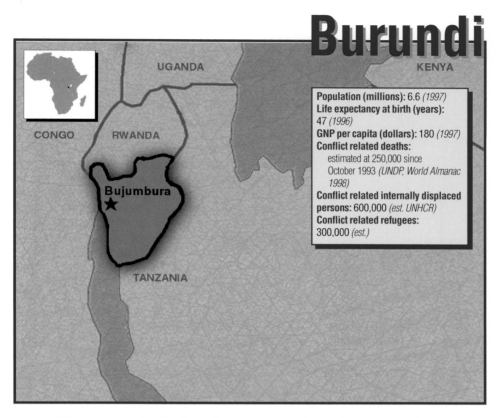

UGANDA

KENYA

CONGO

RWANDA

Bujumbura
★

TANZANIA

Population (millions): 6.6 *(1997)*
Life expectancy at birth (years):
47 *(1996)*
GNP per capita (dollars): 180 *(1997)*
Conflict related deaths:
   estimated at 250,000 since
   October 1993 *(UNDP, World Almanac
   1998)*
Conflict related internally displaced
persons: 600,000 *(est. UNHCR)*
Conflict related refugees:
300,000 *(est.)*

Peace-Initiatives Help Stem the Violence

The small central African country of Burundi has been tormented by civil strife in which an estimated 250,000 people have been killed since 1993. The conflict triggered a series of official diplomatic efforts to bring peace to the country, as well as a number of non-governmental peace-making and reconciliatory initiatives. The interventions may have helped prevent the Burundian conflict from developing into the kind of large-scale genocide that took place in neighbouring Rwanda in 1994. The Burundian government and civil organisations have taken a significant step by implementing some preventive policies. However, the peace efforts have not stopped the violence altogether. Small-scale killings continue to occur. Peace initiatives continue to be pursued as lasting peace between Hutus and Tutsis has yet to be achieved ◆ *By* Jos Havermans

The principal problem in Burundi is the 'ethnic' conflict between the majority Hutus and the minority Tutsis, who have historically held power and still control the military. Tutsis also dominate educated society, and their position is sometimes vehemently defended by

militant elements among them. During massive clashes in the 1970s, for instance, militant Tutsis targeted educated Hutus. The ethnic clashes are fuelled by a continuing power struggle between Hutu and Tutsi political elites who are trying to secure access to scarce economic resources through control of state power. Strife among factions within the two ethnic groups is also vehement. Major massacres took place in 1965, 1972 (100,000-200,000 people killed), 1988 and 1993.

The violent ethnic confrontation of 1993 can be seen as the starting point of the current phase in Burundi's civil war. In response to the installation of a Hutu majority government, brought to power by the first democratic elections earlier that year, elements in the Tutsi-led army staged an attempted coup in October 1993. Their attempt failed, but they killed the democratically elected Hutu president, Melchior Ndadaye and many other senior Hutu members of government. The events triggered ethnic massacres of Tutsis by Hutus in revenge while the Tutsi army killed many Hutus in retaliation. At least 100,000 people were killed, among them many children and elderly, often slaughtered in an extremely brutal fashion.

The Belgian Africa expert Filip Reyntjens has dubbed the coup attempt 'the most successful failed military take-over' of African history. Although the military did not take power, their attacks weakened the government, leading to significant concessions to militant Tutsi demands. After October 1993 minor ethnic clashes continued to occur, killing dozens of people every week. The government of Hutu president Sylvestre Ntibantunganya stood powerless in the face of attacks and killings by the young radical Tutsi militia, the Tutsi-led army and Hutu militias and rebels.

The spiralling violence and the diminishing influence of the government, which was run by moderate Hutus and Tutsis, triggered a bloodless *coup d'etat* in July 1996, bringing Major Paul Buyoya to power. For Buyoya this was a return to the highest office. He had been responsible, as then-president, for the introduction of democracy and a multiparty system in Burundi in the early 1990s. After his return to office in 1996, he dissolved the National Assembly and banned political parties. Neighbouring countries decided to isolate Burundi from the outside world by imposing economic sanctions.

Since Buyoya's take-over, the intensity of the conflict has decreased. While the conflict

between the Burundian army and rebel movements continued, with concomitant casualties, the selected killings of Hutus and the general level of fear amongst Hutus decreased. Although violence considerably diminished in 1998 and 1999, massacres still occur. Buyoya tried to defuse the tension by the mass recruitment into the army of young unemployed Tutsis. These recruits were formerly the rank and file of uncontrollable militias, the so-called '*Sans Échecs*' and '*Sans Défaites*'. Buyoya also decided to concentrate Hutu farmers in camps dispersed over the country, supposedly to protect them against militia and rebel attacks.

The armed Hutu opposition consists of three political movements: The National Council for the Defence of Democracy (CNDD); the Parti pour la Libération du Peuple Hutu (Palipehutu); and Umbumwe.

Each movement has its own armed branch. For the CNDD this is the *Force pour la Défence de la Démocratie* (FDD), established in 1994. This organisation also has some Tutsis in its ranks. Palipehutu/FLN, established in 1980, mainly operates from former Zaire and Tanzania, while Umbumwe's *Front de Liberation Nationale* (FROLINA), which appeared in the late 1980s, operates mainly in the south and the west of the country.

In 1998, the CNDD and its military wing split, when military commander colonel Jean-Bosco Ndayikengurukiye tried to oust Leonard Nyangoma as the CNDD's political leader. However, Nyangoma still claims the presidency and is still recognised as the CNDD's formal representative by foreign diplomats, including the coordinator of the Arusha peace talks, Julius Nyerere. Ndayikengurukiye controls a considerable part of the FDD ranks.

On the other side of the spectrum are the militias of young Tutsis, recruited among educated but unemployed urban youths. These militias are reportedly funded by the PARENA party of Jean-Baptiste Bagaza, a former dictator, militant Tutsi, and rival of his cousin Buyoya.

The national army of Burundi is still dominated by the Tutsi minority, despite plans developed under ousted president Ntibantunganya to recruit more Hutus. Buyoya's decision to absorb militant Tutsi youngsters into the armed forces strengthened its Tutsi dominance. The Burundian army had a reputation of lacking professionalism until the mid-1990s. Since then, its discipline and combat capacities are said to have improved, largely as a result of an increase in armed attacks by its Hutu opponents and under pressure of international criticism of its human rights records. However, random killings and other human rights violations are still reported to be occurring on a regular basis.

Since 1998, the rebels have reportedly coordinated their actions with Hutu forces in Rwanda and the Eastern Democratic Republic of Congo (DRC). Burundi Hutu-rebels fought alongside the army of Laurent Kabila after he came to power in the DRC. The Angolan rebel movement, UNITA, allegedly supported the Burundi rebels of the CNDD by providing them with weapons and training. The Burundi national army became involved in the armed struggle in the DRC and stationed troops in the eastern DRC to prevent Hutu rebel infiltration.

The following factors are among those mentioned in literature as causes of the Burundian conflict.

- Past discrimination: since independence in 1962, Tutsi-dominated regimes have discriminated against Hutus.
- Weight of violent history: Burundi's post independence history is strewn with recurrent coups or attempted coups and inter-communal violence. Clashes took place in 1965, 1966, 1972, 1987, 1988, 1989, 1991, 1993 and 1996. This sequence of massacres has created a culture of violence which is hard to dissolve.
- State monopoly of resources: the population is preponderantly rural and engaged in subsistence agriculture. The country's small industrial sector is confined largely to local production or uncompetitive exports such as coffee and tea, produced until recently by state industries. Control of state power almost entirely coincides with control of economic resources.
- Divisive leaders: the leaders of the countries political camps have engaged in demagogic rhetoric, which has sometimes incited violence.

Conflict Dynamics

War weariness seemed to be at the basis of a major political initiative which occurred in the spring of 1998. What has been described as a 'security impasse', or stalemate, forced the antagonists towards political dialogue. Neither of the two main ethnic groups appear to have the capacity either to physically destroy the other, or to ensure total protection for themselves. A central issue is the mutual suspicion of Hutus and Tutsis, who both genuinely fear that the other group, or at least some extremists within it, is plotting their physical extermination.

The Buyoya government agreed on a political agenda for transition with the re-established National Assembly, thereby partly resolving a long-standing political impasse. The political agreement provided for two vice-presidents, assuring a senior position for each of the main political parties. The National Assembly was enlarged to include more opposition parties and independent representatives from 'civil society'. Moderates on both sides seemed to gain considerable ground in the political arena. This resulted in a breakthrough. Several rounds of peace talks were held in the second half of 1998 and in 1999 in Arusha. In the summer of 1999, the coordinator of the peace process, former Tanzanian president Julius Nyerere, said he expected an accord between rebels and the government to be signed before the end of the year.

At a summit in January 1999, East African leaders decided to suspend economic sanctions against Burundi which had been imposed following the coup in 1996. The measure was taken to encourage the peace negotiations. Meanwhile, the situation in the country remains volatile, with the risk of a renewed escalation of the conflict still being a reality.

The conflict has had a devastating effect on the economy. Due to the recurring attacks, production of tea and coffee - Burundi's main export crop - has diminished, leading to reduced revenues for both farmers and trading companies. In the late 1990s, the country's brewery, which is majority owned by the Dutch Heineken company, was Burundi's only fully functioning industrial plant and the government's major source of tax revenues. Most other economic activities had come to a halt. After the economic embargo was lifted, the economic situation improved only slightly. The majority of people rely on subsistence agriculture and foreign humanitarian aid for their survival.

Approximately ten per cent of Burundi's rural population lacks secure access to food. While food production has steadily declined since the onset of the crisis, market prices of staple foods have more than doubled. Though the country was food self-sufficient in the late 1980s, Burundi had to rely on an annual average of US $21 million in food aid between 1994-1997.

The government tried to separate the population from rebel groups by initiating a policy of forcible resettlement of rural populations into 'regroupment' camps in 1996. At its peak, this policy resulted in the 'regroupment' of nearly 300,000 people into 40 to 45 camps. The vast majority of persons in these camps are Hutu, although some are Tutsi. In 1997, the government allowed some of the regrouped persons to return to their homes. Half of the regroupment camps were dismantled by the end of 1997 but an estimated 150,000 people still live in the camps. Human rights organisations, including Amnesty International, have expressed their concern about the 'regroupment' operations. Hundreds of people were allegedly killed by the army during the 'regroupment' operations. Houses have been destroyed, crops burnt and farming activities greatly reduced. Conditions in the remaining camps continue to be appalling with high levels of disease and malnutrition. The military has been responsible for the rape of women and children inside the 'regroupment' camps and incidents of summary executions of civilians continue to be reported. Armed opposition groups have continued attacks on villages and on camps for the displaced.

In the summer of 1999, the government unveiled a ten-year transition plan which envisaged the enlargement of the National Assembly to include the groups taking part in the Arusha peace process which are currently not represented in parliament. The plan also announced the establishment of a senate whose composition would be ethnically and regionally balanced. President Buyoya was to remain in office for another five years, and would be succeeded by a Hutu president who would lead the country in the last five years of the transition period.

Official Conflict Management

Since the massacres of October 1993, the international community has mounted many efforts in preventive action. The response included the appointment of a UN and several other special envoys, a UN commission of inquiry and an OAU military observer mission.

The *United Nations* involvement in Burundi partly evolved through humanitarian organisations such as UNICEF and UNHCR. These agencies came into the country to help internally displaced persons and Rwandan refugees who fled into Burundi during the 1994 genocide. After the October 1993 massacres, the UN sent a special envoy to Burundi as well as a UN commission of enquiry. The UN's efforts came to be closely coordinated with actions taken by the *Organisation for African Unity*. The OAU sent an observer mission to Burundi in 1994 with the task of trying to reduce tension by monitoring, among other things, the national army's conduct. The coordination between UN and OAU efforts was implemented mainly by entrusting a senior diplomat with the status of both UN and OAU envoy for the region, a position held by Mohamed Sahnoun.

UN special envoy Ould Abdallah strongly influenced the UN's initiatives during his mission in Burundi, which lasted until October 1995 and he reached his goal of avoiding a repetition of the Rwandan massacre. His efforts were focused on democratisation, good governance and development as peace tools. Ould Abdallah was a staunch believer in quiet healing instead of mediation. In September 1994, he brokered a political accord on a new concept of power sharing between the Tutsi led UPRONA party and FRODEBU, the party associated with the Hutu majority. The accord, which became known as the Convention of Government, also encompassed a national debate, which was to include all parties in the conflict in order to bridge the gap between the two ethnic communities.

Since then, the UN's role has attracted

BURUNDI, *Killing fields*

Rob Hof

somewhat less attention, as its activities have increasingly focused on supporting peace initiatives led by other actors, such as the negotiation process coordinated by the former Tanzanian president Julius Nyerere.

In August 1998, the UN Humanitarian Coordinator assembled UN agencies and NGOs in Burundi to review the humanitarian situation and discuss the future course of action. The consultations resulted in a joint strategy for humanitarian assistance and sustainable integration in Burundi. This strategy calls for continued emphasis on timely and effective humanitarian assistance and, simultaneously, increased investment in sustainable reintegration and the foundations of community development in order to solidify the progress towards peace. The strategy was formulated in the Consolidated Inter-Agency Appeal for Burundi by the Office for the Coordination of Humanitarian Affairs (OCHA) in December 1998.

The UN Humanitarian Coordinator plays an important role in the coordination of the activities of the UN system and international NGOs. The weekly Contact Group meeting, led by the Humanitarian Coordinator, brings together UN agencies, donors, and NGOs to exchange information and initiate activities which effect the entire humanitarian community. In addition, provincial and sectoral committees are organised to ensure that efforts are well coordinated, and feed information into the Contact Group.

In early 1999, the UN Humanitarian Coordinator for Burundi presented a broadened community assistance programme that would complement and help strengthen the peace process at grassroots level.

Regional

Official African initiatives were abundant. South African archbishop Desmond Tutu and former Tanzanian president Julius Nyerere were among senior African officials invited by the Carter Center to start a peace effort for the Great Lakes region in 1995. A first meeting in Cairo was followed by a second round in Tunis in March 1996. In subsequent years, this regional approach died down, and Nyerere was assigned the task of attending the Burundi conflict, which at that time had become the most dominant crisis of the region. In 1998, a new series of talks aimed at resolving the ethnic conflict opened in

Arusha (Tanzania) under the chairmanship of Nyerere. He succeeded in scheduling a series of peace conferences to be held between June 1998 and August 1999. Five committees, headed by non-Burundians, must make progress on the following five subjects:

1. the nature of the conflict;
2. democracy and good governance;
3. reconstruction and economic development;
4. peace and security;
5. guarantees for implementation of a peace accord.

The negotiations were proceeding according to schedule in 1999. Each committee has to produce a strategy or plan that will be presented to a plenary meeting in June or August 1999. The main obstacle in Arusha was representation. The army said it was not a warring faction and as such could and should not be included in a cease-fire. The Hutu opposition CNDD was divided after it expelled its vice-president Sendegeya from its ranks. Its armed wing CNDD-FDD reportedly went through a leadership crisis and was not bound by its current leader's signature under the Arusha agreements. The Tutsi-dominated UPRONA party was internally divided over Arusha and was not officially represented. The Hutu party, FRODEBU, previously divided over government appointees inside the party, was fairly united over Arusha and abided by the decision of its leader-in-exile, Jean Minani.

Bilateral

Some foreign powers have been active in supporting diplomatic initiatives as well as in encouraging non-governmental peace initiatives and human rights interests. The Belgian (Van Craen) and US (Krueger) ambassadors were frontrunners in confronting the army with its actions. EU ambassador Johnstone also dared to address the problem but with quiet diplomacy. This was also translated into donor policies that supported various peace-building initiatives, such as the establishment of an impartial radio production studio (Studio Ijambo) aimed at objective news coverage and reconciliation.

In early 1996 the EU appointed Aldo Ajello, an Italian diplomat and former UN envoy to Mozambique, as special envoy to the region.

Ajello partly coordinated his efforts with the special US envoy for the region, Howard Wolpe.

Domestic

Burundi has a longstanding domestic tradition of reconciliation attempts. As early as 1988, after an outburst of ethnic violence, then-president Pierre Buyoya launched a reconciliation process and issued a Charter of National Unity intended to reduce ethnic rivalries. Although these initiatives never succeeded in defusing ethnic tension, subsequent governments continued to develop similar approaches aimed at stabilising the country.

After the 1994 events in Rwanda, president Ntibantunganya and his ministers toured the provinces for months delivering speeches on reconciliation, however the campaign did not prove successful. The Ntibantunganya government had announced that a national debate would take place on the future of the country in which all sections of society could participate. As part of this plan, a round table talk took place in the town of Gitega in March 1998, offering a platform for dialogue between Burundi actors, without interference of mediators.

Since his return to power in 1996, Pierre Buyoya has been convinced that he can reconcile the Burundi people and in his book *Mission Possible* he wrote that he is committed to moving the political battle away from the traditional Hutu-Tutsi rivalry.

As part of the official national campaign for stability, the government launched a campaign in April 1998, aimed at enabling civilians to defend themselves against Hutu militia. As part of the campaign, the government began to arm villagers with rifles and grenades. Some villagers accompanied the military in surveillance.

An improved climate emerged from the new political 'partnership agreement', signed in 1998 between the two main parties in the coalition government, FRODEBU and UPRONA. Buyoya also reached an agreement with the FRODEBU-dominated parliament. According to this agreement, Buyoya gave up his right to dissolve the National Assembly, while the legislature gave up its right to veto presidential decrees. In another move, Buyoya cracked down on human rights violators in the military. More than two hundred soldiers who were found responsible for violations were jailed.

In June 1998, the government decided to make a traditional mechanism of conflict resolution - the *Abashingantahe* institution of arbitration (see section on Multi-Track Diplomacy) - part of the new (transitional) constitution. In the same year, a round table meeting took place in Gitega, which amounted to a significant boost to the still weak internal peace process. The Gitega meeting involved an open political dialogue between a number of leaders of ethnic and political groups, which helped forge consensus on the new transitional constitution. According to some observers, including Christian Scherrer of the Ethnic Conflict Research Project (ECOR), these initiatives amounted to a significant adoption of preventive policies by the government and other major actors in the country. In their judgement, since early 1998 tangible progress has been made on the road towards domestic conflict resolution in Burundi.

Multi-Track Diplomacy
Domestic

Domestic non-governmental initiatives vary from the activities of human rights organisations to initiatives taken by peace organisations such as the Apostles for Peace, also known as the CAP group. The *Compagnie des Apôtres de la Paix* works for a peaceful resolution of the conflict through education, training and dissemination of basic values associated with traditional local authorities (*Abashingantahe*). In 1997 and 1998, the Apostles for Peace organised a series of debates, called '*séances verités*', on important themes (including the Arusha talks, the origins of the present crisis, and refugee issues) throughout the country. One of its key objectives is to see whether South Africa's record of peace initiatives applies to Burundi. Proposals have been written and discussed to set up a type of modernised version of *Abashingantahe* which will function in a similar way to the 'Truth and Reconciliation Commission' on a national level.

The current *Abashingantahe*, or *Bashingantahe*, initiative is a revival of traditional pre-colonial groups of men who were renowned,

as mythology has it, for their sense of truth, justice and responsibility. They settled disputes and reconciled individuals and families. Moves to restore the institution originate from the late 1980s, following ethnic massacres in two communities in northern Burundi. In March 1997, the government of president Buyoya decreed the establishment of a National Council of *Bashingantahe*, consisting of forty men and women drawn from all ethnic and social groups. The council has discussed national issues, including the negotiations between the government and rebels. It issues recommendations. So far the debates are said to have had little impact on the wider population of Burundi.

In early October 1998, the *Human Rights League* ITEKA organised a consultation on the peace process, involving 25 local NGOs. The themes discussed were institutional reforms, integrated development, security, justice and impunity and the role of civil society. Militant extremists, both Hutu and Tutsi, have threatened the lives of people investigating human rights violations.

Grassroots church organisations, such as *Communautés Ecclesiales de Base*, have played a significant role in helping internally displaced people back to their homes, in preaching inter-ethnic peace and in trying to create a sense of security in the hills. They have received substantial support from the Conference of Catholic Bishops and international NGOs.

International

Many international NGOs are engaged in efforts to boost peace in Burundi. They increasingly collaborate with each other, with local organisations as well as with governments and international donors.

International Alert was the first foreign organisation that tried to implement preventive programmes in Burundi. It attempted to bring people from different ethnic background together for an open dialogue. With the help of sponsors, the organisation sent 1,000 footballs to Burundi, a symbolic act to show Burundian youth that there are alternatives to violence and militia enrolment.

In 1995 International Alert facilitated a study

tour to South Africa for 25 senior figures from all sectors of Burundi society. This tour aimed at connecting Burundians to the encouraging example of South Africa's peaceful transfer to democracy and reconciliation. As an immediate consequence of this initiative, the 25 participants formed a Burundian peace group, known as the Company of Apostles of Peace, or the CAP Group.

In collaboration with the CAP Group, International Alert facilitated a visit to Burundi for two local South African community leaders belonging to opposing political groups. The UN Special representative and the South African NGO *African Centre for the Constructive Resolution of Disputes* (ACCORD) also contributed to these events.

International Alert established the *Burundi Steering Committee* which coordinates peace-building initiatives taken by NGOs, the UN representatives and other actors, such as foreign parliamentarians. The London-based organisation also tried to help setting up local Peace Committees, in which civilians and local elders were invited to participate. On the international level, International Alert initiated the establishment of the *International Steering Committee for Burundi*, comprising representatives of NGOs, donor governments and UN representatives, and responsible for the overall policy direction of IA's peace initiatives in Burundi. An International Working Group, representing international NGOs, was set up to exchange information and coordinate advocacy programmes on Burundi. Both groups exchanged information in teleconferences.

The American NGO *Search for Common Ground* opened a field office in Bujumbura in 1995 and initiated three programmes aimed at creating mechanisms for ethnic reconciliation. It established the first independent radio studio in Burundi, Studio Ijambo, in March 1995. Ijambo produces unbiased news programmes, and cultural and social magazines. It also produced a soap opera for radio - Our Neighbours, Ourselves - depicting a Hutu and a Tutsi family living next door to each other.

Common Ground has also opened a women's peace centre in Bujumbura and started a political dialogue project. The Centre for Women, opened

in 1996, works to foster increased cooperation and understanding between Hutu and Tutsi women. It brings women together for debates and, in collaboration with International Alert, helps women who are local leaders to become acquainted with conflict resolution skills. The Political Dialogue Project addresses the ethnic conflict via quiet diplomacy among the Burundian political players. Negotiations are conducted by Jan van Eck, a former South African parliamentarian, who brings the South African experience of transitional politics to the peace process in Burundi.

In 1995, Common Ground, in collaboration with Refugees International, the Council on Foreign Relation's Center for Preventive Action and the Africa-America Institute established what is now called the *Great Lakes Policy Forum* (originally dubbed Burundi Policy Forum). A year later, the *European Forum on the Great Lakes* was inaugurated in Brussels. These forums are strategic coalitions of concerned NGOs, government agencies and international organisations focusing on the Great Lakes region. Members meet regularly to discuss the latest issues and exchange information. They are unique in that they foster a culture of communication and coordination between NGO and government communities.

In March-July 1997, the Italian *Communita di Sant Egidio*, based in Rome, played an important role in bringing the adversaries to the negotiation table. Highly confidential talks in the Italian capital between Burundian government and opposition representatives resulted in the signing of a memorandum outlining the principles of a peace process and political agreement. After details of the memorandum and the very fact that the government had met rebel representatives became public, radical Tutsi politicians protested and the Rome process stagnated.

Sant Egidio continued its role as a mediator. Mateo Zuppi, one of the organisation's leading figures, is closely involved in the official peace process of Arusha. He is the coordinator of one of the five commissions that have been established to make proposals for a permanent peace accord.

Several other NGO initiatives have been taken. The *Dutch Relief and Rehabilitation Agency*

(DRA) started a programme that focuses on peace, reconciliation and development projects in Kinama, Kamenge and Ciboteke zones of Bujumbura.

In 1995, international NGOs engaged in Burundi decided to nominate a NGO security officer to be assigned the task of providing NGOs with information on the security situation in Burundi. Based in Bujumbura, this NGO Security Liaison Officer was considered to be a key factor in enabling NGOs to work in the country.

The *International Crisis Group* (ICG) is active in the region and in 1997 recommended the establishment of a Truth Commission in Burundi, based on the South African model, or a Research Commission tasked with investigating all massacres since independence. The *Forum on Early Warning and Early Response* (FEWER) is deeply engaged in the Great Lakes region and supports the Great Lakes network. It provides a forum for information-sharing and advocacy activities by several NGOs in the region.

Synergies Africa, in collaboration with *Femmes Africa Solidarité* (FAS), has focused on the potential role of women in building peace in the Great Lakes region and organised a seminar to discuss the crisis in the area which was attended by women from Burundi across ethnic lines. A FAS delegation of women visited Burundi and organised a three-day workshop with the Ministry of Women's Promotion and Social Action and the Association of Women's NGOs in Burundi (CAFOB). The participants were Burundian women drawn from various political parties and social groups who tried to identify effective conflict resolution techniques for the country. Recommendations were made to the government aimed at mobilising the potential of women's organisations for peace-building.

Evaluation

According to experts from the US Institute for Peace, the Centre for Preventive Action and other observers who have studied the failure of international interventions to stop the violence in Burundi, some mediators and arbitrating organisations fail to see that the conflict is in fact a life-and-death struggle among competing individuals and factions within Burundi's small

governing elite who use coercion and armed force against each other to obtain or retain wealth and power.

Most of the external attention to the conflict, the observers say, tends to focus on the killings and their humanitarian effects, but not on its basic political and military causes. As a consequence the enormous human and financial resources have not been targeted effectively on the specific causes of instability and violence. According to some observers, several opportunities have been missed. There was also a lack of regular contacts between the monitors on the ground from the academic community on the one hand and high-level diplomats who make decisions about conflict responses on the other.

Two important lessons were drawn from experiences in Burundi. The first is that knowledge about ethnic conflicts, early warning of conflict and crisis, and the array of policies in the 'toolbox' for preventing or managing conflicts is still not being sufficiently disseminated to policy-makers with decision-making authority at high level. The second is that early warning and the implementation of programmes to address the conflict should be better linked. Establishing a permanent policy-planning unit specifically dedicated to prevention has been suggested as a good step to avoid such shortcomings in the future.

Prospects

The suspension of the economic embargo and the return of development assistance in 1999 was expected to contribute to a stabilisation of the new government. This could prevent the biggest danger to the ongoing peace, a new military *coup d'etat* by hard-liners.

Developments in Burundi are closely linked to developments in the Democratic Republic of Congo and in Rwanda. With continued outside support, Hutu extremists may continue to believe that they have more to gain by sticking to their guns than by sitting at the negotiation table. A continuation of the Congo stalemate could act as a magnet for extremists on both sides, with more Tutsi 'volunteers' joining rebel groups fighting President Kabila and more CNDD activists reaching out to Kabila for support. An escalation of the conflict would become even more likely if

CNDD and Interahamwe/FAR 'veterans' become major recipients of weapons and money from Kabila and his allies, while a similar alliance is formed between the RPA (Rwandan Peoples Army), the Burundi army and the major Congolese rebel movements.

The chances of bringing an end to violence are highly dependent on the continuation and outcome of the new rounds of the Arusha peace talks planned for 1999. Much will depend on the sense of compromise and wisdom exercised by the bilateral commissions in working out the conditions of national reconciliation. Items likely to have a significant affect on the peace process include the judicial proceedings against the assassins of President Ndadaye, the issue of impunity of soldiers responsible for the killing of civilians, the withdrawal of Burundi troops from the Democratic Republic of Congo, and educational reforms aimed at the inclusion of more Hutu elements at all levels. A transition of the national army under some form of international supervision and cooperation will be necessary to ensure physical protection for both ethnic groups.

Recommendations

The peace process to date has been characterised by a top-down process. In order to create a sustainable peace, observers say, it will be necessary to supplement it with a bottom-up approach, to organise grassroots support for the process and promote local capacity building. To the extent that bottom-up activities have already been deployed, it is obvious these should be strengthened, according to the Ethnic Conflicts Research Project (ECOR) and other organisations. Most obvious in this regard is the necessity of a campaign for peace education on the value of democracy, national reconciliation and respect for human rights, from the primary schools upwards. Donors should use their influence, says ECOR, to help introduce the notion of basic respect for the well-being of citizens.

In December 1997 the European Parliament echoed recommendations from human rights organisations aimed at a better control and greater transparency of arms trafficking to the region, including the reactivation of the UN

International Commission of Inquiry (UNICOI) on arms trafficking in the Great Lakes region, and the extension of its mandate to include Burundi. In April 1998 the UN Security Council reactivated UNICOI but did not extend its mandate to Burundi. NGOs have pressed for the rectification of this omission.

The International Crisis Group, in a report released in April 1999, recommended action to be taken by Burundian actors and the international community in order to increase the chance of lasting peace in Burundi:

. Organisations that are active in the realm of what ICG describes as the three R's - Rehabilitation, Reconstruction and Repatriation - should not attempt to recreate the Burundian situation of before the beginning of the current crisis, but should try to encompass a deep understanding of the causes of the war in their operations and long-term goals.

. Foreign aid should only be resumed on the condition that the Burundian government decides to implement economic reforms that will fight 'clientelisme' and create a strong structure that will reduce the country's dependency on aid in the long-term. In order to avoid the risk that funding might be diverted into military or security-force budgets, donors should seek to distribute aid at a local level.

- Economic recovery is a major prerequisite for ending a conflict, which is partly fuelled by unemployment and the socio-economic exclusion of part of society.
- International initiatives should not focus exclusively on victims, but also address those responsible for the violence in the country.
- Despite its frailty, the national dialogue should be supported. An internal dialogue between all the parties in Burundi's conflict is an essential component of the wider peace process.

Providing assistance to strengthen the judicial system in order to enable Burundians to address the issue of impunity. The constant recall of past killings and exchanges of accusations of atrocities is a major obstacle to reconciliation and dialogue.

Facilitating the repatriation of Burundian refugees in Tanzania would remove an important source of tension in the relationship between Burundi and Tanzania.

The Dutch chapter of *Medicins sans Frontieres* recommends making human rights monitoring one of the highest priorities because of the destabilising effect of violations. The organisation urges international organisations present in Burundi to report on violations on a systematic basis. The installation of an international tribunal for Burundi is also recommended by the medical aid organisation.

Background document provided by Lucas van den Broek/Doctors without Borders Netherlands

Service Information

Reports
Minority Rights Group International
- Burundi - Breaking the Cycle of Violence, by F. Reyntjens. 1996

International Crisis Group
- Burundi - Proposals for the resumption of bilateral and multilateral cooperation. Report No 4, 1999 (also available in French)
- Burundi - Internal and Regional Implications of the Suspension of Sanctions, 1999
- Congo at War - A Briefing on Internal and External Players in the Central African Conflict, 17/11/98
- Burundi's Peace Process: The Road From Arusha, 20/7/98
- Burundi Under Siege, 28/4/98

Amnesty International
- War Against Unarmed Civilians, AI Index: AFR 16/34/98, 23/11/98

United Nations
- Conseil de Sécurité, Lettre datée du 25 juillet 1996, addressée au président du Conseil de Sécurité par le Sécretaire Général, S/1996/682, 22 août 1996

Other Publications
Burundi, J.P. Harroy. Bruxelles, éd. Hayez/Bruxelles, 1987
Burundi 1972-1988 - Continuité et changement, F. Reyntjens. Bruxelles, Cédaf, 1988
La crise d'août 1988 au Burundi, J.P. Chretien, A. Guichaoua, G. Le Jeune, Cahiers du CRA, nr 6, Paris, Karthala, 1989
Burundi - Le non-dit, D. Hakizimana. Verniers (Genève) éd. Remesha, 1991
Burundi - Au royaume des seigneurs de la lance tome I, R. Ntibazonkiza. Bruxelles, éd.

Bruxelles Droits de l'Homme, 1991
Burundi - Au royaume des seigneurs de la lance tome II, R. Ntibazonkiza. Bruxelles, éd. Bruxelles-Droits de l'Homme, 1993
L'Afrique des Grands Lacs en crise - Rwanda-Burundi, F. Reyntjens. Paris, Karthala, 1994
Les crises politiques au Burundi et au Rwanda (1993-1994), A. Guichaoua. Université des Sciences et Technologies de Lille. Karthala, 1995
Diplomatie Pyromane, Ahmedou Ould Abdallah. Paris, Calmann-Lévy, 1996.
Terreur Africaine. Burundi, Rwanda, Zaire - Les racines de la violence, C. Braeckman. Fayard, 1996
Burundi, Ethnic Conflict and Genocide, by René Lemarchand. Cambridge, Woodrow Wilson Center Press, 1996.
Democratization and Violence in Burundi - The Failure of Preventive Action, by M. Lund and K. Austin. Brookings, 1997
Elements of the Burundi Peace Process, C.P. Scherrer. Tegelen, The Netherlands, ECOR, 1999

Resource Contacts
Jan van Eck - former South African MP, deeply involved in Burundi peace efforts, e-mail vaneck@cni.cbinf.com
Collette Braeckman - journalist *Le Soir* (Belgium), fax +32 2 2255 914
Filip Reyntjens - Centre for the Study of the Great Lakes Region of Africa, University of Antwerpen. Email freyntje@ruca.ua.ac.be
Christian Scherrer - senior researcher at the Ethnic Conflicts Research Project (ECOR), e-mail cscherrer@copri.dk

Selected Internet Sites

www.searchforcommonground.org/burundim.htm
(Search for Common Ground)
www.international-alert.org (International Alert)
www.santegidio.org (Sant Egidio)
www.fewer.org/greatlakes/main htm (FEWER
site with info on Great Lakes region)
www.aktioncourage.org (Germany based group
of Burundi friends connected to Franciscan
Mission community; information on recent
developments)
www.bsos.umd.edu/cidcm/mar (University
project on ethnic groups and their concerns,
including Hutus and Tutsi in Burundi)
www.crisisweb.org (International Crisis Group -
Central Africa Project)
www.incore.ulst.ac.uk/cds/countries/burundi.html
(Overview of sources of information on
conflict in Burundi conflict)
www.burundi.gov.bi (Official site of Burundi
government)
www.geocities.com/capitolHill/Senate/8080/
(Great Lakes Monitor, a weekly electronic
clipping service focusing on political events in
Africa's Great Lakes region, including
Burundi) published in online newspapers and
magazines.

Organisations

ITEKA Human Rights Organization
Bujumbura
Burundi

Association de Réflexion et d'Information sur
le Burundi (ARIB - Belgian based organisation
run by Burundian exiles)
Rue du Porion 24
6200 Châtelet
Belgium
tel/fax + 32 71 402554

European Forum on the Great Lakes
To be contacted through:
European Center for Common Ground
Avenue de Tervuren 94
B-1040 Brussels
Belgium
tel. +32 2 7367 262
fax +32 2 7323 033

DRA
Laan van Meerdervoort 192
2517 BH Den Haag
The Netherlands
tel. +31 70 345 2255
fax +31 70 356 0753

ECOR
Brachterhof 38
5932 XM Tegelen
The Netherlands
tel/fax +31 77 374 0290
  or +45 3332 6432
email cffkjm@inet.uni-c.dk
  or cscherrer@copri.dk

*Data on the following organisations can be found
in the Directory section:*
Great Lakes Policy Forum
Compagnie des Apôtres de la Paix
Search for Common Ground Burundi
Centre of the Study of the Great Lakes
International Alert
African Centre for the Constructive Resolution
of Disputes (ACCORD)
Communita di Sant Egidio
International Crisis Group
The Forum on Early Earning and Early
Response (FEWER)
Synergies Africa
Femmes Africa Solidarité

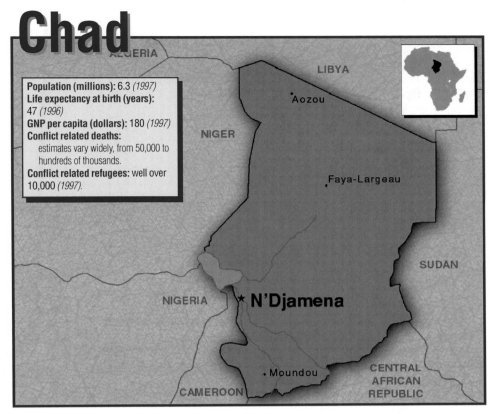

Chad

Population (millions): 6.3 *(1997)*
Life expectancy at birth (years):
47 *(1996)*
GNP per capita (dollars): 180 *(1997)*
Conflict related deaths:
  estimates vary widely, from 50,000 to
  hundreds of thousands.
Conflict related refugees: well over
10,000 *(1997)*.

ALGERIA
LIBYA
Aozou
NIGER
Faya-Largeau
SUDAN
NIGERIA ★ N'Djamena
Moundou
CENTRAL
AFRICAN
CAMEROON
REPUBLIC

Can the Cycle of War be Broken?

Chad, which links both West and North Africa with Central Africa, has known
little peace since its independence in 1960. A succession of civil wars, interference
from Libya - its powerful neighbour to the north - and violent changes of regime
have left the country devastated and destitute. Elections which passed relatively
peacefully may however herald a new period of greater stability. One further cause
for optimism is the emergence of a small but active civil society which is intent on
bringing an end to more than three decades of clientelism and violence. The need
for change is becoming more urgent in the light of the expected oil boom in the
country from 2000 ◆ *By* Bram Posthumus

Chad is one of the many oddities left behind
by colonial cartographers and perhaps one of
the more striking examples of what Basil
Davidson called 'The Black Man's Burden': the
artificial nation state in Africa. Under French
colonial rule, which only lasted from 1891 until
independence in 1960, the territory was part of
French Central Africa. With nothing more than a
set of lines defining the independent state of
Chad, a concept of national unity had to be
invented. The heavy-handed way in which this

was done by the first post-independence
government fed and fanned the succession of
civil wars that have ravaged the country.
Aggravating factors were regional differences
within Chad, clashing politico-military
personalities at the top of the various groups
vying for power, clientelist politics in the capital
city N'Djamena, and outside interference.

Chad can be roughly divided into the mainly
pastoral, Muslim and Arabic-speaking north and
east (called the north) and the mainly

agricultural, Christian/animist, African and Francophone south-western tip of the country (known as the south). Before French rule, northerners would carry out raids in the south for slaves. Under the French, the southerners were quick to spot the advantages of western education, and since education automatically led to jobs in the civil service, southerners came to dominate the state apparatus.

Unsurprisingly, a southern activist and MP, François Tombalbaye became the first president of independent Chad. Political intolerance, enforced nationalism through a one-party state system, exorbitant taxation and the erratic nature of his government turned existing but surmountable differences between north and south (language, religion, culture) into irreconcilable divisions. In 1965, the first northern rebellions took place. Tombalbaye was killed in a violent coup in 1975 and replaced by General Felix Malloum, also a southerner.

The 1970s saw three significant changes. First, the north gained a foothold in the capital. In the face of a major military offensive from the north, Malloum was forced to sign a so-called *Chartre Fondamentale*, which guaranteed a degree of power sharing. He signed the Charter in August 1978. The other signatory was Hissène Habré, a Toubou from a northern clan, a man of letters turned rebel who had crashed onto the world scene by holding a French anthropologist, Françoise Claustre (and, later, also her husband) hostage between 1974 and 1977. With Habré and his troops, the north-south divide was transferred to and ultimately destroyed the capital.

Secondly, the wars became less political and began increasingly to reflect the personality clashes among the country's leaders. This was most prominently the case in the long-standing rivalry between Habré and another northerner, Goukouni Oueddei, the son of the traditional leader of the Toubou in the Tibesti Region. Their rivalry would prove to be the undoing of the entire country. The issue that divided them most deeply was the question of how to deal with Libya.

Libya's involvement represented the third change: the beginning of active outside interference with Chad's violent conflicts (see also the section on the Chad-Libya conflict).

Habré saw the Libyans as invaders and considered himself a true Chadian nationalist, the guardian of national unity. Oueddei on the other hand, favoured Libyan involvement - indeed Libya had backed the northern rebellion since 1977.

But there was wider interference. In the early 1980s, the civil wars briefly took on a Cold War hue with Habré receiving extensive American support brought to him via Liberia, Egypt and Sudan. Ultimately, this helped bring him the presidency in 1982. The American support formed part of the US strategy of the time which was aimed at containing Libya. Ironically, Sudan was instrumental in the success of the uprising that brought down Habré in 1990. It was led by his former commander, and the current president, Idriss Déby. Another major personality clash developed between these two men.

The former-colonial power, France, was frequently called upon to save sitting governments from imminent defeat, which it did on three occasions. First, the French fought against northern rebels on behalf of Tombalbaye and did so reasonably successfully. They pulled out in 1971, leaving 900 men in N'Djamena. Seven years later, they were back, on the side of Malloum in an ultimately futile bid to stem the northern take-over of the country's political system. The French were also called upon by Habré to help fight off the Libyans, a campaign which was ultimately crowned with success in 1987.

Loose factions opposing the government of the day, coalescing into bigger groups, fragmenting into new splinters became a well-established pattern in Chadian politics. Some opposition groups grew into 'national' factions, while others remained under the control of local warlords with no ambition beyond control of their turf. These armed organisations are deemed to be symptomatic of the pervasive culture of violence, which is compounded by the wide availability of small arms. As the chairman of the Human Rights Commission within the Transitional Council told the *EU-ACP Courier* in 1994: 'In this country, people who are disconcerted pick up a weapon, go off into the bush and start organising rebellions'.

According to Chadian political activists and intellectuals, this cycle of rebellion, repression, new rebellions and more repression can only be broken if the political culture of the country undergoes radical change.

On close inspection, the presidents, from both north and south, have much in common. With the exception of Tombalbaye they are all military men who have come to power through the barrel of a gun and maintain position by combining charm offensives with brutal repression. None have shied away from mass violence in order to demonstrate their hold on power. All have attempted to legitimise their presence by either holding (usually rigged) elections or changing the constitution. All have promoted a climate of clan-based clientelism. The state apparatus has been filled first by southerners, and then by people from the north and east. Personal and clan loyalties have proved more important than competence. In a special feature on Chad, published in the *EU-ACP Courier* of May-June 1999, opposition politician Jean Bawoyeu Alingue remarks that 'The so-called north-south conflict is exacerbated by all the injustices this country has known.'

It was not until the early 1990s that some space became available for human rights groups and other members of civil society who tried to promote non-violent and reasonable ways of doing politics. Their freedom to operate appears to be increasingly restricted as 1999 progresses. For example, parliamentarians and journalists who questioned Chad's disastrous adventure in the Democratic Republic of Congo on the side of President Kabila (274 soldiers were killed in a single battle in 1998) have been harassed and intimidated. The latest controversy regarding the country's future oil revenues (see Prospects) will show how hard Chadian civil society will have to fight if it is to defend the ground it has gained in the past decade.

Conflict Dynamics

The very first rebel group called itself *Front de Libération National Tchadien* (FROLINAT). With distinctly left-wing sympathies and intending to redress the imbalances that had grown up between north and south and build a truly national state, it was the only Chadian rebel movement with a political programme. FROLINAT split as early as 1966 and became one of three groups, of which the FAN (Northern Armed Forces), led by Hissène Habré, was another. The various northern rebel groups remained active in the north and east and another group, claiming to be the 'Third Army' of FROLINAT, began operations in the area where Chad borders Nigeria.

In 1976, the FAN itself split, as a result of the rivalry between Goukouni Oueddei and Hissène Habré. Their dispute was fought out in the vast Bourkou, Ennedi and Tibesti areas (known as BET), which comprise one-third of the country but contain only six per cent of its population. Oueddei, with Libyan aid, was victorious in 1977 and threatened N'Djamena. Habré formed a Sudan-mediated coalition of convenience with president Malloum and the French. The result of this exercise was the *Chartre Fondamental* (1978). Malloum kept the presidency and Habré became prime minister.

Any hopes that this arrangement would last vanished when on February 12, 1979, N'Djamena was destroyed in battles between troops loyal to Malloum and Habré. Muslims and southerners were massacred and fighting continued in N'Djamena and the rest of Chad throughout the year. At least eleven factions were at war. Libya once again intervened and threatened to capture the capital, having already taken possession of the Aouzou Strip (see the separate section on this conflict). In the southern town of Moundou, more than 800 Muslims were killed, for which Malloum's police-chief, Wadal Abder Kamougue, was blamed.

This all-out war prompted the first pan-African peace initiative. There were protracted OAU-mediated negotiations, resulting in a Government of National Unity and Transition (GUNT), briefly headed by Oueddei and also involving Habré. Nigerian peacekeepers were sent to N'Djamena. However, fighting among the various factions flared up regularly. In the south, Kamougue carved out his own fiefdom.

After a brief period of relative peace, the GUNT collapsed under the weight of its own internal divisions. In March 1980, Oueddei again asked his friends, the Libyans, for help when Habré began making military progress in

N'Djamena and elsewhere. Fighting raged throughout much of 1980 and the French, who had kept essential services going in the capital, left altogether. With massive Libyan support, Oueddei managed to get rid of Habré for the time being. He took power; the Libyans stayed on, until they were replaced by another ineffective OAU peacekeeping force.

With American aid, Habré launched an offensive from Sudan, in January 1982. Six months later, he chased Oueddei out of N'Djamena. The northern take-over of the country was complete. During nearly seven years in power, Habré pursued a carrot-and-stick policy, holding reconciliation talks with a variety of faction leaders on the one hand while conducting merciless punitive campaigns on the other. In August 1982 one such campaign ended Kamougue's fiefdom in the south. In June 1983, Oueddei repeated his first rebellion, seizing parts of the BET region. Fighting in the south continued through 1983-84, between government forces and local commandos, known as codos.

Chad was now effectively divided by the 16th parallel, with Goukouni Oueddei, his allies and Libya above it; and Hissène Habré, his allies, and the French below it. There was a tense truce, during which the two sides, both consisting of volatile and unpredictable alliances prepared for the next war. Meanwhile some physical and economic regeneration took place.

In February 1986, Oueddei and Libya crossed the 16th parallel, triggering a French response. N'Djamena airport was bombed, as were Libyan air bases in northern Chad. Habré was greatly helped by a dramatic falling-out between Oueddei and his Libyan allies. When, in October 1986, word came out that Oueddei was prepared to make peace with his arch-rival Habré, his house in Tripoli was surrounded and he was shot and wounded. His fighters then decided to side with Habré and Libya was comprehensively defeated in 1987. Most faction leaders returned to Chad to join Habré's government, leaving Oueddei as a lone figure of opposition in exile, now living in Algiers.

Another period of relative calm followed. A referendum was held for a new constitution in December 1989. Its democratic credentials are doubtful, to put it mildly, but Habré was

endorsed for another seven years. However, he was not to complete his time in office. Incursions were mounted from the east by the president's former commander Idriss Déby who was joined by the re-grouped codos. In 1990, Déby, with Sudanese aid, launched his biggest offensive and took N'Djamena on December 1, sending Habré into exile.

'I don't bring gold, or money - but freedom' said Déby on taking over the presidency. But the 1990s have seen more rebellions, clashes, talks, deals and double-deals. It must be added, however, that the scale and intensity of the fighting have certainly not reached the catastrophic levels of the 1970s and 1980s. Nevertheless, very serious human rights abuses, including mass executions, rapes and beatings, continue to be reported, especially in the south. Déby has faced coup attempts and there have been at least five armed-opposition groups operating at any one time in the west, east and south. The biggest challenge to the Déby government to date was posed by FARF (Armed Forces for a Federal Republic). FARF posed a threat for two reasons: it openly harboured federalist aspirations and it operated from an area where oil had been discovered. In May 1998, FARF surrendered to the government; its leader, Laokein Barde, reportedly fled the country. In early 1999 another rebellion took place in the BET area, led by a disgruntled former minister in the Déby government, once more vindicating the words of the Human Rights Commission's chairman, quoted above. In August 1999, president Déby sent a delegation to the BET to open talks with the rebel leader, Youssouf Togoimi, in order to, as one government official put it, 'find out what he wants'. It was hoped a settlement could be reached.

Official Conflict Management

In 1981, the *United Nations* was formally requested to help finance the African peacekeeping efforts, but the Chad delegation at the UN blocked the request. In 1995, the UN visited Chad in a mission reporting on arms proliferation in the West African region. It described the country as 'a potential powder keg', awash with arms, and beset by 'staggering political instability'. The mission met with the

FAYA OASIS, CHAD

head of state and recommended increased support for the demobilisation effort.

Chad provoked the *Organisation of African Unity*'s first major peace initiative. In 1979, when the entire country was suffering from grave factional fighting with heavy loss of life, the OAU requested Nigeria to convene several peace conferences, none of which proved particularly successful. The OAU also attempted to settle the subsequent war of early 1980. Secretary-General Edem Kodjo presented the factions with a simple peace plan, worked out with Liberian president Tolbert (five days before he was murdered in a coup). The plan included proposals for cease-fire, talks, a peacekeeping force and a monitoring commission. A multinational force was going to be sent, but for a limited time and with a limited mandate, because the OAU had no money to pay for the operation, estimated to cost US$ 62 million.

However, none of the main faction leaders in Chad had time to discuss the latest OAU peace plan. Not until November 1981 did the first OAU-sponsored peacekeepers enter Chad, and then in a force far smaller than the 6,000 originally planned. Their mandate was unclear, their financial base very shaky and they could not

stop the fighting. Three months before Habré's military takeover of the country, Nigerian troops started going home, effectively pulling the plug on the entire exercise, which formally ended in June 1982. Since then, the OAU has limited itself to mediation attempts.

Neighbouring and other African governments have made a number of efforts to settle the conflicts. All of them took place in the midst of battles between government and one or more of the factions. Between 1977 and the late 1990s, countries and actors as diverse as Niger, Nigeria, Sudan, Libya, Togo, Guinea, Senegal, Egypt, Gabon and the Central African Republic have played their parts in trying to bring the fighting groups to the negotiating table. They acted either in tandem with the OAU or - in the case of the Togolese and Gabonese presidents - individually. Invariably, the cease-fires that resulted were short-lived. Sudan, Libya and Niger pushed the idea of the Government of National Unity (GUNT), which was laid down in the so-called *Chartre Fondamental* of March 27, 1978. The other tangible result of mediation on the part of Sudan, Nigeria (and France) at the height of the February 1979 fighting was the series of four OAU-sponsored conferences in Nigeria.

In August 1978, France helped mediate peace talks between Malloum and Habré, which contributed to the establishment of the short-lived first GUNT. In February 1979, the commander of the French troops in N'Djamena, Louis Forest, participated in mediation efforts, initiated by Sudan, between Malloum and Habré. Later that month, the French government offered its good offices to settle the Habré-Oueddei conflict.

France and the US paid modest sums into the maintenance of the OAU peacekeeping force that was in Chad between November 1981 and June 1982. During a press conference in February 1979, the French president at the time, Giscard d'Estaing, first raised the idea of Chad as a federation. This has remained a taboo with southerners favouring federation and northerners rejecting it. With Déby in power and the prospect of unprecedented windfalls from future oil exploitation (currently being prepared in the south), federalism is never likely to be contemplated by the central government.

On February 20, 1997, the *European Parliament* passed a motion expressing its concern over reports of human rights abuses emanating from Chad and cautioning EU member states against providing the Chadian government with political, financial and military support - a reference to, among others, France.

All *Chadian governments* have attempted to make peace with rebels, only to either renege on their own promises or to find that they themselves had been double-crossed or overtaken by events. As early as 1968, secret negotiations were held with the Toubou rebel leaders in the north and in 1971 the government reached an Accord with rebels in the east and with some six FROLINAT leaders. None of these initiatives bore any fruit. Following every violent change of regime, attempts were made at reconciliation. In 1982, president Oueddei set up a short-lived National Reconstruction Committee. Hissène Habré did something similar after his takeover in 1982, and so did his replacement Idriss Déby in 1990. There have been occasional successes: some factions have disbanded, integrated their soldiers into the army and become political parties. With others, agreements continue to be reached and broken. Following the old tradition of secret talks,

Kamougue, now speaker of the National Assembly, approached FARF leader Laokein Barde, in order to work out a negotiated settlement. These talks were once again overtaken by events in May 1998.

Government attempts at peace and reconciliation have frequently taken the form of compensation and job-offers to those who are willing to come out of the bush. In a sense, reconciliation was frequently 'bought', leaving former rebels with the option of returning to the bush if they decided they did not like the terms of the deal any more. This system is still by and large in place: particularly successful rebel leaders (i.e. those that become president) can reward the loyalty of their fellow rebels, immediately giving rise to resentment among those excluded from preferment. Perhaps the more substantial changes that the Déby government has made, including reinstating the multi-party system in 1992, after exactly thirty years of one-party rule, will open the way for a non-violent method of opposition. The National Conference, which was held in 1993, and in which, forty opposition parties, twenty other organisations and six rebel movements took part, represented a move in that direction.

An office in the transitional parliament was set up and tasked with creating a mechanism to deal with complaints of human rights abuses. Human rights organisations in the country have accused it of being ineffective.

In 1993, the government set up a *National Disarmament Commission*. It has met with considerable success, retrieving 11,000 weapons. Nevertheless, the large variety of rebel movements and the upsurge of bandits (*'coupeurs de route'*) suggest that there remains a lot to be done. There are still an estimated 30,000 guns unaccounted for in Chad and for many people the gun has become the primary means of production.

Multi-Track Diplomacy
Domestic

During the February 1979 massacres in Moundou, Chad's most senior imam and bishop travelled from the capital to the southern town to try and defuse the situation in what was one of the few religiously inspired attempts to intervene in the conflict.

Since the early 1990s, human rights organisations have sprung up and from 1992 onwards they have staged successful stayaways and demonstrations in N'Djamena. The first occasion was prompted by the murder - allegedly by soldiers - of the vice-chairman of the *Ligue Tchadienne des Droits de l'Homme (LTDH,* Chadian Human Rights League). This was one of the few signs of public outrage at the numerous human rights violations that have been perpetrated with apparent impunity virtually since independence.

The LTDH, which was set up in 1991, has kept up its campaign for the respect of human rights on the part of the security forces. In February 1993 it accused the Republican Guards of conducting a genocide campaign in the south. Other human rights groups, like the *Association Tchadienne pour la Promotion et la Défense des Droits de l'Homme* (ATPDH, Chadian Association for the Promotion and the Defence of Human Rights) also reported massacres of civilians in the south. The Chad Non-Violence organisation even recalled its representatives from the transitional parliament that had been put in place pending elections.

Finally, there was a modicum of success: the Centre pour la Recherche et la Coordination des Renseignements (CRCR, the government intelligence service) was dissolved in May 1993. As under Habré, this branch had been responsible for gross and widespread human rights violations.

In March 1998, an alliance of human rights groups and labour unions called a two-day strike to protest against killings committed by all fighting forces in the country, especially the government and the FARF rebels. This was the first report of such mass popular action.

All human rights organisations in Chad are subjected to various forms of repression: people are arrested and tortured - torture is routine in Chad - or raped. In late March 1998, police surrounded the offices of major human rights institutions in N'Djamena, in response to the protests against the killings in the south.

The *Association Tchadienne pour la Non-Violence* (ATNV) is a human rights organisation, mainly active in the south. Its chairman, Julien Beassemda, was attacked in Europe in November 1997, following an assault on the compound next to his house, where former FARF fighters were also staying. Beassemda was deeply involved in the negotiations between FARF and the government. He regarded the attack on his house as the end of the peace process. ANTV has 61 local committees and 5,000 members in the south. The organisation is engaged in activities of reconciliation, mediation between nomads and farmers, settling the FARF issue by involving all players - including traditional leaders - in the peace process. It uses a non-violent method of action well known throughout Francophone Africa: the *'villes mortes'*, or 'dead cities', where everyone stays indoors and nothing opens for one or two days. It has training centres for non-violent conflict resolution and has helped set up a seminar in Donia on the oil project, which was attended by all stakeholders (see the Prospects section below).

At a different level, the Al Mouna Centre in N'Djamena organised colloquia in 1996 and 1998 on the real or perceived linguistic and religious differences between the north and the south. Its publications include a book of essays, entitled *The North-South Conflict: Myth or Reality?* This kind of work could prove very useful for building a more inclusive political culture in the country.

International
French military involvement received far from unanimous backing from French opinion leaders. French intellectuals, among them Jean-Paul Sartre, made their opposition to the French adventures in its former colonies publicly known.

Amnesty International has issued reports on human rights violations since the 1980s, which have been even-handed in their approach. Government and rebel forces have either denied or ignored the charges. Since the early 1990s, however, Amnesty has been one of the channels that local human rights and peace groups can use to further the causes of non-violent conflict resolution, respect for human rights, an end to clientelism and an equitable distribution of the wealth the oil may produce as of 2001/2.

The breakthrough, as Eirene-Chad's coordinator Hans Determeyer has argued, came when e-mail arrived in Chad, enabling international NGOs to lobby vociferously against the proposed oil project, acting on information coming from the country. This is the case in the proposed oil project (see Prospects), against which development and environmental groups like *Friends of the Earth, Oxfam*, and other British, Dutch and German groups have been lobbying their governments. They want them and the World Bank to study that project's social, environmental and economic impact. The lobby has so far resulted in a Dutch governmental commission, which was gravely worried about the possible consequences. Indeed the World Bank has many questions it wants to see answered before any money is made available. Both inside and outside Chad, the actions and behaviour of the international NGOs have come in for criticism. They have been accused of bully-boy tactics, aimed at stopping the project altogether, while Chadian groups want the oil to start flowing with guarantees for fair distribution of the proceeds.

Prospects

The next big test for Chad's ability to hang together and develop a new, non-violent, and more equitable politics, is imminent. The south is the economic lifeline for the entire country. It produces the cotton that earns Chad its little foreign exchange and it feeds the country when the rains are good. But Chad stands to gain a great deal more foreign exchange when the Doba oilfield, also in the south, is opened for exploitation. This windfall, combined with continued northern domination of political life and the long-standing tradition of clientelism, is the perfect backdrop for the next conflict. However, conflict is not inevitable and may yet be averted.

Oil was first discovered in Doba in 1974. In January 1995, agreement was reached between a consortium consisting of Exxon, Shell and Elf-Aquitaine and the governments of Chad and Cameroon to build a 1,050 km pipeline from Doba to Kribi on the Cameroonian Atlantic Coast. A parliamentarian, Yorongar Ngarlejy, who alleged that Déby got a kickback out of the project, was thrown in jail but later released on the personal orders of the president. The oil consortium will invest US$ 3 billion in the project and has extracted generous tax breaks

from both African governments in return. The World Bank is discussing a loan to the Chadian government to let the oil project go ahead, providing the oil companies with the political backing they need. A decision is expected in September 1999. Meanwhile the consortium assures all who care to listen that every possible precaution has been taken to avoid creating a second Niger Delta: pollution, people displacement and social disruption will be absolutely minimal or non-existent, they claim.

The Chadian government is projected to earn a total of US$ 8.5 billion from the exploitation, about US$ 100 million per annum. Minorities at Risk writes: 'How the revenue from the oil is distributed and how the people of the region are affected by the building of wells...will determine whether [people] remain content'. In December 1998 parliament passed a law stipulating how the money will be spent (mainly on health, education and infrastructure). It will also be kept in a separate bank account, theoretically assuring transparency. Time will tell if the old ways have indeed been replaced by new ones.

Recommendations

The UN mission is very worried about the free flow of arms in Chad and recognises that the problems here and in Niger are probably the most intractable in the region. The national Disarmament Commission was seen as a positive development. More along these lines needs to be done but it is unclear how this can be brought about in a cash-strapped nation with a foreign debt of close to US$ 1 billion. All these problems were acknowledged by the mission.

In the Netherlands, there is a small working group on Chad within the Dutch Labour Party. In a modest 1998 publication on the oil issue (Dutch only) it recommended the oil consortium to behave responsibly and minimise impact on local biodiversity, agricultural land and drinking water quality. It also recommended more civil society participation in Chad itself, thus ensuring better distribution of oil and other revenue, a watchdog function for the World bank (although the group doubted whether this was feasible) and a modest role for international NGOs.

Service Information

Reports
Amnesty International
- Chad - Hope betrayed. 1997

Minorities at Risk
- The Southerners in Chad. 1994, regularly updated

Other Publications
Country Survey: Chad. In: EU-ACP Courier, May-June 1999. Published by DGVIII, Brussels
Conflits et violences au Chad, by Bernard Lanne. In: *Afrique Contemporaine, numéro spécial, 4e trimestre* 1996
Between Sand Dunes and Savanna - Chad and its Environment. Panos Institute, London
The North-South Conflict: Myth or Reality? Al Mouna Centre, N'Djamena

Selected Internet Sites
www.eia.doe.gov/emeu/chad/chadlinks (offers a variety of links to political and economic organisations - including those who are at both sides of the debate about the Chad-Cameroon oil project - Amnesty information on Chad, the US State Department statements on human rights in Chad and many more)
http://antenna.nl/aseed/oilwatch (NGO site which carries news on oil companies and their behaviour)
www.exxon.com/essochad (comprehensive site with the oil company's side of the oil story)

Resource Contacts
Jan van Criekinge - National Development Cooperation Commission of Belgium . Email: Jan.Van.Criekinge@ncos.ngonet.be
Hans Determeijer - hans@antenna.nl

Best gateway organisations to Chad:
- Centre de l'Information et de Liaison des Organisations Non-Gouvernementales, CILONG. Email: cilong@intnet.td
- Eirene/Chad. Email eirene-int@eirene.org

Organisations
Association Tchadienne pour la Promotion et la Défense de Droits de l'Homme (ATPDH)
B.P. 4082
N'Djamena
Chad
Tel. +235 51 58 33
Fax +235 51 58 84

Ligue Tchadienne des Droits de l'Homme (LTDH)
B.P. 2037
N'Djamena
Chad
Tel. +235 51 61 35
Fax + 235 51 61 09

Data on the following organisations can be found in the Directory section
Amnesty International
Oxfam

Chad and Libya
Good Neighbours, Enemies, Brothers - But Never Trusting Friends

Having oscillated between plans for a complete merger on the one hand and outright war on the other, the relationship between Chad and Libya merits special mention. In addition to the almost perennial dispute over the Aouzou Strip, Libya has interfered directly in the internal politics of its much poorer southern neighbour (the income gap is 42:1). This interference finally resulted in a concerted - almost national - effort on the part of the Chadians to encourage their Libyan brothers and friends to return to their own country. Relations currently appear to be stable.

Conflict Dynamics

In 1969, Libya offered to mediate between the government of president Tombalbaye and the FROLINAT rebel armies. The Chadians refused. There were suspicions - later vindicated - about Libyan aid to the northern rebels.

Five years later, Libya occupied 114,000 square kilometres of Chadian territory, known as the Aouzou Strip, citing old claims to the area as justification. Under a 1935 treaty favouring Libya, the Strip had been divided between Italy and France. Following World War II, however, a new treaty was signed favouring what was then French Central Africa. Libya also claimed, with some justification, that the peoples living in the volcanic deserts of the BET region would probably prefer being part of Libya. However, Chad suspected - equally correctly - that Libya was intent on the annexation of the entire country.

Libya provided those Toubou rebels who were led by Oueddei with military and logistical support, enabling them to run large tracts of the BET region virtually unopposed from 1965 until 1988. This led the Chadian government to break off diplomatic ties with Tripoli completely, in 1978 and lodge a complaint with the UN Security Council. This was solved by neighbourly mediation.

In 1979, Libya took advantage of the turmoil within Chad to again invade the area. Because of his rapprochement with the Government of National Unity at the time, Goukouni Oueddei and his FROLINAT forces chased the Libyans out of the country, with some help from Habré. But a year later, in 1980, Oueddei again appealed to Libya to save his position against the onslaught of Habré's FAN. Another Libyan ally at the time, the Chadian Minister of Foreign Affairs and faction leader Acyl Amat extended a welcome to any friendly help in times of crisis. The Libyans were ready to comply. No reference was made to the Aouzou Strip. In the course of 1980, Libya sent up to 15,000 troops into Chad and defeated Habré in December 1980.

Later, the issue of Libyan assistance led to serious rifts in the anti-Habré camp. This came to a head when in January 1981, Colonel Ghadaffi proposed a full-blown merger between the two countries. It appeared that both president Oueddei and Kamougue rejected the idea outright, while Amat and the southern Muslims were all in favour. Not only the Government of National Unity but also the anti-Habré alliance disintegrated over this issue. In April 1981, Oueddei's and Amat's troops fought out their differences in eastern and central Chad, while the Libyans themselves organised mutinies in the south in order to destabilise Kamougue's position there. Libyan troops began to behave more and more like an occupation force, amidst growing resentment from the Chadians, not least their president, who was powerless to do anything about it. When the Libyans pulled out in November 1981 under intense OAU and Chadian pressure, they retained control of the Aouzou Strip. Seven months later the Oueddei government was over and his US-backed rival Habré marched into N'Djamena.

Libya once again entered deep into Chadian territory when it helped Oueddei to his victories in the north in 1983. Since the French were helping Habré with 3,000 troops, a direct confrontation between the two countries was inevitable and both sides used their air power to bomb each other's airfields, near N'Djamena and Ouadi-Doum respectively.

By 1985-6 it was clear that Oueddei was too close to the Libyans for his own comfort, unlike Amat, his successor Acheikh Ibn Omar and other faction leaders in the northern alliance. Consequently the alliance around Oueddei split, leaving the Libyans and a few smaller factions to fight Habré and the French. This was to result in their biggest defeat. Habré's troops, now assisted by elements from the old GUNT and with French backing attacked the Libyans, using nimble four-wheel drive trucks, driving them out of the country, including the Aouzou Strip by June 1987. The Strip, however, was retaken in August. The Libyan armed forces left behind up to US$ 1 billion worth of Soviet equipment and had more of their hardware destroyed when Habré launched a retaliatory attack into Libya, destroying a major airbase. A peace process was then started which led to the resumption of normal relations in October 1988. Habré remained wary of the Libyans, and asked the French to maintain their presence in Chad.

Indeed, this was by no means the end of Libyan-Chadian antagonism. Libya continued to occupy the Aouzou Strip and it used proxies such as the Islamic Legion to destabilise the government. The Islamic Legion was a group of West African and Middle East mercenaries, operating from Sudanese soil. The incursion that brought Idriss Déby to power was backed by Libya, through Sudan. Since then, the situation has calmed considerably. Libya and Chad agreed to hold talks and in April 1998, Ghadaffi came to N'Djamena on an official visit, amidst a great deal of public protest. However by mid-1999 there were signs that this new honeymoon period was drawing to a close.

Official Conflict Management

The *United Nations* has at times discussed the issues between Chad and Libya in the Security Council. The organisation also sent an observer mission to the Aouzou Strip. Called UNASOG (United Nations Aouzou Strip Observer Group), it was established in 1994 to verify the withdrawal of Libyan forces in accordance with the verdict reached at the International Court of Justice in The Hague (see below). To this end, it sent nine observers and six international civilian staff to the area between May and June 1994. According to UN documentation, UNASOG achieved its objective when both countries declared withdrawal to be complete.

Chad and Libya finally agreed to lay the case before the International Court of Justice, which on February 3, 1994 rejected Libya's claim to the territory. This was followed by an April 5 agreement on full Libyan withdrawal by May 30, to be followed by treaties on friendship, good neighbourliness and cooperation.

The *Organization of African Unity* (OAU) has undertaken numerous attempts to settle the disputes between Chad and Libya. In 1977, it set up a commission to look into the border dispute. In 1981, following Libya's de-facto occupation of Chad in the wake of Habré's defeat, the OAU attempted to have the Libyans replaced by an pan-African peacekeeping force, without much success.

When the fiercest fighting between the two countries was under way, in 1987, the OAU mediated a cease-fire between the two sides which came into effect in September. Diplomatic moves towards rapprochement continued when Malian president Moussa Traore, as chairman of the OAU, arranged a direct meeting between the two leaders, Hissène Habré and Colonel Ghadaffi, resulting in an 'historic handshake'. The Nigerian, Algerian and Gabonese heads of state were present at the occasion. Nevertheless, fighting continued on the ground, while a commission, headed by president Bongo of Gabon tried to work out a settlement. Despite sporadic clashes, the cease-fire appeared to hold but neither side was willing to accept neutral arbitration on the matter of the Aouzou Strip. Then, on May 25, 1988, Ghadaffi demonstrated a complete change of mind at the summit celebrating the 25th birthday of the OAU, recognising the Chadian government and expressing his wish to settle all disputes in a brotherly fashion. Talks began in Gabon in July, and the peace process actually gathered pace with the handing over of prisoners of war to the OAU, in September and the restoration of full diplomatic relations, in October.

Individual governments have also made contributions to negotiations on various occasions. The first mediation attempt was undertaken by Sudan which intervened when Chadian-Libyan relations were almost at breaking point in early 1978. The two countries restored diplomatic ties and promised to search for a peaceful solution for the Aouzou problem. All this was confirmed at a mini-conference in southern Libya, in the presence of high-level representatives from Sudan and Niger. In various later stages, personal interventions by the presidents of Gabon, Tunisia and Togo - among

others - resulted in the two sides restoring diplomatic relations.

Prospects

A definitive solution to the Aouzou problem has still to be found. It is doubtful whether Libya has indeed completely terminated its occupation; reports in 1997 claimed that it still held at least some parts of the Strip. Chad certainly does not want to reclaim the strip by military means. For the time being, Libya seems to have frozen its designs on the country as a whole.

Chad will also remain stuck with the problem of an unknown number of landmines in the northern BET region, which have been placed there by the Libyan armed forces.

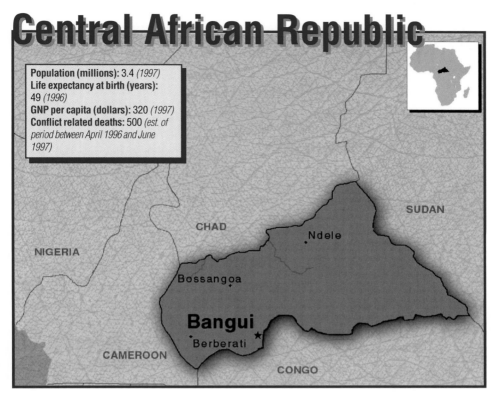

Central African Republic

Population (millions): 3.4 *(1997)*
Life expectancy at birth (years): 49 *(1996)*
GNP per capita (dollars): 320 *(1997)*
Conflict related deaths: 500 *(est. of period between April 1996 and June 1997)*

CHAD
SUDAN
NIGERIA
Ndele
Bossangoa
Bangui
Berberati
CAMEROON
CONGO

Ethnic Strife in a Democratic Setting

The Central African Republic was hit by a series of mutinies in the mid-1990s. Fuelled by anger over arrears in pay, the army's discontent coincided with a democratisation process and turned into a political conflict between ethnic and regional groups. President Ange-Félix Patassé was pitted against former dictator André Kolingba in this confrontation. Calm was finally restored only after a peace process brokered by the OAU and taken over by the UN. In November and December 1998 elections took place. There is doubt, however, whether the root causes of the conflict have been adequately addressed ◆ *By* Jos Havermans

The Central African Republic (CAR) gained formal independence from France in 1960, however, French interests continued to determine the course of events in the republic. French economic and political influence is perfectly exemplified by the case of Valery Giscard d'Estaing, the French politician who was elected president of France in May 1974. By the 1930s, the Giscard family had built up a considerable stake in a French company (SOFFO) that was engaged in rubber trade in colonial French Africa, which included the area

now known as the Central African Republic. Valery Giscard d'Estaing forged a warm personal relationship with Jean-Bedel Bokassa, the dictator who ruled the CAR from 1966 to 1979, and throughout his term of office continued to pursue his family's, as well as France's, economic and political interests in the Republic.

French control of the Central African Republic reached its apotheosis in the *coup d'etat* which ended the regime of Bokassa in 1979. Observers and historians agree that the coup (Operation Barracuda) was wholly organised and coordinated by French officials from French government offices in Paris. Even the speech in which the new president David Dacko presented himself as the new leader to the Central African people is reported to have been written by French officials.

The Republic remained central to France's African policy as it was the site of its main military base on the continent. France used this base to intervene in former colonies in the region, including the Central African Republic itself.

As one of the poorest countries in the world, the CAR was - and still is - highly dependent on foreign aid. By providing most of this aid itself, France was able to use the Republic's dependency to influence political developments and protect its interests in the country. For their part, CAR leaders could sometimes exploit France's high political and economic stakes in their country to increase financial aid. They did this by threatening to leave the French political camp and seek patronage and assistance from other foreign powers such as Libya.

Dependency on French aid and the presence of French troops in Bangui meant that France was able to exert a great influence on developments in the republic, including the turmoil that broke out in 1996. In April of that year, soldiers of the national army of the Central African Republic took to the streets in Bangui to demand the immediate payment of overdue salaries. The military had not been paid for three months, a recurring negligence on the part of the CAR authorities attributed to a combination of economic collapse and bad governance. The mutiny led president Ange-Félix Patassé, who had been elected in 1993 in free and democratic elections, to mobilise his presidential guard. French troops stationed in the country also took up positions in Bangui with the mandate to protect French nationals and to help defend the presidential palace and other key installations. After president Patassé had promised swift payment of the stalled salaries, the mutineers returned to their barracks. The rebellion lasted for only a few days and some nine people, including civilians, were said to have been killed.

In May 1996, a second mutiny took place. This time, however, signs of political motives were more evident. The mutiny followed shortly after a mass rally, which had been organised by the opposition parties to demand the government's resignation. The mutineers took five hostages, including the army's chief of staff and a cabinet minister. France brought in about 500 reinforcements and after five days of fighting, suppressed the rebellion. Eleven soldiers and 32 civilians were reported to have been killed and at least 200 people were wounded.

Despite French financial support to help pay overdue salaries and the installation of a government of national unity, opposition dissatisfaction continued to smoulder and a third mutiny shook the country in November 1996. Rebels occupied a large area of Bangui and again took hostages. During fierce fighting in late November and early December, more than 100 people were killed. France deployed its 1,450 resident troops in the streets of Bangui once more. This time, regional African leaders intervened and helped broker an agreement, which became known as the Bangui Accords.

The confrontation in the Central African Republic is said to be fuelled by a power struggle between political elites engaged in competition for the country's scarce economic resources. This struggle has an ethnic dimension in that it pits several ethnic groups against each other. These groups are the Sara-Kaba of President Patassé in the north on the one hand, and the Yakoma, the southern ethnic group of former military dictator General André Kolingba on the other. Although the Sara and Yakoma are minorities, their longstanding ties with other ethnic groups puts them at the forefront of the internal conflict.

Both camps are dominated by militants, leaving little ground in the political spectrum for moderate forces. Each camp has its own military component: the presidential guard for President Patassé, and factions within the national army for Kolingba and his allies.

According to the French lawyer and expert on Central Africa, Régis Lafargue (see bibliography), the confrontation between the two groups resulted from the tendency to strive for ethnic exclusivity. Lafargue says that Kolingba, who came to power in a bloodless coup in September 1981, established an 'ethnocracy' by only nominating people of his own or affiliated ethnic groups to important positions. When Patassé came to power in 1993 he took revenge by excluding the Yakoma from all major positions in political, military and judicial institutions. He was able to do this because he had extensive executive powers assigned to him under the new constitution that was adopted as part of the democratisation process. According to the new constitution, the president nominates the premier, his cabinet, and all civil servants, and has the right to overrule and dissolve parliament. In addition, the president has control over powerful institutions such as the presidential guard and the secret service.

These unbridled presidential powers are considered to be at the root of the conflict. The country's heritage of dictatorship, manifesting in the politicians' penchant to exploit their prerogatives to the fullest, adds to the tense situation.

Conflict Dynamics

The mutinies and subsequent clashes in Bangui caused the death of about 500 people. About 70,000 people were forced to flee Bangui. Material damage was severe. In a report published in 1998, the Central African Chamber of Commerce estimated that the mutinies had caused damage to the private sector of about CFA 41 billion, a huge amount, considering that total state revenues amounted to CFA 55 billion in 1995. About one third of trading companies had gone bankrupt. The insecurity related to the rebellions reduced national transport by some 20 per cent. The mutinies had a devastating effect on public finance and foreign investments and caused a sharp increase in unemployment.

The crisis ended in January 1997 with the signing of a political agreement, the Bangui Accords, brokered by Burkina Faso, Mali, Gabon and Chad. The Franco-African summit in Ouagadougou had called for these regional mediation efforts. The Bangui Accords were sustained by the deployment of an African peacekeeping force, MISAB. The African force, which leaned heavily on French logistical support, was replaced by UN peacekeepers (MINURCA) in April 1998. The Bangui Accords resulted in parliamentary elections in November and December 1998. Presidential elections were scheduled for late 1999, although a date for the ballot had still not been set in mid-1999. The UN Security Council extended MINURCA's mandate until November 15 of the same year.

Parliamentary elections held in late 1998 ended with a narrow victory for the opposition. The *Union of Forces for Peace* (UFAP), a coalition of opposition parties, won 55 seats in the 109-seat National Assembly. With Patassé's *Movement for the Liberation of the Central African Republic* (MLPC) winning 47 seats, independent legislators held the balance of power. Horse-trading over their loyalties revived deep-seated bitterness and rivalry. President Patassé persuaded at least one independent legislator to join the government camp in January 1999, thereby regaining a majority in the National Assembly. The president allegedly frustrated opposition activities by banning political rallies, including a UFAP meeting in February 1999 convened by the *National Unity Party* of Jean-Paul Ngoupandé, a former prime minister. This led to many opposition members boycotting the National Assembly.

Current developments suggest that the government and opposition camps have taken irreconcilable positions in a setting that is formally democratic but lacks the necessary internalisation of democratic values and practices.

Official Conflict Management

A *regional peace initiative* helped to end the crisis in the Central African Republic. In December 1996 the presidents of Burkina Faso, Chad, Gabon and Mali brokered a fifteen-day truce, which was extended by a month until January 1997. The truce was supervised by the former transitional president of Mali, Amadou Toumani Touré. The mediation of Touré and the other regional leaders eventually led to the signing of the Bangui Accords, or National Reconciliation Pact, in January 1997. The accords set the stage for a reconciliation process, which was still continuing in 1999.

The accords provided for amnesty for the mutineers, the formation of a new government of national unity, which was installed in January 1997, and the replacement of the French military force by an African peacekeeping force.

In February 1997, the regional peacekeeping force, *Mission Inter-Africaine de Surveillance de l'Application des Accords de Bangui* (MISAB) was deployed in Bangui, consisting of 800 troops from Gabon, Burkina Faso, Chad, Mali, Senegal and Togo. MISAB was logistically and financially supported by France and the Organization of African Unity (OAU). MISAB was mandated to maintain peace and security in Bangui, supervise the process of disarmament of mutinous soldiers and militias and monitor the implementation of the accords, including national elections. In June 1997, MISAB troops were attacked by army factions, leading to clashes in which several hundreds of people died, but renewed all out civil strife was prevented. Amadou Toumani Touré travelled to Bangui again, this time in his position of chairman of MISAB, to successfully negotiate a cease-fire and broker an agreement on the disarmament and reintegration in the army of the former mutineers. A pattern seemed to develop of recurring troubles, followed by recurring - successful - mediation efforts.

The *United Nations* became deeply involved in the peace process in April 1998, when MISAB was replaced by a 1,350 strong UN-peacekeeping force named *MINURCA (Mission des Nations Unies en République Centrafricaine)*. The replacement was prompted by signs that France was planning to reduce its military presence in Africa and wanted to cut most of its financial and logistical support for the African peacekeeping force. MINURCA has contingents from Canada, France, Senegal, Togo, Burkina Faso, Gabon, Chad, Mali and Ivory Coast. The Security Council initially determined that MINURCA's deployment should end after the parliamentary elections scheduled for 1998 but later extended its mandate to last until after the presidential elections of 1999.

MINURCA is charged with keeping order and monitoring the preparation of elections. It also supervises programmes aimed at reducing the risk of recurring violence, such as a short-term police training programme and providing advice on building a multi-ethnic Central African army. Under the protection of MINURCA, an electoral commission representing several ethnic and political groups was established *Commission Électorale Mixte et Indépendante* (CEMI) in June 1998. The commission represented more than thirty political parties, the government and civil society. France, Japan, Canada and the EU provided funding for organising the elections.

MINURCA had its own radio station in Bangui, Radio Minurca, broadcasting 24 hours a day to inform the population about MINURCA's mission and the electoral process. The station was run by six professional radio producers, and was modelled on a similar station working to reduce tension in Vukovar, former Yugoslavia.

MINURCA's activities are sustained by UNDP, which runs the so called *Programme Nationale de Démobilisation et de Réinsertion (PNDR)*, aimed at the reintegration of rebellious soldiers in the army. This programme is closely connected to efforts of UN special envoy Oluyemi Adeniji to reform the armed forces by including all major ethnic groups.

President Patassé was known to be very keen on prolonging the presence of the peace-keeping force in his country. In order to win US approval in the Security Council for prolonging MINURCA's deployment, Patassé showed himself sensitive to western demands, including the call for forging peace and stability. Patassé organised a national reconciliation conference in March 1998, which resulted in an accord. In this agreement, Patassé and various political groups, including the army, parliament and the Association of Mayors, agreed to accept elections as the sole means of determining access to government power. All sides also agreed to ban the use of weapons and to practise good governance, excluding nepotism, clanship, tribalism, political patronage and misappropriation of funds. The accord may have helped create an atmosphere in which the national elections were possible.

Multi-Track Diplomacy

Few NGO activities aimed at sustaining peace and reconciliation are known to have been undertaken. This is largely because the crisis in the Central African Republic is dominated by a conflict within the higher echelons of society, a conflict which has been addressed, with some level of success, by regional mediators and the international community. The relative calm in the country and the fact that a programme of democratisation and reconciliation is already under way may have kept (international) non-governmental organisations specialised in conflict management from becoming deeply involved in the country.

In 1994 the *International Assembly of French Speaking Parliamentarians (AIPLF)* organised a seminar in Bangui intended to contribute to the democratisation process in the CAR and other African countries. The seminar focused on the role of parliament and civil society in a democracy. It was attended by parliamentarians from the Central African Republic and other African countries. A follow up seminar took place in Togo.

Professor Zokoue, a scholar and leader of the protestant churches in the Central African Republic (*Alliance des Évangélique de Centrafrique*) staged a reconciliation campaign after the mutinies of 1996. In a well-organised action, the churches urged all protestant communities in the country to address the conflict and discuss ways to boost reconciliation between opposing groups at community level.

In the diocese of Bangassou the *Roman Catholic Church* has been very active in creating a climate of reconciliation. The diocese, under the charismatic leadership of bishop Manikus, organised local meetings and Bible-reading sessions aimed at increasing awareness of potential upsurges of ethnic tension and the need to meet that challenge in a way that would prevent regional ethnic groups allowing themselves to be lured into violent confrontations. The diocese actively tried to bring about a change in mentality with regard to ethnic identity. In prayer and study meetings, the inhabitants of the region were also prepared for a possible refugee crisis, which, the local Catholic Church believed, could result from both domestic strife as well as from the war in neighbouring Congo.

Other non-governmental initiatives were scarce, if not absent, due to the active role played by the OAU, and subsequently the UN and its agencies, in the peace process.

There are some western-based organisations which concentrate on French foreign policy towards Central Africa in general. The most important are *SURVIE, Group Urgence de Rehabilitation et Développement* (URD) and the *European Institute for Research and Information on Peace and Security (GRIP)*. These groups provide analyses of the domestic situation and try to monitor France's Africa policy with regard to the Central African Republic.

Prospects

Journalists and analysts characterised the situation in 1999 as 'armed peace'. The Central African Republic has embarked on a peace process, but this process has, to a great extent, been imposed on the country by the UN and its peacekeeping force.

Potentially rebellious sections of the armed forces kept in check by MINURCA may take up arms again as soon as the UN troops have left. This raises doubts about the inner strength of the country's reconciliatory and democratic tendency. It also feeds qualms about the degree to which democracy and peace are sustainable.

Dissolution of the UN peacekeeping force MINURCA, which will come sooner or later, is expected to be the litmus test for the peace process in the Central African Republic. It remains to be seen whether democracy will by then have established deep enough roots to prevent renewed violent outbreaks. The harsh and confrontational political climate of 1999 is not very promising in this respect.

An external threat to peace is the ongoing unrest in the Central African Republic's neighbouring countries. The DR of Congo, Sudan and Chad are coping with rebellions and its south-western neighbour, Congo Brazzaville, is also experiencing an era of deep instability and violence.

Weapons are abundant in the Central African region. It is feared they will flood into the CAR should a new round of internal violence break out. The instability in the region has already led to an influx of refugees, which in itself has the potential to add to domestic tension.

According to some observers, many citizens in the country fear the outcome of the elections scheduled for late 1999, saying they fear that the two main parties may not accept the outcome if they're on the losing side and could resort to violence. In the event of this scenario proving accurate it is feared that the war in the neighbouring Democratic Republic of Congo might spread to the Central African Republic, particularly because president Patassé is said to be a close ally of Congo's president Laurent Kabila.

Recommendations

The French Africa expert Lafargue suggests that, in order to increase the chance of establishing a sustainable democratic system based on power sharing instead of ethnic exclusivity, the executive powers of the president should be curbed. This implies a discussion on whether the state system should be a presidential democracy (modelled, for instance, on France or the United States), or a parliamentary democracy.

Both assessments seem to imply that any reconciliatory interventions should primarily be directed at the senior political and military echelons. Opening up government institutions, especially the army, to people from all ethnic backgrounds, a measure that has already been chosen as an official policy goal but is far from being realised, is recommended as a starting point by most analysts.

Service Information

Newsletters and Periodicals

Le Citoyen (French language magazine covering Central African Developments)
L'Autre Afrique (Paris-based African weekly with excellent coverage of sub-Saharan Africa)
Jeune Afrique (Paris-based weekly with good coverage of sub-Saharan Africa)
Billets D'Afrique et D'Ailleurs (monthly newsletter of SURVIE on developments in the relations between France and Africa)

Other Publications

De l'autocratie impériale à la dictature d'une ethnie: au-delà du discours démocratique, réalités et pouvoirs en Centrafrique, Régis Lafargue. In: Droit et Cultures, 35, 1998/1 (Meticulous and critical analyses of the current democratisation process)
La Francafrique - Le plus long scandale de la République, François Xavier Verschave. Paris, Stock, 1998 (critical analysis of French Africa policy)
Chronique de la crise Centrafricaine 1996-1997 - Le syndrome Barracuda, Jean-Paul Ngoupandé. L'Harmattan, Paris, 1997 (Ngoupandé - himself deeply engaged in Central African politics - gives an account of the crisis of 1996 and its political aftermath)

Selected Internet Sites

www.agora.it/politic/central-africa.htm (index of Central African Republic political sites on the internet, with links to parties, organisations, media and the government)
mbendi.co.za/cycrcy.htm (Country profile including data and map)
www.sangonet.com/Centrafrique.html (website with extensive information on CAR, including current political developments)
members.aol.com/ens67 (website of *Espace Nord-Sud*, an organisation representing three French development NGOs with extensive relations in Africa)
www.energ.it/development/ac28htm (Italian website listing NGOs operating in the CAR)
www.clw.org/pub/clw/un/minurca.html (concise information on UN peacekeeping operation in CAR)

Resource Contacts

François Xavier Verschave - French researcher and president of SURVIE, specialises in arms trade and role of French foreign policy in Central Africa
Régis Lafargue - French scholar and expert on Africa connected to the University of Nanterre, France
Antoinette Delafin - Journalist, excellent and extensive coverage of CAR peace process, via L'Autre Afrique
Andreas Mehler - German scholar and senior researcher for the Conflict Prevention Network (CPN) and *Stiftung Wissenschaft und Politik* (SWP), email Mhl@swp.extern.lrz-muenchen.de

Organisations

SURVIE + Observatoire Permanent de la Coopération Française (Monitors aid relations of France with developing countries, especially in Africa)
57 Avenue du Maine
75014 Paris
France
Tel. +33 1 4327 0325
Fax +33 1 4320 5558

GRIP
Van Hoordestraat 33
B-1030 Brussels, Belgium
Tel. +32 2 241 8420
Fax +32 2 245 1933
Email grip@infoboard.be
www.ib.be/grip

Groupe Urgence de Rehabilitation et Developpement
Le Cypres-Les-Guards
26110 Nyons, France
Tel. +33 4 7526 2271
Fax +33 4 7526 6427
Email cpirot@aol.com

Congo Brazzaville

CENTRAL AFRICAN REPUBLIC

CAMEROON

EQUATORIAL GUINEA

GABON

CONGO

Brazzaville

Pointe Noire

CABINDA

ANGOLA

Population (millions): 2.8 *(1997)*
Life expectancy at birth (years):
51 *(1996)*
GNP per capita (dollars): 660 *(1997)*
Conflict related deaths:
10,000 *(est.)*
Conflict related internally displaced persons: 800,000

A Democratisation Process Scourged by Violence

About 10,000 people are reported to have been killed and about 800,000 displaced during a civil war in the Republic of Congo (Congo Brazzaville) that lasted from June to October 1997. Since the end of the war clashes have continued to occur. Mediation efforts by a joint representative of the UN and OAU have remained fruitless. Reconciliatory initiatives by grassroots organisations and foreign NGOs meet considerable resistance in a situation dominated by violence-prone warlords and where donor response to emergency appeals is poor ◆ *By* Jos Havermans

nalysts have interpreted the turmoil in the Republic of Congo as a civil war fuelled by the struggle for control over the country's rich oil resources. According to this analysis rival factions within the country's elite have tried to grab the financial revenues for themselves and their dependants. The conflict has pitted three politicians, each with their own militia, against one another. These are: Pascal Lissouba, who has

his stronghold in the south and exerts military and political pressure through his Cocoye, or Zulu, militia; Denis Sassou Nguesso, who has his stronghold in the north and depends on his Cobra militia; and Bernard Kolélas, whose power-base lies in the capital, Brazzaville, and who relies on the Ninja militia. The regional divisions coincide with different ethnic loyalties, giving the conflict an ethnic dimension.

When he came to power in 1992, after the first democratic elections in the history of Congo Brazzaville, Pascal Lissouba attempted to play oil companies off against each other, hoping to channel a bigger share of their profits into his own treasure-chest. He invited American companies such as Exxon, and Occidental, as well as British-Dutch Shell, to enter the long-term Congo Brazzaville oil-game. By offering these relative newcomers the opportunity to exploit Congolese oil fields, Lissouba jeopardised the decades old privileges of the French oil company Elf Aquitaine. Elf's strong position in Congo Brazzaville had been built up under the rule of Lissouba's predecessor, Sassou Nguesso. Lissouba's moves were particularly disturbing for Elf since the French company's revenues relied heavily on Congo Brazzaville. According to Belgian and French press reports (see: *De Standaard*, October 18, 1997, and *Le Monde*, October 17, 1997), Elf hoped Nguesso would be victorious in the elections scheduled for July 1997 and decided to support his militia when the elections were aborted and fighting erupted in June 1997. *Le Monde* quotes 'sources in the French secret service' as saying that Elf helped the Cobra militia to get supplies from Europe through the financing circuits of the oil company. Sassou Nguesso is reported not only to have enjoyed the support of Elf Aquitaine, but also of a much larger informal group of French businessmen with economic interests in Africa.

Lissouba's sour relations with Elf seem to have weakened his position. Lissouba's presidency was further undermined by Angola's decision to support Sassou Nguesso. Angola favoured Sassou Nguesso's side because it maintains close ties with Elf, which is also the main company exploiting oil resources in Angola, and, more importantly because an intervention in Congo allowed it to deal with tough domestic problems. Its military presence in Congo Brazzaville enabled the government in Luanda to crush the remaining UNITA forces still operating from this country and to deal a blow to the Cabinda nationalist rebels (FLEC, *Front de Libération du Cabinda*) operating from Congo Brazzaville. Angola's troops are reported to have been crucial in ensuring Nguesso's victory in October 1997.

Shortly after his defeat, Lissouba began legal proceedings in France in which he accused Elf of complicity in the overthrow of his democratically elected administration.

Apart from being a new phase in the struggle for access to oil resources, the civil war that broke out in Congo Brazzaville in June 1997 also represented a new phase in the turbulent process of democratisation that had started in 1990. The introduction of a multiparty system and the reshuffle of power resulting from the 1992 elections increased tension among rival factions within the country's political elite. Due to mutual mistrust between the major political factions and their inability to form strong coalition governments the democratic mechanisms installed in 1992 never functioned properly.

The three major factions began to form their own militias. In late 1993, clashes occurred between Lissouba's Cocoye and Koléla's Ninjas causing the death of between 1,000 and 5,000 people. In 1994 President Lissouba and the two opposition leaders - Sassou Nguesso and Kolélas - signed an agreement providing for the disarmament of the militias and the formation of a coalition government. This reconciliatory process failed as Sassou Nguesso's political alliance refused to participate in the government. A similar peace pact signed in 1995 failed as Sassou Nguesso hindered the dissolution of his militia.

The civil war of June-October 1997 broke out despite the signing of a tentative cease-fire agreement on July 14, brokered by the International Mediation Committee headed by the president of Gabon, Omar Bongo, and the joint UN/OAU Special Envoy for the Great Lakes region, Mohammad Sahnoun. The war came weeks before a new round of elections scheduled for July 27 but which, due to violence, never took place. In October 1997 Sassou Nguesso's forces, assisted by Angolan government troops, won control of Brazzaville and the country's seaport city, Pointe Noire. Subsequently, Sassou Nguesso ousted Lissouba and was declared president.

Conflict Dynamics

After his military victory and inauguration as president, Sassou Nguesso installed a transitional government in November 1997. He declared himself committed to national reconciliation and revealed plans to secure peace and stability. In January 1998 he convened a forum consisting of 1,420 delegates representing most political parties, although Lissouba's political party (ERDDUN) refused to participate. The Forum approved the beginning of a three-year transition period, which should end in presidential and legislative elections in 2001. During this transition period, a new constitution should be written. A 75-member transitional council, elected by members of the Forum from lists compiled by the Forum and the government, would act as the transitional parliament.

The first stages of the plan seem to have been completed on schedule. In November 1998 President Sassou Nguesso inaugurated a constitutional commission charged with the preparation of a draft version of a new constitution. The final version was scheduled to be submitted to voters in a national referendum in 1999.

In spite of these official reconciliatory efforts, violence continued to erupt in Brazzaville and elsewhere in the country. During the autumn of 1998, Lissouba's and Kolélas' militias carried out guerrilla style sabotage attacks in southern Congo, mostly against civilians who were thought to be Sassou Nguesso loyalists from the north. Sassou Nguesso's security forces, for their part, carried out mopping-up operations in an effort to eliminate Lissouba loyalists. These actions reportedly lead to large-scale human rights violations. Human rights abuses led several international donors, including the European Union, to suspend all non-humanitarian aid in 1998.

Violence flared up again in December 1998 and early 1999, when the Cocoye militia of Lissouba seized control over the Moukoukoulou hydroelectric dam, cutting off power to Pointe-Noire. In the summer of 1999, when electricity supply to most regions had been recovered, the fighting concentrated on control of the railway connection between Brazzaville and Pointe-Noire. Clashes in Brazzaville lead to heavy artillery attacks by the national army against militiamen and citizens supposedly loyal to Kolélas in the southern districts of the city and in the Pool region. Thousands of people were killed

in these attacks, which were described by foreign observers as 'ethnic cleansing'.

Sassou Nguesso' security forces were reportedly assisted in carrying out the counter-attacks by Angolan and Chadian troops. Sassou Nguesso was also said to rely on members of the former Hutu-dominated army of Rwanda, who fled to Congo Brazzaville after 1996. These Hutu-militiamen are being paid as mercenaries. The Ninjas of Kolélas and the militia under control of Lissouba were said to enjoy active support of the Angolan rebel movement, UNITA. In fact, the conflict in Congo Brazzaville has a significant regional dimension, as other states in the region have their eyes on the oil-rich enclave of Cabinda. Sassou Nguesso continues to be supported by the Angolan government, which not only backed him in the war of 1997, but still had troops deployed in the country in the spring of 1999.

The situation in Congo Brazzaville was further destabilised by the situation in neighbouring Congo DR (Congo-Kinshasa). Rebels who used to have their base in Congo-Kinshasa were forced to leave that country after the Kabila take-over, adding to the tension and increasing the number of armed people in Congo Brazzaville. Moreover, Rwandan and Ugandan troops were also said to be present in Kinshasa in June 1997, shortly after the Kabila take-over, and some of these troops reportedly joined the fighting in Brazzaville when clashes broke out there.

The regional involvement, therefore, follows the logic of economic interests, as well as of political manoeuvring on the international level. Rwandan forces were said to be intent on reducing French influence in Central Africa, resulting in a Rwandan tendency to support those rebel forces in Congo Brazzaville that were seen as anti-French. Informal alliances developed between certain governments and rebel groups in the region. As a consequence, a shift in the balance of power in neighbouring countries could have significant effect on events in Congo Brazzaville. For instance, Angola's support to Sassou Nguesso has been jeopardised by the weakening of the Angolan government's position following the escalation in the civil war against UNITA.

Meanwhile, Sassou Nguesso's position was said to have been weakened by a lack of support from France, which, according to analysts, was less inclined to indulge in controversial political deals with African partners in the late 1990s under the socialist government of Lionel Jospin.

The ongoing militia activity and the fierce government reaction in 1998 and 1999 illustrates that all three major factions adhere to the use of force as the prime means of reaching their political and economic goals.

In January 1999, according to Congolese press reports, a new rebel group was formed, the *Mouvement pour la Libération de Congo*. Led by Paul Muleri, a hitherto unknown figure the Congolese political scene, the organisation reportedly wanted to negotiate with the government and called for a round-table discussion outside the country, sponsored by the international community.

The people of Congo Brazzaville are suffering the devastating consequences of the civil war. The fierce fighting in the streets of Brazzaville, including indiscriminate bombing of crowded neighbourhoods, caused massive population displacements. During the June-October 1997 civil war, approximately 500,000 out of the 858,000 inhabitants of Brazzaville fled their homes. Humanitarian sources said clashes in January 1999 led to 30,000 displaced people in Brazzaville alone. At that time, large parts of the population were dependent on foreign humanitarian aid, including a WFP airlift, for food and medical supplies. Malnutrition and other emergency situations had dissipated in most parts of the country.

The infrastructure of the country was left in ruins by the civil war. Serious looting and the widespread destruction of shops, homes and offices left a large part of the economy in ruin. The conflict led to the dispersal of thousands of handguns among the youth of Brazzaville and other cities, causing a sharp increase in crime.

Official Conflict Management

Since the start of its turbulent democratisation process in 1990, the Republic of Congo has developed a tradition of domestic mediation on the official, political level. After he allowed the introduction of a multiparty system, president Sassou Nguesso convened a national conference to debate the country's future. This conference, which was established in February 1991, included opposition representatives and was chaired by the Roman Catholic bishop of Owando, Ernest N'Kombo. The bishop continued to play a key role in the process, as he also presided over a 153-member legislative higher council established by the conference to supervise the writing of a new constitution and prepare elections. This higher council adopted a draft constitution in December 1991, which was approved in a national referendum in March 1992.

In December 1994 the government and the opposition held reconciliation talks, resulting in the formation of a coordinating body which was to oversee the disarmament of opposition militias. In December 1995, parties from the *Mouvance Présidentielle*, the political coalition of Lissouba loyalists, and the opposition signed a new peace pact. It provided for the disarmament of militias and their members integration into the armed forces. Although approximately 4,000 militiamen were integrated into the national armed forces between late 1994 and early 1996, the process did not lead to stability and peace. Armed militias continued to be active.

Bernard Kolélas played an unexpectedly interesting role during the civil war in 1997, as he refrained from using force and appointed himself as mediator. However, his efforts bore no result and in a late stage of the civil war Kolélas aligned himself with Lissouba, thereby, as it turned out, choosing the losing side.

A few years before the 1997 clashes, in July and August 1993, growing ethnic tension had triggered a mediation effort by the *OAU, France and President Bongo of Gabon*. The foreign mediators urged the government and opposition to settle a dispute over the validity of elections held earlier that year giving president Lissouba's political group an absolute majority in parliament. An agreement was signed that an international committee of arbitrators would investigate the elections. The committee ruled in 1994 that the results in eight constituencies were unlawful. However, the external intervention did not divert the Congolese parties from their path toward violent conflict. These efforts may have had little relevance for the events of 1997, but they show that the country's political leaders can be made to yield to pressure of foreign mediators.

The involvement of the *United Nations* in efforts to stem the conflict in Congo Brazzaville for the most part consisted of monitoring human rights and providing humanitarian aid. UN agencies such as UNHCR, UNICEF, WFP, FAO, and OCHA were engaged in humanitarian relief and aid operations. A UN humanitarian report issued in January 1999 stated that efforts to promote reconciliation in the period after the 1997 five-month civil war were hampered by 'very poor donor response' to consolidated emergency appeals.

The UN has been criticised for not taking the lead in efforts in the political field to de-escalate the conflict. Some analysts said the UN Security Council's decision not to send peace-keeping forces to Brazzaville in the start-up phase of the 1997 civil war actually contributed to further escalation and internationalisation of the conflict, because it cleared the way for Angola to send in troops.

The most clear-cut, although unsuccessful, mediation initiative by the UN came from UN Special representative for the Great Lakes region, Mohammad Sahnoun. Acting as both UN and OAU representative, Sahnoun joined President Omar Bongo of Gabon in June 1997 in an effort to make peace through negotiation. As a result of these talks, numerous cease-fires were reached during the five-month civil war, but none of them lasted. Talks between Sassou Nguesso's and Lissouba's camps took place in Libreville, Gabon's capital, concurrently with the fighting in Congo. The talks came close to an agreement when Lissouba offered Sassou Nguesso five seats in the government. The offer, however, was refused.

Shortly after the end of the civil war in 1997, UN secretary general Kofi Annan ordered the UN/OAU special representative to work for a process of national reconciliation, which should lead to 'the holding of free and fair elections with the participation of all parties'. By the summer of 1999, the elections had yet to be scheduled.

In February 1999, the US ambassador in Brazzaville called on the government and the militias of Nguesso and Kolélas to open a dialogue. President Ange-Félix Patassé of the neighbouring Central African Republic also offered his help in the resolution of the Congo Brazzaville crisis. Neither of these initiatives led to significant results.

Multi-Track Diplomacy

Only a few initiatives have been taken by foreign and local NGOs to stem violence and boost reconciliation in the Congo Brazzaville. The Congolese NGO community maintains a strong focus on general developmental aims. Most NGOs are organised in a consortium which functions as a liaison point in contacts with international donors and UN agencies.

Domestic

Since the turmoil of 1993, local groups have taken initiatives in a number of cases to try to contain the conflict and work for a peaceful solution. One of these groups was the *Association Congolaise pour la Nonviolence*, led by Jean Makoundou.

In October 1998, a committee was set up by the *Ecumenical Council of Churches of Congo* to restore peace and security in the south-western Pool region. The committee consisted of about fifty religious leaders, parliamentarians, top army officials and other dignitaries. Its goal was to establish a dialogue between the committee and militias in the Pool region as well as to encourage police to stop harassing civilians and to obtain the release of people detained illegally. The group also planned to distribute food to the poor.

Although the establishment of the committee was a hopeful sign for the peace process, its status remained unclear and doubts arose about its independence, The government is said to have financially supported the committee with CFA francs 38 million. The army's close involvement in setting up the committee also disqualified it in the eyes of many opposition members.

Two weeks after the committee's inauguration, six members, all priests, were killed in an attack by an armed militia on a multi-denominational gathering in a church in the western town of Mindouli. A foreign news agency attributed the attack to the Ninja militia, the rebel group loyal to Bernard Kolélas, but later most observers judged the Cobra militia to have been responsible. The attack dealt the deathblow to the committee's possible reconciliatory role.

Another religious organisation *Lavico*, which stands for *'Laissez vivre le Congo'*, played an active role in efforts to create a reconciliatory atmosphere during the aftermath of the 1997 civil war. Lavico is a broad evangelical movement with roots in the Evangelical Church. The organisation held mass rallies with up to 50,000 people advocating peace and reconciliation in the country. Due to the recurring violence in the country, Lavico's activities have become increasingly focused on relief aid.

The *Congolese Observatory of Human Rights (Observatoire Congolais des Droits de l'Homme - OCDH)*, is a human rights organisation based in Port Noire and Brazzaville which monitors and criticises human rights violations of both rebel militias and government security forces. Apart from its human rights work, OCDH issues reports containing analyses of the current situation in Congo Brazzaville and advocates political moves toward reconciliation and democracy. OCDH maintains contacts with similar organisations abroad and received financial support from a Swedish human rights foundation, giving the organisation some degree of credibility and protection at home. OCDH has been accused by government officials of being an organisation which 'encourages banditry' and the government has threatened to arrest its members.

The *Fondation NIOSI*, a small NGO based in Brazzaville, has been working at the middle and upper levels of decision making since the mid-1990s in an effort to close the gap between protagonist groups in Congo Brazzaville. Under extremely difficult circumstances, the organisation, led by S. N'Sikabaka, tries to facilitate dialogue between opposing factions.

International

During the spring of 1997, the parties in the conflict had shown signs of being susceptible for mediation by a neutral, non-governmental foreign actor. Steps were taken by *Responding to Conflict* in the UK to launch a mediating

initiative. However, due to lack of funding, the organisation did not manage to start the mediation process in time before war broke out in June 1997 and had to call off its intervention.

The *Association Solidarité Internationale (ASI)* is a support group based in northern France which collects medical supplies and educational material for the population of Congo. ASI, which was established shortly before civil war broke out in Congo in June 1997, adheres to its non-political position. It sends its aid in containers to Pointe Noire, is familiar with developments at the local level in several regions and has some good contacts in the country.

Shortly after the civil war started in June 1997, Congolese living in the French city of Rennes took the initiative of establishing an aid organisation that seeks to contribute to building peace in Congo. The *Collectif SOS Congo Brazzaville*, which now comprises Congolese and other sympathetic individuals living all over France, sends medical aid to Congo Brazzaville and tries to induce the Congolese and French governments to increase peace-building and preventive activities 'in order to prevent repetition of the tragedies that happened in Congo'. It organised rallies, including a peace manifestation at the Place de Brazzaville in Paris. Collectif SOS Congo Brazzaville is also interested in launching reconstruction programmes in Congo.

Prospects

Violent clashes continue to erupt. The risk of renewed civil war is real, especially as long as the powerful Lissouba camp remains outside the reconciliatory process. The conflict in Congo Brazzaville seems to become an integral part of a complicated but integrated quagmire of violent conflicts in Central Africa and the Great Lakes district characterised by wars between warlords and national armies. The increased international character of the conflict is illustrated by the presence of foreign combatants from countries such as Angola, Chad and Rwanda, the influx of refugees from war-torn neighbouring countries and Congolese civilians fleeing abroad. However, the prospect of foreign intervention aimed at increasing the chance of a reconciliation and peace process seems remote. Some analysts point out that western powers can be expected to remain aloof as long as oil production in Congo Brazzaville's coastal waters continues unhindered.

Recommendations

The Congolese human rights organisation OCDH urges the government in Brazzaville to adopt a realistic strategy to create mutual confidence among the different ethnic and regional groups. In particular, the organisation calls for the disarmament of all militias and the establishment of social programmes to enable reintegration of militia members in civil society.

OCDH urges all foreign governments and international organisations to include a clause concerning the protection of human rights and democracy in all aid and cooperation agreements with the government in Brazzaville. OCDH also urges governments to channel humanitarian aid to the Congolese people through non-governmental organisations specialising in health-care and education.

Contributing to building a culture of peaceful coexistence of ethnic, regional and political groups seems to be most efficient at the level of the political and professional echelons because most violence seems to be instigated by political and military leaders, both at local and national levels.

According to Sue Williams, an INCORE staff member who is closely acquainted with the civil war in Congo Brazzaville, at the grassroots level religious communities may be found suitable to work with. While individual churches are often perceived as being aligned with one of the parties in conflict, ecumenical reconciliatory initiatives could bear fruit since they may be seen as genuinely non-partisan.

Service Information

Newsletters and Periodicals
Le Chemin - Newsletter of the Evangelical Church in France, contains information on activities of the Evangelical Church in Congo Brazzaville on a regular basis
Lumière - Information bulletin of the Congolese human rights organisation OCDH
L'Autre Afrique - Paris-based weekly with excellent coverage of sub-Saharan Africa

Reports
Amnesty International
- Annual Report 1998: The Republic of the Congo (entry on Congo Brazzaville in AI's yearly report covers human rights assessment for January-December 1997)

OCDH
- Entre Arbitraire et Impunité: Les Droits de l'Homme Au Congo Brazzaville. April 1998

Other Publications
Ethnic war and ethnic cleansing in Brazzaville, by Kasja Ekholm Friedman and Anne Sundberg. In: From post-traditional to post-modern? Interpreting the meaning of modernity in Third World urban societies, by Preben Kaarsholm (ed.) - Roskilde, International Development Studies, Roskilde University, 1995
Du processus démocratique au Congo, by Eric Dibas-Franck. In: *Revue juridique et politique* (1997), annee 51, no 2
La Françafrique: le plus long scandale de la République, by François Xavier Verschave. Paris, Stock, 1998 (critical analysis of French Africa policy)
La Sécurité au Sommet, l'insécurité à la base. Agir ici et Survie. Paris, L'Harmattan, 1998. (Contains chapter on French-Congolese relations)

Selected Internet Sites
www.congoweb.org (site claiming to be independent of government and opposition with links to several Congolese political and news organisations)
www.multimania.com/jecmaus/congo.html (links to numerous oppositional Congolese organisations, including political parties)
http://services.worldnet.net/adele/page1.html (website of the Evangelical Church in Congo Brazzaville)
www.indigo-net.com/canaux/ai/canal-congob.htm (Africa Intelligence site with links to local and international press reports on Congo Brazzaville)
members.aol.com/ens67 (website of Espace Nord-Sud, an organisation representing three French development NGOs with extensive relations in Africa)
www.energ.it/development/ac28htm (Italian website listing NGOs operating in Africa, including Congo Brazzaville)

Resource Contacts
François Xavier Verschave - French researcher and president of NGO SURVIE (specializes in arms trade and role of French foreign policy in Central Africa), tel. +33 1 4327 0325
Sue Williams - staff member of INCORE, UK (familiar with developments in the Republic of Congo, including mediation and reconciliation efforts), tel. +44 1504 375525

Organisations
Lavico (Laissez Vivre le Congo, Group with close ties to *Eglise Evangélique du Congo* working for reconciliation).
BP 3205 Bacongo, Brazzaville
République du Congo
Tel. +242 814 364

Fondation NIOSI
B.P. 1063 Brazzaville
République du Congo
Contact S. N'Sikabaka, secretary general
Tel. +242 412 138 or 810 346
Fax +242 811 909

Observatoire Congolais des Droits de
l'Homme (OCDH)
Bureau National (Head Office)
23, Rue Soumba - OCH
B.P. 4255 Pointe Noire
République du Congo
Contact Christian Mounzeo, secretary general
Tel. +242 949 623/9052
Fax +242 941 915

Bureau de Brazzaville (Field office)
32, Avenue des 3 Martyrs
Station de Bus Jane-Vialle
B.P. 4021 Brazzaville
Republique du Congo
Tel +242 814 130
Email ocdh@mygale.org
www.multimania.com/ocdh

Collectif SOS Congo Brazzaville
25 rue de Vouziers
35000 Rennes
France
Tel. +33 299 504 237
Fax +33 299 417 962/332 528

*Data on the following organisation can be found
in the Directory section:*
Responding To Conflict (RTC)

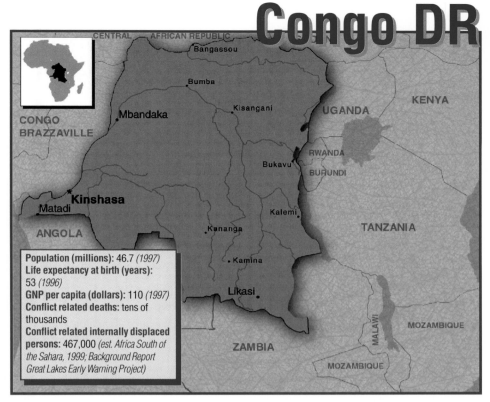

CENTRAL AFRICAN REPUBLIC

Bangassou

Bumba

Kisangani

UGANDA

KENYA

CONGO
BRAZZAVILLE

Mbandaka

RWANDA

Bukavu

BURUNDI

Kinshasa

Matadi

Kalemi

ANGOLA

Kananga

TANZANIA

Kamina

Likasi

MALAWI

MOZAMBIQUE

ZAMBIA

MOZAMBIQUE

Congo DR

Population (millions): 46.7 *(1997)*
Life expectancy at birth (years):
53 *(1996)*
GNP per capita (dollars): 110 *(1997)*
Conflict related deaths: tens of
thousands
Conflict related internally displaced
persons: 467,000 *(est. Africa South of
the Sahara, 1999; Background Report
Great Lakes Early Warning Project)*

Africa's Most Worrying Battle Field

The Democratic Republic of the Congo, as the former Zaire is now officially
called - is in the midst of one of the most sweeping and wide-ranging conflicts in
post-colonial Africa. The war, which has escalated into an international conflict,
has been described as Africa's most African war this century, as western powers
and the UN seem unwilling or unable to influence the course of events. Amid
the gruesome turmoil, special envoys, human rights activists and vulnerable local
NGOs try to keep alive a feeble tradition of reconciliation and peaceful conflict
settlement ◆ *By* Jos Havermans

After the Tutsi-led Rwandan rebel movement, RPF, conquered Kigali in July 1994, some 1.2 million Hutu refugees fled across the border into what was then Zaire. The exodus included members of the defeated Rwandan army and militias that had perpetrated the mass killing of up to 800,000 Rwandans. The massive relocation of people exported the Rwandan ethnic and political conflict into Zaire. The presence of armed Rwandan Hutus in Zaire, exacerbated tensions between Hutus and Tutsis who had been living for many years in the

province of Nord-Kivu and between the local Zairean population and the Banyamulenge Tutsis in South-Kivu.

The imported Rwandan conflict intermingled with a domestic conflict that was already simmering in Zaire. In the eastern Zairean Kivu provinces, which border on Rwanda, Burundi and Uganda, ethnic clashes had erupted in the early 1990s between - on one side - the so called Banyamulenge, a community of people of Rwanda Tutsi origin, and - on the other side - local communities of other ethnic origins, mostly

Hunde. In 1993, several hundreds of people are believed to have been killed in such clashes in the Masisi region in North-Kivu. The clashes were reportedly connected to a struggle for control over land and other economic resources in the region. Regional strongmen are alleged to have deliberately fanned the ethnic hatred to chase away rivals. The dynamics of this domestic conflict and the confrontation imported from Rwanda had an escalating effect.

The war in Zaire further intensified in the early autumn of 1996, when Zairean Tutsi militia. - formed in response to plans of the government in Kinshasa to take away their Zairean citizenship - gained momentum and were joined by dissidents intent on deposing the regime of Mobutu Sese Seko in Kinshasa. This development added another dimension to the conflict and crisis in the country. The conflict in the east developed into a national rebellion aimed at the overthrow of the central government. The whole country now became involved, with the entire population having a stake in the conflict.

As mentioned above, the ethnic boiling pot in the east exploded again in 1996. In October of that year, Tutsi-led militias supported by the Rwandan army attacked Hutu refugee camps. This resulted in massive refugee movements in two directions: hundreds of thousands of Rwandans returned to their home country, and hundred of thousands of other refugees, among them the armed Hutu insurgents, marched west, deeper into Zaïre, some of them as far as the Central African Republic and Congo Brazzaville. The latter group was chased by the militias, by then fighting under the banner of the rebel movement of Laurent Kabila, the *Alliance des Forces Démocratiques pour la Libération du Congo-Zaïre* (AFDL). In this dramatic stage of the conflict, another episode of mass killings took place, out of sight of the international community, with the Hutu refugees and alleged militia members as victims and the AFDL rebels as alleged perpetrators.

The AFDL campaign, which was reportedly supported by Rwanda, Uganda, Burundi and Angola, proved successful. The rebels conquered city after city in their march on the capital and on May 17, 1997 the AFDL troops took over

Kinshasa, shortly after Mobutu had fled the country. Kabila renamed Zaïre the Democratic Republic of Congo (DRC).

After the fall of the Mobutu regime a new situation emerged, raising hopes among the Congolese and the international community that a democratic and well functioning government would be installed. Instead, Kabila clamped down on political rights, banned all political activities, except for those of the AFDL, and failed to install efficient administrative institutions in the provincial capitals. The pro-democratic domestic opposition, centred around the UDPS party of Etienne Tshisekedi, a convinced proponent of non-violent political reform, found it particularly hard to accept that a movement that took power by force should gain international recognition and the benefit of the doubt from such powerful democracies as the US and many European countries.

After he had been in office for only a few months, Kabila's relations with the governments of Rwanda and Uganda began to turn sour as Kigali and Kampala concluded that Kabila was unable to pacify rebel movements based in eastern DRC. In August 1998, a new rebellion started in eastern DRC. This time, the conflict developed into a major international war. Kabila gained support from Zimbabwe, Angola, and Chad, who sent troops to support the DRC national army, as well as from Sudan and Namibia. The rebels were openly supported by Rwanda and Uganda. This second Congolese war, in which eight countries were involved, continued well into 1999, despite several diplomatic attempts by African powers to arrange a cease-fire.

Conflict Dynamics

By the summer of 1999 the situation in the DRC was one of military stalemate, with little progress being made by either party on the battle field. A series of political initiatives has been undertaken to stop the war.

The war has domestic roots, but an even stronger regional character, with foreign powers seeking both to gain access to the mineral riches of the DRC and to control part of DRC territory in order to prevent rebel movements attacking across national borders from bases in the DRC.

In the spring of 1999, the rebels, organised in the *Rassemblement Congolaise pour la Démocratie* (RCD), seemed to be making some progress in their march towards Mbuji-Mayi, the diamond-rich centre in the Kasai province and a major strategic focal point in the war. They dealt a severe military and psychological blow to the government coalition by conquering the town of Manono, Kabila's home town in Katanga/Shaba province, in June 1999. Despite its apparent self-confidence, the rebel camp also suffered a political backlash. There are growing signs of internal discord, with increased irritation between the RCD and the *Mouvement de Libération Congolais* (MLC), as well as within the RCD, which has reportedly split into Uganda-supported and Rwanda-supported factions. Uganda was also said to support Jean-Pierre Bemba's MLC, while losing interest in the Rwanda-supported RCD faction. The split within the RCD rebel movement was also said to reflect tension between non-Tutsi Congolese members of the RCD and the Banyamulenge-Tutsi. Ugandan President Yoweri Museveni appeared to distance himself from the rebel movements in April 1999 when he joined Kabila for talks on a cease-fire in the Libyan town of Sirte. Kabila said he and his Ugandan rival had signed a peace agreement in the absence of rebel representatives. Museveni's move seemed to indicate a souring of relations between Uganda and Rwanda and was reportedly motivated by pressure from international donors on Kampala to stop Ugandan involvement in conflicts abroad.

The Libyan agreement turned out to be one of the foundations for an accord that was signed in the summer of 1999, during talks presided over by Zambian president Chiluba in the Zambian capital of Lusaka. Participants in these negotiations - senior representatives of eight countries engaged in the war - finally agreed to a cease-fire agreement.

Kabila is continuing to put considerable effort into strengthening his ties with the foreign powers he relies on for the survival of his regime. In April 1999 he signed a collective defence pact with the presidents of Angola, Namibia, and Zimbabwe, in Luanda, committing the signatories to a joint response if any one of their countries is attacked. The DRC president

sought to strengthen his position domestically by dissolving his AFDL party, which he accused of corruption and opportunism, and installing so called *Comités du Pouvoir Populaire* (CPP), a manoeuvre that seemed to be inspired by a similar Libyan political infrastructure. Repression of political opponents was intensifying.

The current humanitarian situation in the DRC is characterised by chronic low-intensity problems related to the country's long-term socio-economic decline, compounded by acute humanitarian emergencies arising directly from the war. The country's main human rights organisation, African Association for the Defense of Human Rights in Congo/Kinshasa (ASADHO), described the human rights situation as 'deplorable'. It said that both the rebels and Kabila's regime were responsible for this situation. The UN special rapporteur for the DRC said a 'climate of hatred' persisted in the DRC, where most victims of the war were civilians.

Official Conflict Management

In 1993, ethnic clashes erupted in the North-Kivu province which can be seen as a prelude to the current conflict. Those clashes, if noted at all internationally, did not give rise to any significant peacemaking initiatives on the part of the *United Nations* or the OAU. It was the refugee crisis resulting from the Rwandan genocide in 1994 which led to a massive involvement of the *United Nations* and major foreign powers, a group of actors often dubbed 'the international community'. UNHCR and OCHA (formerly DHA) implemented and coordinated relief operations. Calls by analysts and some NGOs to separate armed militia members from other refugees in the refugee camps in order to prevent militias using international aid to prepare for war, were rebuffed by the Security Council and individual countries showing lack of political will to intervene.

The UN tried to broker negotiations between the warring parties in 1997 and 1998, mostly through its special envoy in the region, Mohamed Sahnoun, but without success. UN secretary-general Kofi Annan helped broker a cease-fire agreement in Paris in December 1998, but this agreement failed to stop the fighting. A UN team sent to the DRC to investigate reports of massacres by forces fighting with Kabila's AFDL had to abandon its efforts in 1998 as a result of obstruction by the Kabila regime.

In April 1999, Kofi Annan appointed the former Senegalese foreign minister Moustapha Niasse as his special envoy for the DRC peace process. Niasse was assigned the task of establishing contacts with DRC political and civic leaders and sounding out a possible UN role in promoting ongoing talks between countries involved in the conflict in Lusaka on reaching a cease-fire in the war. The UN's efforts were sustained by a Security Council resolution adopted in early 1999, calling for peace talks, free elections and deploying the presence of foreign troops in the DRC.

After the refugee crisis became apparent in 1994, the *Organization of African Unity* (OAU) dispatched a number of fact finding missions to the DRC but appeared to be unable or unwilling to take a decisive role in the crisis. In 1998, after the second rebellion in the east had erupted, the diplomatic efforts to stop the war were being run through regional organisations. Western countries were standing back, leaving the diplomacy work to the *Southern African Development Community (SADC)* and the OAU. The SADC/OAU initiatives were chaired by Zambian president Frederick Chiluba. Nelson Mandela, as president of the major power in the SADC-region, also took an active interest in the crisis, as well as the Libyan leader Moammar Gaddafi.

Efforts by president Chiluba to hold a summit in Lusaka in early December 1998 to discuss details of a cease-fire were frustrated by Kabila's refusal to meet representatives of the rebel movement RCD. But military and diplomatic officials of the countries involved in the DRC war gathered in Lusaka in April 1999 for preliminary talks on a cease-fire and a month later in South-Africa. Delegations from the rebel movement RCD did not officially join the talks, which was dubbed 'the Chiluba process', but were intensively consulted. In July 1999, after a new round of talks in Lusaka, the Kabila government, rebel groups and the governments of the neighbouring countries involved in the conflict reached an agreement on a cease-fire. Initially, two of the three rebel groups refused to sign the

document due to disagreement on who were the real representatives of the rebel forces fighting Kabila, but in late August they all put their signatories onder the agreement. The agreement on a cease-fire was considered to be an important, but certainly not the final step towards peace in the region. Implementation of the accord, which included the disarmament of Hutu militias in eastern Congo has not yet started.

In 1995 *The Carter Centre* in Atlanta facilitated a summit in Cairo attended by the presidents of Burundi, Rwanda, Tanzania, Uganda and Zaïre to discuss actions to be taken by their countries and the international community in order to bring peace to the region. Apart from Jimmy Carter, the presidents invited former Tanzanian president Julius Nyerere, former Mali president Amadou Touré and South African archbishop Desmond Tutu to act as mediators. A second meeting was held in March 1996 in Tunis. The heads of states made several commitments, including a promise to prevent cross-border raids into any country and to halt arms flows to rebel groups. However, the initiatives did not lead to lasting stability and peace and were taken over by the SADC-led peace process, supervised by Zambian president Chiluba.

Canada was at the forefront of a diplomatic initiative to lead a multinational intervention force to the Zaire in 1996. It played a crucial role in generating support for such a force, however, events in Zaïre changed course in 1996 and the multinational military intervention failed to materialise.

Several attempts at mediation between the rebels and the Mobutu-regime, most notably by South Africa, occurred in February, March and April 1997 during the AFDL's military campaign, but failed to halt the escalation of the conflict.

At the *Franco-African summit* in Paris in December 1998, French president Jacques Chirac and UN secretary general Kofi Annan brokered a cease-fire, which did not materialise. In January 1999, Rwanda, Uganda, Namibia, Zimbabwe and Angola agreed on a cease-fire at a meeting in Windhoek, but, with the rebels of the RCD left out, it did not stop the fighting.

The *European Union* sought to sustain peace efforts through its special envoy for the Great Lakes region, Aldo Ajello, who continued his peace efforts through travel diplomacy in the

KISANGANI, CONGO, Returning refugees

region in 1999.

In early 1999, the *Liby*an leader colonel Gaddafi set himself up as mediator and allegedly brokered a cease-fire accord signed by Kabila and Museveni. The talks in the Libyan town of Sirte were shrouded in mystery but were also said to be attended by the presidents of Chad and Eritrea. The Congolese rebel movement did not participate in the Libyan talks.

The Sirte agreement may, however, have contributed to boosting the peace process led by SADC as the accord signed in Libya was referred to as one of the buildings stones of peace during talks in Zambia and South Africa led by SADC mediator Chiluba in June 1999. These talks were gaining momentum in the summer of 1999, when the countries involved and the rebels seemed to be getting close to a far-reaching peace agreement. As part of the envisioned accord, Nigeria, South Africa, Libya and Eritrea reportedly had pledged to deploy peacekeeping troops in the Democratic Republic of Congo.

Domestically, a peace initiative was taken in the summer of 1998 by opposition leader *Etienne Tshisekedi*, who stressed his neutrality during the second rebel campaign of 1998/99. However,

Kabila's government stopped him from travelling to Brussels to propagate his plan.

In the spring of 1999, Kabila proposed holding a national debate on the future of the country. Opposition leader Tshisekedi supported the plan and called for participation of the UN, OAU, EU and SADC, as well as the rebel movement RCD. Kabila reportedly contacted the Italian organisation Sant' Egidio to ask for assistance in organizing a first stage of dialogue between the government and domestic opposition groups. In the summer of 1999, Kabila was said to be still interested in setting up such a debate. The release of political opponents, including Joseph Olengankoy, leader of the opposition Fonus party, was interpreted as a move to encourage the opposition to enter into such a dialogue on the country's future as soon as a peace agreement with the rebels could be reached.

Multi-Track Diplomacy
Domestic

Local civil society in the Democratic Republic of Congo is strong when it comes to economic survival strategies and meeting basic needs such as food and housing, but bears little weight in the fields of social, political and human rights activities.

During the last decade of the Mobutu regime, numerous local non-governmental groups were established by people who got together to improve their small-scale economic activities, such as small soap factories, bakeries, poultry farms and vegetable gardens. This practice has not changed under Kabila. The number of non-governmental organisations that focus on promoting democracy, social justice, human rights and reconciliation, however, is small. Civil society in many instances fell prey to ethnic and regional animosities inculcated by political elites. A low point was reached in early 1999 when the leader of the national umbrella organisations of all NGOs in the DRC (CNONGD), Badouin Hamuli Kabarhuza, was arrested and held for a few days by Kabila's secret police under charges of collaborating with the rebels in eastern DRC.

It should be pointed out here that it would be an oversimplification to present the non-governmental civil society as being completely separated from and in opposition to the world of Congolese officialdom. There are in many instances close ties between the acts and interests of Congolese politicians and members of non-governmental organisations. Civil society cannot be regarded as wholly divorced from the problems in the DRC.

In terms of peace building and conflict prevention, a key role was played by the *Conseil Régional des Organisations Non-Gouvernemental de Développement/Nord Kivu (CRONGD/Nord Kivu)* in the early 1990s. This umbrella organisation managed to bring together more than thirty small NGOs that were organised along ethnic lines to work for peace and reconciliation. CRONGD/Nord Kivu organised what was called a Campaign for Peace in North-Kivu. Churches and some unions joined the initiative and about sixty small regional NGOs eventually supported the campaign. Its main goal was to set up a dialogue between the ethnic communities in the region. In addition, the campaign aimed at establishing contact between the Kivu, the civil society as a whole and the government in Kinshasa. The latter initiative led, among other things, to a peace

conference in the town of Mweso in 1993 between CRONGD representatives and the government, resulting in an agreement on the disarmament of militias and the government's promise to withdraw its troops to barracks. The agreement did not materialise. The activities in the region continued and in 1996, the Campaign for Peace in North-Kivu launched a publicity campaign calling on communities to ignore manipulative efforts to arouse ethnic hatred and violence.

The national NGO umbrella organisation, the CNONGD, supported local initiatives and in June 1997 organised a Civil Society Meeting on the Reconstruction and Democratisation of the Democratic Republic of Congo in Kinshasa. At the meeting, which was supported by Synergies Africa and the International Human Rights Law Group, more than two hundred representatives called on Kabila to engage in a continued dialogue with members of civil society.

With the outbreak of the rebel war in 1997, most initiatives of local NGOs in the Kivu and other regions in eastern Zaïre were suspended. Many NGO offices were looted by army soldiers or militias and deprived of scarce resources such as faxes and computers. Many NGOs lost contact with the foreign partners who funded them. The working conditions for NGOs deteriorated even further following the second rebel campaign which began in 1998.

In early 1999 the CNONGD launched another campaign for peace in the DRC. Leaders of DRC civil society toured western countries, including Canada and Belgium, to gain international support for their initiative. The aims of the campaign included a cease-fire, the deployment of a peacekeeping force, an inclusive roundtable process with international guarantees, and establishing democratic institutions. This intervention by civil society is said to have contributed to president Kabila's announcement in April 1999 that he intended to organise a national debate between government, opposition and civil society to seek a peaceful solution to the crisis. Although this debate had not started by mid-1999, Kabila's move implied that his position could be influenced by the interventions of civil society.

With the collapse of state services and

infrastructure during the last years of the Mobutu regime, the *Roman Catholic Church and other churches* in the DRC played a crucial role by providing the only remaining infrastructure which allowed civil society to organise itself and communicate. The churches' radio service enabled local NGOs to be aware of developments in other regions and the capital as well as to maintain relations with the outside world. The Roman Catholic Church helped raise awareness about political and civic rights, through dispersal of leaflets in anticipation of national elections scheduled for June 1997. (The elections were cancelled after the Kabila take-over in May 1997). Many priests played a key role in local NGO activities. An example of such an NGO is the *Groupe Jérémie*, led by a Congolese Jesuit priest. This organisation is engaged in efforts to boost respect for human rights.

Church activities amounted to capacity- and civil society- building as well as consensus-building and did not touch on diplomacy or upper level negotiations, although members of the upper hierarchy of the Roman Catholic Church were involved in the democratisation process on a national level in the mid-1990s. The NGO and church activities could be described as efforts to promote long term, structural prevention. Almost all local domestic activities to sustain peace and promote reconciliation had to be abandoned during the two rebel wars of 1996/97 and 1998/99.

Human rights organisation *ASADHO*, based in Kinshasa, has been one of the few NGOs that has continued to operate through the several phases of political and military turmoil. It has become a focal point for, and to some extent a mouthpiece of, other Congolese NGOs and players in civil society. In its zest to boost human rights in the DRC, ASADHO does not abstain from making statements and recommendations on political developments and calls for negotiations and the establishment of a democratic government.

International
A considerable number of international NGOs have addressed the crisis in the DRC. Most organisations approach the conflict in the DRC as part of the complex crisis of the entire Great

Lakes Region. As many initiatives of international NGOs, such as the involvement of the Italian catholic organisation *Sant'Egidio*, are closely intertwined with official diplomatic actions, it is hard to distinguish between pure non-governmental contributions and the peace process as such.

A group of European NGOs, including Oxfam (UK), Novib (Netherlands) and NCOS (Belgium), supported local NGOs that work for peace in eastern DRC and elsewhere in the country. These western NGOs exchange information on their individual programmes through the *Reseau Européen pour le Congo/ex-Zaïre (REC)*. Efforts have been seriously hindered because of the ongoing civil war.

The Carter Center took action in 1995 to get a mediation process going on the regional African level. Jimmy Carter brokered two summits attended by former Tanzanian president Julius Nyerere, former Mali president Amadou Touré and South African archbishop Desmond Tutu, prominent Africans with a high profile as mediators. (See also Official Conflict Management in this survey).

The *International Crisis Group (ICG)* has been working to organise a major advocacy effort aimed at developing a regional crisis prevention plan for Central Africa.

In April 1998, *The Forum on Early Warning and Early Response (FEWER)* established an Early Warning Network for the Great Lakes Region, consisting of representatives of local organisations in Rwanda, Uganda, DRC, Burundi, Kenya and Tanzania. FEWER has continued to support this Network, which is supervised by the *Africa Peace Forum* and produces situation analyses on a regular basis. It also organises meetings to review the conflict situation in the region.

Synergies Africa and the *International Human Rights Law Group* helped the CNONGD to organise a meeting of civil society representatives in June 1997 to promote constructive dialogue between civil society leaders and the national government on reconstruction of the country.

Some analysts have criticised international institutions for lack of support to and understanding of the domestic DRC opposition, while being biased towards Uganda and Rwanda.   ***243***

The Italian Roman Catholic organisation *Sant'Egidio* managed to persuade the DRC government to take part in peace talks scheduled to be held in Rome in early May 1999. The talks were postponed and later cancelled, as the SADC peace process started to develop into a forum which could bring rebels, the Kabila government and foreign powers together around the negotiating table.

Sant'Egidio remained active, however, and in June 1999 it announced through a representative in Kinshasa that it was working to set up an all-inclusive committee to organise the proposed inter-Congolese national debate between government and opposition.

Conclusion

As all-out war was raging, brokering a cease-fire and negotiating a political solution at the top military and political level was an obvious first priority to get closer to peace and stability in late 1998. It appeared that local NGO contributions to peace building would only become feasible in the post-conflict rehabilitation and reconstruction phase. Local reconciliatory activities at civil society level, which had not been able to prevent escalation of the conflict, came to a halt during the fighting. Many local NGOs are under pressure from the parties in the conflict to choose sides, making it hazardous for international NGOs to decide whether or not to support these organisations. However, analysts and experts working for international NGOs think that the weakened local NGO-structures can be used as a basis for further development as soon as the country stabilises.

Prospects

The signing of a cease-fire agreement in the summer of 1999, constituted a real prospect for bringing an end to the violent conflict in Congo DR. The agreement included the establishment of a joint military commission made up of African countries to monitor the implementation of the agreement and disarmament of the Interahamwe militia, another major goal included in the accord. The agreement also included the deployment of a UN peacekeeping force in the DRC. In the late summer of 1999 it was not yet clear if the accord would hold, nor

what the timetable of its implementation would be. Analysts agreed that the accord was only a first step, though a significant one, towards a final settlement of the conflict, both regionally and domestically.

The democratic opposition of the DRC, which for years tried to depose Mobutu's regime through non-violent means, was still in a tight corner as Kabila's government was still hindering its activities. The political landscape was in a state of flux. One of the most concrete steps to establish peace domestically were moves to set up a dialogue between the government and several opposition parties. Plans to set up such a dialogue were boosted by the cease-fire agreement and foreign organisations, including Sant'Egidio, seemed willing to facilitate such a process.

Recommendations

Stopping the war, obviously the first priority in the DRC, requires first- and other track diplomacy aimed at convincing the Kabila government, the rebel movements and the relevant foreign powers to stop fighting and implement the agreement reached in Lusaka in July 1999. As long as the fighting continues, supporting peace-building initiatives on the local level remains extremely difficult. However, both local and international NGOs working for peace and reconciliation call for support in order to develop plans to boost national and regional reconciliation and the strengthening of civil society.

The Africa Peace Forum recommends two courses of action

- Local civil society organisations should be supported. Over 400 local NGOs have been effective in promoting peace and reconciliation at the local level in the eastern DRC. They need financial, material and moral support to continue.
- Regional mediation efforts of the Southern Africa Development Community (SADC) should be supported. SADC has regional convening powers. This 'African Solutions for African Problems' approach should be encouraged and extended to long term economic and social cooperation.

Service Information

Periodicals and Newsletters

Le Soft - Congolese daily, fairly reliable and independent information. Available at some universities' departments for African studies and on the internet (www.lesoftonline.com)
Periodique Des Droits de l'Homme - Periodical of human rights organisation ASADHO.

Reports

Amnesty International
- Congo (Democratic Republic of) - A Year of Dashed Hopes, 1998

Human Rights Watch
- World Report 1999. Entry Zaire. 1999

Africa Peace Forum/FEWER
- Background Report Great Lakes Early Warning Project. August/September 1998
- Country Early Warning Report - Great Lakes Early Warning Network. Report on DRC, October 1998

International Crisis Group
- Congo at War: A Briefing On the Internal and External players in the Central African Conflict. November 1998

Other Publications

Zaïre, la Transition Manquée 1990-1997, Gauthiers de Villers (ed.). Cahiers Africains no 27-28-29, L'Harmattan, Paris, 1997
La Françafrique, François-Xavier Verschave (ed.). Stock, Paris, 1998. (role of French Africa policy on current events in region).

Selected Internet Sites

www.congonline.com/ Congonline - The most complete website on the Democratic Republic of Congo. Based in Belgium, it offers recent and complete news on the situation in the DRC, suggests many links, provides reports related to the situation, etc. However, Congonline is more than a news agency, it also presents a wide variety of information on subjects such as geography, history, sports, weather forecast, cooking, etc. on DRC. Payed subscription required.
drcongo.org/frames/index.html (government site with information relating government, the Congo Press Agency and contact details)
www.jps.net/rdcongof (information on current affairs in DRC provided by DRC Lumumbist political party)
www.afdl-congo.com (site of the AFDL party)
www.udps.org (information on position of party of opposition leader Etienne Tshisekedi)
www.congorcd.org (site of the rebel movement RCD)
www.ned.org/page_3/asadho (information on human rights)
www.marekinc.com/NCN.htm (extended information on DRC provided by New Congo Net)
www.synapse.net/~acdi20/country/greatla1.htm (information on Central African conflict)
www.crisisweb.org/projects/cafrica/Default.htm (projects run by International Crisis Group)
www.international-alert.org (extended information on Great Lakes Region)
www.lesoftonline.com (newspaper *Le Soft*)
www.heritiers.org (site of *Héritiers de la Justice,* organisation of the protestant churches, about human rights and peace efforts)

Resource Contacts

J. A. Odera - author of an early warning report on the situation in the DRC in August 1998, published under the auspices of the Africa Peace Forum and FEWER (contact via FEWER)
Guillaume Ngefa Atondoko - President of l'Association Africaine de Défense des Droits de l'Homme, ASADHO
Hamuli Kabarhuza - Executive director of CNONGD
Stefaan Marysse - scholar and Africa expert at the Centre for Development Studies at the University of Antwerp, Belgium. Email stefaan.marysse@ufsia.ac.be
Filip Reyntjens - professor at Centre for Development Studies at Antwerp University, Belgium, author of several publications on the Great Lakes area.
Email freyntje@ruca.ua.ac.be

Eric Kennes - scholar at Centre for
Development Studies at Antwerp University,
Belgium.
Jules Devos - Coordinator of Réseau Européen
Congo (REC), located at NCOS, Brussels,
Belgium.

Organisations
Group Jérémie Sud Kivu - c/o CISS Bukavu
via CISS Palermo
coordinator Rigobert Minani
Via Benedetto D'Acquisto 30
Palermo
Italy
Tel. +39 091 340276
Fax +39 091 345707

Reseau Européen pour le Congo/ex-Zaïre
(REC) - Brussels-based DRC civil society group
run by European NGOs.
c/o NCOS
Vlasfabriekstraat 11
1060 Bruxelles
Belgium
Tel. +32 2 5392620
Fax +32 2 5391343
Email jules.devos@ncos.ngonet.be

*Data on the following organisations can be found
in the Directory section:*
CNONGD
ASADHO
The Carter Center
International Crisis Group
Forum on Early Warning and Early Response
(FEWER)
Synergies Africa
Sant'Egidio
Africa Peace Forum
Héritiers de la Justice

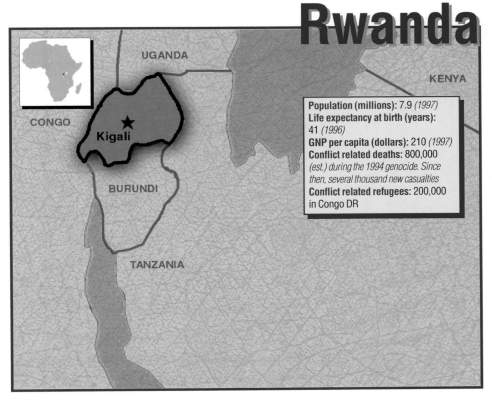

Rwanda

UGANDA

KENYA

CONGO

Kigali

BURUNDI

TANZANIA

Population (millions): 7.9 *(1997)*
Life expectancy at birth (years):
41 *(1996)*
GNP per capita (dollars): 210 *(1997)*
Conflict related deaths: 800,000
*(est.) during the 1994 genocide. Since
then, several thousand new casualties*
Conflict related refugees: 200,000
in Congo DR

Rwandan Crisis Lingers On

After the genocide of 1994 a wide range of humanitarian and peace-building
activities sprouted in Rwanda. Led by international and non-governmental
organisations, these initiatives have placed most parts of the country on a course
toward reconciliation and post-war reconstruction. However, these initiatives are
continuously being jeopardised by destabilisation of the country caused by
ongoing clashes between Hutu-dominated militia and the Rwandan army in the
north-west. Rwanda's involvement in the civil war in the neighbouring
Democratic Republic of Congo (ex-Zaïre) also constitutes a threat to the domestic
reconciliation process ◆ *By* Jos Havermans

The civil war in Rwanda began in 1990 with
an invasion of Tutsi rebels from Uganda. The
armed Tutsi, who had organised themselves into
the Rwandan Patriotic Front (RPF), were the
sons and daughters of Tutsi exiles who had been
chased from Rwanda in 1959. The Tutsi exiles
had been waiting for a chance to return to their
country for a long time. A first attempt to return
and stage a coup against the Hutu majority
regime failed in 1963, shortly after Rwanda
gained independence from Belgium. The Tutsi

exiles and their allies within Rwanda had to wait
until 1990 to stage another, more successful,
offensive.

In August 1993, the civil war into which the
offensive had developed appeared to come to an
end. Under international pressure, the
government of president Habyarimana and the
RPF rebel movement had opened negotiations in
the Tanzanian town of Arusha and reached a
political agreement. The accords provided for the
establishment of a broad-based transitional

government, the repatriation of refugees, the integration of all military forces into one national army and the holding of democratic elections. The implementation of the peace accord was to be supervised by a UN force (UNAMIR), which was deployed in Rwanda.

However, extremists in the Hutu camp refused to accept the formulated power-sharing proposal and prepared a genocidal plan to eliminate all of the RPF's potential supporters. The plan started to unfold on April 6, 1994 after the shooting down of the presidential aircraft which killed president Habyarimana. A major role in the genocide was assigned to the Interahamwe militias, consisting of young Hutu men armed with machetes and clubs. While Hutu militia and armed civilians perpetrated the killings, the RPF stepped up its military campaign. The rebel movement succeeded in quickly conquering the country and seized control of the state in July 1994. Within a few weeks the genocidal killings stopped.

However, the violent conflict between the now Tutsi-led national army and Hutu-militias continues. In the second half of 1997 Hutu rebels from Rwanda, Burundi and the eastern part of the Democratic Republic of Congo entered into an alliance and began infiltrating Rwanda from across the border with the aim of attacking the national army and civilians. In the second half of 1997 alone, an estimated 5,000 people were killed in these attacks. These incursions continue. A harsh repression of Hutu civilians, who are perceived as potential allies of the new rebellion, has been imposed by the Rwandan army, particularly in the north-west.

The conflict in Rwanda can be interpreted as a power struggle along predominantly ethnic lines between the Hutu majority, constituting 85 percent of the population, and the Tutsi minority which comprises 14 percent of the total population. The roots of this rivalry lie for a large part in the colonial era when Belgian authorities exacerbated ethnic divisions. The foreign power perceived the Tutsi minority as an aristocratic people with a natural aptitude for ruling and nominated large numbers of Tutsis to leading positions within the administration. The Hutu majority was perceived as a class of workers and farmers.

This division between Hutus and Tutsi is still perceived as a reality, but is not the only clue to understanding the conflict.

Firstly, there are other affiliations and rivalries, mostly within the Hutu majority, which add a more refined raster to the rough Hutu-Tutsi divide. Under the autocratic regime of Habyarimana, a Hutu opposition had already developed, with the Republican Democratic Movement (MDR) as its major political force. This Hutu movement opposed Habyarimana's Hutu-led National Revolutionary Movement for Development (MRND). Later, divisions also developed between, on the one hand, radical elements who were against democratisation, power sharing and the Arusha Peace Accords, and, on the other hand, moderate forces who supported a peaceful solution to the conflict and were open to power sharing with the RPF. These divisions partly crossed the ethnic lines. Analysts suggest that the downing of Habyarimana's plane in April 1994, the event that triggered the mass killings, may have been perpetrated by radical Hutu groups who wanted to block the Arusha Peace Accords from being implemented, instead of by the Tutsi-led RPF, as the then government claimed.

Secondly, behind the ethnic strife between Hutus and Tutsis lies a conflict between elites over access to the country's scarce resources. Since the scarce resources are most easily accessible for those Rwandans who control state power, the struggle has developed into a violent political conflict about government control in which the radical parties adopted an 'all-or-nothing' approach. The political affiliations of the rival groups are closely intertwined with their business relations and interests and also with their ethnic identity, but not to the full extent.

Thirdly, on the level of the general population, the Rwandan conflict is also to a large extent about access to land, housing and jobs, a conflict deeply immersed in sentiments of ethnic belonging. Tutsi exiles who returned to Rwanda as RPF fighters claimed a place for themselves. In many cases they were able to occupy land and houses of Hutus who had fled Rwanda ahead of the RPF offensive, but when these Hutu refugees returned in large numbers in 1996 they reclaimed their possessions. The massive wandering of people, including the migrations of internally displaced persons, created a complicated Gordian knot of land claims. Nevertheless, the Rwandan conflict should probably not be interpreted as being triggered by demographic pressure, as some analysts and media have suggested. Research has shown that the relationship between demographic pressure and genocide is much more indirect and complex than outside observers tend to believe.

Conflict Dynamics

Since the RPF take-over in Kigali in 1994, the movement is still the principal political force in Rwanda. It controls a government of national unity which has both Hutus and Tutsi in its ranks. Pasteur Bizimungu, an ethnic Hutu, is president, but vice president and minister of defence Paul Kagame, an ethnic Tutsi, is the strongman. Pierre Célestin Rwigyema, an ethnic Hutu, is prime minister. A large majority of deputy ministers are ethnic Tutsi. However, despite the presence of Hutu officials in the government, many Hutus still consider the RPF leaders as foreign occupiers.

The current government has demonstrated a lack of interest in establishing a broad political power base and in processes leading to power-sharing. Instead, gradual exclusion of Hutu, and also Tutsi, opponents from the top political levels, as well as in the administration and in the judiciary, in addition to the continued mono-ethnic nature of the national armed forces, add to the current conflict potential. International conflict mediation efforts have tended to ignore this key issue.

This autocratic tendency within the government may have impaired its policy of playing down the Hutu-Tutsi divide, restoring law and order and prosecution of genocide perpetrators, which have been stated as its main priorities for the first years after the genocide trauma.

One of the means to get over the traumatic past and to create conditions for reconciliation are the trials of suspects in the genocide. In November 1994, the International Criminal Tribunal for Rwanda was established by the UN, and Rwandan courts also try genocide suspects. The judicial system is overwhelmed with more

than 125,000 genocide suspects, detained in overcrowded jails. Several suspects have been sentenced to death by domestic Rwandan courts and have been executed. The International Tribunal, located in Arusha, has convicted a small number of high-ranking suspects. It abstains from capital punishment.

One of the main threats to stability in Rwanda is the Hutu insurgency in the north-west of the country. The attackers are members of the defeated army (the former Rwandan Armed Forces, ex-FAR) and Interahamwe-militias ('Those who work together'). Their hit-and-run actions are targeted against Tutsi survivors of the genocide, local Hutu politicians, foreign human rights monitors and aid workers. The insurgents operate under the name of the Liberation Army of Rwanda (ALIR). Their political wing, formed in June 1996, is known as the Armed People for the Liberation of Rwanda (PALIR). Together they have tried to create a power base in the north-west, the cradle of hard-line Hutu extremism, from where they seek to overthrow the present government or at least to force it to enter into negotiations. The Rwandan Patriotic Army (RPA), which confronts the rebels, has been accused of using excessive force in its attempt to suppress the insurgency. Indiscriminate killings appear to be designed to force the Hutu population to 'choose sides'.

In 1997, Rwandan government forces actively participated in the overthrow of the Mobutu regime in neighbouring Congo/Zaire. Soon after this campaign had led to military victory in May 1997, a rift developed between Laurent Kabila, the new president of the Democratic Republic of Congo, and the government in Kigali. In August 1998, Rwanda decided to support a second military campaign aimed at overthrowing the government in Kinshasa. There are strong indications that Kabila now supports FAR soldiers and the Interahamwe and helps them stage incursions into Rwanda.

The internationalisation of the conflict has coincided with increased international support for both camps, enhancing their ability to keep up their fight for a longer period of time. Additionally, linkages between the domestic Rwandan conflict and other conflicts in the Central African region make it more difficult to reach a peaceful political solution.

Rwanda is trying to recover from one of the worst and most lethal post World War II genocides. The traumatised country is rife with paranoia and suspicion. Much of the nation's physical infrastructure was damaged, while human resources -skilled and educated labour- disappeared. Seventy per cent of the population lives in poverty.

The exact number of people killed in 1994 may never be known but is estimated at 800,000. The genocide led about 1.5 million Rwandans to flee to neighbouring countries, where they were housed in refugee camps set up by the UNHCR and supplied by UN agencies and international humanitarian aid NGOs. In 1996, hundreds of thousands of (mainly Hutu) refugees were forced to return to Rwanda after Zairean rebels backed by Rwandan troops attacked the refugee camps. Hundreds of thousands of Rwandans were displaced internally, including about 200,000 Tutsi genocide survivors who form one of the most vulnerable groups in the country.

As a result of the intensification of the violence in 1997, a new pattern of internal displacement unfolded, especially in the north-west regions of Gisenyi and Ruhengeri. According to an international survey, there were a total of 180,000 internally displaced persons (IDPs) in the country. The government has prevented the establishment of camps or concentrations of internally displaced persons. Guerrilla activity and direct attacks on foreigners forced international NGOs to withdraw personnel and suspend activities in the north-western region.

Despite the ongoing tension and violence in the north-western provinces, Rwanda is making a post-genocidal comeback that has surprised international officials. The government has enabled a gradual return to normality in most parts of the country, partly thanks to massive international aid. Rwanda received more than US$ 2 billion in aid between 1994 and 1999. Two-thirds of the state budget is financed by foreign donors. The conflict in the north-west and Rwanda's involvement in the conflict in the Democratic Republic of Congo is still a drain on the economy, however. An estimated two-thirds

of the internal revenue of the government is spent on the military. Also, allegations of corruption at the top administrative and political levels have become more numerous and better documented during 1998 and 1999.

Official Conflict Management

In the study *The International Response to Conflict and Genocide: Lessons from the Rwanda Experience*, a team of independent investigators concluded that three months before the beginning of the genocide the UN, Belgium, France and the United States had been informed about the impending genocide, but decided not to act upon this information. Non-intervention clearly characterised the attitude of multilateral organisations and foreign powers towards the sudden escalation of the Rwandan conflict. However, they felt compelled to act after the genocide had taken place at which point their energy was spent on humanitarian aid and reconstruction.

The main *United Nations* actors that were active in the immediate aftermath of the mass killings were the Special Representative of the Secretary-General (SRSG), the UNAMIR military force, the UN Department of Humanitarian Affairs (DHA; later dubbed OCHA), the UN Development Programme (UNDP), the UN High Commissioner for Refugees (UNHCR) and the World Food Programme (WPF).

In the absence of a clear international mandate for Internally Displaced Persons, the UN-DHA established the Integrated Operations Centre (IOC), a coordinating body in the Rwandan Ministry of Rehabilitation in Kigali. The IOC, consisting of representatives of UN agencies, NGOs, major donors and the Rwandan government, attempted to foster dialogue and compromise to solve the IDP problem and served as a focal point for repatriation.

One of the major UN contributions to creating a climate for reconciliation was undoubtedly the establishment, in November 1994, of the International Criminal Tribunal for Rwanda, based on a UN Security Council resolution. This court initially planned to bring an estimated 400 suspected ringleaders of the genocide to trial but later had to scale down its ambitions. In early 1999, approximately 35

RWANDA, Reconstruction activities

indictments had been issued. The maximum sentence it can impose is life imprisonment. The first sentencing took place in September 1998.

The UN, in collaboration with the OAU, also appointed a special UN/OAU representative for the Great Lakes region who is charged with the task of promoting initiatives for peace and rehabilitation. The representative's efforts are mainly directed towards ending the conflict in neighbouring Burundi and the war in the Democratic Republic of Congo, in which Rwanda has a great stake.

Many of the UN's activities, such as human rights monitoring and sustaining the development process by UNDP and other agencies, were hindered by sour relations with the Rwandan government. On July 16, 1998, the UN announced it would pull its human rights mission out of Rwanda because an agreement could not be reached with the Rwandan government on a new mandate for the mission. The Rwandan government accused the UN mission of an unbalanced approach by focusing too much on violations by the government army.

Since 1998, the *World Bank* has supported a project run by the Rwandan government

intended to help communities absorb the returning refugees. The initiative, which consists of a large number of local development projects, was spearheaded by the bank's Post-Conflict Unit, created in 1997 to oversee the institution's work to help countries rebuild after violent conflict.

UNICEF is involved in programmes aimed at helping orphans and other children to cope with their trauma and to enable them to participate in education programmes.

The *Organization of African Unity* (OAU) was unable to respond efficiently to the Rwandan crisis. It only became involved after the genocide had taken place. In June 1998, the OAU decided to open an investigation into the Rwanda massacre, in order to draw lessons for future conflict resolution and prevention efforts. The OAU assigned an International Panel of Eminent Personalities, presided over by former president of Botswana Ketumile Masire, to execute the inquiry. It is expected to be published end 1999 or early 2000.

Among *individual states* France, the United States, Uganda, Tanzania, Burundi, and Congo/Zaire played major roles with respect to military and humanitarian efforts related to Rwanda. Belgium was amongst countries that offered a battalion of 400 troops for the United Nations Assistance Mission for Rwanda (UNAMIR). Its troops were withdrawn when the crisis escalated. Since the RPF take-over, Belgium is now pursuing a policy of maintaining influence from a distance. Along with the Netherlands, Belgium is a leading donor to the region.

Canada has been actively involved in peacekeeping in Rwanda and was at the forefront of a diplomatic initiative to lead an intervention force to ex-Zaire in 1996. It played a crucial role, along with the Netherlands, in generating support for a Multi-National Force (MNF) to protect Rwandan refugees. However, it was humiliated internationally as events in then Zaïre changed course and the MNF failed to materialise.

France was regarded by many Rwandans as an ally of the Hutus and is known to have supported the Habyarimana regime, providing it with military equipment and support. Paris played a crucial role in staging the UN-supported 'Operation Turquoise' in the summer of 1994, in which 2,500 French troops were dispatched to Rwanda to protect Hutu refugees. It is believed that the French also used the save havens they created to house ex-government and military personnel and allowed the flow of arms into these havens, thus enabling the Hutu militias to counterattack later. A parliamentary inquiry into the tragedy clarified that France helped the Rwandan regime that prepared and executed the genocide. A telegram from the French ambassador in Kigali to the French government clearly shows that it was well informed at an early stage about the preparations for the mass murder.

The Swiss government ordered an inquiry into the Swiss role in the events. The Swiss enquiry commission came to the conclusion that the dominance of aid and development interests in its relations with Rwanda caused lack of awareness of political developments. In response, Switzerland has decided to nominate a new coordinator for the Swiss development and humanitarian activities who has also been instructed to report on political developments in Rwanda.

The US government was reluctant to intervene during the first weeks of the genocide, fearing another Somalia, where more than twenty American soldiers were killed. However, Washington reacted swiftly once the crisis in Goma (ex-Zaire) broke out and mobilised the US air force to deliver supplies. Since then, the US has established close ties with the Rwandan government and stated promotion of trade, democracy and conflict prevention as its policy objectives in the region. In 1998, the US joined other western donors in providing financial support for strengthening the judicial system in Rwanda and its neighbouring countries, through its 'Great Lakes Justice Initiative'.

Multi-Track Diplomacy

Rwanda's relations with international organisations, both governmental and non-governmental, before, during and after the genocide have been characterised by severe frictions. The Rwandan government strongly resents the international community's failure to prevent and stop the genocide. It has also severely criticised the priorities chosen by international relief organisations. Over the years the government has tried to maintain control over NGOs by forcing them to sign strict working agreements. More than 140 non-governmental organisations entered Rwanda after the 1994 genocide. In December 1995, the government expelled 38 NGOs, freezing their bank accounts and cutting their phone lines. Most of the foreign NGOs work spans humanitarian relief, reconstruction, development, and advocacy activities.

Domestic NGOs faced the same, if not stricter, control by the Rwandan authorities. However, a lively variety of domestic NGOs exist, especially church groups, human rights organisations and civil society debate forums. The foreign NGOs are in the majority of cases working with domestic partners to support their efforts to build peace, justice, and stability.

Domestic
Activities to improve the living conditions of women have been embarked on by several domestic groups. One of these groups is *AVEGA*, an organisation set up in 1997 by

Rwandan widows. It aims to give mutual support and help women to re-build their lives in large parts of the country.

Church members' role in the crisis in Rwanda has been both consoling and accessory to the killings. The church in Rwanda is now fighting to wash off the stigma it suffered for turning a blind eye to the 1994 genocide. The *Rwandan Anglican Church*, which is part of the Nairobi-based Council of the Anglican Provinces of Africa (CAPA) set up departments of reconciliation in all dioceses in the course of 1997. They are holding seminars, inviting people from Europe, America and Africa to speak on the necessity of forgiveness and peaceful co-existence.

Church groups run many of the non-governmental reconciliatory activities. Most domestic church groups active in reconciliatory work are organised in *ACOREB, the Association des Conferences Episcopales du Rwanda et du Burundi*, and in the *CPR, the Conseil Protestant du Rwanda*.

Civil society forums have played an extensive role in increasing awareness of human rights violations. Local organisations such as the *Collective of Leagues and Associations for the Defence of Human Rights (CLADHO)* and the *Association Kanyarwanda*, commissioned an International Investigative Commission into the gross and systematic violations of human rights in Rwanda since October 1990. It played an important role in collecting facts and evidence for the International War Crimes Tribunal. Other forums, such as Profemme-Tsesehamwe and AVEGA, already mentioned above, contribute to the debate on human rights protection and reconciliation.

International

One of the first international NGOs specialised in the field of peace building that started to work in Rwanda was *International Alert*. Since 1995, International Alert has worked on a Great Lakes Conflict Resolution Programme that includes Rwanda. In cooperation with domestic and international partners, the London-based organisation has developed initiatives to encourage dialogue at all levels of Rwandan society.

International Alert especially supports the role of women in peace building. On the level of political infrastructure, International Alert has been trying to boost the functioning of the National Assembly, the Rwandan parliament. It provided computer equipment and training for the legislature's staff. It has also provided support for such simple but indispensable moves as giving parliament members subscriptions to national and international journals. It also supported the establishment of the Assembly's own parliamentary journal. In February 1998, International Alert facilitated a regional conference for parliamentarians on the role of parliaments in conflict resolution. This meeting led to the formation of a regional follow-up committee of regional MPs. International Alert provided the committee with information on constitution-making and different forms of local government, as part of a capacity-building strategy. The initiatives were aimed at strengthening both professional capacity and democratic allegiance, including acceptance of power sharing and the non-violent settlement of disputes.

The UK-based international aid organisation *Oxfam* has addressed gender issues as part of a reconciliation and rehabilitation process in Rwanda. Immediately after the genocide in 1994, Oxfam reopened its office in Kigali and rebuilt its programmes on the principle of working in a way that seeks to bridge the gaps between different groups and to minimise further conflict. Its projects target vulnerable women (survivors and women headed households) and support national advocacy initiatives that promote women's basic rights.

Among the thousands of war refugees now returning to Rwanda are many lost or orphaned children who are suffering great distress. In coordination with UNICEF, several aid agencies, such as *Save the Children*, are offering special psychological support, including play therapy.

In the realm of media, a sector which is of crucial importance considering the dark role played by radio stations in inciting the ethnic violence, the *BBC* has deployed reconciliatory activities in Rwanda. It has broadcast programmes in the local language aimed at strengthening mutual understanding and reuniting those who survived. Other local radio stations, some of them run with support of foreign religious organisations, also disseminate messages aimed at encouraging peace and the prevalence of reason over hatred.

Activities in the realm of advocacy are concentrated in the *Great Lakes Policy Forum*, a unique platform for discussion and exchange of information of international NGOs from various fields, including humanitarian assistance and conflict resolution, and government officials from African and western countries. The Forum, established in 1995, puts its focus in the entire Great Lakes region, including Rwanda.

In the field of mediation, some attempts have been made by *The Carter Center*. During summits in Cairo in November 1995 and Tunis in March 1996, former US President Jimmy Carter brought together heads of state of all countries in the region to address the on-going violence in the region and the need to repatriate 1.7 million Rwandan refugees.

Evaluation

The massive international relief effort triggered by the 1994 genocide has been evaluated in several studies aimed at improving NGO operating procedures and standards. The most comprehensive is *The International Response to Conflict and Genocide: Lessons from the Rwanda Experience. Joint Evaluation of Emergency Assistance to Rwanda*. While this study, facilitated by the Danish government, evaluates the (failed) conflict management and preventive efforts of international official diplomacy, its analyses of the role of non-governmental organisations is, understandably, very much focused on the humanitarian activities most NGOs were engaged in. The study calls for a role for NGOs, especially human rights organisations, in early warning, but within a UN-led and coordinated network.

As one study by Taylor B. Seybolt on the problem of the coordination of the various responses by different organisations concluded, the case of Rwanda indicates that 'a consensus process aimed at achieving shared information and analysis, common representation, and a common framework for action is the most desirable form of humanitarian coordination in a complex emergency.' All coordination efforts for the first ten months following the 1994 genocide were made by international agencies and organisations rather than the government of Rwanda, reportedly due to lack of competence and resources.

One of the most important lessons learned from the Rwandan experience is that the intermingling of humanitarian and military issues can put NGOs in hazardous situations that should be avoided at all costs.

Some analysts claim that international mediation efforts failed to address the alleged tendency of the current government to exclude Hutu, but also Tutsi opponnents, from top positions, a development they say could add to the current conflict potential.

Prospects

Following the severe setbacks for the Hutu extremists in the second half of 1998, it remains to be seen whether they will be able to sustain their military campaign. This will be highly dependent on fresh supplies of arms, regional alliances and the continued possibility of relying on their bases in northern Kivu in neighbouring Congo/Zaire.

Many observers hold that the insurgency in Rwanda, and those in neighbouring countries can only be tackled through a regional strategy. The significant internationalisation of the conflict in the Democratic Republic of Congo, has created a very murky situation which makes prediction about a likely outcome almost impossible.

Domestically, the legitimacy of the minority-led government is still fragile. It is undermined by the continuing defections of its Hutu members. If this process continues, the RPF will find it even more difficult to broaden its political base and increase its chances of survival in future elections.

An ominous development is the deteriorating discipline within the armed forces which tripled in size to 55,000 men in 1997. Not only have soldiers begun to kill out of personal revenge, they have also begun killing for purely criminal motives.

In addition to coping with external factors such as weapon supplies and training, any outcome of the conflict will be dependent on eradicating the hate propaganda spread by the Hutu insurgents.

The handling of the problem of the vulnerable Tutsi genocide survivors creates another dilemma for the government. The government feels restricted in trying to step up the aid to this minority as it cannot afford to be seen as favouring one ethnic group over the other.

The danger of Rwanda is that, as one observer concluded, it may start to resemble Burundi, where a simmering civil war has been going on since 1993.

Recommendations

Integration and coordination are the keywords in the recommendations made by experts and NGOs that have analysed the Rwandan crisis.

The Great Lakes Early Warning Project, a project organised by FEWER, recommends that the three east African Community members Kenya, Uganda and Tanzania should admit Rwanda (and Burundi) into this economic network. 'A regional integration framework would provide a forum wherein security issues could be addressed and commitments made, monitored and implemented,' the Project said in a report published in September 1998.

A group of NGOs evaluating Rwandan developments at a seminar in April 1998 (Challenges in Rwanda. Seminar on the dilemmas faced by NGOs and donors. April 28, 1998, The Hague, Netherlands) recommended the development of cooperation between domestic and international NGOs in order to be able to influence the Rwandan government, a task that is considered to be of high priority given the strained relationship between Kigali and NGOs. They also said trauma counselling and education still require more attention as a means to contribute to reconciliation.

Background document provided by Berto Jongmans/PIOOM

Most organisations also agree that land reform is required in order to create equal access to land, preventing one group from getting preferential treatment over others. Adoption of such a reform policy would be enhanced by efficient advocacy of domestic and foreign organisations in Rwandan government quarters.

Most experts also consider a dialogue between the moderates of the different parties as of utmost important and see a role for NGOs in defining people who represent the various groups in society.

CARE International urged the international community and the leaders of the Great Lakes region to begin a new process to achieve peace, rehabilitation and development. The organisation refers to similar, encouraging, initiatives in Central America that resulted in peace accords. CARE specifically urges the UN to promote efforts by presidents in the region to meet and develop a strategy to reduce conflict.

Another call for a coordinated and coherent approach in dealing with domestic conflicts such as in Rwanda was issued by the UN's Lessons Learned Unit. In a report evaluating the UN peacekeeping mission in Rwanda from 1993 to 1996, the unit advised setting up a joint civilian-military operations centre for any future peacekeeping missions, in order to achieve coordination between the military and humanitarian community.

In a report issued in April 1999 evaluating the quest for restoring justice in Rwanda, the International Crisis Group recommends that the international community continues to support the Rwandan justice system for at least another three years and that it support and facilitate debate on how to deal with the 125,000 detainees, including alternative forms of justice, particularly the setting up of so called arbitration tribunals. The ICG also calls for more attention to be paid to the psychological situation of survivors and the compensation of victims.

Service Information

Newsletters and Periodicals
Dialogue (Belgium-based monthly produced by Rwandan refugees and exiles providing broad-ranging information on current developments)

Reports
Danish Foreign Ministry
- The International Response to Conflict and Genocide - Lessons from the Rwanda Experience. Joint Evaluation of Emergency Assistance to Rwanda. 1996

International Crisis Group
- Five Years After the Genocide in Rwanda: Justice in Question. April 1999

Carnegie Commission on Preventing Deadly Conflict
- People in Peril. Human Rights, Humanitarian Action, and Preventing Deadly Conflict. John Stremlau. New York, 1998. (Includes chapter on Rwanda/eastern Zaïre)
- Preventing Genocide. How the Early Use of Force Might Have Succeeded in Rwanda, by Scott R. Feil. April 1998

Lessons Learned Unit, UN Department of Peacekeeping Operations
- Comprehensive Report on Lessons Learned from United Nations Assistance Mission for Rwanda (UNAMIR), October 1993 - April 1996. December 1996

Republic of Rwanda Ministry of Rehabilitation and Social Integration, Humanitarian Assistance Coordinating Unit (HACU)
- Humanitarian Aid - Results of Non-Governmental Organisation Action in Rwanda (July 1994 - February 1996). 1996

Human Rights Watch
- 'Leave none to tell the story.' Washington/New York, 1999

Article 19
- Broadcasting Genocide. Censorship, Propaganda & State-Sponsored Violence in Rwanda 1990-1994. London, 1996

African Rights
- The Insurgency in the Northwest. London, 1998

Other Publications
We Wish to Inform You That Tomorrow We Will Be Killed with Our Families, by Philip Gourevitch. 1998

Seasons of Blood - A Rwandan Journey, by Fergal Keane. 1997

The Angels Have Left Us - The Rwanda Crisis and the Churches, by Hugh McCullum. 1995.

The Cohesion of Oppression - Clientship and Ethnicity in Rwanda, by Catharine Newbury. 1993

The Rwanda Crisis - History of a Genocide, by Gerard Prunier. 1997

Analyse des crises et pistes pour une prévention - Conflits en Afrique. Dossiers du GRIP 215/217. GRIP, Brussels 1997 (with a case-study on Rwanda)

The End of a Culture of Impunity in Rwanda? Prosecution of Genocide and War Crimes before Rwandan Courts and the International Criminal Tribunal for Rwanda, by C. Cissé. In: *Yearbook of International Humanitarian Law 1998*. The Hague, T.M.C. Asser Press, 1999

The International Dimension of Genocide in Rwanda, by A.J. Klinghoffer. Macmillan, 1998

Selected Internet Sites
persoweb.francenet.fr/˜intermed/ (International Criminal Tribunal for Rwanda)

www.inter-media.org (regular coverage of the International Criminal Tribunal Africa for Rwanda, in English and French).

www.assemblee-nationale.fr/2/2rwanda.html (site of the French parliament containing elaborate information on the French role in the 1994 genocide)

www.jha.sps.cam.ac.uk/policy/pb025.htm (the full 1996 report from the Joint Evaluation of Emergency Assistance to Rwanda, the indispensable source on the international reaction to the genocide and its aftermath. Also available at *www.ing.dk/danida/rwanda.html*

Resource Contacts

Filip Reyntjens - Scholar and Central African Expert at University of Antwerp, Belgium. Email freyntje@ruca.ua.ac.be

Colette Braeckman - Journalist of the Belgian daily *Le Soir*, 21 Place de Louvain, 1000 Brussel Belgie, fax +32 2 225 59 14

Bernardin Ndashimye - Coordinator of the Rwandan umbrella human rights organisator *Collectif des Ligues et Associations des Droits de l'Homme au Rwanda* (CLADHO), via NCOS Brussels, Belgium.

Jan van Criekinge - NCOS, Belgium, e-mail jan.vancriekinge@ncos.ngonet.be

Organisations

AVEGA
B.P. 1535
Kigali
Rwanda
tel + 250 75124

Data on the following organisations can be found in the Directory section

Collective of Leagues and Associations for the Defence of Human Rights (CLADHO)
International Alert
Great Lakes Policy Forum
The Carter Center
Oxfam
FEWER
International Crisis Group

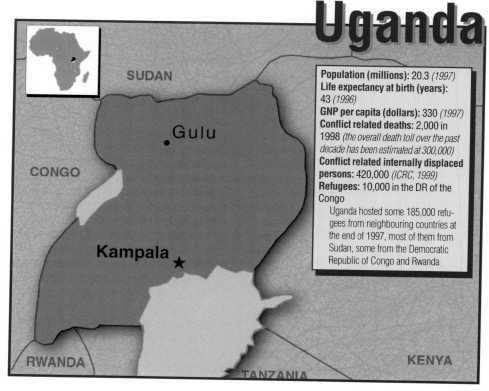

Uganda

Population (millions): 20.3 *(1997)*
Life expectancy at birth (years): 43 *(1996)*
GNP per capita (dollars): 330 *(1997)*
Conflict related deaths: 2,000 in 1998 *(the overall death toll over the past decade has been estimated at 300,000)*
Conflict related internally displaced persons: 420,000 *(ICRC, 1999)*
Refugees: 10,000 in the DR of the Congo

Uganda hosted some 185,000 refugees from neighbouring countries at the end of 1997, most of them from Sudan, some from the Democratic Republic of Congo and Rwanda

Explosive Mix of Problems could re-ignite Civil War

In the twelve years since president Yoweri Museveni's revolutionary forces marched into Kampala, Uganda has shed its shameful reputation for state violence and the government has succeeded in stabilising and pacifying large parts of the country. Sadly, however, the situation in recent years has deteriorated, partly due to the fact that Uganda borders three countries that are involved in armed conflict. It is also argued that Museveni rules a divided country in which many people and regions have yet to benefit from Uganda's turnaround. In the meantime, the civilian pro-peace lobby in Uganda is rapidly gaining strength ◆ *By* Hans van de Veen

Under the Idi Amin, Milton Obote and Tito Okello regimes, Uganda had a long history of civil conflict and gross human rights violations, particularly in the 1970s and 1980s. Out of seven major political changes since its independence in 1962, four ended in large-scale bloodshed. However, a period of political stabilisation and economic recovery started when the National Resistance Army (NRA) marched into Kampala in 1986.

Since that moment, Uganda has shed its shameful reputation for state violence and the government has succeeded in stabilising and pacifying large parts of the country. Of the more than twenty armed groups active in the 1980s, only a handful have survived to continue their armed struggle.

President Museveni has been hailed as the architect of Uganda's successful recovery. Uganda had gradually become one of Africa's

58

most hopeful examples of reform, boasting growth rates of seven per cent or more, year after year. In the beginning of 1998 a confident Museveni told journalists: 'There isn't anything we can't solve. The big problems are behind us.' Today, however, it looks as though he may have spoken too soon.

The humming economy has started to sputter, the army is fighting deep in the Congo, tourists have been attacked by rebels, and bombs have exploded in the capital, Kampala. Uganda's much vaunted political stability is looking shaky, and confidence in president Museveni and his government has taken a serious knock.

Several observers regard the decision to send some 15,000 troops into the Congo in 1998 in support of a rebellion against Museveni's erstwhile prodigy, president Laurent Kabila, as a major error. 'Launching one rebellion in the Congo in 1996 looked audacious, launching a second was foolhardy', *The Economist* magazine argued (May 1, 1999). The attempt by Uganda and Rwanda to topple Kabila by flying hundreds of troops and rebels across the Congo to attack the capital, Kinshasa, ended in disaster. The rebellion drew little support on that side of the country. The intervention also brought most neighbour countries into the war on Kabila's side.

The Ugandan government argues that it is forced to keep troops in the Congo because the Kinshasa regime encourages Ugandan rebel groups to infiltrate Uganda's and Rwanda's western border from eastern Congo. This may be a valid argument, however, the western border remains insecure. In early 1999 Ugandan and Rwandan rebels crossed into the country and killed at least 90 civilians, including eight foreign tourists at Bwindi. This was a major blow to Uganda's tourism industry.

In Kampala, rebels have carried out some twenty bomb attacks in the past two years, killing some 45 people. In the north, war against the messianic LRA is entering its twelfth year. As yet, the government has failed to crush it militarily or to find a political solution. This war is also fuelled by Uganda's foreign adventurism; the LRA is helped by Sudan in retaliation for Ugandan support of rebel groups in South Sudan.

As a result of growing insecurity and

Uganda's active involvement in the neighbouring Democratic Republic of Congo the army had to recall disarmed soldiers in 1997. In early 1998, the government announced a reorganisation of the armed forces in an attempt to create a more effective force. The reorganisation was also intended to create a better ethnic balance within the armed forces. The stepping-up of military operations resulted in increased military expenditure.

Today, most Ugandans - forty per cent of whom are categorised by the UN as living in poverty - are unhappy at the cost of the wars. More worrying for the government is the fact that aid donors - who pay more than half of the government's running costs - are losing sympathy with the regime. While Uganda in 1998 qualified as the first country to profit from an international debt-reduction scheme (HIPC), the IMF in March 1999 delayed a US$18m loan because of the increased defence spending.

After holding power for longer than any other Ugandan leader, Museveni's popularity seems to be waning among the population. From a minority group in the south-west, he fought his way into power in 1986 with a popular, well-organised guerrilla movement. He promised democratisation but retained military control. At the same time, he set up a broad government based on his 'Movement', although it also included opposition leaders. The old political parties were not banned; they were, however, prevented from operating. Arguing that first-past-the-post, winner-takes-all democracy exacerbates religious and ethnic tensions in Africa, the Ugandan government introduced a 'no-party system'.

Museveni was elected in 1996 for a five year term, in elections that were peaceful and orderly. Since then, the government's base has narrowed and critics argue that the 'Movement' now looks more like a one-party affair. Pressure has built up for more democracy and Parliament has proved to be no lap dog. A referendum will be held in 2000 on whether to retain the no-party system or allow multi-partyism.

In the meantime, constitutional changes have been introduced to guarantee greater degrees of participation and transparency at local levels, based on districts and village councils. Observers agree that this decentralisation of power has provided a degree of stability by contributing to security, improving the infrastructure, helping settle disputes and initiating small self-help projects, although with considerable regional variation.

Conflict Dynamics

Uganda has a total of 56 ethnic groups. In an attempt to accommodate ethnic sentiments, the government has permitted the re-establishment of traditional monarchies. However, the 'if-people-so-wish' clause in the monarchic restoration bill prevented the Ankole people for instance from recreating their kingdom, due to ethnic sentiments. It remains an open question if ethnic disputes can be accommodated via re-establishing kingdoms.

The north-south division remains an important factor in Ugandan politics. After some twenty years of rule by northern ethnic groups, the NRA-victory in 1986 meant that for the first time southern ethnic groups took state power.

The government has been accused of amassing wealth in the south and the west at the expense of Nilotic ethnic groups in the north. Northerners claim they suffered more than the rest of the country when the World Bank demanded a reduction of Uganda's public service. The majority of the remaining state-owned companies are headed by people from around Museveni's home area. The Museveni-regime has also failed to prevent persistent human rights abuses by the army in the northern region.

The Holy Spirit Movement first became active in the north-western region in 1986. In 1989 it was replaced by the Lord's Resistance Army (LRA), led by Joseph Kony, which operates from Sudan and is actively supported by the Sudanese government. The LRA's stated goal is to rule Uganda on the basis of the ten biblical commandments. Although the LRA claims it has a political agenda and aims to overthrow the government, its support base seems too limited. Most Acholi people in the region are opposed to the violence employed by the LRA. Since 1994, the LRA has been able to increase its strength to about 2,000 men. When it allied itself with the West Nile Bank Front in 1994, the Ugandan

government began cross border operations in Sudan giving the conflict a regional dimension.

In 1997, the army had 20,000 soldiers deployed in the northern part of the country along the border with Sudan in order to combat the LRA. This represents nearly half of the army's personnel. Escalation of the conflict over the past two years has resulted in the displacement of some 300,000-400,000 people, around fifty per cent of the population of Kitgum and Gulu districts. According to Amnesty International, up to 8,000 boys and girls have been abducted in the past few years. Children have reportedly become the main source of recruitment for the various rebel operations in Uganda. The high level of insecurity has had a devastating impact on the health and education systems in the northern districts.

The Western Nile Bank Front says it wants to create an independent Islamic West Nile state. This group sprang from a number of Amin loyalists active in the 1980s. When Museveni came to power, several guerrillas regrouped in Sudan and offered their services to the Sudanese regime. In 1993, the group was reactivated and dedicated itself to exacting revenge for Uganda's activities in southern Sudan. It suffered severe losses in 1995. After further reorganisation and being resupplied by the Sudanese government it made an alliance with the LRA. In 1997 the Front's forces reportedly were depleted by combat in southern Sudan. In February 1998, the Ugandan army also reported a string of successes against the organisation. However, a few months later the Front began new incursions from bases in the DRC. New activities of another small armed opposition group, the Ugandan National Rescue Front, have also been reported in the north-west.

The north-east of the country is inhabited by the Karamojong pastoralists, a marginalised minority of about 100,000 people. Since the Karamojong acquired automatic weapons the region has become a virtual no-go area. The area is suffering from environmental degradation and is periodically struck by famine. The military has been involved in regular punishment expeditions in the fight again cattle-raiding. Vigilantes have taken the law into their own hands, resulting in a breakdown of law and order. Guns are plentiful and gangs have terrorised the local population. An estimated 30,000 illegal weapons are in circulation which are used to rustle cattle and ambush and raid vehicles. These raids extend across the borders into Kenya and Sudan and on numerous occasions have provoked serious incidents with neighbouring countries.

The *Allied Democratic Forces* (ADF), active in the south-western districts of the country, is held responsible for hundreds of deaths in 1997 and 1998. The ADF is engaged in large-scale abuse of civilians, including killing, rape and abduction. It has planted mines extensively, attacked civilian locations and targeted local officials for abduction and murder. The ADF was founded in the autumn of 1994 and is lead by Herbert Itongwa. The group is opposed to the political programme of president Museveni and claims to favour federalism, multi-party democracy and respect for human rights. It is also opposed to the 'Ugandan adventures' in Rwanda and the Congo. The ADF mainly recruits from the Hutu Rwandan Army and from late president Mobutu's forces, the Armées Zairoises, but has limited support among the local population. It is estimated to have between 600 and 1,000 members, but its membership is growing. In the beginning of 1999 the situation in the western part of the country deteriorated rapidly. Relief organisations decided to withdraw from Bundibugyo, due to the increased rebel activities. Some 50,000-80,000 people were forced to flee their homes to larger towns.

Also in this area, remnants of the *National Army for Liberation of Uganda* (NALU) are active. The movement, which dates back to the 1950s, is no longer considered a major threat but there is a fear that it will be used by outside powers. In 1998, NALU claimed responsibility for a number of bomb attacks on buses.

In August 1998, a large deployment of troops began in eastern Uganda, where the army is trying to quell a mutiny by a little known rebel group, the *Ugandan Salvation Front* (USF). The army had been deployed in the Mount Elgon area on the border with Kenya to check the USF. The deployment came a week after the rebel group attacked the Mutufu local administration prison and abducted 70 inmates.

Militant muslims have been recruiting exclusively among the minority Shi'ite community with local sheiks establishing small groups of activists. When the extremists extended their activities, the Ugandan authorities called on sheik Luwemba to help stop the development. Luwemba condemned the so-called Tabliqs and ordered the destruction of two mosques thought to be headquarters of the extremists. In 1995, the government ordered an operation against a training camp in the Halkum Kaira region. Several hundred guerrillas were killed or captured. The Islamic terrorist threat still exists. The strength of the Tabliqs is estimated at about 400 men. In 1995, a new branch of the Tabliqs appeared under the name of the Liberation Tigers of Uganda. It is reported to be supported by influential circles in Arab countries. In 1995, Muslim deserters from the army established the *Uganda Muslims Salvation Front* (UMSF). Following the bomb attacks on the US embassies in Kenya and Tanzania in the summer of 1998, Ugandan authorities have stepped up efforts to monitor the activities of Muslims, who in total constitute some ten per cent of the population.

In order to stem a rise in crime the government has taken drastic measures in the form of mass arrests. In an operation in November 1998, a total of 5,000 people in the capital Kampala and the northern town of Gulu were taken in for questioning by the security forces in an operation the Internal Affairs Minister said was directed at 'elements who are using robbery to cause insecurity'.

Official Conflict Management

Uganda's growth is highly dependent on foreign donor funding. The country received a total of US$ 750 million from foreign donors in 1997 and demanded US$ 1 billion in 1998. Despite its political weakness, Uganda was a favoured recipient of Western donors. In the past year, foreign investors and donors have begun to worry about the growing level of corruption and Uganda's involvement in the war in the DRC.

As a sign of the growing corruption, Salim Saleh, Museveni's brother and the second most powerful man in the country, resigned. Salim and other Ugandans have financial interests in the exploitation of gold in Congo DR, which is probably one reason for Uganda's support of the rebel movement. Western donors demanded the government show a stronger political commitment to fight corruption. The demand was made by the World Bank, the IMF, UN agencies, the EU-countries and a number of banks, non-governmental organisations and Asian countries.

A report published in 1997, drawn up by Robert Gersony, an expert in civil conflict, for the US Embassy and *USAID*, marks the first time a foreign government has endorsed peace talks between the Ugandan government and the LRA. The US government in particular sees Uganda as an important ally in preventing the spread of Islamic fundamentalism in Africa, as well as in extending the US sphere of influence. Uganda therefore has received substantial amounts of military aid.

Since 1997 the fact of conflict in northern Uganda, and especially the brutalisation of children by the LRA, has become more widely recognised at the international level. In April 1998 the *UN Commission on Human Rights* took the unprecedented step of passing a resolution dealing specifically with child abduction by the LRA. The Sudan government has come under pressure from governments and UN officials to take action against human rights abuses by the LRA by stopping the provision of arms supplies and bases for the armed group as long as it continues to abuse human rights. International observers say there is little sign of really significant action by the Sudanese.

The emergence of a de facto military stalemate in the north has resulted in both the government and the rebels taking the first tentative steps towards finding a political solution to the impasse. In February 1998 the LRA proposed a negotiated settlement of the conflict. In July, president Museveni also proposed peace talks. At the end of that year, the Ugandan minister of state for Defence said, during a visit to Kitgum, that the government would help facilitate initiatives by 'anyone' who wanted to talk about peace with the LRA. In May 1999 Museveni offered amnesty to LRA's leader Joseph Kony and his followers, 'if they come out peacefully' and settle in the Ugandan community. Although these initiatives show some

softening of the government in its long-standing position that negotiations with the LRA are out of question, there is still little sign that the government is itself prepared to take the lead in setting-up such a negotiated peace process. There is equally little sign that the LRA would be prepared to respond if it did. The road to peace has proven to be a rocky one and there are hawks on both sides of the divide who are opposed to a negotiated solution.

Multi-Track Diplomcay
Domestic

The pro-peace lobby in Uganda is mainly oriented toward the conflict in the north and has gained considerably in strength recently. Local leaders in the north, the churches, NGOs and many others have been making calls in recent years for a negotiated resolution to the war.

Students and universities have sponsored wide-ranging political debates in open forums, including an interdisciplinary conference on human rights in the Great Lakes Region at Makarere University in December 1997. In October that year, over 5,000 students marched in the streets of Kampala, urging the government to talk with the rebel groups and end the bloodshed. At the *Kacoke Madit* in London in July 1998 many exiles strongly opposed to the government spoke out in favour of a negotiated peace.

Ugandan church leaders have also urged the government to stop seeking a military solution to the conflict and talk with the guerrillas instead. The call was made during a 'Peace March and Prayer' in October 1998, which was attended by 10,000 people. The event was organised by the Catholic Church's *Peace and Justice Commission* and the *Uganda Joint Christian Council*. Earlier in the year, the Church leaders had bowed to pressure from Museveni to postpone the demonstration, because it was too close to a parliamentary resolution which called for stepped up military operations. The October demonstration was explicitly organised as a non-political event. Politicians who attended the peace march and prayer explained that they did so in their individual capacities. The government chose to stay away and was charged by some participants with indifference.

MBARARA, UGANDA, Boys school

The *Church of Uganda* conducts a Peace and Human Rights Programme, which started in the north and north-east but has been extended to west-Uganda. Several peace and human rights training sessions to raise the consciousness of civil society have been conducted. The Planning, Development and Rehabilitation Department of the CoU is associated with Responding To Conflict, based in Birmingham, UK, and works closely with Action by Churches Together (ACT) in Geneva.

A community peace-building programme in the Gulu district in northern Uganda is run by the NGO *People's Voice for Peace*. Here, trainers in conflict resolution help victims to cope with conflict and to build peace. Support for income-generating activities is part of the programme. The coordination of the community peace-building activities is being done through its Peace and Oral Research and Testimony Documentation Centre. Networking and collaboration with other peace actors within the civil society (local groups, churches, social movements, and traditional institutions) is seen by PVP as essential. Presently the Gulu-based organisation is expanding its activities to neighbouring districts, due to the high demand especially in the area of support to women victims of war.

Under its Popular Human Rights Education project, the *Foundation for Human Rights Initiative* (FHRI) has made several interventions aimed at the peaceful resolution of conflicts in the country. In July 1997 it organised a three-day conference at the Gulu District Council Hall on the conflict in northern Uganda.

Yamii Ya Kupatanisha (JYAK) is the Ugandan branch of the International Fellowship of Reconciliation (IFOR). It has set up the Gulu Vocational Community Centre for boys and girls. Many of the pupils are returnees from Sudan who had been abducted by LRA rebels. At the Gulu Centre, they are offered vocational training and peace education is also part of the programme. JYAK is also preparing trainers for peace initiatives at the individual and community level. The organisation emphasises the role of youth and women as peacekeepers.

A number of NGOs have begun trauma counselling programmes for the children caught up in the conflict. The *Concerned Parents of Abducted Children* (CPAC), for example, have worked with UNICEF and the church in Uganda to get their children back. The CPAC campaigns nationally and internationally for the release of the children and draws attention to the plight of all children in Uganda caught up in war. In December 1998 Angelina Acheng Atyem, a member of the organisation, won the UN Prize in the Field of Human Rights.

The *Centre for Conflict Prevention* is an Uganda-based NGO seeking alternative and creative means of preventing, managing and resolving conflicts. The Centre trains key figures and professionals in conflict prevention and resolution skills, besides other skills like community development, office management and decision-making. The trainees are encouraged to transmit the same skills to people in the community and workplace in turn. Many of the trainers are women who held influential positions in society. The Centre also provides counselling services to traumatised children and young people

ACORD Uganda has been running extensive programs in the north for at least a decade. In March 1997 it organised a two-day conference in Kampala on conflict resolution in the north, with a host of national and regional invitees.

Uganda has a wide variety of NGOs operating in the country. They are obliged to register with the Nongovernmental Organisations Board. NGOs thought to be opposed to the government have sometimes had difficulties in obtaining their registration.

Numerous human rights groups are active in Uganda, including the FHI, the Uganda chapter of FIDA; the UPAF, which monitors prison conditions; the National Organisation for Civic Education and Election Monitoring, which deals with problems related to civil society and political rights; Human Rights Focus; the National Association of Women's Organisations of Uganda (NAWOU); the Human Rights and Peace Centre, HURINET, Ugandan Human Rights Education and Documentation Centre (UHEDOC), Amnesty International and the National Association of Women Judges of Uganda (NAWJ).

The *Uganda Human Rights Commission*, a permanent independent body established by the Constitution, has begun a number of

investigations of human rights abuses and has participated in NGO conferences and seminars. In Amnesty International's view the UHRC has an important and potentially powerful role to play in respect of human rights in the northern area. 'It could fulfil the need for a vigorous, independent body with the capacity to follow up reports of human rights abuses in order to ensure that action is taken.' AI recommended the opening of UHRC offices in the northern area.

International
Between 1996-1997 the *International Labour Organisation* (ILO) conducted its Action programme on Skills and Entrepreneurship Training for Countries Emerging from Armed Conflict in Uganda. Several re-integration activities for ex-combatants and their families were sponsored. All of them included young people affected by conflict. Several programmes combined economic activities with peace education, based on the conviction that when young people have alternative sources of income they are less likely to be recruited into the army or join rebel forces as an occupation. Specific programmes were run by the Volunteers in Overseas Activities (VOCA), the Mennonite Central Committee, DANIDA, USAID, World Vision Uganda, World Learning Incorporated and Heifer Project International. Amongst the Ugandan counterparts were the Ugandan government, the Uganda Veterans Assistance Board (UVAB), CECORE, and the Gulu Vocational and Community Centre.

Since the international recognition of the northern Uganda conflict, and specifically the brutalisation of children by the LRA, several organisations have intervened. In particular, trauma counselling programmes for the children caught up in the conflict have been set up. Donors find these kind of programmes attractive because they do not require expensive infrastructure costs, have a limited running time, are easy to set up and use a language that the Western audiences are familiar with. Consequently it is easy to attract funding.

Recently, representatives of some Ugandan NGOs have questioned the effectiveness of these programmes. They claim that responding to an

African conflict with Western psychiatric care is inappropriate. Programmes should, in their opinion, concentrate on enabling people to leave behind the past and get on with their life, and should therefore concentrate on rebuilding houses, and getting markets and trading going again.

The *Nairobi Peace Initiative*, the all-African peace resolution group, is helping to set up networks of peace advocates in the Great Lakes region. There is one such network in Uganda.

Prospects

Rising inequality and a growing urban-rural gap combined with continuing high levels of insecurity in many parts of the country are an explosive mix that could re-ignite a civil war. Museveni's government has been explaining that the fighting in the north is about to finish for so long that few people believe this any more. According to the Relief and Rehabilitation Network (Nov. 1997), 'Privately, government officials admit that the Ugandan people's Defence Forces profit from the war, that corruption has removed much of the donor money given for the north and the merchants there benefit too'. 'It looks like another case of the phenomenon identified by David Keen in the "Benefits of Famine" - enough people do well out of the war that it continues until there is nothing left.'

There are no signs that the military has the capacity or commitment to bring the war to a conclusion through military means. The government has not shown itself very willing to initiate peace talks. It has assured its critics that talks are under way with the LRA, despite its commitment to a military solution in the north. Neither has it reacted to foreign endorsements of peace talks. The violence has yet to reach a level which endangers the survival of the government. Worsening relations with neighbouring countries may further destabilise the region.

How the situation in the south-west will develop depends largely on whether peace will be restored in the neighbouring DRC. If so, it should be possible to control the activities of the relatively small groups operating in the border area. A clear sign of Uganda's eagerness to find a solution for the Congo crisis was the April '99

agreement in Libya, in which it agreed to pull out its troops.

The outcome of the attempt to create a greater degree of democracy without allowing political parties on a national level, is difficult to predict. There is much speculation inside Uganda as to whether president Museveni will allow the referendum to go ahead in 2000. However, the president has repeatedly said that he intends to push ahead with the referendum, adding that he might leave political life afterwards. This in turn raises the question of his successor. What are the prospects for conflict resolution in Uganda in the absence of such a flawed but also larger than life character who has dominated the political scene in Uganda and the immediate region for so long?

Recommendations

Robert Gersony, the American researcher who wrote an extensive report about the situation in the north in 1997, formulated some recommendations. He argued that the moment was opportune for a resumption of negotiations. In earlier stages of the conflict direct talks had been possible with the involvement of the parties which contributed to a mitigation of the violence. New talks should therefore again be arranged without intermediaries. Gersony expected that negotiations between the two sides would enjoy a great degree of support among the Acholi people because it is a conflict without a constituency or a beneficial purpose.

Gersony argued further that there are several Ugandan organisations that are well placed and in some cases eager to support the peace and reconciliation process. Within the leadership of both parties there will be elements who will oppose such a process. This will remain a significant obstacle. The international community should actively encourage the resumption of the negotiations. A greater degree of attention to the conflict and the negotiation process could have a positive effect.

To overcome another obstacle to the peace process, Gersony recommended the establishment of an independent, impartial, authoritative international Panel of Inquiry. This panel would investigate incidents of large-scale human rights violations in order to end the confusion over the identity of the party responsible for these incidents. Once the obstacles to the negotiations have been removed and the peace process gets under way, international donors should be prepared to provide rapid economic assistance specifically designed and targeted to accelerate post-conflict rehabilitation, reconstruction and economic reactivation in the north. Gersony recommended that donors should consider at an early stage what type of assistance they might provide to support the consolidation of peace should talks succeed, and described a series of options.

Hussein Solomon, working with the South African based NGO ACCORD has argued ('Prospects for Peace in Northern Uganda', in the organisation's magazine Conflict Trends, Oct. 1998) for a three step approach to facilitate a peaceful settlement to the conflict in the north. In the first instance, he wonders if there is a chance to transform the LRA into a political entity: 'This would give the LRA a stake in any

new political dispensation, and if that dispensation also incorporated an element of federalism for the Acholi people of northern Uganda, all the better.'

'Second, both sides need to utilise the positive energies of civil society, both inside and outside Uganda, to assist the process of dialogue and reconciliation. For instance, the Acholi elders have expressed their preparedness to peacefully reintegrate LRA combatants into their communities.' This suggestion is in line with previous Ugandan experience, which suggests the importance of involving civil society at many levels, including traditional leaders, business and exiles (as in the Kacoke Madit).

Finally, Solomon agrees with Gersony, 'the success of the peace process is also dependent upon the support of the international community at the level of post-conflict reconstruction. Peace, after all, is a meaningless concept, in the context of socio-economic deprivation, which in many instances is the root cause of the conflict.'

Background document provided by Berto Jongmans/PIOOM

Service Information

Newsletters and Periodicals
The Human Rights Dateline - A Newsletter of the Foundation for Human Rights Initiative
The Defender - A Bi-Annual Human Rights Journal of the Foundation for Human Rights Initiative

Reports
Amnesty International
- Uganda: Breaking the Circle - Protecting human rights in the northern war zone. March, 1999

Human Rights Watch
- Children Abducted by the Lord's Resistance Army in Uganda. Sept. 1997

International Labour Organisation
- A Study on the situation of conflict-affected youth in Uganda and their reintegration into society through training, employment and life skills programmes. Geneva, 1997.

Other Publications
The Elusive Promise of NGOs in Africa - Lessons from Uganda, by S. Dicklitz. Macmillan, 1998
The Anguish of Northern Uganda - Results of a Field-Based Assessment of the Civil Conflicts in Northern Uganda, by Robert Gersony. Submitted to the United States Embassy, Kampala; USAID Mission, Kampala; August 1997.

Selected Internet Sites
www.imul.com/muk (Makerere University (Uganda)
www.imul.com/vision (The New Vision)
www.uganda.co.ug (Kampala Newsupdate)
www.africaonline.com.ug (AfricaOnline)
www.bsos.umd.edu/cidcm/mar/ugacholi (Minorities at Risk project from the University of Maryland, US offers a complete chronology of the conflict in the North)

Resource Contactss

Rosalba Oywa - Director People's Voice for Peace

Hussein Solomon - ACCORD, South Africa. E-mail hussein@accord.co.za

Frank Rwakabwohe - Church of Uganda, Head of Programmes

Livingstone Sewanyana - Executive Director Foundation for Human Rights Initiative

Organisations

Mennonite Central Committee
Contact: Mrs. Ron and Pam Ferguson
Plot 37 Acacia Av., Kololo
P.O. Box 6051, Kampala
Uganda
Tel. +256 41 258 597
Email: MCC@mcc.uu.Imul.com

World Vision Uganda
Contact: Kofi Hagan
15B Nakasero Road
P.O. Box 5319, Kampala
Uganda
Tel. +256 41 345 758/251 641
Fax +256 41 258 587
Email: Hagan_Kofi@wvi.org

Gulu Vocational and Community Centre
Contact: Michael Ocan Ongom, director
P.O. Box 927 Gulu
Uganda

Uganda Joint Christian Council
Contact: Ms. Jenny Ottewell
P.O. Box 30154, Kampala
Uganda
Tel. +256 41 270927
Fax +256 41 251927
Email: counet-tr@mukla.gn.apc.org

ACORD Uganda
Contact: Sam Aisu
Gaba Road, Kampala
Uganda
Tel/fax +256 41 267 668
Email: ngoforum@starcom.co.ug

Ugandan Human Rights Education and Documentation Centre
Contact: Regina Mutyaba
Plot 25 Lumumba Avenue
P.O. Box 7183
Kampala
Uganda
Tel. +256 41 255 899
Email: UHEDOC@imul.com

Data on the following organisations can be found in the Directory section:
People's Voice for Peace
FHRI
JYAK
RTC
CECORE
Amnesty International
NPI

West Africa

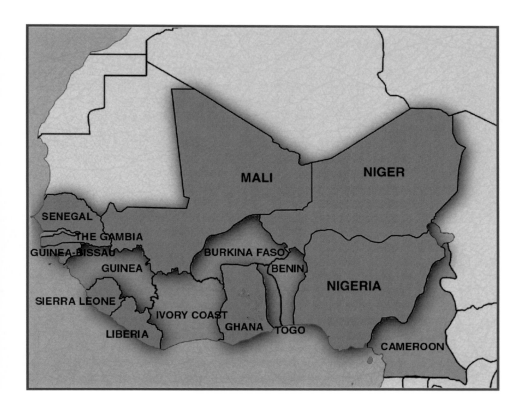

West African Patterns of Conflict Resolution

Without exception, all of the countries in the West African region are either implementing peace agreements or engaged in desperate attempts to negotiate an enduring consensus that will make the political management and resolution of conflicts possible. Without exception they are either recovering from civil war or state power conflicts, or establishing frameworks for preventing reoccurrence

◆ *By* **Prof. John M. Amoda***

According to PIOOM's 1997 World conflict map, West Africa is host to:

- nine low intensity conflicts with fatalities between 100 and 1,000 - Nigeria (five different conflicts), Cameroon, Liberia, Senegal, Sierra Leone:
- six violent political conflicts involving less than 25 political killings per year - Cameroon (Bakassi), Ghana (North), Mali (Tuareg), Mauritania-Senegal (border), Niger (Tuareg), and one more in Nigeria.

Most of today's low intensity conflicts were in yesterday's high intensity category. Liberia is a case in point, while Sierra Leone has traded places with Liberia, being a high intensity conflict arena with conflict related deaths in the thousands, before the signing of the recent peace accord.

The significance of these statistics lies in the fact that in all of West Africa, constitutional conflict management and resolution institutions are dangerously ineffectual and parallel the impracticality of the attempts of international state-craft to anticipate and prevent conflict in this sub-region. Everywhere we find both official and multi-track conflict resolution interventions which become relevant only after the parties in conflict have reached a stalemate. Thus, with governments and international organisations demonstrating an incapacity either to contain or prevent mass violence, a radical concern for conflict appreciation capacity-building is eminently practical and urgently needed.

Theorising the Incidence of Conflicts

We need to be able to classify categories of conflict rather than treating them as discrete events. While it is true that individual national conflicts are discrete historical events, it is becoming apparent that we can recognise a family resemblance between cases. There are, for example, aspects of the conflicts in Mali, Niger about the Tuareg that call to mind the North-South divides of Cameroon, Nigeria, Ghana, Liberia and Sierra Leone.

The success of the Rawlings government's mediation in the 1994-1995 civil war in northern Ghana is an example that can be examined for its applicability to the communal and sub-regional conflicts in Sierra Leone, Cameroon, Nigeria and Mali.

Nigeria can learn from Niger's civil war experience with the Tuaregs who were forced to seek self-determination as a result of their structural marginalisation - they are forced to live in poverty while the south, through control of the government, grows richer from the mining and export of the uranium found in Tuareg lands.

The communal civil war in Nigeria's Delta State and the demands of oil-producing communities in Nigeria's riverine areas have the same structure as the Tuareg demand for the restructuring of the state, government and economy of Niger. In Senegal, the agitation of the *Movement des Forces Democratiques de Casamance* (MFDC) goes to the heart of the problem flowing from nationalist legitimisation of imperialist colonial state structures. The MFDC's agitation for the independence of the Casamance from Senegal exposes the contradiction of the nationalist demand for independence from colonial metropoles. The MFDC argues against the imperialist appropriation of their sovereignty and, through such arguments, challenges the legitimacy of the colonialist state. The MFDC protested against Portugal's annexation of Casamance, until the Portuguese made a gift of Casamance to France in 1866. They then protested against the rule of France and their intransigence led to the exile of the Diola ruler, Queen Diatta in 1943.

When Senegal became independent in 1960 and assumed ownership of the country created through imperialism, the Diola of the Casamance, saw in the new ruler of Senegal the double reincarnation of Portuguese and French usurpers. The Casamance is thus of paradigmatic importance. It raises the ethical issue of the legitimacy of conduct of one of the victims of a thief who now seeks to keep what is stolen from him and his neighbours solely on the basis of a deal he has struck with the thief.

Peace in the Casamance has stalled because the government in Dakar considers the demand of the MFDC treasonable and the MFDC considers everything open to negotiation except independence. Senegal and Guinea-Conakry have been at war with the present government of Guinea-Bissau over the Casamance; Senegal's relations with Mauritania, Gambia, Libya and Guinea-Bissau reflect its neighbours' policy on the Casamance. Senegal's intransigence parallels Nigeria's iron fist attitude to minorities protesting central government claims based upon the laws of the colonial state.

In the civil wars of Liberia and of Sierra Leone we can see that similar patterns to those evident in Senegal's conflicts, stemming from historically rooted disadvantages, are being denounced and new contracts are also being demanded as a basis for more equitable post-conflict arrangements. In Liberia it is apparent that the politics of envy are proving superior to the politics of equity. President Doe's first objective was to take the place of Tolbert and to substitute Krahn domination for that of the Americo-Liberians. Charles Taylor's NPFL government appears more eager to defend the winner takes the 'Executive Mansion' politics. However, the marginalisation of the Americo-Liberians and the Krahns, does not make the Manos and Gios more secure. Will Sierra Leone follow the path of Liberia or will peace involve a re-examination of the historical arrangement which is presently delegitimised?

This is also the nature of the border disputes between Nigeria and Cameroon, and is replicated in the ongoing war between Ethiopia and Eritrea. History thus becomes a political issue everywhere in Africa, and even more so where ethnicity, religious differences and political domination are reinforcing attributes. The Casamance reveals the dynamics of the state-power politics of Rwanda and Burundi; the intransigence of the MFDC and the Senegalese governments gives perspective to what hard-line 'self-righteousness' has effected in Rwanda. Much is therefore to be gained from theorising national cases of state-power politics in West Africa.

Elite versus Communal Power Politics

An apparent pattern can be recognised in the disconnection between elite and communal power politics. But this is deceptive, as we see a Ken Saro-Wiwa internationalise local or communal politics through demands for self-determination. Elite rivalry for control of governments has been essentially economic. Reports of conflicts and their dynamics rarely reflect the character of governments in Africa. What we see are the wars to control governments or to set up rival governments.

In Liberia and Sierra Leone we see what can accrue to governmental power once the grasp of central governments is broken and control of territories and resources decentralised. During the Liberian civil war, Charles Taylor's NPFL turned the port of Buchanan into its gateway to the world. Through this port, Taylor's group exported timber, diamonds and iron; In Sierra Leone we see South Africa's Executive Outcome trading their services for diamond concessions; while, in 1992, the Revolutionary United Front crippled the government of captain Valentine Strasser when it captured the diamond rich territory of Kono.

We see the same relationship of power to control of resources evident in the civil wars in Angola and the Democratic Republic of Congo. What this makes plain is the advantage that accrues from control of governments. In West Africa we also see the relatively young gaining

LAKE CHAD, CHAD, Election registration   EDGAR CLEIJNE/LINEAIR

control of governments through coups and then being able to dominate seasoned statesmen and to bring leaders of the indigenous private sector to their knees. Doe of Liberia, Strasser of Sierra Leone, and Jameh of Gambia took control of government and found themselves in control of their country's economy.

General Abacha of Nigeria, who developed control of governments into an art form, taught this lesson to the world. The economic structure of Nigeria approximates the structure of all West African countries. Colonial laws have vested control of the mineral wealth of the country in central governments; the same governments make the legislation that controls exports and imports; control of governments thus implies control of the wealth-producing resources of countries.

The above is a simplification of a complex of skills resulting in deft political mobilisation of issues and sentiments. Yet it explains the focus of politicians, civilian and military, Christian, Muslim and Animist; it explains wealth accumulation by office holders and the attraction of office holding. It explains why the armed forces of every country are critical to the control of governments. What the above helps identify is

effectively the structure of society in Africa. Force has been pervasive in the construction of society in Africa. Colonial powers moved populations around in the interests of minerals or raw materials. Post-colonial governments are still in the business of moving populations around. In all of these cases, every one recognises that the ownership of government, or of a piece of it, is power. The Casamance wants its own government but the non-Diolas of the Casamance are not eager to exchange the southern yoke for a northern one!

This rivalry amongst groups is most evident at the grassroots level. There the struggle for resources is both elemental and imitative. Elemental because land is literally life. The 1994-95 civil war in northern Ghana with its roots in the colonial period, was essentially about land and its economic potential. But the land issue was camouflaged by issues of traditional governance. The colonial government endorsed the structure of society in which ownership of land was vested in paramount chiefs.

This right has been endorsed by the post-colonial governments. Groups like the Dagombas, the Manumbas, Gonjas and Mamprusi have paramount chieftains; thus they not only own lands but are also host to tenants who - not having the same governance structures - can never own land. Thus these groups, like the Konkomba who are acephalous, now recognise the disadvantages stemming from their traditional republican cultures. They demand their own paramount chiefs. Around this apparent culture conflict a civil war was waged. But by an usual coincidence the Nairobi Peace Initiative was attracted by this problem and through analyses and reconciliation workshops the truth of the quarrel was revealed. Peace was possible because those who were originally averse to chieftains will now have their own.

As events in Ghana show, there is a growing awareness of the need to throw open the process of conflict resolution to all who can help. The Nairobi-based organisation with its expertise in reconciliation and state-craft found a welcome because desperation had given rise to the humility necessary to drink from what would otherwise have been rejected as a foreign well.

The civil war in northern Ghana also reflects the imitative politics of the grassroots. It teaches that government is power; and the lesson taught by national elites has been well learnt at the grassroots. Konkombas know that they are excluded from the Northern and National House of Chiefs because they are republican. So they demand to be monarchical. But when offered three chieftaincies by their opponents, they stick to their original demand for one paramount chief. The problem is not to divide a unified house by tempting sons to compete with their fathers but one of eliminating a structural disadvantage. Much has to be learnt about conflict management from grassroots politics. The greed for power which militates against rational limitation of ambition at the national level has obvious limitations at the grassroots.

Yet this is not the lesson that the national elites learn from those who are at the bottom. As the RUF controlled areas in Sierra Leone show, the greed of the elite finds equivalent expressions at the bottom of society. The poor are not necessarily more virtuous than the rich; their poverty is primarily a poverty of power opportunity. In Nigeria's Itsekiri-Urhobo-Ijaw (Delta), the Modake-Ife, and Kanfanchan communal wars, former neighbours have

'With governments and international organisations evincing an incapacity both to contain or prevent mass violence conflicts, a radical concern for conflict appreciation capacity building is eminently practical and urgently needed.'

become demonic opponents. These are echoes of Rwanda and thus Rwanda should not to be regarded as an aberration.

Economic Community of West African States Monitoring Group

The most important innovation in the West African region in this decade has been the creation of ECOMOG. It appeared as an anticipation of a need; the necessity was preceded by the invention. As if anticipating the deflection of the attention of the West to Eastern Europe and to the Gulf, ECOMOG was invented to address the problem of state power discipline in the West African sub-region. Liberia and then Gambia had produced in a West African sub-region what the elite officer class saw as an aberration limited to Ghana and exorcised by the second incarnation of Rawlings. Coups led by non-officer cadre were distasteful enough. Much more so was the importation of the example of Museveni into the ECOWAS subregion. The imminent routing of the Armed Forces of Liberia by the 'rag tag' crowd led by Charles Taylor had therefore to be prevented because of the lesson his success could teach. Thus ECOMOG landed in Monrovia when only a street kept Taylor from victory in a winner-take-all war. With Doe holed up in the Executive Mansion, ECOMOG proceeded to roll back Charles Taylor's forces and to prevent the NPFL gaining control of Liberia.

Nigerian inspired and for the most part Nigerian financed, ECOMOG has been transformed by circumstances beyond the narrow sympathy for a beleaguered friend that motivated the government of General Babangida. In Liberia, the Nigerian Armed Forces have spawned an organ that they cannot assimilate into their domestic structure. Although it was Nigerian inspired and led, ECOMOG has been shaped by its fields of operation just as all fighting forces are defined by the wars they fight. It is estimated that since 1990, ECOMOG has cost Nigeria over a million dollars a day to keep in the field.

This device, without precedent prevented the dissolution of Liberia; created opportunities for anti-NPFL factions to emerge; provided a learning opportunity for the UN observer force, UNOMIL; carried the burden of peace-making without a script and kept a variety of warlords in the same playing field till the reasonableness of a political solution to the civil war was appreciated by all the combatants. What the United States, Operation Restore Hope, UNITAF, UNOSOM I and UNOSOM II could not achieve, ECOMOG effected: a society without central government and effectively divided by warlords was kept together; these warlords, after the 14th Peace Accord, were persuaded to settle the issue of power through elections. True, Liberia is still a society of elected government without a state; true Liberia has yet to squarely face its post-conflict peace-building chores and challenges. Nevertheless it has one advantage; it has been brought out of anarchy into a civil order and this by a force that delivered victory to one it came to limit.

What ECOMOG learnt in Liberia it has applied in Sierra Leone. It has again provided international security capacity for its elected government. As that government wages a civil war against the RUF it has reinstated the elected government toppled by a coup after a brutal bloody campaign. In so doing, ECOMOG directly enforced an UN and OAU mandate to use the combination of force, sanctions and dialogue to effect a change of government.

All of the above, ECOMOG did while its primary financier and motivator, general Abacha held the winner of the Nigerian presidential election in jail, and was himself a head of government by virtue of a coup! The point, however, is the emerging force called ECOMOG.

It continues to strengthen its claim to legitimacy while, to many onlookers, it is as yet unable to remove the taint of its own bastard origins. ECOMOG has found yet a third terrain of activity - filling in the gap created both by the inability of the OAU and the unwillingness of the UN - in Guinea-Bissau. Here it came with a strategy clearly evolved from its earlier experiences in Liberia and Sierra Leone as a peace-making force with a three-fold strategy: conflict management dialogue, backed by sanctions and embargo, with the option of force as a final resort.

Its record in Guinea-Bissau may yet prove to be ECOMOG's exoneration, having been invited into the country by the combatants to help with peace making. What then are ECOMOG's prospects, what lessons can it teach us? We ask these questions because of all the sub-regional organisations such as SADC and IGAD, ECOWAS has been the most daring and most tested. It has succeeded where both the UN and the OAU have feared to venture. Faced with the possibility of its dissolution if the electoral pronouncements of the Nigerian's elected president are implemented, a case for its institutionalisation can be made, albeit in a revised sub-regional context.

The Re-invention of ECOMOG as a Standby Force of ECOWAS

The case for the institutionalisation of ECOMOG as a standby peace-making force is based upon a confluence of events and resources. The first is the commonsense fact that a force that has been in existence for almost ten years and at a great expense of man-power and financial resources has undertaken two epoch defining operations ought not to be casually cast away. Its experience is precious and its successes unrivalled in the African region. Its third assignment in Guinea-Bissau will test its diplomatic capacity as the crisis of the Casamance requires great tact and ingenuity to resolve.

This is where the second factor in the strengthening of ECOMOG is relevant. The argument is that if this task can be done, this is the opportunity. The present Executive Director of ECOWAS, Ambassador Lasana Kouyate of Guinea, comes well equipped to lead the transformation of ECOWAS into an effective organisation dedicated to developing its expertise in the state-craft of civil war conflict resolution. Kouyate was appointed Acting Special Representative by the Secretary General to Somalia in February 1994. During his tenure he began to heal the relationship between UMOSOM II and General Aidid's SNA. It was Kouyate who brought the two warring factions of Ali Mahdi and general Aidid together in Nairobi. It was this Nairobi Declaration that ended Mahdi and Aidid's attempts to hold the Somali Peace Process to ransom. Ambassador Kouyate has brought this wealth of experience to his task as the Executive Director. Here is a skilled diplomatic professional who knows the UN, the OAU and ECOWAS; one who has in his portfolio experiences that match the exploits of ECOMOG.

What is needed for a happy match is a comprehensive framework for conflict resolution that schematises in theoretical terms the relevant data on West African civil war conflict mitigating state-craft.

What follows is a five-point check-list for civil war conflict situation analyses. The intention of this concluding analytical framework is to make the narrative of case histories amenable to conflict resolution state-craft, at the national, sub-regional, regional, and global levels. It is also intended as a tool to enable governmental, intergovernmental, and non-governmental conflict resolution policy-makers and activists:

1) Ascertain what is the conflict resolution state-craft situation (CRSS) of each country in the West African region by outlining the elements of a methodological framework presented as research questions;

2) Develop knowledge of the patterns of CRSS in the West African sub-region as illustrated in the section addressing the issues of family resemblance between crises events;

3) Understand how the conflict resolution state-craft capacity-building necessary for the West African sub-region may be defined;

4) Assess the present capacity of conflict resolution policy-making as evidenced in the contemporary dynamics of conflicts in the West African sub-region;

5) Advocate for the needed investments in conflict resolution state-craft capacity-building at the appropriate operational levels. The case being made for the ECOWAS can be made with equal justification for cognate sub-regional bodies in the West African region.

What then are the requisite policy dimensions that are to be considered in order to make sense of case histories compiled for the West African directory? We must examine the data for answers to the following questions and where the data are incomplete, the questions themselves indicate the data that are requisite for transforming the case histories into sources of policy-relevant information. The following are the policy-informed questions.

A. *What choice of development strategies are made by parties in state power conflicts?* Is it socialism, capitalism, centrist social democracy, or elite wealth accumulation? In most countries of West Africa, ruling groups tend to choose elite wealth accumulation; lip-service is paid to socialism, or capitalism, and - until the advent of the IMF - most governments have used centrist social democratic values to justify their decisions. Now, in the context of IMF conditions, market economies serve as justification for unbridled pursuit of elite wealth accumulation.

B. *What are the divisions over issues of sovereignty in a country?* Are parties organised to defend the status quo, or to effect annexations of neighbours? Are the parties intent on revolution, secession, or power sharing? Are they intent on instituting rule by elites or popular government? In general, parties favouring the status quo, annexation, revolution and secession focus on a monopolist exercise of power, while parties intent on power sharing, elite dominance or popular dominance tend towards the democratic domain, for what they seek can in principle be more equitably shared. Most parties in the West African region justify elite dominance choices with the rhetoric of popular dominance. Conflicts involving a monopolistic exercise of power are settled militarily; while democratisation politics can be resolved diplomatically even when parties have gone to

MONROVIA, LIBERIA, Education for war orphans   Ron Giling/Lineair

war over democratisation issues.

C. What are the contemporary conflict dynamics of each country in the sub-region? We can outline a scale of conflict and place the conflicting parties at the appropriate point. This scale begins with (1) statement of wrongs and escalates to (2) statement of complaints (3) to protests (4) to riots (5) to demand for reforms (6) to intransigent opposition between government and the aggrieved (7) to national security crisis (8) to armed rebellions (9) to full scale war (10) to stalemate or victory by one side. All of the countries in the West African region are either fighting a war or negotiating a peace or are in stalemate. There are few conflicts that have been concluded, like the Nigerian Civil War, with a

clear victory by one side or the other.

D. What are the phases of conflict in each country? Have the aggrieved moved from (1) demonstrations, (2) to riots (3) to strikes (4) to underground insurgency (5) to armed conflicts (6) to victory or stalemate (7) to conflict management (8) to conflict transformation (9) to post-conflict peace building? The phases-of-conflict scale describes the measures chosen by the aggrieved to pursue state power objectives. While the dynamics-of-conflict scale describes the degree of escalation in ongoing conflicts.

In most of the West African cases, parties caught in stalemate, have welcomed efforts at mediation which encouraged them to opt for conflict management. Many who are enslaved to winner-take-all goals have used conflict management to buy time as a prelude to a final push. For example, it took fourteen attempts by Liberian parties to get to elections.

E. What are the national security strategies of Governments in the sub-region? Are they strategies of conflict suppression, management, prevention of escalation to war; what are the strategies of opposition groups? Are they reformist, secessionist, or revolutionary? In the Casamance, the government in Dakar is committed to suppression of the separatists, while the separatists are committed to independence. This is a case of zero sum opposition. To shift both sides to negotiation, equivalent values have to be created to make both sides winners. How may this win - win option be crafted where neither side can win militarily and neither is willing to back down? Is this not reminiscent of Rwanda, Burundi, Sudan, Algeria and Morocco?

F. What is the war process? What price must be paid for victory in war? Each side must destroy its opponent's armies and war-making capacity. In Somalia the opposing armies destroyed farms, livestock, harvests, burned houses, caused the emigration of peoples from their opponent's territories so as to destroy their economic, social and political support base. As part of the war process the enemy's communication and infrastructures, commercial and financial networks are destroyed. The enemy's arms-supply, support, etc. are cut off. In Somalia all institutions of governance and at least sixty per cent of the country's infrastructure were destroyed or became unusable; central governmental security institutions collapsed and the only security available was that provided by armed groups, sometimes outside of any chain of command structure and subject to no political control.

While the enemy's capacity to wage war and defend its position is being destroyed, efforts are devoted to provide sustainable processes of support, supply and reinforcement through war production for one's own side. Morale is enhanced by the provision of a secured military environment in the areas under control; major airports and seaports are protected from enemy action; key installations and food distribution are secured; normality is simulated; costs of war are valorised; hope is encouraged; losses denied or downsized.

The war process provides data on how much is destroyed and how much is left standing. The war process describes how much reconstruction etc. will have to be carried out whenever peace is secured. How much of a secured environment is there in Liberia for post-conflict peace building to be sustainable?

G. What are the humanitarian consequences of continuing conflict? Are populations subject to (1) banditry (2) terrorism (3) human rights abuse (4) internal displacements (5) trans-border emigrations (6) anarchy (7) societal breakdown (8) the rule of warlords (9) collapse of central governments? Are populations afflicted with (10) epidemics and famine (11) genocidal attacks? Many countries in West Africa are dealing with aggravated humanitarian disasters; the war process explains the pattern of these disasters.

H. What are the different peace-process policies and which of these are chosen by parties in specific conflict situations? (1) adjudication (2) arbitration (3) negotiation (4) mediation (5) reconciliation (6) peace-making trusteeship? Most countries in the West African region have welcomed conflict management mediation and seem interested in reconciliation. See Hizkias Assefa's 'The Meaning of Reconciliation' in the European Centre for Conflict Prevention's publication *People Building Peace* for a clear and erudite explanation of these terms. Peace-making trusteeship is included for cases of self-destructive war, unwinnable by either side yet pursued without let-up and with disastrous humanitarian consequences for populations at risk.

I. What is the peace process intervention measure in operation at any moment of the conflict process? Is it (1) preventive diplomacy (2) peace keeping (3) peace making (4) post-conflict peace building (5) reconciliation, state and society building (6) peace making and peace building trusteeship?

The conflict resolution state-craft needed to

promote sustainable peace in Africa, easily the most conflict ridden of the UN regions, will require dealing with the battery of policy making questions itemised above. If we are to make peace we must know what parties do to advance their interests in power with all means at their disposal. There are populations like those of the Casamance who have never known peace. These deserve the most rigorous attention to peace support state-craft if there is ever to be a hope of rest that justify their interest in society.

---

*　　Professor John M. Amoda is the inaugural Director General and Ambassador-in-Residence at the International Training Institute for Peace with its headquarters in Nigeria. He is Professor of Political Science at the City College of New York and presently engaged in coordinating the African Peace Research Association Project on Sub-regional peace making and peace building in Africa. He is the author of Nigeria's ITIP Compendium on Engineering Capacity for Within Nation's Conflict Resolution Statecraft.

Intervention Precedes Legitimacy

West Africa comprises the region from Mauritania in the West to Nigeria in the East. It thus includes a western area comprising Mauritania, Mali, Senegal, and Gambia; a central area with Guinea-Bissau, Guinea, Sierra Leone, Liberia, Burkina Faso, Ivory Coast and Ghana; and an eastern cluster comprised of Nigeria, Benin, Togo and Niger. Historical, cultural and economic factors provide some basis for the degree of integration and cooperation that already exists across the region, and provide a latent foundation for possible deeper cooperation. The former colonies of France, Britain and Portugal share strong linguistic and cultural ties, respectively, and the constant flow of goods, services and people between the interior areas and the coastal areas help to reduce divisions due to territorial boundaries inherited from the colonial period. The ideas of Pan-African unity were first promulgated here. Individual and communal identities continue to be shaped by a multiplicity of overlapping ethnic, religious, and sometimes political units ◆ *By* Michael S. Lund and Ugo Solinas

However, some of the same factors that contribute to cohesion of the subregion militate against the consolidation of a strong single regional identity. The states within the three main linguistic groups have tended to preserve economic and political ties with their former metropoles, at the expense of greater inter-regional cooperation. All the economies of the area rank low in development and must compete with each other for markets.

Significant differences in levels of economic development between the coastal and land-locked states have slowed concrete realisation of the benefits of greater economic integration. Political and military competition over leadership both across the subregion and within individual states remain a conspicuous feature of West Africa's political landscape. In particular, the hegemonic aspirations of the subregion's wealthiest and most populous state, Nigeria, have been vigourously resisted by rival states such as Ghana, Ivory Coast, and Senegal. The resulting persistence of border disputes, arms races, subversion by neighbours, and military intervention in politics resulting in frequent coups all have conspired to reduce momentum toward cooperation. Due in part to these persisting cleavages, although West Africa has not experienced major inter-state wars, it has witnessed a number of political disputes both between states and within states, and some of

these have escalated into bloody wars causing immense human suffering and destruction.

Recent developments

The prospects for greater regional cooperation appeared to receive an unexpected boost at the beginning of the 1990's when the Economic Community of West African States (ECOWAS) created an all West African peace-keeping force in an attempt to end the bloodshed in Liberia. ECOWAS' role in intervening militarily and eventually bringing an end to the civil war in Liberia and, more recently, restoring Sierra Leone's democratically elected government after the 1997 military coup, may represent the most robust and extensive multilateral initiative that has ever been undertaken by Africans regarding internal African conflicts. It has led a growing number of analysts, policy-makers and other observers to consider whether the regional level, and ECOWAS in particular, holds promising approaches to West Africa's immediate and potential conflicts. Thus in 1995, one analyst was led to compare West Africa with other regions such as South America, in order to consider whether this region could be regarded as an emerging 'security community' and 'zone of peace.'

In addition to ECOWAS, several other governmental and non-governmental actors have tried to contain or mediate an end to the region's wars and foster peace processes once the conflicts have erupted and waged on for some time. More recent actions are being taken to prevent conflicts from arising, such as through creating early warning mechanisms and response procedures for monitoring conditions that could lead to violence escalation. This article briefly describes some of the most important recent developments in West African regional cooperation, assesses what these initiatives have accomplished and the obstacles that have limited them, and suggests some direction for improving cooperation regarding conflict in the region.

Three 'tracks' where regional cooperation in conflict management and prevention can operate are worth distinguishing and examining: inter-state economic cooperation, inter-state diplomacy and security cooperation, and civil society activity in 'track-two' conflict management and the promotion of democracy and human rights.

Economic cooperation

Regional economic cooperation in West Africa began in 1959 when the seven states of ex-French West Africa - Benin, Burkina Faso, Ivory Coast, Mali, Mauritania, Niger and Senegal - signed a convention in Paris creating the West African Customs Union (WACU) with its headquarters in Abidjan, Ivory Coast. The Union soon ran into difficulties principally on the grounds that the members were unable to agree on a formula for the distribution of the customs revenue collected on imports. It was replaced in June 1966 by the West African Economic and Customs Community (WAECU) with the same membership. WAECU's lacked vigour and its achievements were less than had been hoped for.

At a summit in Bamako, Mali in 1970, the same seven states formed the West African Economic Community (WAEC). Already sharing a fully convertible currency, the CFA Franc, which was pegged to the French Franc and fully convertible at a rate of 1Ff to 50 CFAf, these countries aimed to promote faster and more balanced growth through a mutual preferential tariff on industrial products, a Community Development Fund aimed at redistributing the fruits of integration, and a Fund for Solidarity

and Economic Development. Between 1965 and 1985, WAEC succeeded in increasing intra-community trade from 5.1 per cent to 7 per cent. In the latter half of the 1980s, however, an economic downturn deprived WAEC of the financing for its compensation mechanisms. In 1994, after the CFA Franc was devalued by 100 per cent, the WAEC was replaced by the West African Economic and Monetary Union, with Togo as an additional member. A number of other small inter-state organisations based on functional concerns like river basin management have been formed as well, such as the Organization of Senegal River States and the Lake Chad Basin Commission.

In 1975, West Africa's most comprehensive sub-regional economic organisation, and one of the largest of its kind in the world, was formed, when fifteen countries - Nigeria, Ghana, Ivory Coast, Senegal, the Gambia, Mauritania, Mali, Burkina Faso?, Niger, Guinea-Bissau, Guinea, Sierra Leone, Liberia, Benin, and Togo - signed the Treaty of Lagos establishing the Economic Community of West African States (ECOWAS). Cape Verde became the sixteenth member in 1977. According to the ECOWAS treaty, its aim is 'to promote cooperation and development in all fields of economic activity, the purpose of which is to increase the standard of living of its people, to enhance and maintain economic stability, to strengthen relations between its members and to contribute to progress and development on the African continent.' (Art. 2) The Community is to bring this about through trade promotion and liberalisation, increased freedom of movement for its populations, transportation development and coordination, coordination of telecommunications, industrial and agricultural growth. A common market was to lead 'in stages' eventually to the unity of the countries of West Africa. A West African Clearing House (WACH) was also set up by the central banks of the ECOWAS states and a cooperation, compensation and development fund was established, the aim of which is to ensure an even distribution of the costs and advantages of integration between the different member states.

Despite the establishment of a framework and some policies and institutions, however, many reports and studies on ECOWAS confirm the organisation's lack of progress in the economic sphere. In 1989, the African Development Bank concluded that ECOWAS' implementation of a system of cooperation and policy achievements were relatively insubstantial, noting that trade within the community had not been stimulated and had even shown a tendency to decrease.

Because ECOWAS has not realised the economic objectives set out in the Treaty, member states have not reaped the potential security benefits that can come from extensive economic interdependence. In certain cases, its policy measures have even created or worsened tensions within the Community. For instance, Articles 2 (2d) and 27 (1,2) of the ECOWAS Treaty recognised the need to maintain and encourage intra-regional migration. In 1979, ECOWAS adopted a protocol on the 'Free Movement of Persons, and the Right of Residence and Establishment'. But as a result, migrant labourers from Niger, Benin, Togo and Ghana were sucked into the larger Nigerian economy and from land-locked Burkina Faso into Ivory Coast and Ghana. Then in January 1983 and April 1985, economic crisis and unemployment prompted Nigeria to unilaterally deport about two million aliens and close its borders until January 1986.

A fundamental economic obstacle to greater progress in regional economic cooperation is the large inequalities in the levels of economic development among the member states. Nigeria, Ghana, Ivory Coast and Senegal are far ahead of the other twelve members, although an intermediate group can be identified comprising Guinea-Conakry, Sierra Leone, Liberia, Togo and Benin. Political rivalries and lingering suspicions between the leaders of the Francophone and Anglophone states also inhibit cooperation. Initially, the several Francophone regional economic bodies were formed to balance Nigeria's hegemony in the sub-region, and the idea of a West African Economic Community was initially resisted by presidents Felix Houphouet-Boigny of Ivory Coast and Leopold Sedar Senghor of Senegal, who feared it would become a vehicle for the consolidating Nigeria's dominance.

Diplomacy and Security Cooperation

Most actors who have become involved as third parties in seeking to mediate the region's conflicts are not multilateral or region-wide in character, but originate in this or that state or society. ECOWAS has by no means become the main African governmental actor involved. Regional diplomacy of a sort has been carried out by various African heads of state, such as in the Senegalese-Mauritanian conflict. Although this particular effort was unsuccessful, perhaps because they acted on their initiative, two eminent persons asked by the Mali government to help resolve its conflict with Tuareg rebels had some success. Yet other eminent persons similarly engaged in the Casamance conflict did not make any progress.

Individual states have also played crucial roles. The neighbouring African state of Algeria pressured northern Tuareg rebels to cooperate with each other and take part in a conference with the Mali government. Guinea-Bissau took advantage of a deadlock to mediate the Senegalese-Mauritanian conflict next door and acted as a guarantor of the peace accord. It failed, however, to achieve meaningful negotiations in the Casamance conflict.

Yet formally-established multilateral organisations, including regional bodies, have occasionally taken on mediating roles. From outside West Africa, the OAU and the Arab Maghreb Union tried to mediate the Senegalese-Mauritanian conflict, for example, although the UN generally has not been involved in its conflicts. By far the most extensive and noteworthy engagement of African organisations in a particular West African conflict - indeed, in conflicts in any region of Africa - was that by the West Africa region's own Economic Community in the Liberia civil war.

In the late 1970's and the 1980's, WAEC and ECOWAS sought to extend sub-regional economic cooperation into the field of security cooperation by signing separate defence agreements. A WEAC protocol enjoined member states to reinforce collective defence and alert each other of potential threats to their security. In 1978, the supreme body of ECOWAS, known as the Authority, adopted a Protocol intended to discourage armed attack among member states and confirm recognition of their mutual boundaries. The subsequent Defense Protocol of 1981 proposed a collective security regime in which member states pledged to meet to consider mutual assistance in the event of an attack by a non-member or if conflicts arose between member-states. In the latter instance, it envisaged the creation of peacekeeping force to restore order. ECOWAS also was to consider military action where a domestic conflict is apparently supported from outside a country and could endanger the region's peace and security.

Such consultation required involvement by the member states affected, but once military action was decided by the Authority, it was immediately enforceable on the part of the Allied Armed Forces of the Community (AAFC). The practical upshot of the Protocol was left in the air, however, because three of the members declined to sign it, and the AAFC and related offices and councils were never set up.

Although a regional security cooperation framework existed in general outline, it often was not applied, as seen with respect to a Mali-Burkina-Faso dispute in 1985 and a Senegal-Mauritania dispute in 1988. Much more often resorted to in West Africa was and remains various negotiated bilateral, trilateral or quadripartite security agreements or consultations focussed on specific inter-state disputes. The latter approaches to conflict prevention and reduction actually have proved fairly effective in containing the escalation of several conflicts between states in the sub-region. Some of the potentially most serious inter-state conflicts involved Nigeria and Cameroon over the sovereignty of the energy-rich Bakassi Peninsula; Senegal and Guinea-Bissau following the latter's support for separatists in Senegal's Casamance region; the Niger and Mali border conflict; and a three-party conflict along the Malian, Mauritanian, and Senegalese borders. Although most of these troublespots persist, diverse diplomatic efforts have been made at bilateral and multilateral levels to manage them.

The tripartite meetings of Senegal, Mali, and Mauritania to reduce border tensions are illustrative. In January 1995, they agreed to establish a mechanism for consultation among border authorities that would involve information-gathering, border administration, and demarcation. The signatories also created a permanent ministerial committee to review collective measures to eliminate insecurity along the common borders, check the upsurge of religious fundamentalism, combat drugs and arms trafficking, and facilitate the movement of goods and services. Likewise, Senegal and Guinea-Bissau have tried to strengthen defence and security cooperation, including joint military exercises to ease the conflict over the Casamance region.

Although the defence agreements signed between West African states had managed to contain the incidence of interstate conflict and firmly establish a regional norm against aggression, however, by the early 1990's it was becoming evident that they had done little to insulate the sub-region from new threats to regional security generated by *intra-state* conflict. This became dramatically clear on December 24 1989, when a full scale guerrilla war erupted as rebels known as the National Patriotic Front of Liberia (NPFL) led by Charles Taylor, a former minister in the administration of President Samuel Doe, invaded Liberia from its border with Ivory Coast. Allegations of genocide soon followed as the Armed Forces of Liberia (AFL) slaughtered civilians from the Gio and Mano tribes accused of supporting Taylor's rebellion, and reprisals by the NPFL brought even greater suffering. The traditionally accepted rules of war were totally ignored as foreign nationals were taken hostage and UN sites as well as foreign embassies came under attack. By October 1990, Liberian refugees outside the country numbered over 600,000, placing serious strain on the already fragile economies of the neighbouring states.

When a wider international response was not forthcoming, many of the West African countries believed they had no other option than to address the Liberia conflict themselves. The crisis was thus officially addressed by ECOWAS in May 1990, with the establishment of a Standing Mediation Committee (SMC) consisting of the Gambia, Ghana, Mali, Nigeria and Togo. At the urging of President Babangida of Nigeria, an emergency meeting of foreign ministers of members of the SMC was held on July 5th, 1990 to work out modalities of a cease-fire and a peace plan, after which a decision was made to deploy a peace-keeping force to Liberia in order to 'seal off the exploding military situation until the basis of a more durable settlement could be established.' The Economic Community Cease-Fire Monitoring Group (ECOMOG) which was deployed to Monrovia in late August 1990, consisted of 4,000 troops from Gambia, Ghana, Guinea, Sierra Leone and Nigeria, which contributed about 70% of the force. Gabon and Senegal added forces later. Although the first ECOMOG force commander was a Ghanaian, Nigerian dominance was obvious from the outset.

The ECOWAS decision in July to dispatch a Force to Liberia had been made under the assumption that it would keep an arranged peace between the warring factions. But changing circumstances on the ground quickly made it apparent that the situation was far less predictable than initially anticipated and that ECOMOG's actual response would differ from what would be expected in classical peacekeeping. The NPFL had opposed its deployment and did not abide by the terms of an ECOWAS plan. When ECOMOG arrived, there was no peace to be kept. Rebel factions and indeed government authorities continued to commit atrocities while ECOMOG suffered constant attacks from the NPFL.

In the face of ECOMOG humiliation and continuing suffering, the force's mandate was changed from peacekeeping to peace enforcement. A shift to limited enforcement action allowed the force to push the warring factions out of Liberia's capital Monrovia. After the signing of the first comprehensive cease-fire in November 1990, ECOMOG then reverted to its original peacekeeping mandate. Throughout the following year, ECOMOG managed to maintain a fragile peace despite the fact that a series of agreements were made and broken with the constant emergence of new warring factions.

However, in October 1992, the NPFL launched a major attack on ECOMOG and Monrovia, code-named Operation Octopus, which created new humanitarian emergencies. In its bid to defend itself and to deny the rebel group the ability to attack Monrovia at will,

ECOMOG again switched to peace enforcement. The enforcement action in response to Octopus came to an end with the signing of the Cotonou Accord in July 1993 and a new cease-fire. This ushered in another peacekeeping phase in which contingents from Tanzania and Uganda were added to the peacekeepers and the UN Observer Mission in Liberia (UNOMIL) was established and deployed alongside ECOMOG.

Despite this broadened operation, however, hopes for lasting peace and stability in Liberia were dashed by the April 1996 hostilities in Monrovia. ECOMOG's enforcement mandate was not brought to bear this time; it limited itself to a show of force, which had little effect on the intransigent rebel groups. In July 1997, the first free elections in twelve years brought Charles Taylor to power. Many observers felt that Taylor was voted in as a necessary evil in view of the failure of other actors to preserve a lasting peace. But UNOMIL began to pull out of Liberia and was completely withdrawn by the end of September 30. The new Liberian government and ECOWAS member states agreed to keep ECOMOG in Liberia for the time-being to provide security assistance to the country as it recovered from war, particularly in keeping order as refugees returned to their homes. Although Nigeria had shown signs since the 1999 election of General Obusango that it would reduce its support for ECOMOG, it has since extended its stay to ensure the disarmament of factions pursuant to the peace settlement.

Judged by several appropriate standards, the performance and upshot of ECOMOG were decidedly mixed. One obvious criterion is its efficacy in restraining the violence. While it clearly did not respond until the conflict had escalated and thus cannot be regarded as a preventive deployment force, ECOWAS did field an unprecedented African multilateral military response to an internal conflict in a relatively short time, thus filling the vacuum in international responsiveness left by the UN and OAU. On the other hand, it could not prevent Doe's subsequent abduction and killing; was able to establish a zone of peace only around Monrovia; and though it quickly transmogrified into a faction in the conflict trying to defeat the NPFL, it did not actually succeed, allowing the war to wage on and more warring factions to be spawned. Finally, it did not keep the conflict from spreading into Sierra Leone. Not until several years of its intervention were there signs the conflict was waning, and the outcome of the effort largely legitimated the apparently fittest survivor.

The extent peacekeepers can effectively contain and terminate a conflict, and their potential for success in establishing an accepted peace, depend both on their political cohesion and military viability. Political cohesion arises from an organisation's willingness to act and the sustaining of its will. ECOMOG was hardly politically unified and determined. Overall, the ECOMOG coalition partners' resolve toward Liberia was fuelled by a common realisation that the vast flow of refugees out of Liberia and dangerous counterflows of national dissidents into the ranks of Taylor's NPFL risked destabilising Liberia's neighbours. But though individual member states had a strong compulsion to intervene in the conflict, the differing ECOWAS states' actual interests continued to undermine the coalition's political unity.

Throughout ECOWAS' involvement in Liberia, national - and sometimes personal - agendas brought out the historic tensions between the organisation's anglophone and francophone members. Within the acting coalition behind the force, for example, Nigeria's Babangida had personal ties with President Doe, and Nigeria wished to assume a leadership role in the region and to check possible Libyan designs in the area. Sierra Leone joined the mission in part because it supported a rebel faction opposed to Taylor, but it opposed the Doe government as well. Mali hesitated to send troops because of Libya's influence, and Togo went back on its promise to participate. Outside the coalition, moreover, several West African states actively tried to block the mission altogether. Both Burkina Faso and Ivory Coast played a role in keeping the Liberian crisis off the UN Security Council Agenda for some time and actually supported Taylor and the NPLF to the extent of transferring arms from Libya through their territories into Liberia. For Ivory Coast, Nigeria's leading role in ECOMOG was reminiscent of its attempt to impose a 'Nigerian peace' on the continent in the mid-1970s.

Still, Nigeria actively persisted to maintain and improve the political cohesion behind ECOMOG. It exploited on-the-ground successes and increased fears of regional 'contagion' to hold the coalition together, while also actively courting the francophone countries. The June 1991 creation of a Committee of Five, which complemented the original Standing Mediation Committee (SMC) and monitored the implementation of the cease-fire then in effect, was such a gesture. The October 1991 addition of a Senegalese contingent to the ECOMOG force was not only a concession to Taylor, who viewed these troops as more impartial than the rest, but also an attempt to increase francophone members' influence within the force.

Military viability is derived from an organisation's and its member states' collective ability to train, equip, organise and deploy forces for combined contingency operations. The absence of a common peacekeeping doctrine among ECOMOG participants was particularly obvious in the Nigerians' and the Ghanaians' differing approaches. Whereas the Ghanaians are trained in peacekeeping and emphasise diplomacy over enforcement, the Nigerians preferred a more activist, combat approach to the operation. This lack of a common doctrine or indeed, any doctrine, among the ECOMOG forces appears to have had both benefits and drawbacks. On the one hand, the coalition was free to respond with flexibility and imagination to the constantly changing military situation on the ground. ECOMOG is the only mission thus far that has been able to switch credibly back and forth between peacekeeping and peace enforcement. On the other hand, the lack of a common doctrine was made patently obvious by the discrepancies between coalition members' approaches and may have contributed to some of the ECOMOG units' undisciplined behaviour.

A second key criterion by which to judge ECOMOG was its ultimate legitimacy as a truly multilateral action that is authorised through agreed-on rules. By this standard, ECOMOG was also clearly wanting. We have seen how its initiation and conduct were heavily imbued with the regional motives of Nigeria and the self-interested support by other states for differing parties in the fight. In addition, the absence of the consultative machinery that was never established as envisioned by the Treaty meant that the decision-making to deploy ECOMOG was ad hoc and irregular. Some conclude it was an illegal intervention into the internal affairs of a state.

All things considered, however, it is quite possible that the flawed ECOMOG precedent in Liberia and its continuation in Sierra Leone could be transformed into a more viable as well as more legitimate long-term structure for conflict management as well as prevention for West Africa. During the same period reviewed, ECOWAS took visible steps towards expanding sub-regional collaboration into other security areas, notably policing and crime control. At a meeting of West African ministers in charge of police and security in Abuja, Nigeria in March 1997, participants proposed a legal scheme for the collective pursuit and prosecution of criminals in the sub-region. Nigerian head of state at the time, General Sani Abacha, saw the prospects of increased cross-border collaboration against criminals as a means to strengthen ECOWAS' security role. The Abuja meeting adopted a wide range of sub-regional policing measures: criminal investigation; extradition treaties; joint judicial programmes for the eradication of illegal circulation of firearms; drug-trafficking; trafficking in stolen vehicles; armed robbery; and theft of works of art.

More encouraging still, on July 21, 1999 it was announced that the European Union is to provide US$2.03 million for the development of an ECOWAS mechanism for conflict prevention and resolution, under an agreement between the two organisations signed in the Nigerian capital Abuja. The envisioned ECOWAS mechanism provides for the creation of a judicial instrument, establishment of an early warning system, conflict prevention observatories, a council of elders, and mediation committees. The command and control structure for a stand-by intervention force has also been outlined.

A number of obstacles will continue to stand in the way of any West African emerging regional security and conflict prevention apparatus. The dependence of a number of West

African states on bilateral agreements with France may still tend to hinder the development of comprehensive sub-regional conflict management structures. But increasingly since the end of the Cold War, French sub-regional commitments have been reduced. Following its effective disengagement from the common currency in 1994, France scaled down its political and strategic agreements in West Africa, lessening the need for sub-regional organisations of exclusively French-speaking countries. As a result, there has been some ebbing of the linguistic divide which undermined the effectiveness of ECOWAS' intervention. The rapprochement between Ghana and Ivory Coast since the mid-1990's, for example, symbolises attempts to overcome the ideological and linguistic differences that had long frustrated meaningful sub-regional interactions. To the extent ECOWAS must rely for its energies as it often has on the regional hegemon Nigeria, this uneven support throughout the region will also hold it back.

A fundamental drawback is the lack of progress towards the establishment of regional norms in support of democratic systems based on the rule of law and respect for human rights. As Deng et al. point out (p. 161):

'Regional organisations will be limited in their ability to promote responsible sovereignty, development and justice and thereby address the root causes of conflicts to the extent that they are composed of member states under the control authoritarian regimes who use their sovereignty irresponsibly.'

Toleration of governments' lack of regard for democratic principles has delayed the emergence of the normative framework needed if ECOWAS is to fully realise its potential as a vehicle for the prevention and resolution of conflicts in the region. Though the end of the Cold War removed a pretext for the provision of support to financial and military support to authoritarian regimes, many regimes are sustained by Western powers who wish to maintain the economic and strategic benefits of continued cooperation. For example, during the Liberian civil war, the glaring contradiction between Nigeria's leadership in security matters on the one hand and the reversals in its transition to democracy on the other helped to undermine the legitimacy of ECOWAS' intervention. The return of the military to Nigerian politics in 1993 may have had a contagious effect on subsequent military coups in the Gambia, Niger, and Sierra Leone. Four years later, the toppling of Sierra Leone's democratically elected government in the May 1997 military coup, raised further doubts about the credibility of Nigeria's sub-regional leadership. Following the coup, the Nigerian military, as part of the ECOMOG contingent sent to restore the democratically elected government, launched a disastrous bombardment of military positions in Sierra Leone and, with ECOWAS, organised a military blockade. Yet the attempts to restore democracy in Sierra Leone contrasted sharply with its own practices at home for which it was under international sanctions for repeated human rights abuses.

In sum, despite ECOMOG's success in promoting the restoration of an acceptable authority in Liberia and Sierra Leone, security cooperation in West Africa is still geared towards the defence of the status quo rather than the acceptance of a new 'common value system in politics and economics.' ECOMOG can be seen as a flawed but significant step towards the establishment of a permanent framework for the resolution of sub-regional conflicts, but its actions so far are not a complete answer to West Africa's security problems.

Civil society activity
An exclusively state-centric basis for regional cooperation within the ECOWAS framework will have a limited impact on the socio-economic, political and institutional causes of conflict within the sub-region. Thus it represents only a partial response to prevention and management of the region's conflicts. The gap this approach leaves could be potentially filled by civil society organisations that are independent of both governments and particular political factions and that can build up a counter-culture to the common practice of using arms to pursue political objectives. Such actors might be able to monitor and promote human rights and democratisation and foster inter-group cooperation and dispute resolution before they can be exploited by rising warlords.

Non-governmental actors rarely operate at the regional level, however. The numerous non-governmental actors that have become engaged in mediating the region's conflicts and promoting peace processes almost always operate from within particular states or in response to an individual inter or intra-state conflict, not at the regional level. Political parties were active in the Liberia National Conference (LNC) that was held in Liberia in an attempt to find an end to the civil war. Acting as a pressure group, the LNC promoted democratic participation in the peace negotiations and shared power with warring factions in the Council of State.

The costs of failing to engage civic groups in conflict management initiatives were patently apparent in the Liberian civil war. In the early stages of the conflict, a religious group named the Inter-Faith Mediation Committee (IFMC) had used its moral authority to establish a dialogue between Charles Taylor's NPFL and the beleaguered government of president Samuel K. Doe. Regrettably, its suggestions for a draft peace plan which called for the immediate resignation of Doe and the inclusion of Taylor in a transitional government were disregarded by ECOWAS. Instead, the SMC decided to proceed with the establishment of an Interim Government of National Unity (IGNU) from which leaders of the major warring factions were excluded. As a result, the neutrality of the ECOWAS peace-keeping force was severely compromised, complicating the task of finding a peaceful resolution to the conflict.

Unfortunately, however, national NGOs action in direct conflict mediation has been occasional, highly varied in the degree of involvement, and judged by the standard of reducing violent conflict, limited in impact. Although political parties played a continuous role through the Liberia National Conference, one of the warring factions came to power, and became a political party. Three political parties participated in the Casamance conflict negotiations in Senegal, and some parties, such as the opposition PDS acted as mediators between the separatists and government, and presented a mediation strategy to the government. But this was ignored. In Mali, political parties were involved only in the first stages of negotiations with the Tuaregs in the North, but the government then suspended their role. In the Senegal-Mauritania conflict negotiations, Senegalese parties were kept informed of developments and they took positions on issues, but they were not consulted.

A few religious organisations have wielded influence at certain points in conflicts. In Liberia, the Christian-Muslim IFMC shaped the ECOWAS Peace Plan, and the Catholic Justice and Peace Commission played an useful human rights watchdog role. A Senegalese church acted as mediator between the separatists and the government. Similarly, some women's organisations were active in mediation and negotiations, voicing views in Liberia and in Mali co-signing the peace accords, and thus with mixed results. Local human rights organisations were also active in the Liberian and Casamance conflicts but with little impact.

As to neo-traditional leaders, they have often been either powerless against emerging warlords or pawns in the strategies of warlords or other major players. In the Senegalese-Mauritanian conflict, Senegalese local leaders hued to the government position and were sidelined in the Casamance conflict. A notable exception was the important contribution that traditional leaders made in fostering a public statement of rapprochement in the Mali conflict, through the public meetings they organised among the Tuaregs and other communities in the north.

Major extra-regional NGOs have achieved occasional breakthroughs. The Carter Center's role in Liberia's conflict demonstrates the importance of international leadership in NGO and private diplomacy. Through the International Negotiation Network (INN), a group of conflict resolution experts, former US President Carter conducted private and public consultations to instill energy in the Liberia peace process. One project created a consortium of American-and Liberian-based NGOs that engaged a wide spectrum of political, religious, and civic groups in finding new methods for reducing tensions during the civil war. One of the NGOs, the Liberian Initiative for Peace and Conflict Resolution (LIPCORE), was at the forefront of re-establishing social trust in local communities and promoting post-conflict peace-building.

One exception to the pattern that few actions by or about civil society have been launched at the regional level is found in initiatives launched at the regional level seek to make a positive contribution to the process of democratisation in West Africa. One of the most interesting in recent years is the Media for a Democratic West Africa (MDWA). Launched in 1988 by the Panos Institute, a London based NGO, the MDWA programme aims to reinforce the role of the media in the democratic process by creating and developing a legal, economic and technological environment propitious for media pluralism. In the initial stages (1990-1993), the MDWA, then designated as the 'Sahel Programme', was limited to member States of the Permanent Inter-State Committee for Drought Control in the Sahel (CILSS). It was subsequently extended to all sixteen members of ECOWAS and is now implemented in the three linguistic zones of the region, i.e. in the Francophone, Anglophone and Portuguese-speaking countries. Its specific activities include: encouraging and facilitating advocacy for new legal and statutory provisions guaranteeing press freedom, airwaves liberalisation and a more equitable access to Information and Communication Technology (ICT); promoting the establishment of mechanisms for enhanced economic viability of the media organisations; promoting the production, dissemination and exchange of media contents on vital issues concerning peace and democracy in the region; developing synergies between organisations at national, regional and international levels; and developing collaboration between media organisations and other entities of the civil society.

Overall, it appears that civil society organisations can help implement peace processes that are moving along, but are rarely able to muster sufficient political power to assume definitive mediating roles that contribute substantially to ending conflicts. In Liberia, while they could criticise human rights abuses and the political machinations of the factional leaders, they were marginalised in the process leading to a specific settlement. In some instances, civil society representatives actually increase polarisation, rather than lessen it, and can retard a peace process. In the Mali conflict, for example, the government was more receptive to Tuareg demands than were the representatives of civil society, who, except for the women's movement, resisted the peace accord that the government negotiated, over the heads of this opposition.

Possible Directions

The normative foundations and political support for ECOWAS regional peacekeeping and hoped-for conflict prevention roles need strengthening. Because in the short run, civil society actors in the region lack sufficient goal cohesion and influence on governments, and most regimes are not competitive democracies, pressure on heads of state and rival elites to hold to norms of non-subversion, human rights, and democratisation must still largely come from outside the region. Third party donors and others who can wield influence on current leaders have to work jointly in setting goals, but also in partnership with incumbents who are open to change. In the long run, however, the circle of actors must be widened beyond the political leaders to include the politically active but politically autonomous peace constituencies that are needed in civil society to press for and sustain democratisation and to avoid destructive conflicts. But these ranks are unlikely to emerge without substantially increased and equitably distributed economic growth.

Thus, measures to increase economic growth and competitiveness through promoting regional commerce and other methods have to be approached as a high priority for conflict prevention in West Africa.

---

*   Ugo Solinas was recently involved in the development of the World Bank's new Post-Conflict Social Sector Reconstruction Programme for Africa. He received his Bachelor of Arts (Honours) in European Studies from the London School of Economics and King's College, London and his Master of Arts in International Relations from the Paul H. Nitze School of Advanced International Studies (SAIS), Johns Hopkins University, Washington, D.C, where he concentrated in International Economics, Conflict Management, and African Studies.

References

Mamadou Aliou Barry, *La Prevention des Conflits en Afrique de l'Ouest: Mythes ou Realites*, Editions Karthala, Paris, 1997

Francis M. Deng, Sadikiel Kimaro, Terrence Lyons, Paul Ejime, *West African Police Chiefs Meet in Nigeria*. PanAfrican News Agency, March 25, 1997

Jim Fisher-Thompson, *Conflict Resolution Means Breaking Old Habits, Experts Say*. United States Information Agency, March 28, 1996

Nicholas Ibewuike, *Abacha for Collective Ecowas Security*. PanAfrican News Agency, March 25, 1997

Arie Kacowicz, *Pluralistic Security Communities in the Third World? The Intriguing Cases of South America and West Africa*. Paper presented at the 1995 meeting of the International Studies Association, Chicago, Illinois, February, 1995

Gilbert M. Khadiagala, *Confidence Building Measures in Sub-Saharan Africa*. In: Michael Krepon, Khurshid Khoja, Michael Newbill, Jenny S. Drezin eds., A Handbook of Confidence-Building Measures for Regional Security, 3rd Edition, The Henry L. Stimson Center, March, 1998

Terrence Lyons, *Can Neighbors Help? Regional Actors and African Conflict Management*. Chapter Four in Francis M. Deng and Terrence Lyons, eds. African Reckoning: A Quest for Good Governance (Washington, D.C.: Brookings Institution, 1998)

Augustine P. Mahiga and Fidelis M. Nji, *Confidence Building Measures in Africa*, Report of United Nations Institute for Disarmament Research, Geneva(New York: United Nations, 1987. 16 pages

Netherlands Institute for International Relations Clingendael, *Project Conflict Prevention in West Africa: Synthesis Report*. The Hague, December, 1998

Funmi Olonisakin, *African 'Homemade' Peacekeeping Initiatives*. Armed Forces and Society, Volume 23, No. 3, Spring 1997

Donald Rothchild, and I.William Zartman, *Sovereignty as Responsibility*. The Brookings Institution Washington DC, 1996

Jennifer Morrison Taw and Andrew Grant-Thomas, *U.S. Support for Regional Complex Contingency Operations: Lessons From ECOMOG*. Studies in Conflict and Terrorism, Vol. 22, p.53-57, 1999

Torduff, William, *Government and Politics in Africa*, Third Edition, Bloomington, Indiana: Indiana University Press, 1997

Charles Valy Tuho, *West Africa and the Future of Relations between the ACP Countries and the European Union*, Friedrich Ebert Stiftung, Bonn, 1996

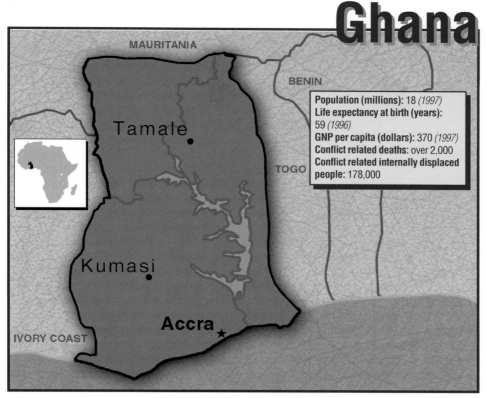

Population (millions): 18 *(1997)*
Life expectancy at birth (years):
59 *(1996)*
GNP per capita (dollars): 370 *(1997)*
Conflict related deaths: over 2,000
Conflict related internally displaced
people: 178,000

MAURITANIA

BENIN

Tamale

TOGO

Kumasi

Accra

IVORY COAST

Ghana

Mediating a Way out of Complex Ethnic Conflicts

Ethnic conflict in northern Ghana has roots which reach back to the colonial period. Heightened tensions during the early 1990s led to the outbreak of civil war in 1994 which continued to 1995. The conflict was largely unnoticed by regional and supra-national organisations, and it was the Ghanaian Government together with domestic and international NGOs who took responsibility for resolving the conflict. Their efforts proved successful and a relative peace has returned to the area, although it is considered fragile by many. As a result of their experiences, conflict prevention has become a core activity of many of the local and international organisations working in northern Ghana* ◆ *By* **Emmy Toonen**

S ociety in the northern part of Ghana is divided along traditional hierarchic and ethnic lines in which the tribe and the chiefs play an important role in day-to-day rural life. It is mainly the chiefs who act as the spokesmen of

*   Several parts of this survey are based on the Oxfam-report 'Building Sustainable Peace: Conflict, Conciliation and Civil Society in Northern Ghana'.

the various ethnic groups and who participate in local and national government. There are, however, also elected local and national politicians and youth association spokespersons are also very powerful.

People from northern Ghana, especially the rural population, identify strongly with their ethnic groups and traditions. The national government in Accra on the south coast is often regarded as very remote and of lesser importance. The distinction is reinforced by the disadvantaged economic position of the north in comparison to the rest of the country. It is difficult to say how far this division has played a role in the genesis of the conflict and, later, in the national conciliation attempts. However, it is certain that the remoteness of some conflict areas and the lack of infrastructure and communication technology has sometimes made communication between the various parties and government mediators difficult.

The roots of the conflicts in northern Ghana are complex and interwoven. Moreover accounts of the origins of conflicts vary among the different ethnic groups. The major points of contention, however, lie in disputes over land rights and political representation. Land rights are ultimately vested in the paramount chief on behalf of the ethnic group. Members of other ethnic groups who live on the land of a chief are expected to live by his or her rules and to show respect or allegiance, sometimes in the form of gifts.

Since British colonial rule, paramount chieftaincy has also been the prerequisite for a seat in the Northern and National Houses of Chiefs, and thus for significant political representation. However, only four ethnic groups, the Dagomba, Nanumba, Gonja and Mamprusi, have paramount chiefs. The other ethnic groups, such as the Konkomba, Nchumuru and Nawuri, have always been 'headless', or acephalous. The Konkomba for example, orginally came from Togo and migrated to Ghana in the early twentieth century. They are generally farmers and often move from one geographical area to another in search of fertile land. Instead of a system of paramount chieftaincy, where the community is governed by several chiefs and headed by a paramount chief, they have a non-centralised political system without secular leaders.

Nevertheless, the Konkomba and other acephalous groups have long claimed they should be entitled to the same political rights as paramount chieftaincy groups. To them, the current system is the unacceptable result of ancient rules. Since all the land belongs to chiefs, Konkomba are forced to live on 'foreign' land. Their refusal to respect the foreign chief's

rule has often led to disputes. In reality, the Konkomba are not completely without political and economic representation. However, a legal recognition of their equal status would enable them to become more involved in local and national government. It would also enable them to gain access to district assembly funds which the government is currently creating to support a decentralisation programme.

Because they form a relatively large part of the population in northern Ghana, the Konkomba feel fully justified in pursuing this claim. According to 1996 figures of *Minorities at Risk*, the Konkomba, with 300,000 to 400,000 people, are the second largest ethnic group in the Northern Region and consequently they feel that they have the right to exercise authority over their own land. However, the land issue is particularly thorny. Fertile lands, which were once sufficient for all, are becoming increasingly scarce and thus increasingly valuable. The owners of fertile land are unwilling to surrender any part of their claim to ownership, particularly as they have the backing of the law.

The conflict over land and political power was a major source of tension among different ethnic groups but the conflict in the region also has other roots. Historically, many of the region's groups have had a good understanding with each other. In some cases, coexistence and intermarriage are common, making it difficult, on occasion, to define which ethnic group someone actually belongs.

However, mutual incomprehension and ridicule, often based on rumours, played an important role in the build up of hostility before and during the conflicts. Rumours of the alleged bellicosity and malign intentions of the other parties were widespread and were frequently fuelled by media reports. In one striking example, the *Ghanaian Chronicle* of January 31, 1993, contained an article predicting a terrible bloodbath in the near future, which would leave as many as 10,000 people dead. This caused such a great disturbance that in the city of Tamale, loudspeaker vans had to be used to calm down the distressed citizens.

Religious differences have also been identified as a source of division, especially over the last ten years. In general terms, Christian missionary activity has been most successful among the acephalous groups, while Islam has had a stronger influence on the chieftaincy groups. However, the Islamic influence is mainly seen among the leading families. The traditional religions still have the largest numbers of followers. At the village level, many people practice an eclectic mix of religion so religious differences are rarely a cause for conflict.

Finally, the situation is further complicated by the fact that conflicts not only occur between the various groups but also within them. Conflicts between the older and more traditional generation of rulers and the younger group members with more modern views on government, sometimes cause divisions within an ethnic group. These internal divisions surface in disagreements on how to solve the problems the group faces, and can subsequently hamper the peace process.

Conflict Dynamics

The 1994-1995 civil war is usually said to have started on January 31, 1994, following a quarrel between Konkomba and Nanumba over the price of a guinea fowl at a market in Nakpayili near Bimbilla. The war is therefore also known as the "Guinea Fowl War".

Relations between the different ethnic groups had been tense all through 1993. Earlier conflicts in the region had never been resolved and there was fear of new attacks. Also, there were a growing number of rumours about Konkomba plans to seize land. From July 1993, these rumours turned into clear mistrust when Konkomba leaders sent a petition to the National House of Chiefs. In this petition, they claimed that, as they were the second largest group in the Northern Region, their most important leader, the 'chief' of Saboba, should have the same status as a paramount chief.

After the incident at Nakpayili - accounts of which vary considerably - fighting broke out between Konkomba and Nanumba and spread rapidly. On February 10, after ten days of fighting the government declared a state of emergency in the town of Tamale and several other districts. A joint Military Task Force was set up. Fighting continued for months with disastrous effect. The numbers of dead and

displaced are still uncertain, however, several observers suggest that there were 2,000 deaths in 1994 alone, that 322 villages were devastated and some 178,000 people were displaced. Farms, herds and produce were destroyed, and the economy severely damaged. Social life in general as well as the interaction between the various ethnic groups was also badly affected, as were medical and educational facilities in the region.

In April 1994 a government delegation held talks with leaders of the warring factions in the capital Accra. Both sides agreed to end the conflict and the violence. On June 9, after a number of quiet, but tense, weeks, a peace treaty was signed. However, it was not until August 8 that parliament revoked the state of emergency, thereby officially ending the conflict.

Although the tensions had diminished, their causes still remained unresolved and in March and May 1995 there were renewed outbreaks of violence. This time, at least 110 people were killed. Health conditions also deteriorated due to a lack of food and clean water. Subsequently, in November, the friction between Konkombas and Dagombas was given a new, religious dimension. As tensions between Muslims and non-Muslims increased in different parts of Ghana, the relationship between the mainly Muslim Dagomba and the mainly animist Konkomba also worsened.

At the end of 1995, the situation in the conflict area grew calmer, which is widely ascribed to mediation attempts and peace talks involving all warring parties. Agreements were made to change the old structure of political representation and land rights. Consequently, the main points of contention seemed to have been tackled. By the end of 1998, the overall situation in the region looked positive. However, problems remain in the (re)building of the area's economy and infrastructure. Moreover, the area was hit by a serious food shortage in 1997. The city of Tamale is now calm but the Konkombas are still too afraid to enter the city for fear of reprisals. Isolated incidents are now and then reported in the Ghanaian press. In May 1999, for example, members of the Konkomba Youth Association in Yendi warned of the threat to peace in the region, following what they claimed as police inaction to attacks on Konkombas.

Official Conflict Management

The northern Ghana conflict, being an internal and local conflict, has received little attention from large intergovernmental organisations. Consequently, official conflict management initiatives have originated mainly from within the Ghanaian government. These domestic attempts were begun in mid-1993, when a delegation of government officials twice visited the area to act as mediators. However, the situation was worsened by rumours and misunderstandings and proved difficult to resolve.

The army is generally regarded as having played an important role in the process of appeasement although its late response has often been criticised. Surprisingly, the army was very constructive in restoring the peace based on a balanced and thorough analysis of the situation. The Task Force dispatched to the conflict area helped NGOs with relief distribution. Other direct government action consisted of an agricultural relief package. However, the government found donor funding difficult to obtain. Ministerial visits to donor headquarters in Europe were unsuccessful as donors preferred to use NGOs as relief activity channels. This is said to have caused tension between the government and NGOs.

In order to negotiate peace, a *Permanent Peace Negotiation Committee* was set up in April 1994 to talk with the various parties involved. The meetings, some of which were set up together with the NGO Consortium discussed below, led to a Peace Treaty on June 9, 1994. At that time, however, the conflicts had yet to be resolved. Negotiation continued and finally two reconciliation ceremonies, both in the presence of President Rawlings, were held in December 1995 and in May 1996. At this stage, a lasting peace seemed to be much more certain.

Multi-Track Diplomacy

With their many different activities, NGOs have played an important role in resolving this conflict. Initially, they focused mainly on relief for the many people who were displaced or had otherwise been affected by the war. As the conflict continued, some NGOs also took up an important role as mediators. Today, their work continues, and often includes conflict prevention activities.

Before the outbreak of the 1994 conflict, several NGOs had already become firmly established in the Northern Region of Ghana. These were mainly social development organisations, both local and international. At the beginning of the conflict, there was hardly any cooperation between the different organisations. Assessment missions were held by several NGOs simultaneously and the first relief aid was donated directly to the various NGOs by their international donors. About a month after the outbreak of the conflict, the first Red Cross relief aid arrived and after two months the government and the various NGO-missions were able to focus on needs assessments.

As the conflict continued, however, the need for more cooperation became apparent. An informal NGO network, the *Inter-NGO Consortium*, was formed. Participants were a mixture of local NGOs, such as Action Aid Ghana, Action on Disability and Development, Amaschina, Assemblies of God Development and Relief Services, Catholic Relief Services, Catholic Secretariat, Council of Churches, Business Advisory Development and Consultancy Centre, Gubkatimali and Penorudas, and international NGOs such as Lifeline Denmark, Oxfam, Red Cross and World Vision. In joining forces, they hoped to obtain and distribute humanitarian aid more efficiently. The independence of the various organisations was kept intact, so that each of them bore the responsibilities for their own projects.

After the first humanitarian aid had arrived, the Consortium also started to focus on conflict transformation and reconciliation initiatives. This was mainly done in cooperation with the *Nairobi Peace Initiative* (NPI), an NGO which, since its foundation in 1984, has built up a lot of mediation experience in several conflicts in Africa. Needs assessment and field visits were started at the end of 1994. The NPI also participated in the Consortium's *Peace Awareness Campaign*. An important part of this campaign was the setting up of a series of workshops, the Kumasi workshops, in which the various parties involved in the conflict were to be brought together. The NPI and Consortium staff

TAKORADI, GHANA, Police officer educates streetkids Ron Giling/Lineair

organised the first two Kumasi workshops in May and June 1995. Participants in these workshops included members from all ethnic groups involved, several chiefs, opinion leaders and NGO staff. In the first two workshops all parties assessed the damage the war had caused. The statements of the different parties were also heard and discussed.

Instrumental in this effort was Hizkias Assefa who based his efforts on a new philosophy 'Peace and Reconciliation as a Paradigm' which is described as a philosophy of peace and its implications for conflict, governance and economic growth in Africa. It attempts to look at the crisis with the hope of providing pointers on how to begin to change behaviour and situations. The paradigm identifies approaches to be utilised in bringing about desired changes. The paradigm also suggests roles for actors leading to the kinds of changes and transformation necessary.

A first step towards reconciliation was made when all parties admitted that mutual hostility should, for the benefit of all, make way for a mutual effort to create a lasting peace. The leaders of the ethnic groups agreed to spread these ideas to their communities so as to

indirectly involve them in the peace process. However, no official agreements had been made at these first workshops. Hostility and mistrust were said to have lessened after these first two workshops, at least at the administrator's level. At village level, however, it was still clearly present. Field visits and meetings with the parties involved continued between the Kumasi Workshops, and in December 1995, a third workshop took place. Once again, all statements were heard. This time, attention was also given to the participant's ideas on how to solve the disputes.

The fourth Kumasi Workshop, in February 1996, concentrated on the composition of a draft version of a Peace Accord. This procedure was the result of more extensive talks held between the NPI and leaders of the ethnic groups, both separately and jointly. In the fifth Workshop, in March 1996, the draft version was officially signed. The main achievement of this Peace Accord was the fact that the acephalous Konkomba were to become a Paramount Chieftaincy group. Also, initiatives to establish peace awareness activities within the various communities were formulated.

Over the period in which the Kumasi Workshops were held, further peace initiatives were launched by the Consortium in cooperation with civil society representatives. Another part of the Peace Awareness Campaign, for example, was the setting up of a *Peace and Reconciliation Working Group* (PRWG). This working group consisted of NGO staff and was established to set up, facilitate and evaluate different reconciliation activities. Another initiative was the *Peace Education Campaign* (PEC). This campaign was aimed at the community level. It involved leaders of the different ethnic groups travelling from one community to the next, acting as peace builders in engaging people directly in the peace process and encouraging them to support it.

In response to a request by a number of local organisations, the UK-based *Conciliation Resources* has formed a team to consult with Ghanaians affected by inter-communal violence to provide an assessment of the conflict and possible constructive responses.

Local organisations

Apart from the peace initiatives taken by the Consortium as a whole, several other, usually local, projects were organised by individual NGOs. These initiatives included, for example, *Action Aid Ghana's* support in the rebuilding of a school by both Konkomba and Dagomba communities. The *Council of Churches*, among others, focused on the coexistence of Muslim and Christian communities by organising mixed prayer sessions and other meetings. Several organisations have set up non-violence workshops, fact-finding missions and peace education programmes for teachers and community leaders. Thus, now that the actual conflict has ended, conflict prevention has become a major concern for a large number of NGOs.

In addition to official domestic and NGO initiatives, another important conflict prevention initiative has come from one of Ghanaian traditional social groups. This is the *Northern Youth and Development Association (*NORYDA). Youth Associations have a long tradition in northern Ghana. They are ethnically or regionally based and are formed by politically active 'opinion leaders'. Though their name suggests otherwise, age does not play a role in the Youth Organisations' membership. As a

body of politically engaged people, Youth Organisations often function as representatives of their community at the national level. With the creation of NORYDA, at the suggestion of the Youth Organisations themselves, this existing model is to be used as a deliberative body on the prevention of new conflicts.

Evaluation

Of the various peace initiatives described above, the organisation and involvement of the Consortium is generally seen as the most influential. It has continued its work after the peace process, changing its main activities from relief, to mediation, to conflict prevention. According to the various NGOs involved, this informal cooperative network has certainly proved useful in times of conflict and humanitarian need. It has enabled the participating organisations to pool their resources and expertise and to cover the widest possible area.

However, this loose structure seems to have had less effect on peace awareness projects set up in the aftermath of the conflict. Here there were frequent complaints about a lack of commitment and means. This is seen as the main reason why larger, coordinated conflict transformation and prevention activities have been difficult to get off the ground and to maintain over a longer period of time. At the end of 1998, the activities of the Consortium and NPI have clearly decreased. Those of the Peace and Reconciliation Working Group have ceased altogether. The small, individual projects of the various NGOs, on the other hand, are reported to be meeting with success. As they are usually local projects, carried out in areas where the NGOs in question had already established themselves, they are having a direct impact in their different communities.

Finally, the future of the NORYDA organisation is generally regarded as positive. Although it faces some problems regarding the unconditional, unbiased and a-political cooperation of the various ethnic groups involved, this same ethnic diversity is also its main source of success. In contrast to the competition that existed between the various ethnic youth organisations before its creation,

NORYDA tries to deal with the interests of the various ethnic groups as a whole. The development of NORYDA is currently being supported by the Consortium and various individual NGOs.

Prospects

In general, the situation since 1995 has been calm. Repatriation and rebuilding activities continue. The government claims to be keeping any possible sources of violence well under control. President Rawlings has stressed on various occasions that violence will not be tolerated and that the government will suppress, with army intervention if necessary, any outbreaks of violence. This policy seems to have had its effect.

Also, the Kumasi Accord seems to have tackled the most direct causes of conflict in admitting the paramount chieftaincy rights for the Konkomba. However, this issue has formed the basis for a new dispute, and possibly for a new conflict. Chieftaincy groups have proposed the appointment of three paramount chiefs for the large group of Konkombas. The Konkombas, however, prefer to have only one. They fear that the proposal for three paramount chiefs is part of a divide and rule strategy of the chieftaincy groups. Peace in the region is always fragile as, with so many different ethnic groups and interests, new conflicts on related issues are always likely to flare up. So too, the general economic situation, which is still feeling the effects of the war and of the droughts, could play an important role in creating new tensions.

Recommendations

The conflict has eased, but some potential causes of future conflict remain. As international fora and separate NGOs have made little study of the situation in northern Ghana, apart from donor policies, hardly any policy and action recommendations have been formulated. The effects of the various peace initiatives, which until now have seemed very positive, will have to prove their value in the long run.

Service Information

Reports

Oxfam
• Building Sustainable Peace: Conflict, Conciliation and Civil Society in Northern Ghana, Oxfam Working paper, Ada van der Linde & Rachel Naylor, July 1999

Other publications
Der Bürgerkrieg in Nordghana 1994, Artur Bogner. In: Afrika Spektrum 31 (1996)

Resource Contacts
Kwesi Aaku - Mediation & Change, Ghana
Charles Abbey - Executive Director African Development Programme, Ghana
Hizkias Assefa - Africa Peace and Reconciliation Network, Kenya. Email: hizkias@africaonline.co.ke
Judith Burdin Asuni - director Academic Associates Peace Works, Nigeria
Seibik-Bugri Jackson - director Partners for Democratic Change, Ghana
Rachel Naylor & Ada van der Linde - through Oxfam UK
Isaac Richard Osei - Action Aid Ghana

Selected Internet Sites
www.ghana.gov.gh/index.html (Ghana government site)
www.icrc.ch/unicc/icrcnews.nsf (ICRC)
www.bsos.umd.edu/cidcm (Center for International Development and Conflict Management/Minorities at Risk Programme)
www.ug.edu.gh/ (University of Ghana)
www.ghanareview.co.uk/ (Ghana Review International)

Organisations
Partners for Democratic Change
P.O. Box 1211
Madina Accra
Ghana
Tel. +233 21 231 021
Fax +233 21 501 279

Inter Agency Consortium & NORYDA
c/o Oxfam Ghana
P.O. Box 432
Tamale
Ghana
Tel./Fax +233 712 2849
Email oxtam@africaonline.com.gh

Data on the following organisations can be found in the Directory section
African Development Programme
Nairobi Peace Initiative
Conciliation Resources
CENCOR
Mediation & Change
ActionAid Ghana

Guinea-Bissau

Population (millions): 1.1 *(1997)*
Life expectancy at birth (years):
44 *(1996)*
GNP per capita (dollars): 240 *(1997)*
Conflict related deaths:
at least 500 civilians, an unknown
number of rebels and government
troops
Conflict related internally displaced
people: 200,000
Conflict related refugees:
5,415 *(Amnesty International)*

MAURITANIA

SENEGAL

MALI

GAMBIA

Bissau
★

GUINEA

Democracy Restored by a Military Coup?

In 1997 the political and economic prospects for Guinea-Bissau - still one of the
poorest countries in the world - looked brighter than they had in a long time. One
year later, however, the West-African country was back at square one. A protest by
a majority of the country's armed forces had turned into a full scale civil war and
destroyed any hopes for a better future. However, the situation in Guinea-Bissau
has not escaped international attention: foreign governments and neighbouring
countries have made several mediation attempts. Civilian pressure groups have
also played an active role. Although renewed fighting broke out in February 1999,
the latest peace accord seems to be holding ◆ *By* Monique Mekenkamp

Although endowed with rich and extensive
fishing grounds and reserves of as yet
unexploited natural resources, including bauxite,
phosphate and petroleum, Guinea-Bissau is one
of the poorest countries in Africa. It is bordered
by the states of Senegal and Guinea-Conakry.
The size of the country - approximately one
million people inhabiting 36,000 square
kilometres - is inversely proportional to its social

complexity. There are about 22 ethnic groups
with political systems ranging from the relatively
centralised patrilineal states in the interior (Fula
and Mandinga) to the acephalous societies of the
coast (Balanta, Manjako, Pepel) and the Bijagós
archipelago (Bijagós, Cocoli, Pajendinca).
Guinea-Bissau also has a sizeable population of
mixed descent.

Effective colonial rule began during the early

299

decades of this century, although the Portuguese presence in the territory dates back to the 1440s. While colonial domination was relatively short, it was nevertheless characterised by harshness and brutality which, together with the stubborn refusal of the Portuguese to grant independence peacefully, inevitably led to war. The protracted conflict that started in 1962 as a guerrilla war, culminated not only in the first unilateral declaration of independence in Africa, but significantly it also led to the downfall of the fascist dictatorship in Portugal and the hasty dismantling of the Portuguese colonial empire.

On 24 September 1973 the *Partido Africano para a Independência de Guiné e Cabo Verde* (African Party for the Independence of Guinea and Cape Verde), PAIGC, declared the colony of Portuguese Guinea independent. After a decade of bloody armed-struggle, hopes were raised that genuine political and economic independence would now be realised. Politics were however quickly monopolised by the ruling party, the PAIGC, which described itself as 'the supreme expression of the sovereign will of the people' and banned all organised political activities falling outside its control. An active national security police ensured that dissent was effectively stifled.

The security forces of President Luis Cabral's government executed about a hundred individuals suspected of collaboration with the Portuguese regime. After a failed coup attempt in 1978, more opponents met a similar fate and were buried in mass graves in the Oio region. In 1980, a successful coup d'état brought Cabral's Defence minister and one of the most prominent guerrilla leaders of the independence war, João Bernardo Vieira ('Nino'), to power.

One of the immediate consequences of the 'Readjustment Movement', as the coup became known, was a considerable reduction in political repression, arbitrary arrests and imprisonment, and flagrant human rights abuses. Nevertheless, the period between 1980 and 1991 was also characterised by political instability, with attempted coups or take-over bids aggravating economic and social crises.

In 1991, at an Extraordinary Meeting of the ruling PAIGC, President Vieira announced the start of a process of transition to multi-party

democracy. With that year officially designated the 'Year of Democratisation', the constitution was amended to allow for political pluralism, with guarantees for freedom of thought, assembly, association, demonstration and the press. Further moves towards the democratisation of Guinean society continued throughout 1992 and 1993, and by the time of the first multi-party elections in July 1994 there were about a dozen legal opposition parties. The elections passed off peacefully, voter participation was high, and President Vieira - whose status as war hero has remained high in the interior of the country - was returned to power with a small majority. The PAIGC won 62 of the National Assembly's hundred seats; Vieira was re-elected as the president of the Republic after a photo-finish rally with the opposition's candidate Kumba Iala (52-48 per cent). Slowly a vibrant civil society, underpinned by the new politics of consensus was beginning to emerge.

President Vieira however started to consolidate his position from early 1998 and decided to postpone the elections of July 1998 to October 1998. He divided key positions amongst his supporters, leaving the opposition parties with empty hands. Moreover, during the Congress of the PAIGC, Vieira succeeded in being re-elected to the presidency of his party. As such he was in contravention of the constitution which prohibits the president of the Republic from holding the position of president of a political party. In response the opposition and the media criticised these undemocratic actions in the strongest of terms.

Conflict Dynamics

In January 1998, Armed Forces Chief of Staff, Brigadeiro Ansumane Mané was suspended by President Vieira and accused of having failed to take measures against the traffic of arms to armed separatist groups in the Casamance region of Senegal. At the same time, more than twenty people including Guinea-Bissau soldiers and civilians and Senegalese civilians suspected of involvement in the arms trafficking, were arrested. This led to increased tension among the armed forces, many of whom were already dissatisfied with the low wages and poor conditions of service. On 7 June 1998, two days after Vieira had appointed Umberto Gomes as the new Army Chief, hereby dismissing Mané, Mané led a mutiny that soon plunged the entire country into civil war.

Two days after the start of the mutiny, on June 9, Mané announced the formation of the *Junta Militar*. During the first week of the conflict, it was demanded that Vieira change his policy and enter into dialogue with the Junta in order to bring about the desired changes. The Junta furthermore called for democratic elections to be held within sixty days. Mané and his men claimed they did not want to take over power, although criticising the regime of Vieira, but called for a dialogue in order to look for ways of improvement. Strong dissatisfaction with the corrupt presidential power and the harsh conditions of life led many people in Guinea-Bissau to side with the Military Junta. Soon the Junta could count on a rapidly increasing support from civil organisations and opposition parties. A few days after the mutiny, politically isolated and abandoned by most of his army, President Vieira was reduced to relying on foreign military force. It is almost certain, that Vieira had already started calling for military support from Senegal and Guinea-Conakry on June 7. Some say it is even very likely, that this foreign intervention was already in preparation before that date. 'Opération Gabou', as the Senegalese intervention was called, became operational with surprising rapidity, and the speed of the decision procedures made in Senegal were 'remarkable' in this respect.

Vieira's rescue by Senegalese and Guinea-Conakry troops led to a situation where the self-proclaimed Military Junta - representing ninety per cent of the armed forces reinforced by veterans of the armed struggle for national liberation - were fighting government forces, representing the remaining ten per cent of the population supported by troops from Senegal and Guinea-Conakry.

In the fifty days following June 7, intense bombardment with heavy artillery took place. The city of Bissau was mercilessly shelled by artillery from both sides resulting in great material destruction. Senegalese troops were reported to have acted as a brutal foreign occupying force rather than the army of the legal government. Generally it is thought that the hasty intervention of Senegal and Guinea-Conakry has prolonged the battle and spread the conflict throughout the country.

The Casamance factor
Relations between Guinea-Bissau and Senegal have improved in recent years, after occasional disturbances in the past. Casamance, the southern Senegalese region was part of Guinea-Bissau until the French took over. One of the structural problems in their relationship was the war in Casamance, where the rebel party *Mouvement des Forces Démocratiques de Casamance* (MDFC) has, since 1982, been engaged in a guerrilla war in the border region of Guinea-Bissau. The majority of the Casamance people have close cultural and historical ties to large groups in northern Guinea-Bissau. For years, Guinea-Bissau gave guerrilla fighters safe passage into the refugee camps just across the border. This was a 'natural' favour as the freedom fighters of Guinea-Bissau of the PAIGC had used Casamance as a refugee basis during their guerrilla war against the Portuguese. The struggle for self-determination for the people of Casamance is one of the causes of tension. Furthermore, Guinea-Bissau has also provided the separatist rebels in the Casamance with weapons for many years, although according to the parliamentary report which was recently published, the amounts of arms sold were not particularly impressive. Responsibility has never been proven but the Senegalese government has always blamed the army of Guinea-Bissau.

Since Guinea-Bissau joined the West-African Monetary union (CFA-countries) in May 1997, President Vieira has embarked on a strategy of normalising relations with Senegal. The dismissal of Army Chief Mané was an element of this strategy. President Vieira had earlier distanced himself from the support of the separatist rebels and an inquiry was set up to investigate the arms traffic across their northern border. Vieira was not very cooperative with the inquiry commission during the execution of their work. However the leaders of both countries have subsequently committed themselves to improving relations. They are now united in their condemnation of both groups of rebels who they believe are helping each other. Some have noted that it is hard to believe that Senegalese president Diouf and Vieira actually *believed* that the Junta and the MFDC were collaborating; it is more likely, that an alleged collaboration between the two rebels was used as an argument to disqualify the Junta on a diplomatic level.

Efforts to restore peace between the Guinea-Bissau government and the rebels started almost immediately after June 7 1998. However, during the first week of the conflict, numerous initiatives from civilian organisations and parliament aimed at opening negotiations, were categorically refused by President Vieira. Also mediation attempts by Portugal, Angola, and Gambia proved ineffective. Diplomats in Senegal's capital expressed concern that the mediation attempts had lost their momentum, while more and more effort was being put into defeating the rebels by military means alone. After three weeks of fighting, Vieira adopted a tough line against the rebels who, he said, had tried to stage a coup d'etat against a legitimate government. He called on the West African military force, ECOMOG, to intervene and help put down the rebellion in his country. In response, the Economic Community of West African States (ECOWAS) adopted a resolution instructing the body to begin preparations to send an intervention force to Guinea-Bissau, if peace negotiations failed. A three-pronged strategy was adopted to try to restore peace in the country: dialogue and negotiation, sanctions and embargoes, and the use of force. Furthermore the body established a special committee on the resolution of the Guinea-Bissau crisis.

While Vieira and his Francophone partners were constantly stressing the rebellious, criminal and illegal character of the Junta, thereby assuring themselves of diplomatic legitimacy, it was after an intervention of Portugal, that the impasse was broken. Portugal supplied Mané with a satellite telephone, and started to criticise Vieira, who was not only fighting his own people, but in collaboration with Senegal, had started to close the country for any commercial or humanitarian transport. It was indeed Portugal, with an important diplomatic

contribution in Cape Verde, that accomplished the first cease-fire of July 26, 1998. This truce was transformed into a formal cease-fire on August 25, but was breached in October. After a few days of fighting, the rebels gained control of most of the country. President Vieira declared a unilateral cease-fire on October 18 and said he was willing to hold talks with Mané. The rebels declared a cease-fire on October 23. At this time the conflict was in a deadlock - Vieira holding the centre of the capital and Mané controlling the rest of the country.

The current peace agreement was finally signed on November 1 in Abuja, Nigeria after three days of talks. The agreement stated that:
1) a government of national unity will be formed, including representatives of the rebels;
2) all foreign troops will be withdrawn and replaced by a 600-man West African (ECOMOG) peacekeeping force; and
3) presidential elections will be held by the end of March 1999.

A glimmer of hope emerged. Delegations from the government, the junta and ECOWAS later reached a draft agreement on the arrival of additional ECOMOG troops and a timetable for the withdrawal of Guinean and Senegalese soldiers, which is envisaged under the peace agreement. However fighting resumed at the end of January 1999 marking the first major incident since the peace accord.

Peace talks were again held under the auspices of ECOWAS including diplomatic representations from Portugal, Sweden and France. On February 17 Vieira and Mané agreed, in the spirit of national reconciliation, to work together to guarantee peace in Guinea-Bissau and resolved never again to resort to arms in order to solve their problems. Later that week Francisco Fadul was sworn in as prime minister of the government of national unity. This seemed to mark the end of the armed rebellion whereby Vieira was able to save his regime at the cost of several hundreds lives, several thousands of refugees and the destruction of the socio-economic infrastructure.

General elections were scheduled to take place in March 1999 under the regional accord signed in Nigeria in November. However delays in implementing the peace process, including the withdrawal of Senegalese troops, made a March election impossible. The Senegalese and Guinean troops finally left the country at the end of March, and have successfully been replaced by a 600-strong ECOMOG force.

By early May however, it had become apparent that Vieira was increasing both his ground forces - particularly the rapidly recruited and trained *aguentas* - and his armaments. The Junta then decided to launch a final assault on the loyalist troops. Witnesses of the talks between president Abubakar of Nigeria and Ansumane Mané stated that Abubakar had strongly recommended this kind of operation. Thus, fighting started again on May 6 when loyalists resisted efforts by the West African intervention force, ECOMOG, to disarm some of the presidential guards. After this, troops loyal to president Vieira surrendered to those backing former Armed Forces Chief Ansumane Mané after a shootout in Bissau. Vieira sought protection in the French embassy but was refused; he then turned to the residence of the Bishop, where he was eventually discovered by the Junta, after which he was handed over to the Portuguese embassy. Finally Portugal granted Vieira political asylum. General and legislative elections are now rescheduled for November 28, 1999.

Official Conflict Management

Neither the *United Nations* nor the *Organisation of African Unity (OAU)* have played decisive roles in the Guinea-Bissau conflict. The role of the UN generally has been weak, and at crucial moments during the peace process they were simply absent.

The UN has been more active in the post-conflict phase. Following the peace agreement the Security Council of the UN called on the parties in Guinea-Bissau urgently to form a government of national unity and to hold elections not later than the end of March 1999. The Council unanimously adopted resolution 1216 (1998) calling for the full implementation of the agreements between the government of Guinea-Bissau and the military junta signed in August, November and December, the UN said in a press release. UN Secretary-General Kofi

Annan also decided to send an electoral needs assessment team to Guinea-Bissau. The Security Council welcomed a meeting of donors to Guinea-Bissau in Geneva on 4-5 May 1999, sponsored by the UNDP, to mobilise assistance for the country's humanitarian needs, its socio-economic rehabilitation and peace-building. At this conference 32 countries and international agencies pledged US $200 million in aid for the next three years.

Furthermore, UN Secretary-General Kofi Annan has appointed Samuel Nana-Sinkam, a Cameroonian national, as his representative in Guinea-Bissau and head of UNOGBIS, the UN Post-Conflict Peace-building Support Office in Guinea-Bissau. This had already been planned some months earlier, however, and the delay has had an impact on the UN's credibility and its capacity. UNOGBIS is mandated, among other things, to help build democracy and the rule of law and to organise free and transparent elections; to work with all involved to facilitate the implementation of the Abuja agreement; and to harmonise the activities of the UN agencies working in Guinea-Bissau. UNOGBIS is to include two officers responsible for monitoring human rights and providing technical assistance for measures to protect human rights, including during the election period.

OAU initiatives have been marginal and the organisation has shown itself powerless to mediate in the conflict. It has happily left the search for a solution to the *Economic Community of West African States* (ECOWAS).

The first cease-fire in August was concluded under the auspices of ECOWAS and the *Community of Portuguese Speaking Countries* (CPLP). ECOWAS, formed in 1975 to promote economic integration among its members, has assumed an increasingly important diplomatic and military role in the region.

While Senegal and Guinea rushed troops to Bissau to help Vieira fight the rebels, the CPLP deployed a contact group to mediate between the belligerents. This mediation resulted in negotiations that led to the first cease-fire. The CPLP contact group also decided on July 31 to send some hundred Portuguese-speaking military observers from member nations to Guinea-Bissau to monitor the cease-fire.

In the search for a solution to the conflict the rivalry between the CPLP and ECOWAS was very noticeable. The CPLP had always advocated an internal solution, and this approach was strongly supported by political parties, civil society and the diplomatic representatives of Portugal and Sweden, who have played an important role. However, ECOWAS preferred a sub-regional solution that involved the mutineers, the government, ECOWAS, Senegal, Equatorial Guinea and later also the CPLP. ECOWAS at first wanted to exclude the CPLP from the peace process, supported by France, which pled for 'having exclusively the West Africans solving problems of West Africa'. Before the mediation, an emergency meeting was called in order to harmonise and coordinate the mediators' efforts. The Cape Verdian Foreign Minister Jose Luis Jesus tried to ease the tensions by highlighting the importance of both institutions in conflict resolution. 'ECOWAS plays a very important role in intervening in conflicts in Africa and in the mediation in the Guinea-Bissau conflict. Like ECOWAS, we are guided by the desire to achieve peace as fast as possible by facilitating dialogue between the two parties.' (Press agency IPS, August 1998)

A special committee of ECOWAS together with Gambian president, Yahya Jammeh, mediated the peace agreement of November. The Government and the Military Junta, the peace negotiators; ECOWAS and the Community of Portuguese speaking countries, the UN and the OAU all signed the agreement.

After the war of May 6-7, *France* actively tried to push both the UN as well as the EU to consider the military action as a *coup d'état* and consequently *condemn* the Junta. France has asked for an economic embargo on Guinea-Bissau. After well formulated protests from Portugal and Sweden - supported by the Netherlands - the EU eventually decided not to issue a condemnation, but, instead, 'to follow the situation carefully and eventually draw its own conclusions'. The French media continue to try and influence international opinion by spreading negative messages about the Junta, suggesting that they are mistreating the population, and that it has various important opponents among political parties and civil society.

Multi-Track Diplomacy

The civil society in Guinea-Bissau, community leaders, prominent individuals, religious groups and non-governmental organisations, has been active in seeking peace and defending human rights, sometimes placing themselves in danger. Their efforts have not been widely reported but they have made a significant behind the scenes contribution. Throughout the period of fighting, many civilians, both from inside the country and living in the refugee community, have tried continuously to bring the parties together for talks and to propose ways to secure a future for Guinea-Bissau in which all human rights are respected.

Domestic

Internal attempts to end the fighting began two days after it started. The major role was played by the *Goodwill Commission* of parliamentarians, representatives of the three main religious groups and of non-governmental organisations. It was led by the late Bishop of Bissau, Dom Settimio Arturo Ferrazzetta, who died, aged 75, on 27 January 1999.

The Bishop has been very active in efforts to achieve peace between the rebels and the government from an early stage in the conflict. He regularly urged both leaders to respect each other and their people and start a peace process. He has made impressive efforts to promote the peace process. In later phases the Bishop has always supported the negotiations and consistently acted as go-between to foster the dialogue between the two parties. Both parties have honoured him as a 'martyr of peace'.

Members of the Goodwill Commission met President Vieira and Brigadier Mané and tried to bring the belligerents to a less extreme point of view in order to expand the opportunities for agreement. For example, they urged the Junta to accept ECOWAS as a mediating partner. They acted in liaison with the CPLP and ECOWAS. In September, when it seemed that the CPLP and ECOWAS had failed to reach a common understanding, the Goodwill Commission decided to pursue internal mediation in liaison with the diplomatic representatives of Sweden, Portugal and

France. They helped pave the way for the Abuja agreement.

Apart from its mediation work, the Commission has also staged 'Marches for Peace' and has sent letters to the United Nations and the European Union to urge them to intervene.

In spite of the country's small size and widespread poverty, Guinea-Bissau's *Liga Guineense dos Direitos do Homem* (Guinean League for Human Rights) has been called one of the most impressive human rights organisations in Africa (University of Minnesota: The Status of Human Rights Organisations in Sub Sahara Africa). The organisation emphasises the rights of women. The bulk of the Liga's work is to inform the people of Bissau of their legal rights and obligations, to monitor the human rights situation in the country, and act as an advocate for those whose rights have been infringed. Before the war, public education was effected through a weekly programme broadcast over the government radio and the publication of a bulletin containing educational articles, information on human rights abuses in Guinea-Bissau, and accounts of the activities of the Liga.

The leading members of the Liga were scattered during the conflict. A few stayed in Bissau throughout, but their work was severely limited by the bombardments and the breakdown in communications systems. Nevertheless, in August 1998 they set up an *International Human Rights Observatory* in Cape Verde, in collaboration with other non-governmental human rights organisations. It aimed to monitor human rights and press the parties to the conflict to respect human rights. It published a monthly magazine, '*Observatório*'. In December 1998, when it seemed that the war had ended, the Observatory was closed and the Liga resumed its normal work in Guinea-Bissau.

The *Instituto Nacional de Estudos e Pesquisa* (National Institute of Studies and Research - INEP) is the largest and most active research institution in Guinea-Bissau. The institute for example has conducted a study on the Guinean democratisation process. INEP has also been a key actor in the country's development, acting as a knowledge centre and the main consulting body for the entire country. The Institute furthermore undertakes a wide range of

activities, including hosting national and international seminars, conferences and colloquia. However, most of its premises and archives were destroyed during the war. INEP is now actively working on its reconstruction and institutional rehabilitation and is already demonstrating its role in Guinea-Bissau society, as it is actively involved in a large-scale habitat rehabilitation programme in Bissau with the Dutch Development Organisation. (SNV).

International
Many international humanitarian organisations are present in Guinea-Bissau and their activities range from organising the return of refugees, to supplying emergency aid and food. The *International Red Cross Committee* and the *International Federation of Red Cross and Red Crescent Societies* are some of the humanitarian organisations active in the country. The ICRC also launches regular appeals and closely monitors the situation in Guinea-Bissau.

A Common Humanitarian Action Plan has been developed by UN agencies to manage humanitarian assistance in a *Consolidated Inter-Agency Appeal for Guinea-Bissau*. Consultations have been held with the government, the military junta and the donor community. The principal goal of the appeal is to facilitate the rapid return to a normal situation for population groups most affected by the conflict and to begin cooperation with the new Government of National Unity as soon as it is constituted.

Several projects have been undertaken within the Action Plan. The *UN High Commissioner on Refugees (UNHCR)* is responsible for relocating and providing basic assistance for the Senegalese refugees in Guinea-Bissau, and for the repatriation and initial reintegration of the refugees of Guinea-Bissau in the sub-region. The *Office for the Coordination of Humanitarian Affairs* (OCHA) is active in the coordination of humanitarian assistance programmes. It facilitates coordination and information sharing among all partners. Furthermore OCHA plays a role in organising agency missions and formulating follow-up recommendations in order to assess humanitarian needs. Both UNCHR and OCHA seek the participation of local authorities and NGOs in the implementation of the programmes.

However, the roles played by the various UN organisations should not be overestimated. WFP, UNHCR, UNICEF did little during the period of conflict, while the relief of tens of thousands of dislocated people was mainly done by the rural population, whose food and seeds stocks have been reduced to a bare minimum. Also the ICRC has often been slow and indecisive. Generally, the multilateral humanitarian organisations have insufficient knowledge of the humanitarian situation in the country before or during the conflict.

A *Solidarity Platform of NGOs with the People of Guinea-Bissau* has been formed. It has met three times since June 1998 to discuss the war and possible solutions. Many European NGOs are present in this platform. The aim of this Platform is to organise meetings to enhance cooperation and to support the peoples of Guinea-Bissau. It has for example drafted an appeal for peace.

ECHO (Office for Humanitarian Affairs of the EU) has developed an action plan for food security, health care and reconstruction. SNV/INEP are executing a habitat rehabilitation project within this framework. Unfortunately, ECHO is hindered by slow Brussels-bureaucracy.

Amnesty International has regularly called both parties to respect human rights. It has issued several reports regarding the implementation of human rights issues in the new constitution and in the peace accords. In its last report it also issued recommendations.

Prospects

In the years before the war the government made little attempt to develop a culture of accountability or to build institutions for the protection of human rights. In 1998, an *Anti-Corruption Committee* and another institution (*Tribunal das Contas*) were created, which can be considered important institutional steps forward. On the other hand, under the Vieira regime, the presidential top never showed any signal of respecting these institutions. Nevertheless, according to the latest Amnesty International report, two factors encourage hope that in the wake of the conflict a new era may begin in which human rights are respected and protected.

On the one hand, the vision and strength of will of NGOs, religious groups and others working for peace and to enhance the range of human rights, is strong. Equally encouraging is the new Government of National Unity's promise to respect human rights and its plans to promote important developments in human rights protection.

The November accord may turn out to be less fragile than its two predecessors. However, political and material reconstruction will only be possible through the establishment of a legitimate democratic regime. The Prime Minister of the transition government, Mr Francisco Fadul has expressed the need for internal reform, but has clearly indicated the need for international responsibility in this matter. He calls for the coordination and transparency of the input of all foreign partners of the country. International aid and assistance is necessary in this post-conflict phase. According to the OCHA, there is an urgent need for donor funding to implement humanitarian programmes.

A positive development is the appointment of human rights officers within the UN Post-Conflict Peace-Building Support Office in Guinea-Bissau (UNOGBIS). Their role is to provide support and technical assistance to the government and to NGOs as well as monitoring the human rights situation.

A recent appraisal of the future is expressed by Roy van der Drift from INEP: 'It is extremely important at this moment, that the international community shows the willingness and intelligence to make a profound analysis of the situation, which will throw a much more positive light on what is actually going on. Until now, all aspects of the Abuja treaty as well as the national Constitution, are respected. The Junta has succeeded in restoring public order, and hardly any incidents are reported. Military presence in the streets of Bissau is every day diminishing. Parliament and civil society are constantly involved in the decision processes. The elections, set for November 28th, have never been questioned (apart from one political party, the PRS of Kumba Iala, which has stated that it is already prepared for *immediate* elections - which logistically is not feasible). Ansumane Mané, who is considered as one of the main persons in the country at this moment, is generally considered as an extremely important factor for the consolidation of peace. Being totally bankrupt, the government of National Unity should be enabled as soon as possible to finance its own functioning, as well as the functioning of Public Administration and Justice. Quick measures to improve the economic and humanitarian situation are to be taken. Moreover, it is important to restore public/government structures on the countryside, and replacing the 'informal' Junta representatives by formal civil officials.'

Recommendations

The Solidarity Platform for the people of Guinea-Bissau organised its first meeting, under the aegis of the *Voluntary Organisations in cooperation in Emergencies,* (VOICE) on July 6, 1998 in Brussels. The aim of this meeting was to exchange information on the political, military and humanitarian situation in the country following the outbreak of the crisis. The Platform also drafted an Appeal to the International Community to call for the opening up of humanitarian corridors and the urgent realisation of aid. This appeal was signed by some thirty organisations.

Another meeting in Paris on September 29, 1998 resulted in a Declaration by the NGOs in solidarity with Guinea-Bissau, to pool their information and their concern, to coordinate their efforts in favour of peace, to consider aid for the victims of the conflict and to alert public opinion. The Declaration, among other issues, called for:

- a peaceful resolution to the conflict and the active building of peace by the people of Guinea-Bissau themselves, removed from foreign interference, and for the participation of the civilian organisations to be taken into account in the negotiations;
- impartial mediation based upon the major interests of the people of Guinea-Bissau;
- the withdrawal of foreign troops.

In a Memorandum of June 1999, the Platform also made some recommendations concerning conditions of stability, a new culture of power, protection of fundamental rights and focused on issues such as transparency and good governance, rehabilitation.

Amnesty International has recently made recommendations to the Government of National Unity, donor governments and the international community. These recommendations focus on measures necessary to prevent human rights violations, particularly during the forthcoming election campaign. They also focus on the longer-term development of institutions and practices for the protection of human rights. Recommendations include the development of a programme of civic education in preparation for the election; the return of key trained personnel; the effective training and posting of national and international election observers; reforming the criminal justice system; the restructuring and retraining of the police; and guaranteeing the independence of the judiciary.

Service Information

Reports

United Nations

- UN Consolidated Inter-Agency Appeal for Guinea Bissau. January-December 1999. OCHA 1998

Amnesty International

- Guinea-Bissau - Human Rights in war and peace, July 1999
- Guinea-Bissau - Protecting human rights - a new Era? April 1999
- Guinea-Bissau - Human Rights under Fire. July 1998

Solidarity Platform for the People of Guinea Bissau

- Appeal for Guinea Bissau and the Situation in Guinea Bissau. July 1998
- Declaration in Paris. September 1998

Sida

- Guinea-Bissau 1997: Going into High Gear - A macroeconomic report, by Renato Aguilar

Other Publications

*Guinea-Bissau 1998 - Democratic Legality versus Democratic Legitim*acy, by Lars Rudebeck. In: Webs of War - Armed Conflicts in West Africa. Africa Study Centre, Leiden/the Netherlands, March 1999
Democracy - Legitimate Warfare in Guinea-Bissau, by Roy van der Drift. In: Webs of War - Armed Conflicts in West Africa, Africa Study Centre, Leiden/the Netherlands, March 1999
Civil War in Guinea-Bissau, by Napoleon Abdulai. In: ACCORD-magazine Conflict Trends, October 1998, Issue 1
Guinea-Bissau - Power, Conflict and Renewal in a West African Nation, by Joshua B. Forrest. Westview Press, Boulder, 1992

Resource Contacts

Renato Aguilar - Department of Economics, Gothenburg University, Sweden. Email Renato.Aguilar@economics.gu.se
Roy van der Drift - INEP, Guinea Bissau. Email van.der.drift@sol.gtelecom.gw
Abdulai Napoleon - ACCORD, South Africa.

Email anapoleon@accord.org.za
Gill Nevins - Amnesty International. Email gnevins@amnesty.org
Lars Rudebeck - Department of Political Science, Uppsala University, Sweden. Email lars.rudebeck@uland.uu.se

Selected Internet Sites

www.bissau.com/ (General information)
guineabissau.forward.net (No Djunta Mon!, meaning Let's Join Hands in the local language Kriol, a website dedicated to assisting efforts to end the crisis in the country)
www.icrc.org/unicc/icrcnews.nsf/$$guinea_bissau ?OpenView (ICRC)
www.imf.org/external/NP/sec/decdo/ecowas.htm (ECOWAS)
www.geocities.com/CapitolHill/Senate/8463/ (Portugese language site on the conflict)
www.uvm.edu/~whawthor/guinea.html (Guinea Bissau links)
africa-research.csusb.edu/countries/gbi01.htm (INEP - in the long term INEP will publish its own website)

Organisations

Instituto Nacional de Estudos e Pesquisa (INEP)
BP 112
Bairro Cobornel
Guinea-Bissau
Tel. +245 251 867, Fax +245 251 125
(Temporarily at SNV-head Office in Bissau, tel. 222 881, 222 882)
Email inep@sol.gtelecom.gw,
snv@sol.gtelecom.gw

Solidarity Platform of the People of Guinea-Bissau
c/o Associação para a Cooperação Entre os Povos (ACEP)
Apart. 24 433, 1250 Lisboa, Portugal
Tel. +351 1 386 5278
Fax +351 1 386 3699
Email: acepongd@mail.telepac.pt

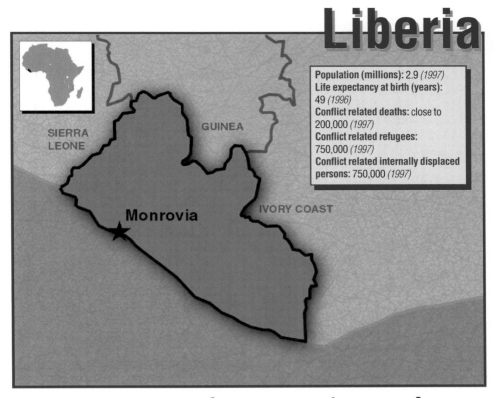

Liberia

Population (millions): 2.9 *(1997)*
Life expectancy at birth (years): 49 *(1996)*
Conflict related deaths: close to 200,000 *(1997)*
Conflict related refugees: 750,000 *(1997)*
Conflict related internally displaced persons: 750,000 *(1997)*

SIERRA LEONE

GUINEA

IVORY COAST

Monrovia

Seven Years of Devastation and an Uncertain Future

Liberia's development has been set back by a series of brutal looting sprees which began as an uprising against a regime that was in moral and physical decline. The wars have left deep scars in Liberian society, but they have also created an opportunity to redefine the country, both in more democratic terms and as an undivided nation. There are groups and individuals willing to assist in that effort. If this succeeds - and the task is immense - the spectre of war may be defeated once and for all. Unfortunately, evidence on the ground has not been encouraging. ◆ *By* **Bram Posthumus**

Liberia was founded in 1822 and declared a Republic in 1847. The founding fathers were mainly a small group of freed American slaves. These 'Americo-Liberians' placed themselves at the top of the social and economic ladder leaving the majority of the (at least) sixteen indigenous peoples living in the interior of Liberia firmly at the bottom. They were considered 'savages' who needed to be 'civilized'. This situation persisted well into the twentieth century until a number of

reforms intended to accommodate the indigenous peoples were introduced under the post-World War II Presidents Tubman and Tolbert.

Despite these reforms, however, the closely-knit Americo-Liberian community continued to profit from the system of patronage which they had built for themselves. Opposition to the succession of unaccountable and intolerant regimes grew until matters came to a head in riots over price hikes in the country's staple food, rice, in April 1979. Dozens were killed by the police. Precisely one year later, Tolbert and other prominent members of the Americo-Liberian elite were killed in a coup. On April 12, 1980, a group of seventeen men, among them the later head of state Samuel K. Doe, stormed into the presidential palace (called the Executive Mansion), stabbed the incumbent William Tolbert to death and took possession of the state. It was a decisive turning point, laying bare the fundamental flaws of the previous 133 years of Liberia's history and sowing the seeds of the war that would destroy the country a decade later.

The new government's promise of hope soon became a record of intolerance. Doe retained the presidency in 1985 only after heavily rigged elections. In the meantime, he had intimidated or alienated most of his erstwhile political allies and driven them out of his government. Civil servants were also dismissed, including the director of the General Services Agency, one Charles Taylor, whom Doe accused of corruption. In the wake of a failed coup attempt by another formerly trusted member of the Doe government, Thomas Quiwonpka, also in 1985, the regime became brutal and erratic. It also introduced a new, tribalist, element into its retribution against the coup plotters. The plotters came from the Mano and Gio people and villages in Nimba County inhabited by Mano and Gio people were attacked and their inhabitants slaughtered by the Armed Forces of Liberia, whose ranks Doe had filled with many of his own Krahn tribesmen.

The international community did little to stop the carnage or prevent further atrocities. Most notably, the United States, midwife to the country, refrained from intervention. On the contrary, Presidents Ronald Reagan and George Bush propped up the Doe regime with aid totalling close to half a billion US$. According to Reed Kramer, in the early 1980s Liberia became caught up in the secret designs of a US government obsessed with ending Colonel Ghadaffi's power in Libya. According to articles published in the *Washington Post* and the *New York Times* in February 1987, the programme was organised by the same people involved in the Iran-Contra scandal. Liberia not only played a pivotal role in the activities directed against Libya, from 1985 it was a stopover for US military and other assistance on its way to UNITA rebels fighting the government of Angola. In the meantime, Charles Taylor secured Libyan, Ivorian and Burkinabe aid for his bid to unseat Doe by force.

Conflict Dynamics

On Christmas Eve 1989, a group of 150 fighters led by Taylor invaded the country from Ivory Coast. Doe swiftly dispatched troops to Nimba County, the area of the incursion, again killing hundreds of people. Taylor's troops of the National Patriotic Front of Liberia (NPFL) meanwhile cut through the country, also causing great loss of life. The NPFL reached the city of Monrovia midway through 1990.

The NPFL pushed its offensive to within a street of Doe's headquarters in the Executive Mansion, but it appears that US pressure dissuaded Taylor from launching an all-out assault on those sections of the city that were still firmly in the hands of Doe and another small faction which had broken away in February, the Independent NPFL. An offensive would certainly have resulted in bloodshed on an enormous scale.

Meanwhile, through the efforts of the regional Economic Community of West African States (ECOWAS), an interim government had been installed and an intervention force (the ECOWAS Monitoring Group, ECOMOG) had landed to enforce peace. However, it too became a party in the conflict. With the then military ruler of Nigeria, Ibrahim Babangida, reluctant to countenance a Taylor takeover of Liberia, ECOMOG dislodged the NPFL from the city and bombed NPFL-held towns elsewhere in the country. ECOMOG again prevented an NPFL take-over of Monrovia in 1992, when the rebels launched their ill-fated operation 'Octopus', which destroyed various parts of the city.

From 1991 onwards the insurgency fragmented into large-scale gang warfare. The NPFL became predominantly a business venture, selling timber, diamonds and iron ore through the port of Buchanan which it controlled, while other groups sprang up, most notably ULIMO (United Front of Liberia for Democracy), which later split into the ULIMO-J faction under Roosevelt Johnson and ULIMO-K under Alhaji Kroma. These and other factions fought each other for control of Liberia's ample resources. At times, as in the case of the predominantly Mandingo ULIMO-K, they painted themselves in tribal colours, but their forces also included mercenaries from Liberia and elsewhere in the region. The use of child soldiers became widespread and the abuse of a wide variety of narcotics resulted in large-scale atrocities and a mass exodus from the country. Men and women were mutilated, raped and killed, towns and villages looted and then burned. In one of the worst incidents, 600 civilians were massacred near the town of Harbel, on June 6, 1993. UN investigations pointed the finger at the remains of the army. War had become, in the words of Tiébilé Drame in the book *Africa Now*, a form of political and economic organisation; the marketplace at its most unfettered.

Only temporarily halted by a series of invariably short-lived peace accords, the succession of fighting, killing and looting sprees continued until the fourteenth peace accord was signed in Abuja, Nigeria, in August 1996. The worst fighting occurred on April 6 1996, when most of Monrovia was destroyed and thousands of desperate people sought refuge in overcrowded compounds such as the US Embassy or on ships such as the Bulk Challenge. Disarmament, first started and then aborted in the buildup to 'April 6', was restarted in November 1996 and overseen by ECOMOG, which in the process earned some respect. Within two months, close to 25,000 people had handed in their weapons and begun a reintegration exercise. Elections were held on July 19, sweeping Taylor to power in a landslide victory.

The elections were duly pronounced free and fair by domestic and international observers. However, the 'free and fair' nature of these elections is disputed. Taylor had a head start in terms of financial resources and media coverage (he owned the only functioning national radio station) and there was large-scale intimidation of voters.

Since then, peace of a kind has prevailed. There are infrequent reports of local skirmishes

in various parts of the interior. Tensions between the various former faction leaders remain and occasionally become violent. The most serious fighting occurred on September 20, 1998, following government accusations earlier that month that it had foiled a coup attempt. There was a shootout on the doorstep of the American embassy, between fighters loyal to former ULIMO-J commander Roosevelt Johnson and president Taylor's troops. The incident was described by some observers as a deliberate attempt by Taylor's forces to gun down Roosevelt Johnson and many of his followers. The clashes left some fifty people dead. Roosevelt Johnson fled into the American embassy and was then transported out of the country. He was charged with treason and convicted *in absentia*, in April 1999. Again in July and August there were clashes in the northern province of Lofa County, which according to unconfirmed reports have put thousands of people on the move yet again.

Official Conflict Management

The efforts undertaken by the *Economic Community of West African States* (ECOWAS) have proved decisive. Although bedevilled by differences in interests and policies among the member states (Burkina Faso and Ivory Coast supported Taylor, while Nigeria in the early 1990s certainly did not), ECOWAS acted as mediator in a long succession of peace negotiations, including the comprehensive Cotonou Agreement of July 1993, which unravelled in early 1994, and both Abuja Accords, of August 1995 and August 1996 respectively.

ECOWAS also set up an intervention force, the *Ecowas Cease-Fire Monitoring Group* (ECOMOG), which began operations in August 1990. In its early days success and failure were evenly mixed. While it succeeded in saving the lives of many refugees it failed to prevent President Doe from being abducted by faction leader Yormie Johnson from under its nose and then tortured to death on its own premises. The initial anti-Taylor sympathies also damaged its image as a peace-enforcing/peace-keeping force, and it lacked the numbers and resources to actually enforce the peace. Its reputation was further damaged by the bombing raids and the behaviour of the Nigerian troops on 'April 6', some of whom indulged in looting sprees while others watched.

Yet in February 1998 an enthusiastic Monrovian crowd bid farewell to the force, shouting 'Thank you ECOMOG, we love you.' The change which earned ECOMOG a modicum of respect may well have come about as a result of the appearance of a new head of the Nigerian government. Relations between Taylor and the former Nigerian military ruler Ibrahim Babangida were largely hostile, while Babangida's successor Sani Abacha and Taylor appeared to understand each other better.

However there was also a growing sense that the Nigerian military and Taylor were mutually indispensable. Abacha needed a success story involving Nigerians to brush up the severely tarnished reputation of his nation. If that entailed accepting Taylor as president of Liberia, then so be it. For his part, Taylor knew that he needed Nigerian approval for his presidency. And so, according to journalist Tom Kamara and researcher Stephen Ellis, a slow convergence of interests took place. All this enabled ECOMOG to oversee the disarmament of the combatants, taking in the guns and handing out a small demobilisation package. In time, Taylor duly won his elections. The ECOMOG mandate expired in March 1998 and the force is currently engaged in operations in Sierra Leone, where it has also relocated its headquarters. It has left a small number of troops in Monrovia to guard the weapons and its own facilities.

The relationship between the newly-elected Liberian government and various ECOMOG field commanders remained edgy, not least because Taylor, in breach of the Abuja II Agreement, denied ECOMOG the opportunity to restructure the Liberian army.

The *United Nations* worked together with ECOMOG for the duration of its mission, making it the first cooperation between the UN and a regional body, even though Security Council approval for the West African peacekeeping operation came only after the first ECOMOG troops were already in Liberia. Following the Cotonou Peace Agreement that was concluded in July 1993, the UN Security Council voted to set up an observer mission in Liberia, named

UNOMIL, the *United Nations Observers Mission in Liberia*. Its brief was to monitor the implementation of the Cotonou Agreement and verify disarmament throughout the country. However, the Cotonou Agreement was short-lived and it was only after various extensions of the mandate and the second Abuja Agreement that UNOMIL could oversee large-scale disarmament, together with ECOMOG. The expansion of ECOMOG, deemed important at the time, was co-financed by the UN Trust Fund for Liberia.

UNOMIL went on to play an observer role during the July 1997 elections. It helped where it could to enable the seriously understaffed and underfunded Liberian Independent Election Commission to do at least some of its work. The mission ended in September 1997. The UN has also maintained a weapons embargo against Liberia since 1996.

At least a dozen other UN organisations are working in Liberia, most notably the *UN High Commissioner for Refugees* (UNHCR), which assists in bringing back the hundreds of thousands of refugees from surrounding countries, together with the Liberian government (in the shape of the Liberian Repatriation, Resettlement and Rehabilitation Commission). Other significant players include UNICEF, which finances the vocational programmes carried out by local NGOs. Other UN actions included sending a high-level commission of inquiry into the infamous Harbel massacre, June 6, 1993 when 600 civilians were killed by the Armed Forces of Liberia and the imposition of an arms embargo against Liberia.

The *Organisation of African Unity* (OAU) sent observers and mediators to various peace negotiations. It also sent some troops in support of the ECOMOG operations. Most significantly, the Liberian crisis compelled the OAU to relinquish its previously unyielding stance on the total territorial integrity of its sovereign member states, thus making support for the ECOMOG efforts possible.

Individual governments, including the United States, the Netherlands, Denmark, Germany and the United Kingdom have given logistical support to ECOMOG, enabling it to better carry out its work. In particular, the United States, under the Clinton administration, has taken

MONROVIA, LIBERIA, Former child soldiers receiving schooling after having handed in their weapons

RON GILING/LINEAIR

more interest in a peaceful Liberia; the special presidential envoy Jesse Jackson is a regular visitor to Monrovia.

The *Government of Liberia* repeatedly makes the right noises about reconciliation, investigations into human rights abuses and respect for the rule of law. It also staged a major public event in July 1998, the National Conference on the Future of Liberia, to showcase the considerable rhetorical talents of president Taylor and many others. Many well-worded statements of intent were issued during the month-long event. Another highly publicised event was the burning of tens of thousands of guns and millions of rounds of ammunition in a massive bonfire in Monrovia on July 26, 1999. It was reminiscent of the Flame of Peace in Mali, but it remains to be seen whether the government of Liberia has the same benign intentions as their Malian colleagues.

In concrete terms, a national Human Rights Commission and a National Reconciliation Commission have been set up but they remain dormant and their mandates unclear. Human rights organisations continue to demand reform, especially of the notoriously violent and corrupt police force. Complaints of harassment and murders of politicians and civilians recur regularly.

The Government has taken an active role in the repatriation of refugees, through the *Liberian Refugee Repatriation and Resettlement Commission,* LRRRC, which works together with the UNHCR.

Multi-Track Diplomacy
Domestic

Many local initiatives aimed at ending the war have been taken. For a long time, these were inspired and to some extent coordinated by the *Inter Faith Mediation Council* (IFMC), a group of religious leaders who wanted to bring the conflict to an end by getting the faction leaders to talk to each other and by mobilising the people against the violence. This last initiative resulted in two hugely successful 'Stay At Home' campaigns in 1995 and 1996. These were acts of civil disobedience in the face of brutal attacks on the civilian population; they were later and more dramatically employed in Sierra Leone where the people staged a long stay-away campaign, following the military coup in that country on May 25, 1997.

There have been other important civil organisations that have contributed to the restoration of some kind of peace. The *Liberian Women's Initiative* (LWI) has brought together women from all walks of life in order to speed up the end of the war. Through a sustained campaign directed at important policy-makers in the peace process (including all ECOWAS Heads of State, the US and the UN), the LWI managed to get a hearing for its proposals. Through constant lobbying, it gained access to some of the peace negotiations. Probably its most important achievement was ensuring disarmament prior to elections, a position it put forward vigorously and which was reflected in the large-scale disarmament exercise of 1996-97. Prior to the elections the LWI was engaged in voter education. It is currently engaged in community work in the poor suburbs of Monrovia and elsewhere in the country. This includes the promotion of non-violent ways to resolve disputes. Civic education continues, in conjunction with the Centre for Democratic Empowerment (see below).

An interesting and at the time important player in the disarmament exercise was *Susukuu*, a development organisation run by the veteran politician Togba Nah Tipoteh. Susukuu devised a 'School for Guns' programme which offered one year of education in exchange for weapons. The programme was part of the successful effort in which well over 24,000 combatants handed in their guns between late November 1996 and early February 1997.

A prominent part in the re-education exercise aimed at ex-combatants is played by the *Liberia Opportunities Industrialization Centres*, (LOIC). It has devised special programmes to deal with the present situation, offering six-month courses to war-affected youths which include vocational and business training, detraumatisation and civic education. Scores of former child combatants have gone through the courses it has set up in various parts of the country.

The *Catholic Justice and Peace Commission* (CJP) has continued to promote respect for human rights and the rule of law by challenging government not to renege on its promises and by offering legal aid to disenfranchised members of the public. It monitors the human rights

situation in the country and publishes its findings in Situation Reports, offering well-documented assessments and recommendations for action. The CJP has consistently asked the government of Liberia to carry through its plans to deal with human rights abuses and reconciliation, two issues it considers inseparable. In October 1998 the CJP asked for a thorough inquiry into the September shootings in front of the US embassy. In May 1999, CJP Director Samuel Kofi Woods received a special honour from Pope John Paul II, in recognition of his service to humanity.

The *Centre for Democratic Empowerment*, (CEDE) headed by former interim president Amos Sawyer, has been engaged in peace-building community activities, promoting disarmament before the elections and national reconciliation thereafter. It is currently engaged in consultations with the government concerning reorganisation of the security forces and national reconciliation.

International

Of the international NGOs, *The Carter Center* has been actively involved in shuttle diplomacy, carried out by former US President Jimmy Carter, who has visited the country five times, on the last occasion, as an observer during the July 1997 elections. The Carter Center has served as a source of information for virtually all parties and mediators in the crisis and has assisted local peace promoting and human rights organisations.

The Swiss-based *Femmes Africa Solidaire* (FAS) had an observer mission in Liberia during the elections, under the auspices of the OAU. Prior to the elections, FAS organised an all-women training course on conflict resolution, reconciliation and the electoral process. Civic education training sessions were continued after the elections.

Another Swiss-based NGO, *Fondation Hirondelle*, set up Star Radio in Monrovia, which is an independent radio station that broadcasts news bulletins in all of Liberia's sixteen languages. It relies on local staff and is studiously non-partisan. Its bulletins are distributed through the Internet.

International NGOs, including *Dutch*

Interchurch Aid and *Oxfam,* have supported local initiatives in Liberia aimed at promoting peace. Others are either stepping up their involvement or starting to assist Liberian NGOs; among them *International Alert.* This organisation supports (together with the government of the Netherlands and USAID) Talking Drum Studio, which produces radio programmes to encourage reconciliation and reconstruction. According to International Alert, survey results show that in the Monrovia area ninety per cent of the population listens to Talking Drum programmes.

Prospects

The tasks facing the government are immense. The country's entire infrastructure has been completely destroyed. Hundreds of thousands of refugees and internally displaced people want to come home. There are still an estimated 15,000 people at large who have not yet handed in their guns and engage in acts of banditry. Tensions among the former warlords who taken up positions in the new government remain and occasional outbreaks of violence cause panic among ordinary citizens. There are persistent reports of harassment of civilians by the police, and various branches of the security forces, both in Monrovia and in the interior. Nor has the long-standing Americo-Liberian versus indigenous dichotomy been resolved. In fact, new tensions among the various peoples of Liberia have been added as a result of the war. Countless numbers of people are traumatised, destitute and lacking in the most basic facilities of life. The first two years of the Taylor government have seen a very steep decline in people's living conditions.

The only redeeming factor is the resilience of the general population, but this is not inexhaustible. There is also a small but vigorous civil society in place which is still willing to work with the new government to ensure that Liberia becomes a viable and democratic nation. This determination may offset the odds for the time being, although scepticism about the government's intentions is increasing, also because the government is not seen to be doing anything to stop the scepticism from spreading.

Persisting regional tensions further complicate the situation. The tragedy in neighbouring Sierra Leone continues and the Liberian government stands accused of aiding and abetting the brutal rebellion against the democratically elected government of that country. Taylor has consistently denied these accusations, and has instead accused his neighbours, most notably Sierra Leone, Guinea and even Nigeria, with harbouring disaffected elements or former warlords who are intent on overthrowing his government. Matters were certainly not helped by the attack on the northern town of Voinjama, in April 1999, in which at least four people were killed, and the brief occupation of three major northern towns, including Voinjama, in August of the same year. Accusations that the attackers came from Guinea were denied by the Guinean government; but there are also rumours in the area that a Guinean rebel group works from Liberia.

With large numbers of people on the move, poor countries like Guinea with enormous refugee populations, a perilous situation in Sierra Leone and Liberia, and the coup in Guinea-Bissau, there are grounds to fear a regional conflagration if tensions and irresponsible rumour-mongering are not checked.

Erratum

Talking Drum Studio, mentioned above, is not supported by International Alert, but by **Search for Common Ground, Washington, USA**

Service Information

Reports
Human Rights Watch
- Easy Prey - Child soldiers in Liberia, London, 1994

Other Publications
Liberia 1989-1994 - A study of ethnic and spiritual violence, by Stephen Ellis. African Affairs, 1995
Liberia - A Casualty of the Cold War's end, by Reed Kramer. Paper issued by the African Studies Program of the Center of Strategic and International Studies, Washington DC, USA, 1995
The International Dimension of internal conflict - The case of Liberia and West Africa, by Emmanuel Kwesi Aning. CDR Working Paper 97.4, 1997
Liberia, the Quest for Democracy, by Gus Liebenov. Indiana University Press, Bloomington, 1988
Regional Peacekeeping and international enforcement - The Liberian Crisis, M. Weller (ed). Grotius Publications, Cambridge
Liberia - Railroading to Peace, by V. Tanner. Review of African Political Economy, 25(75), March 1998
From Civil War to Civil Society - The transition from war to peace in Guatemala and Liberia. - World Bank & Carter Center. Washington/Atlanta, 1998
ACCORD - The Liberian Peace Process 1990-1996, by J. Armon and A. Carl (eds). Conciliation Resources, London, 1996

Selected Internet Sites
www.hirondelle.org (offers quick and easy access to the independent Star Radio station of Monrovia)
www.gis.net/~toadoll/ (news on Liberia, connectivity to other relevant sites, including the BBC's Africa service)
www.emory.edu/CARTER_CENTER/homepage (mission reports on Liberia and the Carter Center's work there)
www.unorg/Depts/DPKO/Missions/Unomil (UN Department of Peacekeeping Operations, information on UNOMIL, also background and all UN Security Council resolutions on Liberia)

Resource Contacts
Samuel K. Woods - fax +31 70 381 8058
Etweda Cooper/Massa Washington - secretary-general and information officer at the Liberian Women's Initiative
Bob Dillon - director LOIC
Stephen Ellis - Africa Studie Centrum, Leiden/The Netherlands. Email Ellis@fsw.LeidenUniv.nl
David Carroll - The Carter Center. Email dcarrol@emory.edu
Addai Sebbo - former program manager International Alert
Bineta Diop - FAS

Organisations
LOIC
Matadi
Monrovia
Tel: +231 226 337

Fondation Hirondelle
3 Rue Traversière
CH 1018 Lausanne
Switzerland
Tel. +41 21 647 2804
Fax +41 21 647 4469
Email info@hirondelle.org
http://www.hirondelle.org

Data on the following organisations can be found in the Directory section
Catholic Justice and Peace Commission
Centre for Democratic Empowerment
Femmes Africa Solidaire (FAS)
International Alert
Liberian Women's Initiative
SUSUKUU
The Carter Centre
Oxfam

Mali

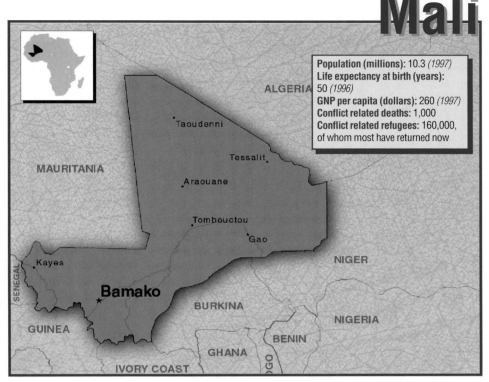

Population (millions): 10.3 *(1997)*
Life expectancy at birth (years): 50 *(1996)*
GNP per capita (dollars): 260 *(1997)*
Conflict related deaths: 1,000
Conflict related refugees: 160,000, of whom most have returned now

ALGERIA

MAURITANIA

Taoudenni

Tessalit

Araouane

Tombouctou

Gao

NIGER

Kayes

SENEGAL

Bamako

BURKINA

NIGERIA

GUINEA

BENIN

GHANA

TOGO

IVORY COAST

Successful Mediation Effort Could Lead to Lasting Peace

Timbuktu, March 27, 1996: a huge pile of burning guns symbolises the end of a small but persistent conflict between successive governments of the landlocked West African state of Mali and armed Tuareg rebels in the North of the country. Local peace initiatives, backed up by an appropriate international response have worked to bring the fighting to an end. This successful peace mediation effort, however, does not hide the fact that the basic problems that underpin the conflict remain. There is still work to do if a real and lasting peace is to take hold in Mali ◆ *By* **Bram Posthumus**

The Tuareg are a nomadic people, about 1.5 million strong, who live in the vast semi-desert area known as the Sahel. The territory that they and their cousins have inhabited and traversed for centuries straddles various present-day states including Mali, Niger, Chad and Mauritania.

About 600,000 Tuareg live in Mali, mainly in the northern part of the country. With the advent of more centralised states in Mali, such as the Bambara empire, traditional Tuareg nomadic lifestyles began to be curtailed. When the French

colonialists arrived, their movements were further restricted through the imposition of borders. Since a nomadic lifestyle is vital for the maintenance of their living standards, these subsequently started to decline. It was under French rule - in 1894 - that the Tuareg turned to armed-rebellion. Like every uprising that was to follow, it was a drought that pushed the Tuareg into action. The French colonisers resorted to force, both in the nineteenth century and again in 1916, to crush Tuareg uprisings with considerable brutality.

In fact, every Tuareg action was brutally suppressed, leaving hundreds dead. This only succeeded in fuelling resentment against central governments that used sticks and guns rather than their ears to solve the problems of the peoples in the North. It was not until the 1990s that there was a change of heart on the part of the authorities.

Under French rule, the Tuareg considered themselves thoroughly marginalised, both economically and politically. Malian independence in 1960 did not change their situation and matters were certainly not helped by the fact that Mali opted for a tightly controlled one-party political system in its efforts to build a nation. As early as 1963, the central government of Modibo Keita found itself faced with the first post-independence rebellion. The government of the day responded once again with a heavy hand. It bombed rebel positions, causing many casualties and even greater resentment among the Tuareg.

The root causes of the conflict are complex. Before borders divided West Africa into nations, the nomadic peoples of the Sahel crossed the vast territory from Mali into what is now Algeria. Confinement in a national state brought no benefits and in fact worsened their situation. There was a total lack of development, the conveniences of modern life - if the Tuareg had wanted them - were not available to them, there was a dire shortage of water and other resources in the region, which was further compounded by the devastating droughts of the 1970s and 1980s. These droughts destroyed traditional family structures. Many young men went away looking for greener pastures (quite literally). The droughts also put severe pressure on the relationships between the Tuareg and the sedentary farmers in the region, who - as Ibrahim ag Youssouf and Robin-Edward Poulton argue in their book *A Peace of Timbuktu* - traditionally relied on each other for economic survival. French colonial legislation that distinguished between the two groups and put legislation in place which favoured sedentary farmers over nomadic people has, however, contributed to the marginalisation of the North.

These structural tensions came to a head in 1990 when the young men who fled the drought,

mainly into Libya and Algeria, came back with revolutionary ideas, acquired in Libya, about how to translate their political under-representation into a cause. The Libyans had also provided them with the guns to pursue that cause. On June 28, 1990, they attacked the town of Menaka in the east of the country, marking the start of the rebellion.

Conflict Dynamics

At first, the response of the military government of General Moussa Traoré, who ousted Keita in 1968, was identical to the repressive actions the previous colonial and independent governments. The activities of the MPLA (Popular Liberation Movement of Azaouad, established in 1988 in Libya and receiving help from Tripoli), were met with the usual iron-fisted response. Most of the scores of casualties were civilians. It was the political situation in the capital, Bamako, which changed this. Widespread demonstrations put the Traoré government under great pressure and in March 1991, a coup swept colonel Amadou Toumani Touré to power. 'ATT,' as he is affectionately known in Mali, held a National Conference to map out the country's political future with a great variety of stakeholders, negotiated a peace agreement with the rebels and prepared the way for democratic elections. Following these elections, Alpha Oumar Konaré became president of the country, in 1992.

Interestingly, the military within General Traoré's government may have already laid some of the foundations for a lasting peace, by negotiating the Tamanrasset Peace Agreement just before he was ousted. Although nobody respected the terms of the agreement, it did contain some of the building blocks for Touré's subsequent efforts. Touré began from the premise that neither the French nor the previous independent governments had found real answers to the Tuareg issue. He directed his efforts towards concluding a National Reconciliation Pact, which was signed by government and rebel representatives on April 11 1992. It provided for a certain degree of autonomy for the North, a special development fund for the region, the reintegration of the fighters and repatriation of the tens of thousands of refugees.

However, the Pact failed to break the cycle of violence, for three reasons. Firstly, lack of financial support sank its implementation in the course of 1993. Secondly, the original MPLA started to show signs of fragmentation along regional, hierarchical, religious and Tuareg-Arab lines, and in 1994 these splinters began fighting among each other. This fighting became so severe that when negotiations finally re-started in the southern Algerian town of Tamanrasset in the same year, the Malian government found itself mediating among the various factions before national peace could actually begin to be discussed. And thirdly, whatever their differences, the Tuareg and Moorish groups continued to feel short-changed in terms of security and representation. They increased the intensity of their rebellion in the course of 1994.

The conflict went through its last phase of escalation before peace could finally prevail. Killings by the rebel groups and revenge killings committed by the armed forces became more widespread. This presented the greatest challenge yet to both Malian and regional stability. Countries like Niger, grappling with a similar problem, were particularly concerned about the escalation. A final complication was brought about by a new vigilante group, called Ganda Koy, meaning Masters of the Land. This was the armed manifestation of the concern of citizens, including non-rebel Tuareg, who simply had enough of the violence and lawlessness around them. Consequently, a peace process needed to be set in motion as a matter of urgency.

The apparent success of that process is largely due to the collaborative efforts of all major players in the conflict: fighters, the military, traditional leaders, the president of the country, local, African and international NGOs, donor countries and the UN.

In the course of 1995, the violence receded. A series of locally mediated agreements feeding into the national process of reducing violence and building peace resulted in the actual cantonment of the fighters and the simultaneous closure of their bases. The exercise began in November 1995 and ended in February 1996 with close to 2,700 combatants being encamped. Of those, over 1,600 have since found jobs in one of the branches of the public security sector or followed courses to diversify into business or agriculture.

As a crowning ceremony of these achievements and a symbolic lesson for the future, it was decided to bring together all the players in the former conflict and burn the weapons of war in their presence. This was done on March 27, 1996, in the northern town of Timbuktu. The *'Flamme de la Paix'*, as the bonfire became known, was attended by representatives from the former rebel factions, Ganda Koy, Ghanaian President Jerry Rawlings in his capacity as Chairman of the Economic Community of West African States, and a host of international observers. Three thousand weapons were burnt. In a meeting between thirteen West African states and 23 arms exporting nations, held in Oslo in April 1998, President Konaré mentioned the instructive character of the Flame of Peace, and its importance for impressing upon people the necessity of having a pluralist, tolerant, just and democratic Mali, in which violence as a means to settle differences would be looked upon as a thing of the past.

Official Conflict Management

The Malian peace efforts seem to have been successful because the local, regional, national and international initiatives somehow managed to interlock successfully and on time. Key elements identified by observers and participants like the UN Resident Coordinator in Mali, Mr. Tore Rose, include the fact that the peace process was essentially home-grown and born out of a genuine desire to end the conflict, that UN support was adequate and timely, and that the government's 'Security First' programme (which will be explained below) was taken seriously and regarded as absolutely crucial - and supported accordingly.

United Nations support for the demobilisation was crucial at a time when none of the donors were ready to provide the required facilitating funds. The UN paid almost half the cost of the cantonment exercise (US$ 2 million) through the creation of a trust fund; significantly, the Malian government paid the other half. A fixed amount was set aside for each gun brought in.

The programme for the reintegration of the

ex-fighters (also partly financed from trust fund money) was another joint effort between the *government of Mali* and the UN. It was part of the government's 'Security First' policy. Essentially, the idea behind 'Security First' is that there can be no development if there is no functional and enforceable system of law and order in a given country. Given the history of banditry in the northern part of the country, the fact that security was foremost in the government's mind was not surprising. But this particular concept is more comprehensive than the presence of large numbers of security personnel on the streets and in the countryside. 'Security First' interlocks good governance, good economic performance with the rule of law, which is enforceable by reliable security personnel. All this is to be realised both nationally and regionally. The arguments put forward by both the Malian government and the UN were convincing enough to persuade the donor community - especially NGOs - to think about ways of supporting the police, customs services and other security personnel in Mali, and indeed elsewhere.

The reintegration programme of ex-combatants was begun in 1995. Essentially, it encompassed first the cantonment and disarmament and then the integration of the 11,500 fighters into either the national army or civilian society. They received pocket money and US$ 100 for each gun handed in. They would then undergo military training or social and economic education. Some 1,600 former combatants have thus been integrated in the security forces while 9,000 benefited from the civilian integration programme.

Another aspect of removing large-scale violence from Malian society is the reform of the military, which was responsible for some of the worst human rights violations. Training and improved communication skills are intended to contribute to a better security force which will earn the trust of the public. It is hoped that people will then also surrender the guns they still possess. Thus far, the funds for this integrated double-edged programme, widely regarded as crucial, have been insufficient to carry it out in its entirety. Funding until recently came from the United Nations Development

Program (UNDP), three EU member states, the USA and Japan.

Because the feeling of political marginalisation was so strong among those who rebelled against the central government in Bamako, the Malian government has also decided to embark on a policy of decentralisation. The aim is to give more discretionary powers to the local authorities. The Konaré government has always stressed the importance of local decision-making bodies and local elections. After all, the peace process itself was started at the local level. If successful, decentralisation will free up local resources for local development and diminish dependence on a distant central government.

In 1994, President Konaré asked UN Secretary-General Boutros Ghali to organise a mission to his country, to study the proliferation of small arms in and outside Mali. The presence of large amounts of small arms wreaks havoc on the region of West Africa, where there is war in Casamance, a shaky cease-fire in Sierra Leone, instability in Guinea-Bissau, Liberia, Nigeria and Niger and where guns circulate from Freetown (Sierra Leone) to Faya (Chad). Konaré, who has described the flow of arms as 'anarchic', therefore wanted UN recommendations relating to their removal. The UN complied and sent two missions to Mali and other countries in the region were also visited. Its recommendations included national committees for disarmament, upgraded legislation, weapons registers and regional exchange of information on flows of arms.

The Malian president has since proposed a three to five-year moratorium on the import, manufacture and sale of light weapons in the region. A three-year moratorium was signed on behalf of or by all heads of ECOWAS member states on October 31, 1998 in the Nigerian capital Abuja. It is the first agreement of this kind in the world and has since been receiving widespread international support from the UN, the Nordic countries and the Chair of the Wassenaar Arrangement, which is a grouping of 33 arms exporting nations that wishes to exercise control on the exports of - among others - conventional weapons. (The Wassenaar Arrangement has grown out of COCOM, which

MALI, pile of guns at the 'Flame of Peace'

HENNY VAN DER GRAAF

was a Cold War instrument to keep sensitive technology out of the hands of the Soviet Union.) The Malian government is looking for financial support for a regional centre which will be tasked with implementing and monitoring the moratorium. Funding has, unfortunately, proved problematic.

The UN has also helped organise several Dutch government-funded seminars on the security situation in the country and the region. These included a Malian seminar on civil-military relationships, which has greatly helped in the redefinition of the role of the military in Mali. It brought generals, members of the civil society and political leaders together in an unprecedented discussion of these topics. The seminar took place in Bamako in November 1996 and has since been followed up by another, in November 1997. A preliminary code of conduct was drafted, in order to define more precisely the role of the Malian military. The other important event was the meeting, in New York, of all sixteen members of the Economic Community of West African States (ECOWAS) on post-violence peace building.

Throughout the peace negotiations, discreet but extremely helpful mediation was carried out by the governments of *Algeria* and *France*. Especially Algeria helped to bring about some unity among the rebels as early as 1991 (they had already started to factionalise by then). There were also briefings by observers at the various series of talks in 1995 and 1996 who briefed the governments of both countries about progress. Together with the UN, France and Algeria were important supporters of the 'Security First' programme.

Multi-Track Diplomacy
Domestic

The foundations for the peace in Mali are local. Tuareg chiefs, religious and community leaders, civil society organisations started convening an impressive series of meetings at the local level from early 1994. When one talks about the 'social capital' used to foster peace in Mali, this is it: embracing the African tradition, where decisions are taken at the village council, where elders preside over a discussion involving the entire community. 'Social capital', defined in *A Peace of Timbuktu* as 'the sum of human cultural and spiritual values and patterns of personal interaction in a society', has been the driving force behind the entire peace process. The national government was keenly aware of this and endorsed it, in fact it had no choice. Participants at the hundreds of meetings that took place from 1994 through 1996 included local leaders as mentioned, social and religious organisations, political parties, the administration, trade unions, NGOs, women's organisations, economic cooperatives and associations. All these meetings stressed the inseparable relationship between security and peace.

The fact that these local initiatives were actually noticed and taken seriously by outside players is a credit to both the UN and the international African NGO *Synergies Afrique*. Firstly, Synergies organised a regional meeting on the Tuareg conflict where politicians and legal experts from the various countries in the region got together to discuss the problem. When Synergies director Hassan Ba visited the region in January 1995, he found that traditional leaders ('chefs') were willing to make their ancient networks available for use as vehicles for national and cross-border deliberations which could lead to peace. The chefs met in Ouagadougou, Burkina Faso in March 1995 and later in the year held local meetings. They succeeded in bringing together the older, more sedate chiefs and the angry young men with the guns, two groups which had until then been difficult to reconcile.

As mothers, wives and sisters, women exercise considerable influence in the various societies that together make up Mali. This fact, embedded in many of the proverbs that oil social life in Mali and elsewhere in West Africa, is frequently overlooked by outsiders, but this part of the country's 'social capital' is of course never lost on actors from within. The *Mouvement National des Femmes pour la Paix* has played an important facilitating role, for instance resulting in local groups beginning to collect arms spontaneously, in a reflection of the government's 'Security First' policy. This and other women's organisations were at the forefront of the peace process.

Various international NGOs have stepped in and started development projects in the North, possibly helping to provide the best guarantees against the return of violence. The African *ACORD*, and European and American NGOs, are all engaging in livestock, fisheries, agricultural and other income generating projects that are aimed to reduce the economic marginalisation of the region.

Together with international NGOs like *Oxfam* and *Novib*, ACORD also helped finance a scientific analysis of the conflict, entitled *Nord du Mali. De la tragédie à l'espoir* (Northern Mali, from tragedy to hope). The analysis was conducted by three West African scholars and published in July 1995.

Norwegian Church Aid has been instrumental in mobilising resources to enable civil society meetings to take place. It is also expected that donor funds that were held back pending the outcome of the conflict will now gradually be released. Tentative moves into the area have been made by development NGOs.

Prospects

Mali provides living proof that peace building on local foundations is a lot cheaper than restoring faith, confidence, bridges, roads and buildings after the fact. What has succeeded here is the combination of the 'social capital' of its people, traditionally available in abundance, with the workings of modern statehood and international mediation. As Amadou Toumani Touré asserted in an interview with a Dutch newspaper in February 1997: 'Mali is a modern democracy with its very own traditions.'

This also applies to the political aspirations of the North, which were not served by the highly centralised forms of government under the French and the first post-independent regimes. Robin-Edward Poulton, senior research fellow at the UN Institute for Disarmament Research, who has worked on conflict resolution for many years in West Africa, describes the Konaré approach as 'ambitious' and 'visionary'.

Observing that 'most of Africa's states will flourish in the 21st century only if they are able to reconcile the need for broader economic or monetary unions with the pressure from local groups to assume their cultural identities,'

Poulton concludes that 'decentralisation is the new framework which will make people responsible for their own lives, for mobilising national resources and using them locally for productive investment.'

There has been political volatility and violent protest in Bamako around the elections that were held in 1997, which led to the arrest of several opposition politicians. In January, a National Forum was held in Bamako, in a government bid to address the political and institutional problems in Mali. There have also been student protests in the capital in 1998 and 1999, although these revolve mainly around bread-and-butter issues. President Konaré appears to take it in his stride, as he told the Guinean weekly *Le Lynx* in June 1999: 'Opposition is not a mistake, it is a demand of democracy.'

The political turbulence does not appear to have had an adverse effect on the peace now existing in northern Mali. In the course of 1997 and 1998 there were reports of violent clashes between Tuareg from Mali and Niger but these appear to be rivalries among local clans over water and grazing rights, without anti-government or rebel overtones. The clashes took place within Niger, where problems persist between the Tuaregs and the very repressive military government of general Mainassara, which was overthrown in April 1999. However, as Dutch brigadier-general (ret) Henny van der Graaf, who frequently visits Mali to help facilitate and monitor the process knows, Tuareg fighters have withheld arms, calling this their own version of the 'Security First' programme. Small arms remain present in the region in large numbers.

Recommendations

Ultimately, it will be the social and economic development of the North that will provide the best insurance against the return of violence.

Mali is fortunate in being, at present, an important destination for donor money and has been able to continue large parts of its ambitious reintegration programme for ex-combatants. Nevertheless, there is a danger that structures and institutions will be built up that bypass precisely those local and other structures that have been responsible for bringing the conflict to an end. These are potential seeds for renewed conflict.

One way of avoiding this is to have the donor efforts coordinated in-country, by a body that is representative of the recipients. The need for donors to conform to realities on the ground, instead of the other way around rises from the pages of *A Peace of Timbuktu* time and again, especially where the authors share their worries about the fact that the various major international organisations carry out their projects but do not seem to be engaged in helping to strengthen the institutions of Mali's civil society.

In *The Weapon Heritage of Mali*, authors Van der Graaf and Poulton argue for a programme tying weapons collection to community development assistance. Instead of providing cash payments to individuals who hand in their weapons, development assistance should be provided to communities for programmes targeting, for example, improved water systems, health care, and education. While a 'Flame of Peace' is in itself both practically and symbolically valuable, development of the weapons programme would not only help to reduce the number of weapons in circulation, but also to bring communities together to provide for both security and development, and quite possibly to prevent those who hand in a weapon from simply going out and acquiring a new one. Funding this project may well be one of the best investments one can make in Mali.

Service Information

Reports
ACORD
- Nord du Mali - De la tragédie à l'espoir. (Information available from ACORD Mali)

UN Centre for Disarmament Affairs
- Sahara-Sahel Mission Report, 1996

Other Publications
Civil Society Takes Responsibility - Popular involvement in the peace process in Mali, by Kare Lode. Oslo, International Peace Research Institute, 1997
A Peace of Timbuktu - Democratic governance, development and African peacemaking, by Robin E. Poulton and Ibrahim ag Youssouf. New York, NY: United Nations Publications, 1998
The Weapon Heritage of Mali, by Henny van der Graaf and Robin E. Poulton. Chapter in publication of the Bonn International Centre for Conversion: 'Weapons Collection and Disposal as an Element of Post-Settlement Peacebuilding.' 1998
A Moratorium on Light Weapons in West Africa, by Sverre Lodgaard and Carsten Rønnfeldt (eds). Published by the Norwegian Institute of International Affairs and the Norwegian Initiative on small arms transfers, 1998
Peacemaking by Consensus in Mali. In: People Building Peace, European Centre for Conflict Prevention, Utrecht, 1999

Resource Contacts
Ousmane Sako - UNDP (PNUD), Bamako/Mali
Tore Rose - UNDP (PNUD), Bamako/Mali
Marianne Maïga - Mouvement National des Femmes pour la Paix, Bamako/Mali
Rita Mba - ACORD, Bamako/Mali
Hassan Ba - Synergies Africa, Geneva, Switzerland. Email hassanba@iprolink.ch
Brigadier-general (ret.) *Henny van der Graaf* - Arms Control and Verification Mission Mission. Email h.j.v.d.graaf@phys.tue.nl
Halvor Aschjem - Norwegian Church Aid

Selected Internet Sites
www.halcyon.com/pub/FWDP/Africa/tuareg.txt (a pro-Tuareg site)
www.worldlynx.net/tamazgha/imucagh.html (a Tuareg information site with links to a large number of documents and other sites on this issue)
www.geocities.com/NapaValley/2111/Mali.html (non-official Malian site with news, history and good connectivity)
www.malinet.ml/palabre/presse/les_echos (Bamako newspapers, regularly updated)

Organisations
ACORD
BP 1969
Bamako
Mali
Tel. +223 220 948
Fax +223 228 216

PNUD (UNDP)
Bamako, Mali
Tel. +223 - 223 694
Fax +223 225820

Norwegian Church Aid
P.O. Box 4544 Torshov
0404 Oslo
Norway
Tel. +47 2222 2299
Fax +47 2222 2420
Email nca-oslo@sn.no

Data on the following organisations can be found in the Directory section
Institut International de la Paix et la Securité
Mouvement National des Femmes pour la Paix
Synergies Afrique
Oxfam

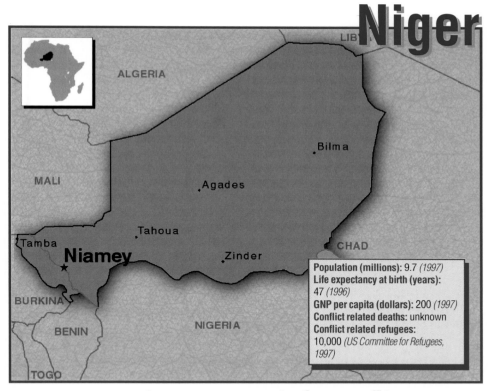

Population (millions): 9.7 *(1997)*
Life expectancy at birth (years):
47 *(1996)*
GNP per capita (dollars): 200 *(1997)*
Conflict related deaths: unknown
Conflict related refugees:
10,000 *(US Committee for Refugees, 1997)*

A Long History, a Brief Conflict, an Open Future

Following the colonisation of West Africa by the French and its independence in the early 1960s, the Tuaregs, former masters of the Sahelian part of this region, found themselves increasingly impoverished minorities in new nation states. One of those states was Niger, where Tuareg perceptions of marginalisation have been aggravated by the fact that the country's economic mainstay - uranium - is extracted from their soil while the economic rewards appear to be reaped elsewhere. Two devastating droughts in the 1970s and 1980s all but destroyed their material support base. When Niger's political system opened up in the late 1980s, the economy went into decline. There was a short but sharp conflict between the Tuareg and the government, which ended peacefully in 1995. However political unrest, continuing poverty and new rebellions make for an uncertain future ◆ *By* **Bram Posthumus**

A nomadic people, about 1.5 million strong, the Tuareg live in the vast semi-desert area known as the Sahel. The territory in which they and their cousins have lived for centuries straddles various present-day nation states including Mali, Niger, Chad and Mauritania.

When the French colonising army arrived in the area now known as Niger in the nineteenth century, wars, Tuareg slave raids and reprisal expeditions had been going on for some time. The French turned the area into their Third Military Territory and managed to 'pacify' it.

325

There was one serious Tuareg uprising in 1916-17, which was the result of famine, a harsh tax regime and the French recruitment drive for its troops fighting the 1914-1918 war in Europe. This rebellion was brutally suppressed.

The French administration also subdivided the population into two distinct groups, nomads -including Tuareg and Toubou- and sedentary farmers, thereby complicating the relationship between these groups who are economically interdependent. The state of Niger was created by a Decree issued in 1920. The colonial regime was highly centralised and came to be dominated by the second largest group in the territory, the Djerma-Songhai. The French provided them with formal education and put them in charge of the state administration and the army, much to the chagrin of the majority Hausa, who comprise about half of Niger's population. In the late 1950s, this political constellation assumed the shape of a one-party state, following the dissolution of the opposition socialist Sawaba Party ('sawaba' is Hausa for Freedom). Hausa elements were blamed for a brief rebellion, four years into independence -in 1964-, which was crushed in a matter of weeks. A period of relative calm followed.

In 1974, Lt.Col. Seyni Kountché seized power in a military coup. Military rule coincided with the golden age of Niger's economy, fuelled by uranium which had been found in Tuareg territory and was mined at the behest of the booming French nuclear industry. Kountché, who headed a regime which was primarily known for its profligacy and its repression, died in 1987 and was succeeded by his cousin Ali Saibou, who opened up the country's political system. This led to a prolonged transitional phase with a National Conference in 1991 - one of the first in Francophone Africa - and elections two years later.

Over the years, the pastoralist lifestyle of the Tuaregs, who comprise ten per cent of Niger's population, changed dramatically. Firstly, state borders restricted their movement. Secondly, droughts in the 1970s and 1980s laid waste to large swathes of the Sahel region. Thousands of cattle were lost and with them, the basis of the Tuareg economy. The droughts sent tens of thousands of Arab and Tuareg herdsmen looking

for opportunities in Niger's oil-rich northern neighbours, Algeria and Libya, where they met Malian Tuaregs who had similar problems. They harboured dissatisfaction with their loss of culture, their poor living conditions, the fact that uranium was taken from their land without proper recompense, and their perceived lack of political influence. While in Libya and with Libyan aid, Nigerien Tuaregs set up a fledgling *Popular Front for the Liberation of Niger* (FPLN) in exile. In 1985, it launched an attack on Tchin-Tabaradene, 500 kilometres from the capital, Niamey. Niger broke off official ties with Libya in 1981. The authorities in Niamey continue to regard the Ghadaffi government in Tripoli with suspicion.

Saibou tried to entice the Tuaregs back into Niger. In the late 1980s, a major repatriation operation took place, involving 18,000 people, one-third of whom were Tuaregs. It suffered from lack of resources -Niger's uranium boom was over, the country had dipped into recession and had been forced to accept IMF-prescribed structural economic reforms- and the returnees were not satisfied with what they found. Neither were they regarded favourably by the other Nigeriens, who saw them as layabouts. The 'Aide aux Repatriées' project never fulfilled its objectives and the government came under attack for alleged embezzlement of the project funds. Dissatisfaction grew and arms were readily available from (among others) war-torn Chad.

In May 1990, Tchin-Tabaradene was attacked again and this marked the beginning of the rebellion proper, which the government tried to suppress militarily, while denying it was a rebellion. Attacks, counter-attacks, negotiations, violent incidents and the fragmentation of the original armed rebellion into various factions marked the progress of the conflict between 1990 and 1994, when a peace deal was signed with most of the rebel groups. The cease-fire held into 1995, while negotiations were extended to include some of the groups that had previously remained outside the peace process.

The military coup of January 27, 1996 put an end to a year-long political standoff between President Mahamane Ousmane and Prime Minister Hama Amadou, which had paralysed the first democratically elected government in

Niger's history. General Ibrahim Baré Mainassara was initially credited with ending the impasse, but the political climate worsened as his hold on power increased. When he was shot and killed by army officers on April 9, 1999, the prevailing public sentiment was one of relief. Civil society representatives hoped that things would begin to improve again. The new strongman, General Daouda Mallam Wanke, has since formed a national transitional government, announced presidential elections for October and a handover of power on December 31, 1999. He has also paved the way for a new Constitution.

Although punctuated by incidents, the peace process has remained largely on track. With the aid of the UNHCR, a few hundred refugees have begun to return to Niger. But there are worrying signs of another rebellion in the southeastern Diffa region which borders Chad. The Toubou who staged uprisings in 1995 and 1997-98, complain about massacres perpetrated by the government army, in which almost 200 people are reported to have been killed. Many Toubou have fled to Nigeria and refuse to return. Low-intensity fighting continues in the Diffa region.

Conflict Dynamics

The Tuareg attack on Tchin-Tabaradene, in May 1990, resulted in 31 deaths, including 25 of the attackers. In response, the army was sent in and, unable to find the attackers, the soldiers turned on the population, killing 63 people (according to the government), at least 600 (say humanitarian organisations) and 1,500 (according to the rebels). This happened while preparations for the National Conference were going on. Unfortunately, the dynamics of the national political process in Niger were not able to prevent violence of this unprecedented magnitude.

An official inquiry into this single biggest incident in the conflict was set up and its findings were presented to the National Conference in September 1991. The Conference censured the army, which had already conducted a purge of its ranks, immediately after the Tchin-Tabaradene events. The army, in its turn, considered itself humiliated by the National Conference-sponsored condemnation. Soldiers staged mutinies in a number of major cities

including Niamey, Agadez and Zinder in the following years. The first of these resulted in the release from prison of the man who had led the government actions at Tchin-Tabaradene. Soldiers also 'arrested' cabinet ministers, especially if they were Tuareg, in clear defiance of the political process towards democracy, as embodied in the National Conference.

The Tuaregs themselves, meanwhile, found insufficient redress in the army censure and while the National Conference was still going on they announced the launch of the *Front de Libération de L'Aïr et de Azaouak* (FLAA). The FLAA existed as a unified force only for a short while. In June 1992, it split along three fault-lines: according to traditional political entities (Tuareg society is divided in a number of identifiable classes), along clan lines, and according to geographical loyalties (there are differences between the Aïr and the Azaouak Tuaregs). This process of fragmentation and re-alignment continued throughout the conflict but the unifying factor remained: the demand for land, cultural dignity and political representation. This was clear from the document released in February 1994, by the newly-formed umbrella organisation, the *Coordination de la Résistance Armée* (CRA). The CRA called for, among other things, the formation of a federation, punishment of those involved in what it called the Tchin-Tabaradene massacre, and constitutional change. A number of observers, including André Bourgeot, note that rejection of these demands by the Nigerien parliament was inevitable, as giving in would have meant signing away much of Niger's landmass - and its uranium.

Between 1992 and 1994, the conflict rumbled on: villages were attacked, people displaced and suspected rebels were arrested by security personnel. A particularly dangerous incident occurred in September 1992, when Tuareg gunmen captured and beat up government soldiers and policemen, whereupon soldiers in Agadez threatened to kill 110 Tuaregs they held captive, if their colleagues were not released. Officers managed to restore order and prevent mass bloodshed.

Talks between the democratically elected government and the rebels had, in the meantime, begun. A truce was reached in March

1993 and one year later peace talks began in earnest. They were held in Ouagadougou, Burkina Faso. In October 1994, an agreement was signed, aimed at ending the conflict within six months. The CRA had meanwhile been subject to more re-alignments and it was the Organisation of the Armed Resistance (ORA) which finally signed the agreement on behalf of most of the rebel groups. This happened in Niamey on April 24, 1995. In the document, provisions were made for demilitarisation, reintegration of Tuaregs into Nigerien society, restructuring of the army, plans for the decentralisation of authority and creating conditions for peace and national reconciliation. Encampment of the groups that signed the agreement was completed in June 1997.

Three groups, united in the Union of the Armed Resistance Forces (UFRA) and a new Toubou rebel group did not sign. Unfortunately, implementation of the Peace Agreement was also extremely slow, due in part to the endless political wrangling between President Mahamane Ousmane and his Prime Minister. These delays led to tensions and fresh violence in the north, involving UFRA. There was a small-scale uprising in September 1997, which killed 27 people and lasted one month. An additional peace accord with UFRA was signed in Algiers on November 28, 1997 by the military government of General Mainassara who had seized power in the meantime. UFRA handed over its remaining weapons in Agadez during a special ceremony in June 1998. This left the Toubou rebel group which continued its activities in the east. It was reported to have attacked a village in July 1998, but barely a month later it was said to have signed a cease-fire with the government. In April 1999, reports of a massacre of Toubou men emerged. The crime was committed under the Mainassara government, posing a new challenge to a fragile transition process. In June 1999, the Toubou leader Issa Lamine accused the new military government of killing civilians. At the same time, peace talks were reported to be under way in Niamey.

Official Conflict Management

The United Nations has not been directly involved in managing the conflict, but the organisation is dealing with a closely related issue: the proliferation of small arms in the region. In 1993, at the request of President Konaré of Mali, it set up an Advisory Mission on the issue. The mission reported its findings to the Secretary-General in 1996. It identified a variety of causes for the unfettered flow of arms, including political instability, poverty, unemployment, ethnic and religious differences and the spill-over of intra-state conflicts into other states. This was said to apply to most of the states visited during the mission, including Niger. It has recommended action to control the flow of arms.

Neighbouring countries as well as the former colonial power, France, have played significant roles in bringing the Tuareg conflict to an end. Especially Algeria, Burkina Faso and France have been instrumental in moving the talks forward. They were asked to mediate in 1992. Burkina Faso offered facilities for the peace talks. First, their combined efforts led to the truce of March 1993 and then to the October 1994 Peace Agreement.

The Nigerien Government, like its counterpart in Bamako, Mali, first tried to solve the rebellion by refusing to acknowledge its existence. During November 1991, however, both governments came together to find ways of ending the rebellions.

In January 1992, the then Prime Minister, Cheiffou, called on the rebels to disarm and the Tuaregs replied with their demands. Talks started between the FLAA and government representatives, and in May 1992, the parties issued a joint communiqué, in which a commitment to creating a favourable climate for negotiations was declared. It did not immediately help calm the situation, but prepared the ground for further negotiations. A truce was reached in March 1993, while the government had in the meantime created a ministerial portfolio to deal with the rebellion and national reconciliation. In spite of continued violence, the two parties decided to extend the truce in June. The constant fragmentation meant that negotiations had to be initiated with each and every new faction that had declared its willingness to engage in peace talks. As a result, in 1993, the government held peace talks with at least five different groups.

NIGER, Resettlement project for Peuhl and Touareg, alfabetisation

In January 1994, just before renewed talks with some of the factions, the government created the *Haut Commissariat à la Restauration de la Paix et la Conciliation de l'Unité Nationale -* whose title neatly summarised its brief: restoring peace and working out an arrangement within the framework of national unity. The official talks, held between March and October 1994, resulted in the Ouagadougou Peace Accord, which - with a few additions - still stands.

Another government action, welcomed by the UN Mission mentioned earlier, was the creation in November 1994 of the *National Commission on the Collection and Control of Illicit Arms.* The government has estimated the number of illicitly circulating guns in the country at 30,000, of which roughly ten per cent have been seized.

The hallmark of all Nigerien governments, military, civilian or mixed, has been their efforts at nation-building, including the integration (some would say 'assimilation') of the nomadic peoples into the nation state and the banning of ethnically-based political parties or movements.

Unsurprisingly, one of the demands put forward by the rebels was that of federalism, which, equally unsurprisingly, was and remains anathema in government circles in Niamey. Successive administrations have made attempts in the past to reflect the composition of Nigerien society by including Djerma-Songhai, Hausa, Tuareg and representatives of other peoples in the administration. However, these attempts at (some would say 'token') ethnic balancing were far outweighed by the centralist tendencies of successive Nigerien governments. Moreover, clientelism took over from nation-building and as a result, the battle for political control between Djerma-Songhai and Hausa was more immediate and relevant than the plight of the marginalised nomads in the far corners of the country. Only when the political system started to be opened up and the Tuaregs started using violence to reinforce their demands, did Niamey sit up and take notice. It was not so much the concept of the nation but the way it was enforced that estranged the nomadic peoples of Niger.

As far as the Toubou conflict is concerned, Chadian officials mediated the 1998 cease-fire between the Toubou rebels in Diffa and the Nigerien government but evidence on the ground suggests that holding fire has not been regarded as a viable option by either side.

Multi-Track Diplomacy

On February 9, 1990, the Niamey police opened fire on a peaceful demonstration of students who were protesting budget cuts in education, killing fourteen students. A week later, there was a 5,000-strong demonstration, protesting against the killings. Civilian organisations have since been a visible presence in Niger, which previously had no tradition of civil society.

In May 1991, one year after the events at Thin-Tabaradene, 10,000 people marched peacefully through Niamey, demanding fair treatment for the Tuareg. The march was organised by human rights groups and individual trade unions. Whether the powerful *Federation of Niger Trade Unions* also put its weight behind the demonstration is not fully clear; it was later reported to have backed army reprisals against Tuareg rebels.

There is a large and active human rights organisation in Niger, *Timidria*, which advocates the defence of human rights and the end to all forms of discrimination and tribalism. Timidria has an 80,000 strong membership. Whether it has played an active role in the peace settlement is not known, but it may well be a force that could prevent future violence.

Prospects

The Peace Accord between the government and most Tuareg groups has generally been honoured since it was signed in 1994. There have been sporadic attacks, the last of which was reported on July 25, 1998. The integration of the fighters of the various factions is under way. The peace plan, agreed in 1995, has a price tag of around US$ 60 million - small beer in a northern context but totally out of reach of a cash-strapped country with a US$ 1.6 billion foreign debt.

Whether the roots of the problem - real or perceived cultural, material and political disenfranchisement - have been removed, remains to be seen. The foreign-dominated

exploitation of uranium continues, but it is doubtful whether this will contribute in any way to Niger's development: demand has dropped and prices have been depressed for decades. Oil exploration is reportedly going on in the same - Tuareg - area.

In the meantime, Niger remains poor and near bankruptcy. *Jeune Afrique* reported in April 1999 that for the past six months, civil servants had received no salaries. In political terms, there remains uncertainty after the April coup: the political parties in Niger were reported, late June 1999, to have rejected the transition plan drawn up by the military.

On July 1, the military adopted a new constitution, providing for an elected president, a prime minister to be appointed by the president, and a General Assembly to whom the prime minister is answerable. Early August, General Wanke proclaimed the new Constitution legal and announced presidential elections, now to be held in November 1999.

Future trouble may come from either Nigeria, with which Niger has a sleeping border dispute, or from Algeria. In December 1998, the Nigerien army was involved in a search-and-destroy mission of a base, set up by Algerian Islamists, in which four soldiers died. In January 1999, the Nigerien police arrested eighteen people, suspected of actively supporting the armed fundamentalist movement in Algeria. Even more worrying is the nascent rebellion in the Diffa region, led by the Toubou group calling itself the *Democratic Front of Renewal* (FDR), which appears to have ties with Chadian rebel groups. Reports of massacres, allegedly committed by the Nigerien army in October 1998 and again in March-April 1999 in the Diffa region will do nothing to diminish tensions in the area. Finally, the continued availability of small arms in the entire region remains a destabilising factor.

Recommendations

The UN Advisory Mission on Small Arms made some recommendation to the Nigerien government - at the time still civilian - and included them in its report. Firstly, it concluded that Niger is among the countries most in need of international assistance. It went on to urge completion of the legislation regarding arms control and recommended an amnesty period, enabling people to hand in non-registered weapons. The Mission then went on to advise the government not to give in too easily to Tuareg demands, and especially not if the resources to match those promises were not in place.

Substantiating this view in his paper on the conflict in Niger, Prof. H.A. Sidikou offers some useful insights in the interrelationships between government policies, international finance and local conflicts. The Tuareg repatriation programme failed in part for lack of finance, which was -in a sense- due to the *Structural Adjustment Program* (SAP) that has just been put in place. The SAP had been necessitated by government profligacy following the short-lived uranium windfall. Sidikou points out that the

dilemma is that while Niger needs financial assistance to ensure a modicum of social peace, the conditions that are attached to the disbursement of that assistance may run counter to people's interests. In a context such as Niger, this may quickly translate into armed conflict.

Sidikou has also, tentatively, moved towards breaking the greatest political taboo in Niger and has cautiously suggested that perhaps a referendum on a kind of federalism might, in the long term, have some benefits. Again, money is an important part of the equation: decentralisation, as envisaged in the peace agreement, is simply too expensive. It would also be better to plan investments more carefully among the various regions in the country creating a kind of economic federalism.

Service Information

Publications

La Rebellion Tuareg au Niger - Du déclenchement du conflit à la signature de l'accord de paix. Harouna Rabi Abdoulaye. Niamey, 1996
Political exclusion - Democratization and Dynamics of ethnicity in Niger. Jibrin Ibrahim. In: Africa Today, 3rd Quarter, 1994
Les Causes des Conflits au Niger. Hamidou Arouna Sidikou (Pr). In: West Africa, Regional report, Clingendael, The Hague, 1999
Revoltes et rébellies en pays touareg. André Bourgeot. In: Afrique Contemporaine, nr. 170, 2me trimestre, 1994
Documentation for the seminar on intra-state conflict and options for policy, Clingendael, The Hague, November 1998

Selected Internet Sites

www.minorityrights.org (Minority Rights Group)
www.halcyon.com/pub/FWDP/Africa/tuareg.txt (a pro-Tuareg site)
www.worldlynx.net/tamazgha/imucagh.html (a Tuareg information site with links to a large number of documents and other sites on this issue)
www.itnet.ne/pnud_fr.html (UNDP site with information on Niger)
www.txdirect.net/users/jmayer/cet.html (Camel Express Télématique - news from Niger, about the only one available)

Nigeria

Transition, a New Opportunity to Transform Nigeria's Numerous Conflicts

Since June 1993, when the military government of Nigeria annulled a free and fair presidential election that was won by Moshood Abiola, the country has seemed poised on the brink of disaster. The suppression by a largely northern military regime of the election victory by a Yoruban candidate from south-west Nigeria intensified regional and ethnic conflict. The Ogoni people in the Niger Delta of the far south also called international attention to Nigeria with their protest against what they claimed was the despoliation of their land by the Shell Oil Company. When Nigeria's military dictator, general Sani Abacha, hanged nine Ogoni leaders, including writer Ken Saro-Wiwa, after unfair trials on murder charges in November 1995, the country's reputation reached its nadir ◆

By **Barnett R. Rubin and Judith Burdin Asuni***

The sudden death of Abacha in June 1998, as he was preparing to de-militarise his rule through a rigged 'transition' process, gave Nigeria another chance. Contrary to many expectations, his military successor, General Abdusalami Abubakar, gradually relaxed military rule and permitted a genuine transition to elected civilian rule. Though the February 1999 presidential election that brought former General and President Olusegun Obasanjo to power was marred by extensive fraud, the opening of political freedom and the election of local, state, and national governments presented Nigerians with one more opportunity to make their unwieldy country work.

Nigeria, created as an administrative convenience by the British empire in 1912, amalgamated many nations and peoples who had no reason to think of themselves as members of a common society. The tensions among these groups exploded into civil war in 1966, leading to the struggle over Biafra in which over a million died.

The subsequent rise in the price of oil and the discovery of more reserves presented Nigeria with further dilemmas. Dependent on the income from this one commodity for eighty per cent of government revenue and ninety per cent of foreign exchange, Nigeria followed the path of other oil states to massive corruption and institutional atrophication. The centralisation created by dependence on the oil revenue of the central government undermined the federalism and decentralisation required to integrate Nigeria's diverse population. Such a situation made the country ripe for military rule, but is also assured the corruption of the military rulers and the deterioration of the military itself, which some wiser generals seem finally to have realised. The revolt of the Ogoni, who demanded greater control of the production of and revenue from the oil extracted from their land, was only one symptom of this broader contradiction.

Nigeria's transition to an elected government under a leader known world wide (indeed better liked abroad than at home) for his work for peace and democracy provides some grounds for hope. The first months of the Obasanjo administration saw the beginning of a crackdown on corruption and the recovery of millions from Abacha's family and associates; the signing of a peace agreement in neighbouring Sierra Leone where Nigerian troops have been fighting as part of a regional peacekeeping force; the appointment of a commission of inquiry into the violations of human rights under the Abacha regime; a mission by the president himself to the tense regions of the Niger Delta; and the emergence of Nigeria once again as a respected and influential presence in the world. At the same time, it has seen a continuation of the high levels of ethnic and anti-state violence in several regions.

Communal killings of Hausa in the Yoruba city of Sagamu, followed by reprisals against Yorubas in the Hausa centre, Kano, left hundreds dead. President Obansanjo's visit to the Delta hardly interrupted the ongoing violence there, and new violence broke out in Aguleri. The transition gives Nigeria the opportunity, but no assurance, of being able to manage and transform its numerous conflicts.

In such a diverse country of perhaps one hundred million people, there are many conflicts, national, regional, and local. Our selection includes two conflicts involving ethnic protest against the central government (Yoruba versus the northern-dominated centralised state, and the Delta minorities against the oil multinationals and the state); a radical religious movement against the state that is concentrated in one large region, the north; and two local conflicts over access to resources, the Aguleri conflict in Eastern Nigeria and the Tiv-Jukun conflict in Wukari, in Nigeria's middle belt. Many more could be added, but these exemplify the many challenges to peace in Nigeria resulting from decades of economic mismanagement and political misrule.

*   Barnett R. Rubin is director of the Centre fot Preventive Action, based in New York. Judith Burdin Asuni is director of the Academic Associates PeaceWorks in Nigeria.

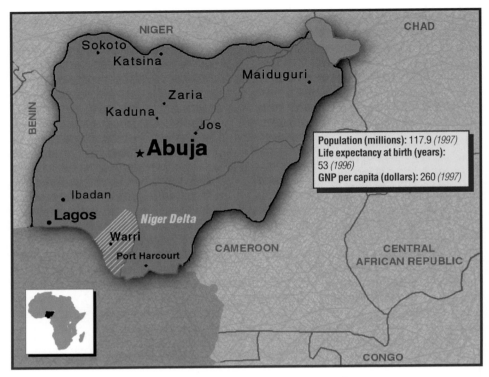

Population (millions): 117.9 (1997)
Life expectancy at birth (years):
53 (1996)
GNP per capita (dollars): 260 (1997)

Defending Nature, Protecting Human Dignity - Conflicts in the Niger Delta

The following article was written by advocates of the position taken by organisations of the indigenous people of the Niger Delta and does not attempt to give a 'balanced' account of one of Nigeria's most intense conflicts. While many groups in the Delta have been pressing for control of their resources and a larger degree of autonomy, the struggle of the Ogoni people is best known internationally, mainly as a result of the work of Ken Saro-Wiwa, the writer who was hanged with eight other Ogoni activists by the military regime of general San Abacha in November 1995. Saro-Wiwa attempted to enlarge the focus of the indigenous peoples' struggle beyond self-determination to include opposition to ecological devastation of the region ◆ *By* **Oronto Douglas and Doifie Ola***

S ince that time, however, other peoples of the Niger Delta have also mobilised, both against the state, and, tragically, at times against each other. Conflict in Warri between the Ijaw, Itsekiri, and Urhobo over control of a new local government established by the military regime has been particularly bloody and shows how the

Nigerian government has aggravated some of these conflicts.

The basic grievance of the peoples of the region is that most of Nigeria's wealth comes out of their soil, yet they gain no benefits and instead suffer much harm as a result. They blame both the repressive, centralised government and the oil companies for their plight, charging that the two are complicitous. The conflicts in the Niger Delta are thus the most visible and violent manifestations of the conflict between oil-driven centralisation and the society's demand for local control.

The oil companies claim that providing services to the Nigerian population is the responsibility of the Nigerian government, not of oil companies. They note that under the memorandum of agreement that permits foreign companies to operate joint ventures with the Nigerian National Petroleum Company, they receive less than US$1 per barrel, with the rest going to the NNPC. Nonetheless, a number of oil companies say they have supported community development programmes. Shell claims to spend about US$30 million per year on such programmes, including building schools and clinics and providing scholarships for youth from the area. Critics of these programmes claim they are little more than disguised bribes for corrupted local chiefs and hardly benefit the people. The oil companies admit to some such problems; Shell, for instance, has proposed implementing such programmes through NGOs.

The companies also argue that the mode of allocating oil revenue between the central government and local populations, as well as the provision of public services, are not decided by oil companies. They have offered, however, to share their experience of revenue sharing in other countries, such as Canada. They also claim that much of the environmental damage is not due directly to their operations but to the sabotage of pipelines by local people who then report the leaks and demand compensation. They have been the targets of some violent attacks, including the kidnapping of their employees, and they have shut down operations in some areas.

Under the military regime, the government executed Ogoni leaders and engaged in massive repression. General Abacha called the protesters 'unpatriotic Nigerians'. The government aggravated conflict in several areas by establishing further subdivisions of local governments. President Obasanjo became the first Nigerian head of state to visit the region, though his statements during his visit there

disappointed many. Incidents of violence continue, including violence by the Nigerian army, in which human rights groups charge Chevron with complicity. The dependence of the Nigerian central state on oil revenues makes decentralisation of control over resources demanded by these movements a sensitive issue for any national government. But resolving these conflicts will be the key test of whether Nigeria can create a genuine nation intent on living together and resolving conflicts peacefully, or whether it will remain a framework for violence among competing groups.

Causes of the Conflict

By popular perception, the exploitation of the peoples of the Niger Delta, the despoliation of their environment and the resultant conflicts have their roots in the discovery of oil in the area by Royal Dutch Shell in the late 1950s. Perception is however not reality as Europe's plunder of the resources of the Delta and the organised resistance of the indigenous peoples date back to the era of the slave trade. Countless men and women were simply plucked in their prime from the Delta and its hinterlands as in most other parts of Africa and shipped to work in North America and the West Indies, resulting in grave economic, social and political costs. With the abolition of slavery, there was a change to trade in palm oil in the first decades of the nineteenth century. Like the slave trade, palm oil trade never benefited the peoples of the Niger Delta as they were consciously cheated by the European traders.

Crude oil has since displaced palm oil as the principal resource for trade in the global market but the Niger Delta remains 'poor, backward and neglected' despite being the richest part of Nigeria in terms of natural resource endowment. There are large oil and gas deposits in the area as well as extensive forests, fertile agricultural land and enormous fish resources. The Niger Delta's potential for sustainable development however remains unfulfilled, and is now increasingly threatened by environmental degradation and worsening economic conditions. Particularly threatened is the mangrove forest of Nigeria - the largest in Africa and sixty per cent of which is located in the Niger Delta. Also facing extinction are the fresh water swamp forests of the Delta which at 11,700 km square are the most extensive in West and Central Africa - and the local people and fauna that depend on them for sustenance.

A 1995 World Bank report estimated that some ten per cent of the area's mangroves have been lost to deforestation triggered by the exploration and production activities of big multinational oil companies such as Shell, Chevron, Elf and Agip. The oil companies as well as government agencies have greatly contributed to agricultural land encroachment and environmental degradation by building hundreds of kilometres of roads in the fresh water swamp forests. These roads block streams and flood plains creating stagnant ponds of water, thereby killing hitherto healthy and thriving forests. The oil companies have also opened up hitherto pristine forests to commercial loggers, with the result that mangrove and rainforest trees are now gradually being wiped out.

Since Shell struck the first oil well in Oloibiri in the eastern Niger Delta in 1956, the oil-producing communities have known only poverty, misery and sorrow. Oil spillage which pollutes farmlands, fishing streams and ponds and the indiscriminate flaring of gas which poisons the air they breath is the brutal fact of their daily lives.

More worryingly, the peoples of the Niger Delta do not even receive any share of the oil proceeds obtained from their land, the bulk of which is appropriated by the Nigerian government and Shell and the other multinational oil companies. Now, oil is the mainstay of the Nigerian economy, accounting for 97 per cent of the country's export earnings and over 80 per cent of public revenue. In this circumstance, oil has become the target of state power. It is in this context that students of Nigerian government and politics refer to the country as a 'rentier' state.

Conflict Dynamics

The Niger Delta communities have been protesting against these injustices peacefully for decades. Civil society groups such as the *Pan-Niger Delta Resistance Movement* CHIKOKO; the *Environmental Rights Action*; the *Ijaw Youth*

Council; the *Movement for the Survival of the Ogoni People* (MOSOP), *Movement for Reparation to Ogbia* (MORETO) and the *Movement for the Survival of the Ijo in the Niger Delta* (MOSIEND) have emerged in the last few years to campaign for corporate responsibility, environmental sustainability, self-determination and democratic development in the Niger Delta.

In the main, the indigenous peoples and forest-dependent communities, like other resource-dependent communities elsewhere in the world, are simply fighting for sustenance and their cultural rights while transnational oil corporations like Shell, Chevron, Elf, Mobil, Texaco are engaged in the brutal exploitation of the oil resources. The Nigerian central government, which for all but nine and a half of the almost 39 years of independence has been headed by the military, is only interested in increased revenue in the form of taxes and rent and a greater jurisdiction.

The broad response of the Nigerian state to these demands has been violence, terror, rape, arrests, harassment, military occupation of the Delta and even judicial and extra-judicial murders as we saw in the case of the writer and activist Ken Saro-Wiwa. Iko, Umuechem, Kaiama, Ilaje, Ekeremor-Zion, Uzere, Opia, Ikenya and in some 800 other communities, multinational oil companies backed by the Nigerian State have spread mayhem, blood, sorrow and tears. It is a case of drilling and killing.

Specifically, in 1987, Iko, a peaceful community in Akwa Ibom State was left in ruins when members of the community protested against the Anglo-Dutch multinational oil giant, Shell over neglect and environmental degradation. A Shell Nigeria manager, Mr Udofia, with permission from Shell top managers in Holland wrote to the authorities of the Rivers State government in 1990 about threats of the people of Umuechem to disrupt economic activities. Shell specifically requested for the deployment of 'the mobile police force' to stop the people from protesting peacefully. That November, the community was bombarded by grenades and shell-fire. Eighty people, including the local pastor and the traditional ruler, were killed and almost five hundred houses were destroyed. In 1993 the company's alliance with the military grew to the level of payment to senior military officers to carry out punitive raids and expeditions into Niger Delta communities.

On October 25 Major Paul Okuntimo was paid by Shell to invade Korokoro village in Ogoni. One boy was killed, an old man was shot through the stomach but survived to tell the gory tale of the murderous propensity of the multinational oil giant and its able ally the military dictatorship.

Elsewhere in the Niger Delta, soldiers and mobile policemen have left stories of sorrow, tears and blood in their oil-directed missions. The deprived and impoverished towns of Uzere, Ozoro and Ekeremor-Zion are a few examples. In the Ilaje community of Ondo State, the American oil giant Chevron procured and flew in armed soldiers who came down very heavily on defenceless peaceful demonstrators who had occupied their Parabe oil facility. Two youths were shot dead and several others injured in that operation that was supervised and directed by Chevron. The Chevron public affairs manager admitted to American journalists that they called in the soldiers and that the protesters were peaceful. The same is true of the French 'area of influence' in the Niger Delta. The people of Egi in Ogba have been on the receiving end of Elf-provoked violence.

It has now been firmly established that some of the multinationals are also involved in the importation of arms and ammunition into the Niger Delta for the purpose of 'protecting our staff and facilities'. Shell, confronted with the evidence of gun running said they 'only imported 107 hand guns'. Claude Ake has beautifully described this development as 'the privatisation of the Nigerian State and the militarisation of commerce'. Not too long ago, Chevron was accused by the Ijaws of supplying weapons to the Itsekiri and by the Itsekiri of giving money to the Ijaws to buy weapons. As they trade these accusations, Chevron issued a weak statement saying they were not involved in the oil-inspired violence that has engulfed the region.

But more worrying still is the damage to the peoples' survival strategies: farming, fishing, and trading. As waters, forests and lands are polluted and as the air is fouled by gas flaring, so there has been a downward trend in the quality of life of the people. There is now an agreement that corporate rule has succeeded in condemning the people to penury, destitution and native imperialism.

Convinced that the multinational oil companies are the principal causes of the poverty and misery in the Delta, a new campaign is now been waged locally and internationally, demanding that all the oil companies quit the Delta until the issue of resource ownership and control is democratically resolved in favour of the peoples of the Niger Delta. Under Nigeria's undemocratic laws, oil in the Niger Delta belongs to the central government and the political structure of the country does not allow the people to participate effectively in governance. Hence, the peoples of the Niger Delta are also demanding a fundamental restructuring of the country to enable them to influence and determine the processes that affect their lives. The most eloquent expression of this position is contained in the Kaiama Declaration issued by Ijaw youths on December 11, 1998. The Declaration proposed resource control and self-government for the Ijaws and other nations, peoples and nationalities in Nigeria as the best way forward to maintain democracy and stability. Rather than attempt to negotiate this urgent demand, the state, supported by the transnational oil corporations opted to visit violence on Ijawland. As it were, this has merely encouraged the Ijaw to continue their determined struggle for self-determination. When the issue of self-determination is raised, some people say it will lead to secession. These people forget that if an ethnic group is treated justly and democratically, it does not usually contemplate secession.

It has also been the tradition for hegemonic forces and their allies to dismiss the struggle of the Ijaws and other oil-bearing communities for self-determination as merely part of 'oil politics'. Whatever that means, it is on record that prior to independence and before oil became Nigeria's principal revenue earner, the Ijaws were among other minorities who expressed fears of domination. This led to the establishment of the Henry Willinks Minorities Commission in 1957.

The commission described the Ijaw country as 'poor, backward and neglected'. It has remained so to date despite various attempts ostensibly aimed at developing the area. For instance, between independence and now, we have had: (I) the Niger Delta Development Board; (II) the Niger Delta Basin Development Authority; (III) 1.5 per cent Derivation Fund and (IV) the Oil Mineral Producing Areas Development Commission (OMPADEC).

Let us briefly look at OMPADEC. As an agency set up by the central government to develop the Niger Delta, OMPADEC has been an embarrassing failure primarily because it has remained a temple of corruption. As such what you see are the agency's signposts, not the projects which the signposts advertise! More fundamentally, OMPADEC represents a major subversion of the tenets of federalism. Why do the Ijaws or Isokos, Urhobos or Ogonis need a federal behemoth to stand between them and their resources? It was the late Ogoni nationalist Ken Saro-Wiwa who compared the creation of OMPADEC to the action of a man who stole another man's shirt and turns round to throw three buttons at the owner of the shirt and yet expects him to be grateful to the thief! No other choice of words could be more appropriate.

Mainstream analysts of the conflicts in the Niger Delta seem convinced that the raging conflicts can be resolved simply by putting in place a social infrastructure and alleviating the level of poverty by making more money available. This is however simplistic because 'the communities of the Niger Delta are poor today not because their land is poor, but because the social and political structures in the country today function to disempower them and make it impossible for them to deploy their natural genius to make the land on which they live to yield its abundance'. It is clear to us that social and political structures can only be truly democratised by means of a Sovereign National Conference where all the ethnic nationalities would have to sit down and define their stakes within the federation. A multi-ethnic state like Nigeria cannot survive under a centralised political system. It has not worked. It never will.

---

* **Oronto Douglas and Doifie Ola are associated with Environmental Rights Action/Friends of the Earth Nigeria**

References

Graf, William, *The Nigerian State: Political Economy, State Class and Political System in the Post Colonial Era.* London, James Currey, 1998

Ijaw Youth Council, *The Kaiama Declaration,* 1998

Okonta, Ike, *Obasanjo and the Challenge of the Niger Delta.* In ERAction, house journal of the Environmental Rights Action, Nigeria, January-March 1999, #2

Okonta, Ike and Oronto Douglas, *Where Vultures Feast: 40 Years of Shell in the Niger Delta.* Benin, Environmental Rights Action, forthcoming.

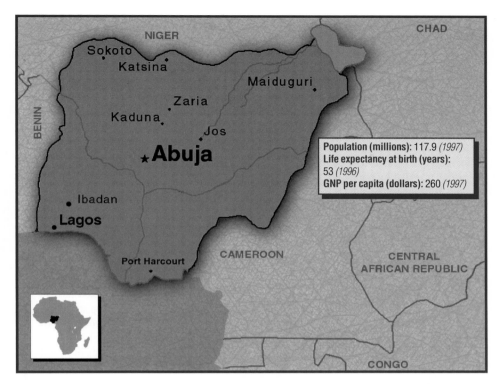

Population (millions): 117.9 *(1997)*
Life expectancy at birth (years):
53 *(1996)*
GNP per capita (dollars): 260 *(1997)*

The Transition to Democracy and the South-Western Opposition

The British colonial administration of the 350 ethnic groups making up Nigeria comprised two separate phases. In the mid-nineteenth century the Protectorate and Colony of Southern Nigeria was established. This was followed by the Protectorate and Colony of Northern Nigeria which was declared in 1900. The British amalgamated the two regions in 1914. In 1947, a colonial constitution split Nigeria into three unequal political regions: north, west and east. The north, dominated by the Hausa-Fulani, was larger and more populous than the other two regions. There is a very significant minority population in the north. The west was, and still is, dominated by the Yoruba, while the Ibos were the largest group in the east. These three regions have now been balkanised into Nigeria's present thirty six-state federal structure. In spite of this departmentalisation, north-south divisions have remained alive in Nigerian politics ◆ *By* **Akin Akinteye**

This paper describes the contemporary opposition of the Yoruba people of the south west of Nigeria to a perceived northern monopoly on power. The conflict is a relatively recent development which intensified following the cancellation of the results of the June 12,

1993 elections by the Nigerian military rulers. The Yoruba saw the cancellation of the elections, which were won by a Yoruban, as the climax of a series of injustices perpetrated by the northern power elite. Under the repressive regime of General Sani Abacha, it was widely speculated that the Yoruba south-west was planning to secede from the federation. Up until the swearing in of Olusegun Obasanjo as president of Nigeria on May 29, 1999, there was open disaffection among the Yoruba. This found expression through various platforms. Recent political reforms in the country executed by the new democratic government, however, seem to have calmed the opposition of the south-west.

Since Nigeria's political independence in 1960, most of its leaders have come from the predominantly Muslim north of the country. In the early 1960s, fears of political marginalisation caused the Eastern Region to attempt to secede from the Nigerian federation. These fears were resurrected during the Sani Abacha era. The south, of which the south-west is only a part, has complained about marginalisation and the prolonged control of political power by the northern power elite. The northern ruling elite is believed to have benefited from all the regimes, military and civilian alike, to the detriment of the south. The clamour for a power-shift to the south became more insistent in June 1993, following the convincing victory of Chief Moshood Abiola at the presidential polls. With Abiola's victory, the south seemed to have achieved its call for a power-shift in its favour. The nullification of these elections led to sustained and organised protest and opposition. The most articulate opposition to this prolonged northern domination came from the Yorubas of the south-west, especially after June 1993.

It should also be noted, however, that the northern power elite ruled Nigeria in collaboration with coopted colleagues from the south, including Yorubaland. The northern ruling class has been condemned by the Yoruba as inefficient, and for utilising state power for massive repression and exploitation. It is also seen as greedy, based on its perceived reluctance to allow power to shift from the north, and given its preference for centralised federalism. A pattern of capital accumulation, the looting of public resources and the subsequent transfer of such resources to foreign countries are some of the ills perpetrated by this group. Even though such abuse of public office cannot be confined to elites from any one region of Nigeria, for indeed they do this along with people from other parts

of the federation, the northerners receive a larger share of the blame by virtue of their position at the core of power. The Yoruba have called for political restructuring, believing that total autonomy offers them the brightest future.

Causes of the Conflict

The north has, over the years, been accused of conniving to permanently control the nation's governance, to the exclusion of others of southern extraction. The Yoruba allege that the north dominates the civil service, the military, the diplomatic service and educational establishments. It is alleged that southerners especially Yorubas, are being removed from top positions in favour of their northern counterparts who are in most cases unqualified and junior to those removed. These allegations are rejected by the northern power elite, who contend that while northerners may hold political positions, the remaining senior, middle-level and other positions are predominantly occupied by others.

The feeling of injustice among the Yoruba reached its peak with General Ibrahim Babangida's annulment of the presidential elections. The Yoruba believed Babangida's move to have been influenced by the upper echelons of the northern power elite. Since the annulment, Yoruba leaders have demanded a restructured federation in which the component states would be sovereign and the ethnic nationalities free. The Yorubas want a situation where the states of Nigeria will no longer be subordinated to the Federal Government, which they see as being a northern monopoly. The Yoruba believe that the north manipulates power, and this is exchanged between the military and its civilian equivalent.

The Yoruba of south-western Nigeria have questioned the operational effectiveness of federalism in Nigeria, which they claim has diminished during the years of northern leadership. This they believe has in turn led to the absence of mutual respect for the values and political peculiarities of the various units that make up Nigeria. Furthermore, the south-west argued that the political powers of various units of Nigeria have been eroded by a central government that is firmly in the grip of the northerners who are intent on advancing their own sectional interests. In summary, the south-west believes that successive governments in Nigeria have only pursued one goal - primacy of the north - which serves as a generic canopy for other interests.

Ironically, when the west and the east advocated independence from the British in 1956, the north strongly disagreed, arguing that it was not ready. The south-west believes it is unfair for the north to be the major benefactor from this independence. Chief Bola Ige, one of the front-line leaders of the Yoruba, (now a minister in the Obasanjo regime), identified two political tendencies and faces in Nigeria. One is 'that of local colonialism of the military in cahoots with a small but closely-knit tribe of conservative and selfish hegemonists' (presumably the northern power elite). The other face is that of 'freedom, democracy, the rule of law and well-being' (presumably the south-west and pro-democracy activists, with their supporters elsewhere).

The unwillingness of the northern power elite to relinquish power was, in the view of a section of Yorubas, symbolised by the statement of Maitama Sule, an orator of the conservative north. He remarked that 'the northerners are endowed with leadership qualities. The Yoruba man knows how to earn a living and has diplomatic qualities. The Ibo is gifted in commerce, trade.... God so created us individually for a purpose. Others are created as kings, servants.... We all need each other. If there are no followers, a King will not exist'. The Yoruba of the south-west interpreted this as an indication that the northern power elite would not relinquish power to other parts of the federation. It is widely believed that the annulment of the election results by the Babangida regime was occasioned by protests made to the general by the deposed Sultan of Sokoto, not to undo the God-given right of the northern power elite to remain permanently in power.

If the south-west feels marginalised, so does the north. There is a wide spread belief in the north that the south controls commercial activities in the economy, banking and the financial sector, education, the public service, etc. The north had held on to political power in

part, to secure itself from complete marginalisation. Spokesmen for the northern power elite have repeatedly made it clear that the north is marginalised economically, educationally, and in all the facets of the public service. Northerners generally perceive leaders of the south-west and their demands as a selfish, and pursuing an ethnic agenda. Indeed, there is very little respect for the position of the south-west among the average northerners, since it is seen as an ethnic position.

Under military governance, issues of socio-economic justice, poverty, restructuring, marginalisation and disparity of varying degrees, became amplified in the conflict between the northern power elite and the Yoruba south-west. They remained unresolved for a very long time. Analysts have argued that the refusal of the northern ruling class to subscribe to addressing the fundamental causes of economic and political crises in Nigeria are as good as erecting the foundation for Nigeria's disintegration.

The Yoruba of the south-west have made a number of demands as pre-conditions for peace and stability in the recent past. Among them are a power-shift to the south, and a sovereign national conference that will bring about a truly federal constitution. Bargaining and negotiated coordination among several power centres, decentralisation, and division of power were also advocated. Also on the agenda was the application of the principle of derivation in the disbursement of the nation's finances, as well as mutual respect among all ethnic nationalities. These demands were made to the government, which was supposedly dominated by the northern power elite. At the official level, nothing was done to bring these demands to fruition. The government's only reaction was to bring about the dialogue between General Abdul Salam Abukakar on coming to power, and leaders of the Yoruba coalition *Afenifere*, and the *National Democratic Coalition* (NADECO). A power-shift from north to south, even though achieved in May 1999, was not negotiated, but came naturally, through the democratic process.

Conflict Dynamics
The cancellation of the June 1993 election marked a turning point in the history of the face-

off between the north and south. In Lagos, which is the nerve-centre of the south, the announcement was followed by rioting which led to a massive loss of life and the mass destruction of property.

Renewing their struggle, the Yoruba forged links with several organisations to help realise their aims. Affiliated ethnic organisations came to the fore in this process. Prominent among the organisations formed during the Abacha regime were NADECO, Afenifere and the Odudua Peoples' Congress (OPC). A 'rebel' radio station broadcasting from an unknown destination was operated by a group suspected to be affiliated to the south-western opposition and proved an irritant to the government.

These organisations, led by notable Yoruba leaders, formed themselves into an opposition, supposedly to free the country from what was believed to be the clutches of the northern power elite. The south-west boycotted the constitutional conference elections of 1994, and also ignored the Abacha transition programme by jettisoning the junta's five self-organised political parties, which they likened to five fingers of a leprous hand. However, the Yoruba were unable to enforce a total boycott. The Abacha regime cultivated a significant following in parts of the Yoruba nation. Strategies employed to promote the south-west position included lectures and seminars, aimed at raising awareness and consciousness of the evils being perpetrated by the northern power elite. A strategic anti-government campaign and mass demonstration was embarked upon. The south-west vowed to make Nigeria ungovernable for the military should they refuse to budge on the issues.

At the same time, the government clamped down on these organisations and individuals behind their formation and activities, in order to neutralise the vibrant civil society and the vocal mass media in the south-west. Successive military governments having inherited a legacy of force and coercion from one another exercised these to the fullest. Patrons who did not support the northern power elite were marked out for political humiliation. One commentator had noted that over the years, those leaders perceived to be threats to the northern hegemony have been dealt with by means of 'corporatism and

entryism or through a systematic policy of withdrawal of rents or development subsidies.'

The June 12 saga was described as a set-back to the plans of the northern power elite. As a result, the Abacha junta embarked on a twin project - attempt to win and retain the power for either himself or at least the north, and crushing parties or individuals perceived as posing a formidable threat to the northern interests. One of the key casualties was Abacha's second in command, the Yoruban General Diya who came from the south-west. Abacha systematically undermined Oladipo Diya who narrowly escaped execution over alleged involvement in a coup to unseat the government.

The Yoruba saw the constitutional conference of 1994 as another example of the north's determination to manipulate and regiment Nigerian politics. There seems to have been a general political consensus that a Sovereign National Conference was essential to the existence of Nigeria as a nation. However, the south-west lost confidence in the conference, believing it was tailored in a direction to favour the aspirations of the northern power elite. The conference left the south-west deeply agitated. The military government later found the leeway to undo major decisions reached at the conference. It must be quickly added that the conflict dimension also changed in that the southern minorities and the Yoruba south-west, by their perennial protests, threatened the corporate existence of Nigeria as one entity.

In 1995, the Nigerian military government, in one of its attempts to crush all opposition, executed eight Ogoni activists despite national and international pleas for clemency. The regime also refused to enter into dialogue with NADECO, the leading opposition group in the country. Anxiety increased following the murder of a number of the regime's opponents. Most of the killers remained free. These attempts were targeted at destroying credible and principled resistance to perceived northern domination therefore forcing them to abandon the struggle to bring about a new Nigeria. Several reports of state-planned bomb attacks and stage-managed inter and intra-communal crises were recorded in the course of the struggle.

This remained the situation until the deaths

of General Abacha and Chief Moshood Abiola. Chief Abiola's death was treated by leaders of the south-west as murder perpetrated by the state. Abiola's death re-ignited the clamour for a government of national unity, restructuring, a power-shift, and a true federal constitution fashioned through a sovereign national conference.

The renewed calls intensified, and took a violent turn with the establishment of another Yoruba platform called the *Oduduwa Peoples' Congress*. The congress, which is a Yoruba socio-cultural organisation led by youths, resorted to the use of direct confrontation with military and police forces. This groups which is strong in Lagos and other parts of the south-west, has clashed with the state forces on several occasions. The group benefited from recruits earlier displaced by the crisis of structural adjustment and its accompanying poverty. These clashes resulted in the destruction of lives and property. On some occasions the Oduduwa Peoples' Congress adopted violation of law and order and instigation of the civil society against the government in carrying out their activities.

Conflict Management

The government's only official attempt at conflict management was the institution of the National Reconciliation Commission. The commission was given the mandate of reconciling all the aggrieved units of Nigeria. However, the commission failed because of lack on sincerity on the part of the government, which prevented it from engaging in dialogue with opposition groups in the country. The fact that this was set up by General Abacha, who was the least enthusiastic about reconciliation, condemned it to failure from the outset.

Genuine moves were made by foreign governments to encourage the government to negotiate with the opposition group. However, these were soon aborted in the face of government recalcitrance. While international organisations and some foreign governments did succeed in imposing sanctions on the Nigeria military government, these sanctions failed to achieve the desired results because crude oil, the principal revenue earner and main attraction for the military government, was exempt.

The activities of certain NGOs are having a indirectly positive impact on the transformation of the conflicts in Nigeria. Organisations such as *Academic Associates, PeaceWorks, Civil Liberties, Human Rights Africa* and the *Constitutional Rights Project* embarked on the training and enlightenment of grassroots organisations on the strategic peaceful resolution of conflicts, systematic identification of injustice and how to seek redress. Some of these organisations also embarked on mass campaigns against violation of human rights and injustice.

Reflection

Nigerian NGOs, however, are far from working together in the pursuit of credible democratic governance in Nigeria. In some cases, NGOs are at logger heads and often fight over the limited resources available from funding organisations. This lack of coordination and a uniform front more often than not creates confusion among the grassroots who look to the NGO sector to bring about change.

Prospects

The weak state of the Nigerian economy and its effects, such as high unemployment, irregular electricity supply, poor telecommunications, healthcare, education, roads, water supply, and the general impoverishment of the larger segment of the population, provides a very fragile and delicate base for the next democratic experiment in Nigeria.

As Amuwo (1998) summarised, the future of the Nigerian Federal System will be determined either by the centrifugal push of ethnic particularism or the centripetal pull of consensual, plural democracy. If the ethnic particularity prevails, arguments about restructuring will be put to rest and if the pluralist or democratic logic triumphs, a Sovereign National Conference will be desirable to negotiate and work out a new type of federal system for Nigeria.

In May 1999, Chief Olusegun Obasanjo, a former military leader of Nigeria was sworn in as the elected civilian president of Nigeria. Even though he is a Yoruba from the south-west, he was not a favourite candidate of the south-west. As such, he gained his winning votes outside the region. With Obasanjo's electoral victory, a power-shift has been achieved, even if by default, meeting one of the principal demands of the Yoruba south-west. Indeed, the Yoruba had dismissed Obasanjo's candidature, believing it to be masterminded by the northern power group, to give them continuous control of state power even under a Yoruba head of state. Events in the early phase of the regime, however, have gone someway to allay these suspicions. Interestingly, the regime has brought on board members of the largely Yoruba political party, Alliance for Democracy. Paradoxically, leaders of the north are now complaining of being marginalised under the Obasanjo dispensation, and are calling on president Obasanjo to reverse the trend.

Finally, the crusade against corruption mounted by the Obasanjo government is an indication of good governance in Nigeria. This will in fact help resolve the issues of political restructuring. Civilian governors have been sworn in for all the 36 states of the federation. This also helps to strengthen an autonomous federalism. Thus, the Yoruba south-west has become relatively calm of late and is no longer so vociferous in pushing many of its earlier demands. Even the Oduduwa Peoples' Congress

has abandoned its confrontation with and attacks on the police and the army. Thus, with good and accountable governance, and under the democratic dispensation which allows states to be independent politically of the central government, many of the issues in this conflict should find a natural resolution.

However Obasanjo's government has encountered a number of problems in its first two months in office. Aside from numerous scandals concerning elected officials, various parts of the country have been plagued by community conflicts. One of the most dramatic is the conflict between the Hausa settlers and the indigenous Yoruba in the south-western town of Sagamu. What apparently started as a fight about a Yoruba traditional festival, expanded into interethnic violence that also spread to the northern city of Kano. In the following days hundreds of people were killed in the two towns. The state governments, traditional rulers, and religious and community leaders stepped in to quell the violence. At the time of going to press, it was still unclear if this violence is part of the larger interregional conflict, or if it is a more limited interethnic skirmish.

*   Akin Akinteye is member of the Oyo State House of Assembly, Ibadan, Nigeria and was Programme Officer at Acadamic Associates PeaceWorks

References

Amuwo, K., A., Suberu, R. and Heranlt, G. (ed) *Federalism and Political Restructuring in Nigeria*. Ibadan, Spectrum, 1998
Amuwo, K. *The Responsibility of the State Legislature and the Party Goals*. A paper presented at the Political Education Forum Among Leaders of Alliance for Democracy in Ibadan. 1999
Kich, G.K. Dr. and Agbese, P.O. *From Politics back to Barracks in Nigeria: A theoretical Exploration*. Journal of Peace Research, Vol. 30 no. 4 pp 409-426, 1993

Marinho, A.O. *If you cannot make the Deaf hear, at least make them see*. A Keynote address during the dinner at the Workshop for Legislators held in Ibadan on 5th May 1999
Olugboji, B. *Military Rule in Nigeria: The High Costs Allies* Constitutional Rights Journal. July-September 1994
The Guardian. *The Price Nigeria is paying for corruption*. Lagos, Wednesday, March 17, 1999
The Guardian *Questions remain over the skewed federation*. Lagos, Wednesday, March 24, 1999

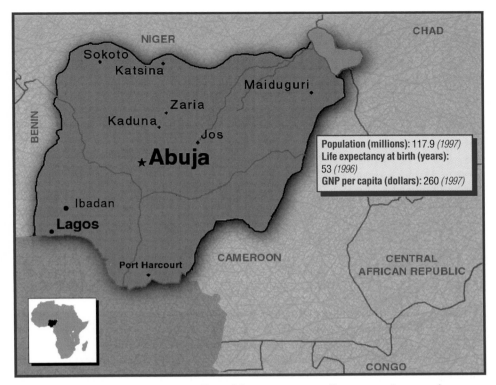

The Islamist Challenge: the Nigerian 'Shiite' Movement

Religion generally, and the radicalisation of Islam in particular, have represented major challenges to the Nigerian state, and to other religious and non-religious groups in recent years. A movement generally described as 'Shiite' because of its ties to Iran, has challenged both the state and traditional religious authorities in northern Nigeria[1] ◆ *By* **Dr. Shedrack Best**[*]

The Islamist challenge and the increasing militancy of religious campaigns, have remained an exclusively northern Nigerian phenomenon, largely due to historical, cultural and geo-political reasons. Southern Nigeria has yet to experience northern-type militancy. Even though there may be people in the south who share Islamist sentiments, they are not linked with the northern movement led by Yahaya el-Zakzaky.

Religious Fundamentalism in Nigeria

Three movements exemplify the intra-Islamic strife in contemporary northern Nigeria. These

are the 'Maitatsine' Movement, the 'Izala' movement, and the 'Shiites'. But Islamic activism and protests against state authority in Nigeria date back to the pre-colonial era. The most significant of these protests occurred during the Dan Fodio jihad, which began and spread through most of northern Nigeria in the early part of the nineteenth century. The objective of Usman Dan Fodio, leader of the jihad, and his fellow reformists, was to depose the ruling Hausa dynasties, who were accused of ruling without adherence to the principles of Islam. The jihad challenged and questioned the management of religion and political power in northern Nigeria. It subsequently removed the ruling group and thereafter planted Fulani-led emirates across the region. From 1900 the British largely replaced these regimes.

Under British rule, the greatest Islamic threat to statehood and the colonial authorities was the rise of 'Mahdism'. This was a trans-Saharan anti-colonial movement. It originated from a messianic doctrine similar to that of Judaism. Muslims believed that at the turn of each century, a Mahdi would emerge with the powers to strengthen Islam and make justice triumph. He would also attract a large following among Muslims. Many Muslims waited for the Mahdi for deliverance. Some Mahdists regarded the forces of Lord Lugard (the first British Governor-General of Nigeria who amalgamated the north and south in 1914) as Satan. They saw any pact with the British and subsequent rule by Christians as worse than death. Thus, after the capital of the Fulani empire (Sokoto) fell to the British, sultan Attahiru fled to Sudan in a 'hijra,' rather than live under 'Christian' rule[2].

In July 1907, some other Mahdists regrouped, appointed a leader, and attempted to re-take Sokoto from the British. Others compromised on the assurance that the British would not interfere with their ways of life. For a long time during the early years of British colonialism, the Emirs and the British officers lived in permanent fear of a Mahdist uprising, basically because of the movement's threats and challenge to the colonial state.

This remained the case up to independence. Other forms of opposition existed between members of the 'Qadiriyya' and 'Tijaniyya' brotherhoods, both of them trans-national Sufi sects. These sects constitute the dominant religious sects in northern Nigeria particularly, and Nigeria in general. Before 1978, when the Izala movement was formed, virtually all Muslims in Nigeria belonged to one of the two sects.

In Nigeria, conflict between these two groups became intense in the 1950s. This, in part, led the late premier of the northern Region, Sir Ahmadu Bello, to establish the Islamic Advisory Council to lessen friction between them. The Council later declined in significance following

the end of Nigeria's First Republic after the military coup of January 1966. Both sects have had close relations with successive regimes in Nigeria. Indeed, the top echelon of the leadership in both sects has benefited from the government in various ways. Unlike radical groups such as the 'Shiites', they seem comfortable with the secular notion of the state and there is little support for an Islamic state and constitution for Nigeria among their members. As such, they have been the targets of revivalist Islamic movements, who tend to identify them with the complacency of the state, and accuse them of moral bankruptcy. The revivalist movements also appealed to youths, and the state is a key subject of attack

At present, there are three prominent religious revivalist and activist groups operating in northern Nigeria: the Izala, the Maitatsines, and the 'Shiites'.

Izala

The Izala, or the Jama'at Izalatil Bidiawa Iqamatus Sunnah (Movement Against Negative Innovations and for Orthodoxy), is principally concerned with the purification of Islam and abolition of practices that are not original to the Koran and Sunnah, the practice of the prophet Muhammad. The movement was begun by sheikh Ismaila Idris in Jos. It later enjoyed the support of important figures such as the late sheikh Mahmoud Gummi. The Izalas do not regard the creation of an Islamic state as a primary concern. They are an ultra-orthodox movement wanting a return to the true practice of the faith. Because a large section of the Izala leadership is drawn from the civil service, the group has not been engaged in any conflict with the state. Their conflict is rather with other Muslims and other Islamic sects.

Maitatsine

The Maitatsine is a radical, anti-status quo movement driven by Islamic fundamentalism and the socio-economic disadvantages suffered by its members vis-à-vis the well-to-do in society. It was founded by Alhaji Marwa Maitatsine, who was killed in Kano during the 1980 disturbances in which 4,177 people perished within less than a month of fighting. The Maitatsines represented a major challenge to the Nigerian state and to other Muslims. It is believed by many Nigerian Muslims that the movement is a heterodox grouping which deviates from orthodox Islam. The members exhibit intense hatred for agents of the state such as the police and members of the armed forces, largely because of repeated violent encounters with the police.

Muslism Brotherhood /Shiite
The Muslim brotherhood movement is popularly described as 'Shiite,' despite the objections of its members. Indeed, the 'Shiite' description is a label given to the movement by journalists and commentators. Rooted in the Sunni Islamic movement, they are linked to Iran through their leader's training in that country and are said to receive some support from Iran, even though it has been suggested that Libya and Sudan are also probable supporters of the movement.

In Nigeria the 'Shiites' are led by Mallam (teacher in Arabic) Yahaya El Zakzaky, whose reputation for radical Islam dates back to his undergraduate days at Ahmadu Bello University, Zaria in the 1970s. At university he led the Muslim Students Society (MSS) for some time, during which period he sponsored some demonstrations in Zaria in the 1970s. He was consequently expelled along with other students by the university authorities in the late 1970s and early 1980s. Given that this period coincided with the Iranian revolution, Iran extended a warm welcome to these students and they were invited to attend conferences, rallies and various training events relevant to Islamic rhetoric and revolution, for a subsequent Iranian-type revolution in Nigeria. A report of the Nigerian Security Organisation noted that the training received by El Zakzaky in Iran included 'planning and executing student unrest.'

The earlier link between the 'Shiite' leadership and university students provided the group with an intellectual and revolutionary foundation, which was superior to the Maitatsine-type movement, for instance. The 'Shiites' quickly became established in key northern universities such as the Ahmadu Bello University in Zaria, Bayero University in Kano, and the University of Sokoto (now Usman Dan Fodio University). This explains why their

strongest operational centres are to be found in Zaria, Kaduna, Kano, Sokoto, and Katsina. The movement's leadership is highly educated and usually young: the typical leader is a university graduate. However, the educated members provide only the leadership.

The 'Shiites' disregard for state authority is exhibited in a number of ways. Among them are the denunciation of the state and government, disregard for party elections, contempt for the constitution and refusal to recognise its laws, refusal to respect the national anthem and national pledge (they will normally not stand as Nigerians do when the national anthem is being sung), and disregard for Nigeria's national flag. In other words, they reject all the symbols of Nigerian statehood.

The earliest manifestation of this movement in Nigeria was seen in 1979, organised under the banner of the Muslim Students' Society (MSS). In that year, El Zakzaky led a demonstration in Zaria. In May 1980, he led another demonstration in Zaria, with ten bus-loads of demonstrators chanting 'down with the Nigerian constitution' and 'Islam only'. These slogans were also written on public buildings in Zaria, Kano and Sokoto, particularly on the walls of university buildings. El Zakzaky later circulated pamphlets titled 'Calling on Nigerian Muslims', through which he condemned the Nigerian constitution and urged Muslims to recognise only the Shari'a, and to rise against the Nigerian state.

Although much had been known about El Zakzaky and his activities, not much was known about the organisation he led before the 1991 fracas in the far northern city of Katsina. In that year, the leader of the 'Shiites' in the ancient city of Katsina led the group in a series of violent demonstrations. The crisis was ignited by the publication of an article in a weekly magazine called *The Fun Times* which suggested that the Prophet Muhammad and Jesus were associated with women of easy virtue. Muslim activists regarded this as blasphemous. Their reaction was similar to that of many Muslims to Salman Rushdie's *Satanic Verses*. They accused the paper of a blasphemy, which they, suggested, could only originate in a Christian-headed paper backed by the government. In spite of the apology offered by the paper, the religionists burnt copies of the *Fun Times*, and set the building housing the magazine ablaze, effectively challenging the military governor of Katsina State to react.

The trial of the 'Shiites' in Katsina was dramatic. They refused to engage the services of lawyers, and yet defended themselves very brilliantly - a reflection of the highly intellectual base of the movement. They displayed contempt for the legal system, the law enforcement agencies, and the law itself, believing them to be contrary to the will of God.

In 1994, the 'Shiites' in Bayero University, Kano, one of their strongholds, caused a major uproar when they passed death sentences on four university lecturers. Their blood was declared halal, meaning it was lawful for Muslims to kill them. The lecturers were accused of boycotting classes and going on strike against a decision of the university, thereby causing students to loiter about, ultimately leading to immoral acts such as female students visiting male hostels. It took three weeks of appealing to the leader of the 'Shiites' before he pardoned the lecturers. The pardon was announced at the same mosque where their death sentences had been passed.

In December 1994, the 'Shiites' again made news in Kano, in what came to be known as the 'Gideon Akaluka episode'. This crisis was caused by the discovery of a page of the Koran on the premises of an ethnic Igbo Christian trader called Gideon Akaluka. The page was said to have been used as lavatory paper and it was concluded that the Igbo trader had desecrated the Koran, and should consequently be given the death sentence. Akaluka was arrested and kept in custody by state agencies. The 'Shiites', not satisfied with the justice system, broke into the prison and beheaded Akaluka. They then impaled his head on a spear and danced round the city of Kano, chanting Allahu Akbar. They also published a picture of the head of Akaluka on a stake in their propaganda paper, *Al Tajdil*, as well as a picture of the leader of the 'Shiites' addressing the faithful after the execution had taken place. Although the government was initially silent, it was later revealed that the military governor of Kano State had ordered the secret execution of those who had executed

Akaluka. It was kept secret to prevent a swift reaction from 'Shiites' in other parts of northern Nigeria. The same military governor who ordered the executions later died in a plane crash, which the members of the movement believed was due to a divine curse.

Perhaps the biggest clash between the 'Shiites' and the state in recent years followed the arrest and detention by the government of the national leader of the movement, El Zakzaky. The arrest followed an attempt by El Zakzaky to step up his movement's campaign by using an unauthorised radio station to propagate the ideals of an Islamic state via revolution. The signals jammed those of the famous Radio Nigeria Kaduna and investigations by state operatives traced the broadcast to the hideout of El Zakzaky in Zaria. With a reinforcement of police from Abuja, El Zakzaky was arrested on September 12, 1996. The arrest, especially under the repressive environment of the Abacha era, led to a spontaneous reaction of 'Shiites' across northern Nigeria, particularly in Zaria and Kaduna. The clashes resulted in the death of twelve persons in Zaria. In Kaduna, the 'Shiites' took on the police and were undeterred by the shooting down of their members, as they picked each corpse, dropped it in a bus, and continued their protest. They killed a police officer, captured a police station, and carted away its arms. The fight was kept alive by the principle of martyrdom and the belief that those who died in such a fight were assured entry into heaven.

In February 1998, there was again 'Shiite' instigated violence in Kano. This followed the attempt by other Muslims in Kano to say their Eid-El-Fitr prayers at the end of their thirty-day fasting period of the holy month of Ramadan. The 'Shiites,' who normally start their own fasting later than others, depending on when they sight the moon in Iran, were opposed to the other Muslims in Kano making their devotions at that time, believing it to be a distortion of the practice of Islam. They accused the emir of Kano, the traditional leaders of the Muslims of the area and an heir of the emirate system of Da Fodio, of misleading Muslims in a manner that led to improper worship. The attempt by the 'Shiites' to disrupt the prayers, and the force used by the police to stop them, led to a clash which culminated in the death of four people and the injury of many others.

El Zakzaky was kept in detention by the Abacha government for two years after his arrest in 1996. The 'Shiites' continued to protest against his detention and demanded his unconditional release. In January (23 to 30 1998), the 'Shiites' observed Jerusalem (Quds) day. This day was initiated by the late Ayatollah Khomeini of Iran, to propagate an Islamic revolutionary approach to the occupation of Arab lands by Israel, in a challenge to most Arab leaders. It is usually observed on a Friday during the month of Ramadan. In Nigeria, the 'Shiites' explain that the day is set aside for all oppressed people of the world to come out and confront their oppressors.

In January 1998, there were mass demonstrations in Kaduna and Katsina, involving large numbers of women and children. The use of these social forces finds justification in the fact that every demonstration is viewed as a jihad, and a jihad is for all. Women and children have to contribute their quota. This is defended by opposition to Bid'a, an Arabic phrase meaning a non-Islamic 'innovation.' A second principle that makes protest inevitable is that of Muzahara, which requires a Muslim not only to merely disagree, but to openly express and show such discontent. Demonstrations are one way of doing so.

The focus of the January 1998 protests was the oppressive nature of the Abacha administration and the open strategy of deceit employed by the government. They pointed to the unfulfilled promises of the Abacha administration, adding that General Abacha had resorted to diverting the attention of Nigerians to alleged coup plotting against his government. The government was also accused of fuelling the many communal and religious clashes in Nigeria. The protesters lambasted the collaborators of the regime, and demanded the release of all detained and oppressed people. They accused the Abacha regime of impoverishing the populace, and added that certain Western nations were working towards the annihilation of Islam in Nigeria.

In Katsina, confrontation between the 'Shiites' and the police led to the death of five persons, including two police personnel. The demonstrations later spread to Kano, using the same methods. In Kano, the Emir was a principal target. The demonstrators wanted to humiliate the monarch, who was supposed to ride round the city of Kano on a horse.

On the eve of the second anniversary of Zakzaky's detention, members of the group across the whole of northern Nigeria protested, and made 'free Zakzaky' inscriptions in red paint on public places: roads, trees, bridges, buildings, billboards, etc. Not long afterwards, Zakzaky was released by the new government, the interim regime of Abdusalami Abubakar. Zakzaky has remained silent since his release, partly due to the fact that the freedom he enjoys is not total. However there are often pro-Zakzaky demonstrations on Fridays at Ahmadu Bello University.

The parties in the conflict over Islam and legitimacy in northern Nigeria are the Islamist movement led by El Zakzaky on the one hand, and the government and leaders of Nigeria and their coercive agencies on the other. The emirate institutions are also included for alleged collaboration with government. Other parties may be secondary. The issues revolve around religion, values, and different approaches to and philosophies of the state and laws that should govern the Nigeria. The 'Shiites' want an Islamic revolution. They opt for an Islamic Republic, hoping that the godlessness and Satanism which characterise governance will be abolished.

The 'Shiites' particularly hate members of the Nigerian police and the law enforcement agencies. They use the principle of Hisba (an Arabic word which recognises and supports public duties in Islam). It provides for training in arms, paramilitary services, defence, general policing, all of which are useable for jihad. The 'Shiites' view the Nigerian police with contempt because they are mixed with 'unbelievers', and to the extent that they are corrupt, they cannot be called 'police'. They actually prefer to kill the police in battle than to kill civilians.

Similarly, the 'Shiites' have no regard for elections, multiparty political systems and competitive democracy. Elections are referred to as Taghuti or demonic, another term borrowed from the vocabulary of the Islamic revolution in

Iran, where the word is used for anything related to the regime of the former Shah. The Islamists reason that it is impossible for genuine Muslims to serve in a system in whose constitution they have no faith. Participation in elections is therefore, seen as part of unbelief.

Conflict Dynamics

There is an obvious imbalance in the power relations between the state and the Nigerian Islamist movement. Given that the state, which has been under military rule for a long time, tends not to engage in any form of dialogue with perceived Islamic fundamentalists, the chances for confrontation become enhanced. The state's response has been consistently to employ force. This is especially so in the case of the 'Shiites'.

The 'Shiites' possess an enormous amount of intangible power. This includes a great organisational capacity, a resolve to drive on the conflict, a sound intellectual base, a fairly widespread base of support across northern Nigeria, with possibilities of stretching to the south, an ever-growing number of adherents, and a determination to defy the state and its apparatus of coercion. These ingredients of power have to be balanced against the more visible power base of the state. It also explains why the state, in spite of its possession of the means of violence, has failed to resolve the problem by use of force.

A key strategy of the 'Shiite' campaign is the provision of leadership by the person appointed and recognised as leader. In Nigeria, El Zakzaky provides the leadership and inspiration for the group, as the late Ayatollah Khomeini did for the Iranian revolution. This trend has expanded and spread since the escalation of the conflict. In keeping with a common pattern among Sunni movements, however, El Zakzaky is not a scholar (Alim), but a lay leader. Here lies the crisis of attempting an Iranian-type Islamic revolution without the corresponding cultural ingredients, such as a hierarchically organised clergy.

There is no means of ascertaining the casualty figures arising from this conflict - mainly because inquiries are not usually conducted into the figures claimed by each group. What can be said for certain, is that the conflicts represent a dangerous trend capable of undermining peace in northern Nigeria. Most escalations in the situation do result in death and the destruction of property.

The sudden death of General Sani Abacha in June 1998 led to some changes in the conflict. This was followed by the release of many political prisoners and prisoners of faith by the Abubakar administration, among them the leader, El Zakzaky. Elections have been held, and the administration of Nigeria has been handed over to elected President Olesegun Obasanjo, ending years of military governance. Though democracy in Nigeria may ease the tension, it is simplistic to assume that democracy will resolve the questions raised by the Islamist movement in northern Nigeria. This is because the Islamic model of governance and democracy advocated by the 'Shiites' bears no resemblance to the liberal notion of democracy. In addition, the poor performance of the Nigerian economy, which shows no immediate sign of improvement, may deepen crises of this nature rather than resolve them. The present silence of the 'Shiite' leadership may also mean that they are thinking of strategies for future militant struggle. There is evidence at the moment, that the group is busy training its supporters and disciples in different parts of northern Nigeria. The support base is also growing. The change in the Iranian domestic environment, which seems to be leading to a slight opening up of the society to Western allies, may however limit the external support that the 'Shiites' enjoy now, and expect to enjoy in the future.

Official Conflict Management

This conflict is confined to northern Nigeria, the region with the fewest international links, especially to the West. It has attracted much less international attention than the issues raised by democratic activists in Lagos, though its popular base and potential for conflict may be at least as large. There has been little or no international involvement. Although the Islamist movement receives some external inspiration and funding, it has failed to forge useful foreign networks that may be relevant to conflict resolution. Similarly, regional organisations such as the OAU and ECOWAS have had nothing to do with the conflict.

However, local civil society groups like the *Civil Liberties Organisation, Campaign for Democracy,* the independent media, and individuals, all moved by the need to uphold human rights against the authoritarian culture of military regimes in Nigeria, condemned the detention without trial, of Mallam Yahaya El Zakzaky, the leader of the movement. They also condemned police high-handedness in responding to the perceived threats from the movement. These acts do not represent support for the 'Shiites' from civil society groups, but a rejection of disrespect for human rights and rule of law. Local Islamic groups have also protested against the treatment of the 'Shiites', even though their responses have not been coordinated. Some do not sympathise with their plight as they regard the 'Shiites' as representing a dangerous brand of Islam.

On the domestic plane, the philosophy of conflict management has been dominated by the government's policy of maintaining law and order and the police and other agents of the state, the prisons, courts, etc., are the instruments for achieving this goal. Government officials feel that the movement and its methods represent a fundamental threat to the state. They therefore, arrest, torture and detain members and imprison their leaders.

Experience, however, shows that the use of force does not resolve problems of this nature. Indeed, the Maitatsine movement in northern Nigeria has probably remained a destructive force because of government high-handedness.

Local and foreign NGOs have yet to become involved in this sort of conflict in Nigeria, which leaves a very wide gap in conflict management. This is largely because the conflict does not fit the typical inter-faith conflict, which may be addressed using inter-faith dialogue and the imparting of conflict management skills. The 'Shiites' have no respect for NGO activities aimed at conflict management. If such groups are external, and if they are rooted in Islamic rhetoric, especially of the brand respected by the 'Shiites', they may succeed in making headway.

The central issues in this conflict are those of ideology and religious values. It is important to recognise that these religious values gain support largely because of widespread destitution and the corruption of the state, which is widely seen as

an alien power, not only by Islamists. This combination makes the conflict difficult to resolve without broad social change.

Another group that could have been useful for intervening in conflicts of this nature is the royal fathers, the emirs and traditional authorities of northern Nigeria. However, the 'Shiites' have no respect for this institution. They believe that the emirs have become greedy and left the ways and laws of Allah, to cooperate with the oppressive and corrupt system of administration in Nigeria. The emirs are uncomfortable with the movement because of the threat it poses to their interests. Consequently, relations between the two groups are characterised by tension and suspicion. Other religious organisations like the Jama'atu Nasril Islam and the Supreme Council for Islamic Affairs are also in a poor position to intervene. They have their own internal difficulties, and are also faced with a crisis of legitimacy as far as the 'Shiites' are concerned. Even though these organisations claim to represent and speak for all Muslims, many of the activists have little regard for them.

Thus, the greatest danger for the future, and the greatest challenge to the Nigerian state in the near or distant future, is not merely the fundamentalist and radical orientations of the Islamist movement in northern Nigeria, but rather the near absence of private and public mechanisms for conflict management, as discussed above. The defiance of the movement to any conventional mechanism on the one hand, and the preference by especially the military leaders of Nigeria, to use force as means of curtailing the perceived excesses of this group, do not represent means of resolving the deep rooted conflict of value. Problems of this nature are perhaps a key challenge to conflict experts and the conflict management community.

Prospects
The events and circumstances leading to Nigeria's democratisation effort in the early part of 1999, coupled with intense protests by members of the 'Shiite' El Zakzaky movement secured the release of the leader of the movement. Many members of the movement, including their leader, have maintained silence

since then, even though it seemed apparent that a showdown with state security agencies was imminent had El Zakzaky been kept in detention beyond a certain period. The silence of El Zakzaky has provided no clue to analysts and conflict managers, with which to make forecasts about the future intentions of the movement.

It may be suggested, however, that the democratisation of Nigerian politics may produce one of two tendencies: a liberalisation that will encourage the 'Shiites' to step up their campaign; or an accommodation - which the military regimes were unable to provide - which will encourage them to discontinue their methods of opposition, or to become more positively involved in the political process. The latter is, however, less probable.

It can also be noted that no clear NGO or official attempts have been made to resolve this conflict. The 'Shiites' do not necessarily have hearts of stone. For instance, the group pardoned those lecturers in Bayero University Kano, on whom they had passed death sentences following appeals from Muslims. They are, therefore, malleable. It is rather the inability of conflict management operatives to address the Shiite question and to attempt to draw them into a conflict management scheme that has caused this big gap.

In the final analysis, there is the possibility that formal and informal channels were used to secure the release of El Zakzaky from detention. If so, then we can conclude that these forces exist both within and outside the government, even though they cannot be easily identified at the moment, and it is to such factors that we may look for a negotiated settlement. Alternatively, the release of El Zakzaky, as has been suggested by others, was simply due to the general policy of reconciliation embarked upon by the Abdulsalami Abubakar regime. If that is the case, then such a soft approach, to the extent that it does not compromise stability, may be looked to for settlement.

* Dr. Shedrack Gaya Best works at the Department of Political Science at the University of Jos, Nigeria and is part-time Research and Intervention Officer at Academic Associates PeaceWorks.

1. In fact the so-called Shiites are a Sunni Islamist movement akin to the Muslim Brotherhood (Ikhwan al-Muslimun) in other Sunni countries. No Muslims in Nigeria follow the doctrines of Imami or Ismaili Shiism, although the so-called 'Shiites' follow the Iranian lead on a few questions, such as the sighting of the new moon for major holidays.

2. 'Hijra,' or emigration, refers back to the Prophet Muhammad's flight from Mecca to Medina in 621 AD when he founded the Islamic community in exile.

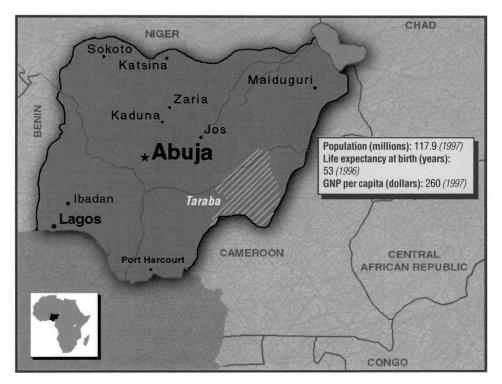

Population (millions): 117.9 *(1997)*
Life expectancy at birth (years):
53 *(1996)*
GNP per capita (dollars): 260 *(1997)*

The Tiv-Jukun Conflict in Wukari, Taraba State

The conflict between the Tiv and the Jukun, two different ethnic groups coexisting in Taraba State in Nigeria, had numerous causes. These included disputes over land, traditional rulership, political authority, fears of domination and marginalisation. While this conflict centred around the issue of settlers and indigenes, which is common in many parts of Nigeria, the Wukari fight was unusually violent. It also received little attention from the government, media or the public, in spite of large-scale loss of property and human lives. Thus it is provides a good example for the study of conflict management ◆ *By* **Judith Burdin Asuni**

Nigeria has a population of about 120 million people, making it the largest country in black Africa. It also has approximately 350 different ethnic groups, although the Yoruba in the south-west, Igbo in the south-east and Hausa/Fulani in the north dominate the national scene. The Middle Belt, which runs west to east between the core north and the south contains numerous small ethnic groups. It has been marginalised politically and economically. Few people in other parts of the country even know where Taraba State and Wukari are located. Wukari is not of strategic importance to any government, hence the neglect which it has suffered.

Anthropologists tell us that in the past there was great movement of people around Africa. Indeed the Jukun, who are probably the older settlers in Wukari, state that they came from Yemen, along with the Kanuri, who settled in the Chad Basin. The Jukun established the far-flung

Kwararafa Kingdom, which reached its peak in the seventeenth century. The Jukun state that they lived peacefully with their neighbours until the Tiv migrated from Cameroon into the Benue Valley in the eighteenth century. The Tiv and Jukun appear to have coexisted peacefully in pre-colonial times for several reasons: the Aku Uka (the Jukun king) was the only paramount ruler, whom everyone respected; there was plenty of land; the Tiv were mainly rural farmers who did not interfere with Jukun administration; and there were no party politics.

However, things began to change in the early twentieth century, as the Tiv continued to expand in population and the farmlands became more densely occupied. By the 1940s the Tiv were not only the largest ethnic group in the Middle Belt, but also three times more numerous than the Jukun in the Wukari Division, which the Jukun considered as their home. The British colonialists were worried about the influx of Tiv farmers into what they considered Jukun territory and tried to curtail it. An example is the establishment of the Wukari Federation Local Council, which included all the other main ethnic groups, but excluded the Tiv as they were considered immigrants.

The agitation for inclusion by the Tiv started in the 1940s and remains a source of conflict between the Jukun and the Tiv to this day. Nearly all of the Tiv and a section of the Jukun trace the conflict back to the introduction of party politics in Nigeria. In various elections since 1954, the Jukun and the Tiv have been in different political parties. Violent clashes, such as the Tiv riots of 1959-60, the 1964 'head breaking' during the First Republic and the Second Republic fights of 1979-83, ceased during the military periods of 1966-79 and 1983-87. Trouble resurfaced with the local government elections of 1987 when the Tiv gained powerful positions at the local and state levels. This of course made the Jukun uncomfortable. After the fracas of 1990-92 in which most Tiv were chased out of Wukari, elections held in 1996 and 1997 were peaceful primarily because the Tiv were not there to voice dissent. However deep fears of political marginalisation remain a major cause of the Tiv-Jukun conflict.

The political dimensions of the conflict are two-fold: traditional and modern. The former concerned control of the local government council and political appointments and other resources. The latter centred around the Jukun's refusal to include any Tiv person on the Wukari Traditional Council, where decisions are made that affect them.

Land is another issue which is frequently named as a cause of the conflict. However, while land is frequently mentioned, it is in reality only a vent for political and other forms of conflict. Although it is often said that the Tiv are encroaching on the farmlands owned by the Jukun, it turned out that the real issue is that the Tiv do not follow the traditional laws of land administration, which require them to obtain permission from the village head, ward head, district head and paramount ruler before starting to farm on a piece of land. Instead the Tiv would not accept that they are settlers and did not recognise the Jukun as the original indigenes. Thus land is not only a pragmatic need but also a symbol of prestige.

Another factor in the conflict is the high population growth of the Tiv, which creates a need for more and more farmland. The Tiv also often invite relatives from neighbouring Benue State, which increases the demand for land, as well as the numerical strength of the Tiv. The Jukun feel that their culture, of which they are extremely proud, is being undermined by this influx of Tiv and have embarked upon a 'rejukunisation' process.

These various causes led to an extremely violent confrontation between the Tiv and the Jukun in 1990-92. No one, including the government or the groups involved, can give exact figures of casualties. However there was massive burning of houses, business premises, and schools, accompanied by looting of property. The methods of killing people were extremely brutal and included beheading, setting victims ablaze, the killing of pregnant women and children. The government has failed to assist the victims in rebuilding their property and eight years later, the destruction is still visible.

Conflict Dynamics
When Academic Associates PeaceWorks (AAPW) began working on the Tiv-Jukun conflict

in 1997, the two groups were clearly separated, both physically and psychologically. Most of the Tiv had been chased out of Wukari; indeed few Tiv felt comfortable about even spending the night in the town. At AAPW's workshop for Wukari elders in January 1998, the Tiv elders refused to stay together in the hotel, as they believed they would be an easy target for attack. The Jukun were fairly happy with the situation, as they now had undisputed control of both traditional and modern political power. However the economy was sluggish, as the Jukun had fewer customers for their wares as well as limited sources of food, which had previously been supplied by Tiv farmers.

In 1997, many Jukun were reluctant to follow a peace process, as they did not want the Tiv to return to Wukari and re-establish their numerical strength. The Jukun were also reluctant to negotiate a peace, as they felt that the government had betrayed them in previous negotiations and would allow high-ranking Tiv military officers to manipulate government decisions in their favour. Many Tiv had been displaced from the lands on which they had lived for decades or even centuries, and had no place to go. The Jukun had vowed not to let themselves be encircled by Tiv farmlands, as was the case in the pre-1990 era. Therefore the Tiv were forced to camp in distant, undesirable areas. Their schools, churches and health facilities had also remained closed since 1990. There was a graveyard peace. The military had stopped the fighting, but underlying issues had not been addressed. Most residents knew little about conflict management and felt that only the government could find solutions to the conflict. Each side felt that the other side was extremely stubborn and difficult, and felt that the people themselves could never sort out their own problems.

In the past two years, things have improved considerably. Some of the Tiv have moved back into Wukari town, tension has reduced, and parties on both sides have resumed interaction. Of course there are still hard-liners who would like to derail the peace process, but there is now a Wukari Peace Committee which tries to prevent future outbreaks of conflict.

Official Conflict Management

The Tiv-Jukun conflict in Wukari was the most violent dispute since the Nigerian Civil War, yet there was no international intervention and virtually nothing was done by the government, apart from using state power and force to stop the violence, without addressing the underlying issues, according to the traditional authoritarian model. Steps taken up to 1997 included:

1. A peace committee set up by the Wukari Local Government Council in 1990, which consisted of half Jukun and half Tiv. The members attempted to calm the situation but these efforts ended after a renewal of violence connected with the 1991 elections.

2. The Gongola State Government (Gongola was later divided into Taraba and Adamawa States) promised to set up a commission of inquiry, but nothing was done. Such commissions are often established, submit a report to government and nothing further is heard.

3. The sultan of Sokoto and other top traditional rulers visited the area and appealed for calm. This helped to stop the violence but did not address the underlying issues

4. The two civilian governors of Benue and Taraba States in the Third Republic reported the conflict to the presidency. Top Jukun and Tiv leaders were called to Lagos, where they met with the vice-president and discussed some of the issues. However the effort was not sustained and no resolution was reached.

5. The Taraba State house of assembly set up an ad-hoc committee to look into the conflict. However, a coup soon ended the government and the investigation died there.

6. The police, then the mobile police and finally the army were called in and brought the fighting to a halt. However the army remained in Wukari long after the end of the fighting and only served to exacerbate the problem by demanding bribes from the local citizens.

Multi-Track Diplomacy

According to reports from local citizens, Academic Associates PeaceWorks is the only NGO to have made an intervention in Wukari. AAPW has been working there for the past two years, using a multi-prong approach which includes:

1. *Peace education in secondary schools.* This training was conducted in June 1997 and involved teachers, principals and students from fifteen schools in Wukari and neighbouring areas. Peace education is a constructive, non-controversial way of entering the community, gaining cooperation and getting people to start thinking about the possibility of peace.

2. *Case study of the Jukun-Tiv conflict.* This was conducted in July-August 1997 by a team from AAPW which included a neutral team leader, one Tiv scholar and one Jukun scholar. By using this team make-up AAPW was able to gain good cooperation from both parties and neutral members of the community. The case study was thoroughly analysed in September by a group of AAPW staff and members of the Corps of Mediators to determine the issues and possible points of entry .

3. *The National Corps of Mediators*, established in 1997 by AAPW, is a group of senior and very respected persons from all parts of Nigeria, who were trained in conflict management and mediation in particular. Two members were selected to work on the Wukari conflict: Chief Ason Bur, a Tiv from Benue State who is a former deputy governor and federal director general, and George Maiangwa, a Chamba (a group aligned with the Jukun) from neighbouring Takum who is an education specialist and former chairman of Takum local government. These two gentlemen made extensive conciliation and shuttle mediation efforts. At first each worked with his own ethnic group and later they worked together. They continue to monitor any budding conflicts in Wukari and support the local peace committee in dealing with these issues.

4. *Conflict Management and Leadership Workshop for youth leaders.* From the case study and activities of the two mediators, AAPW identified the 'soldiers' from the conflict and brought them together in the neutral town of Jos, for a leadership workshop. After initial aggressive stances, members of the two sides remembered their boyhood ties and by the end of the three-day workshop, had sat down together to learn conflict management skills and analyse and find solutions to their own problems. Two youth leaders, one from each side, practiced mediation skills, using the Wukari conflict. They set up a Wukari Reconciliation Forum, which they implemented upon their return home.

5. *Conflict Management Workshop for Elders.* The next activity was a similar workshop for Tiv and Jukun elders, which was held in Wukari in January 1998. It had been scheduled for December, but had to be postponed due to interference by elites living outside Wukari who wanted to be present. By the end of the January workshop, the elders themselves had identified that the two groups had different and non-conflicting need and fears. The Tiv had pragmatic needs of land to farm, schools and health facilities reopened, certificates of indigenisation and inclusion in the modern political process. The Jukun on the other hand, had fears of loss of respect for their culture and authority. The group concluded that the problem could be reduced by the Tiv acknowledging and respecting the traditional Jukun authority, while the Jukun cooperate in reopening Tiv facilities and access to farmland.

6. *Local peace efforts.* After the AAPW workshops, the people formed the Wukari Peace Committee, which consisted of youths and elders from both the Jukun and Tiv. The youths were active and enthusiastic, while the elders were sluggish at first, perhaps due to a few but powerful sceptics among them.

7. *Further Conciliation Efforts.* Although the elders reached an agreement at the end of the workshop, certain issues which had not featured prominently in the sessions were later identified and discussed by the mediators and AAPW staff. The most important of these issues concerned a dispute over a piece of land, in which a rich Tiv farmer had taken the Jukun king to court (an abomination in itself), and to make matters worse, had won the case. It was agreed that this matter was capable of aborting the whole peace process. As a follow-up conciliation effort, Chief Ason Bur visited the Tiv farmer and others, seeking a possible solution.

8. *Follow-up Visits to Wukari.* AAPW staff have made repeated visits to Wukari, to inject more life into the peace process and address issues that need attention. A visit in June 1998 resulted

in progress finally being made on the issue of the farmer and the king.

9. *Efforts of the Wukari Peace Committee.* After the AAPW visit in June 1998, the peace committee finally took action on the issue of the king's land. Between June and September 1998, two members of the committee made frequent visits to the parties in the dispute. They were the chairman, who is a senior Jukun retired civil servant, and the secretary, a Tiv youth leader who happens to come from the community in dispute. These two met with other Tiv village heads from surrounding villages, who put pressure on the wealthy farmer to drop the court case and give the land back to the king, thereby making it possible for the king to in turn give the Tiv what they wanted. This was a face-saving solution for both the king and the farmer.

10. *Further Conciliation Efforts.* In early 1999, more analysis of the peace process and visits to Wukari and the Jukun king were made. It was discovered that in spite of settlement of the land issue, the Jukun had not yet reopened the Tiv schools and health facilities, nor had many Tiv been given the promised indigenisation certificates. Visits were made to key leaders, to ensure that the peace process continued successfully.

The methods used in this intervention include fact-finding, facilitation, consensus-building, use of good offices and informal contacts to facilitate communication among parties, conciliation, negotiation and mediation. It is our hope that the Wukari conflict can be not only managed but also transformed. In the process of finding a win-win solution, both sides have become aware of the conditions from which the conflict has arisen and now know what must be changed in order to prevent violence from reoccurring. Many of the youths and elders have also gone through a cathartic exercise, which has allowed them to go beyond their own resentments and anger, to a point of being able to work together to build a future peace for Wukari.

The Wukari Intervention by Academic Associates PeaceWorks can be considered successful in that it has not only dealt with some of the underlying causes of the Tiv-Jukun problem, but also empowered local citizens with skills of conflict analysis and management which will help them deal with other problems as they arise. The peace process will rely mainly on local action, with support from AAPW only when necessary. Five representatives from Wukari are members of the national Peace Support Network, which was formed in February 1999, bringing together people from six communities which have experienced violent conflict but where some degree of peace has been established. These representatives sat down and drew up an action plan for furthering the peace process in Wukari, reflecting our belief that peace is long-lasting only when the people themselves own the process.

An interesting side-effect of this intervention is that some of the people trained in Wukari have been active in helping to solve the conflict in Takum, a town an hour's drive from Wukari, where fighting between the Chamba/Jukun and Kuteb ethnic groups resulted in US$100 million destruction. It is important that, in the absence of positive government or international intervention, members of the civil society can take the initiative in managing conflicts which affect them. Indeed in the past the government has been an active party in creating community conflicts, often as part of a divide and rule strategy. While there was no government interference in Wukari, our peace activities in nearby Takum have been terminated twice by government, seemingly because some highly placed people do not want to change the status quo. At this point, the people themselves must determine what is their goal and not let anyone or anything divert them from it.

Prospects

As stated earlier, there has been tension between the Tiv and Jukun for a hundred years. It is unrealistic to expect the tension to completely disappear within a few years. However, a start has been made in helping the two groups to understand the others' positions, interests and needs. Efforts have also been made to turn it from a win-lose confrontation into a win-win story. These efforts will have to be continued and supported by the Wukari people themselves.

Recommendations

Based on the experience of the Wukari intervention, several actions can be recommended:

1. Use a multi-pronged approach, which incorporates many sectors of the community in the peace process.
2. Gain the cooperation and support of the top people, be they traditional rulers, elites, religious leaders, or government officials if possible.
3. Use the right person or group: neutral outsiders as mediators, insiders from the right ethnic group or religion or age category who can gain entry and accurate information.
4. Anticipate the role of spoilers. Decide whether to include them in the peace process or purposefully marginalise them.
5. Be flexible, in time schedules and budgets. The peace process seldom follows a tight timetable.
6. Continuously monitor and support the peace process, to prevent backsliding.

References

Adda, Samuel *For Posterity: The Roles of Governor Nyame, Others and Myself in the Tiv-Jukun Conflict*. Jos: Target Publicity, 1993

Adi, Atohinko *Jukun-Tiv Communal Clashes: A Reconsideration*, Adi Atohinko, Wukari, 1993

Atoshi, Grace *The Story of the Jukun-Tiv Crisis: Why and How They Happened*, Amune Printing Press, 1992

Best, Shedrack Gaya, Alamveabee Efhiaim Idyorough, and Zainab Bayero Shehu, in: *Community Conflicts in Nigeria: Management, Resolution and Transformation*. Ed. Onigu

Otite and Isaac Olawale Albert, Academic Associates PeaceWorks, Ibadan, Spectrum Press, 1999

Dent, M. *A Minority Party: The United Middle Belt Congress*. In J.P. Mackintosh (ed.), *Nigerian Government and Politics*, London, Allen and Unwin, 1992

Hogben, S.J. and Kirk-Greene, A.H.M. *The Emirates of Northern Nigeria*, London: Oxford University Press, 1996

Takaya, Bala and Tyoden, Sonny (eds.) *The Kaduna Mafia: The Rise and Consolidation of a Nigerian Power Elite'*, Jos, Jos University Press, 1987

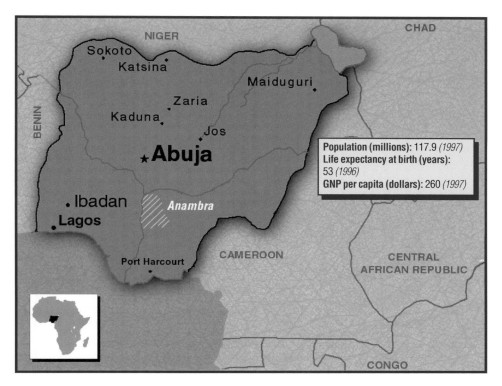

Population (millions): 117.9 *(1997)*
Life expectancy at birth (years):
53 *(1996)*
GNP per capita (dollars): 260 *(1997)*

Aguleri-Umuleri Conflict - The Theatre of Fratricidal War

The incidence of land disputes among rural communities in eastern Nigeria is increasing. Such disputes have become a regular feature of the interaction of rural communities irrespective of whether they belong to the same, or different states or local governments. The centrality of land to rural existence makes this inevitable. In a 1988 survey, some three hundred inter-communal disputes were recorded in the six southern states alone ◆ *By* **Raphael Chima Ekeh***

Not only is the incidence of land disputes increasing, they are becoming increasingly serious too. Many lives have already been lost while property with a value running into hundreds of millions has been destroyed. The stress, bereavement impoverishment, disruption of social life and insecurity caused by these conflicts is enormous and is inimical to the development of the communities concerned. This article presents a critical analysis of one such conflict - the ongoing dispute between the Aguleri and Umuleri. It aims to show how these conflicts can be explained with reference to the pre-colonial era, to describe their nature and intensity, to present an account of the intervention strategies that have been tried, and to make recommendations.

The Aguleri and Umuleri are of the same Igbo ethnic extraction and are predominantly Christians. The Aguleri and Umuleri towns are located in the southeastern part of Nigeria in Anambra State, close to the large town of

Onitsha, which lies on the Niger River. In the southeastern part of Nigeria, they are considered to be among the most highly educated as a result of their early contact with the missionaries.

The question 'who owns the land?' is at the root of communal clashes in several theatres across the country today. The same question also explains the bloody fights between Umuleri and Aguleri communities. The crisis goes back to the beginnings of each community's recorded history as it centres on the question of which community first settled its current territory and which community has the prior claim to the area known as *Otuocha*. To understand the source of the conflict however, an historical overview of the changing dynamics of the land dispute between the Aguleri and Umuleri is necessary.

Pre-colonial boundary conflicts
The central importance of land to the peoples of pre-colonial Nigeria, especially those occupying the equatorial rain forests, cannot be doubted. They were essentially farmers and aside from its direct economic importance, land also served variously for the payment of dowries, reparation for murder and other serious crimes and as a means of exchange. Consequently, land came to be the symbol of wealth and social standing in these societies. Land was also the principal cause of war. A class of warlords emerged and became consolidated in most parts of pre-colonial Igboland. This materialist perspective seems to us a more plausible explanation than the usual reference to the absence of clearly demarcated boundaries between pre-colonial communities. Boundaries were mostly settled on a balance of coercive forces. Thus, it is less a question of whether boundaries exist than it is a question of the ability to enforce their demarcation. This ability depends to a large extent on the development of a warrior class which is able to defend the land already in its possession and to capture more land. This was clearly the case during pre-colonial times.

The colonial era
The colonial state exacerbated the contradictions already existing in these societies by supporting some communities over and against others. Records show that captain O'Connor, the district officer of the area in the 1930s partly engineered the problem by encouraging the Umeleri to make claims to the whole of the Otuocha land, and promised to support them in this war (Chinwuba 1981:1). This, apparently increased the bitterness in the region and bottled it up for the future. Partisan policies of this type led to a substantial loss of faith in the colonial legal system. It is this lack of faith, partly carried over from the colonial state, that accounts for the inability of the post-colonial state to resolve the problem.

The acquisition of land by European traders, and the colonial government for various purposes provided the land necessary for trading and residential purposes, missionaries, churches, schools and farms, government residential quarters and administrative infrastructures. Ibeanu and Matthew's survey of 1995 shows that these lands are usually located in border areas. It was this land, which was either granted or seized, that was to become the most common source of conflict among neighbouring communities. This conflict was also aggravated by competition among European communities, particularly among different churches and levantine companies. In some places, neighbouring communities became divided among two missions. A grant of land to one meant a counter-grant to the other. Where disputed territory is involved, a spiral of conflict is immediately unleashed. The Otuocha land dispute between the Aguleri and Umuleri communities clearly illustrates the role of Europeans in creating and intensifying land disputes. This is a case of grant and counter-grant, sale and counter-sale to Europeans of land that had, historically, been used by the two communities in common without problem.

For one thing, the colonial dispensation created a local class of petty-bourgeois who sought property in land for various reasons. This group of social agents became the 'champions' of the interests of their communities chiefly for the purpose of securing political backing for their interests. The burgeoning of town unions, that became the stepping stone for petty-bourgeois political aspirations, is a remarkable feature of this era. Politically and economically marginalised by colonialism, this was the only platform readily open to the petty-bourgeoisie. They therefore became the vanguard of their communities in the various land disputes. Lawyers were particularly important in this regard. In Aguleri for instance, the youth association continues to play a central role in the dispute with Umuleri.

The post-colonial period
The post-colonial period has seen a worsening of the Aguleri-Umuleri conflict. There is no doubt that to a large extent these disputes were carried over from the colonial era. Land became a rallying point for villages, town and communities. Ibeagu and Matthew conclude that these disputes are difficult to resolve because they tend to become a vehicle for the expression of communal sentiments. The Aguleri-Umuleri dispute over the Otuocha land assumed alarming proportions after the civil war (Chinwuba 1981:25). The dire economic condition of post-colonial Nigeria fuelled the tensions already latent in the situation. However, the conflict was expressed in terms of litigation. The two communities' claims over the Otuocha and Agu-Akor lands have even reached the Supreme Court.

In 1993, the Umuleri sued the Aguleri over the rest of the land outside Otuacha but lost the case because they had earlier sold the land in question to the then Royal Niger Company Ltd. In 1935 and 1950 they also lost their appeals to the then West African Court of Appeal and Privy Council, London.

In 1964, the amendment of the instrument which constituted Otuocha, the headquarters of the then Anambra County Council, by altering the name to 'Otuocha Aguleri' occasioned another suit from the Umuleri which was, however, overtaken by the civil war. However the East Central State Government restored the name to 'Otuocha'

In the landmark judgement of 1984, the Supreme Court ruled that 'neither the Aguleri, nor the Umuleri have been able to establish that they are exclusive owners of Otuocha land'.

After 1984, the Aguleri community took a belligerent and provocative posture and began claiming Otuocha as its exclusive property.

Conflict Dynamics
Despite their close historical ties, the people of the Aguleri and Umuleri communities have been at each other's throats for centuries. The two communities have for decades lived and farmed side by side but with mutual distrust and enmity. In September 1995, the situation exploded. That year, public property including schools, banks, post offices, town halls and even churches were razed to the ground, further, some 200 private houses were destroyed and countless people killed.

The recent clashes of April 1999 followed the death of Mike Edozie, an Aguleri indigene, who was incidentally the chairman of the local government council of the area during the 1995 crisis. During his funeral some young men identified as Umuleri youths swooped on the mourners. There was pandemonium as the Umuleri youths allegedly dispersed mourners, gunning down some of them in the process. Exact casualty figures are disputed, but more than one hundred persons were killed.

Such is the intensity of the Aguleri-Umuleri conflict that both communities are deserted except for those actually prosecuting the war. Most of the indigenes of the feuding communities are now refugees in neighbouring villages while hospitals in Onitsha and environs are overflowing with victims of the communal clash.

Conflict Management
There have been no NGO initiatives in the area apart from the Red Cross Society's provision of emergency aid for refugees and displaced persons in the conflict. This is however considered a reactive rather than a pro-active measure toward transformation of the conflict.

In terms of official government intervention, the Nigerian state has taken three main types of action in an attempt to check the Aguleri/Umuleri disputes: peace enforcement, acquisition of disputed areas, and via court actions over disputed land. State intervention has mainly taken the form of court actions over disputed land.

The government has also constituted a number of commissions of enquiry to look into the causes of conflicts, identify stakeholders and make recommendations. Following the disturbance and killings of 1995, a commission of enquiry was set up to inquire into the circumstances and to ascertain the role played by different parties in the conflict. Although the government released a white paper in February 1997 with far reaching recommendations, nothing was done to defuse the situation until the latest conflagration of 1999.

The apparent failure of the Nigerian state to control the conflict arises from the people's lack of faith in the ability of the state to further their socio-economic aspirations. Thus, state intervention in land disputes is viewed with suspicion. Even the judicial system has failed to command the confidence of the Aguleri/Umuleri people. Despite having numerous lawyers and access to ample external legal advice, both communities have interpreted the various court pronouncements to suit themselves and these distorted interpretations have been largely responsible for the bad blood between the two communities.

Recommendations

Land disputes in general remain a serious threat to national security. The resilience of these disputes calls for a comprehensive national security formulation. This should also take into consideration structural violence arising from poverty, exploitation and inequality. However, state interventions have only served as temporary rather than lasting solutions. Indeed in many cases, these strategies have only deepened and intensified the conflicts.

A meaningful intervention in the Aguleri-Umuleri conflict therefore requires an in-depth, integrated and comprehensive conflict transformation strategy by a third party NGO. This will be aimed at building the capacity of the people in the community towards reconciliation and the re-humanisation of themselves. This could be achieved through bringing together all parties in the conflict to a problem-solving workshop which will create the necessary psychological space for them to begin to talk about their needs and fears thereby re-humanising themselves. This will also empower them to take their fate in their own hands and to take control of the peace process. This however must be preceded by a prejudice-reduction workshop for each of the groups to work on their identity towards healing and reconciliation.

Because of the Nigerian government's power over all aspects of the people's lives, and the NGOs lack of capacity to effect structural changes, it is necessary to have a synergetic peace-making effort involving the government and the NGOs. It is here that the church can play a role. In order to preserve the sainthood attained by one of the indigenes of Aguleri, Rev.Fr. Iwene Tansi, the Catholic church can be prevailed upon to constitute an advocacy group that will lobby the government to put in place the necessary structural changes needed to sustain any peace effort in the area. It is also necessary that a mechanism or structure created and owned by the people for anticipating and managing subsequent disputes be put in place in the area.

* **Raphael Chima Ekeh is Project Officer Training at Academic Associates PeaceWorks**

References

Chinwuba R. *Legal essay on the Otuocha Land Case*, Enugu Star Printing and Publishing Company, 1981
Clubb, L. Iboland Tenure. Ibadan University, Press, 1961
Ibeanu O. and Matthews The Refugee Situation in Nigeria - Paper presented at the conference of the African Studies Association of the United Kingdom (ASAUK). Cambridge University. September 14-16, 1988

Ibeanu O. *The State and Population in Displacement in Nigeria; Politics, Social Stress and Displacement in Rural Anambra State.* Ph.D. Dissertation. University of Nigeria, 1992
Vanguard Newspapers Monday April 19, 1999
This Day - The Sunday Newspaper May 2 1999.

Service Information

Reports

Amnesty International
- Nigeria - Release of Political Prisoners. March 1999

Human Rights Watch
- Nigeria - Crackdown in the Niger Delta. June 1999
- The Price of Oil - Corporate Responsibility and Human Rights Violations in Nigeria's Niger Delta. Febr. 1999
- Transition or travesty - Nigeria's Endless Process of Return to Civilian Rule. October 1997

Other Publications

Stabilizing Nigeria - Sanctions, Incentives, and the Support for Civil Society, by Peter M. Lewis, Pearl T. Robinson, and Barnett R. Rubin. Center for Preventive Action, New York, 1998

Selected Internet Sites

www.ndirect.co.uk/~n.today/mirror.htm (weekly newspaper Abuja Mirror)
www.kilima.com/mediamonitor/ (weekly publication Nigeria Media Monitor, edited by the Independent Journalism Centre in Lagos)
www.postexpresswired.com/ (daily newspaper The Post Express)
www.ndirect.co.uk/~n.today/today.htm (weekly newapper Today)
http://tribeca.ios.com/~n123/nigerldr (Federal Republic)

www.FreeNigeria.org (Free Nigeria Movement, grassroots based global mass movement)
www.igc.org/kind/fon5.htm (Friends of Nigeria)
www.nigeria.net/nigeria.nsf (General news and information)
www.odili.net/nigeria.html (NigeriaWeb)
www.cldc.howard.edu/~ndmorg/ndmpage.html (Nigerian Democratic Movement)

Resource Contacts

Judith Burdin Asuni - director Academic Associates PeaceWorks
Barnett R. Rubin - Director Center for Preventive Action. Email BRubin@cfr.org

Organisations

Environmental Rights Action/Friends of the Earth Nigeria
13 Agudama Avenue, D-line, Port Harcourt, Rivers State, Nigeria
E-mail: disera@infoweb.abs.net

Data on the following organisations can be found in the Directory section:
Academic Associates PeaceWorks (AAPW)
International Women Communication Centre (IWCC)
Centre for Conflict Resolution and Peace Advocacy (CCRPA)
Committee for the Protection of Peoples Dignity (COPPED)

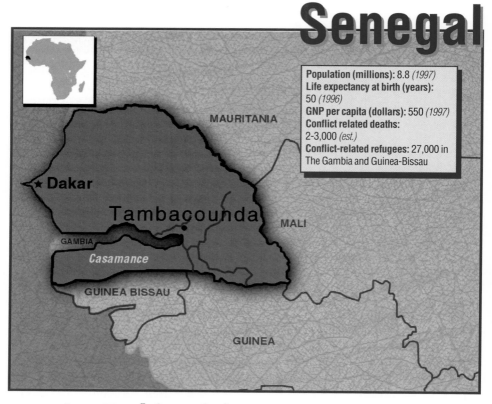

Senegal

Population (millions): 8.8 *(1997)*
Life expectancy at birth (years):
50 *(1996)*
GNP per capita (dollars): 550 *(1997)*
Conflict related deaths:
2-3,000 *(est.)*
Conflict-related refugees: 27,000 in
The Gambia and Guinea-Bissau

MAURITANIA

★ Dakar

Tambacounda

MALI

GAMBIA

Casamance

GUINEA BISSAU

GUINEA

An End in Sight to Casamance Violence?

Now in its seventeenth year, the Casamance problem, which began as a contest between a single-issue independence movement and the Senegalese authorities, has become increasingly complex. The independence movement has fragmented while neighbouring countries - especially Guinea-Bissau - have become more deeply enmeshed in the conflict. Signals are conflicting: the consistently hard line of the Senegalese government does not prevent it from attending peace negotiations, and while one part of the rebel movement escalates its violence, another talks peace. The civilian population, meanwhile, remains the principal victim ♦ *By* **Bram Posthumus**

Casamance is the name given to the southern part of Senegal which is separated from the rest of the country by the river and the mini-state of the Gambia. It differs in a number of respects from the rest of Senegal: it gets more rain, its landscapes - including areas of rain forest - and beaches are a major tourist attraction, while, culturally, it leans more towards the south and

Guinea, rather than the north and Senegal itself. The Diola people are the majority group in Casamance, but the ethnic mix is varied. Although the Casamance region has been Islamicised like the rest of the country, there are a significant number of people who practice Christianity and/or traditional beliefs. Their egalitarian political system and rejection of any central authority has, from a government point of view, made the Diola difficult to govern.

The Casamance was a Portuguese colony until 1866, when the Portuguese gave it to the French while keeping a slice of Guinea for themselves. Diola resistance against the French was quick to emerge and as late as 1943, the French sent the traditional Diola ruler, Queen Diatta into exile.

In 1947, well before national independence, the *Mouvement des Forces Démocratiques de Casamance* (MFDC) was set up and immediately declared the territory independent. When Senegal became a nation state in 1960, the calls for independence continued. This occasionally resulted in violence between local protestors and the police. As far as the Casamançais were concerned, Senegalese national independence simply meant a change of the force occupying their territory: first the Portuguese, then the French, now 'immigrants' from the north of the country.

Whether real of imagined, there has been a perception that the region has been short-changed by the government in Dakar, both in terms of political under-representation and in economic underdevelopment. 'Outsiders' are perceived as dominating the economy: the area does not receive sufficient benefit from the revenues from tourism and income from fish exports it generates. These feelings, and the right to self-determination were eloquently expressed by a Catholic priest, Father Augustin Diamancoune Senghor, in a lecture given in the Dakar Chamber of Commerce in the early 1980s, entitled *Message de la Reine Alinsiitowe Diatta ou hommage à la resistance Casamançaise* (Message from Queen Diatta, or in praise of the Casamance resistance). Senghor was attempting to radicalise public opinion in Casamance, using a Diola cultural organisation as his vehicle, and he subsequently became the leader of the militarised MFDC.

A large demonstration in the provincial capital Ziguinchor on December 26, 1982, marked a turning point in the relationship between Senegal and Casamance. It was organised by the MFDC and started at the sacred groves near the town. According to anthropologists, sacred groves are an important institution in Diola society and the symbolism of the demonstration may be related to the fact that administrative reforms, introduced by the government at the time, ran counter to traditional structures of governance in the region. Protesters attempted to remove Senegalese flags from government buildings and replace them with their own. Police moved in and in the following days there were serious clashes between protestors and police. Tensions remained and surfaced again a year later. December 1983 began with more violent confrontations between the police and protesters and on the December 18 there was a battle between separatist demonstrators and the police, which left 25 people dead. The day came to be remembered as 'Red Sunday'. Opposition continued throughout the 1980s, characterised by, sometimes violent, demonstrations and more government repression, including, detentions, the banning of the MFDC and human rights violations.

The nature of the smouldering conflict changed radically, with the official declaration of the armed struggle for independence, issued by the MFDC in May 1990. Since then, the MFDC, a Diola-dominated rebel group, has waged a guerrilla-type struggle against the Senegalese police and security forces. Their stated aim was - and is - to achieve independence for Casamance. For the government in Dakar, this has never been an option. In the course of the 1990s, the movement split into a moderate and a radical faction; it is said to have fragmented even further in the late 1990s. Repeatedly, neighbouring countries, most notably Guinea-Bissau (formerly Portuguese Guinea) have been dragged into the Casamance conflict by either side.

Conflict Dynamics

From the beginning of the rebellion the government adopted a hard line. President Abdou Diouf made it clear that he intended to deal vigorously with 'the dangers of separatism and fundamentalism of all kind', as he put it. He was following a tradition, firmly established by his predecessor Leopold Senghor, of strict nation-building which made no allowance for regionalist tendencies let alone movements or political parties of that nature. The government defines the Casamance issue in terms of 'law and order' and prefers to refer to the separatists as *'bandes armées au Sud'*, armed bandits in the South. It sends varying numbers of security forces to Casamance, according to the situation. These consist of army personnel, the police (Gendarmes) and Customs Services.

The Senegalese army prides itself on its high standards of professionalism and its track-record of UN peace-keeping operations, carried out in various parts of the world, including Africa. It does suffer, however, from a lack of resources and, according to Amnesty International, self-discipline in dealing with citizens. Amnesty has repeatedly accused both sides of gross human rights violations, but president Diouf has repeatedly rejected calls for investigations into human rights abuses by the security forces.

As early as June 1991, news came of a peace agreement that had been signed in Guinea-Bissau between Diouf and the MFDC on May 31, leading to the release of hundreds of Casamançais who had been held without trial for periods up to months. But the ensuing negotiations in a peace commission, set up to bring violence to an end faltered, because the government was not prepared to discuss independence for Casamance and the MFDC was not prepared to give up that idea. The commission could not engineer a breakthrough. This pattern was to repeat itself: violence - calls for peace - cease-fire - talks - impasse - renewed violence.

In September 1992, reports started coming in of fresh clashes between the two sides, leaving dozens of guerrilla fighters, civilians and military personnel dead. Particularly bloody was an MFDC attack on Cap Skiring, a major tourist resort, where they killed 31 people. As of September 1992, the whole region had been sealed-off by security forces. Even the Red Cross was refused entry. Refugees left in their thousands, including MFDC leader, Father Diamacoune Senghor.

An important reason for the upsurge in violence lies in a split within the MFDC which occurred in August 1992. There were now a north front, led by Sidy Badji, and the south front, led by Senghor. Both wanted independence, both alternated between the

negotiating table and the battle field. There were deep differences in opinion in terms of strategy - the political option favoured by the south versus the military option of the north. An additional explanation is that the north front feared Diola domination of the entire movement and decided to go its own way. The north front collapsed the same year but did not entirely disappear.

Fighting continued in 1993, despite calls for peace from Senghor, and violence was particularly heavy around the February presidential elections. After more than 250 people had been killed between February and July, another cease-fire was worked out. It came into force on July 8, 1993 and was signed by Senghor, now back in Senegal, and Madieng Khary Dieng, the minister of the armed forces of Senegal. Under its terms, the government and MFDC agreed to have an independent academic, French historian Jack Charpy, investigate the origins of the status of Casamance. He finished his work in November and confirmed that the region was Senegalese, a conclusion that was immediately rejected by the separatists.

By early 1995, it was quite clear that the cease-fire was moribund. In April, troops were ordered into Casamance, to search for four missing French tourists. They were never found but it provided the army with a pretext to launch a major cleanup operation in the border area with Guinea-Bissau. Senghor was placed under house-arrest on April 21, 1995. Other leaders were arrested too. In June, the MFDC annulled the cease-fire.

Serious clashes punctuated the year, but the creation, by the government, of the *Commission Nationale pour la Paix en Casamance*, in September 1995, combined with repeated calls for a cease-fire by Senghor led to new talks and the easing of tensions. The government even allowed consultation between MFDC personnel in Senegal and their office in France, in 1997.

However later in the same year, tensions began to inexplicably rise again. In January 1998 the aging Senghor (he turned seventy that year) made one of his numerous appeals for peace which again fell on deaf ears. His influence was reported to have waned in the movement, which appeared to be further

SENEGAL, Meeting of women group Ron Giling/Lineair

splintering into gangs of armed bandits, thus vindicating the government's original description of the rebels as *bandes armées au Sud*. But he still carried great symbolical value: his release remained an important MFDC condition for talks with the government. Meanwhile, tourism went into decline, deforestation became noticeable. According to *Le Monde Diplomatique* (October 1998) the ecological and economic collapse of the Casamance is only a matter of time. The various factions have reportedly resorted to deriving their income from extracting food from the villagers and the cultivation of cannabis for which there is a large market in Dakar, the Senegalese capital, and beyond.

Amnesty International contends that because both sides realise they cannot win the war militarily, they take it out on the civilian population, which has been subjected to arbitrary detention, murder, rape, extortion and intimidation from both sides. 1998 saw a rapid worsening of their plight with the rise in violent armed robberies, the introduction, by rebels, of landmines into the conflict and the Senegalese intervention in the civil war in Guinea-Bissau. Tens of thousands of Bissau Guineans and

Casamançais found themselves trapped between two vicious conflicts.

From January 1999 onwards, two contradictory developments have taken place. First, there was a meeting between Senghor and president Diouf, in which both men pledged to end the fighting and seek dialogue. But two months later, serious violence broke out once more, in which the authorities are said to have killed 22 rebels. One month later, fifteen rebels, four civilians and two soldiers died in clashes and a rocket attack on a house in Ziguinchor. The MFDC strongly condemned the rebel attacks on both the army and civilians, blaming it on 'uncontrolled elements'. Local traders quoted by the French news agency AFP said that the origins of the attack lay in the lucrative cashew nut harvest: whoever controls that trade has a secure income. The fighting coincided with talks in Banjul, the Gambian capital, among various rebel factions, principally the ones led by Senghor and Badji, aimed at arriving a common position during peace talks with the government, which had been brokered by the Gambian president Jammeh and the prime minister of Guinea-Bissau. In June 1999, the Senegalese government relocated a battle-hardened unit into the region, to flush out what it continued to call 'the bandits'. In spite of the increased military activity, the final declaration of the rebel movement, issued June 25 at the end of their Banjul meeting, was remarkable in that the demand for full independence was absent from the text. Senghor, who read the declaration, was confirmed as head of the rebels. The government expressed satisfaction with the fact that the rebels were speaking with one voice and were willing to negotiate.

Regional dimension

The regional dimension has always been latent within the conflict in Casamance. The start of the armed rebellion coincided with the aftermath of the April 1989 massacres of an estimated 2,000 Senegalese in Mauritania and the massive tit-for-tat expulsions between the two countries. International agencies attempted to help with the resettlement of tens of thousands of refugees and deportees. The seeds of this tension had been sown in 1987 when African Mauritanians staged a failed coup against the country's Arab rulers. This occasion marked the birth of an organisation called the *Forces of Liberation of the Africans in Mauritania* (FLAM), which went on to operate from Senegalese soil (some 60,000 Mauritanian refugees remain in Senegal).

Not surprisingly then, the Senegalese government and the press were quick to suspect a Mauritanian hand behind the outbreak of open hostilities in its troubled southern province. It gave the conflict a regional dimension which from time to time came back to claim centre stage, with accusations levelled against Mauritania, the Gambia - both countries allegedly transship Libyan arms to the MFDC - and military action in Guinea-Bissau. Relations with this last neighbour were tense at first, during a very uneasy period after Guinea-Bissau's independence (1975) under a strict Marxist government which Senegal had actively opposed. However, after a brief conflict over oil resources in 1989 which was amicably settled and the softening of Bissau's Marxist position, there have been improvements in Bissau Guinean-Senegalese relations, resulting in close military cooperation against the MFDC as of 1995. Even before that time, Senegalese planes

were bombing the São Domingos region inside Guinea-Bissau in December 1992, claiming it was destroying rebel bases there. The Senegalese had sufficient ground for their claim: because of cultural and kinship ties, the MFDC insurgents were able to operate from northern Guinea Bissau, although it is not entirely clear whether this has been the case from the very beginning of the conflict.

In fact, the direct cause for civil war in Guinea-Bissau had its roots in Casamance. The government of President Joao Bernardo Vieira, which had a standing agreement with Senegal not to support the rebels, accused the military of aiding the MFDC. This accusation was answered by counter-accusations and a military uprising. On the basis of a secret mutual assistance agreement, Senegal intervened within a day to combat the rebellious army and rout the rebels from their suspected bases in Guinea-Bissau. The rebels quickly aligned themselves with the mutinous military of Guinea-Bissau under the leadership of General Ansumane Mané, which made sweeping gains in the countryside and ousted Vieira from power.

Official Conflict Management

Although the *United Nations* has not been directly involved in managing the conflict, it is dealing with a closely related issue: the extreme proliferation of small arms in the region. In 1993, it set up an Advisory Mission on arms proliferation, at the request of President Konaré of Mali. The mission reported its findings to the Secretary-General in 1996. It identified a variety of causes for the unfettered flow of arms, including political instability, poverty, unemployment, ethnic and religious differences and the spill-over of intra-state conflicts into other states. This was said to apply to most of the states visited during the mission, including Senegal.

There have been various intergovernmental meetings in the West African region, in which means of curbing the flow of arms were discussed. A conference on the subject held in Banjul in 1994 even produced an accord on the matter. It is unclear whether any tangible action has been undertaken to implement this accord. *Individual governments* have tried to mediate, most notably Guinea-Bissau, which resulted in the signing of the 1991 peace accord and acted as a guarantor. It also mediated in the establishment of the Peace Commission in 1992 and was involved in the preparations for the short-lived 1993 peace accord, which the Bissau Guinean Minister of Defence, Lamine Mane, also signed. Guinea-Bissau hosts 24,000 refugees from Casamance.

In 1998, the Gambian president Jammeh declared himself willing to mediate. Although a Diola himself, the Gambian leader has remained neutral in the conflict, despite occasional accusations in the Senegalese press.

France also offered to mediate, in 1997. This was announced by prime minister Lionel Jospin when he visited Senegal, who stressed his role was mediation, not interference. The French ambassador was successful in facilitating the meeting between MFDC cadres in Casamance and the foreign representatives of the organisation, in France itself.

The *Senegalese government* has been a partner in the various peace negotiations but has always balked at even beginning to discuss the fundamental demands of independence. Nevertheless, some attempts at increasing Casamance incorporation in the national political process have been undertaken. Following the 1982-83 disturbances, some Casamançais were appointed as ministers and proposals for administrative reform were floated. While attempting to address some of the concerns among the Casamançais, the moves have also carried the element of isolating and de-legitimising the separatists of the MDFC. (For its part, the MDFC has pronounced Casamançais officials in the central government as traitors to the cause.) From its responses to outside allegations of human rights abuses, it remains clear that as far as the Senegalese leadership is concerned, the Casamance situation represents an unpleasant but manageable law and order problem, not a politically-motivated movement. The preference for the military option has therefore remained.

On the recommendations following the UN special mission mentioned above, Senegal has put in place a *National Committee on Light Weapons*, which has attempted to detail the circulation of arms in and out of the country. Arms flows originate in civil war areas in the vicinity of Senegal - mainly in Liberia and Sierra Leone - and pass through the neighbouring countries into the Casamance conflict. They also fuel criminal activities in Senegal itself, most notably poaching and drugs trafficking. A few dozen weapons have been confiscated but tangible action to stem the circulation of arms has clearly not yet moved beyond the stage of preparing legislation concerning possession, importation, licensing and registration of arms, which was going on in 1996. Whether the Commission has any influence other than providing the opportunities for meetings, remains unclear.

Multi-Track Diplomacy
Domestic
The MFDC has been as intransigent a partner in the peace negotiations as the Senegalese government. Most notably, the frequent calls for cease-fires by one of its most radical leaders - Senghor - have in the earlier stages of the conflict led to negotiations that were never fully concluded. There are signs, however, that his influence is diminishing, leaving the man who almost single-handedly radicalised the Casamance increasingly isolated.

There have also been reports of the local clergy getting involved in mediation, most notably the bishop of Saint-Louis, who is a Casamançais himself. According to the independent local daily, *Sud Quotidien*, there were meetings between Senghor and Senegalese bishops in the second half of 1997, even though the MFDC leader was still under house-arrest. Events on the ground have since superseded the Church's mediation efforts and the Senegalese government, having previously made no comments on these particular mediation efforts, denounced the bishops' activities early 1998, closing that avenue.

RADDHO (Rencontre Africaine pour la Défense des Droits de l'Homme), a Senegalese human rights organisation, has helped Amnesty International to compile its reports on human rights abuses in Casamance and has repeatedly asked the government to disclose the fate of people who have been arrested by the security forces and have never subsequently been seen.

There have been various popular calls for peace, starting in 1993 when the violence was at its worst. In March of that year, youth associations organised a major demonstration for peace in Ziguinchor. Two more demonstrations were held in 1995. The last, in December, was organised by the local civilian organisation, *Association pour le Développement de la Casamance* and ended with a huge concert in the Ziguinchor stadium in which all the big names of Senegal's show-business participated. (Senegalese superstar Youssou N'Dour has adapted the lyrics of one of his songs, to protest against the violence in Casamance.)

International

Although not involved in direct mediation, Amnesty International has made public a series of reports in which it has accused both sides in the conflict of serious human rights abuses and has asked for inquiries into these. In the course of its investigations, it did have the opportunity to discuss these matters both with president Diouf and Diamancoun Senghor, in January 1997.

Prospects

At present, the outcome of the conflict in Casamance is unclear. In the words of the UN Mission reports, it looks set to 'fester on', chiefly because of the hard-line stance taken by both sides, i.e. the unwillingness on the part of the government to define the conflict in any other terms than a 'law and order' problem, and the unwillingness on the side of the MDFC (or factions within it) to compromise its stance on independence. Now that some windows to talks have again been opened, there may be other options, although the situation on the ground is still marked by violence. Should peace prevail, then the regeneration of agriculture looks to be a priority, in order to diminish the region's dependence on illicit narcotics. The Senegalese government is also considering moves towards decentralisation, although what form this would take is not yet clear. It has, once again, ruled out the possibility of a referendum on greater autonomy. The prime minister of Guinea-Bissau, who had mentioned this option when he visited Dakar for talks with the government, had to retract his statement.

Service Information

Reports
Amnesty International
- Climate of Terror in Senegal. London, 1998

UN Research Institute for Social Development
- Discours et réalités des politiques participatives de gestion de l'environnement: le cas du Sénégal, Genève, 1998

UN Advisory Mission on Arms Proliferation
- Sahara-Sahel Advisory Mission report. New York, 1996

Other Publications
Comprendre la Casamance: chronique d'une intégration contrastée, by Barbier-Wiesser, François George (ed.). Paris, 1994 (comprehensive set of essays concerning the conflict)
Casamance et Sénégal au temps de la colonisation française, by Jacques Charpy
Intrastate Conflict and Options for Policy, by Pyt Douma, Georg Frerks, Luc vd Goor. Seminar document, Clingendael, The Hague, The Netherlands, 1998
Causes of the Casamance rebellion in Senegal, by Ferdinand de Jong. In: West Africa Regional Report, Clingendael, The Hague, The Netherlands (forthcoming)
MFDC: Casamance - pays de refus. Réponse à Monsieur Jacques Charpy. Ziguinchor, 1995

Selected Internet Sites
http://primature.sn/lesoleil (Le Soleil - government newspaper)
www.metissarana.sn/sud/sudqu.html (Sud Quotidien - independently produced)
www.ucad.sn/websen.html (excellent entry point to information pertaining to Senegal)

Organisations
Rencontre Africaine pour la Défense des Droits de l'Homme (RADDHO)
tel. +221 8246 056
fax +221 8246 052
email raddho@telecomplus.sn

Data on the following organisations can be found in the Directory section
Amnesty International

Sierra Leone

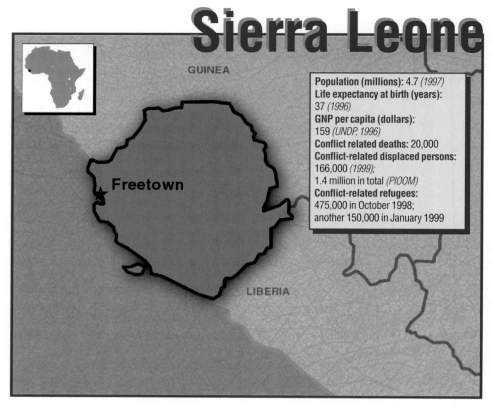

Population (millions): 4.7 *(1997)*
Life expectancy at birth (years):
37 *(1996)*
GNP per capita (dollars):
159 *(UNDP, 1996)*
Conflict related deaths: 20,000
Conflict-related displaced persons:
166,000 *(1999);*
1.4 million in total *(PIOOM)*
Conflict-related refugees:
475,000 in October 1998;
another 150,000 in January 1999

GUINEA

Freetown

LIBERIA

Seeking a Way out of the Abyss

Sierra Leone, a small country wedged between Liberia, Guinea-Conakry and the sea, made headline news in the 1990s by virtue of a conflict between rebel and government forces which is distinguished by the brutality of its impact on the civilian population. Since the rebel incursion in 1991, the war has zigzagged its way through the country's densely forested interior, reaching the capital, Freetown, on two occasions, with devastating results. With the latest rebel advance on Freetown, which was once again repulsed with the decisive help of the Nigerian-led intervention force, it is becoming increasingly clear that a continued preference for the military option on both sides will only lead to endless warfare. The majority of Sierra Leoneans favour neither side, and are increasingly vociferous in their calls for a negotiated settlement that may lead the way out of the seemingly self-perpetuating cycle of violence and away from the bottom spot on the Human Development Index. A cease-fire, effective since May 1999 and largely holding might - just might - bring this about ◆ *By* **Bram Posthumus**

S ierra Leone owes its name to the Portuguese explorers and conquerors who first came to the land in the late fifteenth century when it was under the influence of the Malian Empire. The Portuguese, and later the British, were engaged in the trade of slaves and local commodities. Having dominated the slave trade, the British banned it in 1807 and began resettling slaves from Canada, Jamaica and the United Kingdom itself to a new town, appropriately named,

Freetown. These were joined by slaves from other parts of West Africa who had been recaptured at sea by the British navy and set ashore in Sierra Leone. The ex-slaves coalesced into a community that came to be known by its language: Krio. Freetown flourished and became a centre of education. The Krio ruled supremely and complacently until independence from Britain in 1961.

The post-independence governments were characterised by ever increasing levels of corruption and nepotism. The first democratically elected government was replaced by a military regime, which proceeded to take corruption to previously unimagined levels. The late 1960s saw a number of elections, two coups and finally the installation of the third government, headed by the former Freetown mayor, Siaka Stevens. He ushered in a period of one-party rule, which in the view of the analyst Lansana Gberie, sowed the seeds of Sierra Leone's present troubles by its tendency towards the political and economic exclusion of the majority of Sierra Leoneans. Joseph Momoh, who took over in 1985, headed the fourth in the series of kleptocratic governments. Momoh was forced by donors to carry out a structural adjustment programme that brought what remained of the country's economy crashing to its knees. He also announced a return to multiparty-ism, thus fulfilling the second major donor demand.

In December 1989, a major conflict broke out in neighbouring Liberia between the military dictator there and a movement calling itself the *National Patriotic Front of Liberia*, led by Charles Taylor. This conflict was soon to spill over into Sierra Leone.

In March 1991, the first incursion took place, allegedly by Taylor's forces in retaliation for the fact that Sierra Leone had participated in the Nigerian-led West African intervention force, which at the time was acting as an anti-Taylor army in Liberia. Momoh enlisted the aid of Guinea-Conakry and Nigeria and sent his ill-equipped and poorly trained army to the border area. By June, however, it was clear that the army intervention had been unsuccessful.

Moreover, by this time there was a Sierra Leonean dimension to the rebellion. The rebels had set up base in Pendembu, in the north-east of the country and had named themselves the *Revolutionary United Front* (RUF). The RUF had its roots in a radical student movement in the 1980s, which had denounced government corruption and demanded change. They were headed by Foday Sankoh, an ex-army corporal who had been jailed in 1971 for a minor part in an alleged coup against Momoh's predecessor.

The RUF's political programme extended little further than the overthrow of Momoh - a desire which was by now universal in Sierra Leone - although Sankoh's remarks to the effect that the RUF believed in a multiparty democracy and free trade might be construed as a kind of political agenda. Whatever its political character, the RUF was able to capitalise on the widespread and deep-seated frustration in the Sierra Leonian population particularly among the many young people who felt short-changed in their education, employment and living standards. Whether abducted or serving as volunteers, disenchanted youngsters provided the core of the RUF fighting force. The RUF also developed a strategy of conducting a reign of terror in the areas they controlled, for which they would become notorious.

Before independence, the British colonisers created an artificial division between the coast and the interior with positions of power and influence going to members of the coastal community. However, the corrupt cliques who came into power after independence have been predominantly from the interior. The new elites in Freetown stripped the country bare leaving the rest of the population with little apart from their frustration. Paul Richards argues that 'frustration' is one of key words for understanding the conflict in Sierra Leone. However, it should also be said that, for the average Sierra Leonean, the 'issues' of this struggle seem pretty indistinguishable. Both sides have shown themselves adept at the profession of lofty ideals - perhaps a legacy of Freetown's distinguished educational past - but the problem is that the ideals proclaimed by both sides are constantly betrayed.

Hundreds of thousands have voted with their feet and left the country until such time as the violence comes to an end. Most of those who remain inside Sierra Leone identify with neither of the sides in the conflict and simply want peace as soon as possible.

Conflict Dynamics

The coup that brought 27 year-old captain Valentine Strasser to power on April 29, 1992 will probably be remembered as the action of a young man who came to collect his wages and found himself in charge of a country. Strasser and his men had not been paid and were frustrated by the lack of progress made by the counter-insurgency measures. Strasser set up the *National Provisional Ruling Council* (NPRC), which consisted of six civilians and seventeen members of the military. It was hoped that the NPRC would change the old corrupt ways and end the conflict through dialogue as Strasser had promised. However, in late 1992, RUF forces overran Kono, the country's main diamond area, dealing a further blow to the already crippled economy. The RUF continued to receive assistance from Liberia but there was also evidence of local support, particularly from some traditional chiefs.

NPRC and RUF forces were dragging the country into a vicious circle of violence, as was illustrated in the July-September 1993 issue of the BBC's *Focus on Africa* magazine. One picture showed a head on a pole, surrounded by smiling soldiers. 'Government handiwork', the caption read. The other showed three corpses that had spilled out of a car. 'Rebel handiwork', this caption read. Soldiers and rebels both engaged in extensive looting of the countryside, they illegally harvested cocoa and coffee, illicitly mined gold and diamonds and committed acts of terror against the population. Reports suggested that they actually worked in unison, in order to prolong the war. The people could no longer make any distinction between the two and gave the English language a new word for this phenomenon: 'sobel'.

In the first half of 1993, the government regained most of the territory it had lost and the rebels retreated to Kailahun in the north-east. The rise of an anti-Taylor faction in the part of Liberia bordering Sierra Leone cut off most supply lines, making the RUF more dependent on gathering what it needed from the local population. In

1994, the Sierra Leonean and Nigerian governments established a defence pact. Meanwhile the *Economic Community of West African States* (ECOWAS) extended the mandate of peacekeeping troops in Liberia to include Sierra Leone. These troops are known by their acronym: ECOMOG (ECOWAS Monitoring Group).

Strasser was ousted by his second-in-command, brigadier Julius Maade Bio in January 1996. Bio opened direct talks with Foday Sankoh and promised elections. Strasser had never initiated the promised dialogue with the RUF; instead he had enlisted the military assistance of the Nepalese crack fighters, the Ghurkhas. When this initiative failed he had hired the South African firm *Executive Outcomes* (EO) in May 1995, in order to dislodge the rebels who were by then on the outskirts of Freetown. EO forced the RUF into retreat and was paid handsomely in diamond-mining concessions for its efforts. The South Africans also started training a new anti-rebel force that was to emerge in the course of 1996: the Kamajors. These are traditional hunters, mainly of Mende origin, and surrounded by a degree of mythology about their invulnerability.

Thanks to this outside help, the elections could be held as planned in February 1996. They were won by Ahmad Tejan Kabbah, a retired UN official. Following more talks that were facilitated by both official and non-governmental mediators (see Conflict Management), Kabbah and Foday Sankoh signed a peace agreement in Abidjan, Ivory Coast, on November 30, 1996. The agreement provided for the demobilisation of the fighting forces, the recognition of the RUF as a political force, and the withdrawal of Executive Outcomes, a key demand made by Sankoh.

However, it became increasingly apparent that President Kabbah did not represent a radical departure from the old ways, despite protestations that his government was tackling corruption. Moreover, the war did not end. In breach of the Abidjan agreement, Kabbah intensified his cooperation with Executive Outcomes. The IMF blocked further financial support, effectively stating that it was not prepared to pay for privately hired state-security. EO had to leave in January 1997; five months later, on May 24 1997, major Johnny Paul Koroma staged a coup and chased Kabbah out of the country. Koroma set up a junta called the *Armed Forces Revolutionary Council* (AFRC). The coup was intensely unpopular among the civilian population. The international community slapped an economic and military embargo on Sierra Leone. Koroma invited the RUF into Freetown and for the first time the rebels visited their brand of terrorism on the capital, putting thousands to flight. The RUF/AFRC were dislodged in a major ECOMOG operation in February 1998. There was again mercenary involvement in the restoration of Kabbah to power: the British mercenary outfit Sandline International supplied arms to the Kabbah government.

The RUF/AFRC force and their leaders went back into the bush, pursued by ECOMOG and the Kamajors, now officially regrouped into the Civil Defence Force. According to CDF leader Hinga Norman, his forces also incorporated traditional hunters from non-Mende origin. Kabbah returned from Guinea in March. His government showed no appetite for dialogue, deciding to rely instead on a triumphalist attitude and sheer force. Sankoh, who had been arrested while on a visit to Nigeria, was handed over to the government by the Nigerian authorities. He was tried, found guilty of treason and sentenced to death in October. Twenty-four other executions were carried out during 1998. The rebels developed their own tactics in the wake of this reversal: *West Africa* magazine claims to have seen a report in which the RUF vowed to wreak havoc on the Sierra Leonean people in an operation dubbed Disrupt Civil Life. Sankoh's sentence incensed them into taking parts of Freetown, which they lost again in an extremely messy and ugly battle in January and February 1999, which left up to 5,000 people dead and the city in ruins.

The people, in whose name the conflict is taking place continue to be its victims. They have fled into the countryside, and over the border to Liberia and Guinea-Conakry in their hundreds of thousands, finding sanctuary in camps or among relatives and taking with them countless tales of starvation, rape, murder, gruesome mutilations and pillage, committed mainly but certainly not exclusively by the RUF. The perpetrators are predominantly uprooted undisciplined teenagers under the influence of hard drugs. Interior towns such as Makeni, Kailahun and Kenema have been looted and burned and economic activity has come to a complete standstill. Weapons flow freely around the country; in 1993 an AK47 could be bought for US$ 40. The relative popularity of the government/ ECOMOG/Kamajor side among the population seems to reside largely in the fact that they are perceived as the lesser of two evils. As one man told the *International Herald Tribune* in an article published February 1, 1999: 'The politicians do their own, the rebels do their own, and you're caught in the middle.' Rebels also take their war into Guinea, killing both refugees and Guinean civilians. In early June, the Guinean authorities claimed to have killed 400 rebels in a retaliatory raid inside Sierra Leone.

Nevertheless, as of March 1999, there were faint signs of hope. Firstly, President Kabbah allowed Foday Sankoh out of jail to talk with his rebel commanders about ways to end the conflict. Secondly, Kabbah and Sankoh signed a cease-fire agreement in the Togolese capital Lomé, which came into effect on 24 May and enabled humanitarian organisations to enter the country to help countless desperate people. Thirdly, real peace talks were announced. Since then, Sierra Leoneans have been hovering between hope and fear. Despite one or two minor incidents, the cease-fire has been holding, proving beyond doubt that Sankoh is still in command of his troops.

The Kabbah government and the RUF signed a peace deal on July 7, which incorporated amnesty for the RUF rebels, four cabinet posts for the rebels and further talks on the position of Sankoh. Disarmament began later that month, overseen by UNOMSIL. Estimated cost of this exercise are US$ 35. The rebels have been coming into Freetown, this time to hand in their weapons. Apart from a few skirmishes - one even involving Guinean troops who claimed to chase RUF fighters from their territory - the cease-fire has been holding for three months at the time of writing. Even a brief hostage crisis in

August 1999 in which Europeans and locals were held by the AFRC faction have not derailed the tenuous beginnings of what one might call a peace process. The rebels have yet to release at least 5,000 Sierra Leoneans they are holding in various parts of the interior.

Official Conflict Management

The *United Nations* Secretary General sent a representative to Sierra Leone in 1995 to help mediate a peace deal between the government and rebels. UN representatives also played a mediating role during the talks in Ivory Coast in 1996 and again, in February 1999, Secretary General Kofi Annan instructed his envoy, now Special Representative Francis Okelo, to help start a new dialogue between government and rebels. Okelo was present at the talks in Lomé.

When the Abidjan peace agreement was signed, Annan requested a small peacekeeping force for Sierra Leone. The Security Council failed to consider his request, following objections voiced by the RUF and lack of appetite on the part of the United States.

Two years later, acting on a proposal of the Secretary General, the Security Council created the *UN Mission of Observers in Sierra Leone (UNOMSIL)* on July 13, 1998. It was tasked with monitoring the demobilisation and disarmament of former combatants and training and restructuring the police force. The mission also assists the government in matters concerning human rights. The mission has 61 personnel, a US$ 22.6 million budget and was expected to run until March 13, 1999. UNOMSIL has had little chance to carry out most of its mandate and it had to withdraw its personnel in January 1999. Rebels torched the UNOMSIL headquarters in the same month. Following the return of the Kabbah government and the ensuing peace talks, UNOMSIL returned. It had its mandate extended further and is currently overseeing the disarmament of all fighting forces.

Other UN representatives have visited the country, for instance in 1998 to assess relief needs after ECOMOG had run the RUF/AFRC junta out of Freetown. In June 1999, the UN High Commissioner for Human Rights, Mary Robinson, visited Sierra Leone and called the human rights violations committed in the country 'the worst in the world'. Her remarks briefly turned the spotlight of media attention from Kosovo to Sierra Leone.

The UN Security Council imposed military sanctions, an oil embargo and travel restrictions on the RUF/AFRC junta on October 10, 1997. It also took the unprecedented step of authorising ECOMOG to enforce the embargo. After the violent removal of the junta in February 1998, it lifted the embargo on March 13, 1998. The UN went on to host a post-conflict reconstruction conference at its New York headquarters. In December 1998, the Nigerian delegate to the Security Council called a meeting with the five permanent members, to discuss the deteriorating situation in Sierra Leone.

The *Organization of African Unity* (OAU) authorised ECOWAS states to bring back the Kabbah government after it had been ousted in May 1997. Previously, the OAU had played a mediating role in the government-RUF talks in Ivory Coast and was doing so again in the Lomé talks in June 1999.

In 1998, the OAU created an advisory body called the *African Women Committee on Peace and Development*. Its aim is to foster full participation of women in the continent's efforts to prevent, manage or resolve conflicts. On February 4, 1999 the group issued a statement condemning human rights abuses in Sierra Leone and strongly endorsing both Kabbah's government's efforts to resolve the crisis and the initiatives taken by an organisation called the West African Women's Crusade for Peace and the various Sierra Leonean women's groups.

The *Commonwealth* played a mediating role in the government-RUF talks in Ivory Coast.

The *Economic Community of West African States (ECOWAS)* has played a pivotal role in efforts to bring the conflict to an end, using a mix of military and non-military means. It gave the Nigerian peace-troops, already in Sierra Leone since 1991, increased legitimacy by affording them the same status as those operational in Liberia, under the banner of ECOMOG. This was done in 1994. ECOMOG has continued to enjoy a virtually unlimited mandate, enabling it to wage war against the rebels on behalf of the government of Sierra Leone

FREETOWN, SIERRA LEONE, Psychiatric hospital

EDGAR CLEIJNE/LINEAIR

ECOMOG was also asked to provide security for UN personnel working in the country for UNOMSIL. On the negative side, the UN accused ECOMOG of summarily executing citizens during the battle for Freetown in February 1999. However, its report blamed most atrocities on RUF rebels and advocated continued support for ECOMOG.

Nigeria has carried the lion's share of the burden of the 15,000-strong ECOMOG force, in terms of manpower and cost, estimated by diplomats to be around US$ 1 million per day. This is chiefly because it is the only power in the region with the money to bankroll such an operation, something that the international community is not willing to do. Sierra Leone was in a sense a logical follow-up from the Liberia action and, finally, there were also domestic political reasons for Nigeria's involvement. The country, severely discredited by a period of disastrous military dictatorships, was in great need of some kind of success to bolster its battered image.

Following the May 1997 coup, ECOWAS adopted a three-pronged strategy to restore the elected government to power: the imposition of regional sanctions against the junta in Freetown, continued support for the ECOMOG forces that were enforcing the ban, and talks with the junta. This resulted in the Conakry peace plan, agreed between ECOWAS and the junta in the Guinean capital on October 23, 1997. It provided for the hand-over of power to the Kabbah government on April 22, 1998, a deal the junta proceeded to ignore.

The Nigerian contingent in ECOMOG has also been engaged in training what should eventually become the new Sierra Leonean army.

With a civilian government in power since May 29, 1999, it is clear that changes are on the cards. Nigeria had already indicated that it wants a radical redistribution of the burden to be shared both within ECOWAS and with the international community. The new president Olesegun Obasanjo has made it clear that Nigerian troops will not stay in Sierra Leone forever. In January 1999, the Malian government confirmed that it was prepared to send troops into Sierra Leone to strengthen ECOMOG. The Gambia was also reported to be willing to send in peacekeepers. Ghanaian and

Guinean troops are already in Sierra Leone.

West African governments have been involved in the various series of peace talks as mediators. Between May 1996, when it hosted peace talks in Yamoussoukro, and November 1996, when the peace agreement was signed in Abidjan, the government of Ivory Coast acted as a facilitator and a mediator in the talks between the government of Sierra Leone and the RUF. Currently, Togo is hosting the talks. Its president, Gnassingbe Eyadema is currently chairman of ECOWAS, while his foreign minister, Kokko Koffigou, chairs the talks. Representatives from Guinea and Nigeria are also present. Should the June 28 breakthrough materialise, the new Nigerian president Obasanjo is likely to take the credit for its success as a result of his personal mediation.

Various governments in *Europe and North America* have provided financial support to the ECOMOG effort: the United States (close to US$ 4 million in 1998), Britain (US$ 6.5 million in all), the Netherlands (US$ 10 million), Canada (under US$ 1 million) among them. Britain has pledged US$ 10 million for a projected Disarmament, Demobilisation and Reintegration (DDR) programme, on which the participants in the Lomé talks were briefed by World Bank officials in late June 1999. The Bank has pledged US$ 9 million and manages the trust fund that will pay for DDR. On the diplomatic front, both Britain and the US are present at the Lomé talks. In fact, Jesse Jackson, as US President Bill Clinton's special envoy for the promotion of democracy in Africa, can be credited with having played a major role in brokering the May 1999 cease-fire and securing the release of 2,000 prisoners of war, mostly children. He had already prepared some of the ground in November 1998, when he tried to persuade the Kabbah government into talks with the rebels, with apparent success.

Another diplomat who has been closely connected with the restoration to power of Kabbah in February 1998 was the British High Commissioner, Peter Penfold. His role became controversial when the British government found itself in a full-blown political row over alleged Foreign Office knowledge of a US$ 10 million arms delivery to the Kabbah government

by Sandline International. Investigations made public in February 1999 established the fact that the United Kingdom had breached the UN arms embargo against Sierra Leone, in order to restore Kabbah to power. No ministerial heads rolled.

The Sierra Leone government was a partner in the peace talks in Ivory Coast in 1996 and a signatory to the peace accord that was signed in November of that year. In January 1999, when Kabbah and Sankoh were both at Lungi International Airport from where they could see Freetown burn, they agreed to try and re-institute the Abidjan agreement.

In January 1998, the government announced it was compiling data on people who had committed crimes against humanity and would present these to an international court for prosecution. No follow-up on this activity has been reported.

Multi-Track Diplomacy
Domestic

There has been a great deal of civil action aimed at persuading the country's warmongers to find more peaceful ways to settle their differences. During the February 1996 elections, which were held under extremely difficult circumstances, people literally risked their lives to go and vote by disregarding a RUF threat to kill anyone seen in or near a voting station. The turnout was understandably low, but the RUF goal of enforcing a boycott certainly failed. Civilians protected the ballot boxes with their bodies as they were transported to the counting centres, preventing rebels from taking and destroying them. One report called these actions 'an impressive demonstration of their desire for peace'.

It was by no means the only action. Sierra Leonean trade unions, women's groups, students, clerks, civil servants and many others have been very active in the civil disobedience movement that brought the entire country to a standstill in protest against the May 1997 coup of Koroma. Various groups sprang up, including those with self-explanatory names such as the National Movement for the Restoration of Democracy and the National Salvation Front.

There have been other local peace initiatives and those undertaken by women's groups merit special attention. Since 1994 women's groups have been holding peace demonstrations and prayer sessions and have had a number of meetings with representatives from both sides, in an effort to persuade them to reach a negotiated settlement. In January 1995 they formed the *Womens Movement for Peace*. Women were critical contributors to the relative success of the 1996 presidential election and the massive civil disobedience against the Koroma junta. In as much as they have been able to keep an organisation together, they are very strong advocates for peace and a representative government. Those who have survived the Freetown mayhem in 1999 will be crucial in the reconstruction of the nation.

Sierra Leone has an impressive list of local human rights and other organisations, which, depending on the state of the conflict, have worked either from within the country or from abroad, in an effort to promote human rights and/or a peaceful solution to the conflict. They include the local chapter of Amnesty International, the Civil Liberties Congress, Prison Watch, the National Commission for Democracy and Human Rights, the Society for the Advancement of Civil Rights.

The *Christian Welfare and Social Relief Organisation* is a rural development organisation which has worked in many conflict-affected areas. Inside the conflict areas it runs mainly relief programmes but it also has a Department of Education in Conflict Prevention.

Given the chaos prevailing in the aftermath of the second battle for Freetown, it is impossible to say which of these organisations is active at present and the same is true of the international organisations. Given the climate in the country since the May 1997 coup, work of this nature can be life-threatening. The same can be said of the *media*: the death penalty spree of the Kabbah regime in late 1997 and the rebel onslaught in Freetown have led to the death or disappearance of at least eight journalists. International media and individual journalists have played a role, however small, in bringing the situation to international attention.

A special place may be reserved for the more mystically grounded movements, including the hunter-militias, which have in some places succeeded - albeit temporarily - in fending off both rebel advances and government troop movements by claiming supernatural powers, which are deeply respected by all sides in the conflict. One remarkable example is that of 72 year-old female magician, Marama Keira, who is highly regarded locally and who claimed to have retaken her birthplace, Koidu Town, with her Tambaboroh fighters, using juju. The Kamajors are a similar group but on a larger scale. A number of these groups have been merged into the Civil Defence Force.

International

In early 1995, the Sierra Leone government invited the *International Committee of the Red Cross* to mediate in the conflict. The ICRC played a key role in the release of a number of European hostages. The RUF had taken to abducting Europeans in order to ensure that the conflict was put on the political agenda outside Africa. The ICRC accompanied the hostages to Guinea following protracted negotiations.

One of the more eye-catching efforts at conflict-resolution was undertaken by *International Alert* (IA). IA originally became involved in 1995, also as a result of the hostage crisis. IA's role in the release of the hostages has been controversial: the organisation claims it helped bring about their release while others maintain that IA's involvement has merely complicated negotiations already under way. By the time the hostages were freed, IA was deeply involved in mediation efforts between Strasser and Sankoh. Originally intended as a 'multi-track' effort, its focus came to rest almost exclusively on moving the negotiations forward. The special envoy of IA developed a special relationship with Foday Sankoh, and these efforts are likely to have played an important role in bringing the RUF to the negotiations that led to the November 1996 peace agreement.

IA's role has been severely criticised by a team of researchers from the Chr. Michelsen Institute based in Bergen, Norway, which was commissioned by the Dutch Ministry of Foreign Affairs to evaluate the work of IA in three selected countries, including Sierra Leone. The researchers commended IA for being in Sierra Leone at a critical juncture, but contended that -

while IA may have had a point in agreeing that the RUF had a political agenda to pursue - the position the organisation took on matters during the negotiations made it vulnerable to accusations that it was not an 'honest broker' but played an advisory role and was even on the side of the RUF. IA has admitted to having made mistakes.

The Swiss-based organisation *Africa Women Solidarity (FAS)*, which is closely linked to Synergies Africa, has conducted training sessions with conflict settlement techniques, at the invitation of Sierra Leonean women's organisations. The organisation has also contributed to the OAU-linked African Women Committee on Peace and Development.

The *International Crisis Group* helped fundraising efforts to finance the 1996 elections that brought Ahmad Tejan Kabbah to power. The ICG has supported civil campaigns for good governance and regularly publishes situation analyses of Sierra Leone with recommendations aimed at actors in the conflict.

Amnesty International and *Human Rights Watch*, although not directly involved in mediation, continue to report on human rights abuses committed by all sides in the conflict. More specifically, Amnesty has publicly deplored the evacuation of UNOMSIL in January 1999, as a result of the assault on Freetown and has urged the continuation of the work of the human rights officers who are part of the UN mission. Human Rights Watch has urged an end to the use of child soldiers in the conflict and has also urged the UNHCR to move refugees inside Guinea away from the border area, for pressing safety reasons. On July 8, 1999 HRW issued a statement severely criticising the UN for endorsing the peace deal signed the day before. It said that the kind of atrocities committed by the RUF should never have been pardoned in a general amnesty as per the deal.

FORUT is a Norwegian-based NGO which runs programmes in Freetown, for instance with disabled street children. In 1998, FORUT stated its intention to get involved in conflict resolution through peace education, training, community-based trauma healing and reconciliation.

Other internationally connected groups, such as the *Netherlands Christian Women Farmers Association* have invited people from Sierra Leone over to inform the world about what was going on there. In November 1977, at the invitation of the Women Farmers group, two female teachers made the perilous journey to the Netherlands, and described not only the harrowing atrocities in the country, but also the groundswell of support for the civil disobedience campaign that was at that time being waged against the Koroma-RUF junta.

Prospects

A number of analysts, including anthropologist Paul Richards, have pointed out that the war has been fed by a culture of violence that feeds upon itself: violent acts beget more violent acts and the cycle appears unbreakable. Greed, which has been the preponderant characteristic of Sierra Leone's ruling elites has spawned a particular mind-set among angry and disenfranchised youths in the country: gun + terror = power + income. The RUF-junta rebels, between 10,000 and 17,000 Kamajor militiamen (who have now effectively replaced government soldiers) mainly consist of these youths. He further argues that the RUF may resemble a sect-like structure run by an almost mystical figure (Sankoh), from which escape is impossible. The kind of violence meted out to civilians can be seen as retribution for helping the enemy that is threatening to dismantle the sect.

The only regular armed force in the country are the estimated 15,000 Nigerian and Guinean ECOMOG troops. Also remaining are the various mercenary outfits that have turned Sierra Leone, according to one report, into their 'happy hunting ground', fighting on either side of the conflict. These are all factors in the continuation of the conflict, which has once again gone back to the countryside. The civilian population does all it can to steer well clear of anyone with a gun: hundreds of thousands refugees remain in Liberia and particularly Guinea-Conakry.

Perhaps the diplomatic opening that Kabbah and Sankoh created in early 1999 and which have led to the Lomé peace agreement in July, will provide the much-needed breakthrough in thinking.Two factors may have proved decisive in the adoption of a new line, if that is what it is:

renewed public pressure on the Sierra Leonean president to open dialogue, and the likelihood of the withdrawal of the Nigerian ECOMOG troops, following that country's return to civilian rule. Meanwhile, Sierra Leone has been laid to waste. The infrastructure is gone and the scale of human suffering in the interior has only become apparent with the arrival of emergency aid. Even if the country recovers from its material and psychological traumas - and the required international help to do this is not forthcoming - it will take much longer to solve the basic issues that have underpinned the conflict. After all, if peace is here to stay, there is still the frustration factor to deal with.

Recommendations

The researchers who evaluated the work of International Alert made a number of recommendations to the organisation. Having indicated that IA's problem in Sierra Leone lay in the fact that its actions lacked transparency, the researchers recommend that IA create space for dialogue by developing and strengthening local peace constituencies, rather than facilitating dialogue itself. They also recommend that IA be engaged in advocacy and lobbying around issues of political, social and economic justice - the absence of which breeds conflicts, as the Sierra Leone example amply demonstrates. Finally they recommend that IA maximises the use of the rather limited resources it has and concentrate its actions geographically.

The Centre for Democracy and Development Briefing paper states quite clearly that the lifting of the arms embargo against Sierra Leone following the return of Kabbah was a mistake. All transfers of weapons to Sierra Leone should be immediately stopped, it urges. It also urges dialogue between the two main parties in the conflict, to be guaranteed by OAU and UN. These talks should basically constitute the reactivation of the Abidjan and Conakry peace agreements and involve a cease-fire, the release of Foday Sankoh (in order to avoid him becoming a martyr for his cause), a broadening of the base of the Kabbah government to include more ethnic groups and civil society, an internationally supervised demobilisation process, national reconciliation and elections.

The International Crisis Group has made it clear that the vacuum created by the absence of a reliable professional army must be filled. Furthermore, the civil society sector needs expansion, since it contributes to reconciliation and finally, there needs to be an improvement in the quality of governance in the country.

Taking up that point, Kamar Yousuf, a research intern at ACCORD in South Africa, recommends a comprehensive government strategy aimed at improving the quality of administration, economic revival (especially in the areas of financial accountability, investment and employment creation) and nation-building through a South African-style truth and reconciliation process, with the international community at the ready to promote human rights and the rule of law.

It was Jesse Jackson who singled out the disparity between the world's response to the crises in the Balkans and West Africa. 'It is a tale of two continents. There has been no budgetary commitment to rebuilding this war-torn nation as we heard in Europe.' The *International Herald Tribune* picked up that point in an editorial entitled 'Kosovo and Sierra Leone' in its June 16 edition: 'The contrast can be explained by circumstances, but that is not good enough. A fair and sustainable policy must tap the energies and resources that ease rather than aggravate the lingering question of why the United States sometimes appears readier to help a distressed white country than a distressed black one.'

Background document provided by Berto Jongmans/PIOOM

Service Information

Reports

Amnesty International
- Sierra Leone Reports. London 1995, 1996
- Sierra Leone - A disastrous setback for human rights. London, 1997

Centre for Democracy and Development
- Briefing paper on current developments in Sierra Leone. Kampala, 1999

FAS (Femmes Africa Solidarité
- Women's participation in the peace process of Sierra Leone. Geneva, 1997

International Alert
- Peace Mission to Sierra Leone - Taking steps to advance the peace process, London, 1996

International Crisis Group
- Sierra Leone - Report to the Japanese Government. 1996

Other Publications

War and State collapse - The case of Sierra Leone, by Lansana Gberie. Waterloo, Ontario, Canada, 1998
African weak states and commercial alliances, by William Reno. In: African Affairs vol. 96 no. 383, April 1997
Corruption and State Politics in Sierra Leone, by William Reno, Cambridge University Press, Cambridge, 1995
Fighting for the Rain Forest - War, youth and resources in Sierra Leone, by Paul Richards. London, 1997
NGOs in conflict - An evaluation of International Alert, by Sorbe et al. Chr. Michelsen Institute, Bergen, Norway (incorporates International Alert's response to the case study), 1997
Conflict and Conflict Resolution in Sierra Leone, by Kamar Yusuf, research intern at ACCORD, Durban, South Africa
Kamajors, 'sobel' and the Militariat - Civil society and the return of the military in Sierra Leonean politics, by Zack-Williams. In: Review of African political economy, no. 73, 1997

Selected Internet Sites

www.prairienet.org/acas/panafrican.html (Centre for Democracy and Development)
www.intl-crisis-group.org/projects/sierra/reports (International Crisis Group)
www.crisisweb.org/projects/sierral/Default.htm/ (extensive information on the current situation in the country)
www.fasngo.org (African Women Solidarity)
www.unorg/Depts/DPKO/Missions/Unomsil (UN mission in Sierra Leone)

Resource Contacts

Paul Richards - University of London, Department of Anthropology. Email paul.richards@tao.tct.wau.nl
Bineta Diop - Africa Women Solidarity
Addai Sebbo - former program manager Int. Alert

Data on the following organisations can be found in the Directory section
FORUT
Campaign for Good Governance
Africa Women Solidarity/Femmes Africa Solidarité
International Alert
International Crisis Group
Human Rights Watch
ACCORD

Southern Africa

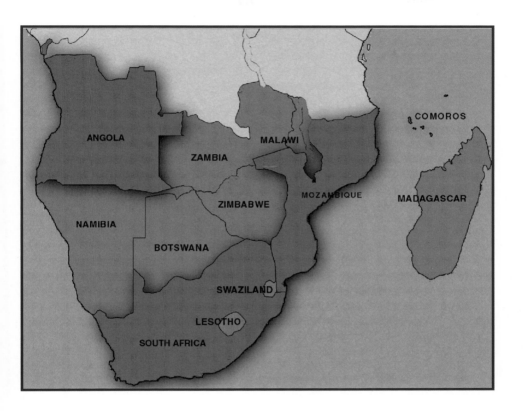

Revisiting the Politics of Peace and Security in Southern Africa

Three years ago, whilst lecturing in Japan on peace and security in southern Africa, I felt like a prophet bearing witness to all the positive developments in the sub-region with the conviction that peace and development was assured. In the space of these three years however, southern African peace and security has deteriorated rapidly and the region as a whole could be said to be facing a crisis. How did this come about? What were the trigger mechanisms that led the sub-region down the path of death, destitution and despair? ◆ By **Hussein Solomon***

Essentially, my lectures in Japan focused on the end of apartheid-destabilisation and how the new South Africa has become a force for peace in the sub-region, especially after Pretoria's successful interventions in Mozambique and Lesotho. The lectures also focused on the growing pro-democracy movement from Dar es Salaam to Cape Town and from Windhoek to Maputo. 1996 was also the year in which several states in the region were witnessing positive economic growth and regional economic integration was becoming a reality with the Maputo Development Corridor and the Lesotho Water Highlands Project illustrating the fruit of closer economic cooperation.

In this period, it seemed that the South African Development Community (SADC) was coming into its own with protocols from the free movement of people to free trade on the cards. In this context, the collapse of the Somali State, civil strife in Algeria and Sudan and the conflict in Liberia and Sierra Leone seemed remote indeed. True, the situation in Angola and the former Zaire was cause for concern, but there was tremendous confidence in the region that the crises in both these countries could be brought to a peaceful resolution.

So what happened in this short period of three years? In attempting to answer this question I will provide a brief overview of some of the threats facing the region. For the purposes of conceptual clarity, each of these will be discussed separately. In reality though, these sources of southern African insecurity overlap

and reinforce overall regional insecurity. The article will conclude with a few recommendations.

The politics of identity and exclusion - The case of ethnocentric nationalism

Since 1998, there has been an upsurge in ethnic nationalism throughout southern Africa. In the cases of South Africa and Malawi, its form is more muted and linked to political parties and voting patterns. In South Africa, Afrikaners concerned about their language and cultural rights as well as what they perceived to be their economic and political marginalisation in post-apartheid South Africa mobilised to form a new political party before the June 1999 elections - the *Afrikaner Eenheids Beweging* (the Afrikaner Unity Movement).

In Malawi, meanwhile, there is a close correlation between ethnic identities and voting patterns. Thus the Malawi Congress Party (MCP) derives its support largely from the Chewa tribe in the central region, whilst the Alliance for Democracy (AFORD) receives most of its support from the north, and the United Democratic Party (UDP) always leads the polling in the southern region.

But, ethnic nationalism can also take more virulent forms, which could threaten the territorial integrity of southern African states as the development of the secessionist movements in both Zambia, and Namibia indicates. In Zambia Akashambatwa Mbikusita-Lewanika, president of the opposition Agenda for Zambia, has since November 1998 been advocating a free and independent Barotseland in western Zambia.

In the Caprivi Strip of northeastern Namibia, the ethnic secessionists have taken a more militant turn in the formation of the Caprivi Strip Liberation Movement (CSLM). Following reports that the CSLM intends to formally declare the secession of the Caprivi Strip from the rest of Namibia, the Namibian Defence Force (NDF) were sent into the Caprivi. This, in turn, resulted in the mass exodus of several thousand people from the Caprivi Strip to northern Botswana where they sought refuge. Following the decision of the Botswana government to grant political asylum to fifteen leading secessionist members, relations between Windhoek and Gaborone grew tense. This tension only served to further sour relations between the two countries in the context of their unresolved contest over ownership of the disputed Kasikili/Sedudu islands as well as use of the waters of the Okavango Delta. The case of the CSLM is instructive since it indicates that ethnic movements not only threaten the territorial sovereignty of the host state but can also contribute to interstate tension.

The politics of illiberal democracy

Illiberal democracy describes a situation in which a multiparty democratic dispensation exists with all the trappings of democracy in name only, at the rhetorical level. In reality however, such a state often functions as a one-party state.

In Malawi, the United Democratic Party faced a serious challenge from opposition parties in the run up to the June 1999 elections due to what the opposition terms the 'legal rigging of the elections'. Essentially what the ruling party has done is to increase the number of constituencies in southern Malawi. As noted above, it is from the south that the UDP draws the majority of its support. Effectively this, according to opposition parties, makes the election results a foregone conclusion - the UDP will remain the ruling party with a comfortable majority.

Such legal gerrymandering, however, is not confined to Malawi alone. In Namibia, on November 4, 1998 the ruling South West

African People's Organisation (SWAPO) made use of its parliamentary majority to change the constitution to enable president Sam Nujoma to run for a third term of office.

The rise of illiberal democracy is also accompanied by human rights abuses as the ruling party responds to criticism by utilising its security forces. Thus, on January 27, 1999 a journalist, Fernando Queinova, was arrested and detained by police in the Cabo Delgado province of Mozambique for reporting on police brutality. In illiberal democracies, even criticism emanating from within the ruling party itself is silenced. Hence on November 27, 1998 Namibia's former High Commissioner to Britain, Ben Ulenga, was suspended from the SWAPO Central Committee after objecting to plans to allow president Nujoma to seek a third term in office.

But it is Zimbabwe that provides the quintessential example of an illiberal democracy sliding down the path to authoritarianism. Tensions in Zimbabwe have arisen as a direct result of economic decline, perceptions of corruption on the part of the ruling Zimbabwe African National Union - Patriotic Front (ZANU-PF), as well as the escalating costs of Zimbabwe's war effort in the Democratic Republic of the Congo which is currently estimated to be costing Harare US $1 million a day. In the face of growing economic hardship, trade unions have demanded a twenty per cent wage hike and embarked upon a stay-away action. In the face of mounting pressure the government has embarked upon a series of repressive measures. These include a government ban on strike activities as well as the harassment of opposition political parties and the arrest and torture of journalists.

Trapped between the politics of traditionalism and modernity: the case of Swaziland

Faced with the ever-increasing pace of globalisation, as we approach the dawn of a new millennium, many African states are trapped between more traditional forms of government and modern ones. Within the southern African sub-region, Swaziland clearly reflects this dilemma.

The spark which served as a catalyst for the

Angola: T-shirt with warning against landmines

PHOTO ANDERS GUNNARTZ/LINEAIR

minister for the country. Despite popular protests the poll went ahead, albeit with a low voter turnout. This together with the state's strong-arm tactics set the tone for the next phase of the conflict. On November 20, 1998, a bomb ripped through the offices of Swazi deputy prime minister Arthur Khoza. Three weeks prior to this a blast destroyed a bridge at Matsapha, east of the capital, only hours after the king had passed by. These incidents point to the fact that the current struggle between the forces of traditionalism and modernity in Swaziland is following a more violent trajectory.

The politics of vengeance: the case of Lesotho

Following the May 1998 elections that witnessed the ruling Lesotho Congress for Democracy (LCD) being returned to power, opposition parties contested the fairness of the elections. Following the Langa Commission Report on the election that acknowledged electoral irregularities, opposition parties began to mobilise. Strong-arm tactics on the part of the state met with strident militancy on the part of the opposition parties and the way was paved for Lesotho's slide to civil war. A southern African Development Community (SADC) force, comprising soldiers from South Africa and Botswana intervened. After a few violent skirmishes, the mutineers of the Lesotho Defence Force (LDF) surrendered to the SADC intervention force and stability was restored to the mountain kingdom.

By October 2, 1998, the various political

current crisis relates to the October 16, 1998 House of Assembly elections. In the run-up to the elections Swazi police raided the homes of pro-democracy activists and arrested forty people. These pro-democracy activists were campaigning for a boycott of the elections on account of the fact that under the Tikhundhla system, no political parties were allowed in the kingdom. Moreover, the Tikhundhla system also concentrated tremendous power in the hands of King Mswati III and the Swazi Royal House. For instance, whilst the House of Assembly elects ten senators, the king appoints the remaining twenty. The king also chooses the prime parties agreed to hold a fresh round of elections in fifteen to eighteen months time. However tensions arose between the government and opposition parties on whether prime minister Pakalitha Mosisili's government should remain in power over that period or whether a more inclusive power-sharing arrangement should be established in the run-up to the election.

Feeling secure in the knowledge that the SADC intervention force remained in Lesotho, the Mosisili regime has rejected the path of national reconciliation and instead embarked on the path of vengeance. This has taken various forms. Firstly, on October 11, 1998, the government stopped a broadcast of a speech King Letsie III was to make to the nation. The Royal Palace announced that it could not understand why the King's address was stopped, as the message was one of reconciliation. Secondly, soon after this, the government threatened those civil servants that participated in demonstrations against the current government with dismissal. Thirdly, by October 15, 1998 the LDF confirmed the arrest of thirty mutineers. Opposition parties immediately expressed concern for the lives of the arrested mutineers due to the fact that they were taken to undisclosed places at night for interrogation and have been denied the right to private consultations with their lawyers.

Vengeance, however, is known to sow bitter fruit and on November 16, 1998 the first of those fruit were harvested when the opposition alliance boycotted the first electoral structure meeting in protest against the arrests of rebel soldiers. The situation remains tense and the future political stability of Lesotho remains in doubt.

The politics of incapacity: the case of organised crime in South Africa
All over southern Africa, organised crime syndicates are rearing their ugly heads engaging in such nefarious activities as drug-trafficking, gunrunning, vehicle hijacking and prostitution. But it is in the new South Africa that over 481 organised crime syndicates are prospering at the expense of the ordinary citizen. Consider in this regard the following statistics. South Africa has an average of 53.4 murders per 100,000 people;

the international average is 5.5. In addition, it has the most reported rapes - 99.7 per 100,000. In this situation, police officers become victims of criminals just as easily as do ordinary citizens. According to statistics recently released by the South African Institute of Race Relations, in 1998, 223 police officers were killed in South Africa. Put differently, these statistics also note that three members of the South African Police Services (SAPS) have been murdered every week for the past fifteen years.

In the face of such rampant criminality, the government seems powerless. In the face of vigilante violence in the Western Cape, the government's response has proven ineffective. In the face of violence in the midlands region of KwaZulu-Natal, the government's response has proven inadequate. As the crime wave sweeps the nation and undermines many of the gains accomplished by the post-apartheid government, an important lesson is gleaned: democratic governance in the absence of effective governance does not contribute to human security. One of the primary functions of government is to provide security to its citizens. Where a government proves incapable of doing this, the erosion of society and the gradual disintegration of the state result.

Zero-sum politics: the case of the Democratic Republic of the Congo and Angola
In both the Democratic Republic of the Congo and Angola the politics of reason and dialogue have been superseded by the politics of the gun. The war raging in both these countries also constitutes the gravest threat to the sub-region. Two reasons account for this. Firstly, as neighbouring states are sucked into the civil war a regional conflagration results. The unfolding war in the Democratic Republic of the Congo is a good example of this where one finds Angolan, Namibian, Zimbabwean, Chadian and Sudanese forces supporting the regime of president Laurent Kabila whilst Rwandan and Ugandan troops support the Congolese Rally for Democracy (RCD). Secondly, its spill-over effects also affect states not participating in the conflict as the 160,000 Angolan refugees settled in the western and north-western regions of Zambia vividly illustrate.

'Democratic governance in the absence of effective governance does not contribute to human security.'

In both Kabila's Congo and in Angola it is difficult to see how the conflict can be resolved in the near future in any permanent way. In the case of the Congo, several factors converge to make durable peace elusive. First, both the Kabila camp and the RCD rebels consist of fractious sub-groups pursuing different agendas at times from their partners. The Mai Mai militia and Dr. Emile Ilunga's Katangan Tigers are good examples of this. The fractious nature of alliance politics in the DRC means that should the main protagonists sign a truce or cease-fire, it may not be regarded as binding by constituent parts of the alliance. Second, the mineral wealth of the country has served to further fuel the war as certain groups have a vested commercial interest in the instability of the Congo. The presence of mercenaries in the country is also partly explained by the mineral wealth of this Central African State. Third, reports have surfaced that Uganda, Rwanda and Burundi are collaborating in installing Tutsis in the Itombwe high plateau in areas surrounding Mavenga in the Uvira region of eastern Congo. If true, this means that this eastern part of the Congo is effectively colonised and further complicates any future peace settlement.

In my view, any conflict resolution strategy embarked upon would need four distinct elements. First, direct negotiations between Kabila and the RCD leadership. Second, such a strategy needs to address the security concerns of Rwanda, Uganda, Burundi and Angola. Third, other political players such as veteran opposition politician Etienne Tshisekedi need to be included in any dialogue concerning the future political dispensation of the country so as to make the process as inclusive as possible. Finally, economic development as well as measures to improve good governance is essential to aid post-conflict reconstruction.

Similarly in Angola, a peaceful resolution to the conflict between the National Union for the Total Independence of Angola (UNITA) and the Popular Movement for the Liberation of Angola (MPLA) is fraught with difficulties at three levels. Firstly, who to negotiate with? The MPLA government has refused to negotiate with Jonas Savimbi's UNITA, preferring instead to negotiate with a tiny breakaway group called UNITA Renovada which consists of some former UNITA members in the Angolan National Assembly. In my opinion, the MPLA has painted itself into a corner. By refusing to engage in dialogue with Savimbi's UNITA, the MPLA has no option but a military confrontation with Savimbi that it is currently losing.

Secondly, there is the problem of who would be able to act as an impartial mediator in the conflict. The UN disqualified itself from acting as mediator when the UN Security Council declared in March 1999 that Jonas Savimbi was the cause of the current conflict in Angola. Similarly, SADC had disqualified itself as a mediator by declaring Savimbi a war criminal at its 1998 Summit in Mauritius.

This, however, leads us to the third problem of resolving the Angolan conflict - is there willingness on the part of both sides to settle this conflict? Here one could answer that no such willingness exists on account of two factors. First, the conflict has gone on for so long, it has become personalised. As such, there can be no rapprochement between the parties as long as Dos Santos and Savimbi are the main protagonists in this unfolding African tragedy. Second, the lack of willingness on the part of UNITA can also be explained by the fact that there is currently nothing that UNITA can derive from sitting at the negotiating table that it cannot take by means of the battlefield.

Conclusion

As I survey the crises facing southern Africa, my hope is that when I give a lecture on peace and security to students in some far-away country three years from now I am able to once more adopt a positive tone. For this to be realised however, several things need to happen:

- Southern African states need to realise that because insecurity anywhere threatens security everywhere and since many of the threats facing the region are transnational in nature, more power needs to be devolved to SADC.

- A concomitant of this, however, is that the organisational tensions inside SADC need to end, specifically insofar as they relate to the duality of leadership in the organisation between the Chair of SADC and the Chair of the SADC Organ on Politics, Defence and Security.
- Greater coordination between SADC, the OAU and the UN is imperative.
- An SADC-wide early warning system needs to be established inside the SADC Secretariat. This would require skilled personnel and the requisite financial resources.

- The on-going carnage in Angola and the Democratic Republic of the Congo suggests the urgent need for the further strengthening of the regional security system. In this regard, the decision by the SADC Inter-State Defence and Security System (ISDSC) in March 1999 to establish a SADC Brigade-level peacekeeping force is to be welcomed.
- Mechanisms for promoting democratic institutions and human rights needs to be strengthened and these need to have in-built punitive measures against transgressors.
- Dynamic partnerships need to be fostered between states, civil society and the private sector.

* Hussein Solomon is currently Research Manager at the African Centre for the Constructive Resolution of Disputes (ACCORD). In this capacity his primary responsibility is to manage ACCORD's Early Warning System and generate Early Warning Reports. Previously he was Senior Researher at the Institute for Security Studies and Research Fellow at the Centre for Southern African Studies.

An Emerging Security Community

Southern Africa narrowly defined includes Namibia, South Africa, Botswana, Zimbabwe, Malawi, Mozambique, Swaziland and Lesotho, but it could also include Angola, Zambia and Tanzania. While this region was divided for decades by bellicose rhetoric and active hostility between the South African apartheid regime and many of these countries, in February 1990, President de Klerk called for a new era of reconstruction and reconciliation in the region. The region's hegemony would shift from a policy of destabilisation and instead seek partnerships with its neighbours. This African region is alone in having no major active violent conflicts at the present time ◆ *By* Michael S. Lund and Enrique Roig*

Despite the ensuing policy of good neighbourliness and the new willingness to cooperate, however, the potential for violent conflicts remains, arising from several short-term and longer term sources. Within these states, a regional trend toward multi-party democracy is still incomplete and such political changes themselves can be destabilising. Domestic sources of insecurity and possible violence stem from ethnic, religious and language differences; the unequal development of areas within the countries; alienation of ethnic groupings from government; the political legitimacy of certain regimes; and economic mismanagement. The uncertain role in politics of the armies leaves the prospect of military coups. The political and economic stability of their neighbours are now concerns for states given the cross-border impacts of state collapse and fratricidal violence.

Inter-state issues with potential for escalating tensions include differences over the equitable usage of the region's water resources; illegal trafficking in drugs, arms, and people; reduced demand for migrant labour; problems in absorbing refugees; trade disputes; and the persistence of territorial disputes. The region's governments have lined up on differing sides in the war in Central Africa. More fundamentally, the level of development throughout the region as a whole is very uneven. An array of non-military threats can weaken a sense of security: large scale unemployment, resource scarcity, lack of food security, and severe environmental degradation. Weak financial institutions and lack

of foreign exchange in a number of countries continue to constrain intra-regional trade.

Recent developments

The foundations for regional cooperation in southern Africa were built prior to the current era of rapprochement. In the early 1970's, Tanzania and Zambia initiated the formation of an informal grouping called the Front-Line States (FLS) in order to coordinate and support the liberation movements of Angola, Mozambique, Namibia, South Africa and Zimbabwe. Angola and Mozambique joined after their independence in 1975 as did Botswana in 1978 and Zimbabwe in 1980. The FLS was partly instrumental in the success of the Lancaster House talks regarding the peace process in Rhodesia (now Zimbabwe) by bringing unity to the National Liberation Movements. The FLS's discussions of ways to promote economic cooperation and reduce the extreme economic dependence, especially of the landlocked states, on the apartheid regime of South African led in 1980 to the formation of the southern African Development Coordination Conference (SADCC), to which were added Lesotho, Swaziland, and Malawi. The region's countries possessed energy resource, minerals, and abundant land, but needed finance, technology and skilled workers to take advantage of these assets. Trade among them was limited. SADCC embraced all the majority-ruled countries of southern Africa - Angola, Botswana, Lesotho, Malawi, Mozambique, Swaziland, Tanzania, Zambia and Zimbabwe. It thus overlapped with the Preferential Trade Area (PTA) and Common Market for Eastern and southern Africa (COMESA), but stuck to the view that smaller economic regions were more workable. Western countries and donor organisations were widely supportive of SADCC, although concerned that its political activities could intensify the region's tensions.

The negotiations and changes going on in South Africa at the outset of the early 1990s encouraged SADDC to rethink and review its objectives given the new political climate. Namibia joined in 1990. In 1992, the SADCC became simply the southern African Development Community (SADC) with the aim of promoting economic progress in the region and harnessing the power of South Africa. The 'New Diplomacy' promoted by South Africa with its commitment to the removal of apartheid, even though viewed suspiciously by other southern African states, eventually resulted in South Africa becoming the eleventh member of SADC in 1994, once its legislative elections put the ANC in power under Nelson Mandela. Now a regionwide organisation headquartered in Gaborone, Botswana, SADC was determined to reduce its members' dependence on aid. They increased the subjects on which they cooperated in three directions relevant to conflict prevention and management: the original concern of economic cooperation and development, diplomacy and security cooperation, and common values of democratic governance.

Economic coordination and cooperation
SADCC had adopted an approach to economic cooperation that differed from the neo-liberal orthodoxy adopted by the EC, ECOWAS, and other regional economic organisations, including many such as the East African Union that had failed badly. Rather than emphasising as they had tariff reductions and customs unions that would likely reinforce uneven development, SADCC focused on improving transport and communications in non-industrial areas in order to stimulate production as well as increase trade, and it established development funds through external aid to initiate projects in fields such as tourism, mining, and energy. This required close

political cooperation. Unfortunately, its high dependence ultimately on donor financing and technology left many of its initiated projects undone. Also, countries such as Zambia responded to their economic self-interests by increasing their trade dependence on South Africa, rather than expanding trade with other SADCC members.

The redirected SADC with its new economic partner relies on the conviction that with the increasing interdependence of the region, South Africa cannot prosper in a sea of deprivation. Without a growing regional market, underdevelopment would impede profitable economic activity in the strongest economy as well and raise the spectre of conflict. Thus, security is viewed as much in economic as in military terms, and economic development is seen as a strategy for preventing conflict and regional instability. Consequently, South Africa is looking to forge economic partnerships in a range of areas, particularly transport, water, and power supplies to assist with long term development. Agreements have been signed to commit its members to share water resources in a drought-prone area.

The SADC is also committed to the gradual elimination of all internal trade barriers by the year 2006. In order for free trade to avoid the imbalances experienced in the other regions, South Africa is likely to need to reshape its asymmetrical regional trading relationships, in which its exports outweigh imports by a factor of almost 5:1. A more equitable trading deal may have to be worked out in which regional exporters are allowed greater access to the South Africa market and regional tariffs are kept in place for South African exports.

Diplomacy and security Ccooperation
The changed climate in South Africa also allowed SADC to envisage more cooperation and coordination in the broader fields of security and political affairs. By providing a regular venue in which important issues affecting member states can be addressed, SADC had established a process of dialogue whereby actual agreements might even be negotiated. At a summit in 1996, SADC decided to go further by creating a new institutional process for handling security

concerns, the Organ for Politics, Defense and Security (OPDS).

Set up separately from SADC per se, the aim of the OPDS is to keep political-military issues from festering and eventually erupting into conflict by ensuring they are addressed in a pro-active, systematic manner. The objective was to go beyond having simply another intergovernmental forum where heads of state could discuss issues, at least in principle. The OPDS put in place machinery for the prevention, management, and resolution of conflicts that could thus ensure that issues do not boil over and erupt into conflicts. The new procedures include an early warning system to identify potential sources of conflict within and between states; a regional preventive diplomacy unit to encourage compromise; the development of regional arbitration procedures or a commitment to seek World Court adjudication on territorial disputes; and mechanisms to guarantee an equitable sharing of the region's scarce water resources. Other threats without enemies such as drugs, HIV/AIDs, and environmental degradation also required a multilateral response.

In conjunction with SADC, the OPDS represented a step beyond the international relations of crisis management toward an integrated vision of comprehensive and cooperative security. The two processes ensure that potential conflicts are addressed in a systematic manner; the SADC through long-term economic cooperation and coordination concerns, and the OPDS for more overt political-military issues.

In its first meeting in October 1996, the OPDS asked three eminent statesmen to put pressure on the Angolan parties to accept a peace agreement that was on the table. In other conflicts such as in Angola, however, the OPDS has failed to play a prominent role in ending the conflict, particularly during 1998 when Angola intervened militarily in the DRC.

Certain difficulties have occurred in trying to use the OPDS machinery regularly. The final communiqué establishing the OPDS in July 1996 seemed to imply that 'military intervention of whatever nature' would be decided upon when all other remedies had been exhausted, in accordance with UN and OAU principles. Thus, reference to

SADC norms was used when South Africa, Botswana and Zimbabwe used coercive diplomacy in August-September 1994 to secure reversal of a coup which had deposed the elected government of Lesotho. This seemed to set the tone for the way SADC would handle military intervention - preceded by a period of sanctions or coercive diplomacy. But one dilemma for the OPDS is deciding at what point dialogue has been exhausted and when it should move toward more punitive measures such as suspension of membership, economic sanctions, or military actions.

In September 1998, in response to a revolt of junior military officers in Lesotho, South Africa and Botswana took matters into their own hands when they sent in a large number of troops to quash the rebellion and restore the government which had received 60 per cent of the vote. But the military action unfortunately devastated the capital, Maseru, and set economic development back by many years. Criticism of South Africa was harsh, especially for its failure to use non-military measures such as economic strangulation by closing the Lesotho border. SADC's commitment to exhausting non-lethal means as outlined in an OPDS communique were bypassed in favour of direct military intervention.

Still, political, diplomatic, economic, and other non-military measures may be effective only if the use of force poses a serious threat. Thus, efforts have been made to create a multilateral regional crisis force that might act after diplomacy or sanctions have failed. This effort, too, has encountered some obstacles. One is gaining the cooperation and participation of as many countries in the region as possible. The idea was somewhat stymied by Angola's concern that regional forces might intervene in its own conflict. The outbreak of conflict in the DRC in 1997 created alliances in southern Africa that further complicate efforts at establishing a regional force.

The role of South Africa is critical in designing and financing such a force. Its military capability and status as a leading African power has also required South Africa to come to terms with the notion of playing a role as 'first among equals' within the SADC's structures, and thus to oversee planning in the area of military intervention and peacekeeping. Many within the defence community in South Africa maintain there is a need for strong armed forces ready to meet a conventional military threat from within the region. The challenge lies in ensuring that South Africa has the capability to lead peace-keeping efforts without allowing it to build up its military capabilities simply for its own self-serving reasons.

In September 1996, the South Africa National Defense Forces (SANDF) took part in the peacekeeping training operation 'Exercise Morning Star' held in South Africa in collaboration with the Norwegian government and the British Army Staff. This kind of support by European governments and the US for enhancing the region's peace-keeping capacity under South Africa's tutelage is viewed with some suspicion by African states who feel that the external powers are continuing to seek control by proxy. But more broadly, a partnership was formed between the European Union and SADC as a whole to work on three priority areas: strengthening democracy, enhancing cooperation for conflict prevention and peacekeeping; and intensifying the common fight against organised crime, by tackling illicit trafficking in small arms.

Discussion about creating a common regional African security policy has often failed to tackle the key problem of the need for political legitimacy in a common policy. To some, South Africa's seeming obsession with preparations for inter-state military conflict have made it incapable of responding in a balance way to the new challenges. This may call for a firmer South African commitment to the peaceful resolution of inter-state disputes within the region. It may also imply a unilateral reduction in South African military expenditure accompanied by a general downsizing of the SANDF.

Though a major constraint to the regional force is the active participation by all southern African states, some progress has been made among South Africa and other regional countries toward developing a regional peacekeeping capability. In February 1997, Aziz Pahad, the deputy Foreign minister announced a joint peace-keeping exercise with Zimbabwe, involving 250 South African troops, as well as

expanded ties with the Tanzanian military, with the long term objective of creating a regional peace-keeping force. Operation Blue Hungwe held in April 1997 was the first major attempt to plan for future regional peace-keeping operations. SADC countries also participated in Operation Blue Crane, a major training exercise held in South Africa at brigade strength with the aim of bolstering regional peace-keeping/peace-making capacity. In October 1997, South African representatives participated in a peace-keeping conference at the Zimbabwe staff college and in January 1998, Denmark offered US $3.3 million over three years to help establish a southern African peace-keeping force.

The efforts at protecting regional security are important but also need to be coupled with real commitments by South Africa to limit its involvement in the arms trade. Regional security stands the danger of being jeopardised by South Africa's arms lobby - an area where SADC must push for reform.

Norms of governance

The growing influence of common regional norms concerning domestic affairs has been a noticeable outgrowth of SADC. Increasingly, as more and more countries have held multi-party elections, SADC has been assuming the role of upholding democratic norms in the region by watching for sources of possible deviations and acting promptly toward possible crises. This is best illustrated by the pressures exercised on Lesotho to re-establish the democratically elected government overthrown in August 1994. A summit of leaders from Botswana, South Africa, and Zimbabwe condemned the royal coup by Lesotho's King Letsie III. The king was later presented with an ultimatum by southern African leaders to restore democracy or face trade sanctions. Pressure from southern African countries were made effective by reference to SADC norms. Eventually, the king restored the ousted government. Similarly, pressures were put on Mozambique's RENAMO leader Dhaklama to participate in the crucial 1994 elections, and SADC leaders showed up in force to endorse the Lusaka Accords in Angola that year, although the rebel leader Jonas Savimbi was boycotting.

SADC still has to straddle the divide between its commitment to advancing human rights and democracy, on the one hand, and sovereignty, on the other. The admission of the Democratic Republic of Congo to SADC in 1997 highlighted this dilemma. The authoritarian style of Laurent Kabila and the subsequent revolt against his regime led to the eventual involvement of five member states in that conflict, some ostensibly to protect Congo's sovereignty and some ostensibly to advance democracy. Because national sovereignty has been a major issue for SADC members, it is unlikely that the quasi-juridical mechanism envisioned by the OPDS, which is similar to the Commission of Mediation, Conciliation and Arbitration proposed and left unused by the OAU many years ago, would be utilised by the member countries.

Further directions

The promising start SADC has made was possible because of a supportive South Africa, the stature of Nelson Mandela, and the spreading of democracy through the region. International encouragement and support is needed to take continuing and full advantage of the current momentum toward building and using regional institutions. Otherwise, South Africa and its neighbours could become preoccupied with their own problems and gradually neglect the regional channels which could otherwise serve as inspiring models for other African regions.

*   Enrique Roig is Senior Program Officer for Mercy Corps International, Washington, D.C.. He has worked in the fields of civil society programming, post-war reconstruction, and conflict resolution in Latin American, Africa, and the Balkans

References

Hamill, James.. *From Realism to Complex Interdependence? South Africa, Southern Africa and the Question of Security.* International Relations, vol. XIV, no. 3. 1998

Kouassi, Edmond K. *Africa's Regional Security in a Changing World.* The Paul H. Nitze School of Advanced International Studies, John Hopkins University. No date.

Micou, Ann McKinstry. *Guide to Regional Networking in Southern Africa.* Institute of International Education, Working Paper Number 32. 1996

Prendergast, John and David Smock. *NGOs and the Peace Process in Angola.* United State Institute of Peace. Special Report. 1996

Thompson, Carol, *African Initiatives for Development: The Practice of Regional Economic Cooperation in Southern Africa.* Journal of International Affairs, Summer, 1992

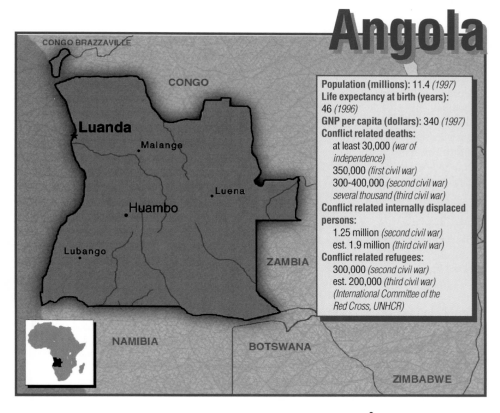

Angola

CONGO BRAZZAVILLE

CONGO

Luanda

Malange

Luena

Huambo

Lubango

ZAMBIA

NAMIBIA

BOTSWANA

ZIMBABWE

Population (millions): 11.4 *(1997)*
Life expectancy at birth (years):
46 *(1996)*
GNP per capita (dollars): 340 *(1997)*
Conflict related deaths:
  at least 30,000 *(war of
  independence)*
  350,000 *(first civil war)*
  300-400,000 *(second civil war)*
  several thousand *(third civil war)*
Conflict related internally displaced
persons:
  1.25 million *(second civil war)*
  est. 1.9 million *(third civil war)*
Conflict related refugees:
  300,000 *(second civil war)*
  est. 200,000 *(third civil war)*
  *(International Committee of the
  Red Cross, UNHCR)*

War Returns Yet Again

The second Angolan peace process died with the launch of a government offensive against UNITA rebels on December 4, 1998. While the offensive marked the official beginning of the fourth war in 38 years, the peace process had already been severely battered by the time that the UN replaced its third verification mission with a smaller-scale monitoring operation in June 1997. Indeed, some argue that Angola has been the scene of one continuous war, punctuated by brief spells of military inactivity. Meanwhile, international NGOs and the remaining UN organisations keep humanitarian relief efforts going and support what is left of health and education facilities. Some among them continue their support for the few civil society organisations, including independent local media, that attempt to formulate possible alternatives to the protracted violence ◆ *By* **Bram Posthumus**

Large-scale bloodletting has been a feature of the wars that have raged in Angola throughout history. The bloodshed began with the slave raids that prompted the wars between the peoples of the interior and the coast. It continued apace in the many uprisings against the Portuguese colonisers, most famously those of Queen Nzinga in the seventeenth century and Mutu-ya-Kevela in the nineteenth century. The sheer brutality the colonisers used to suppress African nationalist aspirations can only be explained by the fact of Portugal's increasing economic reliance upon the vast natural resources of its Angolan colony. In 1961, one of the first major actions against the emergent Angolan nationalist movement by the Portuguese army cost an estimated 20,000 people their lives.

The term 'nationalist movement', however, can be misleading in the Angolan context, disguising the fact that in Angola there has never been a single powerful organisation fighting for independence. Factionalism has existed right from the beginning of the independence struggle in the early 1960s and spilled into civil war when independence was secured in 1975. The three major parties in existence at the time of independence were later reduced to two. The original three were:

- The People's Movement for the Liberation of Angola (MPLA), which was headed by Agostinho Neto, who is generally perceived to be the founding father of independent Angola.
- The National Front for the Liberation of Angola (FNLA), which went into decline in the 1970s but was in charge of a government in exile in Leopoldsville (Kinshasa) in the 1960s.
- The National Union for the Total Liberation of Angola (UNITA), created by the former FNLA shadow Foreign Minister, Jonas Savimbi.

Ethnic and ideological considerations have played a definite, although frequently exaggerated, role in the conflict. The factions recruited fighters from all major peoples in Angola, with the possible exception of the FNLA, which was a mostly BaKongo affair. UNITA was based in the Angolan Central Highlands, home of the Umbundu people, of whom Savimbi is one. The MPLA was mostly urban and counted whites, people of mixed race, Kimbundu and (after the incorporation of the remains of the FNLA) BaKongo people among its ranks.

It would, however, be wrong to characterise the two main parties in the wars in terms of the ethnic origins of their supporters. Although Savimbi has attempted to portray UNITA as a true 'African' movement, he has in the past countered his own anti-white and anti-'mestiço' (mixed race) rhetoric by pointing out that he has non-Africans among his high ranking officials. So too, UNITA has support beyond the Umbundu, while the MPLA can count Umbundu people among its followers.

The ideological stances of the various factions were primarily born out of a combination of conviction and pragmatism. The MPLA started as a Marxist party, which in style and rhetoric moved towards hard-line Stalinism, especially after an attempted coup which was crushed amidst much bloodshed in 1977. UNITA was originally a Maoist movement but developed a pro-Western anti-communist rhetoric when it started receiving massive aid from the United States. Both parties contained in their ranks a complex mix of true ideologues, pragmatists, sycophants and opportunists and both were adept at speaking the language of whoever was prepared to provide them with - mostly military - assistance.

In the course of the 1970s, the two main antagonistic clusters took shape: the MPLA/Soviet Union/Cuba on the one side and UNITA (/FNLA)/United States/apartheid-South Africa on the other. Angola had become a Cold War battleground.

Ethnicity and ideology have subsequently taken a backseat. When the Cold War ended, the conflict became more localised, and when the Cubans and South Africans pulled out this process intensified. The war has been transformed into a battle for control of Angola's abundant resources, fought by two totalitarian movements whose leaders have to this day continued to cash in Angola's considerable assets on the global market in return for military equipment and services.

A more or less separate part of this equation has been the small liberation movement in Angola's oil province Cabinda. The movement, FLEC - Front for the Liberation of the Enclave of Cabinda - has carried out attacks since the early 1960s but since they have failed to make a significant impact on the chain of events in Angola, they will not be mentioned elsewhere in this survey.

Conflict Dynamics

November 11, 1975 saw the birth of two Angola's: the MPLA in Luanda announced the birth of the People's Republic of Angola while roughly 500 kilometres to the south-east in Huambo, UNITA and the FNLA announced that of the Popular Democratic Republic of Angola. There had already been fighting in various parts of the country during the months leading up to independence. South African forces had invaded Angola with the approval of the United States and were heading for the capital city, which the MPLA only managed to hold with Cuban military aid.

For much of the 1970s and 1980s, there was a low-intensity bush war. Major turning points occurred towards the end of the 1980s. Most significant of these was the battle for Cuito Canavale, a town in the south of Angola. This, the largest conventional battle ever fought in southern Africa, raged in the first six months of 1988 and put an end to South African military superiority. At the same time, Communist rule began to crumble in Moscow, diminishing Soviet enthusiasm for involvement in a distant war. Only the US remained constant in its support for UNITA, both overt and covert. (This only changed when Bill Clinton became president in 1992.)

Peace negotiations began under the guidance of the so-called 'troika', consisting of the US, the Soviet Union and Portugal. A series of talks in Lisbon and various African capitals, involving MPLA and UNITA, resulted in the historic handshake of Savimbi and the Angolan president Eduardo dos Santos, in Gbadolite, Zaire, June 22, 1989. Two years later, the Bicesse Peace Accord was signed. Some of the key planks in that accord were an end to the presence of all foreign troops in the country, mutual troop withdrawals by the government and UNITA, and presidential and parliamentary elections.

However the accord failed to take into account the high level of distrust that had built up between the MPLA and UNITA in eighteen years of civil war. This became apparent during the elections, which were held on September 29 and 30, 1992. The results gave the MPLA a parliamentary majority and tied the presidential outcome between Dos Santos and Savimbi, making a second round necessary. But before that round could be held, Savimbi called the elections fraudulent and left Luanda. MPLA forces then shelled the UNITA party headquarters in the capital. The war had resumed.

UNITA made massive gains at the beginning of this second civil war. Two theories have been propounded to explain this initial success: 1)

UNITA had failed to disband troops while the government forces had begun returning to their quarters; 2) UNITA had been able to continue stockpiling arms by smuggling them in through Zaire while the government had been unable to circumvent the ban on arms imports. At any rate there was no shortage of arms and Angola was to live through its second, and most savage civil war.

Among others, the cities of Huambo, Kuito, Malanje, N'Dalantando were besieged and strafed by either side, with heavy civilian casualties. Most of the provincial capitals were either severely damaged or totally destroyed. In 1993, the UN's special representative in Angola stated that with over 1,000 people dying every day this was the bloodiest conflict in the world. A new peace process had to be started. Agonisingly slow negotiations took place in Lusaka, Zambia, which finally resulted in the Lusaka Protocol, which again covered (among other issues) mutual troop withdrawal and quartering, making the country safe for ordinary citizens, and reconciliation. Again it was frequently alleged that UNITA was intent on stalling the peace process, withholding troops, stockpiling arms and keeping Savimbi in its capital, Bailundo. UNITA incurred the wrath of the UN because of its continued procrastination and sanctions were imposed in October 1997.

Meanwhile the MPLA-dominated government continued with its - now legalised - arms buying spree, mortgaging its future oil revenues to pay its arms suppliers. (Estimates suggest that the next 6 to 15 years worth of oil revenue have already been lost in this way.) Cease-fire violations continued throughout.

Between 1996 and late 1998, the continuous unravelling of the peace process reached its inevitable conclusion. First, the government attempted to isolate UNITA militarily, politically and diplomatically by helping to install sympathetic regimes in Congo Brazzaville and ex-Zaire and warning Zambia not to allow UNITA to use its infrastructure for supplies. Luanda was effectively building a 'cordon sanitaire' in the hope that UNITA would no longer be able to solicit help from neighbours. In spite of all this and the UN embargo, UNITA continued to sell its diamonds and buy mostly Eastern European arms in the world's illicit arms bazaars. By late 1997, it had all it needed to continue the war.

On the domestic political front, the Angolan government took similar steps to isolate Savimbi, helping to set up an alternative UNITA and preparing moves to have him removed from Angolan soil altogether, although it remains to be seen how this can actually be achieved. Savimbi was sidelined diplomatically when a SADC conference declared him a war criminal, placing him outside the peace process.

Secondly, it became clear that UNITA had been lying about its compliance with the terms of the Lusaka Protocol when it announced, in March 1998, that it had demobilised, as stipulated by the Lusaka Protocol. Even the UN was forced to admit that UNITA had in fact a standing force of some 30,000 men and very large arms caches in the various parts of Angola's interior still under its control.

The third setback was the death, on June 26, 1998 in a plane crash near Abidjan, of the UN special envoy Maître Alioune Blondin Beye. The inspiringly optimistic special UN representative for Angola was at times criticised for his leniency towards both the warring parties, but his efforts towards moving the peace process forward, were widely regarded as impressive. He was briefly replaced by an Algerian diplomat before the Guinean UN official, Issa Diallo, took over as the new special representative.

At the time of Beye's death, fighting had already seriously intensified in several provinces, including Lunda Norte and Lunda Sul, Malanje, Moxico and Kwanza Norte, displacing tens of thousands of people. Violent recruitment by both parties resurfaced, sending thousands more across the border into Zambia, the DR Congo, and Namibia. UNITA re-captured territory it had returned to the government and the Angolan army launched a number of heavy attacks on UNITA positions. Roads and other areas were re-mined. On December 4 1998, one day before a major MPLA congress in Luanda, the Angolan army launched a major offensive in the centre of the country, marking the beginning of the third civil war.

Since then UNITA has fought back hard, laying siege to Huambo, Kuito, Malanje and Luena and has briefly occupied and extensively looted the northern town of Mbanza Congo. The rebels are engaged in a rural depopulation campaign, committing terrible atrocities against what they themselves consider 'their own people' in Central Angola. Out of the nearly two million people displaced by the war, an estimated one million have been forcibly removed by UNITA. The cities are rapidly becoming death traps as a result of food shortages, disease and UNITA shelling. On June 22 1999, UNITA lobbed grenades onto a market in Malanje, killing more than thirty people. Relief agencies are fast running out of money; they are unable to cope with the catastrophe that is rapidly unfolding. The war itself, meanwhile, appears to have stalled and the population is once again caught in a violent conflict that neither side can win.

Official Conflict Management

Of the three *United Nations Verification Missions* to Angola, the second and the third, UNAVEM II and III, were the most important. The first, UNAVEM I, simply verified the departure of Cuban troops from Angola between 1989 and 1991. The main causes of the failure of the 1991-1994 UNAVEM II mission were located in its mandate and resources. The mandate effectively sidelined UN personnel, only allowing them to watch what was going on without enabling them to intervene. In terms of personnel, it had at best 350 military observers, 90 police observers and 400 election observers in a country the size of France, Spain and Great Britain put together, with a virtually non-existent infrastructure and two large armies that were eyeing each other with utmost suspicion.

The UN's special representative at the time, Margaret Anstee, in a reference to Security Council Resolution number 747 which created UNAVEM II, once likened her mission to 'flying a Boeing 747 with only enough fuel for a DC 3.' UNAVEM II was bound to fail in three key areas: quartering all combat troops, collecting arms, and verifying whether arms embargoes and other sanctions were effectively carried out. It also suffered from an unrealistic time-frame. When the hostilities spiralled out of control in late 1992, the Secretary-General advised the reduction and then withdrawal of all UN personnel.

The UNAVEM III mission (February 1995 until June 1997) did prove to some extent that lessons had been learned from earlier mistakes and from a similar mission to Mozambique. It had a clearer and larger mandate; at its peak it had over 7,000 personnel at its disposal and cost well over US$ one million a day. Large numbers of African troops from countries that had a standby arrangement with the UN and were acceptable to both parties, particularly UNITA, were made available.

Confidence was boosted by the face-to-face meetings of president Dos Santos and UNITA leader Savimbi, personally mediated by the new UN special representative, Blondin Beye. A further incentive was given by the EU which in late 1995 pledged close to US$ one billion, if the peace process would turn out to be irreversible. Finally, the old 'troika', now consisting of the US, Russia and Portugal and the UN actively maintained the pressure upon UNITA to honour its promises. With hindsight, it can be argued that the pressure on UNITA was not matched by hard sanctions, allowing the rebels to re-arm. It can also be argued that the UN time frame, although more realistic than before, was stretched beyond its limits by UNITA procrastination and government intransigence, compounded - some might say encouraged - by UN leniency towards both sides.

In June 1997, the UN went back to a UNAVEM II-style operation, called MONUA, the UN Observer Mission to Angola. It had a greatly reduced observer force of some 1,500 troops, who worked with the remaining police and military observers. The start of MONUA coincided with a serious deterioration in the military situation in the country. MONUA was supposed to have ended its mission in November 1997 but had its life extended to March 1999, during which it could do little more than oversee another slide into civil war.

On June 21, the UN announced its intention to send a new smaller scale mission to Angola. Details of this mission (composition, duties) are still being worked out. Whether the two sides in the war will agree to a renewed UN presence is unclear.

Beye's successor, Issa Diallo, was banned by the Angolan government from seeing Savimbi and went on long regional trips to garner African support for his efforts. MONUA became a political football played by both the government and UNITA. Both made it clear that as far as they were concerned, the peacekeepers could leave altogether. The downing of two MONUA planes by UNITA in December 1998 and January 1999 was the final straw. A gloomy Secretary-General Kofi Annan announced the withdrawal of the mission on February 26, 1999. Diallo left Angola on March 15 and the mission was officially ended five days later. Diallo briefly returned to Luanda in June for talks but no progress has been reported. The UN maintains a huge humanitarian aid presence in the country.

In June, the Security Council agreed in principle to open yet another, very small, UN peace mission to Angola. Details have yet to be made public.

Heads of *individual states* (Kenya, Zambia, Nigeria) have made various attempts at mediation. So too the heads of those African states with friends on either side of the war encouraged the two sides to sign the Lusaka Protocol. A remarkable absentee from these efforts has been the southern African Development Community (SADC) or its predecessor SADCC, which appears to have done little to stop the carnage in its largest member state. Only in the most recent phase has there been some diplomatic action from SADC, directed against UNITA leader Jonas Savimbi.

By far the most important regional player in this war was South Africa. The arrival of white soldiers in body bags after the battle of Cuito Canavale and later the momentous political changes that brought Nelson Mandela to power have did more to reduce the violence in the run up to the Lusaka Protocol than any amount of pan-African argument and persuasion. As one commentator put it: 'Civil wars are rarely settled by negotiation'.

In the process that eventually led to the Lusaka Protocol, it was the members of the 'troika', the two superpowers plus former colonial power Portugal, who helped the negotiations along, together with Maître Alioune Blondin Beye, who succeeded in resolving many points of deadlock.

DILATANDO, ANGOLA: *Days of hope: release of a dove by President Dos Santos during the election campaign in 1992*   PHOTO PAUL WEINBERG/LINEAIR

Multi-Track Diplomacy
Domestic

FONGA is the umbrella organisation of Angolan NGOs. In March 1997, FONGA cooperated with the American Friends Service Committee, a Quaker organisation, in a training workshop aimed at community workers representing about thirty NGOs. The workshop revolved around non-violent means of conflict resolution at community level and was held in Luanda. Nevertheless, people from Lubango, Huilla, and Kwanza Sul were able to attend. This is one of the very few grassroots peace building initiatives to have taken place (the official churches may in the future use their structures to

set up similar initiatives among their rank and file membership). The political atmosphere existing in government-controlled Angola leaves little scope for such initiatives to truly flourish while the situation of intolerance in UNITA-controlled territory is even worse. Nevertheless, FONGA manages to maintain a presence across the UNITA-MPLA divide and continues to attempt to keep local peace-building efforts operating, in spite of the huge difficulties and dangers surrounding this work.

Among the other local NGOs, *ADRA* (Action for Rural Development and the Environment) has since its inception in 1990 tried to organise local communities around development projects, while at the same time raising their political awareness and self-reliance. Since the second civil war ADRA has had to forego its objectives, in order to concentrate instead on providing emergency aid. ADRA is one of the few local NGOs with a visible presence in many parts of the country that are government-controlled. Like most other national and international NGOs, it has no access to UNITA-controlled areas.

Independent Media: There are at present three publications on the streets of Luanda - *Commercio Actualidade, Folha 8* and *Agora* (Now) - which are produced by independent journalists, often at great risk to themselves. They expose arms purchases, diamond-smuggling rackets committed by the army and question government repression. Their contributions to a future post-war Angola by helping to create an atmosphere of transparency and government accountability, are probably incalculable. No such efforts at transparency are known to exist in the UNITA-controlled territories.

Journalists, intellectuals, churches and others launched a Peace Manifesto in Luanda on June 15, 1999. There is no fixed group backing the Manifesto but the initiators now claim that already thousands of people inside Angola have signed up to it. The Manifesto states that there is no military solution to the conflict and that both UNITA and the government should stop passing the humanitarian cost of their conflict on to the international community. It calls for immediate dialogue and states that this war is not between two conflicting sides but in fact jointly committed mass murder of the Angolan people. The initiative has also been taken up internationally. There is no information about its reception in the UNITA-controlled territory although the rebel leadership has acknowledged the existence of the Manifesto.

International
Among the many de-mining groups still working in Angola are the *Halo Trust, Norwegian People's Aid, Cap Anamur*, and the *Mines Advisory Group*. The UN helped set up a de-mining school, in which former Angolan soldiers are trained as de-miners. Various countries, including the Netherlands, the Nordic countries, the US and UK contribute to de-mining initiatives. Great significance should be attached to the very successful International Campaign to Ban Landmines (ICBL), which in 1997 won the Nobel Peace Price.

Saferworld conducts research and publishes its findings and recommendations for the betterment of new peacekeeping efforts. It has conducted an extensive study on Angola and its recommendations contain a list which is as familiar as it is necessary: demobilisation, the return of refugees and displaced persons, de-mining and arms control, community rehabilitation, economic recovery, better governance and the development of a civil society.

Search for Common Ground has set up a Centre in Luanda and organised a high profile peace concert in 1997, which was attended by all the Luandan glitterati (according to one reporter). A peace song, written by Angolan artists, was performed at the event. The

organisation wants to help build civil society, promote dialogue among government and UNITA supporters on the ground and prepare media productions.

Prospects
A former Cold War battlefield and inheritor of a series of internal power struggles, Angola is deeply divided. It remains to be seen whether it can actually be considered a political unit, having been split for so long into two geographical parts controlled by two different politico-military organisations. Confidence is a very rare commodity and perhaps in even shorter supply now than at any time in the succession of wars that has ravaged the country for nearly forty years. Angola badly needs wholesale demilitarisation, with the priority being given to the demilitarisation of the conduct of politics. It needs demobilisation rather than forced recruitment. It needs jobs for ex-soldiers and soldiers-to-be. It needs to massively reduce the presence of arms and a massive influx of funds to start rebuilding the entire country and restore peoples' lives to some normality. In the current situation this seems a very remote prospect. Instead, the war is likely to drag on with no apparent benefit to anyone, except a few on either side of the divide.

The worst that could happen to Angola and its people is that it slips even further away from world consciousness. With the war in Kosovo receiving saturation coverage, and the UN mission gone, this is precisely what has happened. UNITA has been able to carry out its depopulation campaign of central Angola with no-one to observe the unfolding of events. Given the historical responsibilities of the international community in the country, this indifference has taken the cynicism that envelops this country to new levels. A former commander of the UN forces in Angola, Zimbabwean General Sibanda, told the *Mail & Guardian* in April 1999 that given the right amount of resources, the UN could probably have succeeded in Angola, just as it did in Mozambique. He may be right, but General Sibanda will be realistic enough to realise that while the world is prepared to throw an estimated US$ 25 billion worth of bombs on a small corner of south eastern Europe in a matter of three months, it considers a four year peace-keeping operation in a vast corner of south west Africa at 7.5 per cent of that amount too expensive. Having said that, John Stewart comment on this paper also holds true: no amount of peace enforcement or strong-arm diplomacy will help, so long as the protagonists in the conflict are not prepared to see eye to eye. Stewart, for one, believes that there is a long way to go. Meanwhile, as *The Economist* wrote, Angolans will continue to do what they have done for decades: suffer, starve and die before they are old.

Recommendations

Numerous recommendations were have been made by the likes of Human Rights Watch, Saferworld, independent observers and research institutions, particularly pertaining to the United Nations peace-keeping operations in Angola. The most pertinent among them relate to the mandates, resources and time-frames of UNAVEM II and UNAVEM III. These constructive criticisms now of historical value only, since the UN is no longer there to keep the peace and Angola has returned to full-scale war. Relevant comments have found their way into other parts of this survey. As things stand today, no-one has a clear idea of what to do with Angola and the preferred option appears to be to let the war run its course once more.

UN representatives stress the need to return to dialogue one more. For the time being, this is impossible. President Dos Santos has made it absolutely clear that he will never again negotiate with Savimbi, while the rebel leader, Africa's most battle-hardened survivor, is sitting safely somewhere in Angola's vast interior. It is highly unlikely that any dialogue between these two will take place in the near future.

There is one course of action that is now recommended to be taken up more vigorously: getting serious about enforcing sanctions against UNITA, especially in the field of its single largest source of revenue, diamonds. The UN Security Council will take a decision on this matter later in the year, following a mission to the region to be led by the Canadian chairman of the UN Sanctions Commission on Angola, Robert Fowler.

Service Information

Newsletters and Periodicals
Angola Peace Monitor (see website)

Reports and Periodicals
Catholic Institute for International Relations
- Angola - Peace Postponed. London, September 1998

Human Rights Watch
- Angola - Arms trade and violations of the laws of war since the 1992 elections. London, 1994

Saferworld
- Angola - Conflict Resolution and Peace-building. London, 1994

Other Publications
Wars in the Third World, by Guy Arnold. 1995
Angola - Promises and Lies, by Karl Maier. William Waterman, 1996
The Destruction of a Nation - United States Policy Towards Angola, by Richard Wright. Pluto Press, 1997
Analyse des crisis et pistes pour une prévention - Conflits en Afrique. Dossiers du GRIP, Brussels, 1997 (with case-study on Angola)

Selected Internet Sites
www.anc.org.za/angola (Angola Peace Monitor: produced every month by ACTSA - Action for southern Africa - the successor organisation to the British Anti-Apartheid Movement. It is intended to support the work of the Angola Emergency Campaign, which seeks to highlight the need for international action in support of peace and democracy in Angola.
www.angola.org/news/mission/index.html (Angolan Permanent Mission to the UN)
www.gn.apc.org.sworld (Saferworld)

mg.co.za/mg (Electronic Mail & Guardian, covers Angola extensively)
www.ebonet.net (offers access to Angolan magazines and Portuguese newspapers)
www.kwacha.com (UNITA)
www.snafu.de/~usp/iaadheng.htm (for text Manifesto)

Resource Contacts
Fransisco Tunga Alberto - FONGA
Alex Vines - Human Rights Watch. Email hrwatchuk@gn.apc.org
John Stewart - Cath. Justice and Peace Commission, Harare. Email AFSC@mango.zw
Laila Maji - Search for Common Ground Washington Office
Fernando Pacheco - ADRA

Additional addresses
ADRA, Acção para o Desenvolvimento Rural e Ambiente
Praceta Farinha Lenão, #27
Luanda
Angola
Tel/fax +244 2 396 683

American Friends Service Committee (Quaker)
Tel +263 4 722 168/703 122
Email: AFSC@mango.zw

Saferworld
33/34 Alfred place, 3d floor
London WC1E 7DP, UK
Tel. +44 171 580 8886
Fax +44 171 631 1444
Email Sworld@gn.apc.org

The Comoros

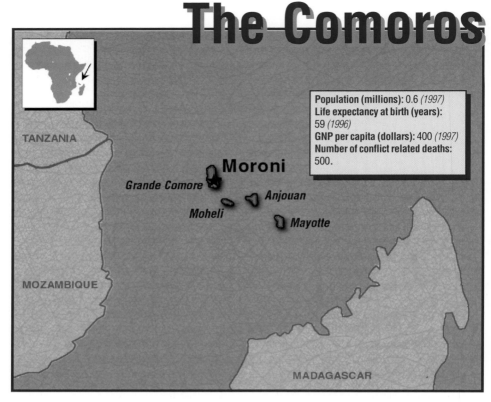

Population (millions): 0.6 *(1997)*
Life expectancy at birth (years):
59 *(1996)*
GNP per capita (dollars): 400 *(1997)*
Number of conflict related deaths:
500.

TANZANIA

Moroni

Grande Comore

Anjouan

Moheli

Mayotte

MOZAMBIQUE

MADAGASCAR

Independence or Back to Colonial Times?

On August 3, 1997, separatists from the islands of Anjouan and Mohéli declared
their independence from the Grande Comoros. This declaration has not only
given rise to considerable political instability, but has also resulted in the deaths
of some hundreds of civilians and military personnel. Moreover it has created a
disastrous humanitarian situation on both islands. To date, only the OAU has
taken some concrete steps towards settling the unrest. An OAU-mediated
agreement signed in April 1999 was on the point of being implemented when it
was derailed by a bloodless coup ◆ *By* Anneke Galama

The group of four islands (Mayotte, Moroni,
Anjouan, Mohéli) that form the Republic of
Grande Comoros were a French colony from
1841 till 1975. They lie between the East African
coast and the north-west coast of Madagascar.
The colonial history of the Comoros is dominated by the struggle for independence from
France. After being ruled by Madagascar - another French colony - the islands gained their internal autonomy in December 1961. It took a referendum in 1974, in which there was a 96 per
cent vote in favour, to gain full independence

from France on the 6th of July 1975. On the
island of Mayotte, the predominantly French
population returned a 64 per cent majority in
favour of continuing under French rule and the
island continues under French administration.
France did not oppose the independence of the
other three islands.

After a successful coup, supported by the
French intelligence service, whose number
included the famous French mercenary Bob
Denard, President Abdallah came to power in
1978. His dictatorial regime was supported by an

alliance of Comorian politicians and mercenaries. Islamic traditions were forbidden and political opposition suppressed. Abdallah was killed in 1989, some say by the presidential guard. Bob Denard was also accused of Abdallah's murder but was acquitted by a French court in May 1999, to the great disappointment of large parts of the Comorian people.

President Mohamed Taki Abdoulkarim, elected in 1996, died in office on November 6, 1998. In accordance with the Constitution, Tadjiddine ben Said Massounde, the President of the High Council was named Interim President. On November 25, he formed a government of national unity and appointed the leader of the opposition, Abbass Djoussouf, as Prime Minister. Although the Constitution calls for the Interim President to hold presidential elections within ninety days of the death of the elected president, an election timetable had not been set by year's end. Both the Interim President and the Prime Minister took the position that the elections should be postponed until the secessionist crisis on Anjouan was resolved.

The shortcomings of 22 years of independence became painfully clear when the Anjouan secessionists acted in August 1997. For 22 years, the political regimes, which were unable and often unwilling to create a stable economy, caused frustration among the civilians. In total eighteen coups or attempted coups took place in the islands of the Republic. France continued to play a political role with the French intelligence service frequently supplying mercenaries to the coup perpetrators. Mayotte, which voted to retain French rule in 1975, has now become an economic and social paradise in the eyes of the poor people of the Comoros. According to the Anjouan separatists, the economic situation will only be improved through true independence. This time, not from France but from the Federal Republic.

The Comoros is one of Africa's poorest countries as it has few natural resources, poor transportation links and a young and rapidly expanding population. The low level of the labour force corresponds with low levels of economic activity and high unemployment. Although agriculture is the leading sector of the economy, the country is not self-sufficient in food production. Rice is the country's main staple and 90 per cent of its supply is imported. Major investments in tourism and the industrial sector are vital to raise the GDP, but thus far have failed to do so. Funds from donors have been used for short-term consumption, not for long-term investments. The Comoros sit astride one of the world's vital sealanes through which super-tankers and foreign warships pass on their way from the sensitive Gulf region to Europe around the Cape of Good Hope. But because of its weak and unstable economic climate the country has not been able to capitalise on its geographical position. There has been no investment in modern harbour-facilities, for example.

The mix of chronic political instability on the one hand and great poverty on the other has made the Comoros a very vulnerable republic. The root cause of the conflict within the Comoros lies in the severe economic deprivation and poverty. When the islands became independent, they were wholly lacking the political and economic basis on which to build a future.

Conflict Dynamics

Two islands in the Comoros group are currently seeking their independence from the Federal Republic: Anjouan, the island of President Abdallah Ibrahim, leader of the *Movement Populaire d'Anjouan* and Mohéli, represented by Muhammad Hasan Ali. Both leaders state that they want to return to French rule with a similar status to Mayotte or become microstates in association with France. They feel themselves economically and socially neglected by the central government. The presidents support their position by arguing that most of the financial aid given by the Development Bank as well as by the UN is claimed by the Grande Comoro. Ironically, France is not interested in any new colonial alliance with the two islands. Despite the rejection of their overtures, Mohéli and Anjouan continue to ask the French government for help.

Although both islands have the same problems and the same view of the future, they differ in their responses to their situation. The president of Mohéli said in the *African Research Bulletin* that the island 'condemns the use of force and does not want an armed struggle'.

Mohéli has consequently tried to seek a solution trough a dialogue with the Federal Government and the OAU.

The political groups of Anjouan on the other hand, have attempted to secure independence through the use of military force. A brief look at the conflict dynamics of the most recent period shows that the federal government as well as the people of Anjouan have reacted in a violent and aggressive way to the problems on the island.

When the Anjouan separatists declared their independence from the central government of the Comoros on August 3, 1997, President Taki immediately sent troops to the island to restore order. The fighting between the government forces and the separatists resulted in the deaths of forty people. During the conflict, President Taki's threat to send more federal troops fuelled the aggression of the secessionists. More skirmishes with fatalities were reported after August. Federal troops had been ordered to suppress the revolts while the rebels were intent on resisting any military authority of the central government. Both the secessionists and the government troops took prisoners.

Within this aggressive and violent atmosphere, President Ibrahim further developed his ideas of an independent Anjouan. The newly created Anjouan government organised a referendum among the islanders to demonstrate the unanimity of the island's desire for independence. The federal government as well as the international community strongly condemned the outcome, 98 per cent in favour, because it contravened the agreement between the opposing parties to seek a solution to the crisis.

In February 1998, the Anjouan government drafted a constitution for the island. The OAU reacted to this very clear manifestation of Anjouan independence by arguing that the secessionists were undermining the fundamental principle of maintaining the territorial integrity of existing states. In the meantime, the humanitarian situation on the island deteriorated. No electricity, little food-production and social insecurity because of unpaid government salaries resulted in numerous strikes.

When the problems on the islands first began, President Taki assumed total power. He asked the OAU, the UN and the Arab League to help him restore order. At the instigation of the OAU, a few conferences were held to try and seek a solution to the conflict situation. All the parties involved strongly condemned the wish of the island people to become independent. They regarded the situation as constituting a threat to peace and security in the countries around the Indian Ocean. The conferences, where Anjouan president Ibrahim continued to refer to the right of self-determination as stated in the UN Charter, ended without any results.

After a few months of stagnation, President Taki tried to regain the initiative in June 1998. Firstly, he promised to improve the disastrous economic situation on the islands. Secondly he tried to re-open the dialogue between the different parties following the failure of the 1997 military intervention and the OAU-mediation efforts. On November 6, however, President Taki Abdulkarim died of a suspected heart attack.

His successor, President Massonde, again requested military assistance from the OAU and France when violence once more erupted in Anjouan in December 1998. More than sixty casualties, destruction of property and displacement of the population were reported. On this occasion the fighting was primarily between two separatist camps. Ibrahim's party, whose main goal is to achieve recognition for his independent state, is now opposed by supporters of Said Omar Chamassi who demand a state constitutionally linked to France. The fighting in December showed that Chamassi's followers are prepared to use violence in pursuit of this goal. Despite the OAU's appeal for military assistance none of its member states volunteered to send troops.

On December 15, however, the two secessionist parties signed a 48-hour cease-fire agreement. During that agreement French diplomats played a mediating role and tried to seek a solution. In February 1999 the OAU launched a new peace-initiative in a twelve-point statement. The statement said that if in a short period of time, the security situation in Anjouan continued to degenerate, regional leaders should consider the use of military force to deal with the situation. It was decided that an inter-island conference should deal with the socio-economic situation in the archipelago and should create a new institutional framework for the country. Although this new framework will respect the aspirations of all the people of the Comoros, the policy of the OAU-ministers seems to ignore the wish for independence.

The inter-island conference was held in Madagascar and led to an OAU-mediated agreement which was signed in April 23. The Madagascar agreement did not grant the wish for independence, but gave greater autonomy to the two islands of Anjouan and Moheli and introduced a three-year rotating presidency between the three islands. However, it led to violence on Grand Comore, with people of Anjouan descent being targeted after the Anjouan delegation to the conference failed to sign the accord on the grounds that they needed to consult their people. Furthermore the violence was said to be instigated by youths who thought the agreement would weaken the position of the Grand Comore.

The violence resulted in a military coup on April 30 1999 in which the army was said to have intervened 'to restore order'. Colonel Azali Assoumani, who seized power in the bloodless coup, said he would hand over to an elected government after twelve months, and would abide by the agreement.

Official Conflict Management

The Federal Republic has more than 24 political parties. Despite its democratic constitution, few of them have the political freedom to provide a serious opposition to the few dominant parties such as the National Union for Comorian Democracy, the party of former president Taki.

The weakness of this political structure became very clear when Anjouan declared its independence. The secessionists of Anjouan and the federal government of the Republic were wholly unable to accept each other's points of view. President Taki's only answer to the problem seemed to be the reintegration of the Anjouan and Mohéli islands within the Republic. To achieve this, he sent his federal troops to Anjouan almost immediately and called upon the OAU for assistance.

The secessionists on Anjouan are strongly opposed to military intervention on their island. They refuse to accept any party or institute at the

negotiating table because no one respects their wish for independence. Only France, seen by the secessionists as their new political ally, has been called on for assistance.

Divisions within the political parties themselves have also frustrated attempts to find a solution to the conflict. For example, the disagreements within the Anjouan secessionist party have lead to new fighting on the island.

The international community continues to recognise the Comorian Government's sovereignty over Anjouan.

The *Organisation for African Unity* is the only body that took the crisis seriously and has sent several missions to the islands. It has played a significant role in the conflict, mainly out of concern for maintaining peace and unity in the Indian Ocean. The Anjouan and Mohéli aspirations for independence are considered to pose a real threat to the unity in the Indian Ocean. In December 1997, observers from Egypt, Niger, Senegal and Tunisia were sent to the islands to help ease tensions after a declaration of independence by the island of Anjouan; the OAU Observer Mission in the Comoros (OMIC). Furthermore, a military assessment mission visited the islands in December 1998 to make a proper, professional assessment of the situation and examine all the options on how to assist in the restoration of the normal situation in Anjouan. The predominantly military composition of the team suggested that peace enforcement would have been, at least, one of the major considerations of the mission.

The representatives of the OAU have also organised two conferences where they tried to seek a solution. One of these, the inter-island conference, resulted on April 23 1999 in the Madagascar agreement which offered each island broad autonomy under a national government and outlined the establishment of an interim government that would rule until the next elections. However as the OAU representative, Mahmoud Kane said: 'The agreement decided to put in place an interim government led by a prime minister. We were about to do that when the coup happened.'

The OAU condemned the coup in the Indian Ocean archipelago on 30 April which it said had set back implementation of a peace deal signed

ANJOUAN, COMOROS: Civil war refugees   PHOTO EDGAR CLEIJNE/LINEAIR

in Madagascar. The OAU withdrew its military observers from the Islands because it did not want to work with the military government. The civilian component of the OAU mission stayed to observe developments and attempt to continue dialogue with the military government.

As old allies of the Comoros, South Africa, Tanzania and Mozambique are the countries most involved in finding a solution to the present conflict.

The *Comoros government* has fostered close relationships with the more conservative (and oil-rich) Arab states from the League of Arab States. But this relationship has transpired to be mainly economic, and the League has not been involved in any peace-initiatives during the conflict.

As the former colonial power, *France* has played a rather interesting role in the conflict. It has refused to respond to repeated requests for political and military assistance from the Anjouan and Mohéli separatists. The idea of resuming political and economic control in Anjouan and Mohéli does not appeal to the French. Effectively, France has no economic interest in the two very poor and politically unstable islands while the latter consider France

as their principal donor nation. Consequently, France has strongly condemned the islands' aspirations for independence. Under pressure from the OAU, France continues to give financial aid to the islands but refuses further involvement.

The *United Nations* has limited its involvement to official statements on the problems of the Comoros. Both the WHO and the Red Cross have given humanitarian aid to the islands.

Multi-Track Diplomacy

According to the available information, no local peace initiatives were taken during the conflict. A UNDP country-report explains why the civil society of the islands has not acquired the dynamism and capacity to play a significant role in social change. The report emphasises the effect of political instability as a hindrance to the development of the islands. Considering the fact that the Comoros is one of the poorest countries of Africa, with a weak infrastructure and poor social conditions, the lack of local NGOs is to be expected, which in turn explains the lack of peace-seeking initiatives within the local community.

The *Comoros Human Rights Association*, established in 1990, is one of the few local NGOs, however,many of its members are unwilling to criticise the Government vigorously for fear of losing their civil service positions. The Government cooperates with international human rights organisations, including the International Committee of the Red Cross.

Prospects

The Anjouan and Mohéli declaration of independence in August 1997 did not come as a surprise. As indicated in this survey, the post-colonial history of the republic is characterised by an unstable political system and weak economy which have in turn led to aspirations of a better future and civil unrest. Given that the society is one of the poorest in Africa, that it lacks any strong social organisation and is poorly represented by political parties or NGOs, it seems unlikely that the struggle can be transferred to the negotiating table. To date the conflict has resulted in the deaths of a few hundred soldiers and civilians and a worsening of the already poor humanitarian situation. Initiatives taken by the ministers of the OAU to find a peaceful solution to the problem and to re-open the dialogue between the different parties have not, thus far, provided any grounds to hope for a successful resolution to the conflict in the near future.

Recommendations

The UNDP report has identified the following priorities which it believes necessary if a course of sustainable and peaceful development is to be successfully pursued:

- Strengthening of governance by strengthening the rule of law, improving the management of public resources, and enhancing the participation of local communities in the development process;
- Improvement of the competitiveness of the Comoros by restoring macroeconomic stability, improving the management of the public sector and creating favourable conditions for productive investment while supporting private initiatives;
- Development of human capital and curbing of population growth by improving the quality and accessibility of education and training and of the health services and creating stable employment on the basis of private initiative; and
- Conservation of the fragile environment of the Comoros by emphasising conservation, increasing the productivity and diversification of agriculture, and promoting land ownership policies and environmental protection.

Also Cedric de Coning from ACCORD, South Africa has emphasised economic development as a prerequisite for a solution of the conflict. The conflict in the Comoros is driven by the poverty and economic degradation that are endemic to the islands. The tensions between the capital island of Moroni and the others are directly linked to their economic relationship. Therefore, according to de Coning, any long-term solution would require an economic cooperation agreement for the Comoran island system that would see all the people of the Comoros benefiting equally from their limited shared economy.

Service Information

Newsletters
Indiana Ocean Newsletter (www.indigo-net.com/africa.html)

Publications
The Politics of Squalor and Dependency - Chronic political instability and economic collapse in the Comoro islands. In: African Affairs, Vol.89, Nr. 357, 1990.
Country Cooperation Framework and Related Matters (1997-2001), UNDP, 1997.
Comoros Country Report on Human Rights Practices for 1998, U.S. Department of State, 1999.

Resource Contacts
Mamoudou Kahn, Special Representative for the Comoros of the OAU, e-mail
oau-ews@telecom.net.et

Cedric de Coning, Programme Manager Peacekeeping, ACCORD, e-mail
cedric@yebo.co.za

Selected Internet Sites
www.chez.com/rita/ (Comoros Online)
www.emulateme.com/government/comorogov.htm (Government of Comoros)
www.chez.com/prc/ (Parti Republicain des Comores)
www.ksu.edu/sasw/comoros/comoros.html (General resources on Comoro islands)
http://lcweb2.loc.gov/glin/comoros.html (offers an annotated list of selected links)
www.undp.org:80/rba/country/ccf/9705416e.htm (UNDP-RBA Country cooperation Framework for Comoros)

Mozambique

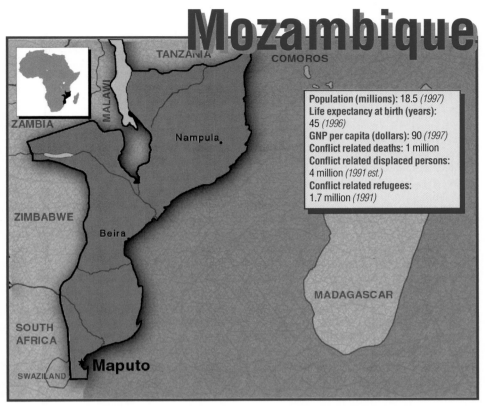

Population (millions): 18.5 *(1997)*
Life expectancy at birth (years):
45 *(1996)*
GNP per capita (dollars): 90 *(1997)*
Conflict related deaths: 1 million
Conflict related displaced persons:
4 million *(1991 est.)*
Conflict related refugees:
1.7 million *(1991)*

An End to an Imported War

After sixteen years of war, Mozambique has now enjoyed more than six years of uninterrupted peace. The war began in 1976 as a destabilisation campaign initially conducted by Rhodesia and then by apartheid-South Africa following Rhodesia's transition to independent Zimbabwe. In the course of the 1980s the war took on local dimensions. Widespread war-fatigue, foreign mediation and a fairly successful UN intervention have brought a durable peace. Money was an important factor in the peace process with large sums being spent on appeasing the two sides in the conflict, particularly Renamo. Since peace began, the economy has performed impressively. Mozambique however has yet to create sufficient wealth to further diminish the threat of violence ◆ *By* **Bram Posthumus**

Mozambique was among five Portuguese African colonies that successfully waged a guerrilla war in pursuit of independence. In Mozambique the Front for the Liberation of Mozambique (Frelimo) was in the forefront of the struggle which began in 1964 and ended when the colonial government in Lisbon was overthrown by the Portuguese military in 1974. One year later, independence was declared. Under the presidency of Samora Machel and as a result of Soviet influence, the country adopted a Marxist-Leninist course, although it was combined with an economic model that mixed free markets with state control.

Mozambique's independence gave rise to considerable unease in the two remaining white minority governments in the region, Rhodesia and South Africa. Particularly worrying for the Rhodesians was Machel's support of the armed wing of the Zimbabwean liberation movement led by Robert Mugabe. In response Rhodesia worked out a strategy with two objectives: destabilising the new Mozambican government and disrupting the actions of the Zimbabweans. The chosen instrument was the Mozambican National Resistance (MNR), brainchild of Ken Flower, the head of the Rhodesian Central Intelligence Organization.

This strategy was a partial success. It did not prevent Zimbabwean independence in 1980, but succeeded in disrupting the development of Mozambique. The MNR was peopled by Portuguese and African soldiers of the old colonial army, ex-Frelimo fighters who had become disappointed by the authoritarian style the liberators had adopted, and mercenaries. It changed its name to the Portuguese-sounding acronym Renamo early in the 1980s and established itself in the Ndau-speaking central region of the country. At the outset, Renamo had no political agenda of its own: this was determined at first in Salisbury and then in Pretoria. It is disputed whether Renamo developed any political programme of its own when it became more of a local force. Its leader Alphonso Dhlakama frequently employed phrases like 'democracy' and 'free market' to defend Renamo's actions. It appears that if there ever was a Renamo ideology, it consisted of a keen sense of the injustice inflicted upon it by a hostile government, as Claudio Mario Betti of Sant' Egidio (one of the principal NGO mediators) has argued.

On the other hand, Frelimo, the victorious liberation movement of the left, turned itself into a 'vanguard party' in 1977. It made itself deeply unpopular by declaring traditional rule and practices 'backward'. Frelimo's criticisms of the traditional chiefs, who were stripped of their traditional powers, gave Renamo an especially good opportunity to score political points. Frelimo's most unpopular move was 'Operation Production', which involved the forced migration of urban dwellers to rural areas and the creation of so-called 'communal villages', which split families and uprooted people. The situation eased when Frelimo moved away from this rigid application of Marxist-Leninism - but by then it had lost most of its goodwill among the rural and some of the urban population of the country.

Renamo found it easy to recruit new fighters, besides its regular practice of press-ganging young boys into its ranks. Beaten into a corner by Renamo's military success which it owed in no small measure to its South African backers, the government entered into negotiations with South Africa, which resulted in the 1984 Nkomati Peace Accord. Under the terms of the accord, Samora Machel expelled the ANC, which was operating from his country. For its part, South Africa was to stop supporting Renamo, which it did not do until 1988, two years after Machel's death in an air crash on South African territory. The new president, Joaquim Chissano, renewed negotiations with the South Africans, and this time the flow of aid to Renamo did come to a virtual stop. However, by this time Renamo could survive on its own and was able to strike virtually anywhere in the country.

In the late 1980s, Eastern Bloc support for Frelimo diminished. The Soviets withdrew, realising there was not much to be gained from heavy involvement in an African country they neither understood nor cared about and facing the imminent collapse of their political system at home. Frelimo initiated moves away from doctrinal Marxist-Leninism. At the same time, the changes towards democracy in South Africa and the removal of the Republicans from the US presidency helped to significantly decrease the destabilising tactics that South Africa had, until then, been able to employ with impunity - if not American approval - against its neighbours to the north.

Indeed, the end of the Cold War precipitated the end of all conflicts in the region, including the one in Mozambique. In addition, the devastating drought in the entire southern African region in 1991-92, which all but wiped out Mozambique's capacity to produce food made it physically more difficult to continue fighting. Finally, there was growing battle fatigue on both sides - fed by the growing realisation that neither side could win the war - and widespread exasperation among ordinary Mozambicans about the never-ending violence and brutality.

It was against this background that peace negotiations were initiated. They were mediated by several African governments, the British multinational Lonrho and the Roman Catholic Church. The negotiations continued for three years and resulted in the General Peace Accord, which was signed in Rome on October 7, 1992. In a massive operation that lasted from late 1992 until March 1995, the United Nations oversaw mass demobilisation and the first elections which returned most fighters to civilian life and Frelimo to power in Maputo, while Renamo did well in Central Mozambique.

Conflict Dynamics

One of the striking features of the dynamics of the Mozambican conflict is that, initially at least, they were not Mozambican at all. Renamo was a Rhodesian invention and without large-scale backing from the whites-only regimes in the region, it is doubtful whether the war would have continued as long as it did. The objective of this support was always twofold: destabilisation and retaliation for Mozambican support for the armed liberation struggle in both countries. During most of the war MNR/Renamo behaved in the manner its founders and backers intended, waging a campaign of terror that earned it the nickname the 'Khmer Rouge of Africa'. Its most notorious act was perhaps the Homoine massacre, where its soldiers killed over 400 civilians.

Renamo set up an elaborate system of forced food provision through slave-labour in the areas it controlled. This, combined with raids on Frelimo areas and neighbouring countries (particularly Zimbabwe and Zambia) kept it alive and operational. It destroyed government installations, especially schools and hospitals, and subjected the rural population to acts of abhorrent cruelty, cutting off breasts, limbs, ears and lips. Rape was used as a weapon of war and was especially directed against women who had previously joined the Frelimo-linked Organisation of Mozambican Women. Renamo made extensive use of child soldiers, who were frequently forced to kill their own families. It managed to get local support, particularly in Central Mozambique because the leadership of the movement came from the region. It received support there and elsewhere also as a result of widespread resentment over Frelimo's arrogance and misguided rural settlement policies.

On the other side, the Mozambican Armed Forces, are known to have committed human rights abuses against the same rural population, albeit not on the scale and with the systematic ruthlessness of Renamo.

The rural population, thoroughly traumatised by the ongoing atrocities and violence, left the countryside in large numbers, swelling the cities. A second preferred area was the Beira-corridor from Zimbabwe to the Mozambican port city of Beira, where tens of thousands found refuge in enormous camps that stretched for miles on either side of the roads and railways that were guarded by the Zimbabwean Army. The Zimbabweans have played a critical role in guarding this economically vital corridor and assisting the Mozambican army in their various offensives against Renamo, at considerable human and economic cost to themselves.

The war was a typical low-intensity conflict in line with the American concept of destabilisation that was also tried and tested in - among others - Nicaragua. It was a guerrilla bush war par excellence, rendering large parts of Mozambique ungovernable and unsafe. All facilities that had been installed since independence, especially local clinics and schools, were destroyed and their personnel murdered. Renamo also destroyed bridges, and roads, sabotaged power and telephone lines and railways. Some estimates place the costs of damage as high US$ 3.5 billion.

Perhaps the most lasting effect of this destabilisation campaign has been the effect on the mostly rural population: the strategy of making people utterly insecure in their own villages has worked very well and people still remain in the towns, unwilling to go back into the bush. An additional problem has been created by the fact that both sides have littered the countryside with landmines, making agriculture a hazardous occupation.

Official Conflict Management

The General Peace Agreement, which was signed in Rome on October 4, 1992, was remarkably comprehensive. It included provision for the formation of political parties; described how elections should be held; stipulated freedom of movement and freedom of the press; prepared the way for the formation of the Mozambican Defence Force - for which both Frelimo and Renamo would make troops available; and it made arrangements for the demobilisation and reintegration of ex-combatants. A number of important state and non-state actors helped mediate in the process that brought about this Agreement. Others have moved in to help consolidate the peace.

The *United Nations* became involved when the General Peace Agreement had been signed. It was tasked with overseeing the transition from war to peace and its response was comprehensive. UNOMOZ (UN Operations in Mozambique) covered the demobilisation, encampment of ex-combatants, preparation for elections - including literally buying both parties, especially Renamo, into the political process -, mine clearance and humanitarian assistance. Despite serious scandals - including child abuse by some of its military personnel, the high cost (US$ one million per day) and the bureaucratic bungling for which the organisation was notorious, the UNOMOZ operation, which lasted from December 1992 until March 1995, more than twice as long as originally intended, was an overall success.

The reasons for this success and for the fact that the political will existed to provide extensive financial backing for UNOMOZ lie in the wider African context. After the disasters of Somalia and Angola, the UN badly needed an African success story. Mozambique provided the occasion, and a number of factors unique to Mozambique contributed to the successful outcome: the belligerents had lost their will to fight, there were no resources over which to fight (unlike in Angola) and the only resource that was abundantly available were the UN millions. Alternating displays of compliance and intransigence by both Renamo and Frelimo opened the UN purse at every turn; in this sense the Mozambican peace was bought. It was also clear that the political will to repeat this feat, for example in another Angolan initiative, did not exist. Mozambique was a one-off.

African governments have been involved in the war and the peace process in various ways. The governments of Zimbabwe and Tanzania provided crucial military and political support to Frelimo and Zimbabwean president Robert Mugabe's personal mediation during negotiations leading up to the General Peace Agreement proved crucial. Zimbabwean troops provided important military backup to the Mozambican army, helping in offensive action and on at least one occasion overrunning Renamo's Gorongosa headquarters, in 1985. Documents seized on that occasion also proved continued South African support for Renamo, in spite of the Nkomati agreement with the Mozambican government.

Apartheid-South Africa, Malawi and Kenya backed Renamo politically and militarily. Support for Renamo by the immediate neighbours only diminished significantly after the rise to power of president F.W. de Klerk in South Africa and the signing of a 1986 agreement between the Mozambican and Malawian governments. In the earlier stages of the talks that finally led to the General Peace Agreement, the Kenyan government carved out a mediating role for itself with considerable success: the first direct talks between Frelimo and Renamo were held in Nairobi in August 1989. Kenyan influence declined when the Rome talks got under way.

Post-apartheid South Africa, Botswana and Zambia have mainly acted as facilitators, providing space for negotiations to take place. Mozambique and South Africa have now signed an agreement aimed at reducing the flow of arms between the two countries. To date, South Africa and Mozambique have jointly destroyed more than 1,000 tonnes of small arms and ammunition in Mozambique, the most spectacular - and worrying - find being a 900 tonnes cache that was destroyed in an action in the first months of 1999. South Africa also co-sponsored a UN resolution adopted in December 1998, which called for an international conference on the illicit arms trade. A date for the conference has yet to be fixed but it should take place within the next two years.

The *Mozambican government's* desire to end the destabilisation of its country led it into negotiations with apartheid-South Africa, resulting in the Nkomati agreement of 1984. Under the deal, South Africa would end its support of Renamo, while Mozambique would expel the ANC from its territory. This it duly did, while South Africa continued supporting Renamo. Under the new president Joaquim Chissano, the drive towards a peaceful solution to the conflict intensified.

One factor which has helped significantly in preventing even further prolonged bloodshed is the fact that in spite of vociferous lobbying by extreme right-wing Republicans and others, neither the Reagan nor the Bush administrations in the US gave overt aid to Renamo. An important factor in the maintenance of this policy was the report by R. Gersony, written for the US State department, which provided a damning indictment of Renamo's murderous tactics. It is difficult to say how much longer the war would have continued if the US had decided to step in on the side of Renamo in the same way as it has helped Unita in Angola. It needs to be added, though, that because of the Cold War psychology, which reigned supreme in Washington, apartheid-South Africa had considerable license to destabilise regimes which were, in the American view, too close to the Soviet Union. Mozambique was one of them.

The *Italian government* covered the cost of hosting the delegations during the Rome talks and provided Renamo with substantial amounts of money, to keep them on board in the peace process. The Italian government is said to have spent up to US$ 20 million on keeping the peace process going. Frelimo was also kept on board; the Italians promised generous aid packages and assistance in the reconstruction of Mozambique's infrastructure.

The *European Union* announced in December 1997 that it had set aside US$ 160 million to facilitate the re-integration of former combatants into society in all southern African nations that had seen violent civil conflict. An assessment of the requirements of each country was to be started in 1998.

Multi-Track Diplomacy
Domestic
Researcher Carolyn Nordstrom of Berkley University in the United States carried out field work in Mozambique between 1988 and 1996 and found a remarkably resilient 'culture of peace', as she called it. Home-grown, informal,

based on age-old practices of welcoming, healing, counselling and reintegration, Nordstrom found these groups all over the country and concludes that the persuasiveness of this particular culture of peace has been responsible for the durability of the peace process in Mozambique.

Civil society in Mozambique did not really come into its own until after the General Peace Agreement was in place and Frelimo had renounced its monopoly on all significant social and political activity. During the war, by far the most important internal player in the country in promoting a climate for peace talks, was the Roman Catholic Church. The *Mozambican Christian Council*, an ecumenical body worked hard to ensure the continuation of the peace talks, especially between 1990 and 1992. Both were heavily engaged in local peace building and community reconstruction, as were some international aid agencies. Traditional beliefs have also played a role, both in terms of individual healing and restoring faith in previously shattered communities.

With peace firmly in place and the one-party state removed from public life, space has become available for other non-state actors to play a role. This is certainly evident in the print media, where there has been a proliferation of newspapers and magazines. Although they cater for a limited, mostly urban, social group, these do include the policy-makers. Through them, the urban elite are kept in touch with events in rural Mozambique. There are human rights organisation in place, including the *Liga Mozambicana de Derechos Humanos* and the (anti-Frelimo) *League for Human Rights (LDH)*, which deals with - among other things - continued police brutality. *LINK* is an umbrella NGO, grouping together a broad variety of Mozambican NGOs, which is currently engaged in civil education, incorporating non-violent methods of conflict resolution. LINK is supported by - among others - the Mennonite Central Committee from Canada.

The Roman Catholic Church in Mozambique, notably in the person of Bishop Jaime Gonçalves of Beira, acted as a mediator by maintaining contacts with Renamo. It began making public appeals for peace in 1983 and issued various

ZAMBEZIA (PROV.), MOZAMBIQUE: Election time

pastoral letters, including one entitled *The Peace that People Want*. Overcoming initial government hostility, the Church gained wider recognition as direct negotiations finally got under way between Renamo and Frelimo and during the protracted talks in Rome, Bishop Gonçalves was present as an observer.

Churches remain active in the effort to persuade civilians to hand in weapons for destruction. The Council of Churches in Mozambique runs a programme entitled 'Transforming Arms into Hoes', of which the weapons destruction exercise is a part.

International

The *Community of Sant' Egidio*, the Italian-based assembly of lay Christian communities, mediated the first contacts between its old friend Bishop Gonçalves of Beira and Renamo, paving the way for mediation by the Mozambican Roman Catholic Church. Sant' Egidio opened up its own contacts with a hostile, anti-church Frelimo and a suspicious Renamo and finally managed to build up a relationship of trust with both sides. Discretion was the hallmark of Sant' Egidio and this has enabled it to keep

communication open. Sant' Egidio went on to host all twelve rounds of talks that were held in Rome from July 1990 until the General Peace Agreement, October 7, 1994. The Community has been criticised for being too lenient towards both sides, but it has at least helped produce the peace desired by the majority. As Ibrahim Msabaha wrote in a comprehensive evaluation of the talks which appeared as a contribution entitled 'Negotiating an end to Mozambique's murderous rebellion' in *Elusive Peace*: 'Delay was the price of success...' And Sant' Egidio's Betti would add that in peace mediation one can only be sure of success if the process is actually owned by those who are involved in it: forced solutions, forced agreements do not work.

Special mention must be made of the *international anti-apartheid movement*, which has kept the Mozambique issue firmly on the international political agenda, through campaigns, lobbies and tangible support to Mozambique itself, even during the 1980s, when South Africa was engaging in its greatest destabilisation efforts. It is especially remarkable, given the prevailing political climate at the time in key countries such as the

US, UK and Germany, whose governments effectively condoned South Africa's activities in the region.

As an endorsement of Mozambique's decision to pursue the path to a durable peace, the South African NGO *ACCORD* conferred its 1997 Africa Peace Award - a biannual event - on the nation of Mozambique. It was presented by a previous winner, Nelson Mandela, whose first official state visit as president of South Africa had, quite significantly, been to Mozambique.

A special position in the run-up to and during the negotiations was held by the British multinational company Lonrho and especially its flamboyant chairman, *'Tiny' Rowland*. Lonrho had significant infrastructure and agricultural interests in Mozambique, including the vital oil pipeline from Beira to Zimbabwe. Initially, Lonrho paid Renamo to leave its assets alone, a strategy that was abandoned in the face of escalating violence. Rowland then started a prolonged shuttle diplomacy exercise, involving key players including Renamo leader Alphonso Dhlakama, Mozambican President Chissano, South Africa's Foreign minister Botha, Kenyan president Moi and Zimbabwean President Mugabe. He personally facilitated meetings, even by flying people to European and African venues in his private jet and mediating directly between Chissano and Dhlakama. Rowland's personal involvement and investment -millions of dollars were poured into Renamo to keep them in the peace negotiations - helped speed up the negotiations and on more than one occasion prevented them from total collapse.

There are some international initiatives to help support the ongoing disarmament in Mozambique. The Japanese cities of Fukui and Itoh have spearheaded a campaign called 'Guns for Hoes', in which bicycles, hoes and other pieces of equipment are gathered in Japan and shipped to Mozambique, where they are plugged into a scheme which gives out these implements for anyone who brings in a weapon. In very much the same vein, the Dutch Foundation *'Vraag en Aanbod'* (Supply and Demand) runs a scheme in cooperation with the church in Zambézia, in which repaired bicycles, sewing machines and carpentry tools are exchanged for guns.

Prospects

Peace has prevailed since 1992. That in itself is a remarkable achievement. Given past events, Mozambicans have demonstrated an extraordinary capacity for reconciliation. 'We have accepted to live with the past', is the way a Maputo street trader put it and she sums up the mood. Almost all of the refugees have returned and have begun to reconstitute their lives as best they can.

The tensions that from time to time still appear between Frelimo and Renamo are confined to the political circuits. Renamo has transformed itself from a guerrilla force into a political party and Frelimo has relinquished its monopolistic hold on power. Renamo has real political power in the centre of the country and hold seats in Parliament. It stages walk outs and boycotts elections, but the realisation that there is more to be gained from political debate than a bush fight appears pervasive. It makes for a modicum of political balance, sometimes shaky, but nevertheless real.

Many of Mozambique's problems are of course still related to the conflict: overpopulated cities, a weak infrastructure (although the trunk roads have all been repaired and the telephone system restored), an unresolved landmine problem (there are an estimated 1.5 million mines and clearance is continuing slowly), and the problem of the thousands of ex-combatants, who feel short-changed by their former masters who spend their time playing politics in Maputo, while they have to get by on a pittance. With the proliferation of small arms, some take their struggle to survive back to the bush and engage in acts of banditry.

Further economic expansion is urgently needed along with a more equitable distribution of wealth in order to include those who have not been able to profit from the impressive growth figures Mozambique has recorded since the mid-1990s. Corruption has, unfortunately, become a major problem. As some commentators have pointed out, the issue of ethnicity could become more pronounced. Although Renamo found its home in the predominantly Shona and Ndau-speaking centre of the country, which it now dominates politically, ethnicity has played its role mostly under the surface. However, these tensions may surface if wealth distribution is not seen to be equitable among the many regions of the vast country.

Recommendations

Perhaps the most important recommendation is that of the Jubilee 2000 debt relief pressure group which emphasises the need to get serious about writing-off the debts of the so-called Highly Indebted Poor Countries, of which Mozambique is one. Debt reduction is on the cards remaining to be played and should bring some relief as Mozambique is one of the most heavily indebted countries in the world. In July, 1999 the IMF and Worldbank announced that Mozambique's annual debt repayment will be reduced from US$ 169 million to US$ 73 million in the period 1999-2005. If acted upon, this initiative will free up considerable local resources for much-needed economic development.

There has been serious criticism of the adopted model of elections. Mozambican journalist Carlos Cardoso has contended that at a cost of up to US$ 70 million - almost half the country's entire export revenue - elections are too expensive an exercise for the country to repeat with every change of government. He has advocated starting the election process locally and then moving it to the national level, which would, in his view, make for a more popularly recognisable and cheaper exercise in democracy.

Also on the subject of money, Alex Vines has raised the question whether throwing money at a peace process in such a fashion encourages the participants to stall in order to extract as much cash from the exercise as possible; a strategy that Afonso Dhlakama in particular has pursued with considerable success.

Service Information

Newsletters and Periodicals
Mozambique Peace Process Bulletin - published by AWEPA, Amsterdam, Netherlands

Reports
Human Rights Watch
- Conspicuous Destruction - War, famine and the reform process in Mozambique. 1992
- Landmines in Mozambique. London, 1994

Other Publications
ACCORD - The Mozambican Peace Process in Perspective, by Jeremy Armon, Dylan Hendrickson and Alex Vines (eds.). Conciliation resources, London, 1998
Managing Arms in Peace Process - Mozambique, by E. Berman. UN Institute for Disarmament Research, Geneva, 1996
The State, Violence and Development - The political economy of war in Mozambique, by M. Chingono. Avebury, Aldershot, UK, 1996
Le cause des armes en Mozambique - Anthropologie d'une guerre civile, by G. Geffray. Paris, 1990
Evaluation of Norwegian Assistance to Peace, Reconciliation and Rehabilitation in Mozambique, by A. Hallam, K. Halvorsen, J. Lexow (et.al.). Oslo, Royal Ministry of Foreign Affairs, 1997
Peace without profit - How the IMF blocks rebuilding in Mozambique, by J. Hanlon. Oxford, 1997
Apartheid's Contras and the roots of war - An inquiry in the modern history of Southern Africa, by W. Minter. London, 1994
The United Nations and Mozambique - 1992-1995. UN, New York, 1995
RENAMO: from terrorism to democracy in Mozambique?, by A. Vines. James Currey, London, 1996

Mozambique - UN Peacekeeping in Action, 1992-94, by R. Synge. Washington, D.C., US Institute of Peace, 1997
Elusive Peace - Negotiating an end to civil wars, by I.W. Zartman (ed). Brookings Institute, Washington, 1995

Selected Internet Sites
www.mozambique.mz/notmoc (political e-magazine in Portuguese with concise news bulletins)
www.sortmoz.com/aimnews (news-site of the government press agency, in English and Portuguese).
www.tropical.co.mz/~tvn/dirhtm/ (extensive links to both political and non-political topics, in Portuguese and English)
www.sadirecory.co.za/mediacoop (the gateway to prominent Mozambican media, including Savana, Mediafax, Mozambique Inview; extensive information from this site requires a subscription)
www.mozambique.mz/awepa (Mozambique Peace Process Bulletin, in English)

Resource Contacts
Alicia Mabota - Liga Mocambicana de Derechos Humanos
Joseph Hanlon - freelance journalist, e-mail jhanlon@open.ac.uk
William Minter - Washington office on Africa, e-mail wminter@igc.apc.org
Alex Vines - Human Rights Watch, e-mail hrwatch.uk@gn.apc.org>

Data on the following organisations can be found in the Directory section:
ACCORD
Sant' Egidio
Link

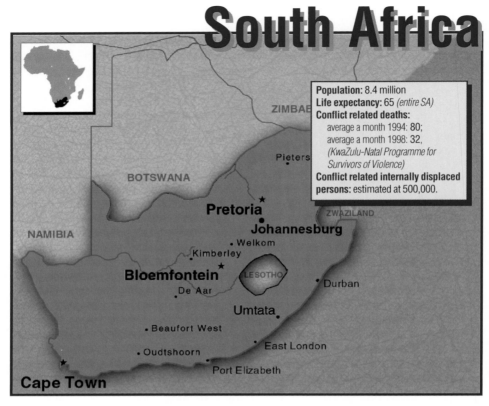

South Africa

Population: 8.4 million
Life expectancy: 65 *(entire SA)*
Conflict related deaths:
average a month 1994: 80;
average a month 1998: 32,
(KwaZulu-Natal Programme for Survivors of Violence)
Conflict related internally displaced persons: estimated at 500,000.

KwaZulu/Natal Province Smoulders

With a turbulent history behind it, saddled with some irresponsible politicians, replete with arms and people prepared to use them, there is little reason to be optimistic about an end to the violence in South Africa's troubled KwaZulu-Natal province. But local efforts continue, aimed at getting one of the country's economic powerhouses off the track of simmering violence and onto the road to recovery and development ◆ *By* **Anne Graumans**

KwaZulu/Natal's recent history has often been brutal. In the early nineteenth century, the area was part of the Zulu Empire, under rulers like Dingiswayo and later Shaka and Dingane. From the 1820s, the empire suffered greatly from an influx of English settlers and Afrikaner Boers of Dutch descent. The Boers were on their trek from the Cape, in order to escape the English whose influence they detested and whose abolition of slavery they resented. Boers and Zulus fought a number of bloody battles in the 1830s in the last of which - the 1838 Blood River battle - the Zulus suffered a crushing

defeat. However, it was the English who annexed Natal in 1843. Most of the Boers in the province then left to establish the Orange Free State and the Zuider Afrikaanse Republiek. For a while the Zulu state continued to pose a formidable threat to both the English and its neighbouring African peoples.

When gold was discovered in the Transvaal, English and Afrikaners engaged in a full-scale war over this new source of wealth, first in 1880/81, then in 1899-1902. Natal witnessed a number of battles on both occasions and in 1897 the Zulu nation was finally destroyed to be followed by the Boer resistance which was brought to its knees in 1902. Bambatha, a Zulu chief, led a short-lived rebellion which was ruthlessly crushed by the English. South Africa became a unified republic in 1910, two years before the precursor to the African National Congress was established and four years before the birth of the Boer-dominated National Party.

The united South African state was every bit as restrictive for Africans as the previous individual smaller states had been, with the possible exception of the Cape. The ascension to power of the National Party (NP) in 1948, which was to entrench the apartheid system for the next 46 years, simply aggravated a situation which put Africans at a structural disadvantage. Successive NP governments pursued the so-called Homelands policy, creating 'native' areas for Africans, under the pretext of recognising traditional authority.

One of these 'Homelands' was KwaZulu, a collection of enclaves scattered throughout the province of Natal. It was only after the political transformation of 1994, which brought the first free elections in South Africa's history, that the first attempts at building a unified and democratic country could be made. One step was reintegrating the Homelands into the provinces; for Natal and KwaZulu, this meant the formation of KwaZulu-Natal.

Conflict Dynamics

This history goes some way to explain the intractability of KwaZulu-Natal's troubles. The recent history of political violence in KwaZulu-Natal dates back to the mid-1980s, when the Inkhata Freedom Party (IFP) sought to consolidate its influence in the province, against the growing support for the Congress of South African Trade Unions (COSATU) and the United Democratic Front (UDF), both aligned to the ANC. Conflict occurred between youth and elders, the Zulu Royal House and its chiefly rivals and between the more forward looking, urbanised organisations associated with the UDF and ANC and the rural-based, chief-led Inkatha movement.

The conflict in KwaZulu-Natal, which reached its zenith in the months preceding the 1994 elections, was different in nature to the equally fierce IFP-ANC battles in Gauteng that raged in the streets and hostels. In KwaZulu-Natal the long-standing war between the UDF and the IFP, which re-ignited in ANC-IFP form after the lifting of the ban on the ANC, was fought in many isolated, mainly rural areas where ANC political structures were less well established or as tightly knit as in urban areas.

The presence of a strong regional political party, the Inkhata Freedom Party headed by Chief Mangosuthu Buthelezi, the nephew of Goodwill Zwelithini, king of all Zulus, has proved to pose a great challenge to stability in the region. In the past thirty years or so, Buthelezi has carved out a personal political empire in the province, using the IFP, which purports to represent all Zulus, as his instrument. From an anti-apartheid activist, he has steadily changed into an uncompromising Zulu nationalist, finding himself on a collision course with the ANC for political reasons and also with King Zwelithini for political and personal reasons.

Information has gradually emerged about the plot that was hatched by the apartheid security forces to foment violence among rival black political parties and leaders, a phenomenon that has become known as the 'Third Force'. Former military and security personnel who were put on trial after 1994 on murder charges have revealed that many assassinations were carried out by the security forces and security force-trained hit-squads, notably the KwaZulu police, which acted as the armed wing of the IFP. This was done, possibly with the knowledge and consent of the highest leaders of the country in those days, in order to destabilise and confuse the anti-apartheid struggle and its structures. Given the history and volatility of KwaZulu-Natal, these destabilising seeds fell on particularly fertile ground. The police merit special mention in this respect because of their perceived inaction in the face of widespread communal and political violence. It made them vulnerable to charges of collusion, which turned out to be at least partially true, as its murky background becomes clearer.

The IFP has been accused of throwing its weight behind the effort of the NP to crush the Mass Democratic Movement aligned to the ANC during the 1980s. More recently the findings of the Truth and Reconciliation Commission (TRC) has held Chief Buthelezi responsible for all the gross human rights violations committed under his leadership of the party, the KwaZulu government and the KwaZulu police. The TRC states that the most devastating indictment of the IFP's role in political violence was found in the commission's statistics which identified the IFP as the foremost perpetrator of gross human rights violations in KwaZulu and Natal between 1990 and 1994. Training of paramilitary units in the Caprivi Strip during 1986 by the SADF and the training in 1993 and 1994 of between 5,000 and 8,000 IFP self-protection unit (SPU) members at the Mlaba training camp must be seen as the responsibility of Chief Buthelezi. The TRC went as far as describing the IFP as an ally of the apartheid-state since high echelons within the IFP cadre cooperated with the South African Police and Defense Force, receiving both financial and logistical assistance.

Police attitudes appear to have improved of late but midway through 1998 allegations of law enforcers fomenting violence resurfaced, together with an upsurge in the violence. President Mandela himself said in July 1998 that there were 'rotten elements' within the police that were helping to fuel the violence. Recent reports in the *Mail & Guardian* show that the police service and national defence force choose sides, often along party lines, in conflicts. The police and security forces have also been accused by Amnesty International of ill-treating suspects and prisoners as late as April 1999.

The situation is further complicated by the fact that as a result of the simmering conflict local 'war lords' have managed to carve out small territories for themselves, over which the leadership of both parties appear to have little or no control. Neither the IFP nor the ANC could rely on apartheid's police forces to provide their leaders with sufficient security. This led to the formation of Self Defence Units (SDU) in the case of the ANC and Self Protection Units (SPU) for the IFP. The units consisted of young men who received military training and were provided with small arms. The failure to integrate the units into the post-1994 transformed South African Police Service and national army has led to a contingent of approximately 5,000 to 10,000 young and unemployed people who often rule the townships of KwaZulu-Natal. The breakdown of family life, particularly in rural areas and the appropriation of SDU and SPU structures by criminal elements further aggravated the lawlessness of these 'community serving' units.

The *Mail & Guardian* has reported the existence of camps in northern Natal where white right-wingers and former security force operatives provided military training to IFP loyalists as recently as this year. The TRC furthermore brought to the light that several truckloads of small arms were transported by the apartheid-security forces to the training camps of the IFP in Mlaba.

The 1994 transition to majority rule finally made it possible to put in place some of the conditions that would make the start of a peace-process on a significant scale a viable option. A parliamentary democracy was introduced. A Bill of Rights was adopted that encompassed all citizens of the country. Some of the earliest peace-making efforts were stepped up and new activities begun. However, the pattern of violence has still not been decisively broken. Violence returned to KwaZulu-Natal in the run-up to the 1999 national elections. Especially in the Richmond area, where between June and August 1998 well over fifty people were killed in politically motivated violence. This followed the killing of a regional IFP leader in April and preceded the violent deaths of three ANC activists in October 1998.

A complicating factor in identifying those responsible is the emergence of a new political party, the United Democratic Movement (UDM). Three key figures in the UDM are Bantu Holomisa, the former ruler of the Transkei 'homeland' who was expelled from the ANC because he had levelled corruption charges against party stalwarts; Roelf Meyer, the acclaimed NP negotiator who helped achieve the 1994 transition; and the late Sifiso Nkabinde, a former powerful ANC leader in KwaZulu-Natal, who was expelled from the party following murder charges against him, from which he was later acquitted. Sifiso Nkabinde was killed in a shoot-out in January 1999. A retaliation act killed eleven people. The violence now re-emerging in the province can be seen as a result of either the old ANC-IFP rivalry or the new ANC-UMD animosity.

Electoral Code of Conduct

The shaky KwaZulu-Natal peace process is a product of many months of tough negotiations between the ANC and the IFP following the ANC's rejection of the provincial results of the 1994 elections, which the ANC believed were irregular. Following Mandela's intervention, however, the ANC finally accepted the results.

May 27, 1996 was to be a turning point where all parties would reach a formal agreement denouncing violence. This would be followed by a delegation from both parties to brief their principals in Cape Town.

At the provincial ANC conference in December 1996, a special amnesty for the province was mooted. This was discussed at the presidential level of the two parties followed by one-to-one meetings between Mbeki and Buthelezi. The two agreed on cooperation between the IFP and ANC before a team of three senior leaders from each organisation was appointed to work on the modalities of peace before this year's elections. However, attempts by the IFP and the ANC to cobble together a code of conduct for political parties in the troubled province of KwaZulu-Natal ahead of the 1999 elections collapsed in June 1998. These efforts were resuscitated and led to the signing of an Electoral Code of Conduct in May 1999.

In its election manifesto the IFP promotes itself as a national party on the grounds that it will be contesting all nine provinces. At the same time the IFP wants to consolidate power in KwaZulu-Natal. The objective of establishing a 'Kingdom of KwaZulu' as a federal unit within the greater South Africa seems to have moved to the background.

On the other hand, the IFP seems to have taken a more hard-line approach for the province. At the opening of the provincial legislature in February 1999, the IFP replaced Ben Ngubane as regional premier with former minister of arts and culture, Lionel Mtshali. Premier Mtshali surprised his audience with his party's call for international mediation to define a political role for the Zulu monarchy. The issue, which threatened to derail the 1994 elections,

has been in abeyance, and the ANC had hoped that the forging of closer ties between the parties had forestalled the demand completely. But, as observers note, the demand is closely allied to the continued existence of traditional authority structures in the provinces.

The June 1999 national and provincial elections in KwaZulu-Natal passed without major incident. The IFP won the elections in the province with 42 per cent of the votes, against 39 per cent for the ANC. Power-sharing is a possibility with the IFP offering up to seven provincial cabinet posts to the ANC. While the detente between the two political parties seems to be firmly embedded, a possible danger lies in the fact that the IFP is dependent on support from IFP aligned traditional chiefs in the rural areas, who do not share the same interests and views as the politicians at the national level.

Official Conflict Management

The new *South African government* has on several occasions appealed for peace in KwaZulu-Natal. President Mandela visited the province in 1995, on June 16 - a very important national holiday commemorating the children's uprising in Soweto - and again on June 12, 1998. The government's requests only met with limited success, and in late 1995 troops were sent in by Minister of Safety and Security Mufamadi to quell the unrest. It is ironic that Chief Buthelezi is Minister of Home Affairs in the same government.

A later mediation effort undertaken by vice-president Thabo Mbeki in 1996, in which provincial party leaders Jacob Zuma (ANC) and Frank Mdlalose (IFP) were also involved was more successful.

In July 1998, troops were again ordered into KwaZulu-Natal, to try and combat the resurfacing violence. In August 1998 National Police Commissioner, George Fivaz dispatched senior police officers to close down the Richmond police station. The station was replaced by a National Intervention Unit under Commissioner Andre Pruis. A Joint Operational Centre would coordinate the activities of all units except those of the special investigation units. In close cooperation with the Joint Operational Centre a Priority Committee was to be set up in

Vice President Thabo Mbeki at a meeting of the Truth and Reconciliation Commission   PHOTO GEORGE HALLET

right-wing elements and/or sectors of the IFP, had fomented, initiated, facilitated and engaged in violence which resulted in gross violations of human rights, including random and targeted killings.

The *National Peace Accord* made provisions for codes of conduct for political parties and organisations, codes of conduct for police and the security forces, guidelines for the reconstruction and development of communities, and mechanisms to implement its provisions. It committed parties to a multiparty democracy and to respect for the fundamental rights and freedoms underpinning a democracy, and provided for a system of peace committees at all levels of society to monitor adherence to the Accord and resolve disputes using mediation and arbitration. These committees united representatives from conflicting parties and civil society in one forum. The effectiveness of the Accord was, however, questioned in KwaZulu-Natal where high levels of violence continued. IFP supporters have accused the National Peace structures of providing a stronghold for the ANC.

Richmond. This was effectively an attempt to set up ad hoc committees at grassroots level to deal with issues of violence, counselling, displaced persons, freedom of movement, and related problems.

A significant official contribution to peace in KwaZulu-Natal has been made by the *Truth and Reconciliation Commission (TRC)*, which has been operating across the country since 1994. Confessions made before the Commission have helped uncover the sinister workings of the 'Third Force', the existence of which had previously been doubted. The TRC discovered that a network of security and ex-security force operatives, often acting in conjunction with

Multi-Track Diplomacy
Domestic

Some of the ANC and IFP initiatives have been brought about by the activities of the *Independent Projects Trust (IPT)*, a Durban-based NGO which devotes its efforts to resolving the conflict in KwaZulu-Natal. It endeavours to foster an attitude of non-violent conflict management through extensive community training, media campaigns, research and analysis and political lobbying. Since its inception in 1990, the IPT has worked with urban and rural communities, traditional leaders, schools and local branches of the main political parties to create an environment in which peaceful settlement of problems becomes the norm. It has also worked with the police in conflict management skills training, in order to help them shed their reputation as a force of brutal repression. Recently the IPT started broadcasting on the radio to increase its reach in the KwaZulu-Natal province. The IPT receives government and non-government support from (among others) Norway, the Netherlands, the USA and the UK.

ACCORD (the Durban University-based African Centre for the Constructive Resolution of Disputes) runs a public sector programme which aims to train key members of the public service in conflict resolution methods and strategies. This programme operates in KwaZulu-Natal and the Northern Cape Province. ACCORD also runs a variety of training programmes in KwaZulu-Natal targeted at young people and intended to get them out of the environment of violent crime and into gainful employment. Its Youth Skills Empowerment Programme is aimed primarily at empowering young people in key flash points in KwaZulu-Natal by providing them with the skills to enable them to either initiate or assist in peace and development projects in their local areas. A secondary purpose is to build confidence among various groups of young people, especially those who have been on ACCORD training programmes - and to encourage closer working relationships among them. Furthermore, ACCORD monitors the situation on the ground in KwaZulu-Natal through the Early Warning System.

The *Centre for Conflict Resolution* seeks to contribute towards a just peace in South Africa and elsewhere by promoting constructive, creative and cooperative approaches to the resolution of conflict and the reduction of violence. It provides third-party assistance in the resolution of political and community conflict, equips people with conflict management skills, promotes public awareness of the value of constructive conflict resolution, promotes

democratic values and advocates disarmament and demilitarisation. Mediation, training, education and research are among the Centre's main activities, with an emphasis on capacity-building at grassroots level. Centre staff have been deeply involved in the transition to a democratic South Africa. They served as monitors, trainers, mediators and policy advisors in Peace Accord Structures and several key commissions.

The *Institute for a Democratic South Africa (IDASA)* is an independent NGO which aims to promote democracy and a culture of tolerance by empowering individuals and designing programmes that transform institutions. They have three main programmes in KwaZulu-Natal, a civil society leadership development programme, a councillor support and training programme, and a programme aimed at the integration of *amakhosi*, or traditional leaders.

The *Freedom of Expression Institute* supports media that are attacked by people in authority; for example, it supported the *Mail & Guardian* after it accused the authorities in KwaZulu-Natal of not doing enough to stem the violence and was subsequently and unsuccessfully sued.

The *Provincial Parliamentary Programme* is a joint programme of the Lawyers for Human Rights, the Institute for Multi-Party Democracy, Black Sash and IDASA. It aims to strengthen public participation in the KwaZulu-Natal legislature and trains civil society representatives in lobbying and advocacy strategies.

Some analysts also emphasise the potentially positive influence of *religious institutions*, if only because of their sheer size and consequently the number of people they can reach with a message of peace and reconciliation. In the same vein, local musicians and theatre groups are reaching out to communities with a similar message. Their impact is of course difficult to assess, but there can be little doubt about the value of their potential influence.

The *KwaZulu-Natal Programme for Survivors of Violence* aims to assist and support individuals, families and communities that have been fragmented due to high levels of violence in the province.

The *National Peace Accord Trust* works towards creating a generation of people empowered with skills and deep commitment to work to restore the family cohesion and community relationships damaged by South Africa's violent history.

The *Human Rights Committee* in cooperation with the Network of Independent Monitors has conducted extensive research into the role of the security forces in Richmond, KwaZulu-Natal, and their report was published in early 1999. The Network of Independent Monitors closely monitors political violence.

The *Centre for the Study of Violence and Reconciliation* provides extensive information and research on its website from a broad range of South African and international organisations in the area of conflict prevention. It lists published articles by subject and has links with related websites.

The *Vuleka Trust* is a church-based organisation committed to community development. It aims to promote and enhance justice and reconciliation and empower people through the acquisition of interpersonal skills in order to respond creatively towards themselves, others and the environment. Among its activities are facilitating and promoting conflict resolution and mediation, conducting skills training programmes in basic human relations, handling conflict creatively, developing effective negotiating skills and designing educational events and conducting community services. It also runs a schools project and a youth leadership training programme.

The *Diakona Council of Churches* comprises fourteen member churches and three member organisations and aims to promote peace through active participation in community police forums and local peace structures and through developing skills in handling conflict and trauma. It also promotes the creation of a vibrant democracy through training in lobbying and advocacy and the monitoring of government and the economy. The Diakona Council of Churches also takes part in the World Council of Churches initiated programme 'Peace to the City' for Durban. Sixteen human rights networks and peace organisations take part in this initiative.

International
The *International Committee for the Red Cross*

(ICRC) was particularly active during the local elections. Alongside its customary work of alleviating human suffering, it actively campaigned for calm during the local elections, using the media to appeal for a reduction of the violence. This 'humanitarian message' was disseminated through radio stations and the national press. It also produced a video with the same message.

The Canadian *International Development Research Centre (IDRC)* is involved in a demilitarisation and peace-building initiative aimed at raising the understanding of dynamics and to identify practical policies and interventions, which could support sustainable peace and human development.

Ultimately reconciliation must be home-grown and consequently the international NGOs have only a limited role to play. The African people of South Africa have shown an impressive capacity for reconciliation, as is demonstrated by the extraordinary scenes that have taken place before the Truth and Reconciliation Commission and by the fact that, for example, policeman and mass murderer Brian Mitchell was able to take his place in the Zulu community he had so terribly damaged. Just as the reconciliation efforts in the country at large have been developed in accordance with their own unique dynamics, so too the process in KwaZulu-Natal will run its course. Outside assistance on terms that are defined locally remains welcome.

Prospects
Essentially, the ANC wishes to extend its existing power throughout virtually the entire country including KwaZulu-Natal, while the IFP wants to retain its power base in the province, in the knowledge that it has no other possibility of building such a base. The detente between the IFP and the ANC has been jeopardised by recent developments such as the installation of hard-liner Lionel Mtshali as Premier of KwaZulu-Natal and the ousting of Bheki Cele (ANC) as chairman of the portfolio committee on safety and security. The ANC has even criticised the IFP's conclusions on the Truth and Reconciliation Commission, arguing it would harm the detente policy pursued.

Political violence in KwaZulu-Natal is likely to persist for the time being. A culture of violence based on the rural-urban division, and tensions between the traditional and modern, the young and old seems to be deeply embedded. The ANC is gaining power among the urbanised, modern youth. Traditional structures with chiefs and *indunas* are likely to remain in place, leading to friction over scarce resources.

As for the main protagonists of the present conflict, they are both part of the problem and part of the solution. Consequently it must be stressed that some initiatives have been taken by the IFP and ANC to resolve the problem of politicised violence in the province. Unfortunately, their efforts at talking their way out of the problems have met with limited success. The events surrounding the 1994 elections are partly to blame for this. More recently, the dialogue between the ANC and the IFP has been threatened by Lionel Mtshali appointment as premier.

It has also become clear that the violence in KwaZulu-Natal cannot be explained only through reference to political rivalry. Some observers argue that the division between militant youth and conservative traditional leaders in KwaZulu-Natal was the single most important factor underlying the sectarian violence of the 1980s and that its impact can still be felt. The Protection and Defense Units are also, albeit in different forms, still operational and armed. There is an abundance of arms and the illegal trade in arms flourishes in the region. The infiltration of criminal elements in factions and gangs and the deplorable social and economic situation in both the rural and urban areas further contribute to the continuation of political violence. The Network of Independent Monitors has warned of a sharp increase in political violence as a result of the stockpiling of weaponry in conjunction with paramilitary training camps.

Recommendations

Most NGOs in South Africa share the view that South Africa's transition to democracy began rather than ended with the elections of April 27, 1994. The Centre for the Study of Violence and Reconciliation argues that transition and transformation agendas must still be developed and consolidated through building a popular human rights culture, through fostering lasting reconciliation, through the transformation of inherited state institutions and through consolidating democracy and development in South Africa.

The Independent Project Trust emphasises that inter-group stereotyping and animosity have to be overcome. Young people must be targeted through education in order develop trust and create security. Faith in the rule of law and an increase in the respect for human rights is central to this process, according to Amnesty International.

The Constitutional Court, the South African Human Rights Commission and civil society organisations argue that crime needs to be more effectively addressed through improving the criminal justice system by giving its personnel adequate resources and proper professional training.

Service Information

Newsletters and Periodicals
Indicator Project South Africa, based at the University of Natal publishes two quarterly journals: Indicator and Crime & Conflict.
Track Two (quarterly), published by the Centre for Conflict Resolution. (www.un.ac.za/indicator)
The KwaZulu-Natal Briefing, published by the Helen Suzman Foundation's KwaZulu-Natal Monitoring Project at the department of politics, University of Natal, provides analysis of events
The *Mail & Guardian* has regular features on the situation in KwaZulu/Natal

Reports
IPT
- Smoke and Fire in KwaZulu-Natal - Geostrategies behind the Peace Process
- Network of Independent Monitors/Human Rights Committee
- Richmond - Role of Security Forces. March, 1999
- Indicator Project South Africa
- Political and Economic Identities in KwaZulu-Natal, R. Morrell (ed.). University of Natal

Institute of Race Relations
- The Natal Story: 16 years of conflict, by Anthea J. Jeffery. 1997, Institute of Race Relations

USAID
- Managing Conflict - Lessons from the South African Peace Committees, by Nicole Ball and Chris Spies. November 1998, USAID Evaluation Special Study Report No 78

Selected Internet Sites
www.webpro.co.za/clients/ipt (The Independent Projects Trust)
www.truth.org.za (Truth and Reconciliation Commission)
www.accord.org.za (ACCORD)
wn.apc.org (South African NGO network Sangonet)

www.idasa.org.za (IDASA)
www.imssa.org.za (IMSSA)
www.anc.org.za/ (ANC)
www.ifp.org.za/ (IFP)
www.violence.co.za (Natal Monitor)
www.mg.co.za/mg (Mail & Guardian)
www.ananzi.co.za (South African search engine)
www.witness.co.za/witness.htm (newspaper The Natal Witness)
www. wits.ac.za/csvr (Centre for the Study of Violence and Reconciliation)

Resource Contacts
Mary de Haas - School of Anthropology and Psychology, University of Natal. Tel. +27 31 260 2431.
Jenny Irish - Network of Independent Monitors. Fax +27 31 307 2814.
Glenda Caine - director Independent Projects Trust
Hussein Solomon - ACCORD, E-mail hussein@accord.co.za
Jabulani Mabaso, Leah Lethale - Independent Mediation Services in South Africa
Laurie Nathan - executive director Centre for Conflict Resolution
Graeme Simpson - director Centre for the Study of Violence and Reconciliation
Maggie Paterson - Amnesty International London office

Organisations
Diakona Council of Churches
PO Box 61341
4008 Bishopgate
Tel + 27 31 305 6001
Fax + 27 31 305 2486
diak@iafrica.com

KwaZulu-Natal Peace Committee
Development Unit
Private Bag X54356
4000 Durban
Tel + 27 31 309 6530
Fax + 27 31 309 6563

KwaZulu-Natal Programme for Survivors of
Violence
206, Burger sTreet
3200 Pietermaritzburg
tel + 27 331 42 1378
fax + 27 331 94 7841
psvpmv@iafrica.com
www.geocities.com/hotsprings/spa/3028

National Peace Accord Trust
PO Box 40-1144
4071 Redhill
tel + 27 31 23-9344
fax + 27 31 23 9443
kznnpat@wn.apc.org

The Centre for the Study of Violence and
Reconciliation
www.wits.ac.za/csvr
csvr@wn.apc.org
City of Peace programme
www.durbanpeace.org.za
coord@durbanpeace.org.za
Tel + 27 31 305 6001
Fax + 27 31 305 248

International Development Research Centre
(IDRC)
PO Box 477
Wits 2050
tel + 27 11 403 3952
fax + 27 11 403 1417
www.idrc.org

*Data on the following organisations can be found
in the Directory section:*
Independent Project Trust (IPF)
ACCORD
Centre for Conflict Resolution
Institute for a Democratic South Africa
(IDASAS)
Vuleeka Trust

About the Authors of the Surveys

Jos van Beurden studied Law and Peace at the Universities of Utrecht, Amsterdam and Groningen in the Netherlands. He has studied Northeast Africa since 1977, paying regular visits to Ethiopia, Sudan and Eritrea since 1985. He has also visited Somalia and Djibouti. He is the author of country studies on Ethiopia, Eritrea and Sudan for the Royal Tropical Institute in Amsterdam, and of an Ethiopia NGO Country Profile for the Dutch Co-Financing Agencies.

Anneke Galama is currently studying at Bradford University to obtain her MA in Peace Studies Studies. Anneke was an intern at the European Centre for Conflict Prevention from January - May 1999 and has assisted in the survey project.

Anne Graumans worked as an intern at the National Peace Secretariat in Johannesburg in 1994. She has worked with several research institutes and NGOs in Cape Town and Johannesburg and is currently a freelance researcher based in Amsterdam.

Jos Havermans is an historian and freelance journalist covering international developments for several Dutch and international magazines. He has written extensively on Sub-Saharan Africa. In recent years his coverage of Africa has included reports on peace efforts and conflict prevention in Burundi, the decay of the central government in the Democratic Republic of Congo and the democratisation process in Malawi.

Reinoud Leenders is based in Beirut where he is affiliated to the American University as an associate researcher in Political Economy. He reports on Lebanese current affairs for Middle East International. He also writes for a Dutch newspaper and the Lebanese daily An-Nahar on Middle Eastern politics. He is preparing a PhD thesis on the Political Economy of Lebanon for the School of Oriental and African Studies (London). In 1996 and 1997 he worked as a researcher in the North Africa team of Amnesty International in London.

Monique Mekenkamp is coordinator of the survey project undertaken by the European Centre for Conflict Prevention. She has studied International Relations at the University of Amsterdam and majored in peace and conflict studies at the Department of Peace and Conflict Studies at Uppsala University, Sweden. She has travelled through southern Africa and lived in Cameroon, Nigeria, and former Zaire.

Bram Posthumus has worked as a freelance journalist since 1990. Before that he was a teacher of English language and literature in Nyanga, Zimbabwe. His work in journalism concentrates mainly on West and southern Africa and on the themes of conflict and post-conflict situations and migration. He has travelled extensively in both regions, visiting among others Angola, Mozambique, Liberia, Zambia and Guinea, with Mali, Senegal and Chad planned for the near future. He publishes in a variety of international magazines (African Business, New African, EU-ACP Courier) and other monthlies and weeklies in the Netherlands, Belgium, the UK and South Africa.

Emmy Toonen is in the final year of her studies of International Relations at the University of Utrecht, where she is majoring in Human Rights. She has worked as an intern at the European Centre for Conflict Prevention and assisted in the survey project.

Hans van de Veen studied Political Science at Nijmegen University in the Netherlands. He is a senior Dutch freelance journalist, specialising in international political affairs, development issues and the environment, with a focus on Africa. He has travelled the continent many times. He is the author of several studies on tropical forestry and edited the European Platform's Directory. Presently he is coordinating and editing the Conflict Prevention Surveys on Africa.

Part III
Directory

Introduction to the profiles

This supplementary section contains organisation profiles which are intended to provide a quick guide to the African community of conflict prevention and management. Some twenty international organisations have also been included as their field of operation or focus is on Africa (such as Alliances for Africa) or an important part of their focus is on Africa (such as the International Crisis Group). The profiles provide a general idea of what these organisations and institutions consider to be their goals, how they attempt to accomplish them and, space permitting, details of specific activities in which they are engaged.

While not claiming completeness, we have endeavoured to find at least one relevant organisation in every nation except the smallest. We have not always succeeded, but the list of countries without representation is again shorter than in our 1998 International Directory. An important criterion for inclusion was that organisations should devote a considerable amount of their time and budget to conflict prevention and management activities. Where a particular country had only one potential entry, we have been relatively lenient in deciding whether or not to include it, as we thought it important to provide the users of this book with at least one local 'bridgehead'.

The arrangement of profiles is based on the location of their offices. The only exceptions to this rule are the organisations that cover the whole, or large parts, of Africa, both governmental (such as OAU) and non-governmental (Pan-African Women Organization).

Two items of information in the profiles may require some clarification. The Countries or Regions listed at the top of each profile indicate in what parts of Africa the organisation has its main focus.

To the left of these geographic details you will find pictographs, numbered one to four, which symbolise the focal activities of the organisation.

 The person sitting at a desk represents *research*, either office-based or conducted in the field (including fact-finding).

 The group gathered around a table indicates *training* or *education*.

 The person with the giant hand saying 'stop' symbolises *action* in the theatre of events: mediating, negotiating, running projects, observing elections, etc.

 The two chatting shadows signify a *lobbying* or *advisory* function.

Deciding the length of individual profiles proved particularly difficult as we are aware that nobody enjoys seeing their employer's activities (or their own) summarised in a hundred words. Decisive here was a combination of informed judgement by experts in the field of peace and conflict, and a good measure of common sense, with priority being given to those entrants whose activities are remarkable for their success or novel methods.

Finally, we are aware of having left a number of 'i's' undotted and 't's' uncrossed, especially in the practical details at the bottom of each profile. We have been meticulous in supplying an address, a person to contact, telephone and fax numbers and an email address as well as the right pictographs for each organisation. However, because some respondents would not supply this information, you will find that the number of staff and a rough indication of budget are sometimes missing. Where figures are given, we have attempted to make them apply to the amounts spent on, and the number of staff working in, the kinds of activities with which this book is concerned. As we have not always succeeded in this, however, these data should not be regarded as carved in stone, but as rough indications of size and available resources. Similarly, where no publications are listed, books, reports or a newsletter may, nevertheless, exist. Again, we just were not told.

Finally, collecting the data for this directory has proven a gigantic task, not least because of unexpected (tele)-communication hitches. To our surprise, some major organisations were very slow in replying, or never bothered to do so at all. It is true that these large groups tend to have web-sites, but in some cases these had not been updated for two years.

We hope that this section proves helpful to you and your colleagues in locating and coordinating activities with other organisations. If so, please help us to keep it up-to-date by reporting any changes, especially changes of communications data: electronic and snail mail addresses, telephone and fax numbers and website details.

African Organisations

 Sub-Sahara Africa

ACCORD

The African Centre for the Constructive Resolution of Disputes (ACCORD) seeks to encourage and further constructive resolution of conflicts by Africa's peoples and to help achieve peaceful coexistence, political stability and economic progress within societies where justice and democracy prevail.

For its research, ACCORD draws upon fifteen universities in southern Africa under its Conflict Policy and Research Group (CRPRG). Its Preventive Diplomacy Forum enables ACCORD to intervene in conflicts. ACCORD conducts training in preventive diplomacy and peacekeeping.

ACCORD is based in South Africa, but it is involved in a variety of programmes far beyond South Africa's borders, in other parts of southern Africa, the Great Lakes region, the Horn of Africa and West Africa. ACCORD's successes have been rooted in two principles. The first of these is that peace-making models that yield positive results in one context can be utilised to help bring about successful resolutions of conflicts in quite different contexts. And secondly, peace-making skills and insights can through training be transferred to other individuals and organisations to broaden the base of peace makers and empower individuals to play active roles in resolving conflicts in their own regions.

ACCORD has developed a Comprehensive Peace Model, based on four pillars: intervention, education & training, research and communication. These pillars are reflected in the organisational structure, which has a programme division including Peacekeeping, Preventive Action, Women, Youth, Public Sector Management, Intervention and Rural programmes; and a Resource Division with Training, Communication & Information, Research and External Institutional Support Units. ACCORD is currently involved in setting up a permanent Conflict Resolution Centre, a retreat, conference, training and research facility.

The organisation presents the biennial Africa Peace Award recognising individuals, communities or nations actively promoting respect for human rights, peaceful settlement of disputes and good governance of public affairs. It also brings out a newsletter, Conflict Trends, which is regarded as a leading publication in the field of African conflicts.

---

c/o University of Durban-Westville
Private Bag X018
Umhlanga Rocks
4320 South Africa

tel +27 (31) 502 3908
fax +27 (31) 502 4160
email info@accord.org.za
http://www.accord.org.za

Contact
Vasu Gounden, executive director
Number of staff
27, 5 in the field of conflict prevention/management
Budget
> $1,000,000

Publications
African Journal in Conflict Resolution, bianual journal
Conflict Trends, newsletter
Occasional Papers
Preventive Diplomacy Series

Great Lakes Region, Sudan, Sierra Leone, Lesotho

All Africa Conference of Churches

Because of the escalation of conflicts since the end of the Cold War, conflict prevention and resolution have become the main priority of the All Africa Conference of Churches. The Conference responds whenever member churches invite it to help. In the field of conflict prevention and resolution, the major activities are mediation, citizen diplomacy, fact-finding and early warning. In Rwanda, Burundi and Congo, the Conference carries out a specific programme concerned with initiating a dialogue amongst conflicting parties, in order to search for common ground. This programme is supported by churches from all over the world.

P.O. Box 14205
Nairobi
Kenya

tel +254 (2) 441 483/441 338
fax +254 (2) 443 241
email mulunda@insight.com

Contact
Ngoy D. Mulunda-
Nyanga, executive
secretary
Budget
$100,000 - $500,000

 Africa

African Association of Political Scientists

The African Association of Political Scientists (AAPS) is a pan-African organisation of scholars whose mandate is to promote basic and primary research by African scholars in political science, public policy, political economy and related fields. It pursues its goals by conducting critical research and disseminating its findings through publication, by organising a biannual meeting of African scholars, by offering educational programmes to the university community and the general public, and by providing services and expertise to both governments and NGOs. Its programmes have included research and advice on conflict issues and advocacy.

P.O. Box MP 1100
Mount Pleasant
Harare, Zimbabwe

tel +263 (4) 739 023/5
fax +263 (4) 730 403
email aaps1@samara.co.zw
http://www.aaps.co.zw

Contact
Kwane A. Ninsin,
executive secretary
Number of staff
5
Budget
< $25,000

Publications
African Newsletter, 3 times a year
Journal of Political Science, bi-annual
Occasional Paper Series, 3 times a year
The State and Democracy in Africa, 1998

Southern and West Africa, Horn of Africa

African Women Committee on Peace and Development

The African Women Committee on Peace and Development (AWCPD) was established in 1998 to increase the effective participation of women in peace and development processes on the continent. The committee embraces as its guiding principle the view that war cannot be an option for resolving conflict. The committee seeks to support the networking of women's peace-building mechanisms in Africa and to identify, articulate and seek ways and means of addressing women-specific experiences of conflict. It also works to ensure that the needs of refugees, returned refugees, and displaced women and children are adequately addressed.

c/o **Organization of African Unity**
P.O. Box 3243
Addis Ababa
Ethiopia
tel +251 (1) 517200
fax +251 (1) 514416/512785

Contact
Mrs. H. G. Sellassie
Number of staff
2 in HQ, 16 committee members
Budget
$500,00 - $1,000,000

 Africa

AFSTRAG

The Africa Strategic and Peace Research Group (AFSTRAG) is an independent research and consulting organisation focusing on strategic and human security problems in Africa. The organisation engages scholars, experienced diplomats and retired senior military officers to undertake in-depth study of continental and global strategic developments and their impact on the prospects for peace, security and human development in Africa, and to formulate in-depth policy options. AFSTRAG also organises seminars, workshops, conferences, roundtables and similar gatherings of scholars, military experts, policymakers and implementers to further discussion on peace and security issues.

PMB 12839
General Post Office
Marina, Lagos
Nigeria

tel +234 (1) 492 5535
email afstrag@gacom.net

Publications
Newsletter
Monographs
Occasional Papers

 West Africa

CODESRIA

The Council for the Development of Social Science Research in Africa (CODESRIA) is a pan-African NGO serving African research institutes, the social science faculties of African universities, and professional organisations. Its primary objectives are to facilitate research, promote research-based publishing, and to encourage the exchange of information among African scholars.

One important manner in which research is encouraged is the establishment of 'multinational working groups', which co-ordinate the research activities of 20 to 30 scholars, in a variety of disciplines, whose studies investigate common themes. Findings are published in CODESRIA's Working Paper series. A similar program of 'national working groups' has been launched to encourage research at the national level. The organisation also organises conferences where social scientists and policy-makers meet to discuss important current issues of concern to all African countries, including democracy and human rights; democratisation; conflict resolution in the Great Lakes Region; academic freedom, research and social responsibility; and a variety of other economic, social and development themes. The organisation has been involved in the 'Conflict Prevention in West Africa' (CPWA) programme and 'The Causes of Conflict in West Africa' (CCWA) programme, and played an active role in activities examining the regional conflict in Liberia, the conflict between Senegal and Mauritania, and the Touareg conflict in Mali and Niger.

An important initiative of CODESRIA has been the establishment of an Academic Freedom Unit which monitors academic freedom, documents and publicises cases of violation of academic freedom, acts to support individuals and professional organisations facing harassment, and promotes research into academic freedom and human rights in Africa.

Angle C.A. Diop et Canal IV
B.P. 3304
Dakar
Senegal

tel +221 825 9822/3
fax +221 824 1289
email codesria@telecomplus.com
http://wsi.cso.uiuc.edu/CAS/
Codesria/Codesria.htm

Contact
T. K. Biaya, coordinator
and senior researcher
Budget
$25,000 - $100,000

Publications
The CODESRIA Bulletin, quarterly
newsletter
CODESRIA Working Papers
CODESRIA Monograph Series
Directory of Research Projects and
Training Institutes in Africa
Annual report of 'Academic Freedom in
Africa'

 West and Central Africa

GERDDES/IRCD

The Research Group on the Democratic, Economic and Social Development of Africa (GERDDES-AFRICA) is a non-partisan, pan-African NGO, established in 1990 by African senior managers and intellectuals. Its mission is to promote democracy in the service of social and economic development, and to cultivate African expertise in conflict prevention and management.

The GERDDES programme organ, the International Research Centre on Democracy and Development (IRCD), participates in election - organisation and - monitoring, and engages in social and political mediation. It has intervened as a mediator in past conflicts in the Ivory Coast, Togo, Congo, Benin, Chad, and Niger, and is currently involved in mediations in Nigeria, Liberia, Burundi, Senegal, and the Congo. Furthermore, it is engaged in educational and training activities which are offered under the auspices of its Institute for Democratic Studies and Development.

GERDDES-AFRICA also organises training seminars and conferences focusing on such target groups as the press, trade unions, women, and the military. In 1997, it brought together more than 150 participants from Africa, Europe and the United States for a 3-day international seminar in Ouagadougou, Burkina Faso on the role of the military in the democratisation process of Africa.

GERDDES has established RANGAPC (Reseau Africain Non Gouvernemental d'Alerte Préventive des Conflits/African Non-Governmental Network for Conflict Prevention), which is building and maintaining a database identifying social and economic events that threaten social stability, and African resource people specialised in political and social mediation at the national and regional level in Africa.

GERDDES publishes 'Development & Democracy', a quarterly newsletter, as well as publications addressing democracy and sustainable development in Africa.

01 BP 1258
Cotonou
Benin

tel +229 334 333
fax +229 334 499/334 332
email
gerddes@bow.intnet.bj
http://www.gerddes.org

Contact
Me Sadikou Ayo Alao,
director
Budget
$25,000 - $100,000

Publications
Democracy & Development, newsletter
Africa Democracy & Development,
political science review
Prévention des Conflits en Afrique,
seminar report, 1998
Election, democracy & governance,
conference report, 1999

Africa

Ass. of Evangelicals in Africa-Commission on Relief and Development

The Association of Evangelicals in Africa-Commission on Relief and Development (ARDC) is involved in programmes of national reconciliation, conflict prevention/transformation and community reconstruction through its network of member and partner groups across the continent. It has been active in conflict areas including Rwanda, Burundi, Liberia, Mozambique and the Horn of Africa. The organisation is currently involved in a situation assessment in Northern Uganda and Southern Sudan to assess the vulnerability of various sectors of the civilian population.

PO Box 49332
Nairobi
Kenya

Contact
Stephen Mugabi,
executive secretary

tel +254 (2) 722 769/714 977
fax +254 (2) 710 254
email AEA@MAF.org

Horn of Africa

Inter-Africa Group

The Inter-Africa Group is a non-partisan regional organisation working to advance humanitarian principles, peace and development in the greater Horn of Africa region through programmes which combine research, dialogue, public education and advocacy. Through expert consultations, brainstorming sessions and efforts to sensitise public opinion, the Inter-Africa Group promotes greater awareness and understanding of victims of disaster and armed conflict and assists in developing national and international consensus to effect coherent and timely responses.

P.O. Box 1631
Addis Ababa
Ethiopia

Contact
Abdul Mohammed,
chairman
Number of staff
15 at HQ

Publications
The Monthly Update, newsletter
The Humanitarian Forum, quarterly

tel +251 (1) 518 790
fax +251 (1) 517 554
email iag@telecom.net.et
http://www.interafrica.org

 Africa

Nairobi Peace Initiative

The Nairobi Peace Initiative (NPI) is developing and practising a multi-disciplinary, holistic approach to conflict in Africa, with the view that conflict prevention is an integral element of peace-building and conflict transformation.

The Nairobi Peace Group, as NPI was known prior to 1990, sought to raise public awareness of the nature and consequences of African conflicts, sensitise people and institutions to the need for peaceful settlements, stimulate discussion on peace and development, and engage in informal diplomacy. It saw its principal role as that of a catalyst for motivating and inspiring churches, ecumenical organisations, academic institutions, NGOs and government agencies to take up peace-making.

With time, the Group became more and more aware of the need to go beyond raising awareness of the devastating effects of violent conflict and to engage directly in assisting parties to search for peaceful solutions.

In 1990, therefore, NPG embarked on a new course and changed its name to NPI to reflect this. Since then, it has developed into an indigenous African peace resource organisation directly involved in peace-making, peace-building and conflict resolution training, both at grassroots and political leadership levels. NPI also seeks to build local capacity through training people in conflict situations in peace-making and peace-building skills relevant to their respective communities.

Obviously, the organisation is not engaged in partisan advocacy, but provides its services only in the context of a mediation or conciliation framework or in pre-negotiation processes leading to mediation. To date, it has worked in Angola, Burundi, Ethiopia, Ghana, Kenya, Liberia, Mozambique, Rwanda, Somalia, South Africa and Sudan.

NPI networks extensively with civil society organisations throughout the continent. These include NGOs, church-based and community organisations and specialised conflict resolution organisations in Africa. The organisation also co-operates with the Eastern Mennonite University in the USA and Justapaz in Colombia.

P.O. Box 14894
Nairobi
Kenya

tel +254 (2) 441 444/440 098
fax +254 (2) 442 533/445 177/440 098
email npi@africaonline.co.ke

Contact
George Wachira, director
Number of staff
4
Budget
Fluctuating

Publications
Peacemaking and Democratization in Africa: Theoretical Perspectives and Church Initiatives, 1996
'Peace and Reconciliation as a Paradigm: A Philosophy of Peace and its Implications on Conflict, Governance and Economic Growth in Africa', 1993, Monograph series

 Africa

Pan-African Reconciliation Council

The Pan-African Reconciliation Council (PARC) is a grassroots organisation working for socio-political as well as moral emancipation of Africa on the basis of nonviolence and 'self-giving love'. Its 700 members include educational institutions, religious organisations and individuals in some twelve African countries and in Europe.

The Council seeks to mobilise public opinion and signature campaigns to eliminate threats to peace, not only in Africa, but throughout the world. It forwards written responses to threats to peace to civil, religious and political authorities. It sets up information, research and communication programmes to help political authorities take the right decisions. In the past, PARC played a crucial role in the monitoring of the Nigerian elections of 1993. It was the co-ordinating organisation and served as secretariat for the 'Hague Appeal for Peace 1999' for Anglophone and Lusophone (Portuguese) West Africa.

The projects of the Council focus on the areas of social and economic justice, nonviolence, refugees, social conflict, interfaith activities, and youth and women. In the area of nonviolence it organises workshops on peace, social justice and reconciliation in African countries. As far as refugees are concerned, it organises relief materials and welfare services for displaced persons.

In the field of social conflicts, PARC conducts research and collects data on the causes of inter-communal conflicts. It plays a mediator role in resolving social conflicts and provides early warning on conflicts within and amongst African communities.

As part of PARC's interfaith activities, it initiates faith-oriented educational resources on active nonviolence, peace, social justice and reconciliation. It also undertakes grassroots campaigns for peace, human rights, self-determination and self-reliance.

Special activities are carried out for youth and women. PARC organises youth leadership training activities and co-ordinates an international campaign to eliminate child abuse and discrimination against women. It assists students on issues of nonviolence and peace.

P.O. Box 9354
Marina, Lagos City
Nigeria

tel +234 (1) 835 004/843 578
fax +234 (1) 264 6082/4
(Quote FDS 091)
email
adenekan@nipost.com.ng

Contact
Ade Adenekan, secretary
general
Number of staff
6
Budget
$25,000 - $100,000

Publications
Pax Africana, bulletin
Occasional papers

Africa

Organization of African Unity

In the past decade, the Organization of African Unity (OAU) has taken concrete steps to respond to violent crisis situations by establishing the Conflict Management Division, and the 'Mechanism for Conflict Prevention, Management and Resolution' (MCPMR).

Since its inception in 1993, the Mechanism has deployed observer missions to conflict areas including Rwanda, Burundi, and Liberia, and supported ongoing peace processes in Sierra Leone, the Central African Republic, the Great Lakes Region, the Democratic Republic of Congo, and the Republic of Congo.

To support the Mechanism, the OAU has set up the OAU Peace Fund. Six percent of the OAU budget is devoted to this Peace Fund, which is supplemented by additional voluntary contributions from OAU Member States and donors. Furthermore, the OAU has established an Early Warning System to improve the efficient functioning of the Peace Mechanism.

Additional initiatives taken by the OAU include a multi-facetted commitment to support democratic processes in Africa, by setting up election monitoring teams that are in place at the early stages of electoral processes; and the establishment of the African Women's Committee on Peace and Development.

The OAU is also taking concrete steps through its 'Building Partnership with Civil Society Organizations' programme to strengthen the foundations of civil society in the belief that civil society constitutes an influential force in the processes of democratisation, peaceful resolution of conflicts and socio-economic development. Goals of the programme include stimulation of networking and resource sharing among the diverse participants in civil society (NGOs, grassroots organisations, academic institutions, media, etc.); collaboration between the OAU and civil society organisations to promote good governance, democracy, respect for the rule of law and the promotion of human rights; and greater involvement of civil society in peace-making activities and involvement in the OAU Conflict Management Mechanism to enhance its effectiveness.

P.O. Box 3243
Addis Ababa
Ethiopia

tel +251 (1) 513 822
fax +251 (1) 519 274
http://www.oau-oua.org

Contact
Sam Ibok, head of
Conflict Management
Division
Number of staff
10 (in Conflict
Management Division)
Budget
> $1,000,000

 West Africa

WANEP

The West Africa Network for Peacebuilding (WANEP) is a network of peace-building practitioners and organisations in West Africa. It aims to serve as an enabling and facilitating mechanism for peace builders and to provide a forum for the exchange of experience and information on issues of human rights; conflict resolution/transformation; social, religious and political reconciliation; and peace building. WANEP carries out research on West African approaches to conflict resolution and publishes the results, operates a peace-building internship program, and works to rehabilitate and re-integrate ex-combatants, especially ex-child soldiers, into post-war West African societies.

AMPOMAH House 3rd
37 Dzorwulu High Way
P.O. Box CT 4434
Cantonments, Accra, Republic of Ghana
tel +233 (21) 221 318/221 388
fax +233 (21) 221 735
email wanep@africaonline.com.gh

Contact
Samuel Gbaydee Doe,
executive director
Budget
$100,000 - $500,000

Publications
Newsletter
Training materials

 Algeria

Rassemblement d'Action Jeunesse

Rassemblement d'Action Jeunesse (RAJ) provides human rights education to young people and has lobbied the Algerian government to engage in dialogue with all parties to the Algerian conflict. In 1995, RAJ produced a manifesto for peace and gathered over 20,000 endorsing signatures. It has also organised peace activities, including an all-night 'concert for peace', attended by 11,000 young people. Although RAJ was extended official recognition in 1993, it has been forced to curtail its activities as a result of pressure from government forces.

P.O. Box 77
Algiers, Port Said
Algeria

Contact
Hakkim Added

tel/fax +213 (2) 668 877/898

 Arab World, Mediterranean

URAMA

URAMA (Unité de Recherche Afrique-Monde Arabe) is a non-profit organisation, based in Algeria, which is conducting research into conflict resolution and security issues in the Mediterranean region, the Arab world, and Africa. The organisation, which is affiliated with the University of Constantine, also carries out training programs and publishes Annals de l'URAMA.

Université de Constantine
Route d'Ain el Bey
25000 Constantine
Algeria

Contact
Azzouz Kerdoun, director

Publications
Annals de l'URAMA
La Securité en Méditerranée, 1995

tel/fax +213 (4) 680 272

Angola

FONGA

FONGA stands for Forum of Angolan Non-Governmental Organizations. It has 150 member organisations. FONGA aims to play a facilitating role by organising workshops and seminars on community development and conflict resolution. Despite the difficulties and dangers of working in an area ravaged by civil war, FONGA continues to maintain local peace-building efforts. In March 1997, FONGA co-operated with the American Friends Service Committee in a training workshop for community workers representing about thirty NGOs. The workshop focused on nonviolent means of conflict resolution at the community level.

Rua D. Manuel 1 No 35, Apt F
C.P. 10797
Luanda
Angola

Contact
Francisco Alberto Tunga,
director

tel +244 (2) 322 537
fax +244 (2) 322 637

 Angola

Centre for Common Ground

Search for Common Ground in Washington, USA, has established an Angolan office, which operates from the premise that only when Angolans experience reconciliation in their daily lives can there be a sustainable peace. The Centre carries out five programmes: dialogues between government and UNITA supporters in various social settings; conflict resolution capacity building and training for NGOs and Angolan institutions; production of reconciliation radio and TV; journalistic exchanges to encourage reporters on both sides to cooperate on shared productions; and production and mass distribution of the Angolan Peace Song.

C.P. 1542
Luanda
Angola

Contact
Julie Nenon, project director

tel/fax +244 (2) 330 035
email
105446.436@compuserve.com
http://www.sfcg.org/mainang.htm

 Africa

InterAfrican Union of Human Rights

The InterAfrican Union of Human Rights (L'Union Interafricaine des Droits de l'Homme - UIDH) is a non-governmental, pan-African organisation working for the defence, promotion and protection of human rights, democracy and development. It currently consists of over 32 NGO members. UIDH monitors the observance of human rights, including those human rights viewed as essential for economic, industrial and scientific progress; encourages research on human rights issues, and co-operation among organisations and national institutions dedicated to the promotion of human rights. UIDH also is also involved in mediation in areas of conflict and human rights violations.

01 BP 1346
Ouagadougou
Burkina Faso

Contact
Halidou Ouédraogo,
president

tel +226 316 145
fax +226 316 144
email uidh@fasonet.bf
http://www.multimania.com/uidh/

 Great Lakes Region

Compagnie des Apôtres de la Paix

Compagnie des Apôtres de la Paix (CAP - Apostles for Peace) is a non-profit organisation working for the peaceful resolution of conflicts, focusing primarily on the situation in Burundi. CAP promotes dialogue among Burundians living both inside and outside the country, and has initiated a programme called 'Espace Dialogue' to promote discussion among Burundians about peace and reconciliation. CAP also organises training sessions on conflict management. CAP stresses that traditional Burundian mechanisms for conflict resolution have an important place in bringing about the just resolution of the current conflict.

Avenue de France
P.O. Box 2605
Bujumbura
Burundi

Contact
Nbizi Isaïe, acting
director
Budget
$25,000 - $100,000

Publications
Cap-Infos, quarterly newsletter

tel +257 217 409
fax +257 217 408
email cap@cbinf.com

Burundi

Search for Common Ground/Burundi

In January 1995, Washington-based Search for Common Ground launched an initiative to help defuse ethnic conflict in Burundi. It maintains an office in Bujumbura and operates programmes aimed at stopping the killing and preparing the ground for national reconciliation. Projects include a radio station, Studio Ijambo (wise words); and the Center for Women, where some 200 Hutu and Tutsi women meet every week.

Studio Ijambo employs a staff of both Hutu and Tutsi workers and produces about 15 hours a week of news, public affairs and cultural programming. In the past, radio, which is the single most important source of information for many Burundians, was used by authorities as a tool to promote fear and mistrust, but Studio Ijambo serves as an instrument to bridge the ethnic gap and to restore peace. In addition to news, public affairs, and cultural programming, Studio Ijambo also produces a weekly radio drama featuring a Hutu family and a Tutsi family who live next door to each other. The production, entitle Ababanyi Ni Tebwe (Our Neighbours, Ourselves) shows how, despite the potential for conflict, these neighbours are able to reconcile their differences.

The Center for Women, which is based in Bujumbura, promotes co-operation and understanding between Burundi's communities, including a programme promoting reconciliation between women displaced by the conflict and their former neighbours. One of the Center's training programmes provides women with conflict resolution skills to be applied at the community level. The Center also operates a conference centre, providing the infrastructure to bring together women from all segments of society, including weekly roundtable discussions attended by women from all ethnic groups.

Search for Common Ground also sponsors political dialogue between political leaders, co-ordinated by South African former MP Jan van Eck, and participates in the Great Lakes Policy Forum.

Old East Building
Avenue des Etats-Unis
Place de l'Indépendence
Bujumbra
Burundi

tel + 257 241 944/216 332
fax +257 217 408
email shamil@cni.cbinf.com
http://www.sfcg.org/mainbur.htm

Contact
Shamil Idriss, project director

Cameroon

Centre for Action-Oriented Research on African Development

The Centre for Action-Oriented Research on African Development (CARAD) is an academic NGO carrying out research and consulting on policy. CARAD has a special research department engaged in conflict prevention, called Ethnicity and Governance. Current projects relating to conflict resolution include 'Prospects for Democracy in Africa' and 'Resources scarcity, state capacity and civil violence: what path to transition for Cameroon?' The organisation disseminates its information through articles in journals, and books.

Central Post Office
B.P. 13429
Yaounde
Cameroon

tel +237 231 825
fax +237 217 470/235 923

Contact
John W. Forje, director
Budget
< $25,000

Publications
Signs of Hope or Despair, manuscript
State-Building and Democracy in Africa, manuscript
Perspective on Democracy in Africa, manuscript
Cameroon without Poverty, manuscript

 Cameroon, Central Africa

Ecumenical Youth Peace Initiative Commission

The Ecumenical Youth Peace Initiative Commission (EYPIC) was established in 1996 in order to involve youth in solving religious, ethnic and tribal conflicts through peaceful means. It carries out research, organises seminars, sponsors projects on sustainable, more settled farming in areas where extensive farming has led to conflict. EYPIC has several committees that deal with conflict prevention and resolution, including the Justice and Peace Committee, the Conflict Resolution Committee, and the Ecumenical and Religious Studies Committee. The EYPIC also provides training and organises workshops on conflict issues in Cameroon.

PO Box 359
Bamemba
Cameroon

tel +237 362 034
fax +237 362 036
email nambang@douala1.com

Contact
Rev. Nja'ah Peter Toh, executive secretary
Budget
$25,000 - $100,000

Publications
Peace Training Manual, a handbook for peace makers, 1997

 Democratic Republic of the Congo

ASADHO

The Association Africaine de Défense des Droits de l'Homme (ASADHO, previously known as AZADHO) is a group of lawyers, doctors and journalists working for the defence of human rights in the Democratic Republic of the Congo. Led by a trained human rights lawyer, ASADHO gathers information through a network covering most regions of the country. Its special reports on human rights issues, which find a wide audience, have made it one of the country's leading organisations in its field. ASADHO has strongly denounced human rights violations under both president Mobutu's and president Kabila's government, and has been attacked by both.

12 **Avenue de la Paix**	*Contact*	*Publications*
Appartement 18	Guillaume Ngefa	Periodique Des Droits de l'Homme,
BP 16737, Kinshasa 1	Atondoko, president	bulletin
Democratic Republic of the Congo		Press announcements
		Reports on human rights

tel +243 (12) 21 174
fax +243 (12) 21 653

 Democratic Republic of the Congo

Centre Résolution Conflits

The Centre Résolution Conflits (CRC) aims at tackling the roots of violence in the northeastern provinces of the Democratic Republic of the Congo, where it is based, and at rapid intervention to defuse crises. Therefore, CRC trains trainers in the skills of conflict resolution. The Centre encourages people to use their energy constructively, to learn to reduce prejudice and increase tolerance and change from being easily manipulated to actively nonviolent. To these ends, CRC holds 'miniconferences of peace' and 'change of mind' courses.

P.O. Box 21285	*Contact*	*Publications*
Nairobi	Ben Mussanzi wa	Newsletters
Kenya	Mussangu, director	Bulletins
		Annual reports

tel +871 (761) 583 630
fax +871 (761) 583 631
email cmenyan@maf.org

Democratic Republic of the Congo, Rwanda

CNONGD

The Conseil National des Organisations Non-Gouvernemental de Developpement du Zaire (CNONGD) is the umbrella organisation of Congolese NGOs. Through its regional networks, CNONGD runs peace programmes throughout the country. The organisation has conducted surveys on local ethnic conflicts in Shaba, Kasai and North Kivu provinces in order to help local NGOs develop strategies of conflict resolution or post-conflict reconstruction. In early 1999, CNONGD launched a peace initiative calling for a cease fire, deployment of a peace-keeping force, and a roundtable process for establishing peace and democracy.

PO Box 5744
Kinshasa-Gombe
Democratic Republic of the
Congo

tel +243 (88) 26 707
fax +243 (88) 40 918

Contact
Hamuli Kabarhuza,
executive director

 Great Lakes region, West Africa

Heritiers de la Justice

Heritiers de la Justice is a non-profit organisation dedicated to the promotion of human rights and peace in the Great Lakes region of Central Africa. Based in the Southern Kivu area of the Democratic Republic of the Congo, its programme includes training for judicial monitors, training for rural mediators, radio broadcasts and publications to provide information on peace and justice issues, assistance and consultation on local organising for peace and human rights, assistance to victims of violence and human rights violations, and direct mediation in conflicts

B.P. 109 Bukavu,
Sud-Kivu
R.D.Congo
B.P. 234 Cyangugu
Rwanda

tel/fax: +377 (93) 107 249
email heritiers@yahoo.com
http://www. heritiers.org

Contact
Innocent Balemba
Zahinda, executive
secretary
Number of staff
7

Publications
Haki Yetu, bulletin
Salam, bulletin
Nota Bene, information flashes

 Horn of Africa

InterGovernmental Authority on Development

The Intergovernmental Authority on Development (IGAD) coordinates development in the Horn of Africa. Djibouti, Eritrea, Ethiopia, Kenya, Somalia, Sudan, and Uganda are member states. It has established the following three priorities: Infrastructure Development; Food Security and Environment Protection; and Conflict Prevention, Management and Resolution and Humanitarian Affairs, reflecting the need to establish peace and security to assure economic development. IGAD leaders have pursued negotiations to end the civil wars in Sudan and Somalia and given priority to the development of an early warning mechanism for the IGAD region.

P.O. Box 2653
Djibouti, Republic of Djibouti

tel +253 354 050
fax +253 356 994/284
email IGAD@intnet.dj
http://www.igad.org

Contact
Tekeste Ghebray,
executive secretary
Number of staff
2
Budget
$100,000 - $500,000

 The Middle East

Al Ahram Centre for Political and Strategic Studies

The Al Ahram Centre for Political and Strategic Studies (ACPSS) carries out multidisciplinary research and conducts policy advocacy work on issues related to the Middle East in general, and the Arab-Israeli conflict in particular, including international conflict and conflict resolution, and political, economic, and social aspects of Arab society in general and Egyptian society in particular. The ACPSS targets political leaders, policy makers, political parties and organisations, political parties, government and military officials, policy analysts and researchers, and the media, as well as the general public.

Al-Ahram Foundation
Al Galaa Street
Cairo, Egypt

tel +20 (2) 518 6037
fax +20 (2) 518 6833/6023
email acpss@acpss.org
http://www.acpss.org

Contact
Mohamed el Sayed Said,
deputy director
Number of staff
34
Budget
< $25,000

Publications
Strategic Papers, monthly series
Al-Ahram Strategic File, monthly series
in Arabic
Israeli Digest, monthly publication
Lebanon Under Siege: The Crisis of
Peace in the Middle East, 1996

Arab region, Somalia

Arab Organization for Human Rights

Although the activities of the Arab Organization for Human Rights are centred mainly around human rights, conflict prevention is also part of the work, especially in terms of research, fact-finding and publishing. The organisation, which is active throughout the Arab world, has a programme on conflict prevention and resolution in Somalia. It cooperates with the United Nations.

91 Al-Marghany
Heliopolis - Cairo
11341 Egypt

tel +20 (2) 418 1396/8378
fax +20 (2) 418 5346
email aohr@linkcom.eg
http://aohr.org

Contact
Ibrahim Allam,
executive director
Number of staff
10

Publications
Arab Organization for Human Rights,
monthly newsletter
Almonazzama Alarabiya Lihoqouq
Alinsan - Nashra Ikhbariya, arabic
newsletter
Hoqouq Alinsan Filwatan Alarabi,
quarterly
Alkitab Alsanaoui Lihoqouq Alinsan
Filwatan Alarabi, arabic newsletter
Special bulletins

 Arab World

Cairo Inst. for Human Rights Studies

The Cairo Institute for Human Rights Studies (CIHRS) is primarily a human rights advocacy group, involved in research and training. In 1999, it organised, in collaboration with the Moroccan Organisation for Human Rights, the First International Conference of the Arab Human Rights Movement. The advancement of this movement has been a constant concern of CIHRS. The Institute has built up a major network of human rights advocates and experts throughout the region and acted for some time as the secretariat for the incipient Arab Regional Working Group for Human Rights.

9 Roustom Street, Garden City
P.O. Box 117
Cairo 11516
Egypt

tel +20 (2) 355 1112
fax +20 (2) 354 4200
email cihrs@idsc.gov.eg

Contact
Bahey El. Din Hassan,
director

Publications
Sawasiah, bulletin
Rowaq Arabi, quarterly journal
Challenges facing the Arab Human
Rights Movement, 1997
The Peace Process implications for
democracy and human rights, 1997,
conference report

457

Egypt

Egyptian Organization for Human Rights

The Egyptian Organization for Human Rights (EOHR) works as an advocate for full respect for all internationally accepted human rights and personal liberties, be they civil, political, economic, social or cultural rights, for the end of the practice of torture, and the promotion of women's rights. EOHR monitors the human rights situation in Egypt and pursues legislative reform to bring Egyptian law and practice into accordance with international human rights covenants and conventions. It publishes periodicals, pamphlets, new releases, and an annual report on the human rights situation in Egypt.

8/10 Matahaf El-Manyal Street
10th Floor
Manyal El Roda
Cairo, Egypt
tel +20 (2) 363 6811/0467
fax +20 (2) 362 1613
email eohr@link.com.eg
http://www.eohr.org.eg

Contact
Mr. Hafez Abu-Se'da,
secretary general

Publications
Huqooq Al Insaan, human rights
magazine
EOHR News, news bulletin
In Defense of Human Rights, annual
anthology
Annual Report on the human rights
situation in Egypt

 Egypt

National Center for Middle East Studies

The National Center for Middle East Studies carries out research, including research focused on conflict resolution and consults on policy issues. The organisation conducts workshops aimed at creating awareness about conflict prevention and resolution and resolving domestic and regional problems. It is involved in the FORWARD program, providing training for stakeholders and conducting consensus building. In association with Search for Common Ground, the Center plans to establish a Center for Conflict Prevention. A series of Arab language conflict resolution papers is also planned, supported by the government of Finland.

PO Box 18, Bab el Louk
Cairo 11513
Egypt

tel +20 (2) 577 0041/2
fax +20 (2) 577 0063

Contact
Maher Khalifa,
programme & research
director

 Egypt and the Arab World

Ibn Khaldun Center for Development

The Ibn Khaldun Center for Development (ICD) was established in 1988 to promote the linkage of social research and public policy in Egypt and the Arab world. ICD is a non-profit organisation carrying out a program of research and advocacy.

In addition to carrying out research of its own, it conducts commissioned research and provides training services to governmental and non-governmental organisations on issues of development and public policy. Additional activities include the organisation of seminars and conferences, and the publication and dissemination of information.
ICD is involved in a variety of programs aimed at preventing or resolving conflicts. These include:

1) Ethnic, Religious and Racial Minorities in the Arab World - a program which monitors, documents, and analyses information about minorities in the Arab world; creates awareness of issues related to monitoring and protecting the human rights of minority groups; and disseminates information on developments related to the treatment of minorities to opinion leaders and policy makers to effect policy changes.
2) Ibn Khaldun's People Fund - direct assistance to disadvantaged citizens to enhance their ability to confront problems and meet their own needs. The Ibn Khaldun People's Fund is currently proving micro-credits to former Islamic militants with the aim of improving their socio-economic position and creating economic opportunities as an alternative to violence rebellion. ICD plans to expand the program to other communities in the Arab world.
3) Making Egyptian Education Minority Sensitive - preparation of educational materials about Egyptian Christians and advocacy to incorporate materials into school curricula and library collections.

ICD also operates an ongoing program on 'Civil Society and Democratisation', which includes such activities as election monitoring, publication of a monthly newsletter, and maintenance of a database on Civil Society.

17, Street 12 Mokkatam
P.O.Box 13
Cairo
Egypt

tel +20 (2) 508 0662/3
fax +20 (2) 508 1030
email ibnkldon@idsc1.gov.eg
http://www.ned.org/page_3/ICDS/

Contact
Saad Eddin Ibrahim, director
Budget
$25,000 - $100,000

Publications
Civil Society, newsletter
Annual Report

Horn of Africa

Ethiopian Peace and Development Committee

Since its founding in 1992, the Ethiopian Peace and Development Committee's core activities have shifted more and more towards conflict prevention and resolution, focusing on the Horn of Africa. The Committee has a conflict prevention and resolution department. Training, education and research are the main activities. The Committee's office in the United States carries out part of the theoretical work on conflict resolution. The organisation aims to consolidate issues like human rights promotion and democracy and development into civil society, mainly in the marginal parts of Ethiopia.

P.O. Box 41879
Addis Ababa
Ethiopia

tel +251 (1) 511 966
fax +251 (1) 515 714

Contact
Yusuf Hassen Noah,
executive director
Budget
$25,000 - $100,000

Publications
Annual report

 Gambia

People in Action

People in Action focuses primarily on food security and environmental degradation. This non-profit organisation has training and implementation programmes on food security, environmental management, sustainable livelihood, forest management, and women's empowerment. It also organises community workshops. As yet, only a small part of People in Action's efforts have been aimed at conflict prevention and resolution activities, mainly in the area of training.

PO Box 1028
220 Banjul
The Gambia

tel +220 497 771/390 776
fax +220 497 772

Contact
Momodou Jobarteh,
director
Budget
$25,000 - $100,000

Ghana

ActionAid Ghana

ActionAid Ghana is a development organisation that embraces conflict prevention and resolution activities as an integral part of its work. Its Peace and Reconciliation Sector operates a pilot peace education programme in junior and senior secondary schools in Northern Ghana, with the goal of providing the students with conflict resolution skills and attitudes. ActionAid Ghana is also involved in community conflict resolution initiatives, through workshops, seminars and training programmes.

P.O. Box 19083
Accra-North
Ghana

tel +233 (21) 764 931/2
fax +233 (21) 764 930
email aaghana@africaonline.com.gh

Contact
Isaac Richard Osei,
programme coordinator
Number of staff
2
Budget
$100,000 - $500,000

Publications
Teachers' Source Book, manual

 Ghana

African Development Programme

Although the African Development Programme, based in Accra, Ghana is primarily a development organisation, it has shifted a small portion of its resources to conflict resolution activities in response to communal violence in Northern Ghana. Its Governance Programme aims to encourage dialogue as a tool to prevent, manage, and resolve conflict and to promote good governance. The programme operates in the Eastern Region of Ghana. Elements of the programme include mediation, citizen diplomacy, and an early warning system.

P.O. Box 3918
Cantonments
Accra
Ghana

tel +233 (21) 306 345
fax +233 (21) 306 345/662 035
email chasadp@africaonline.com.gh

Contact
Charles Abbey,
executive director
Budget
< $25,000

Ghana, Liberia, Sierra Leone, West African sub-region

CENCOR

The Centre for Conflict Resolution (CENCOR) was established to promote peace in Ghana and other West African countries, mainly through research, education and training. It serves as a secretariat for major peace initiatives and undertakes campaigns together with other networks and institutions. Among the programme focus areas are the participation of women in public life, the role of youth in conflict resolution, and peacekeeping education. CENCOR is taking a leading role in developing and building support for proposals focusing on the control of light weapons in the West African region.

P.O. Box 33
Legon, Accra
Ghana

tel +233 (21) 773 049
fax +233 (21) 761 744
email cencor@africaonline.com.gh

Contact
Arnold Quainoo, executive director
Budget
$25,000 - $100,000

Publications
The Bridge, journal

 West Africa

Centre for Democracy and Development

The mission of the Centre for Democracy and Development (CDD) is to promote democracy, good governance and development in Ghana in particular and Africa in general. In doing so, CDD seeks to foster ideals of liberty, enterprise and integrity in government and society. In this regard, the CDD has organised seminars on conflicts and conflict management in Ghana.

PO Box 404
Legon-Accra
Ghana

tel +233 (21) 763 029/776 142
fax +233 (21) 763 028
email cdd@ghana.com

Contact
E. Gyimah-Boadi, director
Number of staff
10
Budget
< $25,000

Publications
Briefing Paper, occasional paper
Critical Perspectives, occasional paper

 West Africa

Mediation & Change

Mediation & Change is a non-profit NGO specialised in conflict prevention and mediation in West Africa. It also works on human rights and democracy. It organises non-violence workshops conducted by outreach teams, as well as conferences. Besides training, the activities of Mediation & Change include fact-finding, early warning and mediation. One of the activities of the centre is a programme in which Christian and Muslim people from Nigeria and Sierra Leone are brought together. The program tries to create awareness for tolerance and peaceful co-existence through dialogue between the two religious groups. It co-operates with Responding to Conflict in the United Kingdom.

P.O. Box 5945
Cantonments
Accra
Ghana

Contact
Kwesi Aaku, facilitator
Budget
< $25,000

tel +233 (21) 778 507
fax +233 (21) 778 500
e-mail ben@AfricaOnline.com.gh

 Horn of Africa, Great Lakes Region

Africa Peace Forum

The Africa Peace Forum (APFO) is an organisation engaged in research and advocacy around peace and security issues in the Horn of Africa and the Great Lakes Region. APFO encourages collaborative approaches to the pursuit of peace and security and promotes community-based peace initiatives. Its specific areas of research interest include political and constitutional reform, demilitarisation, mediation, community participation in peace processes and conflict management structures. Project activities include collaborative research, workshops, and a recently launched internship program. APFO acts as lead agency in FEWER's Great Lakes project.

P.O. Box 76621
Nairobi
Kenya

Contact
Raymond Kiteva, coordinator
Number of staff
6

tel +254 (2) 574 092/6
fax +254 (2) 561 357
email kilenem@africaonline.co.ke

Budget
< $25,000

463

Kenya, Great Lakes Region

Amani People's Theatre

Amani is Swahili for 'peace'. The Amani People's Theatre (APT) makes use of theatre, performance, and a 'multi-arts approach' in its work as an advocate for peace and nonviolence. APT works at the grassroots level in local communities, at youth conferences and at peace festivals in Kenya, encouraging participants to respond proactively to conflict. It also offers intermediate-level training in leadership and conflict transformation. Over the next few years, the Theatre will be researching Afro-centric models of peace-making which might be applied to conflict situations.

P.O. Box 13909
Nairobi
Kenya

tel +254 (2) 576 175
fax +254 (2) 577 892
email apt@maf.org

Contact
Babu Ayindo
Number of staff
5
Budget
< $25,000

Publications
Mbiu, the Call of the Artiste-
Peacebuilder, quarterly newsletter

 Kenya

Centre for Conflict Resolution

The Centre for Conflict Resolution promotes constructive, creative, co-operative approaches to the prevention, management and resolution of conflicts. It carries out public education and awareness campaigns, assesses the scope and nature of social conflicts in Kenya, and serves a liaison function in working to improve dialogue, negotiation and mediation services.

P.O. Box 15626
Nakuru
Kenya

tel +254 (372) 12 435
fax +254 (372) 61 442
email eu-cs@net2000ke.com

Contact
Machira Appolos, director

Publications
Ethnicity, Violence and Democracy -
The Kenyan Experience, 1998

 Horn of Africa

International Resource Group

The International Resource Group on Disarmament and Security in the Horn of Africa (IRG), established in 1994 by a group of non-governmental humanitarian and policy organisations, explores peaceful means of resolving conflict and promotes alternative security structures and disarmament measures.

Its strategies are to engage relevant actors in rethinking security issues and to undertake research to create the basis for discussion and dialogue. It also encourages NGOs to develop humanitarian and development efforts so as to create conditions which contribute to peace, facilitate the demobilisation of armed forces and encourage the development of civil society.

One of the IRG's goals is to forge links between the international civil society community and those engaged in ongoing efforts within local civil society to address humanitarian and national security concerns. Such efforts are often impeded by the limited 'political space' in which local civil society can operate, so a key objective of the IRG is the expansion of political space for civil society in the Horn of Africa.

A second key objective is to promote a culture of openness and transparency to challenge prevailing assumptions that secrecy contributes to enhanced security. The IRG therefore encourages the view that information is a public resource rather than the property of the elite, and sponsors workshops and consultations for discussion on security issues based on publicly available information.

A third objective is to enhance local research and analysis capacity, and the knowledge base from public discourse flows.

The IRG's current programmes revolve around a number of themes, including: the creation of mechanisms for addressing the regional arms trade and the flow of small arms; the development of a responsive regional security architecture; the development of accountable civilian governance authority over military forces; and a focus on the links between environment and security.

P.O. Box 76621
Nairobi
Kenya

tel +254 (2) 574 092/6
fax +254 (2) 561 357
email kilenem@africaonline.co.ke
http://www.ploughshares.ca/
content/BUILD%20PEACE/IRG.html

Contact
Josephine Odera,
programme manager
Budget
$25,000 - $100,000

 Horn of Africa

Life & Peace Institute

Sweden's Life & Peace Institute (LPI) is an international and ecumenical centre for peace research and action. Established by the Swedish Ecumenical Council in 1985, LPI aims to further the causes of justice, peace and reconciliation through a combination of research, seminars and publications.

LPI's Horn of Africa Programme, based in Nairobi, combines research with practical support for grassroots peace building initiatives in Djibouti, Eritrea, Ethiopia, Somalia/Somaliland, Sudan, Kenya, Uganda, Burundi and Rwanda.
LPI's Somali Programme offers assistance in developing bottom-up structures of governance and encompasses a civic education programme addressing topics such as participatory democracy and conflict resolution/peace building. The education programme is aimed primarily at women, elders, media workers, artists, and local NGO staff. The Somali Programme also provides support for locally initiated, bottom-up reconciliation efforts, includes an advocacy component, and involves research on conflict transformation issues.
In Sudan, LPI works in partnership with organisations operating in the south of the country, providing conflict transformation training to local staff, who then provide training to peace volunteers working at the community level. It has carried out a study of the causes of ethnic conflict in Ethiopia. With the emergence of Eritrea as an independent state, LPI has undertaken an extensive study of the challenge of repatriating and integrating 400,000 Eritrean refugees who fled to Sudan during the independence struggle. In Burundi, LPI supports research investigating traditional conflict management mechanisms. It has also provided conflict transformation and peace-building training for regional organisations, including the Inter-Governmental Authority for Development. Also on a regional basis, LPI has undertaken a study focusing on the potential for economic and political co-operation among the nations of the Horn of Africa. The findings are presented in 'Trading Places'.

P.O. Box 21186
Nairobi
Kenya

tel +254 (2) 561 158/570 696
fax +254 (2) 570 614
email lpihap@users.africaonline.co.ke
http://www.nordnet.se/lpi

Contact
Johan Svensson,
regional representative
Number of staff
9
Budget

Publications
Research reports
The Horn of Africa Bulletin
Ready and Willing...but still waiting.
Eritrean refugees in Sudan and the
dilemmas of return, Horn of Africa
series
Trading Places, 1997
Building the Peace. Experiences of
Collaborative Peacebuilding in Somalia
1993 - 1996

Kenya

The National Council of Churches of Kenya

The National Council of Churches of Kenya (NCCK) is an umbrella organisation for Kenyan churches and church-related organisations. The NCCK has been an advocate for an open and democratic society for many years, choosing a strategy of 'creative engagement' and serving as the 'voice of the voiceless'. The NCCK has investigated inter-communal violence, provided relief to victims of ethnic clashes, and operates the multi-faceted NCCK Peace and Rehabilitation Project with the objective of helping to prevent communal violence through dialogue, inter-cultural activities, and the establishment of an early warning system.

Church House
MOI Avenue
P.O. Box 45009
Nairobi, Kenya

tel +254 (2) 338 211
fax +254 (2) 215 169

Contact
Rose Barmasai, peace and reconciliation coordinator
Number of staff
300
Budget
> $1,000,000

Publications
The Update on peace and reconciliation, bulletin

 Great Lakes Region, Somalia, Sudan, Kenya

People for Peace in Africa

People for Peace in Africa (PPA) is a voluntary ecumenical association of people committed to initiating and supporting peace activities in East Africa and the Great Lakes Region. It sponsors reconciliation workshops, engages in peace education and awareness raising activities, provides mediation services, and acts as a policy advocate on peace and reconciliation issues.

P.O. Box 14877
Nairobi
Kenya

tel/fax +254 (2) 441 372
email ppa@AfricaOnline.co.ke

Contact
Joseph A'Ngala, director
Budget
< $25,000

Publications
Newsletter
Bulletin
Training materials

 Kenya

Wajir Peace and Development Committee

The Wajir Peace and Development Committee (WPDC) is a network of 27 governmental and non-governmental organizations representing a variety of people including businesswomen, elders and religious leaders, operating primarily in the Wajir District of northeastern Kenya. The region has been the scene of clan-based violence. The primary mandate of WPDC is conflict prevention and resolution pursued via both traditional and modern mechanisms. It conducts community training for leaders, maintains a Rapid Response Team, run by elders, religious leaders, women and government security officials, to diffuse tense situations, and also mediates in conflict situations.

P.O. Box 444
Wajir
Kenya

Contact
Nuria Abdullahi,
coordinator and trainer

tel +254 (136) 21 427/175/369
fax +254 (136) 21 563

 Liberia, Nigeria, Sierra Leone

Africa Peace Mission

The Africa Peace Mission, an international charity based in Liberia, has been involved since early 1999 in three community-based peace transformation projects which incorporate teamwork and conflict management workshops into a more comprehensive program including health and development components. An important element of the organisation's work is to address the psychological traumas resulting from violent conflict. Staff members include a clinical psychologist and a psychotherapist with a background in social work.

c/o Institute for Peace, Health &
Development
P.O. Box 1920
Musu apt. St Edward's Parish
Logan Town, Monrovia
Liberia

Contact
Francis B. Selemo
Number of staff
5

tel +231 225 953/226 804/5
fax +231 227 838/226 805

 Liberia

Catholic Justice and Peace Commission

The Catholic Justice and Peace Commission (JPC) has played an important role in monitoring and reporting on human rights violations in Liberia. It publishes 'Situational Reports' and broadcasts a radio program, 'The Justice and Peace Forum'. JPC provides legal aid and coordinates the Human Rights Fact-Finding Documentation and Reporting Program. The JPC endeavours to work concretely for reconciliation in Liberia through its Conflict Resolution and Peacebuilding programme, which includes training, workshops, and the promotion of dialogue and tolerance at the local level, utilising existing traditional mechanisms where possible.

Ashmun Street
P.O. Box 10-3569
1000 Monrovia 10, Liberia

tel + 231 227 657 / 225 930
fax +231 226 006 / 227 838
email JPC@liberia.net

Contact
Samul Kofi Woods,
director
Number of staff
6 at national head office

Publications
Situation report, regular bulletin

 Liberia, West African sub-region

Center for Democratic Empowerment

The Center for Democratic Empowerment (CEDE) was established in 1994 by former president Amos Sawyer. CEDE organises and sponsors training sessions, seminars and conferences on issues related to democracy promotion, peace building, human rights and sustainable development. It also provides consultancy services at all levels of government on the creation of democratic institutions. The Center operates a Peace-Building & Security Program. Notable activities have included a national conference on reconciliation and healing, a seminar on Liberia's transition to democracy, a post-election roundtable, and a roundtable bringing together representatives of security agencies and the media.

11a Broad Street
Snapper Hill
P.O. Box 10-3679
1000 Monrovia 10
Liberia

tel +231 226 959/393
fax +231 228 003/226 416
email cede@libnet.net

Contact
Conmany B. Wesseh,
director
Budget
$25,000 - $100,000

 Liberia

Liberian Women's Initiative

The Liberian Women's Initiative (LWI) has engaged in a sustained campaign, uniting Liberian women from all sectors of society, to bring an end to the country's civil war. It has directed its activities at major players in the Liberian conflict, including West African political leaders, officials of the United States, and the UN. Prior to the 1997 democratic elections, it played a major role in bringing about disarmament, and engaged in voter education activities. LWI continues to engage in educational activites promoting nonviolent conflict resolution and civic education.

11 Broad Street
P.O. Box 1063
Monrovia
Liberia

tel +231 227 095

Contact
Etweda Cooper, secretary general
Number of staff
3

 Liberia

SUSUKUU

Susukuu is essentially a development organisation designed to help people help themselves. Against the background of the crisis in Liberia in the 1990s, Susukuu established the 'School for Guns' programme, consisting of the offer of one year of education in exchange for a fully functioning weapon. The programme has attracted many thousands of fighters, mostly young, but been hampered by inadequate funding to support longer study periods. Susukuu also operates a Rehabilitation Program with the goal of rehabilitation and reintegrating former fighters, especially children, into civil society.

P.O. Box 10-1517
1000 Monrovia 10
Liberia

tel: +231 226 944
fax: + 231 226 066

Contact
Togba-Nah Tipoteh, director
Number of staff
12
Budget
$500,000 - $1,000,000

 Malawi

Centre for Human Rights and Rehabilitation

The Centre for Human Rights and Rehabilitation (CHRR) was established in 1995 to promote respect for human rights in Malawi through education, training, research, legal assistance, advocacy, and networking. The organisation engages in conflict management and counselling activities and has helped to resolve a potentially violent conflict between returned Malawian refugees and the government. It is also engaged in mediation efforts to resolve land disputes, and is providing civic education and conflict resolution training as a strategy to resolve a variety of political and social conflicts.

P.O. Box 2340
Lilongwe
Malawi

tel/fax +265 741 292
email CHRR@malawi.net

Contact
Ollen Mwalubunju,
executive director

 Malawi, Zambia

Malawi Institute of Democratic and Economic Affairs

The Malawi Institute of Democratic and Economic Affairs (Midea) was originally established for democratic education, training and economic research. When Malawi experienced conflict at both the leadership and grassroots level, Midea was called in to intervene. Since then the Institute' programme has also included conflict prevention and resolution. The Department of Conflict Resolution and Training develops and administers conflict resolution programmes, facilitates mediation processes, conducts early-warning monitoring and co-ordinates fact-finding missions. Training is also an important additional activity. The Institute is also involved in mediation efforts in Zambia's political conflict.

P.O. Box 30465
Kirk Road
Lilongwe 3
Malawi

tel/fax +265 741 562
email Midea@unima.wn.apc.org

Contact
Shyley Kondowe,
executive director
Budget
$25,000 - $100,000

Publications
Report on Mediation Activities During
Parliamentary Impasse, July 1996 -
March 1997
Annual Reports

 Mali, West Africa

International Institute for Peace and Security

The International Institute for Peace and Security was established in 1998 following the peace process that led to the end of Mali's Touareg rebellion, to prevent a recurrence of the violence and to consolidate the gains of that peace process. Individuals involved include leaders of the rebellion, representatives of the government, and other leaders of civil society who participated in a program of disarmament and re-integration of rebels into security forces or society. Important goals include conflict prevention through education and arms for development programs, and research on arms proliferation.

Magnambougou-Est, Plateau no.2   *Contact*
Lot no.1, BP E2539   Rokiatou Ndiaye Keita
Bamako, Mali

tel +223 773 789
fax +223 770 125/204 749
email SKEITA@spider.toolnet.org

 Mali

Mouvement Nationale des Femmes pour la Paix

Le Mouvement National des Femmes pour la Paix (MNFP), a network of Mali women, played an important facilitating role in activities that helped to bring the Touareg rebellion in Northern Mali to an end. It spurred local groups to undertake arms collection activities consistent with the government's 'Security First' policy that reduced the number of small arms in the hands of civilians and rebel groups, and increased confidence in the prospects for peace.

BP E879   *Contact*
Bamako   Marianne Maïga
Mali

tel +223 224 231/230 642/4

 Morocco, Western Sahara

L'Association Marocaine des Droits de l'Homme

L'Association Marocaine des Droits de l'Homme (AMDH) is an independent NGO primarily engaged in monitoring human rights in Morocco. The organisation defends human rights as defined in the Universal Declaration of Human Rights, monitors the human rights situation in Morocco, and publicises information on cases of arbitrary detention, extra-legal execution, and other human rights violations, including violations in the Western Sahara. AMDH has established a human rights documentation centre and library in Rabat.

B.P. 1740
Rabat
Morocco

tel +212 (7) 709 161
fax +212 (7) 707 871

Contact
Abderrahmane
Benameur, president

 Mozambique

LINK

LINK is an umbrella NGO, grouping together a broad variety of Mozambican NGOs, which is currently engaged in civil education, incorporating non-violent methods of conflict resolution. LINK is supported by - among others - the Mennonite Central Committee from Canada.

Fórum de ONGs
Projecto de capacitação em Resolução
de Conflitos e Mediação
Rua Dr. António José Almeida 191
Bairro da Coop
CP 2187 Maputo, Mozambique

Tel. 258 1 496 279/496 280
Fax 258 1 496 304/ 306 / 497 235
Email conflict@link.uem.mz

Contact
Aida Muhai - Project Coordinator
Adriano Júlio Nhamutócue - Principal trainer

Namibia, Democratic Republic of Congo, Southern Africa

National Society for Human Rights

In addition to its programmes focusing on the protection of human rights, the NSHR (National Society for Human Rights of Namibia) has a special Conflict Prevention and Resolution Project. NSHR monitors conditions in potential conflict areas where minorities live on the socio-economic margins of society. It intends to create a special programme on early warning soon. It anticipates the establishment of an early warning system and training programmes to enhance local capacity to manage conflict. In addition to Namibia, the organisation also monitors human rights situations in neighbouring countries.

57 Bahnhof Street
P.O. Box 23592
Windhoek 9000
Namibia

tel +264 (61) 236 183/253 447
fax +264 (61) 234 286
email nshr@iafrica.com.na
http://www.iwwn.com.na/nshr

Contact
Phil ya Nangoloh,
executive director
Number of staff
5
Budget

 Nigeria, Ghana

Academic Associates PeaceWorks

Academic Associates PeaceWorks (AAPW) was established in 1992 as an NGO focused on building capacities for the management of conflict through study, intervention and greater public awareness. The organisation is based in Nigeria and focuses primarily on Nigeria, but has also been active in Ghana.

It offers training programs on conflict management, and peace education workshops for adult and youth community leaders, local government officials and religious leaders. It also offers training to students and academic staff at seven Nigerian Universities, conducts peace education programmes at primary and secondary schools, and provides conflict resolution training to teachers in several conflict-prone areas of Nigeria. The organisation was instrumental in the establishment of the National Corps of Mediators, providing the training of 21 senior Nigerians in mediation and conflict management skills so that they would be able to effectively deal with conflicts in their communities. AAPW also provided conflict management training to 90 Muslim and Christian religious leaders, and to 135 journalists focusing on interpreting violent conflict and election monitoring. It played a facilitating role in establishing the Journalists' Network for Peace and in the launch of the Peace Support Network. This network consists of all those trained by Academic Associates, including adult and youth leaders, peace education teachers and local government officials, as well as others who are interested in joining.

In conjunction with ActionAid Ghana it has also developed a peace education programme for teachers and NGOs in conflict-prone areas of northern Ghana.

In the future, AAPW plans to intensify its involvement in the Niger Delta, especially in programmes focused on youth, and to increasingly emphasise the close relationship between peace and development.

9 Esomo Close   *Contact*
Ikeja   Judith Burdin Asuni, director
Lagos   *Number of staff*
Nigeria   18
                           Budget
tel +234 (1) 774 3203 $100,000 - $500,000
fax +234 (1) 493 7853
email Jasuni@aol.com

 Nigeria, West-Africa

Centre for Conflict Resolution & Peace Advocacy

The Centre for Conflict Resolution & Peace Advocacy (CCRPA) is involved in mediation and training activities with the goal of empowering people to resolve their own conflicts and control their own destinies. CCRPA has trained its own personnel and many other individuals to serve as observers for local and national elections during 1998 and 1999. It also organises workshops on conflict resolution for businesses and university students. The Centre serves consults with people and organisation from civil society on conflict resolution. It produces an educational radio programme called Peace Radio.

2 Isijola Road, Off Ikorodu
Road
Ilupeju, Lagos
Nigeria

tel/fax +234 1 288 1320
email ccrpa@gacom.net

Contact
M. Ozonnia Ojielo,
president
Budget
$25,000 - $100,000

Publications
The Mediator, newsletter
Guidelines for Domestic Election
Observers, 1999

 Nigeria

Committee for the Protection of Peoples Dignity

The mission of the Committee for the Protection of Peoples Dignity (COPPED) is to promote respect for fundamental human rights and dignity. COPPED operates in the Niger Delta where the organisation supports local communities whose environments are under threat as a result of petroleum exploitation activities. COPPED mediates between communities involved in mutually destructive inter-communal conflicts which COPPED views as intrinsically link to the activities of multi-national corporations. In many instances, COPPED has succeeded in bringing peace to these communities. The organisation has established relationships with several international peace organisations.

1A Hussy Street, Yaba
Lagos
Nigeria

tel +234 (1) 584 0288/497 5929
fax +234 (1) 266 2892
email copped@angelfire.com

Contact
Peter Claver Opara
Budget
< $25,000

Publications
Dignity, newsletter

 West African region

International Women Communication Centre

The primary mandate of the International Women Communication Centre (IWCC) is to document the experience of women during periods of conflict, and to campaign for redress of women victims. The organisation is involved in fact-finding, focusing in particular on victims of the Biafra/Nigeria Civil War of 1966-70, publication of its findings, lobbying, and education. IWCC considers networking to be an important aspect of its programme, and has established relationships with similar organisations in Uganda and the Philippines, and with Liberian women who have fled to Nigeria to escape the Liberian conflict.

P.O. Box 1750
Nicon House, Ilorin
Kwara State
Nigeria

tel +234 (31) 225 688
fax +234 (31) 225 805

Contact
Hajiya Goroso Giwa Limota
Number of staff
18
Budget
< $25,000

Publications
Conference papers
Workshop documentation

 Rwanda, Great Lakes Region

CLADHO

CLADHO (Collectif des Ligues et Association de Défense de la Droits de l'Hommes) is a coalition of organisations and institutions working for the defence of human rights. Focusing mainly on education, training, research and data collection, it organises conferences and seminars on conflict prevention and resolution. CLADHO works together with organisations such as UNICEF and Amnesty International.

P.O. Box 3060
Kigali
Rwanda

tel/fax +250 74 292

Contact
Jean-Baptiste Barambirwa
Budget
$25,000 - $100,000

 Sierra Leone

Campaign for Good Governance

The Campaign for Good Governance (CCG) was established in 1996 as an independent grassroots organisation with the goal of strengthening Sierra Leone's democratic institutions by providing training to elected officials, civil servants, members of the judiciary, and journalists. It also targets civic groups and media at village, chief, and district levels, encouraging a spirit of tolerance in addition to transparency and accountability in government. Though not strictly a lobby group, CCG acts as a pressure group by calling attention to practices inconsistent with good governance.

29 Liverpool Street
P.O. Box 1437
Freetown
Sierra Leone

Contact
Zainab Bangura,
coordinator

tel +232 (22) 238 454
fax +232 (22) 228 896
email cgg@sierratel.com

 Sierra Leone

FORUT Sierra Leone

FORUT, Campaign for Development and Solidarity, is a Norwegian NGO engaged in development co-operation in Asia and Africa. Its development projects are implemented in close collaboration with local organisations. In Sierra Leone FORUT works closely with victims of war. For instance, it runs an activity centre for disabled street boys in Freetown, has built a refugee camp for about 200 people, and collaborates with other organisations involved in refugee assistance. FORUT future plans include conflict resolution through peace education, training, and community-based trauma healing and reconciliation.

P.M.B. 17
Freetown
Sierra Leone

Contact
Lucinda Amara, field
coordinator

tel +232 (22) 241 512
http://www.iogt-international.
org/forutnorway/sierraleone

Somalia

Peace and Human Rights Network

The Peace and Human Rights Network (PHRN) is a non-clan based organisation which came into being in February 1997 when some twenty organisations atttended a workshop in order to analyse the conflict situation. Among the participants were human rights organisations, the Somali Olympic Committee, other NGOs, journalists, teachers, community leaders and ex-militia members. They decided on the spot to form this network organisation. Their most conspicuous activity so far has been the organisation of a peace demonstration on March 8, 1998 which was attended by one hundred thousand people.

P.O. Box 71335
Nairobi, Kenya

tel /fax +252 121 5048
email phrn@compuserve.com

 Somalia

Sanaag Agricultural Development Organisation

Training workshops and research are the main activities of the Sanaag Agricultural Development Organisation (SADO) in the field of conflict prevention and resolution. The organisation is based in Djibouti but operates in Somalia. Through these activities, SADO aims to provide NGOs in Somalia with skills for handling and understanding conflicts. The organisation works with trainers from local NGOs. Research topics include trends in pastoral institutions and livelihoods and the social, political and resource conflicts these might entail.

P.O. Box 10012
Djibouti
Djibouti

tel +253 340 749
fax +253 340 751

Contact
Hassan Mohamed Ali,
director

Publications
Pastoral institutions survey, workshop report
Rangeland Tenure Policy, workshop report
Building Partnerships for Peace and Development, workshop report, 1996

 Somalia

Somalia Peace Line

S omalia Peace Line (SPL) is a non-profit organisation based in Mogadishu working to establish a culture of peace in Somalia and throughout the region, and to achieve the economic, cultural and social reconstruction of Somalia. SPL is involved in local and regional mediation activities, carries out research, and provides conflict resolution training workshops for leaders at the grassroots level. It has also brought together leaders from various armed Somali factions for peace consolidation workshops, and has organised peace gatherings among exiled Somalis. It has relationships with numerous international organisations.

Mogadishu, Somalia - S.B.195 - BC   *Contact*   *Publications*
c/o P.O. Box 3313   Abdullahi M. Shirwa,   Newsletter
Dubai   deputy chairman   Activity Reports
United Arab Emirates   *Budget*
                                         $25,000 - $100,000

tel +252 (1) 658 325/ (59) 64 419
fax +252 (1) 657 600

 South Africa

IMSSA

I MSSA is committed to the effective resolution of disputes and the training of clients in 'alternative dispute resolution'. It describes five levels of service: responsive (resolving disputes), preventive (training), pro-active (R&D of new services), structural (dispute and conflict management design) and policy influence (analysis and evaluation of interventions). It employs a variety of dispute resolution strategies to assist clients in business, government, NGOs, trade unions, local communities, etc. Its Special Projects Division oversees the National Land Reform Mediation Panel and administers funding on behalf of USAID to conflict resolution organisations.

P.O. Box 91082   *Contact*   *Publications*
Auckland Park, 2006   Bill Thomson, project The IMSSA Review, quarterly
Johannesburg   director
South Africa   *Budget*
                          $100,000 - $500,000

tel +27 (11) 482 2390
fax +27 (11) 726 7411
email thabon@imssa.org.za
480 http://www.imssa.org.za

 Southern Africa, Great Lakes region

Centre for Conflict Resolution

The Centre for Conflict Resolution is an independent institute, based at the University of Cape Town, which seeks to contribute to a just and sustainable peace in South Africa and elsewhere in Africa by promoting constructive, creative and co-operative approaches to the resolution of conflict and the reduction of violence.

It provides third-party assistance in the resolution of political and community conflict, provides training in conflict management, promotes democratic values and advocates disarmament and demilitarisation. Mediation, training, education and research are among the Centre's main activities, with an emphasis on capacity-building at the grassroots level. Centre staff have been deeply involved in the transition to a democratic South Africa, serving as monitors, trainers, mediators and policy advisors.

In the post-apartheid era the emphasis has shifted to include other African countries, especially in the Southern and Great Lakes regions. A new focus is on training senior African officials in constructively managing conflict.

Current projects include:

- the Africa project, seeking to build conflict management capacity in African countries at governmental and grassroots level
- the Mediation and Training Services Project, which acts as an independent third-party mediator, with a growing emphasis on public participation and conflict prevention in relation to development
- the Project on Peace and Security, which conducts research on defence and security issues
- Project Saamspan ('working together as a team'), which works for peace at a grassroots level in the rural Western Cape
- the Police Training Project, which trains South African, Namibian and Zimbabwean police personnel in methods of problem-solving, conflict resolution and management of diversity
- the Youth Project, engaged in long-term peace building through peace education and conflict resolution programmes for children, youth, teachers and parents.

The organisation has a resource centre with collection of publications, and offers numerous courses and training workshops.

University of Cape Town
Private Bag
7700 Rondebosch
South Africa

tel +27 (21) 422 2512
fax +27 (21) 422 2622
email mailbox@ccr.uct.ac.za
http://ccrweb.ccr.uct.ac.za

Contact
Laurie Nathan, executive director
Number of staff
29
Budget
> $1,000,000

Publication
Track Two, quarterly newsletter
A Case of Undue Pressure: International Mediation in African Civil Wars, 1998
Strategies for Peace and Prosperity in Southern Africa, 1998
Good Governance, Security and Disarmament: The Challenge of Demilitarisation in Africa, 1998
Demilitarisation and Peacebuilding in Southern Africa: A Review of the Literature, 1997

KwaZulu Natal, Southern Africa

Independent Projects Trust

Training in conflict resolution and management skills is the primary mandate of the Independent Projects Trust (IPT). Its main target groups are the educational system and South African Police Service, both predominantly in KwaZulu Natal. Its Schools Mediation and Reconciliation Training provides training to schools to facilitate the development of conflict resolution structures and democratic processes. A more recent initiative is CASS - the Community Alliance for Safe Schools - bringing together multiple stakeholders in order to maximise efforts to improve school safety. Its Police and Community Training programme provides conflict resolution training to create an enabling environment for proactive policing.

1802 Old Mutual Centre
303 West Street
4001 Durban, South Africa

tel +27 (31) 305 8422
fax +27 (31) 305 8420
email iptnet@wn.apc.org
http://www.ipt.co.za

Contact
Iole Matthews, head of
training
Number of staff
11
Budget
$500,000 - $1,000,000

Publications
Public Information Bulletins
IPT Quarterly
Peace begins with me, training material
School Safety Guidelines, guide

 South Africa, Africa

Institute for Security Studies

The Institute for Security Studies is primarily a research institute, but its activities also include teaching and training, policy formulation, analysis and high level consultations. The organisation played a critical role between 1991 and 1994 in facilitating rapprochement in South Africa, but has since expanded its mission to focus more generally on conflict resolution and security issues throughout the continent. Current programmes include a broad-ranging, research-based effort to analyse conflict risk in its Africa Early Warning Programme, and a research programme regarding the principles and praxis of contemporary peace missions.

P.O. Box 1787
Brooklyn Square
Pretoria 0075
South Africa

tel +27 (12) 346 9500/2
fax +27 (12) 460 998
email iss@iss.co.za
http://www.iss.co.za

Contact
Jakkie Cilliers,
executive director

Publications
The African Security Review, bi-monthly journal
The OAU and African Subregional Organisations - A
Closer look at the 'peace pyramid', ISS Paper no. 36,
January 1999
Child Soldiers in Southern Africa, Monograph 37
Nedcor - ISS Crime Index
Society Under Siege: Crime, Violence and Illegal
Weapons, Vol 2, 1998

 South Africa, Southern Africa

Letsema Conflict Transformation Resource

The Letsema Conflict Transformation Resource is a programme of the ecumenical Wilgespruit Fellowship Centre. The programme was launched in 1991 in response to increased violence occurring on the margins of society. It is involved in conflict resolution intervention, training and development consultation in South Africa, as well as in Swaziland, Botswana and Mozambique. Its conflict resolution training activities are aimed at government, business, NGOs and the non-profit sector, and community groups. It also has helped to develop and work together with other conflict resolution networks

P.O. Box 81
Roodepoort 1725
South Africa

Number of staff
7

Publications
Course material

tel +27 (11) 768 1310
fax +27 (11) 764 1468
email Letsema@wn.apc.org

 Southern Africa

Oliver Tambo Chair of Human Rights

The Oliver Tambo Chair of Human Rights of the University of Fort Hare offers university training programmes on human rights and conflict resolution. Its purpose is to sensitise communities and leadership in the Eastern Cape and the rest of South Africa on these issues. The chair also provides training on human rights and mediation skills to police officers and public officials, and is active in the fields of research, policy advice and documentation on conflict resolution. Under the chair, a Human Rights Resource and Documentation Centre has been established.

University of Fort Hare
Private Bag X1314
Alice 5700
South Africa

Contact
N. S. Rembe, professor
Budget
< $25,000

tel +27 (40) 602 2220
fax +27 (40) 602 2544/2605

 South Africa

Quaker Peace Centre

The Quaker Peace Centre, established in 1988, works to encourage creative, nonviolent resolution of conflict through awareness, co-operation and empowerment. Among its programmes are the Conflict Handling Program, which provides mediation services; the Mediation and Skills Training Programme, providing services to government, civic society, and grassroots organisations; and the Peace Education Programme, which targets students, educators, governing bodies of educational institutions, and parents. Other programmes with a conflict resolution component include the Quaker Peace Centre Youth Programme, the Community Development Programme and the Rural Support Programme.

3 Rye Road
Mowbray
Cape Town 7700, South Africa

tel +27 (21) 685 7800
fax +27 (21) 686 8167
email qpc@wn.apc.org
http://www.quaker.org/capetown/

Contact
Jeremy Routledge,
director
Number of staff
6
Budget
$100,000 - $500,000

Publications
Resolving Conflicts Creatively,
workshops
Young People Handling Conflict,
training course
Lifeskills, collection of workshops

 South Africa

Sakha Ukuthula

Sakha Ukuthula (Educating for Peace in South Africa) is facilitated by the Methodist Church of South Africa. It aims to contribute to a peaceful, just society and to assist in the development of people in such key areas as conflict management, interpersonal skills and visioning peace. This is carried out through workshops and the development and implementation of a formal curriculum and other learning materials directed at a range of age groups, from pre-school to adult. Sakha Ukuthula's activities are concentrated in the northern region of South Africa.

P.O. Box 10376
Johannesburg 2000
South Africa

tel +27 (11) 337 5938
fax +27 (11) 333 3254
email nomad@wn.apc.org

Contact
Kathy Lane
Number of staff
2
Budget
< $25,000

Publications
Training materials
Pre-school peace education curriculum

KwaZulu Natal, Southern Africa

Vuleka Trust

The Vuleka Trust is a church-based organisation committed to community development and conflict resolution. Its main focus is on training, especially with a view to empowering grassroots groups. The Trust promotes and enhances justice and reconciliation. It facilitates and promotes conflict resolution and mediation. Besides this, it conducts skills training programmes in basic human relations, handling conflict creatively, effective negotiating skills and the design of educational events. It also conducts community services, a youth leadership training programme and a school project.

P.O. Box 88
Botha's Hill
3660 Durban
South Africa

tel +27 (31) 777 1363
fax +27 (31) 777 1080
email vuleka@dbn.lia.net

Contact
Rev. Gavin Preuss,
director
Budget
$25,000 - $100,000

Publications
Annual newsletter

 Sudan, Horn of Africa

DIMARSI

DIMARSI, the Disaster Management and Refugees Studies Institute is primarily involved in activities related to disaster management, providing training and engaged in advocacy on prevention and mitigation of natural and man-made disasters, but it is also involved in peace advocacy and conflict resolution work. Its Sudanese Peace Support Programme provides training to politicians, community officials, and traditional leaders. It has also launched the Sudan Campaign to Ban Landmines in a country were an estimated 2 - 2.5 million mines have been scattered across the country.

P.O. Box 8300
Imarat
Khartoum
Sudan

tel +249 (11) 465 142/474 712
fax +249 (11) 473 145

Contact
Elhadi Guma Gadal,
head of research and
training department

Sudan

Sudan Catholic Information Office

The Sudan Catholic Information Office is a religious organisation, primarily involved in evangelical activities. Recently, a Justice, Peace and Reconciliation commission has been formed to participate fully in the programme of the New Sudan Council of Churches. The commission will focus on the implementation of peace and reconciliation in the adult Christian community. It will also study traditional ways of achieving peace and reconciliation among Southern Sudanese communities.

P.O.Box 21102
Nairobi
Kenya

tel +254 (2) 577 595/949/616
tax +254 2 577 327
email scio@maf.org

Contact
Justin Makwach, justice,
peace & reconciliation
coordinator

Publications
Sudan Monthly Report

 Sudan

Sudanese Women Civil Society Network for Peace

The Sudanese Women Civil Society Network for Peace (SWCSN) consists of twenty NGOs, CBOs and consultant members, and exists to bring Sudanese women together to consolidate their efforts to attain peace in Sudan, and to promote the concept of civil society as an instrument to bring about sustained peace. Its specific objectives include facilitation of a higher profile role for Sudanese women in peace-making activities and creation of a forum where Sudanese women from all segments of society can share their peace-making experiences.

c/o Dr. Amina A. Rahana
Ahfad University for Women
P.O. Box 167
Khartoum
Sudan

tel/fax +249 (11) 467 957
email baldorabab@hotmail.com

Contact
Ms. Rabab Baldo,
chairperson

 Sudan

Sudanese Women's Voice for Peace

The Sudanese Women's Voice for Peace (SWVP) was established in 1994 by exiled Sudanese women living in Nairobi. SWVP promotes dialogue among all sectors of Sudanese society, but focuses especially on Sudanese women. Its three-step approach is to empower women through training, establish local capacities for peace, and advance participation in conflict resolution and the promotion of a culture of peace. SWVP attempts to forge bonds among women transcending tribal and racial boundaries. It has been active in establishing peace committees at the village level in Southern Sudan.

c/o P.O. Box 21123
Nairobi
Kenya

tel +254 (2) 562 156
fax +254 (2) 570 614
email lpihap@africaonline.co

Publications
New Voice, newsletter
We have to sit down: Women, war and
peace in Southern Sudan, in cooperation
Pax Christi

 Africa

African Dialogue Centre for Conflict Management and Development Issues

The African Dialogue Center for Conflict Management and Development Issues is an independent, non-profit NGO established to undertake research, provide advisory services and offer training on issues related to intra African and inter-African conflicts and development. Its programme goals include the organisation of non-governmental networks in Africa as a line of defence against violent conflict; monitoring of potential conflicts; publication of position papers on good governance and conflict prevention, management and resolution in Africa; and the development of long-term policies on prevention and peaceful resolution of African conflicts.

Arusha International Conference Centre
Serengeti Wing, Room 628/629
P.O. Box 6202
Arusha, Tanzania
tel +255 578 125/577 714
fax +255 578 482
email adc@habari.co.tz

Contact
Felix G.N. Mosha,
coordinator

Kenya, Uganda, Tanzania

The East African Co-operation

The East African Co-operation (EAC) is an inter-governmental organisation with the mandate to promote regional integration and development among its member states. In its Development Strategy (1997-2000), the EAC emphasises the role of the private sector and civil society. In order to achieve economic co-operation, the EAC places a high priority on friendship and solidarity among the member-states. Primarily a vehicle for economic development through regional co-operation, the EAC nonetheless embraces the promotion of peace, security, stability and good governance as an essential part of its mandate.

P.O. Box 1096
Goliondoli
Arusha
Tanzania

tel +255 574 253/8
fax +255 574 255
e-mail eac@cybernet.co.tz
http://home.twiga.com/eac

Contact
Amb Francis Kirim
Muthaura, executive
secretary
Budget
< $25,000

Publications
EAC News, quarterly newsletter
EAC Development Strategy, 1997-2000

Great Lakes Region

ELCT Advocacy Desk

The ELCT (Evangelical Lutheran Church in Tanzania) Advocacy Desk is currently involved in a data collection project to assess conflict situations and conflict resolution capacities in Tanzania. The results will be used to build a database and to guide the organisation as it develops a more comprehensive conflict resolution program with training, research, capacity-building, consultation and advocacy components. Groups in civil society and at the grass roots level are a primary target, with a strong emphasis on inter-religious contacts.

P.O. Box 3033
Arusha
Tanzania

tel +255 578 857/8
fax +255 578 858
email ELCTHQ@habari.co.tz
http://mission.fi/LCS/index.html

Contact
Amani Mwenegoha,
secretary general
Budget
< $25,000

 Tanzania

Tanzania Conflict Resolution Centre

The Tanzania Centre for Conflict Resolution was established in 1997 to promote awareness of the need for nonviolent approaches conflict resolution and to actively work for conflict resolution at all levels through negotiation, mediation, conciliation and other peaceful means. The Centre is involved in educational activities such as workshops, seminars and training sessions on the theory and practice of conflict resolution, including training of police officers. It is researching traditional approaches to conflict resolution in Tanzania. The organisation has acted as a mediator in several interpersonal and political conflicts.

P.O. Box 12069
Dar es Salaam
Tanzania

Contact
Riziki Shahari, secretary
general

tel +255 (51) 184 065

 Arab Countries

Arab Institute for Human Rights

The Arab Institute for Human Rights (AIHR) is primarily involved in educational and training activities, but it is also involved in research, conflict resolution and mediation activities, and the promotion of democracy. It played an important role in the establishment of the Arab Human Rights Information Network, has sponsored internships for members associated with the Network and conducts human rights workshops in Tunisia and elsewhere in the Arab World. AIHR publishes papers, booklets and brochures on issues concerning women, human rights, and children's rights, including some written in simplified language.

14 Rue Jahedh - El Menzah
1004 Tunis
Tunisia

Contact
Abdel Basset Ben
Hassen, director
Budget
< $25,000

Publications
Arab Journal of Human Rights
Al-Rassed - a translation of the UN's
Monitor
Human Rights Periodical (bi-annual)

tel +216 (1) 767 003/889
fax +216 (1) 750 911
email aihr.infocenter@gnet.tn

 Uganda, Eastern and Central Africa

Center for Conflict Resolution

The Center for Conflict Resolution is involved in research, educational and training programmes, active intervention, and networking and advocacy related to conflict prevention, management and resolution. Based in Uganda, CECORE is active in Eastern and Central Africa. It seeks to empower individuals, organisations, institutions and the community to manage conflicts by applying alternative and creative means so as to promote a culture of tolerance and peace. CECORE looks to both creative conflict resolution strategies and traditional methods rooted in African society to reconcile conflicting parties. It has joined with other NGOs in the Great Lakes Region to form a coalition focusing on the region's conflicts.

National Insurance Building　　*Contact*
Pilkington Road　　Stella Mystica Sabiiti,
P.O. Box 5211　　executive director
Kampala, Uganda　　*Budget*
　　< $25,000

tel +256 (41) 255 033
fax +256 (41) 234 252
email cecore@swiftuganda.com

 Great Lakes Region, Kenya, South Africa

Centre for Conflict Prevention - Uganda

The Centre for Conflict Prevention in Uganda is involved in conflict resolution and citizen diplomacy work, policy advocacy, and the promotion of human rights and democratic development. It has programmes on mobilisation, training and rehabilitation in Uganda, Rwanda, Burundi, Kenya and South Africa. The Centre promotes public awareness of the values and practice of conflict resolution and prevention. Besides this, it provides counselling services to traumatised youth. It also mobilises and empowers individuals, especially youth and women, providing them with the skills to manage community, political, economic and social conflict.

c/o Dr. William Kaberuka　　*Contact*
P.O. Box 10857　　Bintu Juliet, project
Kampala　　programmer
Uganda　　*Budget*
　　< $25,000

490　　tel/fax +256 (41) 343 377

Uganda

Foundation for Human Rights Initiative

The Foundation for Human Rights Initiative (FHRI) was established in 1991 as a result of a growing awareness among activists of the need to address more fundamentally and proactively the situation of human rights in Uganda. Key activities include paralegal training workshops at the village level. The Citizens Advice Bureau assists victims of human rights abuses and the Penal Reform Project to improve prison conditions. FHRI also organises regional educational conferences to raise public awareness of human rights broadcasts radio programmes to provide information on human rights.

Plot 77 Makere Hill Rd
P.O. Box 11027
Kampala, Uganda

tel +256 (41) 530 095/6
fax +256 (41) 540 561
email fhri@muklu.gn.apc.org

Contact
Livingston Sewanyura,
executive director

Publications
The Defender, biannual human rights journal
Strategies for Conflict Prevention and Peacebuilding, conference report, 1998

Uganda, Great Lakes Region

Jamii Ya Kupatanisha

Jamii Ya Kupatanisha (JYAK) is the Ugandan branch of the International Fellowship of Reconciliation. JYAK promotes reconciliation, tolerance and common understanding among the different peoples, ideologies and cultures of Uganda, mainly through education and training. The organisation conducts peace education, peace-building and nonviolence training programmes for many different target audiences, including teachers, and is involved in vocational training and empowerment programs for disadvantaged youth, many of whom are returnees who were kidnapped by rebel fighters. It is also developing a centre for peace, vocational and development education and training.

5 km Kampala - Entebbe Road
P.O. Box 198
Kampala
Uganda

tel +256 (41) 343 757
fax +256 (41) 345 597
email jyak@uga.helpnet.org

Contact
Henry Odra-Raga
Budget
$25,000 - $100,000

Publications
Fellowship Tiding Newsletter

Great Lakes Region, Horn of Africa

Peace Inititiative and Research Centre

The Peace Initiative and Research Centre (PIRC) was launched in 1998. Its mission is to promote conflict prevention and peace-building activities through close co-operation and interaction with individuals and organisations working for the promotion of peace at every level of society. The centre trains and stimulates graduate and undergraduate students in conflict prevention/resolution studies. PIRC furthermore organises seminars and workshops on conflict issues for grassroots participants as well as district and national authorities.

Plot 61 Oyam Road	*Contact*	*Publications*
P.O. Box 720	Emmanuel Fortunatus	Training material
00873 Lira	Amai, director	
Uganda	*Budget*	
	< $25,000	
fax +256 (41) 255 556		

Uganda

People's Voice for Peace

People's Voice for Peace focuses on conflict resolution, economic development, human rights initiatives, research and documentation. The organisation was born out of the need to contribute to a more effective post-conflict recovery process and conflict prevention in Gulu District, Northern Uganda, and began in 1995 as an oral testimony documentation centre examining the causes and impacts of the armed conflict in Uganda. The organisation also supports the economic and social rehabilitation of victims of war, broadcasts a radio programme, and participates in peace education workshops and peaceful demonstrations.

P.O. Box 861	*Contact*	*Publications*
Gulu	Rosalba Oywa, director	Arms to fight, Arms to protect, Women
Uganda	*Number of staff*	speak out about conflicts (1995)
	19	Annual Reports
tel + 256 (41) 267 667	*Budget*	
fax + 256 (41) 250 828	$25,000 - $100,000	

 Zambia, Africa

Mindolo Ecumenical Foundation

The Mindolo Ecumenical Foundation (MEF) is a faith-based Pan-African institution working in the area of education, training and mediation. Peace education is incorporated into the curriculum of its four Pan-African training programmes for youth leaders, women, ecumenical leaders and pre-school teachers. The Foundation has recently announced a new nine-month Pan-Africa training course entitled 'Peace Building and Conflict Transformation', focusing on providing participants with conflict intervention skills and the tools to train others in conflict resolution. MEF is also involved in community development and mediation activities inside Zambia.

Box 21493
Kitwe
Zambia

tel +260 (2) 214 572/211 488
fax +260 (2) 211 001
email janetps@zamnet.zm

Contact
Janet P. Schmidt, peace education lecturer
Number of staff
2
Budget
$25,000 - $100,000

Publications
Mindolo World, biannual publication

 Zambia

Zambia Student Christian Movement

The Zambia Student Christian Movement is a faith-based organisation devoted to empowering young people to develop a vision for transformation of society within the life and mission of the church. One of its main activities is the Conflict Prevention and Resolution Programme. Through education, the organisation tries to improve the skills of government officials, members of civil society, and grassroots participants in conflict resolution and peacemaking activities. The organisation also operates a Human Rights and Civic Education Programme. The Movement networks with other similar organisations and has close relations with IFOR.

Ciel Plaza-off Freedom Way
P.O. Box 32834
10101 Lusaka
Zambia

tel +260 (1) 236 803/702 344
fax +260 (1) 236 803/231 394
email zscm@zamnet.zm

Contact
Gilbert Banda, executive director
Budget
$25,000 - $100,000

Publications
Training materials

 Southern Africa

Southern African Regional Institute for Policy Studies

The Southern African Regional Institute for Policy Studies (SARIPS) is an international network of academics, students, researchers and policy makers addressing issues of regional, political and economic cooperation in Southern Africa. Its primary activities in the field of conflict prevention involve data collection, research and fact-finding. The organisation has recently established a peace and security database, which collects information from Southern African Development Community (SADC) countries. The SARIPS has been involved in discussions concerning the conflict in the Democratic Republic of Congo, including efforts to bring all parties together for talks.

P.O. Box MP 111
Mount Pleasant, Harare
Zimbabwe
tel +263 (4) 727 875/726 060
fax +263 (4) 732 735
email docs@sapes.org.zw
http://www.sapes.org.zw

Contact
Ibbo Mandaza, chair
Budget
> $1,000,000

Publications
Southern Africa Political Economy
Monthly
Policy Studies, journal
State and Democracy, book series
Occasional Papers series

 Zimbabwe, Southern Africa

Zimbabwe Human Rights Association

The main priority of the Zimbabwe Human Rights Association (ZimRights) is 'to develop a culture of human rights among individuals and all sectors of society in Zimbabwe'. In 1998, the Association launched the Economic and Social Rights Outreach Programme. It aims to resolve conflicts by promoting development, democracy, respect for human rights, justice and reconciliation using traditional and modern mechanisms. ZimRights is also engaged in a Civic Education Programme to promote human rights awareness, provides para-legal counselling, conducts research, and carries out investigations into alleged human rights violations.

P.O. Box 3951
Harare
Zimbabwe
tel +263 (4) 775 762 / 755 828
fax +263 (4) 755 829

Contact
David C. Jamali, field
officer
Budget
< $25,000

Publications
Monthly newsletter
Quarterly bulletin

International Organisations

 Africa

ACORD

ACORD (Agency for Cooperation and Research in Development) is an international consortium of 155 NGOs active in the field of development co-operation in Africa. ACORD recognises conflict as a strategic issue in development and is convinced that much of the violence raging in Africa is fuelled by poverty and displacement. It believes an important role can and should be played by NGOs in reinforcing conflict prevention and resolution. ACORD's approach is characterised by empowering grassroots organisations and civil society. ACORD also carries out research and organises seminars and workshops.

Dean Bradley House
52 Horseferry Road
London SW1P 2AF
United Kingdom

tel +44 (171) 227 8600
fax +44 (171) 799 1868
email acord@gn.apc.org

Contact
Adam Platt, research &
policy director
Number of staff
41 (Secretariat
Department)
Budget
> $1,000,000

 Southern Africa, Angola

Action for Southern Africa

Action for Southern Africa (ACTSA) researches various aspects of security in Southern Africa and campaigns for peace in that part of the world. In its current Angola Campaign, it is working for the establishment of a lasting peace by lobbying the UK government, the United Nations and the European Union and by raising awareness among journalists and the general public. Its monthly 'Angola Peace Monitor' is available on the internet. In 1997, it organised a major policy conference on Angola. ACTSA is a member of the Working Group of Landmines.

28 Penton Street
London NI 9SA
United Kingdom

tel +44 (171) 833 3133
fax +44 (171) 837 3001
email actsa@geo2.poptel.org.uk
http://www.anc.org.za/angola/

Contact
Ben Jackson, director
Budget
$25,000

Publications
Angola Peace Monitor, bulletin

 Africa

African Rights

Asfrican Rights focuses on human rights abuses, conflict, famine and civil reconstruction, stressing in particular the central role that Africans must play in dealing with Africa's problems. Its projects areas include: Rwanda, to document the 1994 genocide; Somalia, to work for the restoration of civil institutions; Somaliland, to engage in human rights education and research; and Sudan, to gather information on displaced peoples and, in southern Sudan, research civil institutions necessary for peace. Other projects focus on women's issues, access to justice, and the relationship between human rights and famine.

11 Marshalsea Road
London SE1 1EP
United Kingdom

tel +44 (171) 717 1224
fax +44 (171) 717 1240
email afrights@gn.apc.org
http://www.unimondo.org/
AfricanRights/index.html

Contact
Rakiya Omaar, director
Number of staff
10
Budget
$100,000 - $500,000

Publications
Witness to Genocide, journal
Zimbabwe: In the Party's Interest?
Discussion Paper, no. 8, 1999
Rwanda: The Insurgency in the Northwest,
1998
Justice in the Nuba Mountains of Sudan,
1997

Africa

Alliance of African/African American Peacemakers

The Alliance of African/African American Peacemakers (AAAP) is a U.S.-based organisation which seeks to link people of African descent who are working for the peace, freedom, justice and prosperity of African peoples. AAAP is supporting research and conducting workshops on peacemaking and conflict resolution in African and African-American communities, and has established a network called Gathering of African/African-American peacemakers (GAAAP), which offers workshops at the National Conference on Peacemaking and Conflict Resolution. AAAP publishes a quarterly newsletter and is completing work on a directory of African and African-American peacemakers.

P.O. Box 34617
Philadelphia, PA 19101
USA

tel +1 (215) 729 3377
fax +1 (215) 750 9237
email spb2@ibm.net

Publications
Bridging the GAAAP, quarterly
newsletter

 Africa

Alliances for Africa

Alliances for Africa (AfA) is an African non-governmental peace, human rights and development organisation, based in the UK. It operates by establishing partnerships with local, regional and national organisations to bring about linkage between civil and political rights, on one hand, and economic, social and cultural rights on the other hand.

AfA pursues a four-point agenda to achieve its objectives, comprised of: human rights, peace and development; community development; coalition-building, monitoring and networking; and training and capacity building.

In human rights, peace and development, special consideration is given to the support of human rights activists and advocates, electoral and constitutional reform activities, promotion of respect for international humanitarian standards, good governance procedures, community based initiatives on conflict resolution, peace building and development; economic empowerment; prison issues and women's human rights.

Current activities are concentrated in Kenya, Nigeria, Rwanda and Sierra Leone, and on a number of sub-regional institutions, such as the African Commission on Human and Peoples' Rights, the Economic Community of West African States and the Conflict Resolution Unit of the Organisation of African Unity. AfA has focused on the constitutional review process in Kenya, and more recently Nigeria and other countries. In 1998, it organised a three-day conference on the constitutional reform process for mid-level women politicians, NGOs and local councillors in Kenya. Its 'Women in Politics, Decision-making & Peace-building' programme offers training to African women to improve their ability to participate in politics and in peace-building initiatives. Workshops have been held in Kenya, Uganda, Nigeria and London.

AfA serves as a facilitator for the West African Human Rights and Peace Forum. It has extensive contacts with Africa-based organisations and international NGOs, and has compiled a database of African consultants with conflict resolution, peace-building and human rights experience.

Unit 10, Aberdeen Centre
24 Highbury Grove
London N5 2EA
United Kingdom

tel + 44 (171) 359 1181
fax + 44 (171) 354 4900
email afa@alliancesforafrica.org
http://www.alliancesforafrica.org

Contact
Iheoma Obibi, executive
director
Number of staff
5
Budget
$100,000-$500,000

Publications
African Women in Politics & the
Constitution Making Process in Kenya,
conference report, 1998
Training manual

 Global

Amnesty International

With national sections in over fifty countries, Amnesty International is one of the world's leading human rights organizations. Apart from focusing on individual cases of human rights abuse, it also reports on systematic violations, offers recommendations on how to prevent these and put pressure governments through public and lobby campaigns to heed them. For sudden escalations of human rights violations, such as are typical for violent conflict, the organization has a special crisis response team. AI's human rights education work also contributes to the prevention of violent conflict.

1 Easton Street
London WC1X 8oJ
UK

tel +44 (171) 413 5500
fax +44 (171) 956 1157
email amnesty@amnesty.org
http://www.amnesty.org

Contact
Andrew Anderson, director
of Campaigning and Crisis
Response Programme
Number of staff
320 at international HQ
Budget:
> $1,000,000

Publications
Annually over 200 books, reports and
circulars in over a dozen languages.

National sections in African Countries

AI Section	Postal adress	Phone/Fax	Email
Algeria	BP 377 Alger RP 16004 Algeria	P: +213 2 732 797 F: +213 2 732 797	
Benin	AI Benin BP 01 3536 Cotonou Repub. du Benin	P: +229 32 36 90 F: +229 32 36 90	admin-bj@amnesty.org
Côte d'Ivoire	04 BP 895 Abidjan 04 Côte d'Ivoire	P: +225 48 82 20 F: +225 48 82 20	aicotediv@sections.amnesty.org
Ghana	Private Mail Bag Kokoklemle Accra - North Ghana 805	P: +233 21 220 814 F: +233 21 220	amnesty_ghana@notes.interliant.com
Mauritius	BP 69 Rose-Hill Mauritius	P: +230 454 8238 F: +230 454 8238	amnesty@intnet.mu
Nigeria	PMB 3061 Suru-Lere Lagos Nigeria 5619	P: +234 1 470 5619 F: +234 1 470	amnesty@linkserve.com.ng

Senegal	74a, Zone A Face Ecole St Therese BP 21910 Dakar Senegal	P: +221 25 6653 F: +221 822 05 33	amnesty_senegal@ notes.interliant.com
Sierra Leone	PMB 1021 Freetown Sierra Leone	P/F: +232 22 227 354	aisl@sierratel.sl
South Africa*			info@amnesty.org.za
Tanzania	AI Tanzania P.O. Box 4331 Dar es Salaam Tanzania	P: +255 51 131708 F: +255 51 131708	amnesty_tanzania@ notes.interliant.com
Tunisia	67 rue Oum Kalthoum 3ème étage Escalier B1000 Tunis Tunisia	P: +216 1 35 34 17 F: +216 1 35 26 71	admin-tn@amnesty.org

*   Entries marked with an asterisk are not full sections, however Amnesty International groups in these countries can be contacted at the Email address presented.

 Africa

The Carter Center

The Carter Center works to advance peace and health world-wide. Founded in 1982 by former U.S. President Jimmy Carter and Rosalynn Carter, the Atlanta-based Center focuses in its Conflict Resolution Program (CRP) on peaceful prevention and resolution of conflicts, primarily civil wars.

The Center's conflict-resolution work includes activities to improve nations' capacities for sustainable development, promote and protect human rights and strengthen democracy. To marshal the expertise of peacemakers world-wide, the Conflict Resolution Program established the International Negotiation Network (INN) of prominent individuals who can offer process advice or mediate to help resolve disputes.

In Africa, CRP has a played an active role in:

- The Great Lakes Region, where the Center brought together heads of state from Burundi, Rwanda, Tanzania, Uganda and Zaire to address on-going violence in the region and the need to repatriate 1.7 million Rwandan refugees.
- Liberia, where the Carter Center has actively mediated between combatants over several years and held to broker an agreement to hold democratic elections, which the Center monitored in 1997.
- Sudan, where the Center brokered a temporary cease-fire allowing health workers to enter the battle zone.

The Carter Center has also established a human rights committee which undertakes projects to promote human rights, including intervening on behalf of victims of human rights abuse, working with new democracies to establish institutions to protect human rights. Activities in Africa include collaboration with the Ethiopian Ministry of Education to teach children about human rights through mandatory curricula such as civics classes, and the sponsorship of seminars in Liberia on press freedom and responsibility and on human rights education. The Center is assisting the new Liberian Commission on Human Rights to refine its mandate and is working with Liberia's law school to strengthen the rule of law.

One Copenhill
453 Freedom Parkway
Atlanta, Georgia 30307
USA

tel +1 (404) 420 5100
fax +1 (404) 420 5196
email carterweb@emory.edu
http://www.cartercenter.org

Contact
Joyce Neu, associate
director of CRP
Number of staff
7 with CRP
Budget
> $1,000,000

Publications
Education for Human Rights and
Democratic Citizenship: The Liberia
Model, 1998
Human Rights, the United Nations, and
Nongovernmental Organizations, 1997
From Civil War to Civil Society: The
Transition from War to Peace in
Guatemala and Liberia, 1997

Horn of Africa

Centre for the Strategic Initiatives for Women

The Centre for the Strategic Initiatives of Women (CSIW) builds on local initiatives to advance the full participation of women in the cultural, economic and political development of the countries of the Horn of Africa. CSIW organises women's leadership training programs, short-term training workshops, self-sustaining support services, and research and documentation activities. Currently, CSIW has programmes in Somalia, Somaliland, Eritrea, Sudan and Ethiopia. The programmes include 'Conflict Management and Peacebuilding', 'Women's Political Leadership', 'Women's Rights', 'Women in Muslim Societies', and 'The Strategic Initiative for the Horn of Africa'.

1701 K Street NW, 11th Floor
Washington, D.C. 20006
USA

tel +1 (202) 223 7956
fax +1 (202) 223 7947
email csiw@csiw.org

Contact
Hibaaq Osman, director
Number of staff
7
Budget
$100,000 - $500,000

Publications
Country Reports on the Horn of Africa

 Great Lakes Region

Centre for the Study of the Great Lakes Region of Africa

The Centre for the Study of the Great Lakes Region of Africa is a research centre dedicated to gathering and processing information about countries in the Great Lakes Region. One important aim is to accurately assess and monitor the developments in the region's various conflicts. Founded in 1996 and closely affiliated with the University of Antwerp, the Centre favours a multidisciplinary approach, integrating economics, political science and law into its analyses. It acts as an adviser to NGOs and the Belgian government.

RUCA-COL
Middelheimlaan 1 C
2000 Antwerp, Belgium

tel +32 (3) 218 0662
fax +32 (3) 218 0666
email freyntje@ruca.ua.ac.be

Contact
Filip Reyntjens, director
Number of staff
8
Budget
$100,000 - $500,000

Publications
L'Afrique des grands lacs: annuaire
1997/1998
The administration of justice in Rwanda and the international criminal tribunal for Rwanda, 1997

Africa

Community of Sant'Egidio

The Community of Sant'Egidio is a world-wide assembly of Christian communities. Its primary activity is to care for the poor, but it takes the view that war is 'the greatest of all poverties', and it has, accordingly, been involved in conflict resolution activities and unofficial diplomacy.

Most of its members are in Italy, where it was founded, but some 2000 of them are organised into small groups in 23 other countries. Though laypersons themselves, the religious character of Sant'Egidio is an asset in negotiation activities and enhances their credibility, especially among Muslim parties. In Africa, the group has achieved successes in Mozambique and Algeria. The community's mediation strategy is to stress the human aspect, focusing less on the differences between the parties and more on their common interests.

In the case of Mozambique, the Community of Sant'Egidio built up a relationship with both parties to the conflict, which enabled it to assume a third-party intermediary role. The discussions initiated by the community in 1990 ended in a peace agreement and the deployment of a peace-keeping force.

In 1994, its efforts led to the 'Platform of Rome', bringing together, for the first time since violence erupted in 1992, leading figures of the Algerian government and its Muslim fundamentalist opponents.

The Community has attempted to broker discussions with the conflicting parties to the civil war and Sudan, and facilitators from Sant'Egidio have also been working to achieve a breakthrough in the Great Lakes Region. While 'official' diplomacy continues, Sant'Egidio has been working along a second 'track' to persuade the Tutsi-led government of Burundi and its opponents to agree to a cease fire, a first step viewed as crucial by diplomats working through 'official' channels.

Piazza Sant'Egidio 3/a   *Contact*
00153 Rome   Andrea Riccardi, founder
Italy   and president

tel +39 (6) 585 661
fax +39 (6) 580 0197
http://www.santegidio.org

Africa

Conciliation Resources

Conciliation Resources, a non-governmental international service for conflict prevention and resolution, seeks to provide sustained assistance to partner organisations working at community and national levels to prevent or transform violent conflict into opportunities for social, political and economic change based on greater justice. Assistance takes the form of collaborative design and implementation of conflict transformation strategies, support for seminars and workshops, training and education for constructive conflict transformation, media training or support for institutional development. In Africa, CR has been involved in activities in Sierra Leone, Liberia, Gambia, Mozambique and Somaliland.

P.O. Box 21067 London N1 1ZJ United Kingdom tel +44 (171) 359 7728 fax +44 (171) 359 4081 email cr@c-r.org http://www.c-r.org	*Contact* Andy Carl, co-director *Number of staff* 8-10 in London office, 2-4 in field *Budget* $100,000 - $500,000	*Publications* Accord - An International Review of Peace Initiatives. Issues on Liberia and Mozambique

Africa

Femmes Africa Solidarité

Femmes Africa Solidarité (Africa Women Solidarity), aims to create, strengthen and promote leadership among African women with respect to the prevention, management, and resolution of conflicts. The foundation has carried out many lobbying activities and organised training courses. It is currently involved in a peace project in Burundi which aims to promote and increase the involvement of women in the peace process and includes training and capacity building elements. Previous activities included conflict resolution training in Sierra Leone and election observer missions in Liberia and Burundi.

P.O. Box 2100 1211 Geneva 2 Switzerland tel +41 (22) 798 0075 fax +41 (22) 798 0076 email faspeace@iprolink.ch http://www.fasngo.org	*Contact* Bineta Diop, executive director *Number of staff* 6 *Budget* $500,000 - $1,000,000	*Publications* FAS Advocacy News, bi-annual newsletter Women's Participation in the peace process in Sierra Leone, 1997 Report on Election Observer Mission in Liberia, 1997 Report on Election Observer Mission in Burundi, forthcoming

 Africa

FEWER

The Forum on Early Warning and Early Response (FEWER) was established in 1996 as an interdisciplinary consortium of NGOs, academic institutions and intergovernmental organisations, working together to provide early warning and prevent violent conflicts. FEWER is running a pilot early warning project in the Great Lakes Region of Africa, drawing on the many local NGOs working for peace. It aims to bring the complexities of the conflict to international attention and demonstrate that indigenous groups are addressing the issues and formulating policy options that would help the international community as well.

1 Glyn Street
London SE11 5HT
United Kingdom

tel +44 (171) 793 8383
fax +44 (171) 793 7975
email secretariat@fewer.org
http://www.fewer.org

Contact
David Nyheim,
coordinator
Budget
$500,000-$1,000,000

Publications
Early Warning Reports on the Great Lakes
Consultation: Early Warning and
International Responses in the African
Great Lakes and the Caucasus, 1998
A Manual for Early Warning and Early
Response: Analytical Methodology for
Assessing Conflict and Peace

 Africa

Global Coalition for Africa

The Global Coalition for Africa (GCA) describes itself as a 'North South forum dedicated to forging political consensus on development priorities among African governments, their northern partners and non-governmental groups working in and on Africa.' GCA seeks to act as a catalyst encouraging fruitful partnership among its participants. The Forum has identified six priority issues, including 'governance, democracy, conflict management and reduced military spending' and adopted a framework for evaluating the quality of governance. GCA has held workshops on the institutionalisation of democracy, and on post-conflict demobilisation.

1750 Pennsylvania Avenue
N.W. Suite 1204
Washington, DC 20006
USA

tel +1 (202) 458 4338/4272
fax +1 (202) 522 3259
http://www.gca-cma.org

Contact
Ahmedou Ould-
Abdallah, executive
secretary
Number of staff
10

Publications
Promoting Agricultural Productivity and
Competitiveness in Sub-Saharan Africa,
1999
The Role and Functioning of Parliaments
in Africa - Issues Paper, 1998
Official press releases
Annual reports

Great Lakes

Great Lakes Policy Forum

The Great Lakes Policy Forum (GLPF), based in Washington, DC, brings together a broad cross-section of individuals, including representatives of the US government, the diplomatic community, NGOs and international organisations, for monthly meetings addressing conflict in the Great Lakes Region and related humanitarian issues. It serves as an informal meeting place for the exchange of information, an unofficial platform where government officials can discuss policy, and a forum for visiting dignitaries. The GLPF also provides an opportunity, though informal, to co-ordinate activities among humanitarian organisations and advance mediation efforts.

c/o Search for Common Ground
1601 Connecticut Avenue, N.W.
Suite 200
Washington DC, 20009
USA

tel +1 (202) 265 4300
fax +1 (202) 232 6718
email search@sfcg.org

Contact
Heather Kulp

 Africa

Human Rights Watch

Human Rights Watch is one of the world's major human rights organisations. It reports on abuses in over 70 countries and also regularly works to prevent conflict by highlighting human rights abuses that frequently spark violence. Human Rights Watch sends fact-finding missions to countries where abuses take place and maintains its own personnel in several countries to gather information on a continuing basis. Human Rights Watch maintains an African Division and a Middle East Division which together monitor all of Africa. It also maintains an office in Rwanda.

350 Fifth Avenue, 34th floor
New York City, New York 10018-3299
USA

tel +1 (212) 290 4700
fax +1 (212) 736 1300
email hrwnyc@hrw.org
http://www.hrw.org

Contact
Kenneth Roth,
executive director
Number of staff
200 (in all)
Budget
> $1,000,000

Publications
HRW World Report 1999
Sierra Leone: Getting Away with Murder,
Mutilation, and Rape, 1999
Nigeria: Crackdown in the Niger Delta,
1999
Tanzania - In the Name of Security: Forced
Round-Ups of Refugees in Tanzania, 1999
Hundreds of reports on countries and
various issues

Great Lakes Region, West Africa

International Alert

International Alert (IA) is an organisation whose existence is premised on the recognition that in many countries, internal conflicts undermine efforts to protect individual and collective human rights and to promote sustainable development, but that the world lacks the procedures and structures for resolving or preventing them.

It believes that lasting peace and security can only be built on justice and the recognition of the human dignity of all people. IA seeks the consent and trust of parties to a conflict, and urges respect for international humanitarian law and human rights as indispensable obligations of those parties. IA believes that the protagonists in a conflict - and the citizens whom it affects - will be the primary actors in its resolution, and that sustained dialogue is the principal means to this end.

IA has worked to peacefully resolve many of the world's most intractable disputes. In Africa, IA is currently involved in programmes in West Africa and the Great Lakes Region. It is also involved in research and advocacy activities.

In the Great Lakes Region, it operates programmes in Burundi and Rwanda, as well as a programme focussed on regional issues. The programmes offer conflict resolution training, opportunities for dialogue, confidence building activities, and the provision of both financial and human resources.

The West African programme, which focuses primarily on Liberia, seeks to cultivate a climate conducive to dialogue, the development of inclusive social and political mechanisms, a transformation of a culture of violence into a culture informed by human rights, democracy and civic duties, and the use of existing conflict resolution mechanisms for an early warning function.

IA is also involved in a "Light Weapons & Peacebuilding" programme in West Africa focusing on the development of recommendations for the effective control of light weapons transfers in the region.

1 Glyn Street
London SE11 5HT
United Kingdom

tel +44 (171) 793 8383
fax +44 (171) 793 7975
email general@international-alert.org
http://www.international-alert.org

Contact
Kevin Clements,
secretary general
Number of staff
16
Budget
> $1,000,000

Publications
Civil War, Civil Peace: Resolving
Conflicts, 1998
Modern Conflicts and Their Prevention
and Resolution, 1998
Working to Restore Peace in Burundi -
Gitega & Bujumbura, 1996 and 1997
Training Resource Pack for Conflict
Transformation, 1996

 Africa

International Crisis Group

The International Crisis Group aims at reinforcing the capacity and resolve of the international community to head off crises before they develop into full-blown humanitarian disasters.

Founded in 1995, the Group is involved in fact-finding, monitoring, early warning, training, lobbying, and media-focused activities to help bring resolution to conflicts wherever they may occur. African countries where the Group has been active include Algeria, the Democratic Republic of Congo, Burundi, Rwanda, Nigeria and Sierra Leone. The Group has a board, which includes former prime ministers, presidents and foreign ministers as well as prominent figures from business and the media. These include Senator George Mitchell, former US Senate majority leader, Nobel Peace Prize winner and former Costa Rican president Oscar Arias Sánchez, former Belgian prime minister Leo Tindemans and former Mozambican first lady Graça Machel.

In some case, the group endeavours to give greater prominence to information already gathered by other NGOs in the field. At other times, the Group posts staff to a country for a period to consult widely and produce analysis. High-profile visits to potential crisis zones by the Group's board members may also form part of the strategy.

The Group's haws adopted a four-step approach: 1. Identifying countries that are on the road to crisis. 2. Engaging with all relevant players in those countries, including government and military leaders, opposition groups, business, relief NGOs and religious, ethnic and other groups. 3. Developing strategic, integrated policy proposals aimed at strengthening stability and avoiding the development of crisis. 4. Alerting the international community to the risk of crisis and bringing pressure to bear on governments, international organisations and relevant sections of the business community to take preventive and remedial action. The Group maintains an extensive web site with the texts of its own reports and links to over 200 web sites on Africa.

26 Rue des Minimes
B-1000 Brussels
Belgium

tel +32 (2) 502 9038
fax +32 (2) 502 5038
email intcrisis@compuserve.com
http://www.intl-crisis-group.org

US office
tel +1 (202) 986 9750

Contact
Alain Destexhe,
president
Number of staff
6 at HQ, 16 in field
Budget
> $1,000,000

Publications
Africa's Seven Nation War, 1999
Algérie: Assemblée Populaire Nationale:
18 mois de législature, 1999
Burundi: Internal and Regional
Implications of the Suspension of
Sanctions, 1999
Many others, all accessible on web site

 Africa

Minority Rights Group

The Minority Rights Group (MRG) is a human rights organisation working to secure justice for minorities and to achieve peaceful co-existence between majority and minority communities. In Africa, as elsewhere, MRG undertakes regional projects promoting the rights of ethnic, religious and linguistic minority groups and fostering inter-community co-operation, but the Africa programme has been seriously affected by political instability, particularly in the Horn of Africa. MRG nevertheless maintains its involvement in Ethiopia and Somalia in the Horn, and is currently involved in additional activities in Kenya and Uganda.

379 Brixton Road
London SW9 7DE
United Kingdom

tel +44 (20) 7978 9498
fax +44 (171) 738 6265
email minority.rights@mrgmail.org
http://www.minorityrights.org

Contact
Alan Phillips, director
Number of staff
23
Budget
> $1,000,000

Publications
Outsider, quarterly newsletter
World Directory of Minorities, 1997
Eritrea: Towards Unity in Diversity, 1997
Voices from ..., educational material

 Africa

Oxfam

As a development NGO, Oxfam increasingly has to cope with the build-up to the explosion and the aftermath of conflict. Its response includes human rights and lobbying activities. Oxfam's has a three-pronged approach to conflict. Direct victims of conflict - often refugees - are provided with clean water and other basic needs.

Support is given to grassroots community groups working to demand or safeguard their rights, tackle violence and rebuild their societies. And appeals are made to international decision-makers to work to prevent and resolve conflicts and protect human rights.

Oxfam is active throughout Africa, including many of those areas worst affected by violent conflict. Programs reflect the five themes Oxfam has identified: increasing food security; improving the lives of women, particularly vulnerable groups; responding to the needs of people caught in conflict; offering advice and training to local organisations; and providing basic services such as water, sanitation, health and education.

In 1997, Oxfam launched its Cut Conflict Campaign, calling on governments to take action in four key areas to reduce human suffering: curb the arms trade, bring war criminals to justice, promote peace through general aid, trade and economic policies and uphold the rights of refugees. Conflict is one of Oxfam's four thematic priorities, focussing specifically on support for the right of poor people to be protected from violence. In order to achieve this, it seeks to strengthen governmental and multilateral commitments to conflict prevention, conflict resolution and reconstruction.

Oxfam has also been engaged in an ongoing 'Campaign for basic rights'. The campaign stresses the inter-relatedness of the rights guaranteed in international charters and conventions, and singles out what it considers to be the most basic rights of all - the rights to subsistence and security - in its Oxfam Global Charter for Basic Rights.

274 Banbury Road
Oxford OX2 7DZ
United Kingdom

tel +44 (1865) 311 311
fax +44 (1865) 312 380
email oxfam@oxfam.org.uk
http://www.oxfam.org.uk

Contact
Suzanne Williams, policy
adviser on gender and
human rights
Number of staff
600 at HQ, 1300 in the
field (for all activities)
Budget
$500,000 - $1,000,000

Publications
Development in Practice, journal
Gender and Development, journal
Kenya: Promised Land? 1998
Rebuilding Communities in a Refugee
Settlement: A Casebook from Uganda,
1998
Oxfam's Work in Conflict Situations,
workshop report, 1996

Great Lakes, Horn of Africa, Sierra Leone, Nigeria, South Africa

Responding to Conflict

Responding to Conflict (RTC) seeks to support the efforts of people trying to resolve situations of political and social conflict in which they live. It works with local and international NGOs, UN agencies, diplomats, government officials and public service institutions. RTC offers a 10-week course 'Working with Conflict' for practitioners in development, human rights, emergencies and peace-building; and 'Strengthening Policy and Practices in Areas of Conflict', for staff of international agencies. RTC is also engaged in 'Linking Practice to Policy', a project which aims to influence policy-makers of international agencies and governments by providing media and video coverage of African peace-building initiatives.

1046 Bristol Road
Selly Oak, Birmingham B29 6LJ
United Kingdom

tel +44 (121) 415 5641
fax +44 (121) 415 4119
email enquiries@respond.org
http://www.respond.org

Contact
Simon Fisher, director
Number of staff
5
Budget
$100,000 - $500,000

Publications
Various reports on the courses mentioned above

 Africa

United States Institute of Peace, Africa Program

The United States Institute of Peace (USIP) is an independent, non-partisan institution, established under a congressional mandate, involved in a range of activities to promote peace-building and conflict resolution. It offers training, supports research, provides funding for curriculum development on conflict resolution, and sponsors seminars and conferences in conflict resolution issues. USIP focuses on Africa through its Africa Program, which includes a substantial grants program to organisations promoting peace and conflict management, and a publications program. It also sponsors workshops focusing on important issues related to peace-building in Africa.

1200 17th street, NW
Washington, DC 20036-3011
USA

tel +1 (202) 429 3843
fax +1 (202) 429 6063
email ds@usip.org
http://www.usip.org

Contact
David R. Smock,
coordinator

Publications
Peace Works reports,
Peace Watch, newsletter, 6x a year
A New Approach to Peace in Sudan, Special Report Series,
1999
Building for Peace in the Horn of Africa: Diplomacy and
Beyond, 1999
Elections and Conflict Management in Africa, 1998

Africa, West Africa, Great Lakes Region

Synergies Africa

Synergies is a Geneva-based organisation with its roots in Africa which is involved in enhancing the continent's capacities to manage its own conflicts. As a matter of principle, the organisation co-operates closely with local NGOs, associations and institutions.

Its main programme, called Rencontre Régionale de Concertation des Chefs Traditionnels de l'Afrique, aims to set up mechanisms of permanent consultation among the traditional rulers of regions within the boundaries of present-day states, as well as between them and the national government and representatives of civil society. The programme focuses on ten countries in West Africa: Benin, Burkina Faso, Cameroon, Chad, Côte d'Ivoire, Ghana, Mali, Niger, Nigeria and Togo.

Another project, which focuses on Burundi, is concerned with consociational democracy, power-sharing and institutional design in divided societies. Workshops on these issues are held with Burundian politicians and intellectuals. The project aims to create a paradigm meeting the challenge of multi-ethnicity in establishing democracy.

In July 1995, Synergies co-organised a workshop on 'Media, Conflicts and Humanitarian Urgencies', the underlying idea being that African journalists might move away from the so-called 'hate media' to actually contribute to peace and the defence of the real interests of the population and the nation without falling into a narrow-minded nationalism.

Furthermore, Synergies has organised many meetings, workshops and missions. An informal meeting of top-level African personalities on conflict settlement in West Africa, a workshop on the reconstruction of civil society in Rwanda and one on national reconciliation in Mali and Niger and a conference for Burundi youth are just a few examples. In 1996, Synergies set up a special foundation called Africa Women Solidarity (see separate entry).

P.O. Box 2100
1211 Geneva 2
Switzerland

tel +41 (22) 788 8586
fax +41 (22) 788 8590
email hassanba@iprolink.ch

Contact
Hassan Ba, founder
Number of staff
5
Budget
$500,000 - $1,000,000

Appendices

Appendix 1

Useful Internet Sites on Conflicts and Conflict Prevention in Africa

General

International Crisis Group
http://www.intl-crisis-group.org/projects/af_links.htm
execellent website with a directory of 200 internet links on Africa

Africa Index on Africa
http://www.africaindex.africainfo.no/
very complete source of information in any area of African life

University of Pennsylvania African Studies Site
http://www.sas.upenn.edu/African_Studies/AS.html
listings of Africa-related materials such as articles, events, country specific resources

Columbia University, Institute of African Studies
http://www.columbia.edu/cu/libraries/indiv/area/Africa/
virtual library of African Studies; very complete and up-to-date information on universities, people, newspapers, libraries, etc.

Reliefweb
http://www.reliefweb.int/
published by the UN, Department of Humanitarian Affairs, a very well informed website with excellent information (situation reports, press releases, maps, etc.) on the principal crises in Africa.

Africa South of Sahara
http://www-sul.stanford.edu/depts/ssrg/africa/guide.html
very complete site with links to resources on Sub-Saharan Africa, sorted by country, regions and topics

INCORE Guides to Sources on Conflict and Ethnicity
http://www.incore.ulst.ac.uk/cds/countries/index.html
a joint initiative of the University of Ulster, Northern Ireland and the United Nations University, includes annotated guides to Internet sources on conflict and ethnicity in Africa in general, and in Central Africa in particular.

Africa Study Center
http://www.isp.msu.edu/AfricanStudies/ASCs.htm
links to African Studies Centers at Colleges & Universities around the world

Africa Server
http://www.africaserver.nl
excellent Dutch gateway website with resources sorted by subject (institutions involved in
the continent, human rights, gender and sexuality, etc.) and country.

Africa Viewpoint
http://www.oneworld.org/outlook/africa/index.html
OneWorld Online's Africa office; information on and from people working in the field of
sustainable development and human rights.

Africa Policy Information Center (APIC)
http://www.africapolicy.org
includes many links and useful documentation

Peace Net/Conflict Net
http://www.igc.org/igc
Institute for Global Communication

International Peace Academy
http://www.ipacademy.inter.net/links.htm
selected collection of links to the worldwide community of analysts and practitioners in the
area of peacekeeping, peacemaking, and conflict management, and includes several sources
of good analyses and information

War, Peace and Security Guide
http://www.cfcsc.dnd.ca/links/index.html
Internet resources on armed forces of the world, contemporary conflicts, international
relations, peace, disarmament and arms control, and peacekeeping

Contemporary Conflicts
http://www.cfcsc.dnd.ca/links/wars/index.html
Information Resource Centre, Canada

United States Bureau of African Affairs
http://www.state.gov/regions/africa/index.html
features, news and country information and US policy towards Africa

One World
http://www.oneworld.org
network of over 300 organisations; information by country and issue

The Carter Center
http://www.CarterCenter.org
information on Liberia, Central Lakes, Sudan

Organization of African Unity
http://www.oau-oua.org
links to other internet resources and information about African countries

European Platform for Conflict Prevention and Transformation
http://www.euconflict.org
directory of organisations and surveys of conflict prevention and management activities in
conflict areas

Interpost
http://www.interpost.no/africaindex/
a comprehensive guide to the continent on the Net, developed by the Norwegian Council on
Africa

Entwicklungspolitik Online
http://www.epo.de/register/afrika.html
links to other internet resources and information about African countries

CIA World Factbook
http://www.odci.gov/cia/publications/factbook/index.html
country profiles

Human Rights

University of Minnesota, Human Rights Library
http://www1.umn.edu/humanrts/index.html
very comprehensive website for any kind of human rights information, and information on
the status of human rights organisations in Sub Saharan Africa per country

U.S. Department of State
http://www.usis.usemb.se/humanr97/
Human Rights country reports

Amnesty International
http://www.amnesty.org
human rights reports, news releases, and a great selection of human rights links

Human Rights Watch
http://www.hrw.org
human rights reports and country reports

Minorities

Minorities at Risk Project
http://www.bsos.umd.edu/cidcm/mar/
tracking the status and condition of ethnopolitical groups around the globe

News

Out there news
http://www.megastories.com
news stories per country or event

BBC News
http://www.bbc.co.uk/hi/english/world/africa/default.htm
latest news and reports

Le Monde Diplomatique
http://www.monde-diplomatique.fr

Africa News Online
http://www.africanews.org/
up-to-date news on the whole continent.

Inter Press Service
http://www.ips.org/

Africa Confidential
http://www.africa-confidential.com/

Arabic news
http://www.arabicnews.com

Africanews
http://www.africanews.org

Mail & Guardian
http://www.mg.co.za/mg/

Alert Net (Reuters)
http://www.alertnet.org
the Reuters Foundation's news and communications service for the emergency relief
community

CIDA Contemporary Conflicts in Africa
http://www.synapse.net/~acdi2o/news/main.htm
news and urgent action from the United Nations, situation reports

Refugees

U.S. Committee for Refugees
http://www.refugees.org

UNHCR
http://www.unhcr.ch

Selection of Newsletters and Journals on Africa

African, The - Africa Development Communications Network, London, UK
African Affairs - Royal African Society, London, UK
Africa Analysis - UK
Africa Confidential - Miramoor Publications, London, UK
Africa Insight - Africa Institute of South Africa, SA
African Journal on Conflict Prevention, Management and Resolution - OAU Quarterly, Ethiopia
Africa Recovery - UN Department of Public Information
Africa Quarterly - Indian Council for Africa, New Delhi, India
Billets d'Afrique et d'Ailleurs - Survie, France
CAP-Infos - Compagnie des Apôtres, Burundi
Civil Society - Ibn Khaldun Center for Development, Egypt
Conflict Trends Magazine - ACCORD, SA
Defender, The - Foundation for Human Rights Initiative, Uganda
Democratie & Developpement - GERDDES Afrique, Benin
Focus on the EU and peace-building in the Horn of Africa - Saferworld, UK
Horn of Africa Bulletin - Life & Peace Institute, Sweden
Horn of Africa Vision - Horn of Africa Centre for Democracy and Development, Kenya
Mbiu - Amani People's Theatre, Kenya
Mediator, The - Centre for Conflict Resolution and Peace Advocacy, Nigeria
New African - UK
New Routes - Life & Peace Institute, Sweden
Track Two - Centre for Conflict Resolution, SA
Update on Peace and Rehabiliation, The - National Council of Churches, Kenya

Appendix 3
Selection of Literature on Conflicts in Africa

Abbink, J. and Hesseling, G. (eds.), *Election Observation and Democratization in Africa*, Basingstoke: Macmillan, 1999, 272 p.

Airas, M. (ed.), *The Role of International Cooperation in Conflict Prevention in Africa*, Helsinki: KATU, 1998, 120 p.

Allan, T. and Nicol, A., *Water Resources, Prevention of Violent Conflict and the Coherence of EU Policies in the Horn of Africa*, London: Saferworld, 1998, 32 p.

Asmal, K. and Asmal, L., Roberts, R.S., *Reconciliation through Truth: a reckoning of apartheid's criminal governance*, Oxford: James Curry, 1997, 231 p.

Assefa H. and Wachira G. (eds.), *Peacemaking and Democratisation in Africa : theoretical Perspective and Church Initiatives*, Nairobi-Kampala : East African Educational Publishers Ltd. 1996.

Attah-Poku, Agyemang, *African Ethnicity: History, Conflict Management Resolution, and Prevention*, Lanham [etc.]: University Press of America, 1997.

Bayart, Jean-François, Ellis, Stephen and Hibou, Beatrice, *The Criminalization of the State in Africa*, London: James Currey Publishers, 1999, 126 p.

Barry M. A. and Sada, H., *La prévention des conflits en Afrique de l'ouest: mythes ou réalité?*, Paris: Karthala, 1997, 208 p.

Brogan, Patrick, *World Conflicts*, London: Bloomsbury Publishing London, 1998, 682 p.

Bratton, M. and Walle, N. van de, *Democratic experiments in Africa : regime transitions in comparative perspective.* Cambridge : Cambridge University Press, 1998, 307 p.

Chiffe, L., *Regional Dimensions of conflict in the Horn of Africa. Special Issue: Complex Political Emergencies*, Third World Quarterly, 1998

Clingendael, *West Africa: Regional Report*, The Hague: Netherlands Institute of International Relations Clingendael, 1998, 293 p.

Commission on African Regions in Crisis, King Baudouin Foundation, Médecins sans Frontières, *Conflicts in Africa: an analysis of crises and crisis prevention measures*, Brussels: GRIP, 1997, 281 p.

Deng, Francis M. [et al], *Sovereignty as Responsibility: conflict management in Africa*, Washington, D. C.: Brookings Institution, 1996, 265 p.

Deng, Francis M. and Lyons, Terrence (eds), *African Reckoning: A Quest for Good Governance.* Washington, DC: Brookings Institution Press, 1998.

Deng Francis M. and Zartman W. (eds.), *Conflict resolution in Africa*, Washington D.C.: Brookings Institution, 1991, 418 p.

Dicklitz, S., *The Elusive Promise of NGOs in Africa : lessons from Uganda*, Basingstoke: Macmillan, 1998, 288 p.

Engel, U. and Mehler, A. (eds.), *Gewaltsame Konflikte und ihre Prävention in Afrika : Hintergründe, Analysen und Strategien für die entwicklungspolitische Praxis.* Hamburg: Institut für Afrika-Kunde, 1998, 179 p.

Ezell, W.K., *Newspaper Responses to Reports of Atrocities: Burundi, Mozambique, Iraq*, in: Genocide Watch, 1992, pp.87-112.

Fennell, J., *Hope suspended: morality, politics and war in Central Africa*, In: Disasters, vol. 22 (2), June 1998, pp. 96-108.

Foundation for Human Rights Initiative, *Strategies for Conflict Prevention and Peace Building.*

Proceedings of the Great Lakes Region Conference, held at Hotel Africana, Kampala, Oct. 4 -7, 1998, Kampala: FHRI, 1998, 98 p.

Francis D., *Peacekeeping or Peace Enforcement? Conflict Intervention in Africa*, Cambridge, Massachusetts: World Peace Foundation, 1998, 29 p.

Furley, O. and May, R. (eds.), *Peacekeeping in Africa*, Aldershot: Ashgate, 1998, 336 p.

Gessesse B. and Arsano Y. and Haile T. and El-Hardallo A. and El-Battahani A H., *Trading Places, Alternatives models of the economic co-operation in the Horn of Africa*, Uppsala: Life & Peace Institute, 1996

Gibbon, Peter (ed.), *The New Local level Politics in East Africa: studies on Uganda, Tanzania and Kenya*, Uppsala: Nordiska Afrikainstitutet, 1994, Research Report no. 95

Girardet, E. (ed.), *Somalia, Rwanda and Beyond: the Role of the International Media in Wars and Humanitarian Crises*, Dublin, 1995

International Crisis Group, *Africa's Seven Nation War*, Report No. 4, May 21, 1999

Joseph, R. (ed.), *State, Conflict and Democracy in Africa*, Boulder (etc): Lynne Rienner, 1998, 600p.

Kacowics, A.M., *Zones of Peace in the Third World: South America and West Africa in Comparative Perspective*, New York State: University Press, 1998, 267 p.

Kingma, K. and Gebrewold, K., *Demilitarisation, Reintegration and Conflict Prevention in the Horn of Africa*, London: Saferworld, 1998, 42 p.

Laakso L. and Launonen R., *Building Peace in Africa. Diversity of Distress-Diversity of Possibilities*, Helsinki: KATU, 1997, 79 p.

Lautze, S. and Jones, B.D., Duffield, M. *Strategic Humanitarian Coordination in the Great Lakes Region 1996-1997: An Independent Study for the Inter-agency Standing Committee.* New York: United nations, 1998, 117 p.

Lund, M., *Preventing and Mitigating Violent Conflict: a Guide for Practitioners*, Washington, D.C.: Creative Associates International, 1997.

Lund, M. and Austin, K. *Democratization and Violence in Burundi. The Failure of Preventive Action.* Brookings, 1997, 120 p.

Magyar, K.P. and Conteh-Morgan, E. (eds.), *Peacekeeping in Africa.* Basingstoke: Macmillan, 1998, 208 p.

Malan, Jannie, *Conflict Resolution Wisdom from Africa,* Durban: African Centre for the Constructive Resolution of Disputes (ACCORD) 1998, 119 p.

Mandaza I. (ed), *Peace and security in southern Africa*, Harare: SAPES Books, 1996, 183 p.

Marysse, S. and Reyntjes, F., *L'Afrique des Grand Lacs: Annuaire 1996-1997*, Paris: Editions l'Harmattan, 1997, 342 p.

Mengisteab, K. and Daddieh, C., *Statebuilding and Democratization in Africa, Faith, Hope and Realities,* Westport: Preager pub., 1999, 264 p.

Menkhaus, Ken and Prendergast, John, *Conflict and Crisis in the Greater Horn of Africa*, in: Current History, May, 1999

Monga, C., *The Anthropology of Anger: Civil Society and Democracy in Africa.* Boulder: Lynne Rienner, 1996, 219 p.

Ohlson T. and Stedman S.J., *The New is not yet Born: conflict resolution in Southern Africa,* Washington, D.C., : Brookings Institution, 1994, 322 p.

Obasanjo, Olusegun and Mosha, Felix G.N. (eds.) *Africa: Rise to Challenge,* New York: Africa Leadership Forum, 1992

ACORD (Agency for Cooperation and Research in Development), *Development in Conflict: the experience of ACORD in Uganda, Sudan, Mali and Angola*, London: Overseas Development Institute, 1995, 90 p. (Network Paper 9)

Peace Center Burg Schlaining, *Report on the Seminar on Preventive Diplomacy and Peacebuilding in Southern Africa*, Stadtschlaining: Schlaining working paper 3/98, 48 p.

Prendergast, John, *Building for Peace in the Horn of Africa*, Washington, D.C.: United States Institute of Peace, 1999

Prendergast J., *Frontline diplomacy: humanitarian aid and conflict in Africa*, Boulder: Lynne Rienner, 1996, 165 p.

Reno, W., *Warlord Politics and African States*, Boulder: Lynne Rienner, 1998, 257 p.

Rotschild, D. *Managing Ethnic Conflict in Africa: pressures and Incentives for Cooperation*, Washinton, D.C.: Brookings Institution Press, 1997, 350 p.

Saferworld, *Focus on the European Union and Peacebuilding Efforts in the Horn of Africa*, Autumn 1999, Issue 1

Sisk, T.D., Reynolds, A. (eds.), *Elections and Conflict Management in Africa*, Washington, D.C.: United States Institute of Peace, 1998

Smith, S. and Ould-Abdallah, Ahmedou., *La diplomatie pyromane*, Paris: Calmann-Lévy, 1997, 212 p.

Smock, David R. and Crocker, Chester A. (eds.), *African Conflict Resolution: the U.S. Role in Peacemaking*. Washington, DC: United States Institute of Peace, 1995

Spanger, H.-J. and Vale, P. (eds), *Bridges to the Future: prospects for the peace and security in southern Africa*, Boulder, Col.: Westview Press, 1995, 195 p.

Sorbo, G.M. and Vale, P. (eds.), *Out of Conflict: from war to peace in Africa*. Uppsala: Nordiska Afrikainstitutet, 1997, 214 p.

Torduff, William, *Government and Politics in Africa*, Bloomington, Indiana: Indiana University Press, 1997 3 ed.

The Courier, *Dossier Conflict Prevention*, # 168, March-April, 1998, 65-87.

United Nations Publications, *A Peace of Timbuktu: Democratic Governance, Development and African Peacemaking*. New York, NY: United Nations Publications, 1998, 392 P.

Visman, E. and Brusset, E., *Prevention of Violent Conflict and the Coherence of EU Policies Towards the Horn of Africa*, London: Saferworld, 1998, 48 p.

Waal, A. de, *Famine Crimes: Politics and the Disaster Relief Industry in Africa*, London: African Rights, 1997, 238 p.

Welch, Claude E. Jr., *Protecting Human Rights in Africa: Strategies and Roles of Non-Governmental Organizations*, Philadelphia: University of Pennsylvania Press, 1995

Appendix 4
Index of Organisations

This index lists organisations mentioned in Part I-III. Numbers in brackets refer to profiles included in the Directory.

525